GERMANICUS

GERMANICUS

The Magnificent Life
and Mysterious Death of
Rome's Most Popular General

LINDSAY POWELL

Pen & Sword
MILITARY

First published in Great Britain in 2013
and reprinted in this format in 2016 by
PEN & SWORD MILITARY
An imprint of
Pen & Sword Books Ltd
47 Church Street
Barnsley
South Yorkshire
S70 2AS

ISBN 978-1-47388-198-3

A CIP catalogue record for this book is
available from the British Library.

Typeset by Concept, Huddersfield, West Yorkshire.
Printed and bound in India by Replika Press Pvt. Ltd.

Pen & Sword Books Ltd incorporates the Imprints of Pen & Sword Aviation,
Pen & Sword Family History, Pen & Sword Maritime, Pen & Sword Military,
Pen & Sword Discovery, Pen & Sword Politics, Pen & Sword Atlas,
Pen & Sword Archaeology, Wharncliffe Local History, Wharncliffe True Crime,
Wharncliffe Transport, Pen & Sword Select, Pen & Sword Military Classics,
Leo Cooper, The Praetorian Press, Claymore Press, Remember When,
Seaforth Publishing and Frontline Publishing.

For a complete list of Pen & Sword titles please contact
PEN & SWORD BOOKS LIMITED
47 Church Street, Barnsley, South Yorkshire, S70 2AS, England
E-mail: enquiries@pen-and-sword.co.uk
Website: www.pen-and-sword.co.uk

For my Mother,
Valerie Powell.
Fi'n caru ti.

Contents

Foreword
by Philip Matyzsak

The early years of the Roman empire constitute one of the most fascinating periods in history. There exists almost no other period before the early modern era where we have so much information about a particular society. And the thing about the early modern era is that (almost by definition) many of the values and viewpoints of western society were coming into alignment with those of today.

This is not the case with the early imperial period. Here we find a society largely untouched with ideas of chivalry, Judeo-Christian ethics, and even concepts such as romantic love which form the background to our emotional lives, just as technology and medicine have changed our material lives. Yet despite the huge cultural gap between ancient Rome and that of the modern west, we find ourselves drawn to the emotion, pathos and epic drama which filled the lives of the early Caesars. The stories from this era are timeless. They deal with ambition, betrayal, family feuds and violent twists of fortune, often mixed with mystery, intrigue and flamboyant sexuality.

Of the above, all that detracts from the story of Germanicus is the fact that – unlike his adoptive father Tiberius – all that is reported of the sex life of Germanicus is that he was happily married to a loving wife who blessed him with a regular supply of offspring. (Many of whom did not survive – tragically, childhood in antiquity was more dangerous than military service.)

In fact there is little in the life of Germanicus that would not make an inspiring tale in one of the *Boy's Own* magazines of a century ago. Our man was heroic, yet compassionate, intelligent yet sympathetic and if charisma could be bottled, Germanicus would have had enough to corner the entire Mediterranean market. The ancient sources tell us of his energy on the campaigns which he commanded with flair and success. Of how Germanicus personified vengeful Rome after the treacherous destruction of three Roman legions in the Teutoburg forest, and how he stopped a mutiny of the Rhine army by the sheer force of his personality.

Then there is the tragedy of the young hero's mysterious death in the east. Was he killed by illness or malice? Did misfortune or a devious plot bring the career of Rome's most promising general and politician to its abrupt halt? Here at last we find the whiff of scandal which this dramatic tale has heretofore been lacking.

Yet something else has been lacking from the story of the best emperor that Rome never had – and that is a critical examination by a modern historian. There was indeed another side to the legend of Germanicus had anyone cared to look for it, and by the standards of today that side is pretty dark. After the massacre of the legions in the Teutoburg forest, the problem for a Roman general was not to defeat the Germans in battle, but to bring them to fight that battle in the first place. Germanicus achieved this by conducting vast punitive operations over the Rhine 'which spared neither age not sex'. In other words, Germanicus massacred women and children in the hope of provoking their menfolk into fighting.

Nor were those operations without cost to Rome. Gambling that his armies could be transported by sea despite the proven failure of Roman naval technology in that regard, Germanicus repeatedly and recklessly rolled the dice that put his men at peril upon the sea – and finally lost most of his army. Many of the promises made to the (justifiably) mutinous Rhine legionaries were broken or quietly forgotten afterwards.

For reasons such as these, the life and strange death of Germanicus require re-examination by an impartial historian today. Impartiality is needed for another reason – that the most factually trustworthy historian of the Roman empire, Cornelius Tacitus, blatantly and viciously slanted those facts against Tiberius, the adoptive father of Germanicus. In the works of Tacitus, one seldom reads of Tiberius acting except through selfishness, jealousy or ruthless political calculation. From a reading of the *Annals*, one is forced to the conclusion that Tiberius bitterly resented the brilliance and popularity of his appointed successor, and schemed to limit and tarnish these at every opportunity. From Tacitus, one might assume that the jealousy and conservatism of Tiberius were largely to blame for the failure to assimilate Germania into the Roman empire, and Germanicus was yanked from his command just as the realization of that objective appeared possible.

It is a dramatic story – but is it true? At a distance of almost 2,000 years it takes painstaking research to separate fact from fiction, and drama from reality, and all too often the effort is futile. This is particularly true of the Julio-Claudians, a family who combined for contemporaries the modern cult for pop and film celebrities and the enduring fascination with the private life of royalty. One can read descriptions of senatorial debate, and inscriptions which survive on buildings, dedications and statuary, yet the decisions which affected the course of the Roman empire and the fate of its leaders were generally taken in private chambers and closed family discussions. It is impossible to know what was said on such occasions, but that did not stop ancient writers from guessing. And where the facts failed, they did not shy away from wholesale invention.

For all these reasons a modern, impartial study of the life of Germanicus is not only timely but overdue. For, apart from the enduring mystery of his death, Germanicus did come as close as anyone in the attempt to re-establish Roman rule from the Rhine to the Elbe. Had he succeeded, the history of the Roman empire – and therefore of subsequent ages – would have been greatly different. It is worth examining how and why the attempt failed, and learning more about the man who made it.

Philip 'Maty' Matyzsak
May 2012
Kootenay Hills, British Columbia

Preface

In the annals of history, the story of Germanicus stands as a lesson in what happens when passion, paranoia, principle and power collide. It is a tale of contrasts. The ebullient spirit of wildly popular Germanicus clashes with the brooding temperament of his Uncle Tiberius, the reluctant and widely reviled second emperor of the Roman Empire. The enthusiasm and inexperience of youth are pitted against the conservatism and judgement that come with age. Duty vies with self-interest. Acclaimed historical fiction 'whodunit' author Lindsey Davis pithily summed up the two protagonists for me at the first annual dinner of the Historical Writers' Association in London in December 2011 as 'Germanicus good, Tiberius bad'. Usually, the truth is not as black and white. Historians have to distinguish between shades of grey, and in the process of exposing the truth, many of the graded hues are revealed as exaggerations or outright fictions.

Germanicus has received the better press of the two men. During his short life, Germanicus' star shone very brightly. His troops adored him as he led them at the head of the line to glory, while, for many civilians, he embodied their hopes for a return to the democracy of the old Republic. How Germanicus rose to prominence is the inspiring tale of courage, integrity and patriotism, and a remarkable stroke of luck. How he fell is a tale of political errors of judgement, petty jealousies and possibly murder – with his uncle rumoured to be implicated in the crime. It is also the extraordinary story of one of the strongest husband-and-wife partnerships in history. Germanicus and Agrippina did not make an obvious couple when they married, but they proved to be devoted to each other, and she bore him many children. After Germanicus' death, she spent the remaining years of her life seeking justice for what she saw as treachery behind her husband's death and, in so doing, bringing upon herself the ire of Tiberius.

This contrast of light and dark, the tale of a conflicted family, and regret over lost potential, greatly appealed to classically-inclined intellectuals of the seventeenth, eighteenth and nineteenth centuries, inspiring them to write plays about Germanicus and to paint canvasses of scenes from his life – or, more often, his death. Yet, today, he is hardly known, the story of his life having been overshadowed by other Caesars, many of whom were far below him in character and talent. In this book, I hope to make Germanicus' exciting *Boy's Own* life story known to a new generation of readers.

Remarkably, in modern times, no one has published a full biography in English, spanning the birth to the death of this most important and popular Roman, until this one. The Roman biographer Suetonius refers to 'many authors' who wrote about Germanicus, but, alas, little actually survives down to our own time. The nearest thing we have to a biography is the brief opening section of Suetonius' own book on Caius Caligula in his *Lives of the Caesars*. Germanicus' contemporary, Velleius Paterculus, mentions him in his *Roman Histories*, almost incidentally to the main subject of Tiberius' glorious reign. Of the later historians, Tacitus, in his *Annals*, writes a flawed narrative of Germanicus' military exploits – drawing extensively on an earlier work by Pliny the Elder – as well as his travels in the East. But Tacitus has a discernible bias towards Germanicus, so it can be argued that he perhaps paints a rather rosy, overly sympathetic portrait of the man. In contrast, Germanicus has what could be characterized as a bit part in Cassius Dio's sweeping history of the Roman Empire, written some two hundred years after his death, which drew on older material, including Tacitus. Other sources – Ammianus Marcellinus, Josephus, Ovid, Pliny the Elder, and Plutarch among them – provide insights into the man's character. In recent times, archaeology has revealed several inscriptions, amongst the most important of which are the so-called *Senatus Consultum de Cn. Pisone Patre*, the *Tabula Hebana* and *Tabula Siarensis*. Additionally, there are a number of statue busts, cameos, and coins, which give us a very good impression of how he actually looked in life. Like a detective, by critically assembling this diverse source material and teasing out the bias of each reporter (since there are no eyewitness accounts), it is possible to convincingly reconstruct the life story of Germanicus and to create a nuanced portrait of the man and his achievements.

Germanicus is structured to follow the life of the Roman general chronologically, and to draw out key themes that shaped it:

Chapter 1, 'In the Name of the Father', covering the years 16 BCE to 5 CE, describes the impact of Drusus the Elder's death on the boy who assumed his father's name and legacy, his upbringing and how he was suddenly thrust into prominence.

Chapter 2, 'First Steps to Glory', covering the years 6 CE to summer 9 CE, traces Germanicus' emergence as a military leader during the Batonian Wars and the dramatic changes to his life, as Augustus prepared for his own death.

Chapter 3, 'Once More to Germania Magna', covering the period from autumn 9 CE until 14 CE, describes Germanicus' rise to the consulship, and how he dealt with a mutiny of the Rhine army.

Chapter 4, 'Up Against the Angrivarian Wall', covering the years 15–16 CE, describes how he invaded Germania Magna in a war of vengeance against Arminius and the Cherusci, culminating in the great battles of the Weser River, Idistaviso and the Angrivarian Wall.

Chapter 5, 'Travels and Tribulations in Asia Minor', covering the years 17–19 CE, follows Germanicus as he traversed the east *en route* to taking up his position as supreme military commander of the region, and the events leading up to his death.

Chapter 6, 'A Fine Roman in the Best Tradition', describes the extraordinary events which took place in the immediate aftermath of Germanicus' death.

Chapter 7, 'The Fall of the House of Germanicus', documents the fate of his wife Agrippina and their children.

Chapter 8, 'The Germanicus Tradition', illustrates how Germanicus' story was re-invented through the creative interpretations of later ages.

Chapter 9, 'Assessment', reviews the life of the man and attempts to separate fact from fiction in answering the question, 'what manner of man was Germanicus?'

The author and literary critic Lionel Trilling (1905–1975) wrote that 'every man's biography is to be understood in relation to his father' (introduction to *The Portable Matthew Arnold*, New York: Viking, 1949, p. 15). It is an apposite observation here. The life and legend of Germanicus' father, Nero Claudius Drusus (known to history as Drusus the Elder), reached far into his son's. In many ways they were alike – in personality and temperament, tolerance for personal risk, loyalty to family and country, but also in their intractability and recklessness. *Germanicus* is thus a natural successor to my first book, *Eager for Glory: The Untold Story of Drusus the Elder, Conqueror of Germania*, and the reader will find much of interest in it as a 'backgrounder' to the present volume.

Writing about the ancient world involves making several editorial decisions and presentational compromises. Chronology is one of them. The Romans had their own calendar using the names of each year's consuls (see page xxviii), and ancient historians routinely refer to dates in this way. For modern readers, it is cumbersome and very confusing. Our own style of identifying years by serial numbers makes life so much easier! However, in respect of dates, I have adopted the increasingly accepted conventions BCE (Before the Common Era) instead of BC, and CE (Common Era) for AD. I am aware some readers dislike this newer format, but it is common in research literature. Popular historian Mary Beard is on record in *A Don's Life* (26 September 2011) as stating the convention has been around for years and that about half of the academic papers published on Ancient History display dates in this format – and even the BBC now uses it. The events in Germanicus' life described in this book occur in both eras. Thus, Germanicus was born in 16 BCE (or 16 BC) and died in 19 CE (AD 19).

Romans generally had two names, a personal name (*praenomen*) and a family or clan name (*nomen gentile*); but, from the later days of the Republic, it was becoming common to have three, by adding a nickname (*cognomen*). Victorious commanders in battle might also be granted an honorific title (*agnomen*). Modern historians usually call Romans by their *cognomina* or *agnomina*, the last of the three or more names: hence, 'Caesar' for C. Iulius Caesar, or 'Augustus' for C. Iulius Caesar Augustus. (I have used the proper Roman spelling of Iulius for Julius throughout.) The exception is Germanicus himself. The honorary title he assumed from his father later became his personal name, by which he is known to history. In some cases, the Latin name has mutated into an Anglicism, such as 'Livy' for Livius or 'Pliny' for Plinius. For the names of ancient historians, I use the modern form. For the protagonists in the story, I retain the Latin form – hence, M. Antonius rather than Mark Antony – or the Greek form – thus, Kleopatra for Cleopatra, and Roimetalkes for Rhoemetalces – since this is faithful to the original spelling found on coins and inscriptions, and it respects the names by which they themselves were known in their own time ('The beginning of wisdom', a Chinese saying goes, 'is to call things by their right names'). For the same reason, I use 'Caius' for Gaius and 'Cnaeus' for Gnaeus (British historians seem to have a penchant for spelling these names with the hard mutation, despite what coins and inscriptions of the period show).

By tradition, Roman men and women in extended families often had the same name. Germanicus is a particular example. On the ninth day following his birth, he was named Nero Claudius Drusus, in honour of his father. His father is often called by a variety of names, including Drusus the Elder, Drusus I, Drusus Maior, Drusus Senior, Nero Drusus, Claudius Drusus and Drusus Germanicus, to distinguish him from his nephew of the same name (Drusus the Younger or Drusus Minor) and his grandson Drusus Iulius Caesar. With official adoptions came name changes, which, in the imperial family, often meant assuming the name Iulius Caesar, or just Caesar, as was the case with Germanicus later in his life. The reader will be forgiven for thinking that studying the *Domus Augusta* (the House of Augustus) can quickly become very confusing; it is, even for people intimately familiar with the Roman period. With that in mind, I have tried to use the singular name 'Germanicus' throughout, to refer to the man who is the subject of this biography.

Where a place has a Latin name, I prefer to use it, since the modern name creates a false impression of the scale and feel of the ancient place; hence, Ara Ubiorum rather than Cologne, which is more likely, at this time, to have looked like a town of the American Wild West. In other cases, where the modern place name is unfamiliar to most readers, I use the ancient name, such as Antiocheia on the Orontes (in Roman Syria) rather than Antakya (now in Turkey). Some ancient places have both Latin and Greek names, such as Actium and Aktion, or Laodicea and Loadikeia, in which case I tend to use the Latin form. The exceptions are Athens, Egypt and Rome, because to use Athenae (or Athenai), Aegyptus and Roma would be unnecessarily pedantic. For places whose ancient name is not known, I use the modern name, unless there is a well-known Anglicism. I have listed ancient and modern place names on page 231, for convenience.

The names and places used by the indigenous, so-called Germanic, peoples who sided with or fought against the Romans are only known to us through Greek and Latin writings. A few tribal chieftains and kings are known, but only by Romanized names. We do not know what Arminius of the Cherusci nation was called in his own language, or Marboduus of the Marcomanni. Few Germanic place names survive – though, intriguingly, the geographer Ptolemy lists several, and even offers map co-ordinates for them. While attempts have been made to identify their precise locations, they are, at best, tentative.

The Latin version is used for Roman officer ranks, arms, equipment, and battle formations throughout the text, since there is often no modern equivalent. Definitions of the terms are listed in the Glossary.

The job of a biographer is to present as accurate and unbiased an account – warts and all – of his subject's life as possible, but also to make the story compelling reading. Establishing, checking and interpreting facts makes for an intellectually stimulating journey, as lines of inquiry take one this way or that. Like a detective, asking questions, examining evidence, having an open mind and a willingness to follow the leads wherever they go are the essential prerequisites to successfully solving a case. In the final analysis, however, as one strives to make the man come alive on the page, the writing itself is a lonely endeavour, with the inner voice being both constant companion and sternest critic. I hope the result is a truthful and compelling account of the life of Rome's most popular general and a great human being.

To the shades of Germanicus Iulius Caesar *Imperator*, I present this book. *Ex voto posuit*.

* * *

In advance of the bimillennium of the death of Germanicus Caesar in 2019 I am pleased to be able to correct a few minor errors, which inadvertently appeared in the First Edition, and to add new material into this revised edition.

Lindsay Powell
January 2015
Austin, Texas

Acknowledgements

There are several people who deserve my thanks for helping me with this project. I start with family and friends. My partner, mother, brother and, in particular, my friend Sonia St James (self-styled 'muse to creative minds') have all offered much appreciated encouragement throughout the project: they know how much this new book meant to me. Keeping faithful company with me throughout the project have been Tidus, Auron and Leo, who, when not curled up by my feet on the floor of my office, often tried to make their own creative contributions by variously walking across the keyboard or squatting on the mouse of my computer.

To my commissioning editor, Philip Sidnell, who responded enthusiastically to my proposal for this, my second book for Pen and Sword (a.k.a. 'the sequel to *Eager for Glory*') over lunch at the British Museum, under the spectacular glass and steel roof of the Great Court, and then guided it through to completion, I shall again always be grateful.

I feel very honoured that Philip 'Maty' Matyszak agreed to provide the foreword to *Germanicus*. Maty has a wonderful way of making the history of the ancient world accessible to modern readers. As a life-long classicist and the author of *The Sons of Caesar: Imperial Rome's First Dynasty* (Thames and Hudson, 2006), he is particularly well-qualified to compose the opening remarks. I enjoyed our exchanges by email and have incorporated many of his suggestions. For his kindness, I offer my sincere thanks. To Duncan B. Campbell who patiently edited the volume, I also offer my gratitude.

This book tells the story of Germanicus Caesar in both words and pictures. From the academic community, I must thank David S. Potter, Arthur F. Thurnau Professor of Greek and Latin, Department of Classical Studies, University of Michigan, for permission to use his unpublished translation of the *Tabula Siarensis*. For his assistance in helping me understand the text of the Oxyrhynchus papyrus *P. Oxy.* 2435, I must thank Dominic Rathbone, Professor of Ancient History, Department of Classics, King's College, London, and Chairman of the Oxyrhynchus Papyri Management Committee of the Egypt Exploration Society (EES). Curtis Clay, numismatist at Harlan J. Berk, Ltd, sportingly agreed for me to reproduce his comments published on Forum Ancient Coins' Classical Numismatics Discussion Board. Additionally, Dr Vojislav Divljaković enthusiastically shared his insights into the terrain of his native Croatia, the ancient Illyricum; and William Stavinoha, M.D., of Austin, Texas, very graciously read and corroborated the plausibility of my interpretations of medical issues.

For helping me to illustrate the story, I offer my thanks to Shanna Berk Schmidt of Harlan J. Berk, Ltd, Chicago, and Richard Beale of Roma

Numismatics Limited, London, for kindly providing images of coins. From the re-enactment world, I must thank Chris Haines, MBE, Mike Knowles, and members of The Ermine Street Guard, a registered charity, of which I am proud to say I am a veteran member; and Robert Brosch and the members of Chasuari, for use of their photographs. For images of Roman portrait busts, I express my gratitude to Marie-Lan Nguyen, and to Jasper Oorthuys, editor of the excellent *Ancient Warfare* magazine, published by Karwansaray BV. For permission to reproduce the photograph of *P. Oxy.* 2435, I am grateful to Dr Dirk Obbink of Christ Church, Oxford, and Dr Patricia Spencer at the EES, London.

War stories cannot be told without the aid of maps. I sincerely thank Carlos De La Rocha of Satrapa Ediciones, whose work frequently appears in *Ancient Warfare* magazine, for letting me reproduce his map of Germanicus' military campaigns in Germania. Erin Greb of Erin Greb Cartography did a marvellous job of producing the other maps in like style.

I have quoted extracts from several ancient authors' works whose voices lend authenticity to the narrative. For the translations, I used: Augustus' *Res Gestae*, translated by Thomas Bushnell, BSG, and reproduced with permission (1998); Julius Caesar's *Commentarii de Bello Gallico*, translated by Edward Brooks in *The First Six Books of the Gallic War* (Chicago: The Cenn Publishing Company, 1896); Cassius Dio's Ρωμαϊκὴ Ἱστορία (*Romaikon Istoria*), translated by Herbert Balwin Foster in *Dio's Roman History*, Volume 4 (New York: Pafraets Book Company, 1905), and E. Cary, based on the version by H.B. Foster, in *Dio's Roman History* (London: William Heinemann, 1917); Cicero's *Epistulae*, translated by Evelyn S. Shuckburgh in *The Letters of Cicero: The Whole Extant Correspondence in Chronological Order* (London: George Bell and Sons, 1905); Cicero's *Oratio pro L. Murena*, translated by C.D. Yonge in *The Orations of Marcus Tullius Cicero*, Volume 2 (London: Bell, 1891); Cicero's *Tusculanae Disputationes*, translated by C.D. Yonge in *Cicero's Tusculan Disputations* (New York: Harper and Brothers, 1877); Hippokates' Περί Ἀγμῶν (*Peri Agmon*), translated by Francis Adams in *The Genuine Works of Hippocrates*, Volume 2 (London: Sydenham Society, 1849); Josephus' *Contra Apionem*, translated by William Whiston in *The Genuine Works of Flavius Josephus* (New York: William Borradaile, 1824); Ovid's *Fasti* and *Epistulae Ex Ponto*, translated by Henry T. Riley in *The Fasti, Tristia, Pontic Epistles, Ibis and Haleiuticon of Ovid* (London: Bell and Daldy, 1872); Pliny the Elder's *Naturalis Historia*, translated by John Bostock and H.T. Riley in *The Natural History of Pliny*, Volume 3 (London: Henry Bohn, 1855), and Jonathan Couch, in The Wernerian Club's *Pliny's Natural History* (London: George Barclay, 1848); Pliny the Younger's *Epistulae Selectae*, translated by John Delaware Lewis in *The Letters of the Younger Pliny* (London: Keegan Paul, 1890); Plutarch's Οἱ Βίοι Παράλληλοι (*Oi Vioi Paralliloi*), translated by John Langhorne and William Langhorne in *Plutarch's Lives* (London: William Tegg, 1868); Strabo's Γεωγραφικά (*Geographika*), translated by Horace Leonard Jones in *The Geography of Strabo* (London: William Heinemann, 1930); Suetonius' *De Vitae Caesarum*, translated by Alexander Thomson in *The Lives of the Twelve Caesars* (London: George Bell and Sons, 1893); Tacitus' *Ab Excessu Divi Augusti*

(*Annales*), translated by Alfred John Church and William Jackson Bodribb in *The Annals of Tacitus* (London: MacMillan and Co., 1906); Tacitus' *De Origine et Situ Germanorum*, translated by R.B. Townshend in *The Agricola and Germania of Tacitus* (London: Methuen and Co., 1894); and Velleius Paterculus' *Historiae Romanae*, translated by John Selby in *Sallust, Florus and Velleius Paterculus* (London: George Bell, 1889).

To Noel Sadler who designed the book, and to Matt Jones at Pen & Sword Books who patiently oversaw its production, I also offer my gratitude.

Lastly, my thanks go to Bob Durrett, an enthusiastic and engaging teacher of Latin, who kindly provided the evocative translation of Albinovanus Pedo's poem *in navigante Germanico*, preserved by Seneca the Elder in his *Suasoriae*.

List of Illustrations

3. Bust of Augustus Bevilacqua, inv. 317 in the Glyptothek, Munich. (Photo: Bibi Saint-Pol/Wikimedia Commons)
4. Bronze bust of Tiberius in the Museo Arqueológico Nacional, Madrid. (© Karwansaray B.V.)
5. Basanite bust of Agrippa Postumus, inv. Ma 3498 (MND1961) in the Louvre, Paris. (Photo: Mbzt/Wikimedia Commons)
6. Marble bust of Germanicus, found at Cordova, inv. Ma 3135 (MND 968) in the Louvre, Paris. (© Karwansaray B.V.)
7. Young Germanicus on the Ara Pacis, Rome. (Photo: Author)
8. Marble statue of Agrippina Maior, found at Tinadri, Sicily, inv. NI5660 in the Regional Archaeological Museum of Palermo. (Photo: Marie-Lan Nguyen/Wikimedia Commons)
9. Marble bust of Drusus Iulius Caesar (Drusus the Younger), inv. Ma1240 in the Louvre, Paris. (Photo: Marie-Lan Nguyen/Wikimedia Commons)
10. Bust of Claudius from Lavinium, inv. 243 in the Vatican Museum, Vatican City. (Photo: Marie-Lan Nguyen/Wikimedia Commons)
11. Marble bust of Nero Iulius Caesar in the Museu Nacional Arqueològic de Tarragona. (Photo: Ophelia2/Wikimedia Commons)
12. Marble bust of Caius Iulius Caesar (Caligula) in the Houston Museum of Natural Science. (Photo: Ed Uthman/Wikimedia Commons)
13. Reconstruction of a Roman *legionarius* of the early first century CE. (By permission of The Ermine Street Guard)
14. Reconstruction of a Roman *legionarius* of the early first century CE. (By permission of The Ermine Street Guard)
15. Reconstruction of a Roman *legionarius* of the early first century CE on the march. (By permission of The Ermine Street Guard)
16. Reconstruction of a German warrior of the first century CE. (By permission of Chasuari)
17. Reconstruction of *principales* of the early first century CE. (By permission of The Ermine Street Guard)
18. Scene XXVI from Trajan's Column. (Photo: Conrad Cichorius/Wikimedia Commons)
19. City wall of Salona (Solin), Croatia. (Photo: Marcin Szala/Wikimedia Commons)
20. Vrbas River at Banje Luka, Bosnia-Herzegovina. (Photo: Rade Nagraisalović/Wikimedia Commons)
21. Mount Orjen in the Dinarides, Montenegro. (Photo: Pavle Cikovac/Wikimedia Commons)
22. *Gemma Augustea* in the Kunsthistorisches Museum, Vienna. (Photo: Gryffindor/Wikimedia Commons)
23. *Grand Camée de France* ('Great Cameo of France'), inv. CdM Paris Bab 264 in the Louvre, Paris. (Photo: Marie-Lan Nguyen/Wikimedia Commons)
24. *Gemma Claudia* in the Kunsthistorisches Museum, Vienna. (Photo: Gryffindor/Wikimedia Commons.)
25. View of a forest in autumn in eastern North Rhein-Westfalia, Germany. (Photo: Nikater/Wikimedia Commons)

List of Maps

Chronology

	Bellum Germanicum, phase 1: Drusus launches an attack from Batavodurum against the Sugambri, Tencteri and Usipetes. Takes fleet across Lacus Flevo. Negotiates treaties with the Cananefates, Chauci and Frisii. Navigates the Ems River and defeats the Bructeri in a river battle. On the return journey fleet is marooned on the Dutch coast, but rescued by the Frisii.	
	Drusus returns to Lugdunum, spends winter in Rome.	
	Drusus *praetor urbanus*.	
11 BCE	Drusus and Tiberius receive proconsular *imperium maius*.	5
	Bellum Pannonicum, phase 2: Tiberius campaigns against the alliances of Daesitates, Mezaei in the Dinaric Alps.	
	Bellum Germanicum, phase 2: Drusus returns to Tres Galliae. Drusus launches campaign from Vetera along the Lippe River. Drusus engages the Cherusci, Marsi and Usipetes. Reaches the Weser River. Narrowly avoids defeat at Battle of Arbalo at hands of Cherusci. Drusus acclaimed *Imperator* by his troops (assumed by Augustus). Drusus returns to Lugdunum, spends the winter in Rome. Drusus granted an *ovatio* with triumphal insignia.	
	Tiberius divorces Vipsania, marries Iulia.	
10 BCE	Drusus returns to Lugdunum.	6
	Bellum Pannonicum, phase 3: final conquest by Tiberius.	
	Bellum Germanicum, phase 3: Launches new phase of campaign from Mogontiacum. Defeats the Chatti and Marcomanni.	
	Drusus returns to Lugdunum.	
	Augustus and Tiberius return to Lugdunum.	
August 1	Birth of Drusus' son, Ti. Claudius Nero (future emperor Claudius) in Lugdunum. Dedication of Altar of *Roma et Augustus* in Lugdunum before an assembly of the Gallic tribal leaders.	
	Drusus returns to Rome, probably with Augustus and Tiberius.	
	Drusus granted limited triumphal honours.	

9 BCE–6 CE	Germanicus in Rome.	
9 BCE January 1	Drusus elected *consul* with T. Quinctius Crispinus.	7
January 30	Dedication of *Ara Pacis Augustae* in Rome.	
	Drusus dedicates a Temple of Augustus at Langres.	
	Tiberius in Illyricum. *Bellum Germanicum*, phase 4: Drusus launches second campaign from Mogontiacum.	
mid-August?	Drusus reaches the Elbe River. Spooked by dream of a Germanic ghoul. Erects an altar on the banks of the Elbe River, turns back to the Rhine. Troops witness the Pleides.	
	Drusus falls from his horse in an accident.	
mid-September?	Tiberius rides 200 miles in twenty-four hours by vehicle from Ticinum to join Drusus. Thirty days after the accident, Drusus dies. Drusus' body carried to Ticinum, met by Augustus and Livia, and on to Rome for state funeral. Body is buried in Augustus' Mausoleum.	
	Senate votes Drusus and his male descendants the *agnomen* 'Germanicus', erects statues and a triumphal arch over the *Via Appia*.	
	Rhine legions erect the *Tumulus* (Cenotaph) honouring Drusus ('Eichelstein') in Mogontiacum.	
8 BCE	*Bellum Germanicum*, phase 5: Tiberius in Germania Magna, negotiates a peace settlement with all Germanic tribes. Maelo surrenders, Sugambri relocate to region around Vetera, renamed Cugerni, supplying auxiliary cavalry to Rome.	8

7 BCE	Tiberius consul (2).	9
	Tropaeum Alpium (La Turbie) erected marking the complete subjugation of the Alps.	
	Tiberius celebrates his *ovatio* in Rome for his victory in Germania Magna.	
6 BCE	Tiberius granted *tribunicia potestas* for five years; retires to Rhodes.	10
	Armenian revolt.	
5 BCE	Augustus consul (12).	11
	C. Caesar comes of age, made *princeps iuventutis*.	
4 BCE	Death of Herodes (Herod the Great) in Jericho.	12
3 BCE	Birth of L. Annaeus Seneca (Seneca the Younger) in Cordoba.	13
2 BCE	Augustus consul (13).	14
	Iulia arrested for adultery and treason, exiled to Pandateria. Tiberius divorces Iulia.	
1 BCE March 17 or April 24	Germanicus comes of age, assumes the *toga virilis*.	15
	C. Caesar' mission to the East with *imperium*.	
1 CE	C. Caesar consul.	16
	L. Domitius Ahenobarbus *legatus Augusti pro praetore* of Germania, suppresses revolt, crosses the Elbe, engages Hermunduri and negotiates settlement with Marboduus and the Marcomanni. Establishes an imperial cult altar and his headquarters at Ara Ubiorum.	
2 CE	Tiberius returns to Rome.	17
August 20	Death of L. Caesar at Massalia.	
3 CE	Iulia permitted to relocate to Rhegium.	18
4 CE	Germanicus appointed *frater arvalis*.	19
February 21/22	Death of C. Caesar.	
	Germanicus begins work on translating Aratos' *Phainomaina* into Latin (*Phaenomena*) (?).	
June 27/28	Augustus adopts Tiberius (henceforth Tiberius Iulius Caesar) and Agrippa Postumus (Agrippa Iulius Caesar).	
	Tiberius adopts Germanicus, changes name to Germanicus Iulius Caesar.	
	Tiberius in Germania Magna. C. Sentius Saturninus appointed *legatus Augusti pro praetore* of Germania.	
5 CE	Germanicus marries Vipsania Agrippina.	20
	Tiberius in Germania Magna, reaches the Elbe River.	
	Earthquake strikes Rome. Tiber floods.	
	Famine in Rome.	
6 CE	Famine continues in Rome; fire destroys parts of the city.	21
	Germanicus appointed *augur*.	
	Germanicus and his brother Claudius sponsor games in honour of their father.	
	Birth of Nero Iulius Caesar (Germanicus' first son).	
	Augustus establishes the *aerarium militare* and reforms the army's terms of service.	
	Tiberius and Saturninus launch invasion of Bohaemium, but abort it when forces have to be redeployed to suppress a major revolt in Illyricum (Dalmatia and Pannonia). *Bellum Batonianum*, phase 1 begins.	
Autumn	Agrippa Postumus is abdicated by Augustus and banished to Surrentum.	
7–9 CE	Germanicus in Illyricum.	
7 CE	Germanicus *quaestor*.	22
	Birth of Drusus Iulius Caesar (Germanicus' second son).	
	Bellum Batonianum, phase 2: Tiberius and Germanicus with reserves in Illyricum. Ambush at Mons Claudius. Battle at Volcaean Marshes.	

	Germanicus defeats Mazaei.	
	Agrippa Postumus banished to Planasia.	
Winter	Tiberius in Siscia.	
8 CE	*Bellum Batonianum*, phase 3: Tiberius and Germanicus in Illyricum.	23
	Germanicus sacks Raetinium and Splonum.	
August 3	Bato of the Breuci surrenders at Bathinus River, later captured and murdered by Bato of the Daesitates.	
	Famine in Italy.	
9 CE	Germanicus *praetor*.	24
	Bellum Batonianum, phase 4: Tiberius and Germanicus in Illyricum. Battles at Andetrium and Arduba. Bato of the Daesitates surrenders, revolt squashed. Germanicus acclaimed *Imperator*, granted triumphal ornaments.	
September?	Varus and *Legiones* XVII, XIIX and XIX annihilated in Teutoburg Forest by Germanic forces led by Arminius.	
	Germanicus appointed to command Rhine frontier.	
	Tiberius takes conscripts from Rome to Rhine forts.	

10–12 CE	Germanicus in Rome.	
10 CE	Tiberius in Germania Magna.	25
	Birth and death of T. Iulius Caesar (Germanicus' third son).	
11 CE	Germanicus with Tiberius in Germania Magna on military exercises.	26
	Birth and death of C. Iulius Caesar (Germanicus' fourth son).	
12 CE January 1	Germanicus consul (1) with C. Fonteius Capito.	27
August 31	Birth of C. Iulius Caesar (Caligula, Germanicus' fifth son) in Antium.	
October 23	Tiberius celebrates his full triumph in Rome for victories in Illyricum.	

13–16 CE	Germanicus in Tres Galliae and Germania Magna.	
13 CE	Tiberius' *imperium maius* made equal with Augustus'.	28
	Germanicus made *legatus Augusti pro praetore* in Tres Galliae, Germania Magna.	
	Germanicus puts down an insurrection in Tres Galliae (?), acclaimed *Imperator* (?).	
	Birth and death of unnamed daughter (Germanicus' sixth child) at Ambitarvium.	
14 CE	Census of Rome (4,190,117 recorded citizens).	29
August 19	Death of Augustus at Nola.	
September 17	Tiberius assumes role of *princeps*, aged 56.	
	Agrippa Postumus executed. Germanicus granted proconsular *imperium maius*, and appointed one of the first *Sodales Augustales*.	
	Rhine legions mutiny. Germanicus and Drusus the Younger negotiate a settlement with the legions. Leads men on punitive expedition against the Marsi and Bructeri. Fleet shipwrecked off the Frisian coast.	
	Germanicus' family relocate to the Rhineland (Vetera?/Ara Ubiorum?).	
	Death of Iulia (Tiberius' wife).	
15 CE	Germanicus leads new expedition across the Rhine. Attacks on Marsi, Bructeri, Cherusci and Chatti. *Aquila* of *Legio* XIX recovered. Monument erected and bones buried at Teutoburg battle site. Rescues Segestes, takes Arminius' wife Thusnelda hostage; son Thumelicus born in captivity. Fleet shipwrecked off the Frisian coast, army stranded.	30
	Germanicus acclaimed *Imperator* (2).	
November 7	Birth of Iulia Agrippina Minor (Germanicus' eighth child) in Ara Ubiorum.	
	L. Aelius Seianus becomes sole *praefectus praetorii*.	
16 CE	Germanicus appointed to *Flamines Divorum Augustalis*.	31

Germanicus leads amphibious military expedition via the *fossa Drusiana*.
Sails down Ems River. Engages the Cherusci at battles of Weser River,
Idistaviso and Angrivarian Wall – Arminius flees the field. Roman army
scattered at sea.

Tiberius rejects request for troop surge to complete conquest of Germania.

September 16 Birth of Iulia Drusilla in Abitarvium.

Arch dedicated beside Temple of Saturn in Rome for the two *signa*
recovered from Germania.

17–19 CE	Germanicus tours Eastern Provinces.	

17 CE	Germanicus appointed *pontifex*.	32

May 26 Germanicus celebrates full triumph in Rome, displays Thusnelda and
Thumelicus as trophies.

Birth of Iulia Livilla (Germanicus' ninth child).

Germanicus granted *imperium maius* and appointed *Orienti praepositus*
responsible for the eastern half of the Empire.

Earthquakes destroy twelve cities in Asia Minor.

Exile of Reskuporis.

Revolt of Tacfarinas in Africa.

Germanicus sets off with his entourage.

Sojourns with Drusus the Younger and Livia Drusilla in Dalmatia.

Germanicus visits battle site at Actium; receives conformation of
consulship for 18 CE in Nikopolis.

18 CE Mid- Germanicus competes in a chariot race at Olympia and wins; enters Athens. 33
Summer Germanicus consul (2) with Tiberius.

Cn. Calpurnius Piso appointed *proconsul* of Syria.

Birth of Livilla at Lesbos.

Germanicus visits Byzantium, Black Sea, Illium, Assos, Colophon
(receives omens fortelling his death at Claros) and Rhodes.

Germanicus crowns Zenon-Artaxias III, King of Armenia, at Artaxata and
assigns governors to the new provinces of Cappadocia and
Commagene. Senate grants Germanicus an *ovatio*.

Marboduus of the Marcomanni ousted, seeks and is granted asylum with
the Romans.

Germanicus, Agrippina and Caligula winter in Epidaphnae near
Antiocheia on the Orontes.

19 CE Altercations between Piso and Germanicus. 34
Summer Germanicus in Alexandria. Visits Temple of Aesculapius, Memphis,
receives omens fortelling his death. Visits the Colossi of Memnon at
Thebes. Travels as far as Elephantine and Syene.

Germanicus returns to Syria; discovers Piso has been overturning his
directives and instructions. Germanicus formally revokes friendship
with Piso. Piso quits Syria.

October 10 Germanicus dies in Epidaphnae; body transferred to Antiocheia and
cremated in the forum.

Agrippina departs for Rome with Germanicus' ashes.

December 16 Senate votes posthumous honours for Germanicus.

Riots in Rome.

20 CE Agrippina reaches Brundisium, goes in procession to Rome. Germanicus'
ashes interred in the Mausoleum of Augustus.

Riots in Rome continue until March/April.

Triumphal arches surmounted by statues of Germanicus erected in Rome,
Mogontiacum and Antiocheia. Tumulus erected in Antiocheia.

Death of Vipsania Agrippina.

Arminius assassinated (?).

December 10 Senate delivers its verdict in the trial of Piso for treason and the alleged
murder of Germanicus.

List of Consuls

Year	First consul	Second consul
16 BCE	L. Domitius Ahenobarbus	P. Cornelius Scipio
suff.		L. Tarius Rufus
15	M. Livius Drusus Libo	L. Calpurnius Piso
14	M. Licinius Crassus Frugi	Cn. Cornelius Lentulus Augur
13	Ti. Claudius Nero I	P. Quinctilius Varus
12	M. Valerius Messalla Appianus	P. Sulpicius Quirinius
suff.	C. Valgius Rufus	
suff.	L. Volusius Saturninus	
suff.	C. Caninius Rebilus	
11	Q. Aelius Tubero	Paullus Fabius Maximus
10	Africanus Fabius Maximus	Iullus Antonius
9	Nero Claudius Drusus	T. Quinctius Crispinus Sulpicianus
8	C. Marcius Censorinus	C. Asinius Gallus
7	Ti. Claudius Nero II	Cn. Calpurnius Piso
6	D. Laelius Balbus	C. Antistius Vetus
5	Imp. Caesar Divi f. Augustus XII	L. Cornelius Sulla
suff.	L. Vinicius	Q. Haterius
suff.	C. Sulpicius Galba	
4	C. Calvisius Sabinus	L. Passienus Rufus
suff.	C. Caelius (Rufus?)	Galus Sulpicius
3	L. Cornelius Lentulus	M. Valerius Messalla Messallinus
2	Imp. Caesar Divi f. Augustus XIII	M. Plautius Silvanus
suff.	C. Fufius Geminus	L. Caninius Gallus
suff.	Q. Fabricius	
1 BCE	Cossus Cornelius Lentulus	L. Calpurnius Piso
suff.	A. Plautius	A. Caecina Severus
1 CE	C. Iulius Caesar	L. Aemilius Paullus
suff.		M. Herennius Picens
2	P. Vinicius	P. Alfenus Varus
suff.	P. Cornelius Lentulus Scipio	T. Quinctius Crispinus Valerianus
3	L. Aelius Lamia	M. Servilius
suff.	P. Silius	L. Volusius Saturninus
4	Sex. Aelius Catus	C. Sentius Saturninus
suff.	C. Clodius Licinus	Cn. Sentius Saturninus

5		L. Valerius Messalla Volesus	Cn. Cornelius Cinna Magnus
	suff.	C. Vibius Postumus	C. Ateius Capito
6		M. Aemilius Lepidus	L. Arruntius
	suff.		L. Nonius Asprenas
7		Q. Caecilius Metellus Creticus Silanus	A. Licinius Nerva Silianus
	suff.		Lucilius Longus
8		M. Furius Camillus	Sex. Nonius Quinctilianus
	suff.	L. Apronius	A. Vibius Habitus
9		C. Poppaeus Sabinus	Q. Sulpicius Camerinus
	suff.	Q. Poppaeus Secundus	M. Papius Mutilus
10		P. Cornelius Dolabella	C. Iunius Silanus
	suff.	Ser. Cornelius Lentulus Maluginensis	Q. Iunius Blaesus
11		M'. Aemilius Lepidus	T. Statilius Taurus
	suff.	L. Cassius Longinus	
12		Germanicus Iulius Caesar	C. Fonteius Capito
	suff.		C. Visellius Varro
13		C. Silius A. Caecina Largus	L. Munatius Plancus
14		Sex. Pompeius	Sex. Appuleius
15		Drusus Iulius Caesar (January–December)	C. Norbanus Flaccus (January–June)
	suff.	M. Iunius Silanus (July–December)	
16		Sisenna Statilius Taurus	L. Scribonius Libo
	suff.	P. Pomponius Graecinus	C. Vibius Rufus
17		L. Pomponius Flaccus	C. Caelius Rufus
	suff.	C. Vibius Marsus	L. Voluseius Proculus
18		Ti. Caesar Augustus III (January)	Germanicus Iulius Caesar II (January–April)
	suff.	L. Seius Tubero (February–July)	Livineius Regulus (May–July)
	suff.	C. Rubellius Blandus (August–December)	M. Vipstanus Gallus (August–December)
19		M. Iunius Silanus Torquatus (January–December)	L. Norbanus Balbus (January–April)
	suff.	P. Petronius (May–December)	
20		M. Valerius Messala Barbatus Messalinus	M. Aurelius Cotta Maximus Messalinus

suff. = Suffect Consul.

Roman Names

M. Caelius T. f. Lemonia Bononia

This is the official name of a centurion of *legio* XIIX preserved on an inscription, now in the Rheinisches Landesmuseum in Bonn, Germany (*CIL* 13.8648. *ILS* 2244). His name embodies the elements of Roman naming practice. It translates as 'Marcus Caelius, son of Titus, of the voting tribe of Lemonia, from Bononia'. Marcus is his forename (*praenomen*) by which his family and close friends called him. In inscriptions, public records and narrative texts, it was abbreviated. The standard abbreviations for common *praenomina* were:

A.	Aulus	M'.	Manius
Ap.	Appius	P	Publius
C. or G.	Caius or Gaius	Q	Quintus
Cn. or Gn.	Cnaeus or Gnaeus	Ser	Servius
D.	Decimus	Sex	Sextus
L.	Lucius	Sp.	Spurius
M.	Marcus	T.	Titus
Mam.	Mamius	Ti.	Tiberius

Caelius is his clan or family name (*nomen gentile*). Many of these clans such as the Claudia and Cornelia were famous old families of Rome with proud traditions. Then follows the filiation or patronymic of the father's *praenomen*, whose full name would have been Titus Caelius. As a Roman citizen, his family was associated with one of thirty-five voting tribes: in elections, Caelius voted with the Lemonian tribe. The final element is the place of his birth (*origo*) or domicile (*domus*), which is, in this case, Bononia, modern Bologna in Italy. Together, these distinguished this particular Marcus Caelius from another bearing the same name. To clearly tell men apart with the same name, with their warped sense of humour, Romans often adopted a third nickname (*cognomen*) such as Rufus ('red haired'), Paulus ('shorty') or Brutus ('stupid'). Men who had achieved great victories in war might be granted use of an honorific title *agnomen* such as Africanus ('the African' or 'of Africa') or Britannicus ('the Briton' or 'of Britannia'), indicating where it was won.

The House of Germanicus
(*Domus Germanici*)

Nero Claudius Drusus = Antonia Minor   Marcus Vipsanius Agrippa = Iulia Maior
(Posthumously *Drusus Germanicus*)   (Cos. 37, 33, 31 BCE)
Cos. 9 BCE

Germanicus Iulius Caesar = *Vispania Agrippina Maior*
(Née *Nero Claudius Drusus*)
Cos. 12, 18 CE

| Nero Iulius Caesar = Iulia Livia (Iulilla) | Drusus Iulius Caesar = Aemilia Lepida | Tiberius Iulius Caesar d. 10 CE | Caius Iulius Caesar d. 11 CE | Caius Iulius Caesar (Caligula, emperor) = 1. Iunia Claudilla 2. Livia Orestilla 3. Lollia Paulina 4. Milonia Caesonia | Unnamed Daughter d. 13 CE | Agrippina Minor = 1. Cnaeus Domitius Ahenobarbus 2. Tiberius Claudius Nero (Germanicus' brother and emperor) | Iulia Drusilla = 1. Lucius Cassius 2. Marcus Aemilius Lepidus | Iulia Livilla = Marcus Vinicius |

Stemma Drusorum

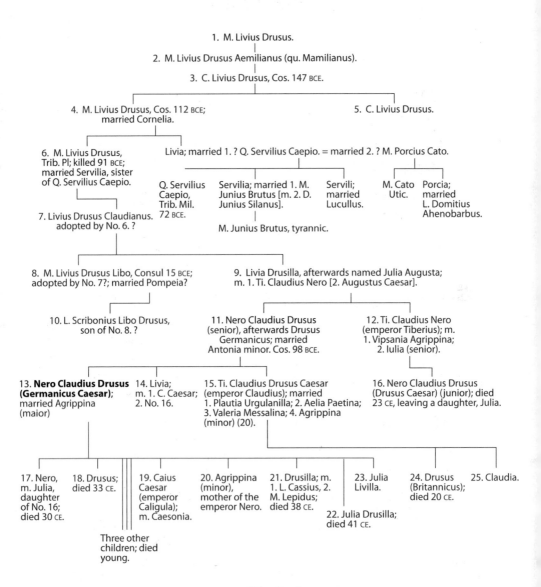

1. M. Livius Drusus.
2. M. Livius Drusus Aemilianus (qu. Mamilianus).
3. C. Livius Drusus, Cos. 147 BCE.

4. M. Livius Drusus, Cos. 112 BCE; married Cornelia.

5. C. Livius Drusus.

6. M. Livius Drusus, Trib. Pl; killed 91 BCE; married Servilia, sister of Q. Servilius Caepio.

Livia; married 1. ? Q. Servilius Caepio. = married 2. ? M. Porcius Cato.

Q. Servilius Caepio, Trib. Mil. 72 BCE.

Servilia; married 1. M. Junius Brutus [m. 2. D. Junius Silanus].

Servili; married Lucullus.

M. Cato Utic.

Porcia; married L. Domitius Ahenobarbus.

7. Livius Drusus Claudianus. adopted by No. 6. ?

M. Junius Brutus, tyrannic.

8. M. Livius Drusus Libo, Consul 15 BCE; adopted by No. 7?; married Pompeia?

9. Livia Drusilla, afterwards named Julia Augusta; m. 1. Ti. Claudius Nero [2. Augustus Caesar].

10. L. Scribonius Libo Drusus, son of No. 8. ?

11. Nero Claudius Drusus (senior), afterwards Drusus Germanicus; married Antonia minor. Cos. 98 BCE.

12. Ti. Claudius Nero (emperor Tiberius); m. 1. Vipsania Agrippina; 2. Iulia (senior).

13. **Nero Claudius Drusus (Germanicus Caesar);** married Agrippina (maior)

14. Livia; m. 1. C. Caesar; 2. No. 16.

15. Ti. Claudius Drusus Caesar (emperor Claudius); married 1. Plautia Urgulanilla; 2. Aelia Paetina; 3. Valeria Messalina; 4. Agrippina (minor) (20).

16. Nero Claudius Drusus (Drusus Caesar) (junior); died 23 CE, leaving a daughter, Julia.

17. Nero, m. Julia, daughter of No. 16; died 30 CE.

18. Drusus; died 33 CE.

19. Caius Caesar (emperor Caligula); m. Caesonia.

20. Agrippina (minor), mother of the emperor Nero.

21. Drusilla; m. 1. L. Cassius, 2. M. Lepidus; died 38 CE.

23. Julia Livilla.

24. Drusus (Britannicus); died 20 CE.

25. Claudia.

22. Julia Drusilla; died 41 CE.

Three other children; died young.

Other Drusi:

26. D. Drusus, Consul suffectus 137 BCE. ? (Dig. 1. tit. 13. g- 2.)
27. C. Drusus, historian. (Suet. *Augustus*, 94.)

Stemma Claudiorum
(Father's side)

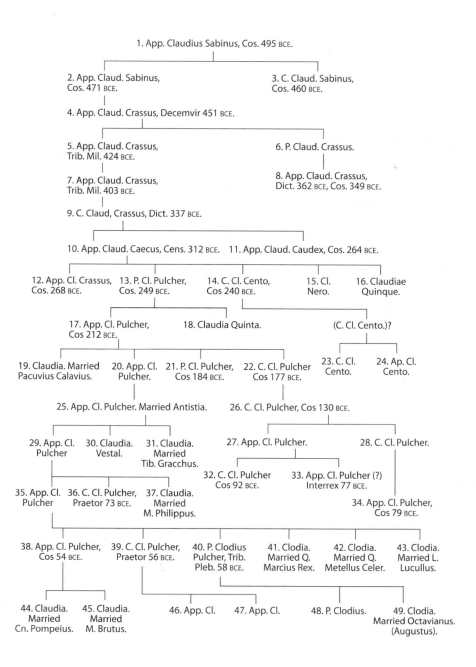

1. App. Claudius Sabinus, Cos. 495 BCE.

2. App. Claud. Sabinus, Cos. 471 BCE.

3. C. Claud. Sabinus, Cos. 460 BCE.

4. App. Claud. Crassus, Decemvir 451 BCE.

5. App. Claud. Crassus, Trib. Mil. 424 BCE.

6. P. Claud. Crassus.

7. App. Claud. Crassus, Trib. Mil. 403 BCE.

8. App. Claud. Crassus, Dict. 362 BCE, Cos. 349 BCE.

9. C. Claud, Crassus, Dict. 337 BCE.

10. App. Claud. Caecus, Cens. 312 BCE.   11. App. Claud. Caudex, Cos. 264 BCE.

12. App. Cl. Crassus, Cos. 268 BCE.

13. P. Cl. Pulcher, Cos. 249 BCE.

14. C. Cl. Cento, Cos 240 BCE.

15. Cl. Nero.

16. Claudiae Quinque.

17. App. Cl. Pulcher, Cos 212 BCE.

18. Claudia Quinta.

(C. Cl. Cento.)?

19. Claudia. Married Pacuvius Calavius.

20. App. Cl. Pulcher.

21. P. Cl. Pulcher, Cos 184 BCE.

22. C. Cl. Pulcher Cos 177 BCE.

23. C. Cl. Cento.

24. Ap. Cl. Cento.

25. App. Cl. Pulcher. Married Antistia.

26. C. Cl. Pulcher, Cos 130 BCE.

29. App. Cl. Pulcher

30. Claudia. Vestal.

31. Claudia. Married Tib. Gracchus.

27. App. Cl. Pulcher.

28. C. Cl. Pulcher.

32. C. Cl. Pulcher Cos 92 BCE.

33. App. Cl. Pulcher (?) Interrex 77 BCE.

34. App. Cl. Pulcher, Cos 79 BCE.

35. App. Cl. Pulcher

36. C. Cl. Pulcher, Praetor 73 BCE.

37. Claudia. Married M. Philippus.

38. App. Cl. Pulcher, Cos 54 BCE.

39. C. Cl. Pulcher, Praetor 56 BCE.

40. P. Clodius Pulcher, Trib. Pleb. 58 BCE.

41. Clodia. Married Q. Marcius Rex.

42. Clodia. Married Q. Metellus Celer.

43. Clodia. Married L. Lucullus.

44. Claudia. Married Cn. Pompeius.

45. Claudia. Married M. Brutus.

46. App. Cl.

47. App. Cl.

48. P. Clodius.

49. Clodia. Married Octavianus. (Augustus).

Stemma Antoniorum (Mother's Side)

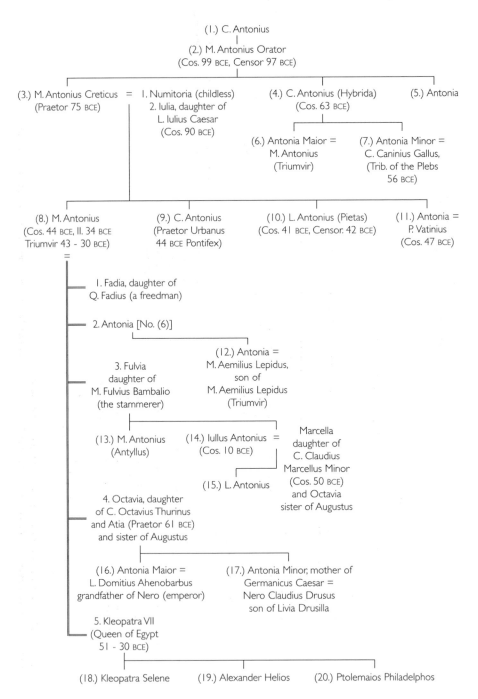

(1.) C. Antonius

(2.) M. Antonius Orator
(Cos. 99 BCE, Censor 97 BCE)

(3.) M. Antonius Creticus = 1. Numitoria (childless)
(Praetor 75 BCE)   2. Iulia, daughter of
                        L. Iulius Caesar
                        (Cos. 90 BCE)

(4.) C. Antonius (Hybrida)
(Cos. 63 BCE)

(5.) Antonia

(6.) Antonia Maior =
M. Antonius
(Triumvir)

(7.) Antonia Minor =
C. Caninius Gallus,
(Trib. of the Plebs
56 BCE)

(8.) M. Antonius
(Cos. 44 BCE, II. 34 BCE
Triumvir 43 - 30 BCE)
=

(9.) C. Antonius
(Praetor Urbanus
44 BCE Pontifex)

(10.) L. Antonius (Pietas)
(Cos. 41 BCE, Censor. 42 BCE)

(11.) Antonia =
P. Vatinius
(Cos. 47 BCE)

1. Fadia, daughter of
Q. Fadius (a freedman)

2. Antonia [No. (6)]

3. Fulvia
daughter of
M. Fulvius Bambalio
(the stammerer)

(12.) Antonia =
M. Aemilius Lepidus,
son of
M. Aemilius Lepidus
(Triumvir)

(13.) M. Antonius
(Antyllus)

(14.) Iullus Antonius =
(Cos. 10 BCE)

Marcella
daughter of
C. Claudius
Marcellus Minor
(Cos. 50 BCE)
and Octavia
sister of Augustus

(15.) L. Antonius

4. Octavia, daughter
of C. Octavius Thurinus
and Atia (Praetor 61 BCE)
and sister of Augustus

(16.) Antonia Maior =
L. Domitius Ahenobarbus
grandfather of Nero (emperor)

(17.) Antonia Minor, mother of
Germanicus Caesar =
Nero Claudius Drusus
son of Livia Drusilla

5. Kleopatra VII
(Queen of Egypt
51 - 30 BCE)

(18.) Kleopatra Selene

(19.) Alexander Helios

(20.) Ptolemaios Philadelphos

The Step-Children of Augustus

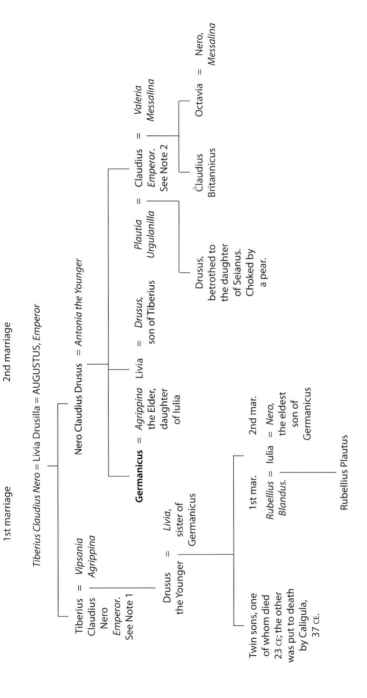

1st marriage

2nd marriage

Tiberius Claudius Nero = Livia Drusilla = AUGUSTUS, *Emperor*

Nero Claudius Drusus = *Antonia the Younger*

Tiberius = *Vipsania Agrippina*
Claudius
Nero
Emperor.
See Note 1

Drusus = *Livia,*
the Younger   sister of
Germanicus

Twin sons, one
of whom died
23 CE; the other
was put to death
by Caligula,
37 CE.

Germanicus = *Agrippina
the Elder,
daughter
of Iulia*

Livia = *Drusus,*
son of Tiberius

1st mar.   2nd mar.

Rubellius = Iulia = *Nero,*
Blandus.   the eldest
son of
Germanicus

Rubellius Plautus

*Plautia
Urgulanilla*
=
Claudius
Emperor.
See Note 2
=
*Valeria
Messalina*

Drusus,
betrothed to
the daughter
of Seianus.
Choked by
a pear.

Claudius
Britannicus

Octavia = Nero,
Messalina

Note 1 – Tiberius was also married to Iulia, the daughter of Augustus.
Note 2 – Claudius was also married to Aelia Paetina and to his niece Agrippina the Younger, daughter of his brother Germanicus.

He was so deeply respected and loved by all his acquaintances that Augustus (to say nothing of the rest of his relatives) wondered for a long time whether to make him his successor...

Suetonius, *Lives of the Caesars, Caligula* 4.1.

Chapter 1

In the Name of the Father

16 BCE–5 CE

The Legacy

The eyes stared back at him coldly and unblinking.[1] The young boy studied the face closely. He recognized in it the features of his father. It was his *imago*, the mask that had been made of him while he was alive, preserving every line and detail of his handsome visage.[2] It was attached to a life-size manequin of the man, dressed in his finest clothes and lying on the funeral bier, which the pallbearers had just placed on the raised speakers' platform in the Forum Romanum in front of the Senate House.[3] The man being honoured was Nero Claudius Drusus (*Stemma Drusorum*, no. 11, plate 1), war hero and consul of the Romans. His seven-year-old son watched the event intently, as he sat in his little *toga* on an uncomfortably hard chair. He was in the front row, sitting among the family and important guests assembled below the *Rostra*.[4] Beside him, his mother Antonia Minor (plate 2), dressed in a black *stola*, fought to hold back the tears. Next to her, a teary trail glistened upon the soft skin of his grandmother Livia Drusilla's cheek. His little sister and other relations were there, too – all except grand-stepfather. Augustus (plate 3) – the inheritor of Iulius Caesar's name and legacy – was waiting for them in the Campus Martius, a couple of miles away, as ancient custom and statute law forbade him, as the head of state in a time of war, to cross the sacred boundary line (*pomerium*) and enter the city.[5]

Seated among the mourners on this chilly winter's day were the *imagines* of the boy's Claudian ancestors and those of the Julian stepfamily. They were worn by male actors dressed in the attire their deceased hosts had worn in life.[6] They had been taken out of the display cabinets (*armariae*) and brought together on this sad day to welcome Drusus the Elder on his journey to the Elysian Fields, their home in paradise across the Styx.[7] Some actors used gestures of the arms, seeming to bring the ancestors dramatically back to life. Stretching out beyond them in the Forum Romanum, from one side of the ancient market place to the other, and from every vantage point in the old court-houses and temples, people of each class of Roman society stood, pressed shoulder to shoulder, eager to see. Seeing the bier (*lectus*) resting on the *Rostra*, the chattering crowd fell silent. This was a day no one had hoped to see – or, at least, so soon.

Some said the signs had been there all along. Omens had warned Drusus not to go to Germania Magna at the start of that year, which bore his and his co-consul's names, but in his eagerness for glory he did not heed them.[8] After a campaign lasting four years, he had finally reached the Elbe River in the summer. Then tragedy struck. While leading his men back to the Rhine River, he had fallen from his horse, his leg having been crushed by his steed when it collapsed on him, and he had died a month later from the ensuing fever.[9] When he perished, consul Drusus was just 29 years old. His body had been carried upon the shoulders of tribunes and centurions of his legions, from deep inside the forests of Germania Magna to the fortress of Mogontiacum, and then upon those of countless *duoviri* and aediles of the cities of Tres Galliae and Italia.[10] At Colonia Copia Munata Felix, the foremost city of the Gauls, which had been Drusus' headquarters for the last five years, Antonia and the family had joined the solemn march. Leading the cortège had been the boy's Uncle Tiberius. In an extraordinary display of brotherly devotion (*pietas*), he had walked every step of the way, from the encampment the soldiers called *Castra Scelerata*, the 'accursed camp', where Drusus had died, to his resting place in Rome.[11]

Tiberius (*Stemma Drusorum*, no. 12, plate 4) now mounted the platform and spoke the *laudatio fenebris*.[12] Young Nero sat quietly, watching and listening to the man who idolized his father. In his practised oratory, Tiberius eulogized his fallen brother, lauding his achievements as a statesman, commander and father, perhaps using similar words to those later written by the poet Ovid:

> To Germania did Drusus owe his title and his death:
> woe's me! that all that goodness should be so short-lived![13]

The crowd applauded his practised declamations and gestures. Many were visibly moved to tears. When Tiberius concluded his speech, he turned and approached the family, embracing each affectionately. It was now time to set off for the concluding part of the ceremony. Following his Uncle Tiberius, the little boy slipped his hand into his mother's and together they walked past the speaker's platform to the broad cobbled stones of the *Via Sacra*. When the 'ancestors' had remounted their waiting chariots, the procession left the Forum.[14] Despite the pathos of the occasion, represented by the hired mourners who tore at their hair and wailed melodramatically, there was a carnival atmosphere, with gaudy clowns making ribald remarks about the deceased consul for the crowd's amusement; men carrying placards bearing phrases and remarks for which Drusus was known; while musicians and dancers displayed their artistic talents.[15]

From the base of the Capitolinus Hill the twisting *Via Lata* became the straight *Via Flaminia* which ran to the Campus Martius. Crowds lined the way.[16] Some, understanding the historic significance of the day, cried as the hearse passed by, while others applauded as they saw Antonia and her son. Flanking the bier, a detail of twelve lictors – each hand-picked by Drusus and dressed respectfully in black – sloped their *fasces*, the bundle of axes and rods that was the distinctive badge of the bodyguard of the state's highest ranking magistrate.[17] In recognition of the death of the consul, their *fasces* were ceremonially reversed.[18] Stopping at the *Circus Flaminius* – the largest building outside the *pomerium* able to hold such a great crowd – Augustus gave a speech in honour of Drusus. It was a very personal eulogy. He spoke in glowing terms of the man who was his stepson. Here was a Roman in the best tradition, he said. Drusus was a bold and fearless warrior. He was a man who had devoted his whole life to the service of the commonwealth. Augustus beseeched the gods 'to make his Caesars like him, and to grant himself as honourable an exit out of this world as they had given him'.[19] The crowd applauded warmly. Then the procession re-assembled and continued on the *Via Flaminia* past the *Ara Pacis*, which had only been consecrated months before, and where in life Drusus had been a honoured guest.[20] Finally, the long line of the colourful courtege arrived at the *ustrinum*, an enclosure located beside Augustus' mausoleum. At its centre was a pyre (rogus) built to resemble an altar with panels painted with garlands of oak leaves.[21] The *princeps* was waiting there and greeted Livia, Tiberius and Antonia. He embraced each one and exchanged some comforting words. To console young Nero, he bent down and placed his hand affectionately on the boy's shoulder. The family then took their designated places before the pyre. The crowd had already assembled a safe distance away, held back by Augustus' Praetorian Cohorts dressed resplendently in their parade armour.

Drusus' decomposing body lay inside a casket on a lower shelf of the bier, and the whole wooden apparatus was now carefully lifted up on the pyre. Antonia said a final, personal farewell. The close members of the family then took turns to throw onto the pyre some of Drusus' favourite things – items from his youth and adulthood, from his family and military life, which he could take with him to the underworld.[22] The family quietly and solemnly stood well back, away from the wooden platform. Presented with a burning torch, Tiberius grasped it firmly with his right hand, lifted it high for all to see, turned about, and thrust it into the pyre. The kindling quickly spat and crackled as flames licked the combustible material. Soon the *ustrinum* was engulfed by fire and curls of acrid black smoke filled the air, rising high above the mourning crowd, where it was blown away by the cold breeze.

Hours passed. When the embers had cooled, the ashes were gathered up, sprinkled with oil and placed in an urn. In a private ceremony, Augustus turned and led the family inside the double door of the mausoleum, and walked solemnly down the dark, high vaulted corridor, the way ahead lit by the flickering light of oil lamps. Standing among the shifting shadows, young Nero watched as his mother carefully placed the urn in one of the niches that had been prepared for him. Above it was a verse composed by the *princeps* himself as a fond tribute to his stepson. The boy's father had finally reached his resting place. *Pater, ave atque vale!*

A few days later – and quite unprompted – the Senate decreed civic honours for Nero Claudius Drusus.[23] An arch of marble was to be erected, which would straddle the *Via Appia*, and statues were to be erected in public places. His peers also voted him a unique *agnomen*, a battle honour which encapsulated his military achievements in a single word that would forever after be a key part of his name: *Germanicus*. It meant simply 'The German', but it conveyed the powerful and emotive image of the great Roman military commander as victor over savage warriors in the wild and untamed land of rivers, swamps and forests of far away

Germania Magna. Significantly, the Senate voted that his surviving sons should be able to inherit the unique war title.

* * *

The boy who would become known through history simply as Germanicus was born nine days before the Kalends of June, on 24 May 16 BCE, probably in Rome (fig. 1).[24] On the ninth day after birth, a cleansing ritual (*lustratio*) was carried out to offer thanks to the gods for his good health, and he was given his father's name, Nero Claudius Drusus. At the time, his father was a junior magistrate and, being based in the city, was able to spend time with his newborn son during the early months of his life. The first of many separations, however, occurred towards the end of the first year, when Drusus the Elder was called to Colonia Copia Munatia Felix Lugdunum to meet his stepfather Augustus and brother Tiberius to discuss a military campaign.[25] Up to that time, he had not yet served as a soldier, and this campaign would provide him with the opportunity to gain the military experience required for his higher political career. The following spring, Drusus led an expeditionary force through the Alps, squashed the Raeti, who had harassed Roman settlements and traders in northern Italy for years, and, with the assistance of his brother, subjugated the Vindelici and annexed the Kingdom of Noricum, in a whirlwind campaign that was celebrated by the court poet Horace.[26] Drusus was rewarded for his skilful leadership by Augustus with a praetorship and the position of *legatus Augusti pro praetore* in charge of the Tres Provinciae Galliae ('Three Gallic Provinces').[27] Soon after, Antonia relocated from Rome to the provincial capital with young Nero Drusus. There, they took up residence in the *praetorium*, a modestly appointed, palatial-sized building designed by Augustus' friend and a former governor of Gaul, M. Agrippa, as a home away from Rome.[28] Already installed there were his grandparents, Augustus and Livia.

Drusus the Elder proved to be an able administrator, but it was his newly-minted military skills that were now pressed into action. Augustus had ambitions for conquering Germania Magna, the great sweep of land across the Rhine that was home to a myriad of warrior nations who often casually raided Roman territory for rich pickings. The most daring of these invasions had occurred in 17 BCE, when an alliance of three tribes led by Maelo of the Sugambri swept deep into Gallia Belgica and overwhelmed *Legio* V *Alaudae*, taking its prized *aquila* standard in the ensuing conflict.[29] It was the catalyst for a complete re-evaluation of Rome's strategy for the north-western frontier and was the reason for Augustus' and Tiberius' visit to Gaul. Between 14 and 13 BCE, Drusus the Elder oversaw the largest build-out of military infrastructure of the period, including the establishment of five substantial legionary fortresses along the Rhine, with several smaller auxiliary forts, and a canal system linking the river to Lacus Flevo (formerly the Zuiderzee).[30] Commencing in 12 BCE, Drusus led a series of annual campaigns by sea and land that systematically annexed Germania Magna eastwards from the shores of the North Sea.

Figure 1. Young Germanicus as imagined for *Wedgwood's Catalogue of Cameos, Intaglios, Medals, Bas-Reliefs, Busts and Small Statues* of 1787.

As campaigning seasons began in the spring and ended in late summer, Drusus was able to return to the Gallic provincial capital and spend several months there with his wife and son. Drusus generally sojourned in Rome during the winter, and the family almost certainly travelled with him. Drusus was in the city in 11 BCE, where he gave the eulogy at the funeral of his aunt Octavia, Augustus' sister.[31]

Two years later, while in Rome on a cold 30 January 9 BCE – Livia's birthday – young Nero took part in the consecration of the *Ara Pacis Augustae*, a great altar erected to honour the personification of the *Pax Augusta*, the world peace made possible by Augustus.[32] It had been commissioned by the Senate on 4 July 13 BCE and had taken three and a half years to build.[33] Erected outside the *pomerium* of the ancient city, in the Campus Martius west of the *Via Flaminia*, it stood on the floodplain of the Tiber River.[34] Carved from gleaming white marble, measuring 11.6m (38ft) by 10.6m (35ft), the altar is considered to be one of the architectural masterpieces of the Augustan age.[35] The altar proper stands on a raised podium within a sacred enclosure in the style of a *templum*. A single opening measuring 3.6m (12ft) wide, approached by ten steps on the west side, allows access to the altar.[36] On the exterior wall of the enclosure, above a lower panel decorated with volutes of acanthus, a procession is depicted in half-relief. The good and the great of Rome are shown here: the Vestal Virgins, the *Pontifex Maximus*, members of the priestly colleges and their retinue of religious attendants, the consuls accompanied by *lictores* with their ceremonial bundles of axes and rods, and many other state officials. Following them are men, women and children who are Augustus' friends and family.[37] The procession is shown on both sides of the external north and south walls flanking the entrance, and forms a single line seen from opposite sides, so that the participants move towards the steps at the front of the altar. The figures are life-size and appear to be the individual likenesses of the actual participants in the event. The frieze is a snapshot, a virtual newsreel, of members of the imperial family celebrating a religious rite on the First Lady's birthday. Among the group at the front of the line is Augustus, shown as *Pontifex Maximus*. Further down stands his close friend and son-in-law, M. Vipsanius Agrippa, clutching a scroll in his right hand. His head is respectfully covered with his toga, perhaps recognizing the fact of his death, which occurred while the frieze was being carved. Behind him is Augustus' wife, Livia Drusilla, whose hand rests upon the head of a young girl.[38] Following her is Tiberius, with a stern look on his face, wearing a *toga* and the ankle-length closed boots of a high-status Roman. After him, Antonia Minor pauses to listen to her husband, Drusus the Elder, who stands at ease behind her. He wears the *paludamentum*, the cloak of a commanding officer, over his left shoulder, and *caligae*, the sturdy boots worn by soldiers, clearly identifying him as a military man. Antonia herself holds the right hand of a very young, well-behaved boy (plate 7), who wears child-size national Roman costume of *tunica* and *toga*.[39] He looks comfortable on this public occasion and is quite unfazed by the gathering of so many major celebrities. He stands facing the viewer full on, but his head is turned slightly to the right, staring out and slightly up. He seems to be concentrating on something in the distance. Around his neck he wears a distinctive *bulla*, the small, round, golden amulet worn by every Roman boy until manhood. This is probably young Nero Claudius Drusus – the future Germanicus – in the earliest depiction of him from life.

What kind of father Drusus was, the ancient sources do not explicitly say, but they consistently describe him as an amiable, respectful and popular man.[40] The evidence indicates that he was sexually faithful to his wife, and keen to establish a family in the best Roman tradition.[41] Nero was very likely not their first child, however. As was common in the ancient world, the infant mortality rate was high. Drusus and Antonia Minor, who married in 18 BCE, may already have tried several times to have children, and some of their issue are recorded as not surviving.[42]

Impatient for progress on the Germanic front, in 9 BCE Drusus set off for Mogontiacum on the Rhine, apparently leaving his family behind. It proved to be a break-through year, with the Roman army finally reaching the Elbe River, which had been an elusive objective for the past four campaigning seasons; but that victory was won at terrible cost. The moment his father died, the young boy called Nero assumed a heady legacy: his father's reputation as a valiant commander (*imperator*), as a fearless challenger for his opponent's rich spoils (*spolia opima*), as a champion of traditional Roman values (*mores maiorum*) and as an upholder of the commonwealth (*res publica*). It was a lot for the diminutive shoulders of a boy of just seven years old to take on. Yet take it on he did. Drusus' son, perhaps at his own request, now changed his *praenomen* from Nero to the honorary *agnomen* Germanicus. Young and small he might have been, but he clearly wanted to publicly celebrate the memory of his illustrious father by taking the name for his own. From that moment on, he would be known as Germanicus Claudius Drusus.

The Early Years

In the absence of his father, Germanicus was raised by his mother. Antonia Minor (Antonia the Younger, *Stemma Antoniorum*, no. 17) was the daughter of Augustus' former friend turned foe. She was born in Athens on 31 January 36 BCE, the child of M. Antonius and Octavia, the sister of Augustus.[43] When Antonius divorced Octavia in 32 BCE, the 4-year-old girl went with her mother and was brought up with the support of her uncle and aunt, Augustus and Livia. She married Drusus the Elder when she was 18 years old, which was later than many of her peers, who were married off in their early teens; but, by then, she had amassed considerable wealth through inheritances, owning property in Egypt, Greece and Italy. Like her mother before her, by reputation, she was a woman of moral virtue and great charm, and portrait busts of the period identified as her attest to her delicate feminine beauty.[44] As a mother, she took an active interest in her children's upbringing. Germanicus' early learning occurred through supervised play, probably in the care of slaves or freedmen and their children. A well-to-do Roman boy had many toys to play with: bricks, with which to build toy houses or forts, a hobby-horse, a hoop and top, and a wooden sword. He also played games with marbles, nuts and counters, or tossed coins, shouting 'Heads' or 'Ships' – a reference to the early images on the obverse and reverse of Rome's early bronze coinage.[45]

While in Rome, Augustus also took an active interest in the education of the young man. As effective head of state, he strove to set an example as a family man. When he dined with his family, he insisted that his adopted sons and grandsons recline beside him on his couch, and when they travelled with him, they rode in the carriage in front or on either side of his.[46] He actively taught all his grandsons how to read and write, showing them how to copy his handwriting, and drilled into them a liking for health and fitness by teaching them to swim.[47] From the age of six or seven, a *litterator* (typically an educated slave or freedman or Greek) was employed for the more tedious parts of a high-status boy's formative training. Learning by rote was the norm for Roman students. They mastered reading and writing by copying passages from the great poets – for example, Ennius in Latin or Homer in Greek – and the rudiments of arithmetic, using the cumbersome Roman number system and the abacus.

Germanicus' education also involved learning about his ancestors, and how each had lived his life in accordance with the several virtues that defined the Roman character. This code of personal ethics underpinned a citizen's ability to fully participate in Roman society. Chief among these was *virtus*, the expectation that a man should display courage, or manliness, in difficult times and when facing tough decisions – it is the origin of the English word 'virtue'. Other valued behaviours were *clementia*, the ability to show mercy; *dignitas*, the virtue of taking pride in oneself; *firmitas*, tenacity or strength of mind; *frugalitas*, living the simple life without being miserly; *gravitas*, the sense of seriousness and responsibility with which a man approached an issue; *honestas*, the projection of a respectable image in society; *industria*, the value of working hard; *pietas*, the respect for the natural order of things, including loyalty to one's country; *prudentia*, the foresight and wisdom gained from personal experience or that of others; *salubritas*, the belief in wholesomeness and cleanliness; *severitas*, the ability to maintain self-control; and *veritas*, the belief in the value of truth over falsehood. Roman citizens were also expected to live up to a set of publicly shared virtues, among which were *aequitas*, the belief that it was morally right to act fairly within government and with the people; *fides*, that in all dealings a man should act in good faith; *iustitia*, that citizens should expect justice and fair treatment before the law; *libertas*, the belief in freedom for all citizens; and *nobilitas*, the expectation that a Roman should strive for excellence in all he did.

Germanicus inherited the traditions of two historic Roman clans – the Claudian on his father's side, and the Antonian on his mother's. The *gens Claudia* figured prominently in Rome's history, and its semi-legendary founder was App. Claudius Sabinus Inregillensis. He was born Attius Clausus in Regillus in the Sabine (*Sabinium*) territories of Latium, and he sought peace with his Roman neighbour after they had overthrown their king and founded a republic.[48] It was not a popular position among the Sabines, but he left his hometown around the year 504 BCE and was joined by others equally dissatisfied with the turn of events. Claudius was received warmly on his arrival in neighbouring Rome. He was made a senator and his followers became Roman citizens. Nine years later, he was elected consul. His enforcement of the debt laws forced a secession of the plebians in 494–493 BCE. Despite his tough autocratic leanings, he established one of the most important and respected Roman dynasties.

Many of Claudius Sabinus' successors held high state office as consuls and censors, defending the commonwealth in times of political crisis and leading armies in wars against the increasing number of Rome's enemies. The family tree of the Claudians was a study in leadership, both good and bad. In the five centuries following App. Claudius Sabinus, 'it was honoured with twenty-eight consulships, five dictatorships, seven censorships, six triumphs, and two ovations', writes Suetonius.[49] The men of *gens Claudia* were principled, bold, and, often-times, bloody-minded and stubborn individuals who had *virtus* in abundance. Many were prepared to take on the vested interests in the name of *aequitas* and *libertas*, and more often than not left Rome a better place than they entered at birth.[50] One such was App. Claudius Caecus, his *cognomen* meaning 'the blind' (c.340–273 BCE). As censor in 312 BCE, he sought to enfranchise the sons of freedmen and the rural tribes who had no land. He commissioned the building of the *Via Appia* that connected Rome to Capua, and the aqueduct that brought abundant fresh running water to the fountains and baths of the City. For the first time in Roman history, he published a list of legal procedures and the legal calendar, knowledge of which, until that time, had been the exclusive preserve of the *pontifices*. Twice elected consul and appointed dictator for one term, he was remembered for a speech he gave against Cineas, an envoy of Pyrrhus of Epirus, in which he declared that Rome would never surrender.[51]

Claudians played a prominent role in the wars against Rome's sworn enemy, Carthage. In 265 BCE, App. Claudius Caudex, whose *cognomen* means 'block-head', was the first to cross the Straits of Misenum with a fleet of ships to come to the aid of the Mamertines, and succeeded in driving out the Carthaginians from Sicily. In liberating the Mamertines, however, he triggered the First Punic War (264–241 BCE).[52] Caudex's nephew P. Claudius demonstrated that he had less humility than he had humour. He was also the first of the *Claudii* to receive the *cognomen* Pulcher, meaning 'beautiful', though it was intended not as a compliment but as a cruelly sarcastic joke of the sort the Romans enjoyed, since he was far from handsome. In 249 BCE:

> when, off the coast of Sicilia, the pullets used for taking augury would not eat, in contempt of the omen, he threw them overboard, as if they should drink at least, if they would not eat. After his defeat, when he was ordered by the senate to name a dictator, making a sort of jest of the public disaster, he named Glycias, his apparitor.[53]

Back in Rome, he was tried for incompetence and impiety, and fined. He died shortly thereafter, probably by suicide.

It was one of the four sons of App. Claudius Caecus who founded the branch of the family known as the *Claudii Nerones*. In 214 BCE, C. Claudius Nero (a relative of Claudius Caecus) was sent to crush Hasdrubal Barca, on his arrival from Hispania with a vast army, before he could unite with his brother Hannibal. Either he lost his way on the journey, or he did not have enough time to arrive in time, but the engagement between the Carthaginian and the consul M. Claudius Marcellus took place without him. Seven years later, as consul, Claudius Nero redeemed himself when he scored a pivotal victory for the Romans in the Second Punic War (218–201 BCE) at the Battle of Metaurus.[54] He cut off Hasdrubal's head and lobbed it provocatively into the camp of the great Hannibal.

Germanicus' own paternal grandfather, Ti. Claudius Nero (a descendent of C. Claudius Nero) had a colourful life story, too. He was married to his cousin, Livia Drusilla (*Stemma Drusorum*, no. 9), from the *Claudii Drusi* branch of the family founded by M. Livius Drusus, but agreed to divorce her at Octavius' (Iulius Caesar's nephew) request and apparently without contest.[55] M. Tullius Cicero, the statesman and orator, described Nero as the sort of man who was effusive and overeager to show gratitude in return for a favour. The result was that his life was a chronicle of poor judgements. In 54 BCE, he beat M. Antonius' brother to be the prosecutor at the impeachment trial of A. Gabinius, the governor of Syria who was alleged to have overseen an incompetent and corrupt provincial administration – and he lost the case. He sought the hand of Cicero's daughter Tullia in marriage, but the orator dithered, his wife made the decision for him, and Nero lost her to another.[56] Nero threw his weight behind the rising star in Roman politics, C. Iulius Caesar. He was rewarded by Caesar with the appointment of *quaestor* and commanded the fleet at Alexandria, and for his services he was assigned a senior priesthood in place of P. Cornelius Scipio.[57] Caesar authorized him to establish colonies in Gallia Narbonensis in 46 BCE, and Arelate (Arles) and Narbo (Narbonne) owed their foundation to him. When Caesar was assassinated, however, Nero made a succession of bad decisions. He switched to the side of the assassins and even proposed special honours for them. When the self-styled liberators' fortunes began to wane, he switched sides again, this time backing M. Antonius of the new triumvirate – the legal cartel of three men that officially ruled the Roman state, comprising M. Antonius, M. Aemilius Lepidus and Octavius, now Iulius Caesar's heir and using the inheritor of the great man's name.

Nero was elected *praetor* in 42 BCE, but when a dispute broke out among the members of the triumvirate, he refused to step down at the end of his term and, by doing so, broke the law. Two years later, after the assassins were defeated at the Battle of Philippi, Iulius Caesar's heir began confiscating lands in Italy to reward his retiring veteran legionaries. Antonius' brother and sister became champions for the dispossessed Italians and tried to foment rebellion against Caesar's adopted son. Nero chose to support their cause, and moved his wife Livia and their young son to Perusia, where the main opposition was gathering. Perusia fell, however, and Tiberius and his family managed to escape just in time, first to Praeneste, before arriving at Neapolis, where a slave revolt was being planned. That, too, collapsed in the face of the forces of Caesar's heir, and Nero pulled off yet another daring escape. In Sicily, he hoped to be welcomed by Sex.

Pompeius, the brother-in-law of M. Libo, but he was disappointed. Nero and his family were dismissed and headed east, hoping to find refuge with M. Antonius. On the way to Athens, they found temporary sanctuary with one of Livia's distant family members, L. Scribonius Libo. They had hardly reached the Greek city when Antonius, who wanted nothing to do with Nero, quickly sent him on his way to Sparta, where the *Claudii* still had supporters. They enjoyed the locals' hospitality for a time but, for reasons that have not come down to us, had to escape from there too.

In 39 BCE, Antonius and Caesar's adopted son reached an accord, signing the Peace Treaty of Brundisium and, a short while later, the Treaty of Misenum with Sex. Pompeius, in which amnesty was granted to those who had sided with him. Finally, Nero and his young family could return to Rome. As a result of the Treaty of Misenum, they may have found that their house on the Palatinus Hill had been confiscated, because, rather than fleeing Italy for their safety, they were proscribed or marked down as opponents.[17] Nero played no further role in public life and probably spent his time with his two boys, since under Roman law the children of a divorced mother were returned to their natural father. There is nothing in the Roman literature to suggest what kind of father he was, but Tiberius and Drusus the Elder at least appear to have respected him. Their time together was short, however. In 33 BCE, Nero unexpectedly died, leaving the five-year old Drusus and his older brother fatherless. Nine-year-old Tiberius was left to deliver the funeral oration at the *Rostra* in the Forum.[58] The boys were subsequently brought up in the household of Augustus and Livia. Germanicus' father was never adopted by Augustus and remained a stepson.

The *gens Antonia* had an equally exotic past. Several *Antonii* reached senior positions in the Roman political system, including *tribunus plebis*, *magister equitum* (a personal aid to a *dictator*), *praetor*, *censor* and consul.[59] There were two branches of the *Antonii*, the patrician and plebian, which were apparently unconnected by ties of blood.

The earliest recorded member of the patrician branch of the clan is T. Antonius Merenda, whose *cognomen* meant 'lunch'.[60] He was elected *decemvir*, one of a board of ten magistrates, which helped draft what later became known as the Twelve Tables of Roman Law in 450 BCE. Merenda was defeated by the Aequi on Mount Algidus.[61] Thereafter, the patrician *Antonii* achieved little of public significance.

The plebian – non-aristocratic – side of the clan, who bore no *cognomina*, came to prominence with the oratorical skills of M. Antonius Orator (*Stemma Antoniorum*, no. 2), son of C. Antonius (*Stemma Antoniorum*, no. 1).[62] He was elected *praetor* in 104 BCE, consul in 99 and *censor* in 97, but was executed during the bloody purges of C. Marius and L. Cornelius Cinna in 87–6. The most celebrated member of the plebian Antonians, however, was Germanicus' own maternal grandfather, M. Antonius the *triumvir* (*Stemma Antoniorum*, no. 8), and Germanicus was proud to call himself a descendant of his.[63] He was the eldest son of M. Antonius Creticus (*Stemma Antoniorum*, no. 3), who was *praetor* in 75, and grandson of the great M. Antonius Orator.[64] He was probably born in the winter of 86 or 83 BCE.[65] Young Marcus was influenced by his uncle, C. Antonius, also known by the *cognomen* Hybrida (*Stemma Antoniorum*, no. 4).[66] He was consul at the time of the conspiracy of Catalina in 63 BCE – the year Cicero famously claimed he had saved the Republic – and in which he was heavily involved.[67] Very much taking after his uncle, in his early life Marcus indulged his passions for sex and gambling and, by the age of only 20, he had amassed a debt of 250 talents – an immense sum for the times.[68] To escape his creditors, he fled to Greece and, once there, he studied rhetoric at Athens, during which he developed his trade-mark Asiatic style of public speaking, which was described as full of florid language.[69] When summoned by the proconsul of Syria to take part in campaigns against Aristobulus II in Iudaea, he then discovered his abilities as a cavalry commander.[70]

In 54 BCE, Antonius became a member of the staff of Iulius Caesar's armies in Gallia Comata and proved to be a competent military leader, showing courage, boldness and chivalry to his enemies, but his personality and temperament often led to upsets.[71] Antonius and Caesar were said to be the best of friends and, despite falling out in 46 BCE over a financial matter, they were later reconciled.[72] He remained a devoted friend and faithful adjutant to Caesar for the rest of his life. After Caesar's assassination, Antonius gave the eulogy in the Forum Romanum and succeeded in turning the populace against the conspirators.[73] As a member of the triumvirate, he hunted down the murderers, finally defeating M. Iunius Brutus and C. Cassius Longinus at Philippi on 23 October 42 BCE.[74] He allied with Kleopatra the following year and became her lover, but never-theless married the sister of Caesar's heir in 41 BCE.[75] The next ten years were filled with personal animosity and political uncertainty, finally ending in the naval battle at Actium in 31 BCE, in which Antonius was roundly defeated.[76] When the younger Caesar invaded Egypt, thinking Kleopatra had already killed herself and seeing all was lost, Antonius committed suicide.[77] The victor spared his sur-viving daughters and son, Iullus Antonius, by Octavia, as well as his children by Kleopatra, but he coldly executed her son by Iulius Caesar.[78]

From the blended genetic code of the Antonian and Claudian bloodlines, which had produced statesmen, soldiers and orators in some considerable numbers over the generations, Germanicus inherited innate abilities, which he would hone in adulthood and define him as a man.

When he reached the age of nine or ten, Germanicus began his higher educa-tion. He was instructed by a teacher called a *grammaticus* who was a specialist in literature.[79] Under his direction, Germanicus was expected to learn passages by heart, prepare spoken and written explanations of them, frame arguments, and declaim them with appropriate flourishes and gestures. Romans read not silently but aloud. In reciting the words, Germanicus learned to enunciate and pronounce them correctly, and to read with conviction and emotion. Greek and Latin epic poems were studied, not only for their intrinsic beauty of language and metre, but because, through them, a Roman student learned about the order of things – about astronomy, geography, social history, natural history, mythology and religion. It must have been an enjoyable period for him, because Germanicus formed a lifelong love of drama, history, philosophy and poetry.

Entering Public Life

On reaching puberty, a Roman boy officially came of age. His Uncle Tiberius was fifteen when he celebrated his own coming of age, which would place Germanicus' rite of passage in 1 BCE. This milestone event was a cause for great celebration. It normally occurred on 17 March, on the day of the Festival of Liber and Libera, at the transition between winter and spring. In the morning, Germanicus took off the *bulla* for the last time and placed it in the shrine of the family gods (*lararium*).[80] He then donned his best white tunic and, for the first time, wore the all-white *toga pura* instead of the *toga praetexta* with its striped edge, which he had worn as a boy. Leading a procession of his family and friends called the *deductio in forum*, on arrival at the Tabularium, the office of public records located under the Capitolinus Hill, he was registered as a full Roman citizen (*civis*) and his name was entered on the roll of his tribe. His special day ended with a coming-of-age party, and congratulations and gifts from the invited guests.[81]

Germanicus continued his education until his late teens. For male members of Augustus' family who were expected to fully participate in government, proficiency in the art of eloquent speaking was a particularly important skill to master.[82] Germanicus enjoyed the services of Salanus, a *rhetor*, who specialized in the art of oratory. His name has come down to us in a poem composed by P. Ovidius Naso (Ovid), who held his friend of 'moderate association' in high esteem, and whose nature he described as 'noble', a quality he found to be in diminishing supply in his day.[83] In one of his poetic letters, Ovid praises the teacher for nurturing Germanicus' skill in the art of public speaking:

> You have been for long his companion, you have been in union with him from his earliest years, finding favour with him by virtue of a talent that equals your character. Under your guidance, as a speaker he forthwith attains fiery eloquence, in you he has one to lure forth his words by your own.[84]

Not much else is known about Salanus. Remarkably, such men often came from quite humble backgrounds.[85] One such was M. Antonius Gnipho, a Gaul rescued from exposure at birth, sold into slavery, and acquired by one of the triumvir's relatives in Rome, who later gave him his freedom. His was said to have been a great genius 'of singular memory, well-read in Greek as well as Latin'.[86] His talent was recognized and he was employed to tutor the young Iulius Caesar, and even Cicero attended classes he taught on rhetoric. Augustus' own teacher of declamation was Apollodorus of Pergamon.[87] Under Salanus' guidance, Germanicus further studied the Greek and Latin authors, and went to the court-houses to listen to advocates for their plaintiffs or defendants, and displaying their practised oratorical skills.[88] In Germanicus, the teacher found a keen pupil. Public speaking would be a skill he constantly drew upon throughout his career.

Germanicus' academic studies did not exist in isolation. As a member of Augustus' family, he would have been learning about real world current affairs, the inner workings of government, and military strategy, directly from his relatives and the visitors and dinner guests at Augustus' house on the Palatinus Hill.[89] The public rooms of his modest property bustled every day during the *salutatio* with a continuous stream of friends, senators, military men, ambassadors, kings, princes, and other clients, seeking to meet the *princeps*, to update him on developments or to present petitions or to seek favours.

Following his settlement with the Senate in 27 BCE, Augustus had gradually taken a less active role in war-fighting, leaving it to his appointed deputies (*legati*) to carry out in his name.[90] Principal among them was M. Vipsanius Agrippa, who became his son-in-law when he married Iulia the Elder; but his unexpected death in 12 BCE thrust his two stepsons to the fore.[91] Following the untimely death of his younger brother Drusus, Tiberius became Augustus' principal man for executing his military policy.[92] The year following Drusus the Elder's death, he attempted to tie up the loose ends left by his brother in Germania Magna. In this task, he succeeded, retaining the good will of the allies and negotiating peace treaties with the principal Germanic nations living along the Rhine, Lippe, Lahn and Main rivers.[93] One of the terms of the settlement was the relocation of the Sugambri nation to the Roman side of the Rhine in the vicinity of the military base at Vetera (Xanten), and the surrender of its warlord, Maelo, who had led the invasion and defeated M. Lollius in 17 BCE.[94] For the first time in decades, it looked like there might be a lasting peace in the northern region. Further south, a great wedding-cake-like trophy, sculpted in marble to celebrate the subjugation of the sixty tribes living across the great sweep of the Alps, was inaugurated at La Turbie, as if to stamp a period on a project that had lasted over a century.[95] On his return to Rome, Tiberius was rewarded with an ovation and a second term as consul, to serve jointly with Cn. Calpurnius Piso in 7 BCE.[96] An indicator of the trust Augustus continued to place in him was the grant of *tribunicia potestas* – the legal power which gave the imperial family control over the Senate – for five years.[97] Furthermore, he assigned him Armenia in the east, where relations between the client king and Rome were deteriorating since rival claimants to the incumbent Tigranes' throne had come forward to challenge him.[98] Tiberius was far from a happy man, however. Something snapped in Germanicus' dour and intense uncle. For reasons that remain unclear, he suddenly announced that he was quitting public life and retiring to the island of Rhodos (Rhodes).[99] This dramatic turn of events unexpectedly left the *princeps* without his most experienced right-hand man.[100]

Had Germanicus' father been alive, it would probably have turned out very differently. Augustus greatly admired his youngest stepson and had even declared before the Senate that Drusus was joint-heir with his adopted sons, come the time of his own death.[101] At the funeral, Augustus had stated publicly that Drusus was an *exemplum*, a role model, for his sons. Despite their unwavering loyalty to him, and their successful military exploits for which the *princeps* claimed all credit, Augustus had adopted neither Drusus nor Tiberius. Perhaps because they were the sons of his wife, Livia, he felt no need to formally adopt them; but the fact that Augustus saw his adopted Julian sons as his natural successors over the Claudians may have galled Tiberius, and, having lost his brother and best friend in the forests of Germania while serving his stepfather, he felt underappreciated and had simply had enough. Adding to the pressure on him, his marriage to Iulia the Elder had also broken down. They had become estranged; so much so that, when he departed for Rhodes, he left her in Rome.[102] Having been abandoned by Tiberius, her lifestyle became increasingly wild, dominated by drinking and partying, which ended in a scandal that saw her accused of adultery and treason. Her punishment was severe. Augustus exiled her to Pandateria (Ventotene), banning her forever from Rome, and even barring her from drinking wine anywhere on her tiny island.[103] For a man promoting wholesome family values, it was an acute embarrassment.

Tiberius' retirement to the eastern end of the Mediterranean meant that Augustus now had to accelerate the promotion of his two adopted sons. They would have to learn fast how to play their part in politics and take over military duties from Tiberius.[104] In 17 BCE, with an eye firmly on his succession, Augustus had adopted the two sons of Iulia the Elder and M. Vipsanius Agrippa privately in a symbolic sale.[105] The older of the brothers was born between 14 August and 13 or 23 September 20 BCE, and named C. Vipsanius Agrippa. On his adoption, he took the name C. Iulius Caesar. His younger brother, Lucius, was born sometime between 14 June and 15 July 17 BCE. Augustus doted over the two boys, lavishing great attention on them and writing to them when he or either of them was travelling.[106] He named a new colonnade and basilica after them in 12 BCE and gave gladiatorial games in their honour.[107] They were promoted as the young Caesars, and appeared together on the most-minted coin of Augustus' reign, shown standing proudly in their togas on either side of two large, round, golden shields and gold-tipped spears – which indicated that they had reached the age at which they could serve in the army – accompanied by various items associated with religious ritual.[108]

Following popular demand for him to be made consul, Caius was given a priesthood and permitted to take a seat in the *curia*, where the Senate met, and was made *consul designatus*, acknowledging that he would assume the high office, but only when he reached the age of 20.[109] Meantime, Augustus permitted him to host gladiatorial games and banquets.[110] When Caius came of age in 5 BCE, he was appointed *princeps iuventutis*, 'prince of the youth', which granted him command of a unit of cavalry.[111] A year later, Lucius was given the same honour.[112] This fawning attention by their father, their public popularity, and the flattery of strangers intent on seeking favours, was having an unintended effect on the boys, however. Augustus became increasingly disconsolate when he found the little princes growing up to behave more like spoilt brats than potential heads of state, a situation he tried to change.[113] In 1 BCE, Caius, now old enough to join the army, was assigned command of a legion stationed on the Danube River (Danuvius, Ister); but, rather than learning the arts of war first-hand, he preferred

Map 1. The World, according to M. Agrippa, c. 12 BCE.

to stay out of harm's way by putting others in it.[114] Lucius saw service in the west.[115]

On the eastern edge of the empire, Armenia (map 1) finally broke out in revolt in 1 BCE.[116] It had always been a tricky region of the world to rule, existing in both Rome's and Parthia's sphere of influence. Augustus was keen to keep it under Roman control, and needed someone to quickly restore order in the region and to secure the frontier with Parthia. This posed a terrible dilemma for the *princeps*: he was too old and infirm, at 62 years of age, to take command in the field in person; his trusty warhorse Tiberius was skulking in Rhodes; and neither Caius nor Lucius had the military or diplomatic experience necessary to handle the situation.[117] The remarkable fact, if Dio's report is accurate, is that there were no other men the *princeps* believed he could trust to carry out the task.[118] Out of necessity, he chose C. Caesar. The 19-year old was given his first official state duty as the grandly named *Orienti praepositus*, 'commander of the East'.[119] To bolster his position, Caius was delegated *imperium maius*, the legal power to carry out orders in Augustus' name, which had been forfeited by Tiberius. Shortly before leaving Rome, there was one last item to attend to. He would not depart Rome a bachelor, but was married off to Germanicus' sister, Livilla, making them brothers-in-law.[120]

Perhaps aware of Caius' reticence to fully engage himself in military affairs, and to compensate for his diplomatic inexperience, Augustus assigned him the services of M. Lollius as official 'companion and guide'.[121] That this was the same man who had been responsible for the disaster in Gaul in 17 BCE shows how forgiving Augustus was of his friends' failings and how trusting he was of their abilities. Despite his apparent maturity in years, Lollius was an odd if unwise choice, having a reputation for avarice, deceit and spite.[122] He also harboured a great dislike of Tiberius, stemming back to 16 BCE when he had been replaced by him as governor in Gaul and then watched from the sidelines as he went on to win victories in Raetia and Noricum. Yet Lollius was still favoured by Augustus.

While island-hopping his way to Asia Minor, Caius received an unscheduled private visit from Tiberius at Chios or Samos.[123] He wanted to pay his respects to Caius and to clear up any suspicion the young man might have had of him.[124] Tiberius received an unexpectedly frosty welcome. Lollius had had plenty of time to poison the mind of his young charge. Caius had been influenced by his advisor's slanders, among which were allegations that Tiberius was inciting revolution.[125] Tiberius' deference did not win over the man, and all he succeeded in doing was to humiliate himself. Caius left soon after and went on to spend time in Syria, Iudaea and Egypt.[126]

The highlight of Caius' two-year tour of duty was the peace treaty he agreed with Phratakes V (Frahâtak) of Parthia, which was signed on an island in the Euphrates River.[127] He was the son of King Phrates (Frahâta) from whom, eighteen years earlier, Tiberius had received back the *signa* lost by Crassus to the Parthians at Carrhae in 53 BCE. The Parthians agreed to renounce their claim on Armenia, but required that the Mede Ariobarzanes be installed to rule over them.[128] Shortly after, a new coin was minted showing the young commander riding a horse galloping past a clutch of army *signa*.[129] News of the agreement contained in Caius' letter was read out to the Senate, probably by his own brother Lucius, who enjoyed reading all his dispatches when he was in Rome.[130] Meantime, Frahâtak revealed that Lollius had been taking bribes, and the Roman deputy was recalled to face charges.[131] He was immediately replaced by P. Sulpicius Quirinius, who had taken care to visit Tiberius in exile.[132]

Through Caius' diplomacy, a war with Parthia over Armenia had been avoided. However, the Armenians resented the choice of regent and now declared war on the Romans.[133] The conflict was not settled until the following year, when Ariobarzanes' position was confirmed, but it was a shortlived solution: he unexpectedly died and was replaced by his son, Artabazus.[134] Caius had shown some promise as a military commander in the East, but he was wounded while campaigning in Syria.[135] In 1 CE, at the age of 21, he was finally elected consul *in absentia* with L. Aemilius Paulus as his co-consul. In one version of the story, an upstart by the name of Addon (or Adduus) now took hold of the town of Artagira.[136] On the pretence that he would reveal the Parthian king's secrets, Addon tricked Caius into coming up close to the city's walls and succeeded in seriously wounding the Roman commander.[137] In another version, while reading documents delivered by Dones, the king's governor of Artagerae, Caius was attacked.[138] The Roman army promptly laid siege to the stronghold, which held out for a while, before finally falling to the Romans. However, the wound caused Caius to fall sick.[139] Dio says that Caius' health was not known for being robust, and the ensuing fever befuddled the clarity of his thinking.[140] He wrote to Augustus pleading to be relieved of duty and to retire as a private citizen, which his father reluctantly agreed to, though with the proviso that he should immediately come back to Italy. Taking a merchant ship bound for Lycia, however, Caius died on reaching Limyra on 21 or 22 February 4 CE, aged just 24.[141] A cenotaph was erected on the Limyrus River to commemorate his brief life.[142] He left no children.

With amazing bad luck, just nineteen months earlier, tragedy had struck when Lucius was taken ill while on his military service in Tres Galliae and Germania, and he died at Massilia (Marseille) on 20 August 2 CE.[143] He was only 19 years old and also left no heirs. The bodies of the two young men were brought separately under military escort back to Rome and met *en route* by the magistrates of the cities they passed through. The Senate voted honours for the young Caesars, and agreed that the golden shields and spears they had received on achieving the age of military service were to be hung in the senate house.[144] The caskets containing their ashes were lodged in the Mausoleum of Augustus (fig. 9), where they joined those of their birth father M. Agrippa, and Augustus' sister Octavia, his nephew Marcellus, and stepson Drusus the Elder.

This remarkable series of misfortunes, which Augustus appeared to treat with more resignation than heartbreak, caused him to completely rethink the succession plan he had carefully crafted over a quarter-century.[145] He cast his eye over the remaining live branches of his family tree. Three names stood out: his grandson Postumus Agrippa, his stepson Tiberius, and his step-grandson Germanicus. Postumus (plate 5), the only remaining son of his daughter Iulia the Elder and M. Agrippa, was an angry young man, but, as direct kin of his best friend, Augustus gave him the benefit of the doubt.[146] Augustus' relations with the now-humbled Tiberius had begun to mend – with some direct intervention from Livia – when his stepson returned from self-imposed retirement in 2 CE.[147] However, he wrestled with Germanicus. The young man was still unproven, having as yet no experience of civil government or the military. Yet he clearly had potential. 'He was so deeply respected and loved by all his acquaintances,' writes Suetonius, 'that Augustus (to say nothing of the rest of his relatives) wondered for a long time whether to make him his successor'.[148] But his doubts persisted, allegedly encouraged by his wife.[149]

The decision Augustus made would change the course of Roman history. By a bill passed in the *curia* on 27 or 28 June 4 CE, he formally adopted Tiberius (whose name changed to Ti. Iulius Caesar).[150] While the adoption was a private affair, it was reported that the arrangement was made for 'the good of the commonwealth'.[151] Tiberius' public career had ended and he was now a private citizen with neither *imperium* nor *tribunicia potestas*. The adoption by Augustus opened the way for him to be rehabilitated and once more to assume the tribunician power.[151] Tiberius expressed his reluctance, publicly, to re-assuming the power, but he relented and accepted it for the good of the state.[153] Seemingly as a precaution against anything happening to – or in his relations with – Tiberius, he also adopted his grandson Postumus Agrippa who adopted the name Agrippa Iulius Caesar.[154] The surprise, however, was that he made Tiberius adopt Germanicus, in turn, as *his* son.[155] It might seem that Augustus was laying out not one, but two generations of his successors in what one scholar has dubbed a *Doppelprinzipat*, in the manner of a dynast.[156] An alternative view is that, by having Tiberius adopt Germanicus, he was reducing the risk of frictions and the rise of factions in the imperial household.[157] It might have also been intended as a way of eliminating the prospect of the younger man as a rival. The son of Drusus the Elder changed his name for the third – and final – time to Germanicus Iulius Caesar. The 19-year-old now found himself thrust very prominently onto the public stage, with a real chance of being the successor to the imperial throne.[158]

All in the Family

Germanicus was growing up to be an attractive young man, both physically (plate 6) and personally. Statues and later representations of him on coins show Germanicus to have been clean-shaven with a pleasantly inverted triangular-shaped face, supported by the muscular neck that was characteristic of the Claudians; a mop of thick hair in a fashionably feathered cut, falling over a broad forehead and worn rather long at the back of the neck; somewhat large ears; and a prominent nose, but small lips. That he was conscious of his physical appearance is revealed in the way he overcame what he felt was a disfigurement. 'His legs were too slender for the rest of his figure', writes Suetonius, 'but he gradually brought them to proper proportions by constant horseback riding after meals'.[159] This dogged determination to overcome a shortcoming reveals great depth of character. Like his father, Germanicus was also blessed with a charismatic personality and empathetic temperament. Tacitus describes him as 'a young man of unaspiring temper and of wonderful kindliness'.[160] Suetonius went further, writing in gushing terms that:

> It is the general opinion that Germanicus possessed all the highest qualities of body and mind, to a degree never equalled by anyone; a handsome person, an unequalled valour ... and a remarkable desire and capacity for winning men's regard and inspiring their affection.[161]

These gifts would prove definitive and of immense value as he entered public life, preparing him well for a high-profile career, in both politics and the army.

Privately, he harboured a specific phobia: an irrational and intense fear of chickens. Plutarch records that 'Germanicus could not abide the sound or sight of a cock', a condition nowadays referred to as alektorophobia.[162] The cause of most phobias is believed to be a traumatic event experienced during childhood, but the exact nature of the incident responsible for it in Germanicus' case, if recorded at all, has not come down to us.

On the verge of turning 20, it was decided that the time had come for him to marry. With his connections to the first family, he was an eligible bachelor, but, in Augustus' extended family, few married for love. Marriage served a political end, either rewarding Augustus' new allies or reinforcing long-standing connections. There were several eligible brides available in Rome, but the young woman chosen for Germanicus was Augustus' own grand-daughter.[163] Born in 14 BCE, Vipsania Agrippina Maior (Agrippina the Elder, plate 8) was the child of Iulia the Elder and M. Vipsanius Agrippa, which made her Germanicus' second maternal cousin.[164] She was just two years old when her father died. However, Iulia the Elder was not a widow for long, and the very next year was married, at her father's request, to his stepson, Tiberius. Though Augustus had a reputation for being a womanizer in his younger days, as *princeps* he sought to enforce a return to wholesome family values, especially among his womenfolk. The control Augustus exerted over his family was considerable.[165] As a result, Agrippina had a closeted rather than a cosseted upbringing in the family home on the Palatinus Hill. Just as he had done with his own daughter, so too he insisted that his grand-daughter learn the two traditional domestic handicrafts of Roman women: spinning and weaving.[166] His own tunics were made of homespun cloth woven by the hand of his wife Livia, or daughter or grand-daughters.[167] The portraits identified as Agrippina the Elder show her to have had a pleasant, well-proportioned face, bright eyes, and a full nose, with hair fashionably parted in the middle and made into ringlets on either side. Yet she was expected neither to be seen nor heard, whether in private or public. Her overprotective grandfather insisted that she record her daily movements in the family daybook, and tightly controlled the access guests and strangers had to her. In one recorded instance, Augustus reprimanded L. Vinicius, apparently a perfectly upright young man, whose only transgression had been to travel to the seaside resort of Baiae and presume to meet her.[168]

Augustus enjoyed a close and warm personal relationship with his grand-daughter. Agrippina grew up to be a quick-tempered, strong-willed, but fiercely loyal woman, standing somewhat in dramatic contrast to Germanicus' cultured, sociable and well-mannered nature.[169] Advising a Roman husband how to cope with his wife's faults, the recently deceased scholar and prodigious writer M. Terentius Varro had said 'put up or shut up', since, in the former case, it made him a better man, while, in the latter, it made her more attractive to him.[170] In Germanicus' case, he did not need to worry. Despite their apparent mismatch, the marriage of Germanicus and Agrippina the Elder would prove to be one of the most remarkable husband-and-wife partnerships in Roman history.

Agrippina was two years younger than her husband-to-be. As a member of Augustus' extended household, she would certainly have known Germanicus, probably from an early age, and they may even have been close friends from childhood. The betrothal ceremony was a simple affair, in which the consent of the fathers was normally secured before relatives and friends; but, since Augustus was both step-grandfather of Germanicus and grandfather of Agrippina, it was a formality. Germanicus offered his fiancée a number of gifts and, most importantly, an engagement ring (either a circle of iron set in gold or a circle of gold), which she immediately put on.[171]

The actual date of the wedding in 5 CE is not known. In keeping with tradition, the *collegium pontificum* was consulted to find an auspicious day. The Kalends, Ides and Nones were considered bad days for weddings. May (the month of the Lemuria) was considered particularly ill-omened, while the first half of June was deemed the most propitious – that was until the Temple of Vesta had been scoured on the fifteenth day.[172] Coming from the patrician class, Germanicus and his bride married according to the sacred rite of *confarreatio*.[173] The ceremony was named after the cake of spelt wheat (*libum farreum*) that the couple shared during the formal proceedings. The event was a blend of solemn ritual and ribald spectacle. To invoke the good will of the gods, the front door and doorposts of the house in which the ceremony took place were decorated with branches of myrtle and laurel and wreaths of flowers tied with coloured ribbons, while fine carpets were laid at the entrance. Family members – alive and dead – were all part of the festive occasion. To that end, the doors of the armoires containing the wax *imagines* of the ancestors spanning generations were opened so that their spirits could watch the happy event.

The day before the wedding was the time for Agrippina to dedicate her childhood toys to the household gods, the Lares and Penates. It marked the end of her childhood and the beginning of her womanhood. Just before going to bed in the evening, she put on her wedding dress, a plain white tunic without a hem reaching to her feet (*tunica recta*) tied at the waist by a girdle of wool in a double knot (*nodus Herculeus*).[174] Rising early next morning, her maidservants attended her to dress and fuss over her appearance, to make her perfect for Germanicus. She draped a saffron-coloured cloak (*palla*) over her *tunica* and put sandals of the same shade on her feet. Her hair was dressed into six plaits (*sex crines*) using the point of a special spear (*hasta caelibaris*) and tied with ribbons (*vittae*). Over this, she donned an orange veil (*flammeum*) that covered the upper part of her face. A wreath of sweet marjoram and verbena was placed upon this head-dress. When she was satisfied with her appearance, she went out to meet and mingle with the invited guests in the high-ceilinged *atrium* of the house. There she welcomed the bridegroom, resplendent in his crisp white tunic and *toga pura*, and his family.

The marriage ceremony commenced with the sacrifice of a pig, or sometimes a ewe.[175] The *auspex* inspected the entrails and, having found them propitious, declared that the marriage ceremony proper could begin. Germanicus and his bride signed a formal marriage contract (*tabulae nuptiales*) before ten witnesses, who affixed their seals to it by pressing their engraved rings into blobs of hot wax.

A matron (*pronuba*), who was required to have been married only once, accompanied Agrippina throughout the ceremony. The *pronuba* then took the bride's and groom's right hands and placed them in each other's. This was the high point of the ceremony (*dextrarum junctio*), in which the young couple silently exchanged vows to live together, and Agrippina uttered the words '*ubi tu Gaius, ego Gaia!*' This concluded the wedding ceremony. The guests burst into applause, shouting '*feliciter!*' to express their warm congratulations, as Germanicus tenderly kissed the *nova nupta*, probably for the first time in public.

The banquet that followed the wedding (*cena nuptialis*) lasted until the onset of night. The finest foods and wines were served to the guests, and, in keeping with the party atmosphere, ribald remarks were exchanged in the spirit of fun and to raise the libido of the new couple. Normally, in a tradition echoing the Rape of the Sabines, Germanicus would then attempt to snatch away his bride from the protective arms of her mother, while she feigned terror and resisted him. Though she had been moved to Rhegium (Reggio di Calabria) on the mainland, Iulia the Elder was still under virtual house arrest, and her banishment meant she was certainly absent from the wedding.[176] Perhaps Livia substituted for her on this occasion.

Having overcome this play-acted resistance, Germanicus took his bride by the arm and walked her to their new home. The couple did not have far to go. Germanicus' house was one of the many buildings that adjoined Augustus' main residence on the Palatinus Hill, or it may have been a wing within it.[177] The music of flute-players accompanied the newly-weds as they were led in a procession (*deductio*) to their bedroom followed by five torchbearers. The guests followed, singing cheerful and bawdy songs. Three boys, whose parents were required to be still alive, accompanied the bride. One of them carried a firebrand of tightly twisted hawthorn twigs (*spina alba*), the charred remains of which were given to the guests as lucky keepsakes. The other two boys – named *patrimi* and *matrimi* – led Agrippina by the hands. The doorway of the room had been decorated with strips of wool and anointed with pig's fat and oil. Once the procession arrived at the door, Germanicus swept her up and carried her through into the bedroom, treading upon a fine white cloth, strewn with green leaves and petals. Three bridesmaids carried her distaff and spindle – symbols of her virtue and motherhood – into the room. In exchange, Germanicus offered her water and fire. The *pronuba* led Agrippina to the marriage bed (*lectus genialis*), where her new husband invited his bride to recline facing the door. Prayers were offered to the Lares and Penates of the couple's home, and then the wedding guests were shooed from the room. When the door closed behind them, the couple were finally left to enjoy the privacy of their own company for the first time. His heart racing, Germanicus lifted off her *flammeum* and removed her *palla*. He carefully untied the *nodus Herculeus* and slipped off the *tunica recta* to share the first of many nights of intimacy with the grand-daughter of Augustus. That night, the couple tried for their first child.

Having woken up together next morning, Agrippina made an offering to the household Lares and Penates and received wedding gifts from Germanicus.

Shortly thereafter, the couple joined Augustus and Livia for a private banquet (*repotia*). Livia was reported to be particularly pleased with the choice of partners because, for the first time:

> the union of Agrippina and Germanicus created a blood connection between herself and Augustus, so that her great-grandchildren were shared with the *princeps*.[178]

The joy of the first family, secreted away on the Palatinus Hill, was in stark contrast with the joyless life of the common families in the streets below. Rome's citizens were beset with one natural disaster after another. An earthquake had recently struck, damaging some buildings, and the Tiber had broken its banks, taking with it one of the bridges and flooding several districts of the city.[179] The flooding probably inundated the emporium and warehouses located along the Tiber River in district XIII below the Aventinus Hill, and spoiled the stores of grain contained in them.[180] Diminishing supplies of the staple of the Roman diet meant that people were going hungry – a problem that, if left unresolved, would lead to urban unrest.

Chapter 2

First Steps to Glory
6 CE–Summer 9 CE

Bread and Circuses
The famine of 5 CE continued well into the New Year. Austerity measures were introduced to reduce the number of mouths requiring to be fed. The courts were shuttered, because trials brought in crowds of litigants, who were now a drain on the city's diminishing food resources. Anyone of means was encouraged to leave Rome and take his retinue with him.[1] Recognizing that many senators had left town, the normal quorum required for passing legislation in the *curia* was suspended, and a bill was passed allowing decisions taken by the house during this period to be declared valid.[2] Even the slave and gladiator markets in the city were closed and their traders required to move a distance of at least 100 miles away.[3] Augustus tried to mitigate the suffering of the poor by digging into his own reserves, and even suspended the public banquets normally celebrated on 24 September, his birthday.[4] Witnessing first-hand the suffering caused by famine to the most vulnerable people in society was a lesson Germanicus would take with him through the rest of his life.[5]

Panem et circenses – 'bread and circuses' – the poet Juvenal would write, a century later, but it applied equally well to Germanicus' time.[6] Blood spectacles kept the people amused yet peaceful in the amphitheatres, but empty stomachs could lead to riots and bloodshed in the streets. To keep the unemployed poor docile and dependent, Roman authorities handed out daily measures of grain (*annona*) with which to make bread or gruel. At this time, some 150,000 – about half of the urban plebs – of a population estimated at 1 million received a distribution of *free* grain.[7] The *modius*, a dry measure equivalent to eight quarts – a quarter of one bushel equal to 8.8 litres (537.6 cubic inches) – was the regulation issue of grain. To make his daily meal, a Roman consumed around 60 *modii* annually.[8] To provide it, as far as possible without interruption, there existed a long but well-run supply chain. Vast estates in northern Africa (supplying 40,000 *modii*) and Egypt (20,000 *modii*) provided a total of 5,095,000 hectolitres (14,009,291.5 bushels) of wheat for Rome every year.[9] Deep-hulled merchant ships ferried the vital commodity under sail across the unpredictable Mediterranean Sea to the safety of the port at Ostia. Unloaded onto barges, the cargo was brought to the great warehouses lining the right bank of the Tiber River in the floodplain below the Aventinus Hill. Distributing it to the people was exacting work. The *mensores frumentarii*, professional corn measurers, used a special scraping tool called a *rutellum* to precisely divide up the measures.[10] But it was too early this year for more grain to be shipped in. The grain transports would not cross the sea for months. Even if there were caches to be bought, the shipping lanes were closed for the winter. This year, as supplies continued to dwindle in Rome, the workload of the *mensores* grew lighter. Yet, as their trade suffered, others gained. Where demand exceeded supply, unscrupulous traders could profit from a black market in the scarce goods. Alert to the problem, Augustus appointed a board of ex-consuls to oversee the fair distribution of the declining supplies of grain and to ensure that profiteering did not take place.[11] These were increasingly desperate times. In case of trouble, the board members were given a bodyguard of lictors.[12]

Exacerbating the situation during the same year, a fire broke out destroying swathes of the city.[13] Many of the city's residential buildings were multi-storey tenements – poorly built, overcrowded and prone to collapse. Made of timber, and wattle and daub, with rubble infill, they were also inherent fire hazards. Fires were frequent occurrences in Rome.[14] After this particularly destructive event, however, Augustus set up Rome's first companies of fire-fighters by recruiting freedmen (*liberti*) and organizing them into seven cohorts under the command of an equestrian *Praefectus Vigilum*.[15] Wearing military issue helmets, they were equipped with axes, buckets, grappling hooks, ropes and water siphons. Though intended to be a temporary solution, the *vigiles* proved popular with the public and continued to operate for centuries after, with barracks located in Rome and salaries paid directly out of the treasury.

The domestic lot of the average unemployed pleb in Rome was not a happy one. Cramped, often insanitary conditions forced tenement dwellers to live their daily lives outdoors in the streets. Distractions were to be found in the *thermopolia*, the fast-food restaurants serving hot meals and drinks by the measure; or the *fora*, the public marketplaces, where the stall-holders hawked their wares while barristers harangued the jury in the adjoining courthouses. Much of this busy exterior life was shut down with the famine and fire. Hungry, and in many cases homeless too, among some of the people there was open talk of rebellion.[16] Fingers of accusation pointed to one P. Rufus – whom Dio emphatically denies was responsible – but the mob now had a scapegoat.[17] To placate the angry public, a board of investigation was set up.[18] Rewards were offered for information, with the predictable result that many came forward with information, both legitimate and bogus. The city began sliding into an unruly commotion, which only ended when the grain supply was finally restored and the thousands of hungry stomachs were sated.[19]

Perhaps hoping to raise the public's morale, Germanicus and his younger brother, Ti. Claudius Nero (plate 10), sponsored funeral games (*munera*) to commemorate their father Drusus the Elder on the fifteenth anniversary of his passing.[20] It was normal practice to honour one's deceased father in this way.[21] Indeed, Drusus and Tiberius had commemorated their father exactly this way, years before.[22] The games were public events, originally intended as religious rites by offering blood-sacrifice offerings to the gods, but the privately-funded *munera* served to raise the profile of the sponsor by providing entertainment for the people.[23] Organizing them was a major undertaking involving the planning of a programme of events and ceremonies, managing a budget, contracting with owners of gladiator troupes (*familiae*) and distributing admission tickets (*tesserae*). The games had become a big business and politically-minded magistrates could exploit them for votes. After the famine and fire, the games would be anticipated with great excitement. Paid for by Germanicus and Claudius as sponsors (*editores*), they would be looking for the best show their money could buy. Hard-nosed negotiating, calling in favours, a certain amount of back-scratching and appealing to good citizenship, all played a part in staging the grand *spectacula*.

The chosen venue was the Circus Maximus.[24] Situated in the plain between the Aventinus and Palatinus hills, the Circus was normally the venue for chariot races. Its enormous 540m (1,772ft) long by 80m (263ft) wide arena provided the single largest enclosed, purpose-built space in which to display all kinds of public sporting events.[25] The great banks that rose up around the sand-covered track could seat up to a quarter of the city's population. Under the *lex Iulia theatralis*, senators and equestrians were assured of seating in the front rows, but the lower social orders, who sat in the higher tiers, received their tickets from their patrons, so the distribution of *tesserae* – the coin-like disks or tokens that permitted entry to the events – was a means to reward political favours and curry others.[26]

The Claudian brothers' games were anticipated with great excitement by all classes of Roman society. As sponsors, Germanicus and his brother took their seats in the VIPs' box. The programme included a varied fare of executions of criminals, wild beast hunts and fights between pairs of gladiators. Novelty and variety of combat techniques fascinated the Roman spectators. They delighted in pitching gladiators against each other where trade-offs were made in the advantages and disadvantages of different equipment and fighting styles.[27] A combatant called a Samnite (*samnis*) equipped with wide brimmed helmet and crest, pectoral plate armour (*pectorale*), a greave on the left leg, a short sword (*gladius*) and large shield (*scutum*), might duel against a Thracian (*thraex*) armed with a heavy helmet featuring a visor with many eye holes and a large crest, arm guard (*manica*), a distinctive curved sword (*sica* or *falx*) and a small rectangular shield (*parmula*) complemented by high greaves. The gladiators fought until one man fell or raised his hand for clemency. The referee (*lanista*) appealed for a decision to the sponsor, who generally looked to the spectators for guidance. Gladiators were expensive assets and the owner of a troupe had every incentive to keep as many of them alive as he could. A gladiator had a remarkable nine-to-one chance of surviving a single bout, though, if he lost, the odds worsened dramatically to four-to-one.[28] Nevertheless, men did die on the sand of the *arena*, with most of them being under 25 years of age. The Romans admired how gladiators faced death. Some fifty years earlier, an awestruck Cicero wrote:

> What wounds will the gladiators bear, who are either barbarians, or the very dregs of mankind! How do they, who are trained to it, prefer being wounded to basely avoiding it! How often do they prove that they consider nothing

but giving satisfaction to their masters or to the people! For when covered with wounds, they send to their masters to learn their pleasure: if it is their will, they are ready to lie down and die. What gladiator, of even moderate reputation, ever gave a sigh? who ever turned pale? who ever disgraced himself either in the actual combat, or even when about to die? who that had been defeated ever drew in his neck to avoid the stroke of death? So great is the force of practice, deliberation, and custom! Shall this, then, be done by a Samnite rascal, worthy of his trade; and shall a man born to glory have so soft a part in his soul as not to be able to fortify it by reason and reflection? The sight of the gladiators' combats is by some looked on as cruel and inhuman, and I do not know, as it is at present managed, but it may be so; but when the guilty fought, we might receive by our ears perhaps (but certainly by our eyes we could not) better training to harden us against pain and death.[29]

Without having been near a battlefield, at just 21 years of age, Germanicus had already witnessed the gory spectacle of death through combat and been hardened to the sight of the spilling of blood of men his own age.[30] Bringing the killing fields into the city was an essential feature of Roman culture and part of a Roman citizen's socialization.

Sponsors of these grotesque sports always hoped to provide novelty with their entertainments, so that they might be remembered and talked about long after they had ended, and, in this, Germanicus and Claudius succeeded. Gladiators and wild beasts were displayed and:

in the course of them, an elephant vanquished a rhinoceros, and a citizen from the equestrian order, distinguished for his wealth, fought in the arena as a gladiator.[31]

The presence of such exotic wild beasts, imported from Africa, was a certain crowd-pleaser. The twelve elephants – six males and six females, dressed as men and women – were trained to perform tricks. As Pliny the Elder records:

In the show of gladiators that Germanicus Caesar exhibited, the elephants were seen to show some disorderly movements, after a manner of dancing. It was a common thing to fling weapons through the air, so that the winds had no power against them; to flourish and meet together in fight like gladiators, and to make sport in a Pyrrhic Dance; and afterwards to go on ropes; to carry (four together) one of them laid at ease in a litter, resembling the manner of women newly brought to bed; and some of them would enter a dining-place where the tables were full of guests, and pass among them with their footsteps so equally ordered that they would not touch any of the company as they were drinking.[32]

These games would not be quickly forgotten and the memorial games had the intended effect. The public still remembered Drusus the Elder with affection and respect, and transferred these positive feelings to his sons, especially Germanicus. Dio writes, 'this mark of honour to the memory of Drusus comforted the people'.[33] Having the love of the people was a tremendous asset to the up-and-coming politician and built up a great reservoir of political capital. Tiberius drew on the good reputation of his brother too. On one of his frequent visits to the city from the front in Illyricum, Germanicus' adoptive father, Tiberius, found time to dedicate the Temple of Castor and Pollux in both his brother's and his own name, using the form Claudianus for his clan, recognizing that he had been adopted by Augustus.[34]

That year, Germanicus took up his first official religious posts. He was appointed to the ancient and prestigious college of augurs. The role of this body of fifteen priests was to find signs in nature which confirmed that the decisions of the Roman state met with the approval of the gods.[35] Specifically, augurs studied the flights of birds, but did not predict the future.[36] Civil, political and military actions were blessed by the augurs. Consequently, it was a highly influential appointment. 'Who does not know that this city was founded only after taking the auspices (*auspicia*)', said elder statesman Appius Claudius, in words attributed to him by Livy, 'that everything in war and in peace, at home and abroad, was done only after taking the auspices?'[37] The presiding magistrate at an augural rite had powers vested in the right of augury (*ius augurii*). Before the ceremony began, certain explicit signs called *auspicia imperativa* would be requested of the god to provide confirmation. Standing within a purified square space or a temple fore-court, with his head covered by a fold of his white toga, he asked Jupiter a question in the ritual formula, 'send me such and such a sign'. While clutching his ritual crooked staff (*lituus*) in his right hand, he then studied the birds as they passed by. Germanicus had to master a complex code of signs, covering the course and elevation of bird flight, carefully noting the region of the sky they were in, as well as the direction and pitch of their song.[38] Only certain species of birds were considered messengers of the gods, the *aves augurales*, among them eagles, owls, ravens and woodpeckers.[39] As he identified the required signs, he called them out. Unexpected signs – *auspicia oblativa* – might be interpreted as being spontaneously offered by the god, and it was Germanicus' right as the prevailing augur to announce and interpret them. It was a skill which would come to play a decisive role later in his life.

He also joined the *Fratres Arvales*, a religious college of twelve members elected for life. The order's duty was to offer an annual sacrifice for the fertility of the fields – particularly important in the wake of the recent famine.[40] Among the distinguished members of the *collegium* for 5 CE were Augustus, Tiberius, L. Domitius Ahenobarbus, L. Calpurnius Piso, and L. Aemilius Paullus.[41] If they appeared all to be from an exclusive 'club', it was because they were – they were all hand-picked friends (*amici*) of the *princeps*. Augustus had revived the institution of the Arval Brothers, after it had fallen largely into obscurity, as part of his 'restoration' of the traditions of the old Republic. The appointment formalized the network of connections Germanicus probably already enjoyed informally, but established the young man as having the approval of Augustus, who was almost certainly the *magister*, or president, of the fellowship and whose choice it was to co-opt new members. Germanicus was probably an ordinary member on his initiation, but he could look forward to promotion to priestly *flamen* or *praetor*, as positions were elected annually, or as they became vacant through the death of a member. Germanicus would have been intricately involved in organizing the annual three-day festival of the archaic earth goddess Dea Dia in May.[42] The rite usually took place in Augustus' house, as *magister*.[43] As his badge of office, Germanicus wore a chaplet of ears of corn fastened to his head by a white band.[44] When the sun rose on the morning of the first day, fruits and incense were offered with prayers to the goddess. A banquet followed, after which the guests were handed gifts and garlands. On the second day, four boys – all sons of senators – each wearing a wreath of corn upon his head, a white fillet and the *toga praetexta*, formed a chorus, who sang the song of the *Fratres Arvales*. The lyrics of this hymn were in a dialect of Latin so ancient that even the Romans of Germanicus' time struggled to understand them.[45] There was a ritual dance in the temple of the Dea Dia, while, in her grove, located about 5 miles south of the city, a purification rite took place. There were elections for the officers of the *collegium* for the next year, followed by races and a banquet. On the third and final day, ritual prayers were offered and solemn oaths were made to the goddess.

With his appointments as augur, and as one of the Arval Brothers and a sponsor of memorial games for his popular father, Germanicus' public life had truly begun. In his private life, too, there had been important developments. Within a year after the wedding, Germanicus' first child was born. He was a healthy boy given the name Nero Iulius Caesar (plate 11).[46] Nero had always been a popular name among the Claudians. It was a good name for a boy descended from a family of such distinguished ancestors. In the Sabine language – once commonly spoken in the region around Rome – the word *nero* meant 'strong' or 'valiant'.[47] As head of the household (*paterfamilias*), Germanicus may have particularly chosen it in honour of his father.

A Gift for Words
Subsumed in the hubbub of the city, Germanicus could enjoy Rome's extensive cultural life. He lived in what modern historians refer to as the 'Golden Age of Latin Literature', that period which spans the years 83 BCE-14 CE. Among the poets and writers of narrative history living during his lifetime were Horace (Q. Horatius Flaccus), Hyginus (C. Iulius Hyginus), Livy (T. Livius), Manilius (M. Manilius), and Ovid (P. Ovidius Naso). Educated under the previous generation of great literary men and orators, who lived during the last years of the Republic, Germanicus' contemporary creative writers were mindful of Augustus' personal tastes and sensibilities.[48] It was possibly for his transgression of these same *mores*, with the publication of his poem *Ars Amatoria* – 'The Art of Love', a lusty celebration of seduction and romantic intrigue – that Ovid found himself banished from Rome on the direct orders of Augustus in 8 CE.[49]

In his spare time, Germanicus turned his own pen to creative writing. 'Among other fruits of his studies', writes Suetonius, 'he left some Greek comedies'.[50] The choice of genre – comedy rather than tragedy – is revealing. Comedic performance greatly appealed to the Romans. Roman audiences first saw comedic shows through the reinterpretation of Greek originals by Plautus (T. Maccius Plautus), who wrote no fewer than fifty-two plays at the turn of the second century BCE. A few decades later, Terence (P. Terentius Afer) adapted – or, in many cases, simply translated – six earlier Greek comedies. The tales of twins separated at birth, of chance encounters, gross misunderstandings, the foibles of the Olympian gods, and the antics of eccentric characters, such as the swaggering soldier, the lusty old man and the desperate parasite, provided the material for all manner of convoluted plots. To write a successful comedy, Germanicus would have had to master the art of creating dialogue rich in verbal humour, from distortions of meaning to puns, and from plays on words to riddles and jokes. Unfortunately, none of the comedies written by Germanicus survives for us to determine how well the young author had perfected his craft.

He also turned his talent to weightier subject matter. Germanicus' education was based in part on the study of the great epic poems of Greece and Rome. Ovid, in fact, regarded Germanicus as a poet in his own right.[51] Pliny the Elder notes, 'the divine Augustus also formed a tomb for his horse, concerning which there is a poem by Germanicus Caesar which still exists'.[52] This commemorative equine *opus* has not come down to us, either. However, ascribed to Germanicus is the work called *Aratus: Phaenomena*, which does survive in large part. At face value, it is a Latin translation of the original Greek didactic poem by Aratos of Alexandria (c. 315/310–240 BCE), written in the 270s or 260s BCE, possibly based on two earlier prose works by Eudoxus of Cnidus (Eudoxos of Knidos) of a century earlier. On closer examination, it appears to be an amalgam of lines by Aratos – 731 verses of the *Phaenomena* ('Appearences') joined to 422 lines from fragments of *Diosemeia* ('Weather Signs') – reworked in places by Hipparchus (Ipparchos).[53] Ipparchos (c.190-c.120 BCE) was a Nicean-born scientist, specializing in astrology, astronomy, geography, and mathematics, who wrote a highly critical commentary on the work by Aratos and Eudoxos. The poem itself describes the constellations and celestial phenomena in turn, and their mythological and zodiacal associations. The Latin translator frequently paraphrases the original Greek, rather than offering a faithful, literal translation.[54] A strong case can be made for the Latin translation having been done by Germanicus, between 4 and 7 CE.[55] He certainly wrote poetry and spoke and wrote Greek fluently.[56] The Roman writers Lactantius (L. Caecilius Firmianus Lactantius) and St Jerome (Eusebius Sophronius Hieronymus) both cite him as the translator.[57] The surviving – but incomplete – title in one extant copy mentions *Claudii Caesaris*; another, however, mentions *T. Claudii Caesaris* (T. but not Ti.). While Germanicus Iulius Caesar was born with the *nomen gentile* Claudius, so was his uncle Ti. Claudius Nero, now Tiberius Iulius Caesar.[58] Yet this raises the possibility that Tiberius, in fact, may have been the translator of the poem. During his lifetime, Tiberius also used the name Germanicus from the exploits of his adopted son.[59] It is also known that he was devoted to studying the literature of both cultures, and he spoke Greek fluently, though he preferred to use a Latin word over the Greek equivalent whenever possible when speaking or writing Latin.[60] During his self-imposed exile on Rhodes, he would have had the opportunity to meet other Alexandrian poets such as Euphorion and Rhianus, as well as having the time to study astronomy and astrology aided by his favourite, Thrasyllus, and to indulge his interest in mythology.[61] A few lines in the Latin version of the poem are sufficiently ambiguous that either candidate could have written the work. In these opening lines, Iupiter is invoked as the inspiration for the poem.[62] Much later in the poem, the death and apotheosis of Augustus are cited.[63] One view is that Germanicus could have written the work and dedicated it to the living Tiberius. Alternatively, Tiberius could have written the body of the poem while in exile, and inserted the deification lines after Augustus' death, in what became a revised version – but then Germanicus could equally have done so.[64] All that can be safely said is that the evidence is inconclusive as to the authorship of the so-called 'Aratus Ascribed to Germanicus', and that Germanicus is a potential candidate for its creation.[65]

Professionally, as a member of Augustus' extended family, Germanicus was expected to work his way steadily up through the political career ladder, the *cursus honorum*, atop which were the two much-coveted offices of consul. On the way up, the aspiring politician served the Commonweath in different elected public service positions, with proper respect shown for the qualifying ages and intervals between officers. While Germanicus' relationship with Augustus meant that some of the rules were relaxed, however, the young man was nevertheless expected to perform his duties responsibly and well. *En route* to the consulship, as had been permitted with Marcellus, Tiberius, and his own father before him, Germanicus started in the first of these official positions five years before the legal age.[66] Normally, Germanicus would have started his career in one of the twenty entry-level judicial or administrative posts – advocating in one of the lower courts, overseeing the minting of coins, or supervising the maintenance of highways inside and outside the city.[67] However, Germanicus started at the next level up, in the post of *quaestor* in 7 CE. Though dating back to the epoch when kings ruled Rome, by Augustus' time the quaestorship had become an elected magisterial position, responsible for managing public finances and auditing financial records. More usually based in Italy, the posting might involve service overseas as a financial assistant to the governor of a province.[68] One of the aims of the formal career ladder was to expose the up-and-coming generation of senators to a wide variety of real world issues. Germanicus' uncle, for instance, had started his position as *quaestor* supervising a department dealing with the problems of the corn supply, and later serving as an investigator into allegations of malpractice in the houses of correction across Italy.[69] A candidate for the office would normally have been expected to serve with the army before taking the office, which Tiberius had done as a tribune in Hispania, yet there is no evidence that Germanicus served in the military before his twentieth birthday. Was a concession made for the eldest son of Drusus the Elder? In the days immediately after Drusus' funeral, the Senate granted his mother Livia certain privileges under the *ius trium liberorum* passed by Augustus.[70] This legislation granted the father or mother of three legitimate Roman children permission for their sons to stand for public office before the stipulated age or without the requirement to observe the interludes between holding offices. This directly benefited Drusus the Elder's two surviving sons in 'fast tracking' their political careers.

No records survive to tell us how he felt as he arrived on his first day at the office. For Germanicus, who had experienced his entire life as a somewhat sheltered high-status citizen, working with people of all levels of Roman society would be an opportunity to learn first-hand about life in the real world. Eighty years later, when Pliny the Younger was about the same age as Germanicus, he had, as one of his first official jobs, the task of auditing the records of an auxiliary cavalry and infantry unit.[71] Being a conscientious fellow, he applied himself to his new job with admirable dedication and thoroughness. He found that most accounts were maintained with scrupulous care, but he was surprised to uncover evidence of deliberate falsification of others. Understanding how the machinery of government worked – and often did not – would stand Germanicus in good stead for when he became a senior official later in life.

Revolts in Illyricum

As Germanicus was beginning his career in domestic politics in Rome, there was unfinished foreign policy business in Germania Magna. Over the thirteen or so years since his brother's death, Tiberius had largely succeeded in pacifying the Rhineland Germanic nations. The process of turning the scattering of farming and warrior communities into urban settlements with centralized administrations – what modern historians call 'romanization' – had begun in earnest. Being erected for the first time on German soil, now considered peaceful, were Roman trading posts, such as at Waldgirmes, founded in 4 BCE in the Lahn Valley, while military installations, such as the watch-tower manned by *beneficiarii* at Billig in Euskirchen, began to take on the role of ensuring security, rather than as installations for making war.[72] Deeper into *barbaricum*, Rome's control was weaker, however. Pushing the limits of Roman influence ever north-eastward, Cn. Domitius Ahenobarbus finally achieved what Germanicus' father had not by crossing the Elbe River with his army in 1 CE. He pursued the Hermunduri tribe, which lived there, and signed a non-aggression pact with them, settling them in the lands above the Main River vacated by the Marcomanni, and was awarded triumphal insignia for his victory.[73] To better manage the province of Germania, he established his civilian and military administration at Oppidum Ubiorum, moving it from the Vetera garrison, where it had been since Drusus founded it.[74]

In 4 CE, Tiberius led a military operation into the still un-annexed regions of Germania Magna. In the far north, the Chauci, with whom Drusus the Elder had signed a peace treaty, were restless. In the east, the fierce Suebi continued to remain outside direct Roman control and represented a threat to the region already under it. New offensives began using the navigable rivers to carry supplies and matériel to strike deep into the heart of Germania as far as the Weser (Visurgis) River.[75] Tiberius stayed in the militarized zone until December, to oversee his expeditionary force digging defensible positions, then left the region in the care of C. Sentius Saturninus and headed back to Rome.[76] He returned to lead a spring offensive in 5 CE, which saw the launch of a mission to engage the Suebi. Following his deceased brother's own model campaign of 12 BCE, an amphibious expedition set off under oar from Batavodurum (Nijmegen) into the Lacus Flevo (Zuiderzee, now the Ijsselmeer). He was able to use the series of hydrological engineering works – comprising a canal and ramparts constructed by his brother and still bearing his name – which connected the Rhine to the freshwater lake beyond.[77] The 'short cut' offered by the *Fossa Drusiana* enabled the fleet to avoid the treacherous North Sea (Mare Germanicum) and to take the relatively calmer Wadden Sea route along the Dutch coast.[78] The fleet sailed to the opening of the Elbe (Albis) River, which brought the army straight to the homeland of the Lesser and Greater Chauci nations.[79] Velleius Paterculus writes:

> The tribes of the Chauci were reduced to submission; all their youth, infinite in number, gigantic in size, strongly guarded by the nature of the country, delivered up their weapons, and, with their leaders, surrounded by troops of our soldiers glittering in arms, prostrated themselves before the tribunal of the *imperator*.[80]

Sailing up-river, the fleet met up with the land army, where they moved forward together to engage the Langobardi, one of the larger warrior tribes making up the confederation of Suebi.[81] Of the ensuing encounter, Paterculus writes: 'the Langobardi, a nation exceeding even the Germans in fierceness, were crushed'.[82] In an example of social engineering, the Romans ejected the Langobardi from the left bank of the Elbe and drove them back to the other side.[83] The army was declared victorious and Tiberius returned to Rome, where, on 27 January 6 CE, he dedicated the Temple of Castor and Pollux in his own and his dead brother's name.[84]

The complete subjugation of Germania Magna now seemed a real possibility to high-ranking Romans. Paterculus writes effusively that 'the whole extent of Germania was traversed by our army; nations were conquered that were almost unknown to us even in name'.[85] The key strategic issue remaining before 'mission accomplished' could be declared was to take a V-shaped wedge of land called Bohaemium between the Rhine and Danube rivers.[86] It was occupied by the Marcomanni, a nation of Germanic origin having allegiance to the Suebi. In 10 BCE, Marboduus (or Maroboduus), who was educated at Rome, returned to his people – or perhaps was taken there under Roman escort – and became their king.[87] He had enjoyed the patronage of Augustus, possibly as a *praefectus* of an auxiliary cohort in the Roman army, and took back with him ideas about how the Marcomanni might benefit from adopting Roman-style law, government and military science. In the years he spent among them, he had come to understand what motivated the Romans. Rather than challenge Rome or be conquered by her legions, Marboduus convinced his tribe to relocate far from Roman temptation. On the migration to a new homeland in Bohemia (Bohaemium), the Marcomanni were joined by the Lugii, Zumi, Butones (or Gutones), Mugilones and Sibini nations – a combined force of some 70,000 men on foot and 4,000 horse. While he had sworn not to take up arms against Rome unless provoked by them to defend himself, the view on the Palatinus Hill and in the *curia* was that Marboduus and his Marcomanni represented a continuing and present threat that could launch attacks on neighbouring Roman interests at will.[88] A pre-emptive strike was called for.

Tiberius, who had shown great care in planning the previous year's campaign, conceived a three-pronged attack on the Marcomanni to be launched in 6 CE.[89] On the western flank, Sentius Saturninus, the new governor of Germania, would lead his army from the Rhine and cut through the Hercynian Forest. In the centre, a second army group would thrust north-east from Raetia under an unknown commander.[90] Tiberius would launch his offensive from his Danubian base camp at Carnuntum on the eastern flank.[91] This co-ordinated pincer movement was designed to envelop and reduce the Marcomanni with overwhelming force. No fewer than twelve legions, each of 5,600 heavily-armed troops, and an unspecified number of auxiliary cohorts, each of between 500 and 1,000 infantry or cavalry, were involved in what was the largest expeditionary force ever mustered by Rome against a single foe, though this number may actually be the sum of units in Germania, Raetia and Illyricum at this point in time, rather than the force committed to the war.[92] Joining Tiberius at Carnuntum was M. Valerius Messalla Messalinus, the governor of Illyricum.[93] The administration and security of the province of Germania, meanwhile, was delegated to P. Quinctilius Varus. He was one-time commander of *Legio* XIX in the wars to subjugate the Vindelici in 15 BCE, had been co-consul with Tiberius in 13 BCE and subsequently served terms as governor in Syria and Africa, and had married the great niece of Augustus, Claudia Pulchra.[94] He was a very trusted pair of hands. Meantime, to bring the units of the expeditionary force up to full strength, levies were raised in the neighbouring provinces. Among the regions supplying men for the war were the Balkans. Yet, as Paterculus reflects philosophically, 'Fortune sometimes frustrates, sometimes retards, the purposes of men'.[95] Even as the massed forces of the Roman army were preparing to cross the Danube and Rhine rivers and move towards their assigned military targets, the planned invasion had to be abruptly aborted when news arrived of a rebellion to the south in the Balkans.

At this time, the western Balkans were referred to as Illyricum.[96] Dalmatian Illyricum ran along the Adriatic coast, stretching from the Drilon River in the south (in modern Albania) to Istria in the west (in modern Croatia) and to the Sava River in the north (in what is now Bosnia-Herzegovina).[97] Landlocked Pannonian Illyricum was bounded by the Sava River to the south, and stretched to 'the crags of the Alps' in Noricum (in modern Austria) in the west, the province of Moesia (in modern Hungary) in the east, and as far north as the banks of the Danube River.[98] Appian noted that:

> Pannonia is a wooded country extending from the Iapodes to the Dardani. The inhabitants do not live in cities, but are scattered through the country or in villages according to relationship. They have no common council and no rulers over the whole nation.[99]

Like so much of Europe before subjugation by Rome, Illyricum was a patchwork of independent native and immigrant communities living side by side. There were no 'Illyrians' or 'Pannonians' before the Romans coined the names for them. There was no coherent group of people, no sense of common identity among them, that could be described as either the Illyrian or Pannonian nation.[100] The region was home to many different independent nations and confederations of tribes with different cultures, languages and politico-economic systems. In the north-west, in the foothills of the eastern Alps, near the Isonzo and the source of the Sava rivers, lived a cluster of tribes who spoke a language called Venetic. Tribes speaking Celtic tongues occupied a broad sweep of the Balkans along the Sava and Drava rivers and their tributaries as far as the Morava. In the hills and valleys down towards the Adriatic coast, Illyrian peoples lived alongside communities who had been heavily influenced by colonies of Greek settlers.[101] Thus, before the Romans arrived, the region did not exist as a single geo-political entity.[102] Pannonian Illyricum did not fully enter Rome's sphere of influence until neighbouring Noricum was annexed in 15 BCE by Germanicus' father, although it had been the object of actual conquest by Octavianus twenty years earlier.[103] Illyricum and Pannonia were Roman inventions for the convenience of its own government and foreign policy.[104] Through pacification and assimilation, the invaders from Italy attempted to re-invent the patchwork of smaller tribal communities as provinces with coherent identities for assimilation into the Roman commonwealth of nations. The Romans almost certainly used established local tribal aristocracies to administer the provinces, while gradually introducing Roman policies and practices.[105]

The Romans had worked remarkably hard to annex the region, only to squander it all through maladministration. They made 'first contact' in 229 BCE after crossing the Adriatic Sea, but it only came under the direct rule of Rome after it had been subjugated by military means in 167 BCE. The following year, it became a protectorate. Iulius Caesar was assigned to govern Illyricum in 59 BCE. Octavianus himself led an expedition to the region in 35–34 BCE, occupying Siscia on the Sava River for a time, the result of which, from 33 BCE, was that it officially became a province administered by a senatorial *proconsul*.[106] Rebellions were common in the region and Rome responded punitively; but, once the military operations had been concluded, the army normally withdrew, leaving the defeated people to scheme and plot new rebellions the following year.[107] On account of the need for constant military suppression, from 11 BCE it was made an imperial province with a *legatus Augusti pro praetore* and assigned a permanent contingent of legionary troops.[108] M. Agrippa was dispatched to the Balkans in 13 BCE to lead an offensive that became known as the *Bellum Pannonicum* – the Pannonian War – and which, after his death, Tiberius continued until 9 BCE.[109] At the end of this first year's campaigning in 12 BCE against the Pannonii, Tiberius had all their young men – the potential next generation of rebel fighters – rounded up, deported, and sold in the slave markets of the empire.[110] It was not a strategy designed to endear the local people to their Roman overlords.

The Romans were drawn to the region because of its coastal seaports, its wealth of natural resources, and the need to connect their Achaean, Macedonian and Asian conquests directly to Italy by a secure highway. The short distance by sea from Brundisium to Apollonia saved time compared to going overland via Veneto and down the length of the western Balkan peninsula.[111] Strabo notes:

> Now the whole Illyrian seaboard is exceedingly well-supplied with harbours, not only on the continuous coast itself, but also in the neighbouring islands, although the reverse is the case with that part of the Italian seaboard which lies opposite, since it is harbourless. But both seaboards in like manner are sunny and good for fruits, for the olive and the vine flourish there, except, perhaps, in places here or there that are utterly rugged. But although the Illyrian seaboard is such, people in earlier times made but small account of it – perhaps in part owing to their ignorance of its fertility, though mostly because of the wildness of the inhabitants and their piratical habits. But the whole of the country situated above this is mountainous, cold, and subject to snows, especially the northerly part, so that there is a scarcity of the vine, not only on the heights but also on the levels. These latter are the mountain-plains occupied by the Pannonians.[112]

As in other parts of the burgeoning empire, this region's natural resources, largely unexploited by its native peoples, could be turned into a profit by the application of Roman organization and technology. The ability to leverage scale in this way was one of the secrets of Rome's success.

In the western Balkans, Rome's treatment of the local peoples was clumsy and unnecessarily punitive, thereby sowing the seeds of discontent and destruction. The Roman appetite for taxation and tribute reached new extremes in the region closest to the Danube.[113] What was clearly lacking – and what the Romans at that time apparently failed to see a need for – was a fair and even-handed treatment of their subjects. Dio sums up the feeling of seething anger in a comment reportedly spoken by one of the rebel leaders. '*You* are responsible for this', he said, 'for you send us, as guardians of your flocks, not dogs or shepherds, but wolves'.[114] Conscription levies were a particularly sore point.[115] For their invasion of Bohaemium, the Romans recruited local men for the auxiliaries to fight along-side their regular legionaries, and the governor of Illyricum (*praepositus Illyrico*), M. Valerius Messalla Messallinus, demanded his quota of conscripts. Dio notes that, when the non-Roman auxiliaries assembled together and realised just how many they were in number and how strong in arms, one among their ranks, a man named Bato of the Daesidiatesi, took the lead to openly incite rebellion.[116] Interpreting the choice as between putting their lives on the line in a war for the benefit of the Romans that they did not themselves want, or fighting the Romans to liberate their own homeland, many decided to join him. The rebellion can be interpreted as an emotional response to an imposed burden, not a premeditated military campaign.[117] With remarkable alacrity, Bato's rebel force succeeded in defeating the first Roman troops sent against them, and, witnessing their victory, many of the other Dalmatian nations then rallied to the cause. Meanwhile, in

Pannonian Illyricum, the chief of the Breuci – also named Bato – and his people took up arms and marched against the Roman town of Sirmium.[118] They failed to capture the place, but it was a painful lesson to the Roman authorities that the rebels could disrupt the peace of everyday life at will. From neighbouring Moesia, the *propraetor* A. Caecina Severus led a counter-insurgency attack, engaging the rebels at the Drava River. The Pannonii suffered great losses and retreated, but not without first inflicting casualties on the Romans, and rallying yet more men to join their cause.[119]

In total, the rebel force now numbered some 90,000–100,000 infantry and 9,000 cavalry.[120] Not much is known about their organization or mode of fighting. Concerning one about which something is known, the Iapodes tribe who lived on the far south-eastern end of the Alps, Strabo writes only 'they are indeed a war-mad people', noting 'their armour is Celtic, and they are tattooed like the rest of the Illyrians and the Thracians'.[121] Related to the Iron Age Celts of central Europe, the Pannonii were a diverse population of individual tribes, each one being a highly-structured society. A king or clan chief (*ri* or *rigon*) ruled in conjunction with a warrior class of nobles, and was advised by bards, diviners and and druids.[122] Below them was the great number of common people, often disenfranchised and existing as bondsmen who could be called upon to fight at any moment. A warrior protected himself with a large, oblong or hexagonal shield, made of wooden planks butted together and covered with leather; used in tandem with other fighters, it could form a shield-wall. Many wore bronze or iron helmets, and an inscription showing Iapodean warriors from Bosnia depicts men with tall crested 'bowler hat'-style headgear.[123] Shirts of chain-mail were worn by the élite, while the commoners often fought without body armour. The most common offensive weapon was the long, heavy spear (*lancea, sibyna*) with a flat, leaf-shaped bronze or iron blade at the tip. The Pannonian warriors who could afford them wielded iron swords measuring 0.55–0.57m (1.80–1.87ft) in length, with a pointed end best suited for cutting not thrusting. In contrast, the Illyrian warriors used arms and armour derived from Greek models, preferring the curved, single-bladed *machaira* or the *sica*, a short, curved sword that Romans associated with assassins.[124] Knives, battle-axes, and bows and arrows were also part of the Illyrian war fighter's armoury.[125] As noted horsemen, many Pannonian and Illyrian nations could field cavalry, which often rode into battle, dismounted and continued to fight on foot. According to Appian, 'they do not assemble in one body, because they have no common government'.[126] Small-scale ambuscades and surprise attacks on troops on the march were common tactics. These hit-and-run tactics were well-suited to attacking heavily-armoured Roman troops, who were most vulnerable while marching in forests, through valleys and over mountainous terrain, but less effective in large set-piece battles, where superior equipment and discipline tipped the advantage to the Romans.

Having joined with the Delmatae, Bato of the Daesidiates led his own men and marched on Salona, in the hope of taking the base from which the Romans administered the province (map 2). The ruins of the ancient city (plate 19), in what is today the town of Solin, lie 6km (4 miles) north of Split on the Dalmatian

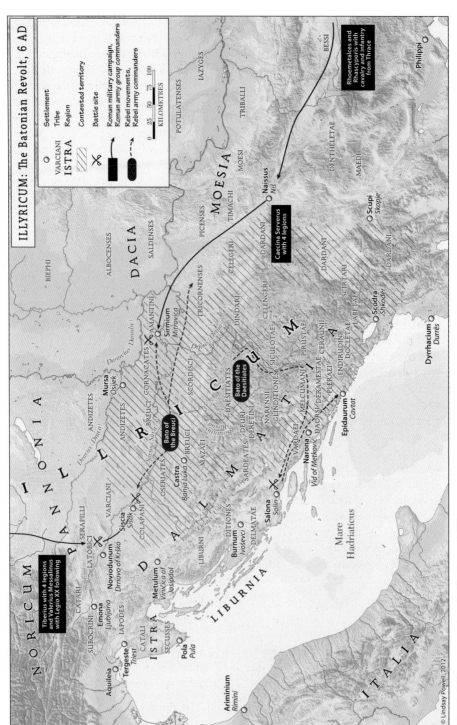

Map 2. Military operations in Illyricum, 6 CE.

ILLYRICUM: The Batonian Revolt, 6 AD

○ Settlement
VARCIANI Tribe
ISTRA Region
Contested territory
✗ Battle site
Roman military campaign,
Roman army group commanders
Rebel movements,
Rebel army commanders

0 25 50 75 100
KILOMETRES

Tiberius with 4 legions
and Valerius Messalinus
with *Legio XX* following

Rhoemetalces and
Rhascyporis with
cavalry and infantry
from Thrace

Caecina Serverus
with 4 legions

Bato of the Breuci

Bato of the Daesitiates

© Lindsay Powell, 2012.

coast. Several advantages favoured its development in ancient times. Its geographic position in the central part of the eastern coast of the Adriatic Sea, lying at the bottom of the crystal-clear Kastelanski Bay, provided shelter to shipping; its proximity to the delta of the Salon river (now called the Jadro River) offered a freshwater supply; and its access to the road network linked the city to the hinterland. All contributed to the accelerated development of the town. Under its founders, Salona had been the coastal stronghold and the port of the Delmatae nation, in the immediate vicinity of the neighbouring Greek colonies of Tragurion and Epetion. Supplementing the native Illyrian population and the descendants of Greek immigrants, Salona was at this time home to a large Italic community. Their arrival followed the civil war between Caesar and Pompeius Magnus in 48 BCE, when demobbed troops were encouraged to adopt Salona as their home, which was then granted the legal status of a Roman colony. The grandly-named Colonia Martia Iulia Salona became the administrative and political capital of the Roman province of Illyricum. From here, roads radiated out south, south-east and north, carrying officials of law and order as well as tax-farmers to the inland regions of the Province.[127] The trapezium-shaped old town was fortified with stout walls and towers, some constructed in the second century BCE.[128] To the rebels, Salona represented the very heart of their nemesis. Taking it would cripple Roman control of the entire region. Attacking it, however, was a declaration of war on the Roman state and would bring its wrath down upon them.

The particulars of the Illyrian attack on the city of Salona are lost. It probably consisted of one or more attempts to directly storm the city-gates and breach the circuit wall with extemporized battering-rams and scaling ladders. Critically, the rebels lacked artillery. The Romans were experienced at siege warfare as attackers, but even with the tables turned, they put up a fierce resistance as defenders. In the ensuing battle, Bato himself was wounded when struck by a stone, perhaps from a Roman sling.[129] Its leader withdrawing from the field to recover, the rebel siege quickly collapsed. The retreating insurgents fanned out along the Dalmatian coast, wreaking havoc on the unprotected communities and settlements as far south as Apollonia. There they engaged the Romans again, initially seeming to suffer defeat before snatching an unexpected victory.[130]

With the Roman army pinned down in Salona and being defeated elsewhere on the battlefields across the region, it looked as though the rebellion could turn into the disaster Augustus feared, after all. The contemporary historian Velleius Paterculus captures the urgency of the Roman response to the news:

> Troops were accordingly levied: all the veterans were everywhere called out; and not only men, but women were compelled to provide freedmen for soldiers, in proportion to their income. The *princeps* was heard to say in the Senate that, unless they were on their guard, the enemy might in ten days come within sight of the city of Rome. The services of Roman senators and *equites* were required, according to their promises, in support of the war.[131]

But who should lead the mission? The cream of Roman society well knew the answer. 'The *res publica*, therefore, requested of Augustus to give command in that war to Tiberius, as their best defender'.[132] Separately, news reached Tiberius in Germania of the rapidly deteriorating situation in the Balkans. He knew the region only too well and understood the toughness of its fighters and their mode of warfare from bitter first-hand experience. There was no time to lose. He sent ahead of him his deputy Messallinus, who was in Carnuntum on the Danube River preparing for the invasion of Bohaemium, with a small detachment from *Legio* XX, and followed up himself with the main army group.[133] The *Bellum Delmaticum* had begun in earnest. Also known by its other moniker, *Bellum Batonianum*, the 'War of the Batos', it was later considered the gravest since Rome's war with Carthage.[134] In this first year of war, eight legions, equivalent to 40,000 men at full strength, plus auxiliary cohorts, were committed.[135]

Bato of the Breuci either anticipated or learned of the Romans' advance and, despite still recovering from his injury, he personally led his force to intercept Messallinus. The men of the Breuci gained the upper hand in open battle, but lost the advantage when later ambushed by the Romans.[136] Realising the only way to beat the Romans was to have numerical superiority, Bato of the Breuci set off to parley with Bato of the Daesidiates.[137] Remarkably, the two men reached an accord to co-operate with each other. They combined their forces and assembled north of the city of Sirmium, on a mountain called Mons Alma (Fruska Gora), hoping to exploit the advantage of terrain. Meanwhile, the army of Severus set off from Moesia to attack them, but, knowing his march would take several days, the Roman commander had taken the precaution of sending ahead a request for assistance from Rome's ally in neighbouring Thrace. Thrace was not a province of Rome but a pro-Roman client kingdom ruled by Roimetalkes (Rhoemetalces). Quick to respond, the lightly-armed, tough Thracian units were the first to arrive on the scene. Later, Severus arrived. The rebels fiercely resisted the Romans, but finally buckled under the added onslaught from Roimetalkes" army.[138] The sweet taste of victory was fleeting. Word then reached Severus that, while the Roman governor had withdrawn his army, the Dacians and Sarmatians had invaded Moesia and he now had to return there to regain control of his province.[139]

Tiberius and Messallinus set off for Siscia to relieve the garrison commander, Manius Ennius.[140] The former cavalry commander and *quaestor*-designate for 7 CE, Velleius Paterculus, set off from Rome to take part in the operations.[141] He passed up the opportunity of a provincial governorship and, instead, seeking adventure and glory, he assumed the post of legate assigned to Tiberius and duly arrived in Siscia with reinforcements.[142] Despite the setbacks, there were Roman successes. Messalinus, leading only half of *Legio* XX – presumably the other half being on campaign elsewhere in Germania or Illyricum – engaged an opponent several times its size.[143] His army found itself surrounded, but Roman discipline held and the Illyrici were routed, with 20,000 fleeing the field.[144] When news of his victory reached Rome, Messalinus was accorded the honour of triumphal ornaments.[145]

Elsewhere, the rebels had overrun the region, daily recruiting more tribes to their cause who saw that they had been able to successfully take on the Romans and beat them. Paterculus places a positive spin on the course of the war, but, at the time, it seemed a very real possibility that the province would be entirely lost.[146] By now, the rebels had learned not to engage the Romans in open battle, but, instead, to use their knowledge of the terrain and light arms to wage a guerilla war and exploit terror tactics, which greatly disadvantaged the heavily-armed legionaries.[147] In this way, they stretched the fight out into the winter – when the legions normally retired to camp – and even invaded the Roman province of Macedonia, causing damage wherever they went.[148] Once again, Roimetalkes and his Thracian soldiers, assisted this time by his brother Riskuporis (Rhescuporis), blocked and tackled the Illyrians' advance southwards and eastwards.[149] As the weather worsened, the other rebel nations retreated to the hilltops, from where they launched hit-and-run raids upon the Romans at will.

Off to War

Augustus watched the 'War of the Batos' from afar with increasing frustration and growing anxiety.[150] Dio records that Augustus thought the campaign should have been over quickly, and suspected Tiberius of deliberately impeding progress, in order to have an army under his direct control.[151] Augustus knew both the terrain and the enemy from personal experience, but probably underestimated the scale of the present threat. Nevertheless, he sent letters of encouragement to Tiberius, in which he extolled him as a consumate general, praised his prudence, and emphasized that the fate of the Roman Empire depended on his continuing good health and safety.[152] This might have been the opportunity for his adopted son Postumus Agrippa to prove his mettle. Instead, he idled his time fishing, drinking, arguing violently and generally acting in ways others interpreted as depraved or mad.[153] When his bad-mouthing of Livia and constant arguing that he had been denied his father's inheritance finally pushed Augustus beyond his breaking point, the *princeps* abdicated him, stripped him of his name and banished him to the small island of Surrentum in the autumn of 6 CE.[154] Any chance that he might succeed Augustus was now extinguished.

The *princeps* turned to the only person left in his family that he could trust. He ordered Germanicus, still at that time holding only the junior rank of *quaestor*, to assemble an army and set off for the front in the western Balkans.[155] This was the 21-year-old's first chance to gain military experience and to prove himself up to the task. From the outset, he faced two major challenges. He had no training as a military man, not to mention as a commanding officer; and he had to build his army from scratch himself.

Debate continues as to what training Roman officers received on taking up their commissions. There does not appear to have been an Officer Training School that Germanicus could have attended. The aspiring military leader was, to all intents and purposes, an 'armchair general' who learned about strategy and tactics from reading histories or actual campaign commentaries.[156] A surviving example of a military handbook from the early Empire is the one authored by Sex. Iulius Frontinus, a general who lived eighty years after Germanicus. He compiled his own file of best practices culled from Roman history and published them under the title of *Strategemata*, a Latinization of the Greek word meaning 'to be a general'.[157] He arranged summaries of narrative examples under headings such as 'on discipline', 'on ambushes', 'on creating panic in the enemy's ranks', and the usefully-titled last resort, 'on escaping from difficult situations'.[158] Better than book-learning was to meet with real soldiers. Based in Rome was a small military force of three Praetorian Cohorts, representing up to 1,500 men-at-arms.[159] The cohorts provided Augustus and the members of his family with an escort when on tour, and a guard-detail while at home. In order not to intimidate the city folk, the guardsmen did not wear armour, but instead wore the civilian white toga, possibly concealing their sheathed swords beneath the folds of its voluminous cloth, though the military-style hobnailed boots would betray their status as military.[160] Germanicus would probably have been able to consult officers of the three cohorts, not least the two *praefecti* drawn from among senior *equites* and under whom the units had recently been placed.[161] He would nevertheless have to be a quick study.

Germanicus also needed to recruit men and train them fast. Distinguishing his special unit would be its unique composition. It was not composed exclusively of Roman citizen volunteers (*volones*), like the legions; nor was it made up of aliens (*socii*), like an auxiliary unit. Instead, it was created by a conscript levy (*dilectus*) of the population, its ranks of free-born Romans supplemented by freedmen – manumitted or *former* slaves – and slaves whose freedom had been bought expressly for military service.[162] This was highly irregular and a last resort in times of extreme national emergency. That Augustus resorted to conscription confirms the very real unease he felt at the worsening situation in the Balkans. Indeed, he is described by Velleius Paterculus as visibly 'shaken with fear'.[163] Yet, ever mindful of the delicate state of public finances, to pay for Germanicus' conscript unit, he levied a two per cent tax on the sale of slaves, and redirected funds from the scheduled gladiatorial games.[164] Furthermore, he suspended the annual review of the equestrians in the Forum Romanum.[165] Everyone had to share in the discomfort. Nothing is recorded of the organization of the unit under Germanicus' command, though it is reasonable to surmise that it was one or more cohorts of 1,000 men, comprising centuries of 80 men like the regular legions or non-Roman auxiliaries, each led by a centurion or decurion. For protection (plate 13), they would probably have been issued with a large, oval shield (*scutum*) and a helmet of bronze or iron (*galea, cassis*) and possibly a chain-mail shirt (*lorica hamata*). A short, double-edged, bayonet-like sword (*gladius*) and a spear (*hasta*) were the weapons most likely provided. Thus equipped, the men would need to learn how to function as a military unit and to use their weaponry.

While the Praetorian Cohorts could have played a role in training Germanicus' 'band of brothers', there is another intriguing possibility. The official suspension of the games was bad news for the owner-managers (*lanistae*) of the gladiatorial schools (*ludi*). There were several of these schools in Rome, and in them could be found all the skills and equipment a commander needed to train novices in basic swordsmanship, defence and attack techniques. There was a precedent. The first to do so was the consul P. Rutilius Rufus, during the emergency of the northern wars of the Cimbri and Teutones, in 105 BCE.[166] In arranging the memorial games for his father, Germanicus had established relationships with the owners of the gladiatorial schools. Though there is no direct evidence for collaboration between Germanicus and the *lanistae*, this was a public emergency and, being a pragmatic people, the Romans would use all resources at their disposal to address it.

With his army trained, Germanicus prepared to leave Rome. For him personally, the timing was unfortunate: Agrippina was pregnant with her second child. However, he had his marching orders. Either by traversing the 700km (435 miles) from Rome to the border of northern Illyricum, or taking the shorter route by crossing the Adriatic Sea from Brundisium (modern Brindisi) to land at Dyrrhacium (Durrës), by the start of the campaign season of 7 CE Germanicus' 'barmy army' had reached the theatre of operations.[167] Roman forces were now deployed in many locations, using the valleys and plains of the Drava and Sava Rivers to advance south-east (map 3). Five legions had meantime arrived from the East under the command of A. Caecina Severus and M. Plautius Silvanus, bringing the total under Tiberius' supreme command to 'ten legions, more than seventy auxiliary cohorts, ten *alae* of cavalry and 10,000 veterans and, in addition, a large number of volunteers and numerous cavalry of the king' – a combined force of some 145,000 men.[168] 'Never', writes Velleius Paterculus, without exaggeration, 'had a greater army been assembled in one place since the civil wars'.[169] Always the cautious commander, however, Tiberius used a strategy of 'advance, hold and defend'.

Yet, large numbers by themselves did not guarantee an easy victory – or victory at all. The weaknesses in the quality of some of Augustus' 'armchair commanders' began to reveal themselves remarkably quickly. Further, they were not helped by their junior officers, who, it appears, could not always be counted on to be of the highest calibre. Writing of his father-in-law Cn. Iulius Agricola's military apprenticeship stationed in Britannia from 58 to 62 CE, Tacitus comments:

> Agricola did not utilize his rank of *tribunus* and his lack of experience either to indulge in vice, like the young men who find military service an opportunity for debauchery, or to idle away his time in pleasures and in being absent on leave.[170]

The discipline and fighting capabilities of the lower ranks of the legions could be squandered by the amateur leadership of their generals and by inexperienced next-tier commissioned officers – which is precisely what happened next in Illyricum. The five legions from the army group brought by Severus and Silvanus, joined by Roimetalkes and his Thracian infantry and cavalry, found themselves suddenly surrounded by the Illyrian rebels. In the ensuing battle, the Thracian cavalry were routed, the auxiliary infantry and cavalry were driven off, and even among the regular legionaries (plates 14 and 15) 'some confusion took place'.[171] The Romans paid a heavy price for their carelessness. A *tribunus militum*, a *praefectus castrorum*, several *praefecti* of auxiliary cohorts, a *primus pilus*,

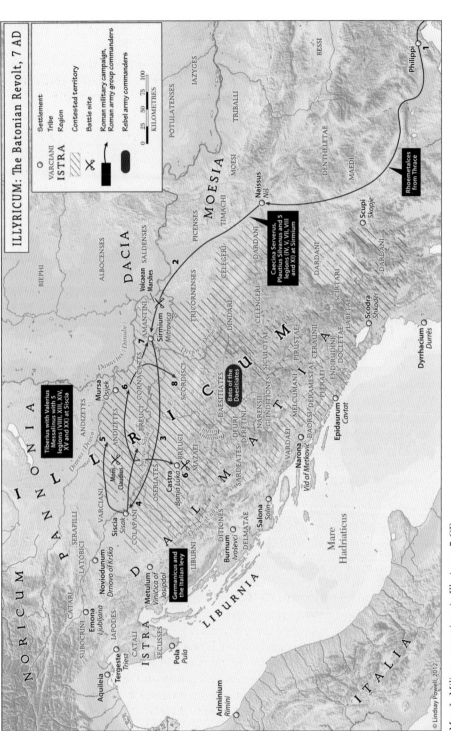

Map 3. Military operations in Illyricum, 7 CE.

and other centurions were killed in the ambush.[172] 'But the courage of the Roman soldiers', writes Paterculus in defence of the ordinary men:

> on that occasion, gained them more honour than they left to their officers, who, widely differing from the practice of the commander-in-chief [Tiberius], found themselves in the midst of the enemy, before they had ascertained from their scouts in which direction they lay.[173]

Under these high-pressure conditions, the centurions (plate 17) – the backbone of the Roman army – kept cool heads and ruthlessly applied the basic combat doctrine. 'The legions, encouraging one another, made a charge upon the enemy', Paterculus writes, 'and, not content with standing their ground against them, broke their line, and gained an unexpected victory'.[174]

Returning from Moesia to the region, Severus marched along the Bosut River, a tributary of the Sava in eastern Croatia, and right into a trap. He was set upon by the combined forces of the two Batos at his marching camp near the Volcaean Marshes in the area of later Cibalae (Vinkovici).[175] Dio describes how the rebels 'frightened the pickets outside the ramparts and drove them back inside'.[176] Once behind the turf rampart surmounted by its hedge of sharpened stakes (*sudes*), however, the Romans rallied, stood their ground, and gradually overwhelmed their besiegers. Learning from this, the Romans changed their tactics, dividing into their cohorts and centuries, so that 'they might overrun many parts of the country at once'.[177] The tactical change, however, proved largely ineffectual. Tiberius, meanwhile, finally broke out from his fortified position in Siscia and began his advance moving east. He trapped many rebels between the Drava and Sava rivers at Mons Claudius (Papuk Hills).[178] It was an important morale booster in what had been a difficult year with little progress to show, thus far.[179]

Germanicus' army, meanwhile, was dispatched to the centre of the conflict zone, with orders to engage any opposition when he encountered it. Soon he met the Mazaei nation.[180] The Mazaei, listed as Pannonii among the tribes by Strabo, was a Celtic tribe who lived along the meandering Vrbas River (plate 20) with its magnificent limestone gorges, as far as the Una to the north and the Bosna to the south, and centred on the transitional plain now occupied by Banja Luka in modern Bosnia-Herzegovina.[181] The region was then, as now, mostly grassy woodland, criss-crossed by the tributary rivers Suturlija, Crkvena, and Vrbanja that flow into the Vrbas, which finds its source on the slopes of the Vranica. The region is hilly and the three highest mountains – Manjača (1,214m, 3,983ft), Čemernica (1,338m, 4,389ft) and Tisovac (1,172m, 3,845ft) – are part of the Dinaric range, which now separates Bosnia from Dalmatia. With his irregular unit, Germanicus was enjoying greater success than his professional peers. The enemy he faced was largely made up of lightly-armed farmer-warriors. Their tactical advantage was their knowledge of the terrain and the fire in their bellies, from fighting for the homeland. Yet the enthusiasm of the young Roman commander and the effectiveness of his soldiers' training made the critical difference. Germanicus 'conquered in battle and harassed the Mazaei', writes Dio, cryptically.[182] It was a promising start for the novice commander and his army, and both were rapidly gaining and improving with experience. A smart man assuming a new military command took the time to get to know the men reporting to him and to familiarize himself with their capabilities. Tacitus' description of Cn. Iulius Agricola could equally apply to Germanicus Iulius Caesar. 'He made it his business', he writes:

> to become known to the army, to learn from the best officers, never to thrust himself forward for display, never to hang back from timidity, and at the same time to combine caution with dash.[183]

But it was just one small victory and the war was not yet won. Germanicus' army probably remained in the country of the Mazaei, in sight of the Dinaric Alps, for the duration of the winter. Whether Germanicus stayed with his men or returned to brief Augustus is not disclosed in the extant records. It is known that, in his eagerness for news of progress in the war, meanwhile, Augustus had relocated to Ariminium (Rimini).[184] It is highly probable that Germanicus resided there with the *princeps* and his father Tiberius, until the new campaign season commenced.

The war to squash the rebels dragged on into 8 CE. During the year, the Romans secured the lowlands (map 4). Germanicus and his troops now moved southwards, up into the mountains. Their target was Splanaum – or Splonum to the Romans – on the Dalmatian side of the Dinaric Alps.[185] This was the centre of Illyrian mining, producing ores for the precious metal industry.[186] The Dinaric Alps – or Dinarides (plate 21) – compare well in importance with the Caucasus Mountains and the Alps, and are considered the fifth most rugged in Europe. They extend for 645km (401 miles) along the Adriatic coast, and rise to their highest point of 2,692m (8,832ft) at the majestic Prokletje. Many rivers have their source in this long mountain range. The crystal-clear waters cascade down brooks and streams, tumbling over karsts such as the Kravice, and combine to become roaring torrents at the lower levels. From their present position, Germanicus and his troops could follow the course of the 235km (146 miles) Vrbas River, which took them along a meandering and increasingly narrow route up the Vranica mountain. If not by this route, he may have approached the target via the 271km (168 miles) Bosna (Bosona) River to Mount Igman.[187] The journey presented a formidable obstacle to the invading Romans. Precipitous cliffs and narrow, tree-covered ledges, beneath steep rock faces, often bare of vegetation and glaring white, made their ascent difficult – particularly for the carts, with their iron-rimmed wheels, carrying the heavy baggage and supplies.

Splonum's remote location, strong fortifications and 'vast number of defenders' posed a considerable challenge to Germanicus.[188] The normal options open to a commander in this situation were to blockade the defenders, in the hope of starving them out, or to assault the stronghold directly and take the place by force. As time was not on Germanicus' side, and being equipped with siege weapons, he attempted a direct assault. On this occasion, tension and torsion technologies did not give the Romans the decisive edge they needed. Dio reports that 'he had been unable to make any headway, either with engines or by assaults'.[189] Isolated from the main army, and relying on provisions they had

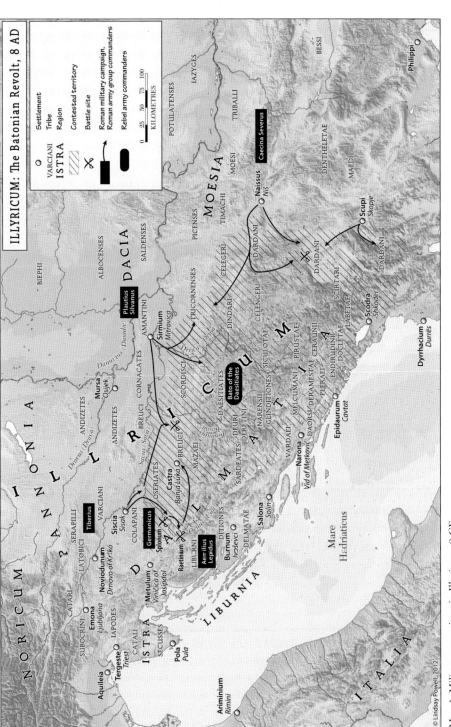

Map 4. Military operations in Illyricum. 8 CE.

ILLYRICUM: The Batonian Revolt, 8 AD

Settlement
Tribe
Region
Contested territory
Battle site
Roman military campaign,
Roman army group commanders
Rebel army commanders

VARCIANI
ISTRA

0 25 50 75 100
KILOMETRES

© Lindsay Powell, 2012

carried with them – since foraging was not an option at this height – the Roman attackers were quickly running out of options. Out of sheer frustration at the stalemate:

> Pusio, a Germanic horseman, hurled a stone against the wall and so shook the parapet that it immediately fell and dragged down with it a man who was leaning against it. At this, the rest became alarmed and, in their fear, abandoned that part of the wall and ran up to the citadel; and, later, they surrendered both the citadel and themselves.[190]

The defenders panicked and retreated to the fortified acropolis. Shortly after they surrendered the citadel and themselves.[191] Buoyed by his successes, Germanicus marched on, capturing other rebel strongholds on the way to Raetinum.[192] On arriving there, his luck – or his judgement – changed. His inexperience in assessing high-risk situations now became evident. The tale of the fall of Raetinum is a harrowing one, recorded in gruesome detail by Cassius Dio:

> The enemy, overwhelmed by their numbers and unable to withstand them, set fire, of their own accord, to the encircling wall and to the houses adjoining it, contriving, however, to keep it so far as possible from blazing up at once and to make it go unnoticed for some time; after doing this, they retired to the citadel. The Romans, ignorant of what they had done, rushed in after them, expecting to sack the whole place without striking a blow; thus, they got inside the circle of fire, and, with their minds intent upon the enemy, saw nothing of it until they were surrounded by it on all sides. Then, they found themselves in the direst peril, being pelted by the men from above and injured by the fire from without. They could neither remain where they were safely nor force their way out anywhere without danger. For if they stood out of range of the missiles, they were scorched by the fire, or, if they leaped back from the flames, they were destroyed by the missiles; and some who got caught in a tight place perished from both causes at once, being wounded on one side and burned on the other. The majority of those who had rushed into the town met this fate; but some few escaped by casting corpses into the flames and making a passage for themselves by using the bodies as a bridge. The fire gained such headway that even those on the citadel could not remain there, but abandoned it in the night, and hid themselves in subterranean chambers.[193]

Raetinum, now a smouldering ruin, fell to the Romans.

His adoptive father Tiberius, a man imbued with a talent for military affairs honed by years of operations in theatre, suffered setbacks, too. In this the third year of the war, ten legions were committed to campaigning in the Balkans.[194] The troops themselves were becoming restless and growing daily more impatient as the war dragged on, seemingly without end. Experience taught Tiberius to listen to the mood of the men. Facing the real prospect of mutiny, he resorted to a radical realignment of the expeditionary army to refocus their energies. He 'made three divisions of them: one he assigned to Silvanus and one to Marcus Lepidus, and with the rest he marched with Germanicus against Bato'.[195] This was a major promotion for Germanicus, who now led his own army group, comprising legions and auxiliaries, as well as his own irregular unit, against one of the two leaders of the rebellion.

With the revolt proving harder to win than envisaged, squabbling broke out among the rebels and, with it, acts of treachery. Bato of the Breuci had betrayed a certain Pinnes with the connivance of members of the tribe and, as his reward, he now ruled alone over the nation, unchallenged. Meanwhile, the two Batos had become estranged and were suspicious of each other. After a struggle, the Breucian was handed over to Bato of the Daesidiates by his own people and summarily executed.[196] Seeing what the Illyrian war-chief had done to their own leader, many Pannonians felt betrayed and rose against their erstwhile allies. This schism was the opportunity the Romans had waited for. Silvanus launched an offensive against them and succeeded in defeating the Breuci and their allies 'without a battle' – a measure of how war-weary many of the rebels had become.[197] Seeing that all hope was lost, the Pannonians sued for peace terms from Silvanus, hoping to save their lives. On 3 August 8 CE, the Pannonians surrendered at a place on the Bathinus (Bosna?) River.[198] Bato of the Daesidiates was not so easily overcome, however. Retreating to the passes leading to central Illyricum, the men still loyal to him ravaged the surrounding lands. They continued to resist Roman attempts to reduce them for several months more.[199]

Gradually, over the course of the following year (9 CE), the war turned in the Romans' favour. Strongholds that had held out against Tiberius and his deputies' armies fell one by one, such as the city of Seretium, which had resisted from the beginning (map 5). Silvanus and Lepidus rapidly overwhelmed the opposition they encountered. However, the going for Germanicus and Tiberius was to prove much harder. Bato of the Daesidiates had moved his base of operations to a fort called Andetrium (Muč) on a rocky escarpment not far from Salona.[200] It was a well-chosen location to build a fort, and all attempts by Tiberius to besiege it failed. Bato had carefully stocked provisions there, so he could afford to wait it out for some considerable time – time that Tiberius did not have.[201] As they attempted to scale or undermine the walls, his men were pelted with rocks and projectiles, and the rebels launched hit-and-run raids on his provision trains. 'Hence, Tiberius', writes Dio, 'though supposed to be besieging them, was himself placed in the position of a besieged force'.[202]

In one key respect, the Romans had clear superiority over the rebels. During the winter months, the Romans' supply lines had replenished the stocks of food and matériel of their combat units, though the supply of corn remained an ongoing issue.[203] In stark contrast, years of war had taken its toll on the rebels. Beyond the special arrangements Bato had made at Fort Andetrium, the rest of the rebel army, lacking food and the means to treat wounds, went hungry and many succumbed to disease.[204] They might have sued for terms, but the voices of those whom the Romans were least likely to spare if they surrendered (the deserters from the auxiliary units of the Roman army) drowned out those – such as one Scenobardus – who were eager to lay down their arms.[205]

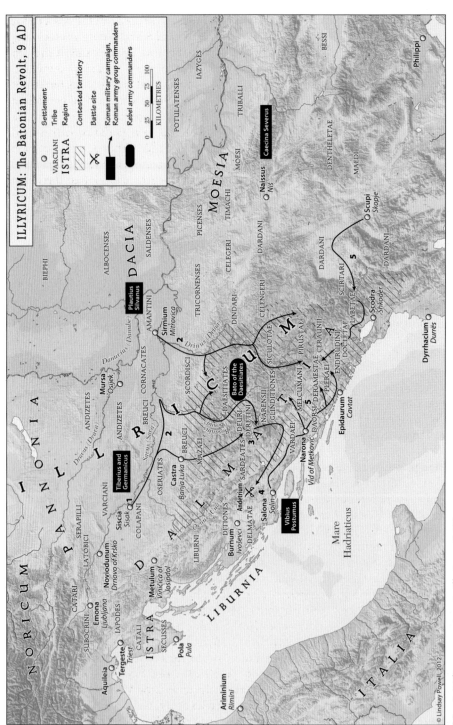

Map 5. Military operations in Illyricum, 9 CE.

© Lindsay Powell, 2012.

On the plain beneath the walls of Fort Andetrium, Tiberius was at a loss what to do. Incensed at the indecision, his own troops broke out into a riot, shouting wildly, the noise of which reached the enemy, who, fearing an attack, retreated into their fort for safety.[206] Tiberius addressed his men, rebuking some and giving others a dressing down, but staying cool-headed during the address.[207] Watching from his vantage point on his parapet, Bato began to panic. What was his opponent planning? Thinking the worst, he dispatched a herald with a message asking for terms.[208] Tiberius was in no mood for negotiating with a rebel and, instead, rallied his men for an attack on the fort.[209] Forming a *quadratum*, a dense square, his men advanced at a walking pace, then raced at speed towards the foe, breaking ranks when they reached the rocky ascent. The rebels deployed outside the walls of the fort, standing higher up the slopes than the approaching soldiers, rained down missiles – Cassius Dio lists rocks, slingshot, wagon-wheels, wagons, circular chests loaded with rocks – upon the advancing Romans.[210] Bato's men clashed with the attacking soldiers, taking full advantage of the rocky upland terrain. For a while, it seemed the rebels were winning, and the men watching the battle from the parapet above cheered their side. The Romans took losses and might have yet lost the battle had not Tiberius brought up last-minute reinforcements.[211] At some point in the chaos of battle, the gates of the fort were closed shut, so that the rebels still fighting outside discovered they could not retreat behind the safety of its stone walls.[212] The rebels tried to escape up the mountainside, throwing down their cumbersome arms, but they were hunted down, many being found in the surrounding forests, and were slain like animals on sight.[213] Witnessing the fate of their brothers, the men inside the walls of Andetrium surrendered. Greater numbers and superior training on the Romans' side finally brought them victory. Tiberius spent the following days in 'arranging the affairs of the enemies who had surrendered'.[214]

To Germanicus fell the prosecution of the war against the remaining rebels.[215] It was to be a gruelling fight. Germanicus marched and laid siege to a stronghold called Arduba. During the course of the war, the rebels had learned much about fortifying their camps. At Arduba, Germanicus faced robust, man-made defences, almost entirely surrounded by a fast-flowing river.[216] His numbers, which were greater than the besieged, did not give him any tactical advantage, faced with this natural obstacle. It was the besieged inside the enemy camp, however, who unexpectedly came to his aid. Many now wanted to surrender. Their anguished pleas were refused by womenfolk who preferred liberty and death over surrender and ignominy. They attempted to leave the place, but were prevented from doing so, and fighting broke out. Many made it to the Roman lines and offered surrender, but those still inside took their own lives, throwing themselves into the flames of bonfires or hurling themselves into the river to be swept away by the fast current.[217] Other rebel strongholds in the vicinity, on learning the fate of Arduba, promptly offered their own surrender. Leaving one Postumius in charge of mopping-up operations, Germanicus left to rejoin the commander-in-chief.[218]

Tiberius, meanwhile, was negotiating the terms of his capitulation with Bato of the Daesidiates.[219] Bato sent his son Sceuas with an offer of surrender in exchange for a pardon. Remarkably, Tiberius agreed.[220] It seems he had learned the lessons of the aftermath of failed Roman policy following the *Bellum Pannonicum*.[221] On a late summer night, Bato went to the Roman camp and, next morning, was led under armed escort before Tiberius, watched by the assembled Roman troops.[222] The rebel leader now showed precisely the kind of courage and dignity the Romans respected in a defeated enemy. He kneeled before the Roman commander, who was seated upon a tribunal, and formally laid down his arms at his feet, and spoke in defence of his fellow rebels, but asked no special conditions for himself.[223] He then bowed his head, baring his neck for the *coup de grâce*. This show of humility saved his life. Germanicus announced victory for the Romans, and the troops acclaimed their leader Tiberius by shouting the word *Imperator!* ('commander') for his achievement. The brutal 'War of the Batos' was finally over. In Rome, senators eager to coin a new accolade in recognition of Tiberius' achievement – among which were 'Conqueror of Pannonia', 'Invincible' and 'Pious' – were overruled by Augustus.[224]

The war had been won at high cost in blood and treasure.[225] The customary benefits in kind accruing to the troops after battle were few, as 'very little booty was taken'.[226] The towns and the economy of Illyricum were shattered, the people were beaten and exhausted, and it would take time, money and a defter touch to restore civility, peace and prosperity to the region. Crucially, the war to rid the threat posed by Marboduus had not taken place. Instead, Tiberius was forced to make a hasty treaty with the king of the Marcomanni, and the potential for conflict along the Rhine-Danube frontier remained.[227] Yet, at the end of the four-year-long war, Augustus could boast publicly that he had conquered 'the nations of the Pannonians, which before my principate no Roman army had ever approached'.[228] Augustus normally added the *imperator* battle honour to his roster, but graciously permitted Tiberius to use the name for the first time, and granted him a full triumph, also.[229] Two triumphal arches were erected to celebrate the victory in Illyricum.[230] After the rebellion, the Romans rethought their administrative policy framework for Illyricum, and sub-divided it into two smaller provinces: Dalmatia, along the coast, and landlocked Pannonia.[231] A comprehensive road-building programme began under the *legatus* P. Cornelius Dolabella, connecting the provinces to their neighbours, and towns populated by veterans were established.[232] In the years that followed, the region became a major recruiting ground for the Roman army. Recognizing their technical skill and bravery in warfare, the Roman army accepted Breuci as recruits, creating eight new *cohortes* of *auxilia*.[233] The Romans had clearly learned that the earlier policy of rounding up and deporting young men did not work.[234] No more rebellions are recorded in the region after 9 CE.[235]

Germanicus had played a significant role in the victory and his contribution was also fully recognized. Velleius Paterculus acknowledged that, in the Dalmatian War, Germanicus had 'been sent into various places of difficulty and danger' and had 'exhibited great proofs of courage'.[236] For this:

> Germanicus received the *ornamenta triumphalia*, a distinction which fell likewise to the other commanders, and also the rank of a *praetor*, as well as

the privilege of giving his vote immediately after the ex-consuls and of holding the consulship earlier than custom allowed.[237]

In just three years, he had come a very long way. Before the conflict, he was a young, naïve civil magistrate, with a talent for creative writing. Now, he was a battle-tested soldier and a commander with honours. He had done well under exceptional circumstances: raised an army, led it into battle, and beaten his foes. Germanicus had front-line leadership experience, and earned a solid reputation forged on the anvil of war. Velleius Paterculus writes:

> In the Dalmatian War, Germanicus, who had been dispatched in advance of the commander to regions both wild and difficult, gave great proof of his valour.[238]

His father (who had earned the honorary war-title his son now bore) and his grandfather (who had served Iulius Caesar and once rivalled Augustus for power) would have undoubtedly been proud.

Chapter 3

Law and Disorder
Autumn 9–14 CE

The New Normal

By September 9 CE, the campaign season was drawing to a close. Four legions would remain in the region formerly known as Illyricum, to ensure that law and order were maintained.[1] Tiberius, Germanicus, and their deputies, however, began their winter preparations by marching their other units back to their garrison camps along the Danube and Rhine rivers. Personally and professionally, they were looking forward to celebrating their hard-won victory in Illyricum in style, according to the public honours just awarded to them by a grateful Augustus and the Senate. The euphoria, however, was short-lived. Five days later, dispatches arrived from Germania.[2] 'Scarcely had these decrees been passed', writes Dio, 'when terrible news arrived from the province of Germania that prevented them from holding the festival'.[3] The first reports received seemed incredible. All Germania was in revolt. There had been an ambush. Roman allies led by a man named Arminius had been involved in an elaborate deception. Three legions, six cohorts and three *alae* of cavalry had been annihilated.[4] Varus was dead. There were few survivors. As more reports arrived, the worst was confirmed. Those who had made it out alive, by struggling back to the forts along the Lippe River and finally reaching the safety of the Rhine, gave their personal accounts in harrowing detail. In short, all Germania over the Rhine was lost. Even the priest of the altar of Rome and Augustus at Ara Ubiorum, Segimundus son of Segestes of the Cherusci nation, had raced off to join the rebels, taking with him the sacred garlands.[5]

Being the most senior man closest to the crisis, Tiberius immediately set off to take command and render assistance, taking with him detachments of the units which had just completed operations in the western Balkans.[6] Even at a forced march covering 25 miles a day, it would be weeks before he would reach the great military camps at Mogontiacum (Mainz), Novaesium (Neuss) and Vetera (Xanten). He would have to rely on the most senior man on the spot to use his initiative. Arriving at the virtually unmanned Rhine fortresses, he found L. Asprenas, a nephew of Varus, already assisting the survivors.[7] Fortunately, Varus had not withdrawn his entire five-legion army from the Rhine, but had been wise enough to leave two in reserve, one of which was *Legio* I. Once on location, Tiberius ordered guard details to be posted at points along the river-bank to intercept the Germanic rebels if they attempted a crossing.[8] With these temporary arrangements in place, and deputizing Germanicus as commander on the Rhine frontier, Tiberius rode off as fast as he could to Rome, to determine with Augustus what to do next.

When news of the catastrophe finally reached Rome, Augustus was mortified. His response was personal, like a father who had lost his own sons. In his despair, he is reported as ripping his clothes and tearing his hair, oftentimes shouting aloud, 'Quinctilius Varus! Give me back my legions!'[9] His hysterical reaction was 'not only because of the soldiers who had been lost, but also because of his fear for the German and Gallic provinces, and particularly because he expected that the enemy would march against Italy and against Rome itself'.[10] He had good reason to be fearful. Knowing the immense military resources available to the Marcomanni, and in an attempt to sway him to their side, the leaders of the rebellion had sent the severed head of Varus to King Marboduus. Remarkably, the Germanic king saw that there was nothing to be gained by breaking his new treaty with Rome and, holding to his obligations, he sent the head directly to Augustus and maintained his neutrality.[11] As the news spread of the catastrophe – which rapidly acquired the moniker *clades Variana*, the 'Varus disaster' – fear of barbarians gripped the city. In Rome, there was a large community of resident Gauls and Germans, and some were armed, including Augustus' own personal bodyguard, the *Germani Corporis Custodes*, and others serving with the Praetorian Cohorts.[12] Wary that they might now turn on their Roman paymasters, Augustus dispatched them 'to certain islands' where they could do no harm, and required those not under arms to quit the city.[13]

As head of state, Augustus had to quickly address the new crisis. Having conscripted all men of military age to fight in Dalmatia and Pannonia just three years previously, there were now few available that could be called up to defend the Italian fatherland.[14] Nevertheless, this was a state of emergency, so he issued instructions for a new levy requesting all able-bodied volunteers to come forward and do their duty. Remarkably, his call to patriotism met passive resistance, and:

> when no men of military age showed a willingness to be enrolled, he made them draw lots, depriving of his property and disfranchising every fifth man of those still under thirty-five and every tenth man among those who had passed that age. Finally, as a great many paid no heed to him even then, he put some to death. He chose by lot as many as he could of those who had already completed their term of service and of the freedmen, and after enrolling them sent them in haste with Tiberius [who had in the meantime arrived in Rome] into the province of Germania.[15]

Effectively press-ganging men into the service, however, would come back to haunt the senior leadership.

When Tiberius finally reached Rome, he found the city plunged into gloom. The shortening hours of daylight and the trees shedding their leaves added to the sense of foreboding. It was no longer 'business as usual' in the city, as people anticipated the worst, fearing that the Germanic 'barbarians' might soon be charging through the streets. In a mark of how grave the public perceived the situation, even the religious festivals were suspended.[16] Aware of the solemn mood, but nevertheless feeling entitled to celebrate his triumph, Tiberius still donned the purple-bordered toga and the victory laurel crown of the *triumphator* and entered the city.[17] In the Forum Romanum, he ascended a tribunal specially erected next to the Saepta and took his place beside Augustus, between the two consuls, while the members of the Senate stood alongside. From here, Tiberius addressed the assembled crowd. He was then escorted out to pay the required religious observances with visits to the temples, as protocol dictated. It was a carefully managed public display of solidarity – a reminder to the people that, despite a military setback, the Roman state and her protecting gods still prevailed.[18] After a brief sojourn in the city, Tiberius took the unwilling band of men that could be assembled back with him to the Rhine.

The winter came and went. With the passing of the New Year, so too did the immediate crisis. The much-feared Germanic invasion did not transpire.[19] The new Rhine frontier held. Augustus' ire had waned and he began to try and understand the situation that had befallen him. He reflected that he had failed to read the omens. There had been plenty to see, had he had eyes to see them.[20] Cassius Dio meticulously records the catalogue of signs and portents. The Temple of Mars in the Campus Martius had been struck by lightning. There was a plague of locusts. There were reports that the Alps exploded like volcanoes. Comets had blazed across the night sky. Yet there had been even clearer signs:

> Spears seemed to dart from the north and to fall in the direction of the Roman camps; bees formed their combs about the altars in the camps; a statue of Victory that was in the province of Germania and faced the enemy's territory turned about to face Italia; and, in one instance, there was a futile battle and conflict of the soldiers over the eagles in the camps, the soldiers believing that the barbarians had fallen upon them.[21]

How could he have been so blind to these signs? In his retrospection, he might have forgotten that it is easy to be wise with hindsight.

Ever cautious but pragmatic, Tiberius decided not to invade Germania, 'but kept quiet, watching to see that the barbarians did not cross; and they, knowing him to be there, did not venture to cross in their turn'.[21] There was no need to provoke the Germanic nations, he thought – at least for the time being. Tiberius would bide his time and use it to formulate a new strategy. Yet the stark fact was that the Rhine River was now Rome's de facto north-western frontier, even if temporarily, and, for the sake of the security of Tres Galliae, Raetia and Italia, it had to be held at all costs. In a cruel twist, the survivors of Teutoburg suffered a second torment. There were numbers of Roman troops still alive, but being held captive by the Germanic tribes, who saw this as an opportunity to raise cash from desperate families. Their relatives willingly paid the ransoms and received back their loved ones, but the Roman authorities intervened and insisted that the returning men were not permitted to return to Italy.[22] It was as though they were cursed and would bring bad luck to the Commonwealth if they were allowed to step on the sacred soil of the fatherland.

With the emergency in Germania contained, for the moment, Germanicus' stint as military commander came to an end. He returned to Rome, where he would stay for the next eighteen months. The mood in Rome was improving and returning to its old extrovert normality. Germanicus, too, quickly resumed his place in society. He was a *praetor* and with that position came the responsibilities of a senior magistrate. Under Augustus, twelve men were elected annually by the Senate, but, despite the outward show of due process, the *praetor*'s function increasingly was becoming one of administration rather than jurisprudence.[23] As a high profile magistrate, rather than overseeing civil actions (*actiones*), Germanicus would have been more likely to be involved in criminal cases (*quaestiones perpetuae*), in particular the so-called 'crimes against the public' (*crimina publica*). In this role, he could appoint judges to act as jurors, voting for decisions of guilt or innocence, with condemnation in the former and acquittal in the latter case. In criminal cases, a conviction could result in the death penalty, though senators and *equites* could be exiled or opt to fight in the arena as a means to save face.[24] To bring a case to a criminal court, in the absence of a district attorney, state prosecution service or public prosecutor, a private citizen acting as the plaintiff would first assemble his case and gather witnesses.[25] He would inform the defendant of his intention and grounds for pursuing a case (*editio actionis*) against him. If the defendant refused to accompany him, the plaintiff was permitted some leeway to bring the accused man to court, including reasonable force.[26] The plaintiff would then petition the *praetor*.[27] The two litigants would present themselves before Germanicus, who would then examine the legal basis for the case, a procedure referred to as *in iure*. They would appear again, this time before a judge (*apud iudicem*) agreed to by both parties or appointed by the *praetor*. Then as now, the outcome would rest on the quality of the evidence, witness' testimony and the performance of the advocates arguing their cases in the courtroom.

In Germanicus' lifetime, the practice of law by the politician, such as Cato or Cicero, looking to build his reputation as he rose through the *cursus honorum*, was changing to a more consistent professional footing. This was the age that saw the rise of the fee-charging legal assistant (*iuris consultis*) and the court advocate (*orator*).[28] The *iuris consultis* would proffer advice to his client, based on an understanding of the statute law, and suggest the best strategy.[29] The *orator* would perform in the courtroom for his client, using his knowledge of the law, his finely crafted skill of eloquent speaking, the practised gestures of the hand, and a lifetime of insights into human psychology, to question the witnesses and to sway the judge or jury to his argument. The element of theatricality in criminal cases, as much as the salacious detail of the evidence, often brought large crowds of bystanders.[30]

Despite his position as *praetor*, Germanicus was quite prepared to offer his services as an *orator*. By now, he had developed a talent for public speaking, a 'surpassing ability in the oratory and learning of Greece and Rome', notes

Suetonius.[31] As a nobleman, Germanicus served the public in the long tradition of offering free defence to the less well-off. Already, his name brought credibility to a case of a capital crime. In the one recorded instance that has come down to us, Germanicus took a brief to defend a certain *quaestor* on a charge of murder.[32] Learning that the grandson of the *princeps* was going to represent the defendant, and fearing his celebrity would sway the presiding judge:

> his accuser became alarmed lest he should, in consequence of this, lose his suit before the judges who regularly heard such cases, and wished to have it tried before Augustus.[33]

The plaintiff's request to be tried in another court was denied. In the event, Germanicus presented the stronger argument and the accuser 'did not win the suit'.[34]

Along with a gift for advocacy, Germanicus was winning public approval for his even-handedness in taking on cases, irrespective of the status of the person he represented and regardless of which judge presided over the trial:

> Germanicus was becoming endeared to the populace for many reasons, but particularly because he acted as advocate for various persons, and this quite as much before Augustus himself as before the other judges.[35]

The *princeps* took his own legal responsibilities very seriously, often staying to judge cases until the onset of night.[36] If he was feeling unwell, rather then miss them, he would arrange for his litter to carry him down to the Forum Romanum and hold the cases at the open-air judicial tribunal. Tiberius had, himself, presented before Augustus in his early judicial career. In that role, he successfully defended Archelaus, a Jewish king, in a case held in private and presided over by the *princeps,* and on other occasions he had also advocated on behalf of the citizens of Thessaly and Tralles.[37] Whether Germanicus found advocating before Augustus a pleasant or nerve-wracking experience is not recorded.

Consul Germanicus
At home, the family of Germanicus and his wife steadily grew. Agrippina the Elder was 'characterized by her outstanding fertility', wrote Tacitus.[38] While her husband had been away in action in Illyricum, Agrippina had given birth to a healthy baby boy and named him Drusus, after either his celebrated grandfather or his uncle.[39] He was already 3 years old. With the return of Germanicus, the couple tried for another child. In the late summer of 10 CE, Agrippina gave birth to a boy, but the poor little mite did not survive the year.[40] While Suetonius does not disclose the name of the child, an inscription found on a sepulchral monument located on the *Via Flaminia* near the Mausoleum of Augustus, in which the ashes of the dead child were buried, clearly identifies his name as Ti. Caesar, after his adopted grandfather.[41] Infant mortality rates in first century Rome, as for all ancient societies, were relatively high by modern standards. Though the mean life expectancy at birth was 25 years or less, those individuals who survived the first several years could live to quite respectable old age.[42] Unperturbed, the

couple tried again and, in 11 CE, she produced another son at Tibur (Tivoli).[43] Named Caius, sadly, he also did not live to see his first birthday.[44] He may be the 'charming child' of 'lovable disposition' to whom Suetonius refers, who captured the hearts and minds of grandparents Augustus and Livia.[45] Livia dedicated a statue of him as Cupid in the Temple of Venus Capitolinus, and Augustus had another statuette made that he kept by his bed and used to kiss fondly every time he entered the room.[46]

Germanicus' young family provided the *princeps* with a model of domestic bliss within his own household. Keen to promote marriage as a cornerstone of Roman society, Augustus brought in laws that imposed fines upon eligible bachelors for failure to marry and raise families. Finding the new requirements intolerable, men of the wealthy equestrian order protested for repeal of the marriage laws during a performance at the theatre Augustus was himself attending:

> whereupon he sent for the children of Germanicus and showed them, partly sitting upon his own lap, and partly on their father's, intimating, by his looks and gestures, that they ought not to think it a grievance to follow the example of that young man.[47]

Many men managed to elude the law by marrying under-age girls, and by divorcing and remarrying several times. Augustus moderated his policy, requiring marriages to be consummated within a set time period and imposing restrictions on divorce.

Tiberius deemed that it was time for the Romans to flex their armour-covered muscles. Germanicus was recalled to take part in the military manoeuvres. In 11 CE, 'Tiberius and Germanicus (acting as *proconsul*) invaded Germania and overran portions of it'.[48] Significantly, Dio reports that 'they did not win any battle, however, since no one came to close quarters with them, nor did they reduce any tribe'.[49] If the Germanic tribes were shying away from a fight, it was matched by the ever-cautious approach of Tiberius, 'for in their fear of falling victims to a fresh disaster they did not advance very far beyond the Rhine'.[50] The aim of this seemingly pointless mission was to demonstrate (as much to the audience at home as to the Germans) that the Romans could still enter the region and march about at will – and that they would be back to reclaim it. It also served a practical function. In place of constant drills on the parade ground and building practice camps in friendly country, this expedition took the army into hostile territory, built up unit cohesion, and kept the men in combat-ready mode. It was not intended to be a reoccupation, for:

> after remaining in that region until late autumn and celebrating the birthday of Augustus [23 September], on which they held a horse-race under the direction of the centurions, they returned.[51]

Roman honour had been satisfied.[52] The Romans went home. Germanicus himself did not spend the winter in Tres Galliae. He had been called to Rome to attend to important state business.

On 1 January 12 CE, Germanicus was sworn in as *consul ordinarius*. Remarkable was the speed with which he had attained it.[53] At just 27 years of age, he had been elected to the position two years before his father Drusus had, and one year earlier than Tiberius. Indeed, he was among the youngest ever to receive the honour. There were always two men in the office at any one time, and his co-consul was C. Fonteius Capito.[54] Little is known about him. He is likely to have been the son of the man of the same name, the *legatus* M. Fonteius in Gaul.[55] In the quaint but cumbersome Roman calender, the year 12 CE would forever be known as 'the Year of the Consuls Germanicus Caesar, son of Tiberius Caesar, and C. Fonteius Capito, son of Caius'.[56]

The consulship by this time was not what it had once been. When Cicero had been elected to the highest position in the heyday of the *res publica* in 63 BCE, the *consules* were elected to carry out three responsibilities: to command Rome's armies, to preside over meetings of the Senate, and to ensure its decisions were implemented.[57] Then, there was a mandated two-year interval between the candidate's praetorship and permitting him to stand for the consulship.[58] Under the settlement with Augustus of 27 BCE, the ancient *comitia centuriata*, which had elected the consuls for hundreds of years, lost their powers, and the Senate chose two men from among its ranks themselves – no doubt with strong guidance from the *princeps* or those who knew his mind.[59] Augustus all the while controlled the army. Without military power, the consulship thereafter became largely honorary.[60]

In his assessment of Germanicus' achievements for the year, Dio notes that at least he held the post for the full term of office.[61] It was becoming increasingly common for a consul to resign from the role after only a few months, and a replacement (or *consul suffectus*) to be appointed.[62] This created a larger pool of ex-consuls, who could be assigned positions as provincial governors – proconsuls and *propraetores* – or legates of legions. Capito did precisely this, and was replaced during his term by C. Visellius Varro.[63] Dio writes, somewhat dismissively:

> Germanicus himself did nothing memorable, except that at this time, too, he acted as advocate in law-suits, since his colleague, C. Capito, counted as a mere figurehead.[64]

His legal and administrative training had prepared Germanicus for this work. Governing the Roman Empire was not only about winning glory through wars of conquest, but as much about the hard graft of enforcing the law and interceding in the more humdrum details of disputes between its citizens and its resident aliens. Nevertheless, Augustus recognized and appreciated his contributions, and wrote a letter to the Senate stating so.[65] The letter was read aloud in the *curia*, not by the *princeps*, whose voice had apparently grown weaker in old age, for he was now 73, but by Germanicus himself.

On the calender of events for the year was a special festival hosted by the city's guilds of actors and horsebreeders; and the *Ludi Martiales*, gladiatorial games held in honour of Mars.[66] As the Tiber had once again flooded parts of the city, including the valley between the Aventinus and Palatinus hills and, with it, Rome's largest sports stadium, the Circus Maximus, these religious games had to be held in the Forum of Augustus, opened in 2 BCE.[67] The games were repeated a second time – as was the custom – with Germanicus as the sponsor and, this time, in the Circus.[68] Unlike the *munera* that Germanicus had co-sponsored with his brother in 6 CE to commemorate his deceased father, these *ludi* were deeply religious in significance. During the days preceding the games, members of the political priesthood (*quindecemviri sacris faciundis*) provided sulphur, tar and torches for the public to carry out private purification rites in their homes.[69] The day of the games combined the pomp and ceremony of a religious rite with the glitz and glamour of a rock concert. A purification ceremony (*lustratio*) took place in which a pig, a sheep and a goat were sacrificed. As the throat of each animal was cut and its lifeblood gushed out, the priest intoned the words *Mars pater, te piaculo* – 'Father Mars, to thee I make atonement'.[70] The ritual took place to the accompaniment of musicians – horns, flutes and even hydraulically-powered organs.[71] The religious formalities attended to, it was showtime.

Germanicus laid on a rich and varied programme of entertainments. In planning his *spectacula*, which would showcase combats between gladiators and exotic wild beasts, he had to work within restrictions imposed by law. In 22 BCE, to mitigate abuses by politically-minded sponsors, Augustus had transferred responsibility for organizing the official *ludi* from the aediles to the praetors, placing a strict cap on public spending and limiting the number of gladiators to 120 individuals, unless express permission was granted for more by the Senate.[72] The high point of Germanicus' show was a display of the skills of the *bestiarii* or *venatores*. A *bestiarius* had a helmet, a shield and a sword, and fought the wild beasts like a gladiator, while the *venator* was armed with a spear and a dagger, and hunted his prey as he would in the wild.[73] The bigger and more exotic the animal, the more likely it was to be killed in a public demonstration of Rome's power over Nature – both in terms of its ability to acquire the beast from the remotest parts of the world and, once captive, of its decision over whether it lived or died.[74] Some 200 lions are recorded as having been killed during the performance.[75] It may have been during these very games, at the noonday show while the gladiators fought, that the spectators witnessed – awestruck – a fiery meteor (*fax caelestis*) streaking with 'a long train of light' across the sky.[76] From this heavenly spectacle, all present would have deduced that Mars approved of Germanicus' games.

There was good news on the family front, too. On 31 August at Antium (Anzio) or Tibur, Agrippina gave birth to a baby boy.[77] He lived beyond the first eight days and, perhaps hoping for better luck, the parents chose the same name for the boy as the one who had died the previous year, who had captivated Augustus and Livia.[78] C. Iulius Caesar (plate 12) was doted on by his family. Germanicus was now the proud father of three boys – Nero, Drusus and Caius.[79] The older boys were, meanwhile, being taught by the eminent poet Carus, who was known to Ovid.[80]

One of the high points of the year 12 CE was Tiberius' Pannonian triumph.[81] Originally awarded in 9, it had been foreshadowed by the terrible events at *saltus Teutoburgiensis*.[82] Germanicus and the other *legati* who had seen service in the Balkans and had also been awarded triumphal ornaments also took part, including Velleius Paterculus and his brother.[83] On 23 October, Rome turned out in force to cheer the 53-year old commander during his celebratory military parade.[84] The last time he had been honoured in this public way was on a cold New Year's day in 7 BCE, as a reward for his victories in Germania.[85] The seemingly interminable season of rain broke that day and the sky was clear, blue and serene.[86] A Roman triumph was the ancient equivalent of the military ticker-tape procession, combined with the spectacle of a Fourth-of-July parade on an epic scale complete with a cast of thousands. He entered the city on a chariot pulled by four horses, and wore the embroidered robe of a *triumphator*, his head bearing the victor's laurel crown.[87] Germanicus and the other generals whose achievements were also being celebrated probably rode on horseback behind Tiberius. Tiberius mounted a tribunal erected in the Saepta Iulia and sat with Augustus between the two consuls, while the senators stood out of respect, and saluted the people. One of the star attractions of the triumphal procession was the captive Pannonian warchief (*dux*) Bato of the Daesidiates.[88] Not for him a long-term incarceration at the Tullianum jail, or the humiliating death by strangulation that had been the grim end of Vercingetorix at Iulius Caesar's triumph in 46 BCE.[89] Bato's life had been spared on account of his noble decision to allow the Roman troops to escape when cornered (perhaps at Andetrium), and of his honourable surrender.[90] After the public celebration of Tiberius' victory, Bato retired to Ravenna, to live a very comfortable, all-expenses-paid life in exile.[91]

The *triumphator*'s chariot (*currus triumphalis*) followed the route of the ancient *Via Sacra* through the Forum Romanum, along which the city's crowds were packed, everyone eager to see the man who had 'reduced to complete subjection all Illyricum lying between Italy and the kingdom of Noricum, Thrace, Macedonia, the Danube River and the Adriatic Sea'.[92] The road turned beside the Temple of Saturn and ascended the Capitolinus Hill where Tiberius stepped down from his chariot and knelt at Augustus' feet in homage and fealty.[93] It may be this moment to which the *Gemma Augustea* (plate 22) – an exquisite cameo believed to have been engraved by master craftsman Dioskurides or one of his pupils – refers.[94] The engraver created two tiers of parallel allegorical scenes from double-layered Arabian onyx. In the upper tier, Augustus appears as Iupiter, seated on a curule chair and holding a long staff. The gem might commemorate Tiberius' victory, but it was won under the auspices of Augustus.[95] He is being crowned with a *corona civica* of oak leaves – for saving Roman lives – by Ecumene (Oikumene) while Oceanus or Neptunus and Gaia sit beside her.[96] To Augustus' right sits Roma, wearing a helmet and clasping a spear, but she is lightly touching a sword, as if to indicate that Rome is always ready to defend herself. To her right stands a man wearing the armour and distinctive *paludamentum* of a commanding officer. Most scholars identify this youthful figure as Germanicus Caesar. To his right, Tiberius descends from a chariot, clutching a staff in one hand, while a winged victory stands behind him. In the lower tier, soldiers heave as they hoist up a *trophaea*, while bound barbarian captives look on dejectedly.

Tiberius' triumph was well-deserved. He had been a loyal servant of Augustus, from the first days he had entered the army in Hispania at the age of 16, and had been fighting his wars in a great many of the years since. A measure of the confidence Augustus had in him is demonstrated in the fact that, the following year, he made Tiberius' *imperium maius* equal to his own and renewed his tribunician power for another five years.[97] Although the act of kneeling before the *princeps* suggested a subservient relationship, in all but name Tiberius was now co-regent of the Roman commonwealth. The exiled poet Ovid speculated on Germanicus' own future as a military commander, and prophesied that he would one day celebrate a triumph of his own.[98]

After the sacrifices and prayers of thanks had been offered, a public feast was laid out on a thousand tables, and Tiberius gave each man a donative of 30 *sestertii*. On this day, he also dedicated, in his and his deceased brother's names, the Temple of Castor and Pollux, which had been paid for by the spoils of the Pannonian War.[99]

Germanicus the Governor
Having successfully completed his term as consul, Germanicus was now legally qualified to take up his first official provincial management position. Germanicus was appointed Augustus' deputy and governor (*legatus Augusti pro praetore*) for the Tres Galliae, the 'Three Gallic Provinces', and Germania, at least what was left of it, and crucially the eight legions stationed on the Rhine.[100] It was an important step on the career ladder bringing with it great prestige. A quarter of a century earlier, his natural father had assumed the very same governorship, which he had held until his death. The word *provincia* originally meant 'appointment' or 'task', and, outside of Rome, it was applied to the 'sphere of action' of elected magistrates.[101] As Augustus' deputy, he was invested with the *princeps'* powers of *imperium* and had complete jurisdiction over the Tres Galliae and the allies still loyal to Rome in Germania, and he could make decisions and lawfully carry them out in his name.[102] Just as Drusus the Elder had assumed the governorship of the provinces from Tiberius, now so too did Germanicus. It was as though the region was the testing ground for the sons of Augustus. In early 13 CE, accompanied by his escort of lictors as his bodyguard, he travelled the 1,000km (621 miles) journey by road to Colonia Copia Munatia Felix (Lyon) located on the confluence of the Rhône (Rhodanus) and Saône (Arar) rivers. While it was nominally the provincial capital, Germanicus would spend most of his time elsewhere in the region. Indeed, it seems that, shortly after arriving there, he departed for Ara Ubiorum (Cologne) on the Rhine.[103]

As governor, Germanicus had several explicit duties to perform. First of these was nation-building. The local Gallic aristocracies were to be encouraged to build self-sustaining urban communities.[104] Augustus had adopted a 'carrot and stick' approach to driving regional economic and political development in the Tres Galliae, which Drusus the Elder had continued.[105] They had actively promoted certain regional capitals, lavishing largesse on them, awarding them privileges and Roman citizenship, and even lending them the prestige of his own name, such as the marketplaces of the Aedui at Augustodunum Aedorum (Autun), the Rauraci at Augusta Raurica (Augst), and the Treveri at Augusta Treverorum

(Trier). Others singled out for recognition included Augustomagus (Senlis), Augustonemetum (Clermont-Ferrand), Augustobona (Troyes), and Augustoritum (Limoges).[106] These centres were the means of encouraging adoption of the Roman way among the élites of the native peoples through civic rivalry, and competition for prestige and the attention of the imperial family.[107] Competition for recognition among Rome's élites had been the ever-present catalyst that had driven it from a small village on seven hills to an expansive empire on three continents. By Germanicus' time, two generations had passed since the Gallic aristocracies had fought Iulius Caesar. Their great-grandsons were now the leaders of their communities. In the most developed form, such community governments were miniature versions of the political system in Rome, with junior magistracies such as quaestors and aediles supervised by two senior magistrates (*duoviri*) who ran the administration and the courts and were advised by a town council or senate (*ordo*).[108] The *ordo* was made up of local worthies (*honesti*), whose membership of the body was qualified by wealth and property limits, since they were expected to pay for certain expenses out of their own purses as a responsibilty of holding office. In some communities, the traditional Gallic magistracies continued, such as the *vergobret* among the Lexovii and Santones, a position which may have been the equivalent of a Roman *praetor*.[109]

Many of the leading men (*primores*) enjoyed wealth or power by mediating between the Roman authorities and the mass of tribal commoners.[110] Writing of the Gauls' British cousins some forty years after the conquest of their island, Tacitus noted how quickly they had adopted the Latin language and were keen to wear the toga.[111] They were oblivious, he said, to the fact that they had been seduced by the comforts of the bath and the dining room, which they called 'culture' (*humanitas*), whereas, in truth, 'it was but a part of their servitude'.[112] It was this life of comfort and indulgence that Tacitus blamed for the Gallic people becoming passive.[113] To build a peaceful commonwealth of nations, Augustus had to create a complaisant population. Tacitus's observations of the behaviour of the Gauls in the first century CE was actually a measure of how successfully the *princeps* and his provincial governors had implemented the policy.

Secondly, there was the task of ensuring internal security. Germanicus was responsible for ensuring the stability of the region and maintaining its borders. To enjoy Roman protection, the local population was expected to pay for it through taxation. The three Gallic provinces were imperial territories under the direct control of Augustus, and Germanicus had very significant military resources under his care to enforce Roman power.[114] There were eight legions on the Rhine – fully a third of the empire's legionary manpower – comprising I *Germanica*, II *Augusta*, V *Alaudae*, XIII *Gemina*, XIV *Gemina*, XVI *Gallica*, XX *Valeria Victrix*, and XXI *Rapax*, and an unknown number of auxiliary cohorts.[115] It was a responsibility that called for a loyal and sober temperament, since an ambitious man could be tempted to use the forces at his command to challenge the government in Rome.[116] Each legion had its own legate, personally chosen by Augustus from men who had served in the Senate, but Germanicus was their commander-in-chief within the region. The fact that he was just 28 years old was not an issue. He had personal credibility (*virtus*) from having served successfully in action during the Pannonian War; he had prestige (*gravitas*) as a former consul; and he had authority (*auctoritas*) as Augustus' personal deputy imbued with *imperium* and the right to make war.

Thirdly, there was the matter of promoting of Roman interests – which, in most cases, meant economic interests. The three Gallic provinces had many natural resources that Roman entrepreneurs were quick to exploit. These resident Roman citizens fully expected that their rights and privileges enshrined in law would be promoted and supported in the provinces. Already in the early first century CE, Roman businessmen ran a very broad range of profit-making operations in the Tres Galliae, from importing wine from Italy by sea to running great estates producing wheat, and from operating mines and quarries to manufacturing fine red tableware. Many enjoyed contracts to provide the army with foodstuffs, animals and raw materials, which it consumed in vast quantities. Germanicus' army of eight legions, representing a total of some 40,000 men, excluding non-combatants, would have consumed an estimated 60 tonnes (132,277lbs) of corn and 240 *amphorae* of olive oil and wine, *each and every day*.[117] The same army would require 4,000 horses and 3,500 pack animals. Horses were required for the cavalry, and mules were used to carry the leather *contubernium* tents and other heavy items on the march.[118] While all animals could feed off the land to some extent, quantities of fodder nevertheless had to be carried whenever the army went on campaign. One estimate is that a single cavalry *ala* with 560 horses required between 560kg (1,235lbs) and 1,680kg (3,704lbs) of barley, and 5,600kg (12,346lbs) of hay each year.[119] As a consumer of resources, such a large army presence acted as a dynamo to the local economy. If the body of the Roman Empire was its cities and institutions, its bloodstream was the flow of goods and money that coursed along its network of roads.

Germanicus had an additional responsibilty that was not typical of a provincial governor: ensuring the security and uninterrupted operation of the mint (*moneta*) in Colonia Copia, which struck coins almost from the moment of its establishment in 15 BCE.[120] It had quickly become the only location in the western empire to produce the *aureus* or 'golden *denarius*', and Augustus may have actually intended the mint in Tres Galliae to prevent the Senate from meddling in the production of high-value coins.[121] The mint also produced the silver *denarius* and small change in copper (*aes*) and bright yellow brass (*orichalcum*), which facilitated the burgeoning markets in traded goods across the region.[122] Every coin was made by hand, by placing a flan of metal in a two-part die and striking it with a hammer. It was a slow and labour-intensive process. Significantly, the mint was located between the mines in the Iberian Peninsula and Gaul, which produced the precious metals, and the troops stationed there and across Tres Galliae, Raetia and Noricum, who needed regular payment.[123] Since coins had to be physically transported to the army in its winter camps three times a year, the location of the mint at Colonia Copia solved the logistical challenges of safely moving great quantities of gold and silver pieces from Rome, by taking the centre of production closer to the points of distribution. Ensuring that the mint was secure and that the die kept striking was now Germanicus' responsibility.

The relatively long period of peace in the region had enabled the Gallic communities to grow economically, but a key component was the *concilium Galliarum*, which promoted its political welfare.[124] It was created by Drusus the Elder during the period 14–12 BCE to bring together the élites of the cities (*primores*), to give them a larger platform from which to express themselves, and to reinforce their status and control in their own communities. Through it, they could bring grievances to the notice of assembly members and the presiding *propraetor*, and proffer advice on measures intended to apply to the entire province. The assembly was also responsible for overseeing the imperial cult of Roma and Augustus at the spectacular cult sanctuary (*fanum*) at Condate, across the valley from Lugdunum, where its chief priest (*sacerdos*) conducted religious ceremonies and instigated gladiatorial games annually on 1 August.

Even with the loss of the territory in Germania Magna, there was still a sizeable Gallo-Germanic community on the Roman side (*Gallia Cisrhenana*) of the River Rhine. M. Agrippa, or one of his deputies, had founded the marketplaces of the Treveri at Augusta Treverorum (Trier) and the Ubii at Oppidum Ubiorum (Cologne).[125] Tiberius had relocated the Sugambri at Vetera. In an attempt to build an identity for these people, Ahenobarbus replicated the successful model set up by Drusus the Elder, by building an altar to the imperial cult in Oppidum Ubiorum and renaming the city Ara Ubiorum.[126] A council was founded with members drawn from the confederation of Germanic tribes. Segimerus of the Cherusci was elected as its first *flamen*.[127]

One of the first tasks Germanicus is recorded as having undertaken as provincial governor was the census. During Caesar's war of conquest and the years of the civil wars, the Gallic nations had been asked to provide men and horses to bolster the ranks of the Roman army. In the era of peace ushered in by Augustus, it was supplemented by the need for cold, hard cash.[128] Augustus needed funds for his Rhine army. Some communities responded to his beneficence and paid Augustus handsomely.[129] Nevertheless, accurate assessments of the assets of the population were needed to calculate the tax basis, and a nationwide *census* was undertaken every five years (a period of time called a *lustrum*). Augustus had, himself, overseen a census of the three Gallic provinces in 27 BCE, while holding assizes in Narbonensis, and Drusus the Elder had done so in 14/13.[130] It was a major undertaking that required careful planning and diligence in its execution. By law, Roman citizens living in Italia were exempt from direct taxes – an entitlement called the 'Italian Right' – but those resident outside were not. Outside Rome, the census was supervised by a team of *censitores* and their assistants (*censuales*) who compiled a complete register of Roman citizens and their property. The governor might assign his deputies to do so, but it appears that Germanicus oversaw the duties himself in 14 CE.[131] Many of the requirements of the census are known from the *Digest* of the jurist Domitius Ulpianus, who lived in the second century CE.[132] He records that the person registering was required to make estimates, himself, of all his estates – acreages of arable, pasture and woodland, numbers of trees, olive trees and vines, ponds, harbours and saltpans – and detail his slaves by number, age, nationality, function and skills. Concessions were made for landslides that took land out of production and for withered vines or dead trees that reduced the total taxable output. It was a heavily labour-intensive procedure. Each registrant had to be interviewed in person and notes were recorded by hand. The entire operation was controlled from Colonia Copia, but registrants may have been required to go to a designated town where the *censitor* had set up his information-gathering operations.[133] The grand scale of the retinue such an official brought with him survives on the tombstone of Musicus Scurranus, who served as an imperial *dispensator ad fiscum Gallicum provinciae Lugdunensis* under Tiberius and died when he returned to Rome. The inscription reveals that accompanying Scurranus was a crew of freedmen and slaves, including a business agent and an accountant, three assistants, a physician, two slaves responsible for silver and one for the wardrobe, two chamberlains, two footmen, two cooks, and a woman of unspecified role and responsibility.[134]

Agrippina joined her husband on the Rhine frontier at Ara Ubiorum sometime in 13 or 14 CE, taking her oldest children with her on the long journey, but leaving her youngest son in the care of Augustus and Livia. She was expecting again. On the journey, at a village called Ambitarvium near Augusta Treverorum, she bore Germanicus a daughter.[135] The baby girl died not long after and was not given a name, as children were only named on the eighth or ninth day of life.[136] The child's memory was, nevertheless, honoured. An altar was erected close by to mark the occasion, with the inscription 'FOR THE DELIVERY OF AGRIPPINA'.[137] Alarmingly for the family, in the spring of 14, little Caius fell ill. Worried by the development, his grandfather wrote to Agrippina on 13 May, informing her that he had immediately dispatched the boy to her, in the care of a physician (*medicus*).[138] Presumably, he felt that the boy would recover more quickly with his mother, rather than his grandparents. Augustus advised her that he had written separately to Germanicus and apprised him of the situation, with the offer that he could keep the doctor, who was a slave, if he wanted.

While Gaul itself appears to have been calm, there is tantalizing evidence that Germans were crossing from the right bank of the Rhine in 13 CE. A surviving document, called by modern scholars the *Tabula Siarensis* (see Appendix), pre-serves the mention that, following campaigns in which he expelled the Germans from the region, he 'set Gallia in order'.[139] As governor, it was Germanicus' job to expel the invaders and restore order. How serious a threat this Germanic invasion was is not explained in the other documentary sources, but the gravity of the matter clearly merited mention in the senatorial record posted in Rome. Paterculus mentions earlier 'dissensions which had broken out among the Viennenses', put down by Tiberius.[140] The poet Krinagoras also cheers a great victory in which Germanicus struck down masses of enemy he identifies as κελτοί living between the Alps and Pyrenees.[141] It may have been after this encounter that Germanicus was acclaimed by his soldiers as *imperator* – a title meaning simply 'commander', but normally granted by the soldiery for acts of valour or for bringing them victory after battle – though the evidence for it is inconclusive.[142] Germanicus, however, had a bigger mission. Velleius Paterculus observes that Caesar Augustus sent his grandson 'to finish the remainder of the war in Germania'.[143] In this, he was following in the footsteps of both Drusus the Elder and Tiberius. Tiberius himself was also due to begin military manoeuvres. In the late summer of 14 CE, he set off for the Dalmatian coast of Illyricum, accompanying Augustus on the journey as far as Beneventum.[144] Augustus continued on his way to Nola in Campania, but contracted a sickness *en route*; a shooting star was seen in the sky, which some took to be a portent.[145]

The World Turned Upside Down
Late in the summer of 14 CE a rider of the *cursus publicus*, the imperial courier service, approached Germanicus, dripping with sweat.[146] He had ridden fast and furiously, carrying a letter intended for the *propraetor*'s eyes only. Saluting the senior officer, the messenger handed over the tightly-rolled scroll of papyrus. Germanicus recognized the seal. It was a profile of Augustus's head, exquisitely carved by the master craftsman Dioskurides: it was the *princeps*' own personal seal.[147] Yet there was something distinctly odd. The handwriting was Tiberius'.[148] Germanicus broke the seal, unrolled the letter, and read the contents. The news it contained was devastating. On 19 August, C. Iulius Caesar Augustus, First Man of the Roman world, had breathed his last breath in Nola. In his last living moments, Tiberius had been chosen by him as his successor, to carry on the great work of leading the Commonwealth.[150] Germanicus' adoptive father now wore the ring that had once graced the finger of the revered leader, and, by dint of it, was the most powerful man in the Roman world. Respecting Germanicus' status, Tiberius dispatched envoys 'to express sympathy with his grief at the death of Augustus'.[151]

The death of Augustus was a major landmark event in the history of Rome. He had lived 75 years, 10 months and 26 days, and been the leading man of the Senate (*princeps senatus*) for almost 41 of them.[152] In Augustus' will, which was read out in the *curia* before the assembled Senate by an imperial freedman named Polybius, Tiberius and Livia were declared his principal heirs.[153] As heirs 'in the second degree', Drusus the Younger received one third of the estate, while Germanicus and his three male children received the rest.[154] Germanicus' children were now and henceforth permitted the use of the name Caesar.[155] Largesse was to be distributed among the Praetorian Cohorts, the troops of the legions, and the citizens of Rome, according to rank and status.[156] Everything had been planned in advance. The arrangements for the funeral; instructions for how the mausoleum was to be furnished, including the attachment of his account of his lifetime's work (*Res Gestae*) on bronze plaques by the entrance; the standing of the army and details about the nation's budget and public spending; as well as personal wisdom and guidance on good government – including the recommendation not to expand the frontiers of the empire – were read out by Drusus the Younger.[157] The succession of Tiberius was a major turning point in the history of Rome. Augustus had cleverly avoided accusations of establishing a dynasty, by not appointing a direct successor – not even in his last will and testament.[158] While Augustus bequeathed to Tiberius the use of his name, as well as his estate, he did not pass on his constitutional powers. He did not need to. The legally-minded Romans recognized that Tiberius had already acquired powers equal to those of Augustus, by virtue of having received the *tribunicia potestas* – renewed in 13 CE – which meant he could convene the Senate; and through the *imperium maius* – also granted the year before – Tiberius had direct control over the imperial provinces and the army (*exercitus*) and their chief executives.[159] Indeed, Tiberius' first official acts were to issue orders to the Praetorian Cohorts, the legions, and the auxiliaries, and to convene the Senate, leaving no doubt in people's minds who was in charge.[160]

The rule of a powerful First Man with the consent of the Senate and Roman people was affirmed. There would be no going back to the unpredictable and unstable democracy of the Republic. Most people in Rome and the provinces accepted the situation without protest, but many intellectuals, traditionalists, and even ordinary citizens had hoped for a restoration of the supremacy of the consuls, the Senate and the popular assembly, but they would continue to be frustrated.[161] One of these would have been Tiberius' brother – Germanicus' own natural father – Drusus the Elder.[162] While alive, he had hoped that Augustus could be persuaded to step down and restore the old way of governing the country.[163] If Tiberius was once sympathetic to this view, now that he had the opportunity to do something about it, he did not relinquish the powers he had gradually assumed from the *princeps*. Ensuring the 'Peace of Augustus' – characterized by the ending of almost a century of civil war, military successes over Rome's enemies, and greater security along the borders – and the *rei publicae causa* were probably paramount in his mind.[164] The price of this was continuing the constitutional autocracy, the form of government founded, shaped and nurtured by the heir of Iulius Caesar.[165] 'The condition of holding empire', he allegedly said, 'is that an account cannot be balanced unless it be rendered to one person'.[166] Yet his decision was not universally welcomed or liked.[167]

Tiberius gave the eulogy at the funeral in the Forum Romanum, and is reported as having said, 'if one wished to enumerate all his qualities mainly one by one, one would require many days'.[168] After summarizing Augustus' lifetime achievements, Tiberius concluded:

> It was for all this, therefore, that you, with good reason, made him your leader and a father of the people, that you honoured him with many marks of esteem and with ever so many consulships, and that you finally made him a demigod and declared him to be immortal. Hence, it is fitting also that we should not mourn for him, but that, while we now at last give his body back to Nature, we should glorify his spirit, as that of a god, forever.[169]

In death, the one they called 'the revered one' was deified.[170] The man who was once 'first among equals' was now a god above men, *Divus* Augustus. Mortals would now swear oaths in his name, make offerings at his temples, and celebrate his feast day. A new religious college, the *sodales Augustales*, was founded in 14 CE to oversee the rites and rituals accorded to the god.[171] Twenty-one members were chosen by lot from 'the chief men of the state'.[172] Tiberius, Germanicus along with his brother Claudius, Drusus the Younger, Cn. Calpurnius Piso, and L. Volusius Saturninus Favonius were added to the number.[173] On 3 or 5 October, games were opened in the Circus in honour of Augustus and ran until the twelfth day of the month, the occasion of his official birthday.[174] Originally inaugurated by the *princeps* during his lifetime and held every five years as the *Augustalia* to mark the Battle of Actium, in death this event now became an annual fixture in the official calender (*Fasti*) under the management of the tribunes of the plebs.[175] They remained popular and continued to be held even in Cassius Dio's day, and not just in Rome, but in Herculaneum, Neapolis (Naples) and other cities across the Empire, too.[176] They were not displays of blood sports, but instead consisted of a horse race, and gymnastic and musical contests.[177] Augustus had enjoyed the format himself and happily mingled with the audience during and after performances, but Tiberius was not such an outgoing personality and, to add to the sombre occasion, the contests of 14 CE 'were disturbed by quarrels arising out of rivalry between the actors', apparently over stipended pay.[178] As the new *princeps*, Tiberius turned a blind eye to their dramatic protestations, but the tribunes urgently convened the Senate and won their plea to spend more than the amount allowed by law, to settle the performers' dispute.[179]

Tiberius sought to consolidate his power base. Publicly, he stated that 'my position is that of master of the slaves, *imperator* of the soldiers, and first citizen among the rest'.[180] The Senate quickly kow-towed to its new boss. That year's *consules ordinarii*, Sex. Pompeius and Sex. Apuleius, were the first men to swear allegiance, and senior senators followed them by fawning obsequiously at Tiberius' feet.[181] Around this time, Postumus Agrippa, who was still in exile on the remote island of Planasia, died, allegedly at the hand of a *tribunus militum*, either on the orders of Tiberius, though he denied any connection with the matter, or his mother Livia.[182] Some now doubt whether it was an assassination, and the rumour was confused with reports that Agrippa's personal slave Clemens, meantime, had gathered a band of men to avenge his master, but was outwitted by a clever stratagem, taken into custody, and never heard of again.[183] The whole affair was quickly forgotten. As for the other exile, Tiberius decided not to recall his wife Iulia from Rhegium, in the toe of the Italian peninsula: indeed, during that same year, she unexpectedly died – presumably of natural causes – aged 53.[184] In accordance with Augustus' wishes, her ashes were not placed in his mausoleum.[185]

The death of Agrippa Postumus now made Germanicus the next heir to the throne. The relationship between the two men underwent a change – at least according to Tacitus. He suggests that Tiberius now feared that Germanicus might oppose him by force and take the throne for himself, 'who had at his disposal so many legions, such vast auxiliary forces of the allies, and such wonderful popularity, might prefer the possession to the expectation of empire'.[186] Consequently, he surrounded himself with armed guards wherever he went.[187] Yet Tiberius' alleged paranoia was not directed solely at his adopted son. Two years after he had assumed the leading role in the state, at a private meeting with a prominent member of the Senate who had been suspected of plotting a coup, quite reasonably, Tiberius insisted on his son Drusus being present.[188] However, Tiberius may have been less inclined to be the autocrat and actually more willing to accept a sharing of governance of the empire than Tacitus implies. At the outset of his reign, Tiberius approached the Senate, humbly suggesting that he would take on whatever administrative duties they might assign him, 'since no man could be sufficient for the whole, without one or more to assist him'.[189] In that, Germanicus could be useful. His young blood relative was eminently qualified to take on some part of that responsibility. Indeed, at the request of Tiberius in the Senate, on 17 September 14 CE, Germanicus was granted the *imperium proconsulare*, whereas he did not ask the same for his son Drusus.[190] It was entirely appropriate to do so. As the regional commander of two consular-grade legates, each in charge of four legions, Germanicus needed a superior title and the authority to match.[191]

If Tiberius really did fear his adopted son, taking power away from his father was very far from Germanicus' mind, and, through his actions, he proved his unswerving loyalty to the new *princeps*.[192] He remained in place as governor of the Tres Galliae and Germania. In the provinces, life continued as normal. The census was not yet complete, however, and Germanicus continued with the project. It was while he was away in Gallia Belgica, overseeing the gathering of tax information, that news arrived of trouble on the Rhine.[193] For once, it was not the Germanic nations causing problems. This time, it was much more worrying. The Roman army of the Rhine had mutinied.[194] As the senior commander, Germanicus decided without equivocation to go to the source of the trouble, and, to ensure that his rear was secure, he made the Belgic nations and Sequani swear their obedience in his presence.[195] Then he immediately set off to deal with mutiny. Unbeknownst to Germanicus at the time, mutiny had already broken out in the army of Pannonia and Dalmatia.[196] The men of one of the legions on the Danube had even tried to murder their legate, Iunius Blaesus, and arrested and tortured his slaves.[197] Drusus the Younger was still trying to regain control of the situation on the Danube and restore discipline among the troops. With a larger army, however, Germanicus had by far the greater problem in finding a quick resolution.[198]

While Velleius Paterculus mentions the mutiny, our main source reporting on the events on the Rhine is Tacitus in Book 1 of his *Annals*. He was not, himself, a witness to the events, and he drew on other sources. One of these was Pliny the Elder, whom he explicitly mentions by name in the text. Pliny wrote the *Bella Germaniae*, an account in twenty books 'of all the encounters in Germania'.[199] Unfortunately, this work is now entirely lost. Pliny served three tours of duty in Germania (41–53 CE) and probably based his account on written reports he found in the archives of the legionary camps, and may have spoken with veterans or sons of veterans to get first-hand accounts. Germanicus would have written up his version of events for his report to the Senate. His deputies, too, may have filed their own reports, in turn. Thus, Tacitus could have drawn on a broad range of source material. The problem for the modern historian is knowing where facts end and dramatic licence or embellishment begins. Unlike a modern historian, Tacitus does not chronicle the events giving exact dates, times and places. He quotes Germanicus' and the other partipants' speeches, but we have no way of knowing if the words are the ones actually spoken – most were certainly not. They may be Tacitus' reinterpretation of recollection from memory of the events by men or their descendants who were there; or they may be pure inventions of the Roman historian, to dramatize the events described – an approach that was entirely consistent with how narrative histories were written in the ancient Greek and Roman worlds. Overlaying the content and style aspects of the reporting, Tacitus is generally considered to have an editorial bias against Tiberius. This means that he may have understated Tiberius' role, focusing instead on Germanicus, in order to emphasize the failings of the tyrant. Cassius Dio may have drawn on Tacitus' work in writing Book 57 of his own history, but he adds several interesting details and nuances not recorded by the earlier historian. Combining the two accounts produces a remarkably detailed story of the turbulent events of 14 CE.

The Roman army of the Rhine frontier was sub-divided into two commands. Germania Inferior, or 'Lower Germany', so-named because it bordered the Rhine River as it flowed downstream from about midway along its length to its mouth at the Mare Germanicum (North Sea), was under the leadership of A. Caecina Severus – now transferred from Moesia – based either at Vetera or Ara Ubiorum.[200] The legions answerable to him mutinied first. The legions of Germania Superior, 'Upper Germany', which bordered the Rhine River from its source in the Alps cascading down to southwestern Germany, were under the command of C. Silius – son of P. Silius Nerva, and consul in 13 CE – based at Mogontiacum (Mainz).[201] The men in his units were closely watching their neighbouring brothers-in-arms, but, at the time of Germanicus' intercession, they were still undecided whether or not to join the mutineers and, for the time being, stayed obedient to their commanding officers. Tacitus' narrative suggests that the mutiny occurred during the summer, and the attempts to address it lasted well into the autumn. The legions are described as being in their marching camps or 'summer camps' (*in aestivis*) when the mutiny broke out, and only later being located back in their 'winter camps' (*in hiberna*, *hibernantium*).[202]

After several days' ride, he arrived at the combined camp of *Legiones* I and XX. Germanicus found the military base in disarray.[203] The troops came out to greet him, but did not form an honour guard or salute him. It was a remarkable display of disrespect to a deputy of Caesar Augustus and their regional commander-in-chief. Germanicus found the men in a gloomy mood with their heads bowed. He passed through one of the gateways and the murmurs became audible chatter, as the men began to recognize who their unannounced visitor was. As Germanicus walked past, some reached out to kiss his hand but, instead, pulled it up to their mouths to reveal toothless gums. He eventually reached the tribunal in the centre of the camp and climbed its wooden steps to take centre stage. The tribunal, like the *Rostra* in the Forum Romanum, was the place around which citizens assembled to hear their politicians and leaders present motions (*contiones*). Just as in Rome, far away on the Rhine, the soldiers gathered round this wooden stage.

Germanicus called upon them to line up in their centuries and cohorts, so that he could see the *signa*, which identified the units.[204] The men shouted back insolently that they could hear him well enough from where they stood, but begrudgingly brought out the standards. He had managed to restore some semblance of order, but it was a potentially dangerous situation. These two legions had, to a man, enthusiastically embraced mutiny, and they were in no mood to be trifled with. Germanicus wasted no time and addressed the soldiers as their commander. He evidently believed that, by speaking to them as reasonable men, and using his skill as an orator, honed as a prosecutor and defender at court, they would respond to an appeal for reason.[205] As recounted by Tacitus, he began his speech with a patriotic evocation of Augustus and the triumphs of their *imperator* Tiberius, who, together with the legions of Germania, had achieved great victories in the recent past.[206] He spoke of the unity of the Italian home-land, of the loyalty of the Tres Galliae, and the peace that currently existed in the Roman Empire. The men listened in respectful silence. Then he asked what had happened to the discipline and obedience of the soldiers, and where they had put their officers? These rhetorical questions were met with an instant and very emotional response by the soldiers. They erupted into a babble of unintelligible words as they slipped off their army tunics to reveal bruises, scars and welts from frequent beatings with the *vitis* and whippings with the lash.[207] It was a pitiful sight. Many centurions had run rackets, taking bribes before allowing men to take time off or work on less arduous duties, and administered casual corporal punishment for the most minor of misdemeanours. When the mutiny broke out, it was the centurions who were the first subjects of the men's fury. Many a *miles gregarius* bore a deep resentment towards his centurion – no doubt borne of deep welts and bruises on their bodies – who was the strict enforcer of military discipline. Venting their fury during the initial uproar, the men of one legion turned on their centurions and beat them up, throwing their bodies – some by now lifeless corpses – over the parapet into the V-shaped ditch or even into the rushing flow of the Rhine River.[208] One *centurio* named Septimius had pleaded for his life at Caecina's feet; but, fearing for his own life, the legate yielded to the legionaries' demand for him to be handed over and, once in their hands, the mutineers slew the officer. Incensed by what he witnessed, a young Cassius Chaerea would not stand for the indiscipline and forced his way through the armed and dangerous mob to safety.[209] Meanwhile, the *praefectus castrorum* and the military tribunes of the mutinous legions had been placed under house arrest in their quarters and were unable to restore discipline.[210]

As Germanicus surveyed the men from the tribunal (fig. 2), he heard their complaints – especially the veterans' – loudly and clearly:

> they spoke bitterly of the prices of exemptions, of their scanty pay, of the severity of their tasks, with special mention of the entrenchment, the fosse, the conveyance of fodder, building-timber, fire-wood, and whatever else had

Figure 2. Germanicus addressing the troops during the mutiny in an engraving from Lucretia Wilhelmina van Merkel's epic poem *Germanicus*.

to be procured from necessity, or as a check on idleness in the camp. The fiercest clamour arose from the veteran soldiers, who, as they counted their thirty campaigns or more, implored him to relieve worn-out men, and not let them die under the same hardships, but have an end of such harassing service, and repose without beggary.[211]

It quickly became evident that the mutiny was not a challenge to the authority of the Roman Commonwealth. These were proud and loyal citizens, but extremely frustrated soldiers. In fact, this was a labour dispute over basic pay and conditions.[212] Specifically:

Their demands were, in brief, that their term of service should be limited to sixteen years, that they should be paid a *denarius* per day, and that they should receive their prizes then and there in the camp; and they threatened, in case they did not obtain these demands, to cause the province to revolt and then to march upon Rome.[213]

Without a complaints or arbitration process, the aggrieved men's patience had reached breaking-point. They vented their fury in the only way open to them: by taking over the camp and hoping someone with influence would come and hear their grievances.

One of the primary causes of the problem of the rank and file was the impact of a series of reforms instituted by Augustus just a few years before.[214] Curtailing his ambitions for new conquests, he first had to wage war on the defence budget. As he was wont to do, he tried to balance public income and expenditure, and in doing so found the finances of the army were in a precarious state.[215] Following Actium, Augustus had demobbed some 120,000 troops and settled many of them in *coloniae* throughout the empire by 29 BCE, decommissioning several legions in the process.[216] In 6 CE, he finally put the finances of the army on a firm footing by setting up a military fund, the *aerarium militare*, which received money through a variety of taxes, including a one per cent duty upon every item sold at auctions (*centesima rerum venalium*) and a 5 per cent estate tax on inheritances and legacies (*vicesima hereditatum et legatorum*).[217] Into it, over his remaining lifetime, he put 170 million *sestertii* of his own money, in both his and Tiberius' names.[218] The fund, managed by two praetors, ensured there were henceforth sufficient monies available to cover the retirement costs of men leaving the army.[219] A lump sum in cash was to be paid to every serviceman on his honourable discharge (*honesta missio*), having completed the required years of service. It replaced the antiquated and outmoded system of land grants. There had been numerous grievances over the years from retirees who were given tracts of barren or unworkable land. Cash was fairer to all and simpler to administer. However, Augustus also amended the terms of service:

It was therefore voted that 20,000 *sestertii* should be given to members of the Praetorian Cohorts when they had served sixteen years, and 12,000 to the other soldiers when they had served twenty years.[220]

Men of the legions would be expected to be available to serve as reservists (*evocati*).[221] 'They constitute, even now, a special corps', wrote Dio in the third century CE, 'and carry rods, like the centurions'.[222] While sound in theory, in practice there were severe administrative failings. The service records, typically handwritten notes on slithers of wood, could be problematical for the task of identifying when men were due for their honourable discharge. Thus, the veterans among the men shouted to Germanicus that they had already served thirty years – a full decade beyond the reformed set term – and they were desperate to be retired and allowed to enjoy what years they had left, in some semblance of good health and comfort (fig. 2).[223]

Yet why should the men choose *this* moment to mutiny? Tacitus states that it began when news of Augustus' death reached the army and:

> a rabble of city slaves, who had been enlisted under a recent levy at Rome, habituated to laxity and impatient of hardship, filled the ignorant minds of the other soldiers with notions that the time had come when the veteran might demand a timely discharge, the young, more liberal pay, and all, an end of their miseries and vengeance on the cruelty of centurions.[224]

The men of *Legiones* V and XXI, already smouldering with a growing sense of injustice, were particularly receptive to these incendiary views, and then quickly convinced their brothers in I and XX to join them.[225] The mutiny was facilitated by the fact that they were all sharing a summer camp together in the territory of the Ubii and, having only light duties, seem to have had too much time on their hands and not enough distractions.[226] Remarkably, the legate did not stand up to the mutineers but, by his inaction, enabled the indiscipline to take over the camp.[227] Soon after, the soldiers were determining their own rosters for guard duties and patrols. The protest had unanimous support and there were apparently no dissenters. 'The Roman world', the men of the legions of Germania Inferior confidently asserted, 'was in their hand; *their* victories aggrandized the State; it was from *them* that emperors received their titles'.[228]

Germanicus was prepared to hear the men's grievances, but not what followed. Someone in the throng shouted out that Germanicus should be the successor to Augustus – not Tiberius – and that, should he announce his intention to claim the title, they would support him.[229] Some in the ranks unashamedly abused the name of Tiberius.[230] Indeed, Tacitus ascribes, as a key motive of the mutineers, 'the confident hope that Germanicus Caesar would not be able to endure another's supremacy and would offer himself to the legions, whose strength would carry everything before it'.[231] Germanicus jumped down from the tribunal. In his mind, this was tantamount to treason. As he tried to push his way through the crowd, the men drew their swords, insisting that he return to the tribunal. He adamantly refused, saying that he would rather take his own life than be disloyal to Tiberius, and theatrically drew his own *gladius* from its scabbard and gestured as if to thrust it into his chest.[232] It was precisely the kind of trick an *orator* would use in the law court, but with the troops on the front line, the melodrama fell flat. The men nearest him grabbed his sword-hand, so that he could not carry out his threat. Men in another part of the crowd, however, urged him to see the task through, whereupon one soldier by the name of Calusidius, who was standing closest to Germanicus, proposed that he take his army-issue *gladius*, saying it was certain to be sharper than the commander's own.[233] The situation was getting ugly. 'Germanicus, accordingly, seeing to what lengths the matter had gone, did not venture to kill himself', writes Dio insightfully, 'particularly as he did not believe they would stop their disturbance, in any case'.[234] The officers, now worried for Germanicus' personal safety, ushered him away.[235]

Germanicus and his leadership team met urgently to discuss what could be done to solve the matters now revealed to them. Even as they were considering ideas, they received word that the mutineers were planning to send a delegation to the legions of Germania Superior, to win them over to their cause.[236] There was also talk of a raid to destroy and plunder the nearby civilian town of Ara Ubiorum, and then a move south to pillage Gallia Belgica.[237] Baser instincts were now taking over the mob. Potentially exacerbating the dangerous situation was the realization that the Germanic tribes on the right bank of the Rhine were becoming aware of the mutiny, and, if the north-western frontier were left undefended, they could cross the river and wreak untold damage. One option would be to use the auxiliary cohorts to face down the legions. Thus far, they had remained loyal to Rome, but to deploy them in this way could provoke a civil war. Germanicus had few options and he needed to come up with a solution fast.

Someone in Germanicus' team conceived a clever ruse. They would produce a letter, he said:

> written in the *princep's* name, to the effect that full discharge was granted to those who had served in twenty campaigns; that there was a conditional release for those who had served sixteen; that they were to be retained under a standard with immunity from everything except actually keeping off the enemy; and that the legacies which they had asked, were to be paid and doubled.[238]

It would have been better left to one of Germanicus' comedies. The soldiers were not fools and saw right through it.[239] They continued to press their demands more emphatically. Facing a situation that could quickly get out of hand, Germanicus backed down and agreed to their demands.[240] The military tribunes were ordered to see to the honourable discharges of those qualified for retirement, and the rest were promised what was owed to them on their return to barracks. The men of *Legiones* V and XXI adamantly refused the proposed settlement, however, and demanded to be paid there and then. 'Most of them', explains Dio, in his account, 'belonged to the city troops that Augustus had enrolled as an extra force after the disaster to Varus'.[241] To them, it seemed fair recompense for the years they had unwillingly served in the army. Out of options, Germanicus pooled the funds he had brought to cover his own and his entourage's travel expenses, and borrowed from those of his fellow officers. The hurriedly cobbled-together settlement worked. The mutiny was over. The disconsolate men of

Legiones V and XXI packed up their kit and headed for their winter camp at Vetera, 103km (64 miles) north-west of Ara Ubiorum.[242] Tacitus pointedly notes that the men of *Legiones* I and XX marched back to their winter camp at Ara Ubiorum in disgrace, their treasure being carried as part of the detail guarding the *aquila* and *signa*, with a humiliated Caecina at the head of the column.[243]

Only now did Germanicus go to Germania Superior. Once there, he secured the allegiance of *Legiones* II *Augusta*, XIII *Gemina*, XIV *Gemina* and XVI *Gallica*.[244] The men of *Legiones* II, XIII and XVI duly confirmed their loyalty to Germanicus, but those of *Legio* XIV apparently hesitated before accepting the offer of pay and discharges for eligible veterans.[245] While this was going on on the left bank of the Rhine, veterans of an unspecified legion stationed among the Chauci nation, who lived between the lower Ems and Weser rivers, now broke into a mutiny of their own.[246] The *praefectus castrorum* M'. Ennius sought to restore order by summarily executing two of the ringleaders. This only served to inflame the mutineers. Ennius fled and hid, but it was not long before he was located and dragged out. The terrified *praefectus*, in fear of his life, argued that it was not he who had issued the order, but Germanicus and Tiberius. During a struggle, he managed to break free of his captors, seized the unit standard and, holding it aloft, cried that anyone who did not follow him to the riverbank would be deemed a deserter. Realizing the consequences if they were ever captured, his men followed his orders with resignation, cowed by the experience.[247]

By this time, Germanicus was in Ara Ubiorum, playing host to a consular deputation from Rome sent directly from the *princeps*.[248] Dio explains that Tiberius:

> had secretly communicated only so much as he wished Germanicus to know; for he well understood that they would surely tell Germanicus all his own plans, and he did not wish that either they or that leader should busy themselves about anything beyond the instructions given, which were supposed to comprise everything.[249]

On this cloak-and-dagger mission, Germanicus would only be told what he needed to know, while creating the illusion that Tiberius was in complete control the whole time. However, word quickly spread of the arrival of the very important visitors. The men of *Legiones* I and XX in their winter camp panicked, thinking the proconsul Munatius Plancus and his associates had arrived to nullify the accord and bring the ringleaders to account for the mutiny.[250] A mob of angry soldiers gathered around the ex-consul and reproached him as the author of the Senate's decree. At the midnight hour, they stormed into Germanicus' accommodations, kicking down the door, and dragged the *legatus Augusti* from his bed, demanding to have the legionary standard.[251] On threat of death, Germanicus let them take it and the rebels raced out into the street. In Dio's account of the same event, the troops seized his wife – who was pregnant again – and the boy, 'both of whom had been sent away by him to some place of refuge'.[252] They only released his wife 'at Germanicus' request', but kept little Caius. The boy was now widely known by his nickname Caligula, 'Little Boot', after the diminutive, hobnailed, army-style shoes (*caligae*) he wore.[253] Both Dio and Tacitus agree that the angry soldiers bumped into the envoys from Rome – who had been alarmed by the commotion and who were on their way to Germanicus to seek sanctuary – and almost killed them.[254] The visitors were subjected to a barrage of insults, but managed to escape to the relative safety of the camp of *Legio* I. Plancus fled to the strong room in the *principia*, where the legion's venerated standards, the *aquila* and *signa*, were kept under guard.[255] The mob, however, tracked him down there, finding him clinging to the staffs of the sacred emblems. The quick thinking of the *aquilifer* Calpurnius saved both the man's skin and the legion the shame of spilling a consul's blood in a Roman military camp at the hands of his own countrymen.

By the time dawn broke the next morning, sanity had returned. Germanicus entered the camp and ascended the tribunal to hold another *contio*.[256] He invited Plancus to join him. The commander addressed the troops directly, berating them for their reprehensible treatment of the envoys and for second-guessing the purpose of their mission. The men of *Legio* XX in particular, he said, had disgraced themselves. He lectured them on the merits of pity, and then sent the envoys on their way with a cavalry escort – a unit of auxiliaries, deliberately not the customary *ala* of a legion of Roman citizens.[257] There could be no mistake about how he felt.

In Rome and elsewhere, Germanicus was later criticized for not having gone to Germania Superior first and used the loyal legions there to end the mutiny in the lower province.[258] They charged, his *imperium* notwithstanding, that he had overstepped his authority in granting the mutineers concessions in payments and discharges. Moreover, they asked: how could he, a family man, keep an expectant wife and small child in the midst of such mortal danger? Hearing of the charge, Agrippina later retorted that she was the grand-daughter of Augustus and could face any peril. Germanicus had complete confidence in his wife, but not all army officers felt the same about theirs. While military commanders were permitted to live with their wives in camp, there were detractors who expressed concerns about the presence of civilian women among the rankers, who were not permitted to have wives.[259] One, in fact, was Germanicus' own deputy, Caecina Severus. He later spoke before the Senate and said unequivocally that:

> no magistrate, who had been allotted a province, should be accompanied by his wife. He explained beforehand at some length that 'he had a consort after his own heart, who had borne him six children: yet he had conformed in private to the rule he was proposing for the public; and, although he had served his forty campaigns in one province or another, she had always been kept within the boundaries of Italy. There was point in the old regulation which prohibited the dragging of women to the provinces or foreign countries: in a retinue of ladies, there were elements apt, by luxury or timidity, to retard the business of peace or war and to transmute a Roman march into something resembling an Eastern procession. Weakness and a lack of endurance were not the only failings of the sex: give them scope, and they turned hard, intriguing, ambitious. They paraded among the soldiers; they had the centurions at beck and call.[260]

Agrippina had not remained at home and *did* accompany her husband on his assignment. Thus, in the camp together and threatened by their own soldiers, Germanicus and his wife embraced each other and little Caius, and broke down in tears.[261] In Suetonius' account, the mere sight of Caligula was enough to quell the troops.[262] Eventually, Agrippina was persuaded to leave the camp and head for the safety of Augusta Treverorum (Trier).[263] The legion was treated to the distressing spectacle of a respectable Roman woman – the wife, no less, of their commander – and his young son, being forced to leave the camp, to the wailing of the other officers' wives.[264] Particularly galling to the Roman soldiers was the idea that their commander's wife felt safer in the company of the Treveri nation than amongst her own people, which says something of their own distrust of newly Romanized populations. Hearing the crying, soldiers emerged confounded from their barracks.[265] Many were bewildered by what they witnessed. Suetonius adds that, as the carriage departed through the camp, some soldiers tried to restrain and stop it from going any further.[266]

Still addressing the troops, Germanicus turned the poignant moment to his advantage. Emotional at the sight of his wife departing, he appealed to the reasonable and the patriotic men among the soldiery.[267] As related by Tactus, using all his oratorical skill, he evoked the names and achievements of Iulius Caesar, Augustus, and Nero Claudius Drusus Germanicus; and spoke of duty, obedience, and of directing their wrath at the enemy. It had the desired effect. Either during the speech or shortly after, the men were moved to action. Responding to his words, the men felt repentant and, hoping to redeem themselves, sought out and handed over the ringleaders of the mutiny.[268] Now that the mood had changed, Germanicus acted quickly. The men charged with mutiny appeared before their legionary legates. As presiding military judge, the legate of *Legio* I, C. Caetronius, summarily tried the offenders in his unit, but did so cunningly, with the active involvement of the soldiery.[269] Each of the accused was made to stand upon a raised platform. Beside him, a military tribune stood ready, while the men of the legion waited around below with their swords drawn. The tribune asked if the man was guilty as charged. If the men shouted back affirmatively, the accused was thrown off the platform and stabbed to death by his former comrades.[270] It was a gruesome and bloody end to what had been a sorry episode in Rome's history. Nobody emerged from the affair without some degree of shame or embarrassment, and the army's reputation for loyalty and discipline had been damaged.

The lessons were not lost on Germanicus, however. He had already addressed the pay and retirement issues. He then removed the older men, who had been quick to side with the mutineers and still had time to serve before they could retire. They were promptly dispatched to Raetia on the pretence that the Suebi were planning a raid.[271] An attempt was also made to get to the root cause of the soldiers' grievances. He purged the centurionate to rid it of the worst offending officers, the very men who had demoralized so many of the troops. Each centurion was required to reinterview for his job. Giving his full name and listing his combat history, brave deeds and military awards, he was judged by a panel of tribunes and picked men of the legion. Those judged worthy of commendation were retained. Those judged unanimously to be cruel or rapacious were summarily dismissed (*missio ignominiosa*).

Restoring the morale of the younger men in the ranks was now of paramount importance to Germanicus. The men of *Legiones* V and XXI were still resentful, unmoved by the punishments meted out elsewhere or the repentance shown by their brothers-in-arms, and they could yet riot again. He was careful to have a contingency plan. In case they challenged his authority, he considered sending a fleet down-river with men of the legions and the allies, to break them once and for all.[272] Enforcing discipline was critical to avoid another mutiny. He allowed an interval of time to pass and then sent a message with a dispatch rider to Caecina.[273] He advised his deputy that he was on his way with a guard, and that he expected him to execute anyone who showed disloyalty, or he would see to it himself. Caecina shared the contents of the letter with the eagle- and unit standard-bearers and the most trusted of the troops. They formulated a plan and determined who was loyal among the soldiers, and who was not to be trusted. When the agreed signal was given, the loyal men, on instructions from Caecina, fell upon the 'vilest and foremost of the mutineers' and slaughtered them.[274] What followed can only be described as sheer butchery as the absent legate and tribunes gave their men free rein to administer the roughest kind of justice. Yet it soon spiralled out of control. In the confusion, even some of the most loyal men were killed, as the men who were the targets of the attacks now took up arms to defend themselves. When Germanicus finally arrived at the camp, he was appalled by the harrowing scene he encountered. 'Exclaiming, with a flood of tears, that this was damage rather than remedy', he ordered the bodies of the dead to be cremated.[275] He had not meant it to end with this extent of bloodshed, but nevertheless he was in large part to blame for it, because his written instructions had been open to interpretation by his deputy and those he had consulted.

The soldiers' demands for their share of Augustus' legacy were met.[276] The men of the other legions were keen to re-establish their good name in the eyes of their commander, and sought to appease the souls of those Romans recently slain by religious means through sacrificing impious beasts.[277] What better way was there to satisfy both needs than to focus their energies and pick a fight with a common enemy?[278] Issuing orders for the legions to assemble:

> Caesar followed up the enthusiasm of the men, and, having bridged over the Rhine, he sent across it 12,000 from the legions, with 26 allied *cohortes* and 8 *cohortes equitata*, whose discipline had been without a stain during the mutiny'.[279]

The Germanic nations of the Rhineland, meanwhile, were celebrating the prolonged absence of the Romans from their territory during the period of mourning for Augustus and the military insurrection. They were not expecting the Roman army to appear on their side of the river any time soon. By forced march, Germanicus' expeditionary force cut through the Caesian Forest (*Caesia silva*), which lay between the IJssel and Lippe rivers (map 6).[280] They marched on until

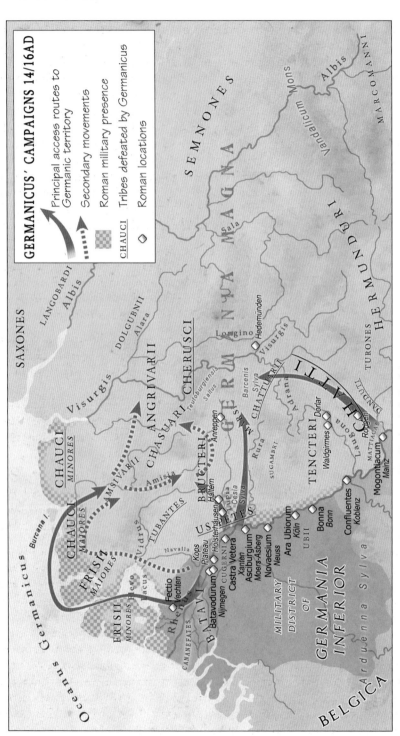

Map 6. Military operations in Germania Magna, 14–16 CE. (Carlos de la Rocha)

they reached 'the barrier which had been begun by Tiberius' and upon which Germanicus' men quickly established a camp, with 'his front and rear being defended by entrenchments, his flanks by timber barricades'.[281] Then, to leverage the tactical advantage of surprise, the army took a long and circuitous route that was known to be unguarded by the Germans, since they were, according to Roman scouts, drunk from celebrating a feast.[282] Caecina had express orders to take his lightly-armed cohorts and clear a way through the woods. Under a clear sky illuminated by the light of the moon, the men made quick work of it and, shortly after, the legions arrived in force. They reached a village of the Marsi nation and surrounded it. They encountered no resistance, but, in the words of Tacitus, 'peace it certainly was not – merely the languid and heedless ease of half-intoxicated people'.[283] Germanicus now revealed a ruthless side to his nature. He gave orders for his legions to form four columns and to devastate with fire and sword the region for 50 miles around:

> Neither sex nor age moved his compassion. Everything, sacred or profane, the temple, too, of Tamfana, as they called it, the special resort of all those tribes, was levelled to the ground. There was not a wound among our soldiers, who cut down a half-asleep, an unarmed, or a straggling foe.[284]

It could hardly be described as a glorious victory, but the point of the exercise was to provide a means for his troops to redeem themselves and, in the process, to rebuild unit cohesion after the divisive events of the previous weeks. In that he succeeded.

The neighbouring Germanic tribes – the Bructeri, Tubantes and Usipetes – soon learned of the general slaughter visited upon the Marsi, and prepared to attack the Romans on their return to the Rhine. Germanicus had, however, also anticipated this risk and:

> he marched, prepared both to advance and to fight. Part of the cavalry and some of the auxiliary cohorts led the van; then came the *Legio* I, and, with the baggage in the centre, the men of XXI closed up the left, those of V, the right flank. *Legio* XX secured the rear, and, next, were the rest of the allies.[285]

As the Romans marched home, the Germans tracked them from a distance, coming closer only when they entered forests and were able to use the trees as cover. They pressed the column lightly on the vanguard and flanks, but attacked in force at the rear, where the Romans were most vulnerable, causing confusion in their line. Germanicus showed courage and audacity by riding up to the men of *Legio* XX who were under attack at the rear and shouting 'advance, and hasten to turn your guilt into glory!'[286] Seeing their commander among them, and roused by his words, the men broke through the dense enemy lines and pushed them back into open country. Meantime, the vanguard had emerged out of the other side of the forest, and began digging a camp for the night in which the expeditionary force then took refuge. The legions returned by daylight to their respective camps for the winter with their honour restored.

At the end of that stressful year, Germanicus returned to Rome.[287] Word of his exploits in squashing the mutiny and invading Germania had raced ahead of him. Even as he was still several miles away from the city:

> all the Praetorian Cohorts marched out to meet him, notwithstanding the order that only two should go; and all the people of Rome, both men and women of every age, sex, and rank, flocked as far as the twentieth milestone to attend his entrance.[288]

This outpouring of popular adulation for Germanicus contrasted with the public criticism of Tiberius for his personal handling of the affair in Germania.[289] Fortunately for him, they were still unaware of the mutiny still in the process of being quelled by Drusus the Younger in Pannonia, which would have only worsened his standing.[290] They accused him of not having been forthcoming with the facts, implying that all was well with the army, while, in fact, it was very far from being so. Further, people remembered that Augustus, even in his advanced years, travelled up to Aquileia and Ticinum to be closer to the front during wartime, whereas Tiberius, in the prime of health, preferred to sit and nit-pick the words of the Senate.[291] In fact, though he made preparations to travel on several occasions, in the event, he spent the first two years of his principate in Rome.[292] On balance, the criticism was probably undeserved. After all, he had given his trusted deputies – his own sons – complete freedom to address the situation as they saw fit, precisely in the manner that Augustus had delegated missions to him before.[293] Indeed, he said publicly, 'in a free state, both the tongue and the mind ought to be free'.[294]

Public censure of this kind gnawed at the conscience of a man widely seen as introspective, complex and increasingly paranoid. For Tacitus, it would come to gradually undermine his relationships with those closest to him and Germanicus in particular.[295] Tiberius faced a difficult balancing act, being both the father and mentor of two boys. Indeed, while Germanicus lived, he maintained an impartial attitude towards the two princes.[296] Nevertheless, Tiberius often showed magnanimity to Germanicus.[297] He wrote to him and to Agrippina, thanking him for his loyalty, and he praised his greatness (*virtus*) in glowing terms before the Senate for having crushed the mutiny – in fact, he gave a longer accolade to Germanicus than he did to Drusus the Younger.[298] In the face of temptation to take power for himself, Germanicus had unquestioningly shown Tiberius unswerving loyalty. 'It is difficult to say', writes Suetonius, 'whether his regard to filial duty or the firmness of his resolve was most conspicuous'.[299] Though privately Tiberius admonished him for having acceded to the wishes of the soldiers, yet he granted the same salary to the legions serving on the Danube as Germanicus had agreed to those on the Rhine.[300] Tiberius would not negotiate, however, on the sixteen-year term of service. When his son Drusus (plate 9) failed to bring before the Senate the soldiers' demand for a restoration of the former service contract, the *princeps* himself issued an edict ignoring the soldiers' request, and reconfirmed the new twenty-year term.[301] In this matter his word was final.

Chapter 4

Up Against the Angrivarian Wall
15–16 CE

Settling Old Scores

Ovid's poetic prediction came true.[1] For his achievements, Germanicus was accorded the public honour of a triumph, with all its pomp and circumstance – that, despite the fact that the war in Germania was technically still going on and not yet officially won.[2] An arch of marble was voted for Germanicus, and ground breaking began for it shortly thereafter.[3] Having proved his ability to keep his cool in a crisis, his brother Drusus was also rewarded with the consulship in 15 CE, fusing his name to the Roman calendar year along with that of C. Norbanus Flaccus. It was a very fine way for the young Caesars to start the year.

Germanicus' love for Agrippina continued to flourish and, in January or February, his next child was conceived. But duty came first and he soon returned to Ara Ubiorum.[4] Uppermost in the governor's mind was ensuring border security and the loyalty of the army. Across the river from Fort Mogontiacum, the Chatti – or Catti or Catthi – represented an ever-present threat. They had become well known to the Romans during Germanicus' father's campaigns in 11 and 10 BCE. Strabo's account is the earliest surviving written source we have that describes these Germanic people. He located them in the mountains and valleys of the Elder, Fulda and the upper reaches of the Weser rivers, in what is now modern Hessen.[5] The best account of the Chatti, however, is preserved in Tacitus' *Germania*. He calls them 'the children of the Hercynian Forest' and describes them as 'distinguished beyond their fellows by their singularly hardy frames, well-knit limbs, resolute eyes and by a remarkable energy of spirit'.[6] Unlike most of their neighbours, who eschewed urban living, the Chatti established at least one urbanized settlement called Mattium (near modern Kassel) located in the defensible Taunus Mountains.[8] Despite their status as barbarians in Roman eyes, Tacitus was struck by the similarities between the Chatti and his own countrymen. In common with the highly-organized Roman army, 'their whole strength is in foot soldiers' (plate 16), he writes, 'who, besides carrying their arms, are loaded with tools and supplies'.[8] As the legions did, they posted pickets by day and dug ditches around their camps at night. Also, like the legions following their *propraetores* (ex-consuls), the Chatti obeyed the orders of their leaders, whom they elected; and they fought in formations, which they kept in the heat of battle. Unlike their barbarian neighbours, who 'came out for a single battle', the Chatti engaged in campaigns, and:

seldom make mere raids or allow themselves to be drawn into a casual encounter: it is cavalry, to be sure, from which one expects a quick success or a
quick retreat; speed goes with timidity, slowness is more allied to steadiness.[9]

The Chatti were an opponent the Romans could understand.

In April or May, Germanicus launched a two-pronged attack against the Chatti
nation (map 6).[10] He ordered Caecina to lead an expeditionary force of four
legions and 5,000 *auxilia*, 'with some hastily raised levies from the Germans
dwelling on the left bank of the Rhine' – probably the Cugerni, Treveri and
Ubii.[11] At the same time, Germanicus himself led a force of as many legions, but
took with him twice as many allies, among them cohorts of Gauls, Raeti and
Vindelici.[12] The advance through German territory was swift. In the Taunus
Mountains forward scouts managed to locate the embankments and ditches of the
old Roman camp built by Drusus the Elder in 11 BCE, and upon it Germanicus
erected a new palisade.[13] With his operations base established:

> he hurried his troops in quick marching order against the Chatti, leaving
> L. Apronius to direct works connected with roads and bridges. With a dry
> season and comparatively shallow streams, a rare circumstance in that
> climate, he had accomplished, without obstruction, a rapid march.[14]

Time was of the essence. Concerned about the risk of heavy rain, which could
slow his army's advance through enemy territory or impede its return to the
Rhine, Germanicus acted quickly to locate the Chatti. The ensuing encounter
was bloody and brutal. 'All the helpless from age or sex', writes Tacitus grimly,
'were at once captured or slaughtered'.[15] They were left defenceless when their
able-bodied menfolk suddenly abandoned them, having fled in the face of the
invaders by swimming across the Adrana (Eder) River.[16] Later regrouping, they
fought hard to impede the Romans, who meantime tried to erect a bridge over
the river, but 'subsequently they were driven back by missiles and arrows'.[17]
Sensing that they were losing the fight and faced reprisals, some of the Chatti sent
emissaries to negotiate for peace. They found Germanicus in no mood to accept
their terms. In the face of the Roman's stubborn resolve, others gave up the fight
and surrendered to him unconditionally, 'while the rest, leaving their cantons and
villages, dispersed themselves in their forests'.[18] Left undefended, the Romans
razed the Chattian settlements to the ground at will.[19] Most important was their
tribal capital of Mattium, which Germanicus ordered burned and the surrounding countryside devastated.[20] It was a calculated attempt at preventing the Chatti
from entering the war later in the season. The Roman army continued on, marching deeper into their territory, temporarily re-establishing its presence at the fortress originally set up by Drusus the Elder at Hedemünden (map 7). Built on a hill
overlooking a bend on the Werra River, it was designed to intimidate and impress.
The defensive enclosure measured 320m (1,050ft) long by 150m (490ft) wide,
encompassing an area of 3.215 hectares.[21] Roman guile worked. Tacitus writes
that the enemy did not dare 'to harass the rear of the retiring army, which was his
usual practice whenever he fell back by way of stratagem rather than from panic'.[22]

Alerted to the plight of their neighbours and allies, the Cherusci meanwhile prepared to come to their aid. Located in the area between modern Osnabrück and Hanover, at the source of the Lupia (Lippe) River and beside the immense ancient forest called Bacenis, the Cherusci first enter the written record in Iulius Caesar's *Commentarii de Bello Gallico* ('Commentaries on the Gallic War'), detailing events of 53 BCE.[23] In his campaign report, Caesar associates them with 'outrages and raids' – *iniuriis incursionibusque* – on their neighbours the Suebi, who retaliated with attacks of their own. Drusus the Elder had waged a brutal war against them in 12 BCE from his base in Mogontiacum, as he struck out towards meeting his goal of reaching the Weser River.[24] In the aftermath of Drusus' death, his brother Tiberius launched a campaign into the Rhineland, which saw the Cherusci become allies of Rome, involving the handing over of hostages as surety. Among them was a son of the nobleman Segimerus, the boy named in the Latin literature as Arminius or his younger brother Flavus.[25]

The location of the Cherusci – approximately in the centre of the contested region of Germania Magna – was strategically important. Caecina's march into their homeland prevented them from coming to the aid of the Chatti, south-east of them, and by the end of his unexpected invasion, he had completely reduced their will to fight.[26] As he returned to the Rhine, the warriors of the Marsi nation (located south-west of the Cherusci) launched their own assaults on the unwelcome Roman invaders traipsing through their lands. Caecina engaged them in a set battle – which almost always favoured the Romans – and overwhelmed them. Their war-chief Mallovendus promptly surrendered.[27] The expeditionary force returned to camp flushed with success. Just months after the mutiny, the old discipline and fighting spirit of the Roman army were back.

On 24 May of that year, Germanicus marked his thirtieth birthday. Whether he was back on the Roman side of the Rhine to celebrate it with his family is not disclosed in the sources. His mind was already working on his next project. With the spring offensive concluded, his new mission would address the continuing threat posed by Arminius, now the undisputed head of the Cherusci nation. The anti-Roman faction led by Arminius and the pro-Roman faction headed by Segestes had grown far apart. Complicating matters, these two men were bound by family ties. Segestes was Arminius' unwilling father-in-law, by way of marriage to his daughter Thusnelda. The disagreement over the marriage notwithstanding, Segestes rejected Arminius' foreign policy stance. He believed that there was more to be gained from an alliance with Rome than remaining independent. In 9 CE, Segestes had learned that his son-in-law was planning a rebellion and had advised Quinctilius Varus of it, but the *legatus Augusti pro praetore* dismissed the tip-off, preferring to trust the word of his younger cavalry commander, Arminius. It was a grave error of judgment and he paid for it with his life. Segestes, however, remained a loyal Roman ally, years after, and continually fed intelligence back to his partners across the Rhine. Emissaries from the German side led by Segimundus, the former priest of the cult of Rome and Augustus at Ara Ubiorum, arrived with a message from his father. In it, Segestes directly appealed for help from

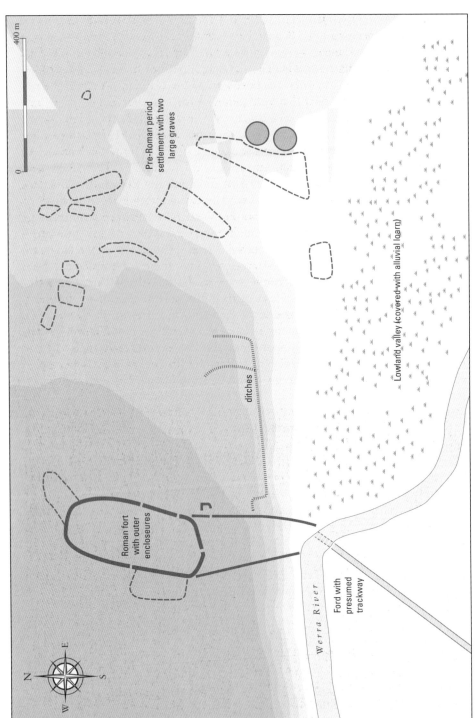

Map 7. Hedemünden Roman Fort, Germany.

Germanicus.[28] Despite his earlier betrayal, Segimundus was received as a friend and formally escorted into the Roman city. Germanicus learned that the old man was living day to day under the constant threat of injury or death by those of his community supporting Arminius, who still sought war with Rome. It was surely only a matter of time until one of those attempts succeeded. Rescuing a loyal Roman ally gave Germanicus his *iustis causis*, if one were needed, to go to war.

To rescue Segestes, Germanicus conceived a daring snatch raid. How large a force he took with him and its composition is not disclosed in the sources, but Roman arms soon clashed with Cheruscan, and, after a bitter struggle, Segestes was located and rescued.[29] Members of his extensive retinue were also taken, among whom was his daughter Thusnelda (fig. 3). She was proud and defiant like her husband, and she neither shed tears at her predicament nor pleaded for release from her captors. Her arrest, however, was a significant coup for Germanicus. He now had not only his main adversary's wife, but as she was pregnant, also his child. To their benefit, also, the common soldiers found plunder and spoils stolen from Varus and his army six years before, and which had then been distributed among the Germanic warriors for services rendered. Segestes offered his thanks to Germanicus, who, in turn, assured him that he, his daughter, and his grandchild would be looked after while in Roman territory.[30] True to his word, they were given a comfortable new home in Ravenna, and it was there that Thusnelda later give birth to a boy. With his very important captives securely under guard, Germanicus led his army back to the Rhine. On Tiberius' personal suggestion, he was acclaimed *imperator* for the second time.[31] It was a prestigious

Figure 3. *Segestes hands over Thusnelda to Germanicus* after the painting by H. Konig.

honour for the young man. His birth father Drusus had been denied an acclamation from his troops by Augustus, and the fact Tiberius proposed it suggests
that good relations existed between adoptive father and adopted son.

The news of Thusnelda's capture quickly reached Arminius. He roused his
council of advisors to wage total war on the Romans. Among the nobles coming
to Arminius' support was his uncle Inguiomerus, a man long respected by the
Romans and whom Germanicus hoped would, at least, remain neutral.[32] This
rallying cry, and the forces assembling in response to it, posed a real danger to
stability in the region. A large massed invasion by Germanic tribes at a single
point along the Roman frontier could potentially overwhelm the available Roman
resources. Timing was critical. Without delay, Germanicus prepared a plan for a
pre-emptive strike. Three army groups would simultaneously invade Germania
Magna from different compass-points to surround and isolate the Cherusci. First,
however, they would need to reduce the ferocious Bructeri and disarm them, so
that they could not come to the assistance of the Cherusci. To that end, Caecina
was ordered to cross the Rhine from the south-west and march to the Ems River,
cutting through their territory. Under his command were forty auxiliary cohorts,
assisted by *praefectus equitum* Albinovanus Pedo leading the cavalry comprising
men of the Frisii nation, representing a combined force of some 48,000 men.
Simultaneously, L. Stertinius would move inland and engage the Bructeri from
the south. Germanicus himself would lead an amphibious invasion that would
deliver his troops directly to the estuary of the Ems River, whence they would
march south-east, following the course of the river. Four legions made up his
army group, among which were auxiliaries from the Chauci nation, through
whose homeland they would advance. Accompanying Germanicus and Caecina
were survivors of the disaster of 9 CE – men who had been denied the right to
return to Italy, and who knew the lay of the land and what to expect when they
traversed it.[33] The war to topple Arminius had begun in earnest.

The inspiration for the amphibious invasion was his own father's campaign of
12 BCE. It had been a daring and bold campaign, in preparation for which Drusus
had built the largest military infrastructure of the time, including the series of
hydrological works that connected the Rhine to the Lacus Flevo (Zuyder Zee,
IJsselmeer) called the *Fossa Drusiana* – 'Drusus' Ditch'.[34] The canal had been
maintained in good working order since that original invasion, and had even been
subsequently used by Tiberius in the campaign of 5 CE. Some ships from that
recent campaign may have still been in existence that could be pressed into use in
the new invasion. Enough ships were found, and from its designated assembly
point on the Rhine, the flotilla passed through the canal onto Lacus Flevo and,
several days later, entered the Wadden Sea. The voyage of Germanicus – *in
navigante Germanico* – was later recorded by Albinovanus Pedo, as a poem that
attracted the admiration of Seneca the Elder for its stirring description of the
North Sea, which, he wrote, no poet until then had expressed 'with such great
inspiration'.[35] It still evokes the peril of the journey faced by the soldiers more
used to feeling earth beneath their hobnailed boots:

Now they see the day and the sun left behind them
– and indeed see themselves as banished from the known bounds of the
    earth,
foolhardy to go through unceasing darkness towards the end of western
    lands and the farthest shores of the world.
They see that Ocean which bears horrid monsters beneath its numbing
    waves, which everywhere bears savage beasts
without reason and the fierce dogs of the sea.
They see the waves to rise up, and having seized their ships,
the waves' breaking and crashing heaps dread upon them.
Now they see their ships settle in the muddy shallows,
and their fleet forsaken by the swift wind,
believing that they are about to be torn to pieces by the ferocious
    creatures of the sea
– abandoned to their woeful lot by uncaring Fate.
And indeed, someone on high, from the lofty, windy prow
– having struggled to break through the dark with striving sight,
so that he could not distinguish anything – with the world having been
    torn away – poured forth from his very soul a cry such as this:
'To what place are we being carried off? The very daylight flees,
and Nature, at her most extreme, hides the world in perpetual darkness.
Do we seek peoples settled even farther beyond – under another turning
    point of the sky –
or do we seek another world untouched by wars?
Surely the gods call us back, and forbid mortal eyes
to know the end of these things. Why do we violate
strange foreign seas and sacred waters with our oars,
and trouble the peaceful homes of the gods?'[36]

As the heaving waves of the grey ocean crashed against their lightly-constructed boats, the soldiers aboard them may have wondered why the lands across the Rhine were of such great importance that Caesar would risk their very lives to retake them.

Eventually, the fleet reached the relative safety and calmer waters of the estuary of the Ems River. Disembarking there, the expeditionary force regrouped and set up camp. The presence of the Roman army of Germanicus' time is attested by a variety of items that have been uncovered at Bentumersiel in the Leer district of Nieder-Sachsen (Lower Saxony), in Germany.[37] Excavations have produced remains of legionary equipment – the distinctive pyramidal head of a *pilum*, various fragments of a scabbard, terminals from a military apron, and belt fittings, as well as parts of a horse's bridle, all dating to the early first century CE.[38] The organic remains have long since vanished. The nearby camp was probably a temporary affair – in operation only during this campaign season – its purpose to guard Germanicus' ships in the estuary or to act as a supply dump, or both.

Stertinius' column, meanwhile, had raced inland from the Rhine, and had already begun engaging the Bructeri.[39] Tacitus locates this landlocked Germanic tribe along the Ems River and says that they were deeply resented by their neighbours for 'their overbearingness'.[40] Drusus the Elder had encountered them in 12 BCE, when his fleet made its way down the river and was attacked by them.[41] They had subsequently joined the alliance led by Arminius in 9 CE and fought alongside them at *saltus Teutoburgiensis*. When Stertinius' troops arrived, the Bructeri were found to be preparing to escape, burning their possessions so that they would not fall into Roman hands.[42] Remarkably, 'amid the carnage and plunder', writes Tacitus, the Romans 'found the eagle of *Legio* XIX, which had been lost with Varus'.[43] Its recovery was a tremendous morale booster for the Roman side and would be a great public relations coup for Tiberius. Now, only two eagles remained to be found. The other groups marched further inland, ravaging the country of the Bructeri between the Ems and Lippe rivers. Thus far, the campaign had proceeded flawlessly and attained its objectives.

The three army groups then joined up. They were now not far from the site of the annihilation of the three legions commanded by Varus six years earlier. Veering from his campaign plan, Germanicus felt compelled to visit the place where so many Romans had fallen and whose bones were thought to still lie unburied.[44] He despatched Caecina to locate the exact site of the battlefield and to clear the way ahead, raising bridges and constructing roadways along the route, so that the main body could follow unhindered.[45] Guided by the survivors of the massacre, they found the battlesite. Germanicus and his army arrived there and 'visited the mournful scenes, with their horrible sights and associations'.[46] He assembled the men and announced that their countrymen would be honoured with a *tumulus*, a sacred mound of earth. Germanicus himself laid the first sod.[47] Suetonius claims that he was also the first to put his hand to the work of collecting and bringing the scattered bones to a place of burial.[48] It was an emotional moment for all gathered at that grim place. 'In grief and in anger', writes Tacitus, Germanicus and his men:

> began to bury the bones of the three legions, not a soldier knowing whether he was interring the relics of a relative or a stranger, but looking on all as kinsfolk and of their own blood, while their wrath rose higher than ever against the foe.[49]

By leading his people in this way, he channelled the collective sorrow and rage of the Romans into an act of communal piety. Yet this simple act of reverence carried with it both political and religious risks. Tacitus comments that Tiberius would later express his disapproval of this unplanned ceremony, because it represented time that Germanicus could have better spent campaigning.[50] He also notes, however, that by engaging in a funeral rite, Germanicus had polluted his sacred status as a religious official of the state and specifically that of *augur*, which required him to keep his hands clean.[51]

With his men unified in common cause, Germanicus gave the order to march. Their mission was to hunt down the man responsible for the slaughter of their countrymen. They did not have far to look. Arminius and his men were close by, but keeping their distance, using the trackless woods and vegetation to hide their movements (plate 25). The preferred tactic of the Cherusci was the ambush. They had used it to good effect against Germanicus' father at Arbalo in 11 BCE.[52] In that valley, Drusus the Elder had almost lost his own army, but the Germans did not press home their advantage and let the Romans go. This time, Arminius did not intend to repeat the mistake. The advantages of timing, cover and surprise were on his side. With the Romans in hot pursuit, but uncertain of the exact location of their adversary, the German war-chief ordered his men to launch an attack from the cover of the forest.[53] The Roman cavalry were first to be taken by surprise. Outnumbered and fearing annihilation, they retreated, but as they did so, they charged straight into the cohorts racing to their rescue. The result was a general panic among all. Arminius' men now drove the Romans towards a bog, just as they had done at *saltus Teutoburgiensis*; but this time they were to be cheated of another muddy victory. Germanicus arrived just in time with his legion marching in battle order. 'This struck terror into the enemy', writes Tacitus, 'and gave confidence to our men'.[54] After a brief but indecisive engagement, the two opposing sides separated. Germanicus' decisive action had saved the day for the Romans.

Mindful that the campaigning season was entering its final days, Germanicus decided it was time to call for the general withdrawal. His expeditionary force was now deep inside Germania Magna and the Rhine was hundreds of miles away. He could take the direct route overland, but his sea transports were still waiting for him on the Ems River. Germanicus led his men back to the rivercraft, ordering part of the cavalry to make for the Rhine via the western seashore.[55] He ordered Caecina to lead his army group by the more direct route.

The Battle of the Long Bridges

On the journey, Caecina crossed a section of highway called *Pontes Longi*, 'Long Bridges'. It was a narrow plank or corduroy road, built fifteen years before by engineers of L. Domitius Ahenobarbus' army, connecting wooden bridges that traversed an as yet unidentified bog.[56] What had once been a secure way through precarious territory now posed a serious challenge to the retreating Romans. In the years since its construction, it had not been maintained. The stagnant water trapped in the muddy swamp upon which the road rested had rotted many of its timbers, making it impassable in places. Caecina's army had to make extensive repairs before it would be safe enough to bear the weight of his heavily-laden troops. Every minute they spent on repairs they exposed themselves to the risk of attack. The bog stayed constantly wet by run-off from the surrounding hills and forests, from where the Germanic warriors were planning their next attack. It was going to be a long and arduous task, and Caecina ordered his troops to set up camp where they stood. While part of the army worked on the infrastructure, the rest formed a defensive shield-wall. It was a high-risk strategy. 'Everything alike was unfavourable to the Romans', observes Tacitus, 'the place with its deep swamps, insecure to the foot and slippery as one advanced, limbs burdened with coats of mail, and the impossibility of aiming their javelins amid the water'.[57]

Figure 4. *The unfortunate campaign of Germanicus in northern Germany* after the painting by
Ferdinand Leeke.

Arminius' men took every opportunity to harass the Romans in their vulnerable situation (fig. 4). As the Roman engineers dug, hauled, cut, and hammered
with their tools, the Cherusci threw their *frameae* and pelted them with stones
from the relative safety of their positions, inflicting casualties and wearing down
their opponents. Only at night did Caecina's men get respite. Cunningly, the
Germans diverted some of the streams to flood the bog below, submerging entire
sections of the renovated highway.[58] After a night's uneasy rest, the Romans
awoke to find that they had to work twice as hard to gain lost ground or face
being stranded forever in that desolate place.

In Caecina, Germanicus had a tough and fearless leader. A soldier with forty
years' experience, he had been through many hard campaigns and he was very far
from broken.[59] Caecina carefully reviewed his options and decided that the best
one was to keep the Germans holed up in the forest, while allowing his heavily-
equipped troops and wounded to leave the scene. As luck would have it, there was
one continuous stretch of the *Pontes Longi* by which these men could escape. He
met with his deputies and assigned *Legio* I to the head of the column, placing
V *Alaudae* on the right flank, XXI *Rapax* on the left, and XX to guard the rear.[60]
He told them to prepare to move out. They would try to break out from their
entrapped position at dawn next morning.

Under the strain of the worsening situation, the morale and discipline of the
rank and file were faltering. Arminius knew well how to wear down his adversaries. His men, encamped on dry ground, made merry around their campfires.
Enjoying themselves noisily, the Germans prevented many of the Romans from

sleeping in their own waterlogged camp in the valley below.[61] For two of the units, it was too much to bear. Caecina awoke the following morning to find that the V and XXI had deserted their positions and retreated to a plain beyond the morass. The remaining legions assembled. As the column began to move, the wagon train (*impedimenta*) became stuck in the mud, and, as the soldiers came forward and tried to push them along, the ordered ranks behind them quickly fell into disarray. They now began to fear an ambush, and many looked to save themselves. Centurions continued to bark out orders, but increasing numbers of soldiers ignored them. The *signa*, too, became separated from the units, and soon the situation dissolved into chaos. It was the moment Arminius had waited for. His warriors unleashed a ferocious attack, focusing particularly on the Romans' horses and pack animals. The startled horses reared up and threw off their riders – among them Caecina himself – and the frightened beasts trampled many men under hoof. Arminius well understood how the Roman army revered its standards and the Cherusci targeted the eagles directly with a storm of missiles. Relief finally arrived when *Legio* I came to their comrades' rescue. Many of the Cherusci turned their attention instead upon the abandoned Roman baggage, to rob it for spoils. Without the Gemans biting at their rear, the Romans struggled on to firmer ground. In the process, they lost their tools and tents. In their new location, they found they could not dig a camp for the night. The soldiers made the best they could of a bad situation, sharing their marching rations 'soiled by mire or blood' among themselves, writes Tacitus, and 'they bewailed the darkness with its awful omen, and the one day which yet remained to so many thousand men'.[62]

With fear and hunger at their highest and morale and comfort at their lowest, Caecina's men became susceptible to panicking at the slightest disturbance. During the night, a horse caused a general panic when it broke free and galloped into a group of men trying to sleep.[63] Many others awoke and, fearing that the Germans had broken into the camp, raced to the *Portus Decumanus*, which was the gate furthest away from the enemy's position. Only Caecina kept a cool head. He quickly established that it was a false alarm and ran to the gate, thrusting himself in the way of the fleeing troops. They would have to step over his body, he cried, if they were intent on leaving. Meanwhile, his officers pleaded with the soldiery, and order was restored. Caecina called his officers about him and set out his vision for the escape plan.[64] In short, they could not continue to flee, he said, to be hunted down by the Germans. They had to stand their ground, engage the enemy in a close-quarters fight using their camp as protection and their arms to their deadliest extent, and only then, with the Germans beaten, could they hope to reach the Rhine. He reminded them of the gravity of the crisis they faced, appealing to their love of their homeland, and rallied their spirits.

The next morning, the Germans launched their assault on the Romans' position. Seeing the wall thinly defended, the Cherusci attempted to fill in the defensive ditch surrounding the Roman camp and breach the parapet.[65] They did not realise it was a trap. As soon as the Germans had breached the defences, the order was sounded and the Roman troops rushed forward. While at a disadvantage outside in the bog, on firm ground inside, the Romans fought with the odds in their favour. With superior arms and armour, and fervour in their hearts, the Romans soon overwhelmed the Germanic warriors. Sensing defeat was at hand, Arminius fled the battlefield. Inguiomerus was wounded as he turned to escape. Sensing victory was theirs, Caecina's men fought on gallantly for the remainder of the day until nightfall. Though almost out of supplies, but now unhindered by enemy assaults, the Romans pushed on and made their way back successfully to the Rhine.

Return to the Rhine

Rumours of another disaster across the Rhine and the impending invasion by Germans swept through the bases on the Roman side of the river. The order was given to destroy the single bridge-crossing at Vetera, which represented the final leg of the escape route.[66] It was the quick thinking and bold action of Germanicus' wife Agrippina that prevented this hasty act. She actively rallied a rescue effort for the troops making their way back from the front. Tacitus writes:

> A woman of heroic spirit, she assumed during those days the duties of a general, and distributed clothes or medicine among the soldiers, as they were destitute or wounded. According to C. Plinius, the historian of the Germanic Wars, she stood at the extremity of the bridge, and bestowed praise and thanks on the returning legions.[67]

Unaware of his deputies' miserable situations, Germanicus Caesar's army group faced perils of its own. To his legate P. Vitellius he gave command of *Legiones* II and XIV, and ordered him to march by the coastline route.[68] Germanicus himself would lead a skeleton crew by sea, taking the fleet anchored in the Ems River, and reach the Frisian coast. His rationale was that, without the extra weight of men and matériel, the fleet could make swift progress in the shallow waters. The fleet would intercept Vitellius' army marching overland and pick them up when it was safe to do so. It seemed a reasonable plan and, while the ground was dry and firm, Vitellius made good progress. However, it seems that he had not taken into account the ebb and flow of the sea at the shoreline (plate 26). When the tide came in, his men became trapped. The ordered lines of men rapidly descended into a shambles, as:

> men were swept away by the waves or sucked under by eddies; beasts of burden, baggage, lifeless bodies floated about and blocked their way. The companies were mingled in confusion, now with the breast, now with the head only above water, sometimes losing their footing and parted from their comrades or drowned. The voice of mutual encouragement availed not against the adverse force of the waves. There was nothing to distinguish the brave from the coward, the prudent from the careless, forethought from chance; the same strong power swept everything before it.[69]

Eventually, the Romans located higher ground and struggled up onto it. With their equipment and rations lost, and no means to make fire, they spent a cold, wet and hungry night, shivering under the stars. When daylight returned and the sea had once again receded, the bedraggled men headed back inland in the direction of the Weser River (Visurgis).[70] Vitellius' men, however, had begun to lose heart and felt that only the sight of Germanicus in person and the fleet would restore their confidence. Tense hours passed until the transports finally arrived and the relieved but battered troops boarded them.[71]

Of Germanicus' three army groups, only Stertinius' emerged from the campaign almost unscathed. He had received the surrender of Segimerus, brother of Segestes, and taken him to Ara Ubiorum.[72] Even Segimundus, who had been suspected of desecrating the body of P. Quinctilius Varus at Teutoburg, was given the benefit of the doubt.[73] These men were pardoned and granted asylum. This was a moment for practical politics, not humiliation or revenge.

When Germanicus finally returned to his base on the Rhine, he took stock of the situation. He reflected gloomily that, during that campaign season, his army had suffered terrible losses in arms, equipment and animals, and had taken significant casualties. Taken together, these attritions seriously reduced his strike capability and combat readiness for the next season. The response of the provincials, however, was heartwarming. On hearing the heroic tales of the Romans' return from *barbaricum*, the provinces of Tres Galliae and Hispaniae, as well as the communities of Italia, were inspired to act patriotically, and assisted the young commander by completely replacing lost weapons and horses and by donating cash.[74] A lesser or venal man may have exploited their generosity for personal profit, but Germanicus showed his humanity and good judgement. 'Germanicus, having praised their zeal', writes Tacitus:

> took only for the war their arms and horses, and relieved the soldiers out of his own purse. And that he might also soften the remembrance of the disaster by kindness, he went round to the wounded, applauded the feats of soldier after soldier, examined their wounds, raised the hopes of one, the ambition of another, and the spirits of all, by his encouragement and interest, thus strengthening their ardour for himself and for battle.[75]

Despite the embarrassing mishaps of the return journey, overall the campaign in Germania Magna of that year had actually been successful. The Chatti and Cherusci had been roundly defeated; arch-villains Arminius had been humiliated and Inguiomerus wounded; and Segestes and his pro-Roman entourage had been rescued. Of particular propaganda value was the capture of Thusnelda and the fact that the child of Arminius would soon be born in captivity among Romans. This victory story would play well with the home crowd, eager to scrub out the shame of the Varian disaster. In recognition of their achievements under Germanicus, *triumphalia insignia* were awarded to legates Apronius, Caecina and Silius.[76]

Meanwhile in Rome it was business as usual. The Tiber had once again flooded its banks, inundating parts of the city; Tiberius had refused the honorary title *Pater Patriae*, 'Father of the Country', offered him by the Senate; and Drusus the Younger had presided over gladiatorial games in his and Germanicus' name.[77] Disturbing to many members of the public was the fact that, away from the battlefield, his brother was beginning to reveal a distinctly sadistic tendency to his nature.[78] It was rumoured that Tiberius had rebuked his son for his unashamed bloodlust, and himself shunned the games. For Germanicus, the distractions of Rome would have to wait. Germanicus appears to have remained among his troops that winter. There was good reason to. On 6 November, Agrippina gave birth to a healthy daughter in Ara Ubiorum.[79] They named her after her grand-mother, Iulia Agrippina. The local burghers of the town were charmed by their little home-grown imperial child, and even added her name to their city's.[80] Germanicus and Agrippina now had four children: 9-year-old Nero, 8-year-old Drusus, 2-year-old Caius and the baby, affectionately known to her family as Agrippinilla, 'Little Agrippina'.[81]

Once More Over the Rhine

At the start of 16 CE, Germanicus was as committed as ever to achieving a decisive victory in Germania Magna. Preparing the new campaign plans, he assessed the relative strengths and weaknesses of his foes. 'The Germans, he knew', writes Tacitus, 'were beaten in the field and on fair ground; they were helped by woods, swamps, short summers, and early winters'.[82] In contrast, 'his own troops were affected not so much by wounds as by long marches and damage to their arms'.[83] The evident weak link in his campaign strategy was logistics. On the supply side, the provinces of Tres Galliae, in particular, had been exhausted by the constant demand for the supply of horses. On the march, long baggage-trains presented obvious targets for ambushes, and Tacitus adds that having to fend off the Germans 'was embarrassing to its defenders'.[84] He needed a better way to deliver men and matériel to the battlefield. Indeed, it was a question his father had carefully considered in the formative stage of his planning for the German war, thirty years earlier. Germanicus arrived at the same conclusion, that:

> by embarking on the sea, invasion would be easy for them, and a surprise to the enemy, while a campaign too would be more quickly begun, the legions and supplies would be brought up simultaneously, and the cavalry with their horses would arrive, in good condition, by the river-mouths and channels, at the heart of Germany.[85]

His mind was made up. That year's campaign would open with an amphibious landing. Compared to going overland, it was, however, the more expensive option. To fund the project, he dispatched P. Vitellius and C. Antius to Lugdunum, to collect cash from taxation.[86] To his legates Anteius, Caecina and Silius, he issued orders to construct a fleet, and gave instructions for a variety of sea-worthy craft (plate 18) to be built:

> It seemed that a thousand vessels were required, and they were speedily con-structed, some of small draught, with a narrow stem and stern, and a broad centre, that they might bear the waves more easily; some flat-bottomed, that they might ground without being injured; several, furnished with a rudder at each end, so that by a sudden shifting of the oars they might be run into shore either way. Many were covered in with decks, on which engines for

missiles might be conveyed, and were also fit for the carrying of horses or supplies, and being equipped with sails as well as rapidly moved by oars, they assumed, through the enthusiasm of our soldiers, an imposing and formidable aspect.[87]

Germanicus' own vessel may have been of the sea-going bireme design, which the Romans called a 'long ship' (*navis longa*). As depicted on Trajan's Column, it had a characteristic long, narrow hull, an upwardly curving prow at water-level, a high bulwark at the bow, an in-swinging bulwark at the stern, and two banks of oars. [88] For the troop transports, recent finds in Oberstimm and Mainz point to a more modest design. In 1986, two ships were uncovered, west of the Roman fort at Oberstimm on a tributary of the Danube River, and have been dated dendro-chronologically to 80–110 CE. One of these ships measured 15.7m (51.5ft) long, 2.7m (8.9ft) wide and 1m (3.3ft) high, and there was evidence for a crew of twenty, with ten oarsmen on each side.[89] The ship could also move under sail. Its planks were made of fir, assembled with mortice and tenon joints secured with wooden pegs, while its keel was made of oak. In tests, a faithful reconstruction of the ship, named *Victoria*, proved very swift, achieving speeds of 5 knots under oar and 7.4 under sail, and remarkably manoeuvrable too, being able to turn a full 180 degrees in just 30 seconds.[90] The remains of five ships at Mainz, dated to the late-third and early-fourth centuries CE, also suggest a more modest appearance for the troop transports (fig. 5).[91] The preserved hulls revealed that the ships measured between 17m and 21m (56–69ft) in length, their maximum height was 90cm (35.4 inches) and the width at midship of the largest vessel was a little over 2.7m (9ft).[92] The dimensions suggest a crew of twenty-seven to thirty-five men, of whom between twenty-four and thirty-two were oarsmen sitting twelve to sixteen in each row. The crew would have probably been joined by a steersman and two additional men to operate the sails. The Oberstimm and Mainz vessels seem to better fit Tacitus' description of ships with a 'small draught, with a narrow stem and stern, and a broad centre'.[93] The soldiers themselves are likely to have provided the power for the vessels, based on Tacitus' comment about 'the enthusiasm of our soldiers' in the use of sails and oars.[94]

Assuming that three ships were required to ferry a *centuria*, and there were sixty centuries to a legion, Germanicus' fleet of 1,000 ships equates to two legions – three at most – and their supplies. To build a fleet of such a size required a massive supply of timber. Recent work around the site of Batavodurum reveals that the Kops Plateau near Nijmegen was once originally densely wooded with oak and birch trees, but these were completely cleared away in the Augustan period.[94] Were they felled to provide the wood required to build the Roman invasion fleet? It seems likely. The cleared land would have also provided a convenient assembly point for the expeditionary force.

For the details of the campaign Germanicus once again looked to his father's example:

The island of the Batavi was the appointed rendezvous, because of its easy landing-places, and its convenience for receiving the army and carrying the

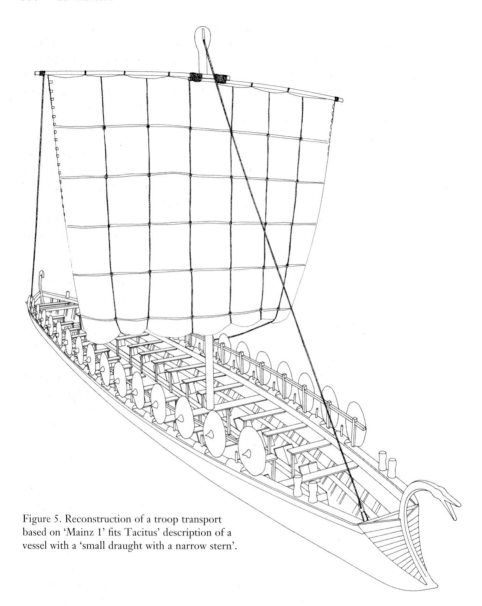

Figure 5. Reconstruction of a troop transport
based on 'Mainz 1' fits Tacitus' description of a
vessel with a 'small draught with a narrow stern'.

war across the river. For the Rhine, after flowing continuously in a single
channel or encircling merely insignificant islands, divides itself, so to say,
where the Batavian territory begins, into two rivers, retaining its name and
the rapidity of its course in the stream which washes Germany, till it mingles
with the ocean. On the Gallic bank, its flow is broader and gentler; it is called
by an altered name, the Vahal, by the inhabitants of its shore. Soon, that
name, too, is changed for the Mosa river, through whose vast mouth it
empties itself into the same ocean.[95]

Before giving the order to start the amphibious invasion, he first sent his forces against the Rhineland nations to take them out of the war (map 6). To the south-eastern section of the river, Germanicus ordered Silius to engage the Chatti.[96] However, this army group's anticipated swift progress was hampered by bad weather. Battle was joined and the Chatti were beaten. During the mopping up operation, the wife of Arpus, the war-chief of the Chatti, and minor spoils, were taken. The offensive achieved little of lasting value in Tacitus' opinion, but the tactical objective was achieved.[97] The Chatti would not now be fighting on the side of the Germans in the forthcoming season. Meanwhile, Germanicus himself marched across the Rhine with an army of six legions, representing a force of approximately 34,000 men, to which should be added auxiliary cohorts.[98] Tacitus gives the reason for committing such a significant number of troops this early in the season as the arrival of news 'that a fort on the river Lupia was being besieged'.[99] The clear implication is that Roman forces were still occupying part of the right bank of the Rhineland region of what is usually considered to be a Roman-free zone. Which fort the Romans garrisoned Tacitus does not reveal, though later in the same passage he cites the fort at Aliso, so this may be the fort under siege. The location of Aliso has eluded historians for centuries. It could have been Anreppen or Haltern Hoffestatt or an as yet undiscovered fort.[100] Before Germanicus' army group arrived at its target, the besieging Germanic warriors fled – his reputation alone, it seems, was sufficient to strike fear into some of his opponents and cause them to withdraw.

A quarter of Rome's entire complement of legions was now active in Germania Magna. Relieving the fort on the Lupia may have been the initial target of the campaign thrust, but the large commitment of troops demonstrates the Roman leadership's intention of permanently changing the balance of political and military power in the region. Rome meant business.

Germanicus learned then that the *tumulus* he had erected only months before in honour of Varus' men had been upturned and desecrated.[101] He decided not to go and restore the mound, deeming it unnecessary at this stage, but instead he made for a structure his own father had established several years before, deep in Germanic territory.[102] It was still the most northerly Roman structure in existence at that time. It was while Drusus the Elder was considering what to do at the end of his campaign of 9 BCE that he gave the order for his men to erect a *tropaeum* using the spoils of the Marcomanni.[103] What came to be known as the *Tropaeum Drusi* was regarded as a highly significant landmark, and its location was recorded by Ptolemy in his *Geographia*, written a hundred years later, at the co-ordinates latitude 33° 45′, longitude 52° 45′.[104] Various modern attempts have been made to identify its precise location, with Dresden or Magdeburg currently the leading contenders.[105] In his description of the structure visited by Germanicus, Tacitus uses the phrase *aram Druso*, 'Drusus' altar', rather than *tropaeum*.[106] While its construction was an act of celebration and piety in the religiously observant eyes of the Romans, it was seen as a provocation to the Germanic tribes. In the intervening years, the local people had sought to scrub out the desecration to their land, and they soon destroyed the alien structure. It was here, on what the Romans considered hallowed ground, that Germanicus ordered the altar restored and re-consecrated 'and himself with his legions celebrated funeral games in his father's honour'.[107] It is telling, and perhaps significant, that the long shadow of Drusus the Elder continued to touch his son a quarter century later. Tacitus recounts that, when Germanicus entered the canal named after his father:

> he prayed to Drusus, his father, to lend him, now that he was venturing on the same enterprise, the willing and favourable aid of the example and memory of his counsels and achievements.[108]

People of the time spoke of Drusus Germanicus – Drusus the Elder – in almost legendary terms. During the extraordinary campaigns in which he had led his men to lands unknown, he displayed personal courage, committed acts of almost reckless derring-do, and yet showed his unswerving patriotism, winning him the love of his troops. It still resonated with Romans of all classes, civilian and military alike. By his deeds, his son was proving to be worthy of Drusus' legacy.

The Battle of Weser River

Germanicus was now intent upon installing a permanent garrison in the region. Everywhere, the men of the legions were deployed in constructing defensive positions, and soon, writes Tacitus, 'all the country between Fort Aliso and the Rhine was thoroughly secured by new barriers and earthworks'.[109] The fleet, meanwhile, had arrived at the estuary of the Ems River, after a trouble-free voyage, bringing with it much needed supplies and matériel.[110] Germanicus assigned ships for use by the legions and auxiliaries. Fatefully, he had the ships disembark on the left bank of the river and remain there, rather than ordering the fleet to continue upstream. Tacitus calls his decision – quite bluntly – an *erratum*, a 'blunder'.[111] With the benefit of hindsight, he writes that 'he disembarked the troops, which were to be marched to the country on the right, and thus several days were wasted in the construction of bridges'.[112] At this point in the campaign, Roman spirits were high, perhaps overconfident. The usual competitiveness between rival units manifested itself:

> The cavalry and the legions fearlessly crossed the first estuaries in which the tide had not yet risen. The rear of the auxiliaries, the Batavi among their number, plunging recklessly into the water and displaying their skill in swimming, fell into disorder, and some were drowned.[113]

Cooler headers prevailed when Germanicus – apparently up to that point distracted by supervising the measuring-out of his temporary camp – received news that the Angrivarii nation had broken out in revolt.[114] Tacitus locates this tribe in the region between the Dulgunii and Chasuarii to the south and the Frisii to the north and west.[115] The insurrection risked delaying the strategic thrust into the heart of Germania, so, to deal with the matter, Germanicus dispatched Stertinius at once with cavalry and lightly-armed troops. Their pre-emptive action, which Tacitus describes as summarily punishing the perfidy of the Germanic people

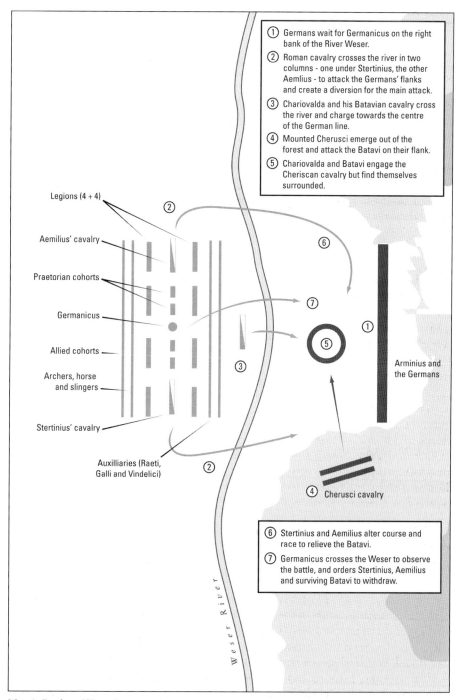

① Germans wait for Germanicus on the right bank of the River Weser.

② Roman cavalry crosses the river in two columns - one under Stertinius, the other Aemlius - to attack the Germans' flanks and create a diversion for the main attack.

③ Chariovalda and his Batavian cavalry cross the river and charge towards the centre of the German line.

④ Mounted Cherusci emerge out of the forest and attack the Batavi on their flank.

⑤ Chariovalda and Batavi engage the Cheriscan cavalry but find themselves surrounded.

Legions (4 + 4)

②

Aemilius' cavalry

Praetorian cohorts

Germanicus

Allied cohorts

Archers, horse and slingers

Stertinius' cavalry

Auxilliaries (Raeti, Galli and Vindelici)   ②

⑥

⑦

①

⑤

Arminius and the Germans

③

④ Cherusci cavalry

⑥ Stertinius and Aemilius alter course and race to relieve the Batavi.

⑦ Germanicus crosses the Weser to observe the battle, and orders Stertinius, Aemilius and surviving Batavi to withdraw.

Weser River

Map 8. Battle at Weser River, 16 CE.

'with fire and sword', contained the revolt from spreading.[116] The way was now clear for an unimpeded march into the heartland of the region, which had for so long frustrated Roman ambitions for outright conquest.

Not many days passed before Germanicus' army reached the left bank of the Weser River. From its source in the Weserbergland of Hannoversch Münden, the Weser River courses through Lower Saxony until it pours into the North Sea at the port city of Bremerhaven. At 452km (281 miles) in length, it is actually Germany's longest river. To the Romans, it was known as the *flumen Visurgis*. Curiously, Strabo's account – contemporary with Germanicus' campaign – makes no mention of the river, though he does acknowledge that 'the Romans [have discovered for us] the entire west of Europe as far as the Elbe River'.[117] Where the Roman army halted exactly is difficult to identify. Tacitus' account gives the barest of topological information, but this has not stopped scholars from suggesting a plain somewhere between Hameln and Minden, possibly at Porta Westfalica, in North Rhein-Westphalia, though it depends on the route Germanicus took heading south.[118] There, the Roman commander found his adversary, standing with his war council on the opposite bank.[119] The Germanic war-chief inquired if Germanicus had arrived, and asked to speak with his brother, Flavus. Germanicus granted permission for the meeting and agreed for his archers to be withdrawn out of range, so they could not strike down Arminius. The Romans were then treated to a bizarre spectacle of two brothers arguing across the fast flowing waters of the Weser. Is the story an invention of Tacitus? Without other sources, it is impossible to tell, yet the story does have a ring of truth about it. There are the seemingly authentic personal details: the Roman historian describes Flavus as 'a man famous for his loyalty, and for having lost an eye by a wound, a few years ago, when Tiberius was in command', and who bore a scar 'which disfigured his face'.[120] Flavus was the kind of 'barbarian' the Romans cultivated. While in the service of her army as a leader (*dux*) of a cohort of his own countrymen, he had successfully assimilated the Roman way, and even spoke Latin with some fluency.[121] There are also other details that lend credence to the story. His loyalty to Rome had been rewarded by increased pay and military awards for valour in battle, including a neck chain, a crown, and other undisclosed gifts.[122] Arminius derided his rewards as a pittance for giving up his freedom. The brothers then traded arguments about their respective situations: Flavus evoked Rome's might and the fact that Thusnelda and the baby boy had been treated with respect, while Arminius spoke of hearth and home, of liberty and local gods. Germanicus and the armies of both sides watched the entire argument from a distance. The exchange in Latin and Cheruscan – which, by now, had become bitter, with Flavus demanding his weapons and horse, and spoiling for a fight – was finally interrupted by Stertinius, who tapped Flavus on the shoulder and ended it.[123] But there would be no battle that day. The two sides parted and retired to their camps for the night.[124]

When the sun had risen next day, the opposing forces took up their positions. The only description of the battle to come down to us is Tacitus', and his accounts of battles are notoriously lacking in detail about tactics and terrain.[125]

He tells us that the Germans assembled across the Weser River from the Romans on the right bank (map 8).[126] The area immediately in front of Arminius' army formed a plain down to the river, while behind it the area was forested. Meantime, Roman scouts were dispatched to gather intelligence on the size of the enemy and its whereabouts. To force an engagement, Germanicus' army would have no choice but to cross the river. In places, Tacitus indicates the river was shallow and there were fords, but, from his vantage point, Germanicus decided that, without bridges, he would be exposing his legionaries unnecessarily to danger.[127] Instead, he ordered Stertinius to take his cavalry and cross the river in a manoeuvre co-ordinated with a contingent of horse led by Aemilius, his *primus pilus*. By distracting the Germanic warriors wth attacks on their flanks, Germanicus intended to create an opportunity for his finest cavalry to strike directly at Arminius' centre. Cohorts of the Batavi under their leader Chariovalda, who were renowned for their exceptional riding skills, drove into the river 'where the stream is most rapid' and made straight for the Cherusci.[128] But Germanicus had underestimated his adversary's insight and experience. Arminius had himself served with the Romans long enough to be familiar with this distractionary multi-pronged attack strategy. Anticipating the move, he had laid a trap. His own men feigned a counter-attack that succeeded in drawing Chariovalda's men onto the plain surrounded by a screen of trees. Suddenly, from out of the cover of the forest rushed the Cherusci infantry. Missiles hurtled through the air and rained down on the unprepared Batavi cavalry, piercing unprotected flesh. Spears thrust menacingly at the horses and the men they carried, cutting skin and stabbing bone. Clubs struck weapons and limbs, breaking arms and legs. Above the shouts and screams of men and the clash of metal and wood, Chariovalda rallied his troops into a tight formation. With a rousing yell, they charged directly at the Germanic horde. Hooves pounded on the soft ground as horses launched their riders forward. The Germans launched another barrage of weapons. In the mêlée, the Batavian chief fell and his horse collapsed under him – both struck down by a cloud of lethal darts. Around him, many of the finest nobles of his Batavian war band succumbed to the same rain of death. They would have been wiped out completely had his men not maintained their strength and resolve, giving Stertinius and Aemilius enough time to arrive at the head of their contingents of cavalry.[129] Germanicus had meantime crossed the river and taken up a position on the right bank. Eagerly, he surveyed the unfolding battle: he soon realized that his opening gambit had failed. Cutting his losses, Germanicus decided against committing additional forces that day, sounded the retreat, and returned disappointed with his men to the camp.[130]

While Chariovalda had been engaging the Cherusci, a deserter from the German side had come into the Roman camp.[131] From him, Germanicus learned that Arminius had picked his place and time for the main battle, and that other tribes loyal to him had gathered in a forest grove, sacred to Hercules. Germanicus' own scouts returned and confirmed the truth of the deserter's information. From the quisling, he also learned that their plan was to attack Germanicus' men while they slept in their tents at night. Thus forewarned, Germanicus considered his options: to hold his ground or retreat.

The young Caesar decided that he needed to get the measure of the morale of his men first. He could seek the counsel of his tribunes and centurions, and risk being told what he wanted to hear; or he could call an assembly of the troops, and risk the shouts of the louder men drowning out the voices of the quieter. Instead, he slipped out of the back of his tent of augury with a trusted companion, and wandered discretely among his men to hear their opinions, unprompted and unexpurgated.[132] Dressed scruffily with the skin of a wild animal draped over his shoulders to look like a camp handler, he apparently moved unnoticed about the camp. He was pleased by what his men said. According to Tacitus, Germanicus:

> enjoyed the men's talk about himself, as one extolled his noble rank, another, his handsome person, nearly all of them, his endurance, his gracious manner and the evenness of his temper, whether he was jesting or was serious, while they acknowledged that they ought to repay him with their gratitude in battle, and at the same time sacrifice to a glorious vengeance the perfidious violators of peace.[133]

Proof of their sincerity was made manifest soon after when, in the dead of night, a Latin-speaking Germanic warrior rode up to the Roman battlements and began taunting the men inside.[134] To each Roman who switched sides, he promised a wife, land and pay of 100 *sestertii* for every day the war lasted. The Roman troops reacted angrily. They jeered the man, shouting back that they would, in any case, take the lands of the Germans and their wives – but as spoils of war. They relished the fight. This was heartening, indeed, for their commander to hear. It was apparently bolstered by a vivid dream the commander had.[135] Though frequently used by ancient historians simply as a literary device, dreams were taken very seriously by the superstitious-minded Romans.[136] Tacitus reports that, while he was sleeping, Germanicus saw himself engaged in a sacrificial rite and, wearing a robe sprinkled in sacred blood, being offered a finer garment by his grandmother, Livia Augusta. His training in religious rites and auguries enabled him to interpret this as a good omen. Thus doubly reassured, Germanicus made up his mind: he would stay and take the fight to the Germans.

The Battle of Idistaviso

Next morning, clasping the ritual crooked staff, Germanicus took the auspices and, determining them to be favourable, he called for the soldiers to assemble. He addressed them and, using all the practised art of the orator, roused his men to wreak havoc upon the poorly-armed Germanic host. As reported – or, more likely, reconstructed – by Tacitus, mindful of the issue that had caused mutiny in the recent past, Germanicus delivered a speech:

> If, in your weariness of land and sea, you desire an end of service, this battle prepares the way to it. The Albis is now nearer than the Rhenus, and there is

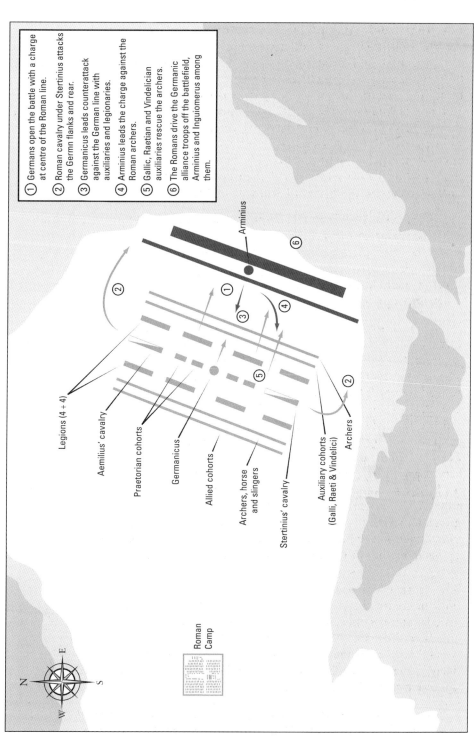

① Germans open the battle with a charge at centre of the Roman line.

② Roman cavalry under Stertinius attacks the German flanks and rear.

③ Germanicus leads counterattack against the German line with auxiliaries and legionaries.

④ Arminius leads the charge against the Roman archers.

⑤ Gallic, Raetian and Vindelician auxiliaries rescue the archers.

⑥ The Romans drive the Germanic alliance troops off the battlefield, Arminius and Inguiomerus among them.

Arminius

②

①
③
④
⑤
②

Legions (4 + 4)

Aemilius' cavalry

Praetorian cohorts

Germanicus

Allied cohorts

Archers, horse and slingers

Stertinius' cavalry

Auxiliary cohorts (Galli, Raeti & Vindelici)

Archers

N
E
W
S

Roman Camp

Map 9. Battle of Idistaviso, 16 CE.

no war beyond, provided only you enable me, keeping close as I do to my father's and my uncle's footsteps, to stand a conqueror on the same spot.[137]

The men cheered, the trumpets sounded, and centurions barked orders to stand to attention. Then they waited for their enemy to arrive. The long hours passed. The anticipated attack did not finally come until midday, but the Romans were ready and waiting.[138] Behind their defensive array of ditch, earthen rampart and parapet of sharpened wooden stakes, the men had formed up tightly in their centuries and cohorts behind their standards. Intimidated by the steely resolve and evident calm of the Roman troops, the skirmishers withdrew as quickly as they had arrived. This was Germanicus' moment. He gave the order and the army marched out of the camp to join battle.

The new battlefield was not far from where the previous action had taken place.[139] Arminius and his alliance army had again picked the location and assembled down onto a plain named Idistaviso (fig. 6):

It winds between the Visurgis and a hill range, its breadth varying as the river banks recede or the spurs of the hills project on it. In their rear rose a forest, with the branches rising to a great height, while there were clear spaces between the trunks. The barbarian army occupied the plain and the outskirts of the wood. The Cherusci were posted by themselves on the high ground, so as to rush down on the Romans during the battle.[140]

Germanicus' army then marched across the river:

The Gallic and Germanic auxiliaries were in the van, then the foot-archers, and, after them, four legions and Caesar himself, with two Praetorian Cohorts and some picked cavalry. Next came as many other legions and

Figure 6. *Field of Idistaviso* in an engraving illustrating *Picture Atlas of German History* by Dr Paul Knötel.

light-armed troops with horse-bowmen, and the remaining cohorts of the allies. The men were quite ready and prepared to form in line of battle according to their marching order.[141]

The standard Roman battle formation was to place the auxiliary cohorts in the centre, with the legions behind them and the cavalry on the flanks. The exact positions of the legions and Praetorians is not detailed in the only extant account of the Battle of Idistaviso, which is again Tacitus'. Not strong on tactical detail, Tacitus has left us with a series of stylized highlights from different parts of the battlespace (map 9). The Cherusci initiated the battle with a charge directly at the Roman centre. Germanicus immediately responded by ordering his finest cavalry and units under Stertinius to move in from the flanks and attack the Germans on their sides and rear. For the moment, Germanicus held his infantry back. His spirits rose when he spotted eight eagles flying towards the woods and sweeping into them. As the bird of Jupiter and the iconic emblem carried by each of the legions, the eagle held great significance for the Romans. As an augur, Germanicus knew how to exploit this vision among his men to his own advantage. 'Go!' he shouted to his men, 'follow the Roman birds, the true deities of our legions!'[142] He could not have played it better.

Emboldened and encouraged by their commander's words, the air filled with the brassy blasts of Roman horns sounding the order to advance. Unleashing their *pila*, the legionaries then charged, probably in a series of wedge formations, with their shields held high and their short stabbing swords ready to thrust. As the infantry advanced, the Roman cavalry was already nipping at the rear of the Germanic lines. The alliance led by the Cherusci responded chaotically. The men who had charged the Roman centre so confidently just moments before now turned and ran towards the wood above the plain. The others, up until then protected by the cover of the trees in the rear, seeking their chance for glory, rushed out and raced towards the Romans. Arminius, meanwhile, was caught up somewhere in the midst of the confusion. He tried to rally his men bravely, gesturing to get his men's attention, and calling upon them to fight gallantly – despite having himself sustained a wound. He led an attack on the unit of Roman archers and almost overwhelmed them, until men of the *cohors Gallorum*, *Raetorum* and *Vindelicorum* arrived in force to relieve them.[143] It seemed that Arminius might be captured, but his luck held. Smearing his face with his own blood, so that he could not be easily recognized, he rode his horse hard and rushed through the Roman lines closing in on him. Tacitus writes, 'some have said he was recognized by Chauci serving among the Roman auxiliaries', adding disapprovingly, 'who let him go'.[144] His Uncle Inguiomerus was also close to being captured, but managed to escape with his life. For those still in the middle of the bloody struggle, the fight was grim indeed. 'The rest were cut down in every direction', writes Tacitus:

> many in attempting to swim across the Visurgis were overwhelmed under a storm of missiles or by the force of the current, lastly, by the rush of fugitives and the falling in of the banks. Some in their ignominious flight climbed the

tops of trees, and as they were hiding themselves in the boughs, archers were brought up and they were shot for sport. Others were dashed to the ground by the felling of the trees.[145]

Although not disclosed in the account, the number of Roman casualties was slight compared to the massacre of the Germans. 'It was a great victory and without bloodshed to us', and to emphasize the point about enemy casualties Tacitus reports that 'ten miles were covered with arms and dead bodies'.[146] It was a moment for Germanicus to savour. The battle over, the troops were permitted to pick up the spoils. Among the finds were lengths of heavy chain the Germans had brought, confident they would be taking back Roman prisoners as slaves. Not for Germanicus was there to be a third acclamation.[147] The troops shouted their praise to Tiberius as *imperator* (whose acclamations now numbered seven) for bringing them victory. It was the politically correct choice, however. On Germanicus' orders, the arms of the Germanic nations were gathered up into a trophy, a mound formed of arms and equipment, into which rose a tree-trunk draped like a scarecrow with captured body armour, crossed spears, shields hanging from the 'arms', and a helmet on the 'head'. An inscription was attached to Germanicus' trophy, upon which were inscribed the names of all the defeated tribes.

The Battle of Angrivarian Wall
The war might have ended there. Defeated, many of the Germanic warriors considered turning homeward or fleeing beyond the Elbe River, far away from the invaders. The raising of the triumphal monument by the Romans, however, only angered the German alliance and emboldened its members' resolve.[148] Humiliated in their defeat, the enraged Germanic warriors spoiled for a new fight to regain their lost honour and to appease the spirits of their fallen comrades. Some spontaneously raced off to engage the Romans and succeeded only in spreading disorder and suffering new wounds. Their leaders under Arminius, instead, thought carefully about their next move, and decided to relocate a short distance away in preparation for making a last stand there.

Their mistake in each of the last two encounters had been to pick the wrong places for battle: the open spaces and firm ground actually favoured the Romans, enabling their soldiers to deploy their combat doctrine to its fullest degree. Arminius had counted on large numbers of highly mobile infantry and concealed reserves to overwhelm the Romans, but the strategy had failed on not one but *two* occasions. To convincingly defeat them, he needed to find terrain that turned Roman strengths into weaknesses, as he had done seven years before at Teutoburg. Close by the Weser River, he found it. Beside the river and a section of forested wetland was a narrow swampy plain. Between the Cherusci and the forest, the warriors of the Angrivarii nation set to work raising a broad earthwork, forming a barrier between them.[149] When it was completed, the infantry assembled by the wall of earth, and the cavalry moved into the cover of the forest. Arminius banked on the assumption that, on approaching them and keen to avoid

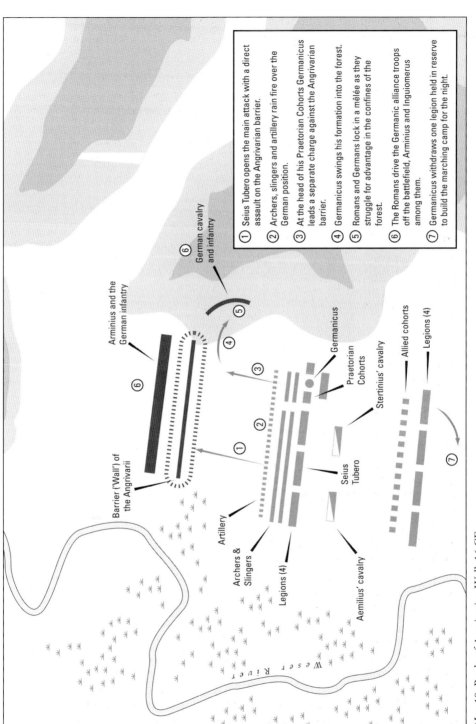

1. Seius Tubero opens the main attack with a direct assault on the Angrivarian barrier.

2. Archers, slingers and artillery rain fire over the German position.

3. At the head of his Praetorian Cohorts Germanicus leads a separate charge against the Angrivarian barrier.

4. Germanicus swings his formation into the forest.

5. Romans and Germans lock in a mêlée as they struggle for advantage in the confines of the forest.

6. The Romans drive the Germanic alliance troops off the battlefield, Arminius and Inguiomerus among them.

7. Germanicus withdraws one legion held in reserve to build the marching camp for the night.

German cavalry and infantry

Arminius and the German infantry

Germanicus

Praetorian Cohorts

Stertinius' cavalry

Allied cohorts

Legions (4)

Barrier ('Wall') of the Angrivarii

Artillery

Archers & Slingers

Legions (4)

Seius Tubero

Aemilius' cavalry

Weser River

Map 10. Battle of Angrivarian Wall, 16 CE.

the swamp, the Romans would be forced into climbing over the heavily-defended wall or entering the woods, whereupon the cavalry would sweep out from the cover of the trees and attack them from their unprotected rear. As they had done in the narrow pass below the range of the Teutoburg hills, Arminius hoped with this ruse to repeat his spectacular victory.

However, Arminius had not reckoned on his adversary discovering the plan. Germanicus' scouts watched the Germans raising their earthwork from a safe distance and couriered reports back to him. From that moment, it was clear to him that the Germans intended to fight again and, in response, he developed a counter-strategy.[150] Germanicus Caesar's plan was to divide up his forces to attack the Angrivarians' defensive wall and the forest, while he led a separate strike (map 10):

> To Seius Tubero, his chief officer, he assigned the cavalry and the plain. His infantry he drew up so that part might advance on level ground into the forest, and part clamber up the earthwork which confronted them. He charged himself with what was the especially difficult operation, leaving the rest to his officers.[151]

The remainder of his forces he held back in reserve. Confident that his preparations were made, he let battle commence. Almost immediately, the differences in difficulty faced by the two army groups in achieving their assigned objectives became apparent.[152] The soldiers attacking on the level ground quickly gained a foothold and forced a passage through the German lines. The troops assaulting the earthwork, however, found progress slow and heavy going, as missiles rained down upon them from the enemy standing on the parapet above. Recognizing the asymmetry of the unfolding battle, Germanicus attempted to tip the odds in his favour. Slingers were brought forward to pelt lead shot and small stones upon the Germanic defenders, while artillery rained down bolts and heavy stones. Having softened the Germans up, the Roman commander now moved in himself at the head of his Praetorian Cohorts, storming the earthwork first, then turning to launch an assault on the forest at speed. The hand-to-hand fighting was intense and every inch of ground was taken only with the spilling of Germanic blood. With the morass now at his rear, the forested wetland Arminius had chosen with such care in which he planned to squash the Romans suddenly presented a peril to his own side. Meanwhile, Germanicus' men were hemmed in by the river and the wall of compacted earth. 'Both were in a desperate plight from their position', writes Tacitus, 'valour was their only hope, victory their only safety'.[153]

It seemed that neither side could bring the decisive blow that would end the battle and so conclude the war. The confined space of the forest hampered both sides: the Germanic warriors could not wield and swing their *frameae*, and the Romans could not fight in formation with their *gladii* and heavy shields. Arminius' resolve began to waver under the stress of command and the pain of his wound.[154] Inguiomerus raced from place to place trying to rally his men. Germanicus pressed headlong into the throng. Like his fearless father before him, 'in battle, he often engaged and slew an enemy in single combat'.[155] Aware of the fragile nature of the situation, Germanicus ripped off his helmet so that his men could see his face. He exhorted the men around him to fight on; they would not take prisoners this time, but continue the slaughter until the Germanic nations were completely destroyed.[156] Fired up by their commander's words and seeing him personally engaged in the fight, despite being weary and bloodied, the Roman troops fought on. The Roman cavalry, too, carried on the struggle, though with less success, on account of the unfavourable terrain. Mindful that the daylight was fading, Germanicus withdrew one legion to erect the camp for the troops later returning from the battle.

Eventually, the persistent Romans cut their way through the enemy lines. Arminius and Inguiomerus finally gave up the fight and fled with their lives, and with them went the survivors of the Angrivarii and Cherusci war bands. When the last of the tribesmen had retreated from the field, the Romans claimed victory as theirs. Technically, it was; but Arminius had got away. Germanicus gathered his men and praised them for their courage, fortitude and loyalty. In the days that followed, his troops gathered up the spoils strewn around the battlefield and erected another trophy. On the pile of arms and armour, they attached an inscription, which proudly announced:

> AFTER THOROUGHLY CONQUERING THE NATIONS
> BETWEEN THE RHENUS AND ALBIS, THE ARMY OF
> TI[BERIUS] CAESAR DEDICATED THIS MONUMENT TO MARS,
> JOVE AND AUGUSTUS.[157]

Conspicuous by its absence was Germanicus Caesar's own name and title. Tacitus offers two explanations for this: Germanicus did not want to cause jealously – presumably of Tiberius rather than Drusus the Younger – and, by dint of it, cause bad feeling; or, the more benign motive of the two, Germanicus considered that the deed was its own reward, 'thinking the consciousness of the achievement was enough'.[158] Either way, Germanicus was publicly demonstrating his loyalty to his adoptive father and commander-in-chief, and that he was not in any way looking to upstage him. He may have led the Romans to victory on the battlefield, but Idistaviso had been won under the auspices of Tiberius. Indeed, Germanicus had set his mind on bringing Germania to heel for the glory of Rome and its *princeps*. There was much yet to do: more battles to fight, many German nations to conquer. To that end, he dispatched Stertinius with orders to crush the Angrivarii. Hardly had he reached their territory than they surrendered.[159] It was a clever move on their part. By offering their surrender voluntarily, they sought and received Germanicus' clemency. The Romans had long believed that it was better to make a friend of a honourable enemy who might prove of use at a later time. But it was a calculated gamble. The Germans, more often than not, merely saw a negotiated settlement as an expedient way to address an immediate problem or buy time, and would quickly break their word as soon as the Romans left.[160]

Homeward Bound

It was now high summer and the campaign season would end in the next month or two. Hundreds of miles lay between their present position, deep in still largely hostile Germania Magna, and their winter camps along the Rhine. Germanicus now had to consider how his large invasion force would make the journey home. The ships were still berthed along the Ems River, but they were not sufficient in number to carry everyone. So, many of the troops would have to march overland and be prepared to defend themselves along the way.[161] For those going by sea, the return journey was to have its own perils. Tacitus stirringly evokes the epic homeward adventure:

> At first, the calm waters merely sounded with the oars of a thousand vessels or were ruffled by the sailing ships. Soon, a hailstorm bursting from a black mass of clouds, while the waves rolled hither and thither under tempestuous gales from every quarter, rendering clear sight impossible and the steering difficult, while our soldiers, terror-stricken and without any experience of disasters on the sea, by embarrassing the sailors or giving them clumsy aid, neutralized the services of the skilled crews. After a while, wind and wave shifted wholly to the south, and from the hilly lands and deep rivers of Germany came, with a huge line of rolling clouds, a strong blast, all the more frightful from the frozen north, which was so near to them, and instantly caught and drove the ships hither and thither into the open ocean, or on islands with steep cliffs or which hidden shoals made perilous. These they just escaped, with difficulty, and when the tide changed and bore them the same way as the wind, they could not hold to their anchors or bale out the water which rushed in upon them. Horses, beasts of burden, baggage were thrown overboard in order to lighten the hulls which leaked copiously through their sides, while the waves, too, dashed over them.[162]

Their travails did not end there. Remarkably, Germanicus or his pilots had miscalculated the tides off the Frisian coast – just as his father had done – and, yet again, the Roman fleet foundered:

> As the ocean is stormier than all other seas, and as Germania is conspicuous for the terrors of its climate, so in novelty and extent did this disaster transcend every other, for all around were hostile coasts, or an expanse so vast and deep that it is thought to be the remotest shoreless sea. Some of the vessels were swallowed up; many were wrecked on distant islands, and the soldiers, finding there no form of human life, perished of hunger, except some who supported existence on carcasses of horses washed on the same shores.[163]

Germanicus' leadership team sailed aboard a sturdy trireme and it, alone of the vessels in the fleet, safely reached the shore of lands inhabited by the Chauci. He blamed himself for the catastrophe visited upon his men. 'Day and night', writes Tacitus, 'on those rocks and promontories, he would incessantly exclaim that he was himself responsible for this awful ruin, and friends scarce restrained him from seeking death in the same sea'.[164] He soon regained his composure, and he ordered his trireme to set sail and go in search of survivors.

The cycle of disaster was finally broken when the weather improved.[165] Calmer seas and softer winds brought the battered boats back to shore. Some of the crews had torn up their tunics and used them for sails to catch the breeze, while others were towed by boats still capable of being propelled by oars. Once back on land, Germanicus assessed the state of the fleet. The vessels in the best condition and those that were repairable were quickly restored, and the rest were raided for salvageable parts or abandoned. Germanicus' sent boats back out to sea to search for survivors trapped on the islands, tidal flats and beaches of the Wadden Sea. Remarkably, many men were discovered still alive. Meantime, the gamble to accept the submission of the Angrivarii now paid off. To demonstrate their good faith, the tribe paid ransoms to neighbouring tribes to buy back captured Romans and returned them to their countrymen. Some of these returned hostages had been tossed upon the sea as far as the island of Britain and sent back by the chieftains to the Continent. Bewildered by their extraordinary adventures:

> everyone, as he returned from some far-distant region, told of wonders, of violent hurricanes, and unknown birds, of monsters of the sea, of forms half-human, half beast-like, things they had really seen or in their terror believed.[166]

Gradually, Germanicus' rag-tag army reassembled, but, as the Romans continued their struggle to go home, word of their demise spread by word of mouth throughout the Germanic communities, and with it calls for action to defeat the invader once and for all.[167] Germanicus, however, was keen to keep the peace, if only to get his men home. The tribes most keen to break the Romans appear to have been the Chatti and Marsi, who had earlier been neutralized, but in the intervening months had recovered and sought satisfaction for their humiliation. Germanicus had to act quickly. He sent C. Silius with 30,000 infantry and 3,000 cavalry against the Chatti. Germanicus himself took an army, which Tacitus describes simply as 'larger', to deal with the Marsi.[168] Faced with these numbers, the Germanic nations were overwhelmed and Mallovendus of the Marsi once again sued for terms. During the surrender negotiations, he revealed that in a forest nearby was hidden an eagle of one of Quinctilius Varus' legions, protected only by a light guard detail. This was an unexpected bonus, indeed. Germanicus immediately sent out troops who recovered it, apparently without a struggle. Energized by his good fortune, Germanicus led his army deep into the lands of the Marsi on a punitive raid. They were taught a severe lesson in Roman justice. Their lands were devastated, and all resistance was met with ruthless force. From the prisoners who were taken, the soldiers were told over and over, 'they were invincible'.[169] It seemed quite incredible to the Germans that, despite:

> having thrown away a fleet, having lost their arms, after strewing the shores with the carcasses of horses and of men, they had rushed to the attack with the same courage, with equal spirit, and, seemingly, with augmented numbers.[170]

Months after they had set out on their mission, the Roman army returned to barracks for the winter. The troops celebrated that their calamity at sea was compensated by the victories they had achieved on land, and the generous cash bonus Germanicus paid out had made up for their losses.[171] Individual achievements were recognized, too. Tiberius had set the example by actively encouraging his legates to reward troops for acts of bravery and courage in battle, and did not require them to seek his permission first.[172] One to receive recognition from Germanicus was C. Fabricius Tuscus, who had been appointed *tribunus* during the general levy (*dilectus ingenuorum*) of 9/10 CE, and had since risen to the rank of *praefectus* of the *cohors Apulae* comprised of Roman citizens. His awards of a *hasta pura* and a *corona aurea* were proudly celebrated on an inscription raised in his honour by the citizens of his adopted town.[173] For his personal loyalty and valour, P. Vitellius was invited to join Germanicus' personal staff (as a *comes*).[174] He would come to play an unexpected but important role in later events.

Amidst the celebration, an officer stationed in Germania Superior may have commissioned an armourer to make a special decorative piece for his kit.[175] The so-called 'Sword of Tiberius', now displayed at the British Museum, comprises the iron blade of a *gladius* and its bespoke scabbard.[176] The scabbard is a typical design for the period, but it is an exceptional piece, on account of the tinned and gilded detail its creator invested in it. It is loaded with symbolism. In the centre is mounted a medallion bearing the profile of Augustus. The supporting bands of the scabbard are detailed to look like the oak leaves of a *corona civica*, perhaps marking the awards received by the owner of the piece. At the lower pointed end is a *lararium*, the shrine of the Roman household gods, and an Amazon, symbolizing wild barbarian enemies. In the upper panel, Tiberius sits semi-nude on a curule chair in the pose of Iupiter. His left hand rests on a round *hoplon* shield engraved with the words *FELICITAS TIBERI*, 'Tiberius' Good Luck'. Behind him stands winged Victory, in front of him the bearded war god Mars Ultor.[177] The *princeps* receives a commander, who stands in full panoply and bears a small figurine of Victory in his left hand. The two men shake hands. The simple scene conveys the message that Germanicus went to war with the protection of Rome's gods, and returned to his patron – the new Augustus – bringing him the prestige of victory.[178]

Farewell Germania

Germanicus returned to Ara Ubiorum later that year and rejoined his growing family. On 16 September, Agrippina had given birth to her second daughter, who survived and was given the name Iulia Drusilla.[179] Germanicus agreed to betroth his eldest son, Nero – now eleven years of age – to the daughter of the repected senator Q. Caecilius Metellus Creticus Silanus, who was one of the consuls in 7 CE. He had been appointed governor of Syria six years later and was still in that position in 16 CE, but was due to return within the year to Rome.[180] Nero and his younger brother Drusus were progressing through junior education. Little Caius, nicknamed Caligula, was already four years old, and Agrippina was two. It would not be long before Agrippina and Germanicus tried for yet another child. They had become quite the model Roman family, just as Augustus had recognized years before.[181]

Contentment with domestic affairs contrasted with frustrations of the foreign policy kind. As he looked back over the last campaign season and prepared his report for the Senate, Germanicus could count among his major achievements the defeat of Arminius and his belligerent Cherusci war bands, and the recovery of the second of Varus' three lost eagle standards.[182] The stain of humiliation of Teutoburg had finally been expunged and Roman honour restored. Moreover, the Bructeri, Chatti and Marsi had been beaten, and the Angrivarii restored to the Roman side. While the job of conquest was not finished, the stage had been set for a complete re-annexation of the lands his father Drusus had conquered two decades before. Germanicus believed he had proved himself the man able to do it. He argued the case in a series of letters addressed in person to Tiberius.[183] His adoptive father, however, responded that Germanicus should return to Rome and celebrate the triumph that had been awarded him the previous year. Germanicus replied that it was time to strike the final blow – the tribes that had held out were wavering, and others were considering suing for peace. Tiberius answered firmly that 'he had now had enough of success, enough of disaster'.[184] He reminded Germanicus that his victories had been won at some considerable cost in lost men and matériel, and, though not directly blaming its commander, nevertheless they 'were still grievous and shocking'.[185] Tiberius pointedly recounted that, when he had been sent by Augustus to deal with the Sugambri, 'he had done so more by diplomacy than by arms', and the Germanic tribe had surrendered.[186] Marboduus and the Marcomanni, too, had been forced into accepting a peace treaty.[187] The other Germanic tribes, the Cherusci included, had been left to fight amongst themselves, because Roman honour had been satisfied – and, by implication, without putting Roman troops in harm's way. Rome's interests could be best served through a proxy war. Unwilling to concede, however, Germanicus wrote back, formally requesting one more year to complete the mission. But he had misjudged the mood of the *princeps*.

Tiberius was looking for an exit strategy, and this was his moment to execute it. He had been advised by Augustus not to expand the borders of the empire, as, in his opinion, it would be hard to police the longer frontier and risked losing the gains already achieved.[188] Tiberius had ignored that advice and let his son have his head, but had now grown impatient with him. He had tried appealing to Germanicus' reason, but that approach had not worked. His latest letter was more explicit. There would be no 'troop surge', no extension of the campaign in Germania: if there was need of further action there, his son Drusus would be assigned the mission, since this was effectively the only theatre of war left where he could garner military honours of his own. Recognizing that this might seem harsh, as an enticement and to soften the blow, Tiberius offered Germanicus a second consulship, but insisted that he must be in Rome in person to carry out his duties. Reading that letter must have been a terrible disappointment to Germanicus. Tacitus writes that he 'saw this was a pretence, and that he was hurried away through jealousy from the glory he had already acquired'.[189] That may be rather more Tacitus' interpretation than Germanicus', whose own personal view is not known from any other source. If, in fact, he did read sinister motives into Tiberius' words, he must have realized that there was nothing to be gained by pushing the matter with the commander-in-chief, to whom, anyway, he was unswervingly loyal. He knew when to stop arguing. Without further delay, he made arrangements to return to Rome. He would never again return to Rome's north-western frontier.

In the Forum Romanum near the Temple of Saturn, the Arch of Germanicus, begun the previous year to commemorate the recovery of the standards lost by Varus, was formally consecrated.[190] It stood just 150ft from Augustus' own arch, erected to mark the recovery of the standards from Parthia in 20 BCE by Tiberius.[191] On the inscription engraved across the attic, Germanicus' leadership was properly noted as having been under the auspices (*auspicia*) of Tiberius.[192] In marble and gilt bronze, the new arch expressed the emperor's view that the war in Germania was finally over. Its proximity to the older arch was deliberate, but its subtext altogether more subtle. As deputy, Tiberius had once shown his *princeps* Augustus dutiful co-operation. The new arch demonstrated that same alignment existed between Tiberius and his subordinate, Germanicus.

Across the Empire, communities were eager to associate themselves with the good fortune of Germanicus. He accepted a number of honorary magistracies, including the post of *praefectus* or *praefectus quinquennalis* at Caesaraugusta, Colonia Augusta Buthrotum, Fulginiae, Hispellum, Interpromium, Priene, and Regium Lepidum; and shared honorary posts with Drusus the Younger at Acci, Aquae Flaviae, Praeneste, and Carteia.[193] He did not take on the duties and responsibilities in person – they were delegated to a local dignitary – but his acceptance of the honours showed an enthusiasm for supporting local communities. It was already normal practice, by this time, and Germanicus could happily reflect on the fact that he had more honorary magistracies than Augustus himself, who had held just five.

Chapter 5

Travels and Tribulations in the Orient

17–10 October 19 CE

Triumph and Treachery in Rome

Germanicus would have to wait a while for the promised second consulship. He did not sit idly, however, during his time in Rome. He continued to offer his services as a popular advocate in court, in the process enhancing his reputation for personal integrity and fiery oratory.[1] To his religious duties as augur and Arval Brother was added the new post of *flamen divorum Augustalis*, a new priesthood of the imperial house, honouring the divine Augustus.[2] 17 CE was the inaugural year for the cult priesthood and, being a lifetime position, it publicly demonstrated the high esteem in which Tiberius held his adopted son. These cults traced their origin back to the centuries-old tradition of ancestor worship – the *di parentes* – celebrated both at home and in public over nine days from the Ides of February.[3] The cult followed the model established several years before for the Divine Iulius, whose current priest was Sex. Apuleius. The new priesthood and its rites established for Augustus elevated his status, and, by reason of his adoption by him, also that of Tiberius. The appointment of Germanicus as *flamen divorum* carried with it great prestige. During the ceremonial rites, Germanicus would don the *apex*, the distinctive spiked cap worn by the *flamen*.

Among his many public duties, Germanicus consecrated a Temple to Spes, the personification of hope, which had been erected in fulfillment of a vow made during the Punic Wars by A. Atilius.[4] Many of the temples in Rome had been built by grateful and victorious generals returning from war centuries before, but their upkeep was often neglected by future generations. The Temple of Hope was one of several sacred buildings that were refurbished under Tiberius, owing to their old age or damage caused by destructive floods and fires.[5] The restorations not only beautified the city, but publicly proclaimed Tiberius' piety to the gods and his commitment to maintaining their good favour.

The series of ancient religious festivals and sacred rites gave the Roman calendar its distinct shape and peculiar character. In celebration of the days and months of the Roman year and the astronomical influences and popular traditions underpinning them, Ovid was busily composing his elegiac poem, the *Fasti*. Each book of the epic poem describes a month and the origins and customs, by day. There is a hint in his writings that he finished it in its entirety, but only six books have survived to the present day, covering January through June.[6]

Originally dedicated to Augustus, Ovid changed it in favour of his adoptive grandson, opening his poem with the self-deprecating personal appeal:

> Receive, Caesar Germanicus, this work with benign aspect, and direct the course of my timid bark; and not disdaining a mark of attention thus slight, be propitious to this act of duty consecrated to you.[7]

Whether Germanicus ever read the poem dedicated to him is not known. As a translator of the *Aratus*, the work would have had obvious appeal. Ovid, by now exiled in Tomis on the shore of the Black Sea, saw Germanicus as a kindred spirit – an educated and cultured man – but, most importantly, as someone who could help improve his lot in life. In Scythia Minor, hardly anyone spoke Latin and brutal barbarian tongues predominated. The *Fasti* was one of several works in which the isolated Roman lauded the young Caesar, in the hope that he might bring his influence upon the emperor and advocate for the repeal of his banishment. The connection with his tutor Salanus might imply that he was at least known to him, but, even if he was an acquaintance, Germanicus probably did not know Ovid intimately. His grandfather's reasons for punishing Ovid with exile in 8 CE are still unclear – he never explicitly says why, in any of his writings – and Tiberius made no attempt to repeal the sentence after his predecessor's death in 14 CE.[8] Ovid had long since become a *persona non grata* in Rome. His appeals to his friends were all in vain.[9] Far from his beloved Rome, his imagination conjured up life in the city, and it is through his writings that we are able to visualize the great celebratory event of Germanicus' life.

On 26 May 17 CE, the long-anticipated triumph of Germanicus Caesar finally took place.[10] Rome was abuzz with anticipation to see its young and dashing hero in his 'brilliant triumph'.[11] It was advertised as a celebration of 'his triumph over the Cherusci, Chatti, and Angrivarii, and the other tribes which extend as far as the Elbe'.[12] In exile, Ovid was stirred into describing the joyful day, imagining the Palatinus Hill as 'decorated with wreaths, and the frankincense is crackling in the blaze, and by its smoke is obscuring the day'.[13] Cheering crowds thronged the processional route from the Campus Martius, outside the walls on a plain north-west of the city, to the Forum Romanum. Germanicus rode in a glittering gilded four-horse chariot (*inaurati carrus*) decorated with ornately carved winged victories and a laurel wreath. As *triumphator*, he wore the purple dyed *toga purpurea*, or *toga picta*, which is known from representations on coins to have been a gown elaborately embroidered – probably with thread wrapped in gold – with borders, tendrils and curlicues over a *tunica palmata*, so named because it was adorned with a palm leaf, the traditional symbol of a victor (fig. 7).[14] According to ancient tradition, his face, and possibly his entire body, was daubed a deep red colour with cinnabar or red lead.[15] Holding the reins of the four horses draped in garlands in one hand, and a sceptre surmounted with an eagle in the other, Germanicus stood proudly in the two-wheeled chariot.[16] As it moved at a sedate pace, a public slave or a chosen companion held a laurel wreath over his head, uttering the words *respice post te! Hominem te memento!* ('Look behind you! Remember that you are a man!'). It had become customary for members of the

Figure 7. Germanicus shown celebrating his triumph on 26 May 17 CE, riding in the triumphator's chariot (obverse) and holding one of the recovered legionary standards lost by Varus (reverse). Drawn by the author.

family of the triumphant commander to stand with him in the chariot or ride on horseback alongside. 'The admiration of the beholders', writes Tacitus, 'was heightened by the striking comeliness of the general and the chariot which bore his five children' – Nero, Drusus, Caius, Iulia and Drusilla.[17] Velleius Paterculus remarked how well 'the magnificence of his triumph corresponded to the grandeur of his exploits' – in part, a tribute to Tiberius' generosity.[18]

Behind Germanicus and his young guests marched the men of the legions who had fought for him and endured hardships during three years of the *Bellum Germanicum*. This was their moment of celebration, too. Held high were the two eagle standards of the legions lost at Teutoburg and recovered by Germanicus. Behind them rolled a long procession of floats and wagons, piled high with magnificent war trophies. 'There were borne in procession spoils, prisoners, and representations of the mountains, rivers and battles', conveniently described on placards, carried aloft on poles so that they could be read by the crowd, all to the lively accompaniment of horns and flutes, while soldiers sang bawdy victory songs.[19]

Paraded prominently among the exhibits of this spectacle were the captives from the myriad nations of Germania, a veritable roll call of V.I.P.s of *barbaricum*:

amongst whom were Segimundus, the son of Segestes, the chief of the Cherusci, and his sister, named Thusnelda, the wife of Armenius, who led the Cherusci when they treacherously attacked Quintilius Varus, and even to this day continues the war; likewise his son Thumelicus, a boy three years old, as also Sesithacus, the son of Segimerus, chief of the Cherusci, and his wife Rhamis, the daughter of Ucromirus, chief of the Chatti, and Deudorix, the son of Baetorix, the brother of Melo, of the nation of the Sicambri; ... There was also led in triumph Libes the priest of the Chatti, and many other prisoners of the various vanquished nations, the Cathylci and the Ampsani, the Bructeri, the Usipi, the Cherusci, the Chatti, the Chattuarii, the Landi, the Tubattii.[20]

Segestes – the father-in-law of Arminius and now seemingly an isolated figure – had a privileged view of the entire event, 'he being held in honour by the Romans', wrote Strabo. Ovid imagines the humiliating scene, contrasting the exhibited and the spectator:

> the countenances of some changed with their fortunes, those of others still firm, and forgetful of their condition. Some of them will be enquiring the reasons, and the circumstances, and their names: some will be telling, although they know little about it.[21]

Who among the cheering onlookers cared who these conquered barbarians were, anyway? This was Germanicus' victory day. The day was made all the sweeter by a gift of 300 *sestertii* to every plebeian from the purse of Tiberius Caesar.[22]

The grand procession wound its way along the route of the ancient cobbled *Via Sacra*, through the monumental Forum Romanum, passing the Temple of Iulius Caesar, the *Rostra* and Senate House, before taking a sharp left turn at the Golden Milestone towards the Temple of Saturn. A narrow street zigzagged up the Capitolinus to the Temple of Iupiter Optimus Maximus. There, Germanicus and his children descended from the chariot. A blood sacrifice and prayers were offered. Imagining the event, the exiled poet wrote, 'the white victim, struck on its neck with the planted axe, is dying the ground with its crimson blood', in fulfilment of vows made by Rome's leaders to the nation's friendly gods to bring them victory.[23] Curls of smoke, spiked with fragrant incense crackled in the fires at the temples, rose skyward. The smell of sizzling choice cuts of meat and offal soon filled the air. In the closing moments of this religious rite, 'the war, seeing that he had been forbidden to finish it, was taken as finished'.[24] 'By this fierce Germany', sang Ovid, 'like the rest of the world, you may have bent the knee to the Caesars'.[25] The message for public consumption was 'mission accomplished':

> There was peace: and the occasion of your triumph, Germanicus,
> The Rhine had now surrendered to you its subservient streams.[26]

At the age of 32, Germanicus' *curriculum vitae* was a veritable list of all the important magistracies and religious positions in the Roman state, and he was the most popular man in the Empire to boot. Publicly, he was being presented as a key figure in the ruling triad with Tiberius and Drusus, not just in Rome, but in the provinces, too. On the coast of western Gaul at Mediolanum Santonum (Saintes), a double arch was dedicated on 1 January 18 CE, surmounted by an equestrian statue of Tiberius flanked by effigies of his 'co-regents', Germanicus and Drusus, both on foot (plate 27).[27] The question now being asked was what to do with Germanicus. Tacitus presents a somewhat cynical view of Tiberius' response:

> Failing to obtain credit for sincere affection, he resolved to get the young prince out of the way, under pretence of conferring distinction, and for this he invented reasons, or eagerly fastened on such as chance presented.[28]

Tiberius was, above all else, a pragmatist, and he needed to deploy Germanicus' talents where they could best serve the interests of the nation. The East provided him with just the place to invest his deputy's skills and intellect. Suetonius asserts that the objective of Germanicus' new assignment was to 'restore order in the Orient', while Josephus explains the mission as to 'settle the affairs of the East'.[29]

The first trouble spot was Rome's arch-nemesis, Parthia. Two years earlier, the Parthians had expelled their king, Vonones, who was the eldest son of Frahâta IV.[30] The Parthians saw him as too Roman. In his youth, he had been handed over to Augustus by Frahâta as a hostage along with his three brothers under the terms of a peace treaty.[31] When Frahâta died, civil war broke out and, at the request of a deputation of nobles from Parthia, Vonones set off from Rome to take the throne.[32] While he travelled east, first Tigranes IV, and then the woman Erato, reigned briefly.[33] In 16 CE, Vonones finally arrived in the capital, Ctesiphon. Tired of years of instability, the reaction of the local people to their new king was initially warm; but then a sense of resentment grew at having been forced to accept a regent, in effect, chosen by their enemy, and during whose exile he had adopted foreign ways. Vonones did not help his own cause by seeming to disdain Parthian traditions – in particular, hunting, preferring to be carried about in a litter and attended to by his Greek staff – and scorning nationally cherished festivals while touring the country.

The Parthians were wrong to think that their chief Roman adversary approved of their new king. Tiberius never officially recognized Vonones as ruler of Parthia. Indeed, his governor of Syria, Q. Caecilius Metellus Creticus Silanus, fretted about the possibility that he might be dragged into an unwanted war with Parthia, in order to defend Vonones' right to rule there.[34] The Parthian nobles secretly turned to a member of the royal Arsacid family to oust the unpopular incumbent. His name was Artabanus. He was a young man who had grown up among the Scythian tribe of the Dahae, and yet was seen as a better embodiment of Parthian ways – or, at least he was not tainted by Roman ways. The rebels rallied around Artabanus, providing him with troops. At the first engagement, Vonones' army defeated his rival, but, in the second encounter, he won, and he was crowned Artabanus II.[35] Hoping to keep him under surveillance in Syria lest he cause trouble, Silanus promptly sent for Vonones, though he let him keep his royal title and the pomp that went with it.[36] Like a wild bird kept in a cage, Vonones would never accept his captivity, no matter how comfortable. He staged a daring escape and fled to Armenia.

Crisis brewed in neighbouring Cappadocia, Cilicia and Commagene, too. The rugged mountainous kingdom of Cappadocia had been ruled for the past fifty years by Archelaus Sisinnes.[37] He was now old and infirm, and he had a history with Tiberius – and not a good one. In 25 BCE, Tiberius had represented the king in court, but, during his self-imposed exile in Rhodes, the regent had failed to show the son of Livia the required respect. Members of the household of Augustus, eager to talk up Caius Caesar's rising prospects, counselled the king to be wary of the *princeps'* disgraced stepson. Now Tiberius was *princeps* and he remembered clearly the way the old king had disrespected him: it was payback time.[38] Livia summoned Archelaus to Rome and, in the letter she sent to him, urged him to show humility. In return, she promised he could expect leniency from her son. On his arrival, however, the old king was received coldly and summarily arraigned before the Senate on what Tacitus describes as charges 'fabricated against him'.[39] Cassius Dio elaborates on the story, telling us that Archelaus was suffering with dementia and gout and had to be brought to the Senate House in a litter, from which he occasionally leaned out to address the conscript fathers.[40] If found guilty, the penalty was death. In the event, he was spared, but, shamed by his treatment or just from the anxiety brought on by the legal process, the poor man died shortly afterwards, some said by taking his own life.[41] Cappadocia was reduced to a province of the empire in the care of an equestrian governor.[42] Mazaca, the principal city of Cappadocia, was renamed Caesarea in Tiberius' honour.[43] With the accretive revenue stream brought by the new province, Tiberius announced that he would reduce the tax levied on the sale of goods, then at 1 per cent, to precisely half that amount.

South and east of Cappadocia respectively, the kingdoms of Cilicia and Commagene also saw trouble. Cilicia was a cleft country, divided into highland peoples, who lived in the Isaurian Mountains partly by banditry, and settled communities living peacefully in the plain below.[44] By an unfortunate coincidence, both Philopator II of Cilicia and Antiochus III of Commagene had recently died. The élite classes there saw a chance to advance their own status and wealth by seeking Roman intervention, but the common people were still loyal to the old dynasties and wanted their new rulers to come from the same trusted royal families.[45] If that was not enough, the Roman provinces of Iudaea (under *praefectus* Valerius Gratus) and Syria (now rid of Creticus Silanus), 'exhausted by their burdens, implored a reduction of their tribute'.[46]

Bringing stability to the region called for a firm and, particularly important for Tiberius, a loyal pair of hands. Those belonged to his adopted son:

> Tiberius accordingly discussed these matters and the affairs of Armenia, which I have already related, before the Senate. 'The commotions in the East', he said, 'could be quieted only by the wisdom of Germanicus; his own life was on the decline, and Drusus had not yet reached his maturity.' Thereupon, by a decree of the Senate, the provinces beyond the sea were entrusted to Germanicus, with greater powers wherever he went than were given to those who obtained their provinces by lot or by the emperor's appointment.[47]

It was another example of Tiberius replicating tried and tested policy established by his forebear. Just as Augustus had first sent his son-in-law M. Agrippa to Syria as *Orienti praepositus* – commander or overseer of the East – in 23 BCE, and then C. Caesar twenty-two years later, so now Tiberius dispatched his adopted son with *imperium proconsulare* to the same region of the Roman world.[48] Germanicus was clearly being sent to get an important job done with the full confidence of the *princeps* and Senate. Velleius Paterculus praised Tiberius for making the appointment, exclaiming 'in what an honourable style did he send his Germanicus to the transmarine provinces!'[49] In contrast, with his slanted editorial bias, Tacitus reads sinister motives into Tiberius' choice:

> The commotion in the East was rather pleasing to Tiberius, as it was a pretext for withdrawing Germanicus from the legions which knew him well, and placing him over new provinces where he would be exposed both to treachery and to disasters.[50]

Studying the statement closely, it seems a dubious claim for Tacitus to make. Germanicus was no stranger to difficult situations. He was parting from the company of the commanders and troops of eight legions along the German frontier, whose loyalty he had earned, but he had once had to win over these men, and risked his own life in putting down the mutiny of 14 CE. In the transfer to the East, he was assuming responsibility for fewer legions – four in Syria and two in Aegyptus – but the greater geographic area with its affluent populations and the strategic importance of the frontier region suggest that his new appointment was clearly a promotion.[51] His reputation for courage and fairness would go before him, so he was more likely than not to be warmly received on arrival, by military and civilian officials alike. Moreover, while any incoming new commander had to establish his credibility with the men reporting to him, his legal power ensured that he would be obeyed. Under the army reforms of Augustus, when Roman troops took the *sacramentum militiae* on enlistment, they swore 'to follow the commanders to whatever wars they may be called, and neither desert the *signa* nor shrink from death on behalf of the *res publica*'.[52] To fail to uphold the oath was mutiny, and Germanicus had already proved he could face one down. Additionally, for the safety of his own person and of his family, Germanicus would take with him his complement of twelve lictors and possibly an allocation of units of the *Cohortes Praetoriae* from Italia.[53]

Suetonius also describes Germanicus' departure for the East as *expulsus*, meaning 'hurried' or 'sudden'.[54] This seems an unnecessarily dark interpretation. The nature and speed of Germanicus' appointment was probably not due to any animosity or odium on Tiberius' part. Firstly, it was in response to the urgency of the perceived deteriorating state of affairs in the region, which appeared to grow more perilous by the day. Germanicus was unquestionably the best man available to carry out the complex mission of restoring order in the Orient, and a man who had proven his unswerving loyalty to the *princeps*, despite multiple temptations to act otherwise. Secondly, the sooner he left for the East, the better: the hazards of travel could delay an official on business from reaching his destination, and Tiberius had already made it clear that his deputies had to be *en route* to their assignments by June at the latest.[55]

The occasion of Germanicus' appointment as special envoy to the East may have been the reason for creating the so-called *Grand Camée de France* (*Gemma Tiberiana*, plate 24), an extraordinary engraved five-layered sardonyx cameo, now in the Bibliothèque Nationale in Paris.[56] Scholars have long debated the significance of the symbolic imagery on the gem – the largest cameo to survive from the ancient world.[57] Many believe that it depicts the central figure of the enthroned

Tiberius, bidding farewell to Germanicus, shown in the panoply of a military commander, as he takes up his new mission. Standing behind Germanicus are Agrippina and Caligula, depicted in a child-size cuirass, *pteryges*, *paludamentum* and greaves. Who commissioned it is also not known, but the quality of the piece and the likely high cost of its manufacture suggest someone very important.

Yet there was a potentially unsettling development. At the same time as Germanicus was due to head east, Tiberius also recalled Silanus to Rome. The vacancy in the governor's office in Syria was filled by Cn. Calpurnius Piso.[58] The character of this man could not have been more different from Germanicus'. Tacitus describes him as 'a man of violent temper, without an idea of obedience, with indeed a natural arrogance'.[59] He came from a patrician family with a known streak of independence and a propensity for superciliousness. During the civil war which followed Iulius Caesar's assassination, Piso's father sided with Brutus and Cassius. When the last of the conspirators had been dispatched, Piso refused to grovel before the victorious Triumvirate and did not pursue political advancement. Only when Augustus offered him a consulship, did he accept it. His son Cnaeus followed suit and felt he was at least the equal of Tiberius. He looked down on the *princeps'* children – which included Germanicus – as ranking far beneath him. As *propraetor* of Syria, Piso would report to Germanicus. It was an awkward arrangement for Germanicus, but Piso had important family connections. He had married the wealthy Plancina, herself of strong character, but, importantly, she was a personal friend of Livia, Germanicus' grandmother.

Alternative explanations for the choice of *propraetor* are that Germanicus was being tested; that it was a safeguard, intended to limit Germanicus' ambitions; or that Tiberius was punishing his adopted son. The long-established family connection between Piso and the imperial family carried great weight. Augustus looked after his friends, but expected loyalty in return. It was an approach Tiberius continued. Tiberius would later state that Piso 'was my father's representative and friend, and was appointed by myself on the advice of the Senate, to assist Germanicus in the administration of the East'.[60] Nevertheless, the choice of deputy ensured that the relationship would be troubled, unless handled with deftness. It might have thus been intended as a test of Germanicus' character: he would have to prove his ability to 'take the rough with the smooth' and learn how to manage rivals, if he was to be Tiberius' successor. Tacitus suggests a more overtly politically motivated reason, however. His appointment was a counterbalance to Germanicus. 'He [Piso] thought it a certainty', writes the historian, 'that he had been chosen to govern Syria in order to thwart the aspirations of Germanicus'.[61] Implicit in that rationale is that Tiberius still distrusted his adopted son, and saw in Piso a man who could rein him in if he became too haughty or ambitious. Perhaps the choice was driven by Tiberius' doubting personality. He could bear a grudge over many years, but delighted in achieving the final revenge. If this interpretation holds true, by appointing Piso, he could take an impish delight, watching from afar as Germanicus wriggled and squirmed in dealing with this pompous and unpredictable patrician.[62]

Perhaps Tiberius was jealous of his popular adopted son. There was a precedent for this. In the literature, there is a rumour that, years before, at one point in their otherwise close relationship, Tiberius hated his popular brother Drusus – Germanicus' birth father. The story reported by Suetonius tells how Tiberius purposely disclosed a letter he had received from his brother, in which he proposed that Augustus should step down for the Republic to be restored.[63] If the inflammatory comments were intended to cause a rift between Drusus the Elder and his stepfather, it did not have the intended effect. While there is no other story that survives to back-up a long-harboured resentment of the older brother towards the younger, yet it is in the realms of possibility. Tiberius was a complicated man. In Germanicus, it could be said, Drusus the Elder was reborn. Not unnaturally, Tiberius would be expected to favour his own son, Drusus, for preferment, yet his deeds more often than not benefited Germanicus. Tiberius' relationship with Drusus the Younger was not an easy one. His son's vices and dissolute lifestyle actually exasperated him.[64] Tacitus asserts that the imperial household sensed this discord and divided into two camps: the supporters of Germanicus faced off those of Drusus.[65] Beyond Tacitus' account, there is no other evidence to support the notion of a family divided; but a fractious, politically-charged hothouse on the Palatinus is nevertheless a possibility. Those supporting Germanicus could point to the fact that he was descended from an illustrious family-tree: his grandfather was M. Antonius, and his great-uncle was Augustus; moreover, he was married to Agrippina, the grand-daughter of Augustus. In contrast, Tiberius came from the *gens Claudia* through his father and *gens Drusi* through his mother: he had come into the *gens Iulia* only through adoption and by marriage to Augustus' daughter. If Tiberius felt inferior to his adopted kin, his own son Drusus apparently did not. Tacitus frankly admits that 'the brothers were singularly united, and were wholly unaffected by the rivalries of their kinsfolk'.[66] Indeed, it was to meet Drusus that Germanicus now headed, since it would be a while before they might have that opportunity again.

The Occidental Tourist
If Germanicus' new appointment was swiftly decided, his journey to the East was leisurely undertaken. Long distance travel in the first century CE was dictated by the vagaries of the weather as much as the mode of transport and route taken. Rather than go by road, he chose to go by sea. The usual departure point from Italy was the seaport of Brundisium (map 11). Accompanying Germanicus was his personal staff of companions, advisors, adjutants and lictors. Between them, these men had many years of combat and administrative experience. Among them were his *comes* P. Vitellius, who had been with him in Germania in charge of *Legiones* II *Augusta* and XIV *Gemina*; *quaestor* P. Suillius Rufus, a man in his thirties and a former *praetor*; the current *praetor* Q. Servaeus; Cn. Sentius, one of the older men in the group; C. Silius, former legate of Germania Superior and recently a tax auditor in Tres Galliae; Q. Veranius, a former *praetor*; and Vibius Marsus.[67] On this trip, only six-year-old Caius went along, his older brothers and sisters probably remaining in Rome in the care of Antonia or Claudius; but another child was

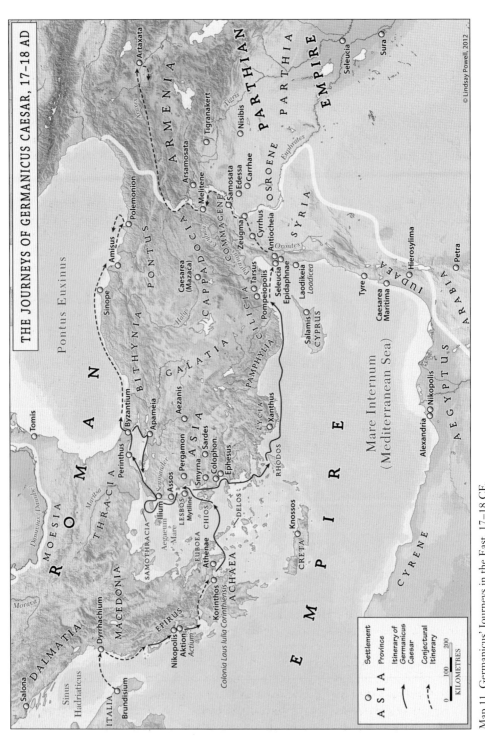

Map 11. Germanicus' Journeys in the East, 17–18 CE.

on the way – Agrippina was pregnant again.[68] The family boarded a sleek trireme with a complement of some 122 oarsmen and modest accommodation for guests on deck.[69]

The first stop on the journey took them to Dalmatia. Drusus was residing on the coast – probably at Salona or Apollonia or Dyrrhachium – before departing to lead a new campaign in Germania.[70] Travelling the Adriatic Sea was a treacherous business. While pirates were no longer a threat, natural hazards persisted. The Italian coast had few recognizable landmarks to navigate by, or places at which to harbour, and there was a multitude of dangerous shallows.[71] In the event, Germanicus' flotilla reached the Illyrian shore without difficulties. For the moment, the brothers and their families could enjoy each other's company in relaxed circumstances. Germanicus likely shared his insights about the lands across the Rhine and lessons he had learned about the officers and men awaiting their new commander. Livilla was probably with her husband Drusus, completing something of a family reunion. Then they exchanged farewells, and the flotilla set sail into the clear aquamarine-coloured sea, following the craggy coastline as it headed south-southeast towards the Greek peninsula.

For long distance voyages, sea captains had many choices of route, but ancient navigators tended to follow well-established shipping lanes (*cursus maritimi*).[72] Currents and winds, however, dictated the ease or difficulty of sea crossings. Mediterranean currents still generally circulate anti-clockwise, while winds generally blow between north-east and north-west.[73] For safety, shipping in antiquity hugged the coastlines and travelled along the chain of islands populating the region, their captains mindful of the unpredictable Maestro, a wind which blows in the summer months when the pressure is low over the Balkan peninsula. At Nikopolis the travellers berthed and entered the city.[74] Here a courier caught up with the travellers and delivered the long-expected news that Germanicus had been confirmed as consul for the second time with Tiberius Caesar as his co-consul on 1 January 18 CE.[75] This was yet more public affirmation of the *princeps'* confidence in Germanicus and of his position as heir presumptive.[76]

The 'City of Victory' in Epirus was fast becoming a tourist attraction in its own right, living off its association with Augustus and panoramic view (plate 28) of the site of the Battle of Actium of 31 BCE. A description of the place as it appeared four decades before Germanicus' visit survives in Strabo's *Geography*:

> Nikopolis is populous, and its numbers are increasing daily, since it has not only a considerable territory and the adornment taken from the spoils of the battle, but also, in its suburbs, the thoroughly equipped sacred precinct – one part of it being in a sacred grove that contains a gymnasium and a stadium for the celebration of the quinquennial games, the other part being on the hill that is sacred to Apollo and lies above the grove. These games – the Actia, sacred to Actian Apollo – have been designated as Olympian, and they are superintended by the Lacedaemonians. The other settlements are dependencies of Nikopolis. In earlier times, also the Actian Games were

wont to be celebrated in honour of the god by the inhabitants of the sur-rounding country – games in which the prize was a wreath – but at the present time they have been set in greater honour by Caesar.[77]

The *raison d'être* of the city was the Actian War monument. Strabo describes it:

> Near the mouth [of the Gulf of Ambracia] is the sacred precinct of Actian Apollo – a hill on which the temple stands; and at the foot of the hill is a plain which contains a sacred grove and a naval station, the naval station where Caesar dedicated, as first fruits of his victory, the squadron of ten ships – from vessel with single bank of oars to vessel with ten; however, not only the boats, it is said, but also the boat-houses have been wiped out by fire.[78]

Modern archaeology has located the victory complex built just two years after the epoch-making battle. Situated below a three-sided covered portico erected on the site of Octavianus' camp, it took the form of a monumental wall displaying the cast bronze beaks from the ships captured from M. Antonius and Kleopatra and consecrated to Mars and Neptune.[79] Perhaps while he was there, Germanicus paused to view the bronze statues of the ass named Nikon and its driver called Eutychus, which the victor of Actium had erected in memory of an encounter with them before the battle, and had since become a draw for tourists.[80]

The visit concluded, Germanicus' ships set off again on the next leg of the journey. It would be prematurely short. A storm suddenly blew up in the Ionian Sea off the coast of Epirus and several ships were damaged during it – sufficiently seriously that the travellers had to pull in to shore to make repairs. These would take several days to complete. Taking the unexpected opportunity for some additional sightseeing, Germanicus set off for Cape Aktion at the mouth of the Ambracian Gulf to view the actual site of the famous Battle of Actium for him-self. The place had a special meaning for the young commander. Here, almost a half century before, his grandfather Antonius had clashed with his adoptive grandfather Augustus: it made quite an impression on Germanicus. A man who appreciated history and was gifted with an artist's eye, 'vivid images of disaster and success rose before him on the spot'.[81]

With repairs completed and taking advantage of better weather, the flotilla departed once again. By mid-summer Germanicus reached the western Pelopon-nese. His party headed inland to Olympia on the Alfeios River. Athletic com-petitions had been held there in honour of Zeus, according to tradition, since 776 BCE and 17 CE was the year of the 199th Olympiad. A limestone block, perhaps of pedestal for a statue, erected by M. Antonius Peisanus, attests to Germanicus Caesar as having entered a race of chariots (*tethrippon*) drawn by four fully grown horses.[82] It is not clear if he drove the chariot himself or had a professional driver represent him. Races were held in the hippodrome and required charioteers to successfully complete twelve laps, a distance of 72 *stadia* or 13,167 metres (43,200 feet). Driving the stripped down two-wheeled racing cart – based on the war chariot of earlier times – required strength, skill, agility and courage. Crashes frequently occurred as chariots sped round the tight bends and drivers momentarily lost control. Amazingly, the name of Germanicus appears – in a corrupted form – in the official list of victors (*Olympionikes*) for that year. There is no suggestion that the result was fixed before the race.

Rather than going around the Peloponnese (map 11), they probably retraced their route and traversed the Isthmus of Corinth using the ancient *Diolkos*, just as young Octavianus had done in 31 BCE, after his victory at Actium, to gain a time advantage over Antonius and Kleopatra *en route* to Egypt.[83] It was also by this shorter route that Ovid travelled to Athens in December 8/January 9 CE on his way into exile.[84] The travellers of Germanicus' party eventually reached the port of Piraeus and triumphantly entered the city of Athens.[85] He considered the visit as a pilgrimage and he paid homage to its people. 'There, as a concession to our treaty with an allied and ancient city', notes Tacitus, 'he was attended only by a single lictor'.[86] Germanicus dispensed with his lictors when entering free towns, a behaviour which demonstrates a personal sensitivity to local custom and a profound respect for those who championed their hard-won liberty.[87] His gesture was warmly appreciated:

> The Greeks welcomed him with the most elaborate honours, and brought forward all the old deeds and sayings of their countrymen, to give additional dignity to their flattery.[88]

The reaction of the Athenians, in particular, was reassuringly favourable to him. Though an unwavering patriot, in Germanicus the Greek-speaking world found a philhellene at the highest level of Roman society. He spoke and wrote Greek and was enamoured with its culture. It was an idiosyncracy his enemies tried to use against him. Just a few days before, Calpurnius Piso, on his own outbound trip, had stopped by and tried to stir up trouble prior to Germanicus' arrival.[89] Tacitus records in detail his adversary's premeditated antics, when he writes of how Piso:

> terrified the citizens of Athens by his tumultuous approach, and then reviled them in a bitter speech, with indirect reflections on Germanicus, who, he said, had derogated from the honour of the Roman name in having treated with excessive courtesy, not the people of Athens, who indeed had been exterminated by repeated disasters, but a miserable medley of tribes. As for the men before him, they had been Mithridates' allies against Sulla, allies of Antonius against the Divine Augustus. He taunted them too with the past, with their ill-success against the Macedonians, their violence to their own countrymen, for he had his own special grudge against this city, because they would not spare at his intercession one Theophilus whom the Areopagus had condemned for forgery.[90]

It was Germanicus' one and only visit to the city of the legendary warrior-king Theseus. Once a world superpower, its glory days were long since over and, by the first century CE, Athens had degenerated into a theme-park of tourist attractions, famous for its exquisite antiquities, painted porticoes, and fine temples, supreme among which was that of Athena Parthenos on the acropolis, with its statue of the goddess created by renowned sculptor Pheidias.[91] Visitors from overseas admired the collections of the finest bronze statues on public display throughout the city and could order faithful marble copies to take home with them to grace their villas. Rich men sent their sons here to be taught by renowned orators, among whom was Germanicus' own grandfather. Patrician benefactors, such as Iulius Caesar and Cicero's friend Atticus, lavished largesse on the city, funding repairs to old structures and commissioning new ones, like the forum located north of the acropolis and east of the older *agora*. On his tour of the Hellenic antiquities, Germanicus made a point of stopping at the tombs of distinguished men and offering sacrifices to honour their memories.[92] The travellers probably stayed for the winter of 17 CE, waiting for fair weather in the spring.

Leaving Attica, Germanicus' flotilla crossed the narrow Euripus Strait to Euboea.[93] From there, the travellers island-hopped across the Aegean Sea to Lesbos, where they rested in its major city, Mytilene.[94] The third-largest island in the Aegean, it had only come under the direct control of the Romans in 79 BCE. It had been home to Sappho the poet and Pittakos, one of the Seven Sages of the Greek World. Pittakos was credited by Diogenes Laertius as coining several notable sayings, among which was 'know your opportunity' – an insight that Germanicus would have done well to heed.[95] On Lesbos, Agrippina gave birth to another girl. The Roman sources give the name Iulia Livia (Livilla) to this baby, the couple's ninth child.[96] The news of the arrival of the little girl was greeted with joy by the local people, who responded by deifying the mother.[97] With Agrippina still recovering from childbirth, Germanicus' entourage departed Lesbos. Rather than heading south, they now went north, following the coast of Asia Minor, which is now Turkey. Tacitus comments cryptically that they 'penetrated to the remoter parts of the province of Asia'.[98] Slicing through the sea that Homer famously described as 'wine-dark', they reached Thrace and the city of Perinthus.[99] For the Romans, it was an exotic world of untamed landscapes, where the mythical tales of Hercules and Jason took place, and was home to ancient races and colourful kings. King Roimetalkes of Thrace, who had come to the aid of the Romans during the Great Illyrian Revolt, had died in 12 CE, and his kingdom had been split up by Augustus between Roimetalkes' son Kotys (Cotys) VIII and his surviving brother Riskuporis (Rhescuporis) II.[100] Despite the division, the region remained stable and pro-Roman. Nevertheless, it seems that Tiberius had designs on the territory and secretly manufactured a subterfuge, which resulted in Kotys usurping and re-uniting the kingdom, only to be murdered by Reskuporis, who, in turn, was arrested and charged with a capital crime by Roman authorities, transferred as a prisoner to Alexandria, and put to death after allegedly attempting to escape.[101] Thrace was again divided, this time between Riskuporis' son Roimetalkes and the sons of Kotys, but, as they were too young to rule, Trebellienus Rufus, an ex-*praetor*, was appointed to govern the kingdom and act as guardian for the children.[102] If Germanicus was involved in any way – and if not, what he personally thought of the sordid affair – it is not recorded in the sources that have come down to us.

The flotilla then moved north-eastwards, passing through the Dardanelles strait into the Propontis (Sea of Marmara), until they reached Byzantium.[103] It was not yet a great world-class metropolis, but a modest trading city, thriving on its unique access to and from the Black Sea. Emboldened to go further, and motivated 'by an anxious wish to become acquainted with those ancient and celebrated localities', the intrepid Roman travellers crossed through the Bosporus and sailed on to the dark, deep sea that Ovid described as 'sinister'.[104] Travelling east, the flotilla would have reached Pontus. If they, in fact, sailed that far, the visitors from Rome may have been the guests of Polemon II of Pontus, who was a trusted client king over lands located north of Armenia.[105] There was good reason to meet him and establish relations in this tightly interconnected region of the world. The thirty-year-old king's full name was M. Antonius Polemon Pythodoros, and he was the second son and middle child of the Pontic rulers Polemon Pythodoros and Pythodorida. His father had died in 8 BCE, and, shortly thereafter, his mother married King Archelaus, whereupon the family moved to Cappadocia. Polemon II was raised there with his siblings at his stepfather's court. Archelaus died in Rome in 17 CE, whereupon Polemon II and his mother moved back to Pontus. His eldest brother was Zenon (or Zeno), and his youngest sister was Antonia Tryphaena, who was married to Kotys VIII of Thrace. Zenon's grandfather had steadfastly supported Germanicus' grandfather, M. Antonius.[106] Through his maternal grandmother, Polemon was a direct descendant of the *triumvir* and his second wife, Antonia Hybrida Maior (*Stemma Antoniorum*, no. 6), and he was the only one in the family still living to bear the famous Roman's full name. The reigning client king of Pontus and the serving consul of Rome were, thus, distant cousins.

Returning through the Propontis, perhaps stopping at Apameia, the fleet of ships with its distinguished passengers attempted to land at the island of Samothrace.[107] It was famous in antiquity for an oracle whose advice Germanicus now urgently sought. Even today, the island is one of the most rugged and mountainous in the Aegean, and it has no natural harbour. At the time of Germanicus' visit, strong winds – perhaps the Meltimi (Etesians) – blasted the flotilla, and the planned visit had to be abandoned. The travellers had better luck, however, when they turned towards the mainland and reached the Troad, on the westernmost coast of Anatolia. On the Scamander River stood the city of Ilium (Hisarlik). This was the true site of Ilion (plate 30), the Troy of Homer's epic poem, which Germanicus – like every other student of his day – had studied closely in the orginal Greek at school.[108] This place had potent meaning for all Romans, as it was from here, according to legend, respun by Vergil in the *Aeneid*, that the defeated Trojans fled the burning city on an epic journey to Italy led by Aeneas, which resulted in the founding of the Roman race. Under Augustus, the town had recently been re-established on the citadel, enjoying its position south-east of the Dardanelles and north of Mount Ida, at a natural crossroads where traders from east and west met. The city now boasted all the amenities of the most cultured of Roman metropolises, including a forum, an odeon, a *bouleuterion* and a Temple of Athena, once visited by Iulius Caesar.[109] From this vantage point, Germanicus surveyed 'a scene venerable from the vicissitudes of fortune and as the birth-place of our people'.[110] He then went down to the wide Plain of Scamander, which stretched out to the shore of the Aegean Sea, where Homer set the ten-year struggle between the Trojans and the Greeks that led to the citadel's fall. Shortly after his visit, Philon, son of Apollonios, dedicated a statue on a round base to Antonia, Germanicus' mother.[111] On it, Philon addressed Antonia as 'the goddess Aphrodite, belonging to the race of Anchises'.

Returning along the southern coast of the Troad, he visited the city of Assos (modern Behramkale), which boasted an academy opened by Aristotle – the teacher of Alexander the Great – and a theatre with stunning sea views. It seems that, here, Germanicus' youngest son, unperturbed or even encouraged by all the public attention, made a speech, for in subsequent years, the citizens of Assos erected an inscription to C. Caesar, which read:

BE IT ENACTED BY THE SENATE AND THE ROMAN MERCHANTS ESTABLISHED AMONG US, AND THE PEOPLE OF ASSOS, THAT AN EMBASSY BE APPOINTED FROM THE FIRST AND BEST ROMANS AND GREEKS TO MEET AND CONGRATULATE HIM, AND TO ENTREAT HIM THAT HE WILL HOLD OUR CITY IN REMEMBERANCE AND UNDER HIS PROTECTION, EVEN AS HE HIMSELF PROMISED WHEN, WITH HIS FATHER GERMANICUS, HE FIRST ENTERED UPON THE GOVERNMENT OF OUR CITY.[112]

While in the region, Germanicus may even have visited other inland cities of Mysia, Lydia and Phrygia, or received deputations from them. Bronze coins bearing Germanicus' profile and name in the Greek form ΓΕΡΜΑΝΙΚΟΣ ΚΑΙΣΑΡ were likely issued by local mints at this time. Among them were the cities of Aezanis and Apameia in Phrygia (plate 29), Pergamon in Mysia, Sardes in Lydia, and Smyrna on the Aegean coast.[113]

It was not only as a tourist that Germanicus had travelled so far, but also as an official benefactor. 'He gave relief, as he went', writes Tacitus, 'to provinces which had been exhausted by internal feuds or by the oppressions of governors'.[114] As the most senior official in the region, he was in a unique position to rally resources, to revive local communities, and to address maladministration where uncovered. Tiberius himself had set the tone, just months before, when earthquakes levelled several cities across Asia. He personally led the appeal for help by digging into his own purse and generously donating 10 million *sestertii*, setting up a board of independent senators to oversee the reconstruction programme, and granting the affected communities temporary tax and tribute relief for five years.[115]

Much as he may have wanted to stay longer, nevertheless, he was due in Syria – and sooner rather than later. The entourage set sail again and 'coasted back along Asia, and touched at Colophon', berthing at its port of Notium, which lay just 15 miles (24km) north-west of the bustling city of Ephesus.[116] The city was named after rosin – κολοφώνιο, in Greek – which was a kind of resin produced by the pine trees that grew in abundance in the region. The city had once been the home of the philosopher Xenophanes and the poet Antimachus. One mile (1.6km) south of Colophon lay Claros, a sanctuary with a massive altar shared between Apollo and Dionysus, a sundial and a temple built over a cave containing a sacred pool.[117] It was here that Germanicus consulted the famous Oracle of Apollo.[118] As Tacitus explains:

> There, it is not a woman, as at Delphi, but a priest chosen from certain families, generally from Miletus, who ascertains simply the number and the names of the applicants. Then, descending into a cave and drinking a draught from a secret spring, the man, who is commonly ignorant of letters and of poetry, utters a response in verse answering to the thoughts conceived in the mind of any inquirer.[119]

Germanicus approached the oracle as a supplicant. What question he asked is not recorded, but its ambiguous answer is. 'It was said', writes Tacitus, 'that he prophesied to Germanicus, in dark hints, as oracles usually do, a timely departure'.[120] It was an unexpectedly ominous turn of events; yet, unperturbed, Germanicus' band departed for their next destination.

The coast of southern Anatolia was then, as now, rocky and strewn with reefs, so the captains of the ships had to approach with great care as they navigated the cluster of Dodecanese Islands.[121] Eventually, the party reached Rhodes (Rhodos). Of it, Strabo writes effusively, 'with regard to harbours, roads, walls, and other buildings, it so much surpasses other cities, that we know of none equal, much less superior to it'.[122] In a region where government so often failed its people, Rhodes provided a case study in good governance, more about which Germanicus was keen to learn. While not a representative democracy, the Rhodian élite understood the importance of benign government to the stability of the state, and provided welfare to the less well-off members of society.[123] The poor received allowances of grain – paid for by the rich – which were properly and fairly distributed by appointed state officials. The result was that the poor knew where their next meal was coming from, and the government could count on their service when called upon, in particular, to man her fleet. The island had become famous for its colossal statue of the Sun, made by Chares of Lindos and considered a Wonder of the World – one of several Germanicus would visit on the trip – but which, by the time of Germanicus' visit, lay broken in giant pieces upon the beach, after having been felled at the knees by an earthquake.[124] The island had also become a centre of excellence for ambitious patricians eager to learn from the leading teachers of philosophy and oratory of the day. One of them was Tiberius himself, who had chosen to stay here during his self-imposed exile from 6 BCE to 2 CE.[125]

Rift with Piso

While Germanicus was visiting Rhodes, Piso coincidentally sailed past. He had probably taken the longer route, sailing from Ostia with his retinue and belongings, and, perhaps after his stay in Athens, had lingered on one or more of the Greek islands. As Piso cruised past the island, a storm had blown up and sent his ships crashing upon an outcrop of rocks, marooning him and his party.[126] Hearing the news, Germanicus immediately dispatched several triremes to rescue his deputy and crew. Tacitus notes that Germanicus was fully aware at that time of Piso's slanders against him, but acted to assist him anyway – such was his good nature, observes Tacitus.[127] If he thought his goodwill gesture would win over Piso, he was to be disappointed. Piso did not stop even to thank him, but sailed directly on to Syria.

Germanicus and his guests probably arrived not long after, at the port of Seleucia on the Orontes. Agrippina went on to Antiocheia (modern Antakya, in Turkey), but Germanicus continued with his diplomatic mission. He had been made aware that there were pressing matters in Armenia that now needed his urgent attention.[128] Since leaving Rome, the situation in Armenia had become dramatically more precarious. It lay strategically between the two great empires and was the focus of politicking by both sides. Vonones, who had arrived in Armenia from neighbouring Parthia, was quickly expelled by the people, leaving them both without a regent and potentially vulnerable to hostile attack.[129] Anticipating trouble, Germanicus issued orders to Piso to march with part or all of the legions under his command to Armenia, or to delegate the mission to his son Marcus.[130] In a remarkable act of insubordination, Piso chose not to, and ignored the order. Germanicus was now forced to go there himself and evaluate the situation in person. The route to Armenia (map 11, plate 32) took him along a 'green corridor', a narrow but passable defile formed by the Euphrates River – marking the natural border between the Roman and Parthian Empires – and connecting the arid desert in the south and the rugged mountains of Armenia in the north. His journey took him through the important and ancient cities of Zeugma, Samosata and Melitene, which was the base of *Legio* XII *Fulminata*.[131] Much to his relief, it rapidly became apparent that military intervention was not, in fact, going to be needed. Popular support had rallied around Zenon, the brother of King Polemon of Pontus. Tacitus informs us that Zenon had been pro-Armenian since his childhood, adopting their manners and customs, and even developing a taste for hunting, which enamoured him to the local people. As an adult, he had formed vital relationships with the chiefs and people, which now stood him in good stead. Thus the way was open to a peaceful transition of power. It was to the city of Artaxata (modern Artashat, near Yerevan) that Germanicus now travelled as the emperor's personal representative to give Rome's stamp of approval to the nobles' choice. His arrival was in stark contrast to the last great Roman, Cn. Pompeius Magnus, who had gone there at the head of an army as a conqueror.[132] Before a vast assembled crowd, Germanicus placed the royal diadem upon Zenon's head.[133] Nobles and commoners alike paid him homage and cheered him as King Artaxias, the name he adopted after the city of his coronation. It was a brilliant propaganda coup for Germanicus. When news reached Rome weeks later, the response was ecstatic. Germanicus was credited with no less an accolade than of 'conquering the king of Armenia'.[134] It was all the more impressive for the fact that he had succeeded without an army. The Senate acclaimed his achievement and decreed that Germanicus should be permitted to enter the city of Rome with an ovation, and that a triumphal arch be erected beside the Temple of Mars Ultor, surmounted with his statue.[135] Tacitus observed that 'Tiberius was the more delighted at having established peace by wise policy than if he had finished a war by battle'.[136] Achieving peace without bloodshed was precisely how Tiberius envisioned that foreign policy should be under his auspices.

With diplomacy becoming the preferred approach of the emperor's regime to foreign affairs, prudence was also being encouraged within the empire's borders. Provincials could now expect to be fairly treated. The enlightened view being ushered in by Tiberius' personal envoy must have come as welcome news to the local people, more used to a succession of oppressive governors and tax collectors. The sources do not record if Germanicus stopped in Cilicia and proceeded to neighbouring Commagene on his return, though their proximity makes it a possibility and when he had left the region, Cappadocia (plate 31) – up to that point without a king following the death of Archelaus – was 'reduced to the form of a province', a fact which was regarded by Suetonius as one of the truly great achievements of his life since its acquisition was peaceful.[137] Q. Veranius now left Germanicus' party to become Cappadocia's first Roman governor and Q. Servaeus departed to administer Commagene as *propraetor*.[138] The new benign policy of government in the Orient was extended to Cappadocia, and the burden of tribute paid to Rome was lightened 'to inspire hope of a gentler rule under Rome'.[139] The importance of these new provinces was that they, like Armenia, were in the sphere of influence of Parthia. Building resilient pro-Roman communities there was vitally important to her interests. Perhaps to demonstrate this trust concretely, a legionary garrison was not placed in Cappadocia, Cilicia or Commagene: if troops were needed to address a security threat, they could be moved up quickly from Syria.

Germanicus now rode to Cyrrhus, north-east of Antiocheia, and the location of the winter camp of *Legio* X *Frentensis*. He had sent instructions to Piso for him to meet him there. Successful as these recent diplomatic settlements with Rome's allies had been, Tacitus observes that 'it gave Germanicus little joy because of the arrogance of Piso'.[140] He decided he now had to confront Piso directly. Before the meeting, Germanicus was briefed by his friends and confidants, 'but friends who knew well how to inflame a quarrel, exaggerated what was true and added lies, alleging various charges against Piso, Plancina, and their sons'.[141] If Tacitus' account of the meeting is accurate – and it is the only one we have – then it was a fraught encounter. The two men sat, 'each controlling his looks, Piso concealing his fears, Germanicus shunning the semblance of menace'.[142] Germanicus chose not to assert his authority but, instead, tried to reason with the older man:

> At last, in the presence of a few intimate associates, Germanicus addressed him in language such as suppressed resentment suggests, to which Piso replied with haughty apologies.[143]

The result was plain for all to see when 'they parted in open enmity'.[144] The opportunity for what modern diplomats term a frank exchange of views had been passed up in favour of verbal posturing. The failure to get the issues out on to the table only exacerbated an already difficult relationship, and made it worse. How bad that relationship had become is illustrated in a later episode related by Tacitus:

> After this Piso was seldom seen at Caesar's tribunal, and if he ever sat by him, it was with a sullen frown and a marked display of opposition. He was even heard to say at a banquet given by the king of the Nabataeans, when some golden crowns of great weight were presented to Caesar and Agrippina and light ones to Piso and the rest, that the entertainment was given to the son of a Roman emperor, not of a Parthian king. At the same time he threw his crown on the ground, with a long speech against luxury, which, though it angered Germanicus, he still bore with patience.[145]

Germanicus seems to have been willing to persevere with his deputy, despite the man's blatant insubordination and unconscionable behaviour. Perhaps he felt unable to reprimand Piso as the older and more experienced man who had been chosen personally for the position by Tiberius. Perhaps he simply felt intimidated by Piso. Yet it could also be interpreted that he preferred to avoid conflict rather than face it head on. It might be seen as weakness, none more so than by Piso, who already looked down on the younger man and took an impish delight in making life uncomfortable for him.

The strained relationship with Piso was in remarkably stark contrast to the successful diplomatic relationships forming around him. Learning that Germanicus was in the region, King Artabanus II of Parthia sent envoys carrying a message of peace.[146] The king reminded Germanicus of the friendship their two nations had enjoyed since Augustus and Frahâta IV negotiated the treaty, and in that same spirit he wished their peaceful co-existence to continue. As a gesture of his sincerity, specifically 'in honour of Germanicus' he said, he offered to meet him at the bank of the Euphrates River.[147] The development reveals an underlying shift in the balance of power. The Great King made the first move because Rome was now in a stronger position than eighteen years earlier. Some speculate that Germanicus was even investigating the possibility of encouraging cross-border incursions.[148] The concern about internal security was of particular importance to the Parthian regent, as reflected in a special request he made to Germanicus. Artabanus pleaded with him to remove Vonones from Syria. The king feared that Vonones' close proximity to Parthia might prove tempting to opponents of his regime, who could visit him there and rally around him and then plot against Artabanus. He had implicitly approved of the regime change in Armenia, overseen by Germanicus – even though Artaxias was Rome's choice – by watching from afar and not protesting it. Germanicus gave a considered response. He consented to continuing the treaty in florid language and he commended the king for the manner of the visit, speaking in 'graceful and modest' terms.[149] However, he declined the offer of a face-to-face meeting, but as a concession to the king Germanicus arranged for Vonones to be transferred to Pompeiopolis, a port city on the Mediterranean coast of Cilicia. It was conveniently bordered by Syria in the east and the inaccessible Taurus Mountains, known as 'Rough Cilicia', in the west. In this quiet province, it was expected that Vonones could do no harm. Yet Tacitus also adds:

> This was not merely a concession to the request of Artabanus, but was meant as an affront to Piso, who had a special liking for Vonones, because of the many attentions and presents by which he had won Plancina's favour.[150]

All did not end well for Vonones, however. He escaped his confinement in Cilicia and made his way back to Armenia, only to be recaptured on the bank of the Pyramus (Ceyhan) River by a Roman cavalry officer, and was killed by the man entrusted with his custody.[151]

Germanicus and his remaining staff finally entered Antiocheia late in the year. The crowds turned out in strength here as they did at all places Germanicus visited.[152] In their ardour, the crush of people seemed almost threatening – causing not a little concern for his lictors, whom he had again asked to stand down – but, as the newest resident, Germanicus preferred to be accessible, not hidden by a screen of bodyguards. The city was no stranger to the great and good. It had been founded in around 307 BCE by one of the successors of Antigonos Monophthalmos, a general of Alexander the Great. It was later captured by Seleukos (Seleucus) I Nikator and, in subsequent years, developed into a fine, free city. Choosing a location beside the Orontes River and beneath Mount Silpios (fig. 8), Seleucid surveyors laid out a main street some 2.5km (1.6 miles) long,

Figure 8. *Antioch in Syria from the North West* from a sketch by Capt. Byam Martin R.N. capturing a landscape barely changed since Germanicus' time.

running south-west to north-east, following the direction of the river.[153] Streets
ran off it in a gridiron pattern, forming regular residential and commercial blocks
(map 12).[154] An island in the middle of the river, to the west of the main city, was
the location of the palace complex that was the home of Roman governors of the
province of Syria, from the time Cn. Pompeius Magnus conquered the remnants
of the Seleucid Empire in 64 BCE, and it was where Piso at present lodged.
Antiocheia was considered one of the great cities of the day ranking alongside
Alexandria, Athens, and Rome. The city's rulers competed to bequeath to their
successors a more beautiful place than they had inherited.[155] Roman benefactors,
too, among them Iulius Caesar, Augustus, Agrippa, Tiberius, and the client king
Herodes, added to the fabric of the urban environment. The amenities the city
accumulated included temples and shrines to Minos, Demeter, Herakles and
Iupiter Capitolinus; a theatre, a *stoa*, a city hall, colonnades, and, in the second
century BCE, King Antiochus IV built the largest bathing complex in Asia,
containing no fewer than ten baths. The city was fed by springs and their crystal-
clear waters were channelled via aqueducts to public fountains, baths and residential neighbourhoods.[156] Under the Romans, the city flourished, prospering
on the back of trade from its location on the east-west trade route and access to
the nearby harbour at Seleucia, also known by the name Pieria.[157] The locality
was fertile, too, producing timber, fish and vegetables in abundance. The second
century CE philosopher Athenaeus noted that in Antiocheia grew the best
cucumbers.[158] The wealth and artistic sensibilities of some of its citizens is
attested by the discovery here of many of the finest mosaics to have been found
anywhere in the Roman world. By the first century CE, it was becoming a leading
centre of Hellenic culture in the region.[159] For a cosmopolitan like Germanicus,
Antiocheia was a very fine place to stay in its own right and the ideal location in
Asia to spend the winter.

Germanicus resided just outside the city in a smart suburb called Epidaphnae
(Beit el-ma or Harbiye).[160] It was an idyllic place and renowned for its pleasant
climate. Located to the west of the city, here were found the springs named after
Ladon, the daughter of the Arcadian river-god, which supplied the city with water,
and the grove sacred to Apollo and Artemis.[161] For his lodgings, Germanicus
chose an historic villa. His grandfather had stayed here in 42/41 BCE *en route* to
meeting Kleopatra, and had received a delegation of 100 influential Jews who
came to accuse Herod, and to which the king himself later fled seeking his friend's
help.[162] By locating himself away from Piso, Germanicus kept a healthy distance
between himself as commander of the Orient and his provincial governor of Syria.

While in the province, Germanicus devoted his time to understanding the
issues peculiar to the provinces and client kingdoms of the East. He quickly discovered that problems of corruption and financial mismanagement were per-
vasive in Asia. He uncovered several matters requiring his immediate personal
attention, not least the poor state of affairs of several city administrations and
their requests for a lightening of the tax burden – even the discipline among the
legions was lax compared to elsewhere.[163] To his deputies and the city fathers,
he issued directions to restore good governance and he put them on notice that

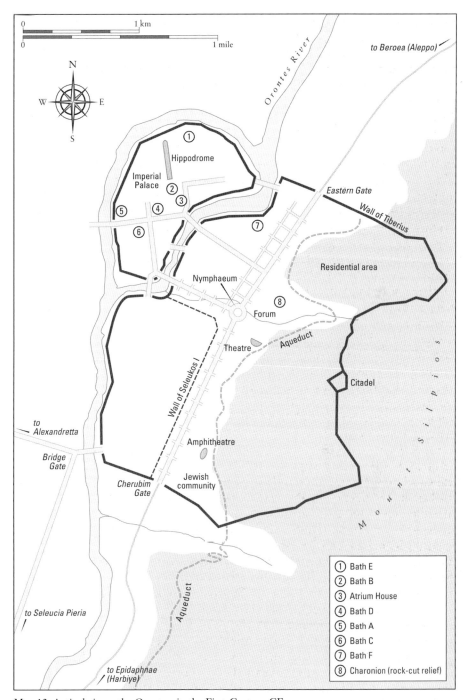

Map 12. Antiocheia on the Orontes, in the First Century CE.

he would continue to keep a watchful eye on their progress.[164] A surviving document, called the 'Palmyra Tariff' and dated to 137 CE, cites a ruling issued by Germanicus that civic taxes were to be calculated in Italian currency (*aes*) to encourage fairness by adopting a common unit of value across the region, where so many different local currencies were in circulation.[165]

Meantime, with his family under one roof, he could spend time being a father and assisting Agrippina with raising their youngest children, in particular young Caligula.

In the Footsteps of the Pharoahs

Roman chroniclers meticulously recorded the unusual events of the day, in the hope of finding clues that would give insight into the minds of the gods and their plans for mankind. Dio writes:

> When M. Iunius and L. Norbanus assumed office [19 CE], an omen of no little importance occurred on the very first day of the year, and it doubtless had a bearing on the fate of Germanicus. The consul Norbanus, it seems, had always been devoted to the trumpet, and as he practised on it assiduously, he wished to play the instrument on this occasion, also, at dawn, when many persons were already near his house. This proceeding startled them all alike, just as if the consul had given them a signal for battle; and they were also alarmed by the falling of the statue of Ianus. They were furthermore disturbed not a little by an oracle, reputed to be an utterance of the Sibyl, which, although it did not fit this period of the city's history at all, was nevertheless applied to the situation then existing. It ran:
>
> > 'When thrice three hundred revolving years have run their course,
> > Civil strife upon Rome destruction shall bring, and the folly, too,
> > Of Sybaris . . .'[166]

Oracular pronouncements could spell trouble for those running the affairs of state. Himself an avid believer in astrology, Tiberius took a direct and personal interest in the matter, denouncing these verses as spurious. He investigated all the Sybilline Books for any that contained prophecies, rejecting some as worthless rubbish and retaining others as genuine, though on what basis he made the determination Dio does not say.

Far away in Syria, Germanicus was oblivious to this ominous sign at the start of the New Year. He spent his time industriously reviewing the administration in Syria, issuing orders to his military commanders and directions to city administrations.[167] By mid-year, he decided he needed a holiday. His mind turned to ancient history. Leaving affairs in the hands of deputies, he set off for Egypt, 'to study its antiquities', though Tacitus adds that 'his ostensible motive, however, was solicitude for the province'.[168] Ever conscientious, on the outbound journey, he may have called into Cyprus, Iudaea, Crete or Arabia Felix, as Tacitus refers to 'visits to several provinces'.[169] It is not clear if Agrippina or the children accompanied him, though Caligula is a possibility. Eventually he reached Alexandria (map 13).

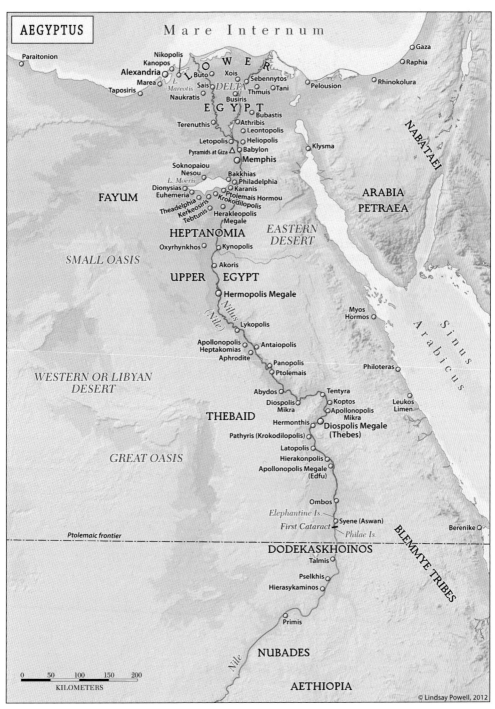

Map 13. Roman Egypt in the First Century CE.

Alexander the Great had personally chosen the site for the city named after him in 331 BCE, just eight years before his premature death. He was struck by the special qualities of the location.[170] The city occupied a narrow limestone ridge, which formed an embankment between the desert in the west and the Nile delta to the east, bound on its north side by the Mediterranean and on the south by Lake Mareotis.[171] A visitor to the city in around the year 25 BCE, Strabo writes that its location so close to water and the cooling Etesian winds meant that 'the Alexandrians pass their time most pleasantly in summer'.[172] Climate apart, Alexander saw the location as an ideal hub for trade.[173] Two harbours were constructed on either side of a natural promontory: the Great Harbour on the eastern side, bounded by a causeway and dominated by the Pharos lighthouse, and the harbour called Eunostos to the west, 'dug by the hand of man', which was surrounded by warehouses and ship-houses.[174] To plan and build the city, Alexander charged Dinokrates of Rhodos, the architect of the Temple of Diana at Ephesus (which became one of the Seven Wonders of the World).[175] His engineers marked out the city as a grid of seven parallel streets running latitudinally, and eleven parallel streets intersecting them longitudinally. The longitudinal streets ran in the same direction as the north-west wind in summer, keeping the city cool. The main latitudinal thoroughfare was a broad street, 30m (98ft) wide, bisected in the middle of the plan by the main longitudinal street, 14m (46ft) wide. In the years after Alexander's death, Ptolemaios, his chief of staff and commander of his bodyguard, took over Egypt and buried his master in a sepulchre there, originally in a sarcophagus of gold, but, by the time of Germanicus' visit, it had been remade in glass.[176] It was said that his body had been mellified to preserve it for all time. Ptolemaios and his successors added to its amenities, including the Serapium, the Library and Museum, the Emporium, the Heptastadium, a theatre and a Temple of Poseidon.[177] Queen Kleopatra had started to build a temple to Iulius Caesar, which was only completed by Augustus after the queen's suicide, when it became known as the Caesareum. The palatial building faced out to the sea. Flanking the entrance to it were two obelisks that had been transported there from Upper Egypt. This became the official residence of the Roman *praefectus*, a man appointed personally by the emperor from the equestrian order. The current administrator was C. Valerius, who had been in the position since 16 CE.[178] From the Caesareum, a mole projected into the middle of the Great Harbour, which was commissioned by his grandfather. On the terminus of it, the *triumvir* had built a royal lodge that he called Timonium.[179] It was probably here that Germanicus and his entourage stayed.

The Egyptians gave the young Roman commander a rapturous welcome. This is confirmed in a document referred to by historians as *P. Oxy.* 2435 (short for 'Papyrus Oxyrhynchus', plate 34).[180] It is a verbatim record of what was said on the occasion of a visit by Germanicus. Addressing the assembled crowd as 'men of Alexandria', he announces that he has been sent by his father Tiberius. He is immediately interrupted when the crowd cheers and shouts greetings and best wishes. Germanicus continues by asking the crowd to let him answer the questions put to him before they applaud. He restates that he has been sent by his father to regulate the provinces overseas, which he describes as a difficult task to accomplish, firstly because of the necessity to travel by sea, and secondly because it has taken him away from his family and friends. He continues saying he had wanted to see the great city for himself – having anticipated seeing a 'dazzling spectacle' – primarily because of the man who founded it, but also because of the hospitality the good people had shown Augustus and his adoptive father during their visits. His remark is met with shouts of jubilation and appeals for his long life by the ecstatic crowd. He continues to comment on the warmth of his reception, at which point the papyrus breaks off. The document vividly captures the rapport Germanicus was able to quickly establish with the public and the sincerity with which he addressed them. It is a character portrait which is consistent with other descriptions of Germanicus' personality.

Germanicus was sensitive to how his popular reception would look back in Rome, however. He would have been acutely aware that his grandfather had been accused of 'going native' – seduced by Egyptomania, or more specifically Kleopatra – and turned his back on traditional Roman *mores*.[181] Without delay, Germanicus issued an edict – the so-called *Acta Alexandrinorum* – in which he berated the people for hailing him and his wife with the same honorary titles reserved exclusively for Tiberius and Livia.[182] Nevertheless, Germanicus felt very comfortable in the city founded by Alexander. 'He would go about without soldiers, with sandalled feet, and apparelled after the Greek fashion', writes Tacitus.[183] In this, it was said that he imitated P. Scipio Africanus, who was reputed to have done likewise in Sicily at the height of the Punic War. It was not the kind of behaviour Tiberius approved of and, when he learned of it, he made his disapproval of his son's dress and manners known – albeit gently – in writing.[184] More gravely, however, by visiting Egypt, Germanicus had broken one of the cardinal rules laid down by Augustus. This was that no high-ranking Roman senator or member of the *equites* was permitted to visit Alexandria without the express permission of the *princeps*. In his subsequent letter to Germanicus, Tiberius issued a pointed reprimand. The reason for the strong reaction was grain. Egypt was Rome's breadbasket. Who controlled Egypt, controlled the grain supply; who controlled the grain supply, controlled the bread dole; who controlled the bread dole, kept the restless plebs of Rome at bay. Augustus, and in turn Tiberius, 'had specially reserved the country, from a fear that anyone who held a province containing the key of the land and of the sea, with ever so small a force against the mightiest army, might distress Italy by famine'.[185] Germanicus' action suggests either he did not understand the rule, or he interpreted his own wide remit to mean he was not bound by it. Significantly, in his speech to the Alexandrians, as recorded in *P. Oxy.* 2435, Germanicus specifically uses the Greek word επαρχία meaning 'province' to describe Egypt, which suggests that he took the broader view, and was unaware – or consciously chose to ignore – that he was transgressing any rules.[186] Moreover, this was a holiday trip, not official business. To Tiberius, however, it appeared that Germanicus was acting on his own initiative and without due regard for long established protocol, verging on insubordination.[187]

Hardly helping his position in Tiberius' eyes was the news that his adopted son had 'reduced the price of grain by opening the granaries, and adopted many practices pleasing to the multitude'.[188] The justification for his unauthorized decision was that on his arrival, Germanicus found Egypt suffering from famine. He had seen the effects of starvation close up for himself back in Rome in 6 CE when 21 years old. The crisis called for tough decisions to be made, and it meant not everyone would receive food. In *Against Apion*, Josephus records an appeal by a Jew to Caesar for having shown loyalty when Augustus fought the Egyptians, though accepting how very desperate the general situation was. 'If Germanicus was not able to make a distribution of grain to all the inhabitants of Alexandria', Josephus writes, 'that only shows what a barren time it was, and how great a want of grain there was then'.[189] He adds, 'for what all the emperors have thought of the Alexandrian Jews is well known, for this distribution of wheat was not otherwise omitted with regard to the Jews, than it was with regard to the other inhabitants of Alexandria'.[190] Racism and prejudice towards its subject peoples were present in Roman society.[191] Germanicus was probably no more or less anti-Semitic than the next Roman; however, this example shows him not to have singled out the Jews *exclusively* for discrimination, as other groups were also denied.

Germanicus' entourage now left the city and travelled eastwards a short distance of 30 *stadia* along the road to Nikopolis, a second 'Victory City' established by Octavianus in a suburb of Alexandria, on the site of his defeat of Antonius' army.[192] In founding the civilian settlement beside the base camp of *Legiones* III *Cyrenaica* and XXII *Deiotariana*, as Augustus he created a sacred area for games and worship of a local deity – for which an amphitheatre and stadium were specially constructed – just as he had done at Actium in Epirus, but this time in honour of his victory at the Battle of Alexandria in 30 BCE.[193] Its impact was profound. In Alexandria proper, the Serapeum and other long-beloved religious buildings were soon abandoned for the new city of his victory cult, and, by Strabo's time, they had already fallen into neglect; it was in this dilapidated condition that Germanicus would have found them.[194] In stark contrast, Nikopolis was a manicured city-space of lush gardens and groves and grandiose public amenities.[195] In Strabo's opinion, the most beautiful building was the Gymnasium with its immense porticoes, 'a *stadium* in length'.[196] In the middle of Nikopolis was 'the Paneium, a 'height', as it were, which was made by the hand of man; it has the shape of a fir-cone, resembles a rocky hill, and is ascended by a spiral road; and from the summit one can see the whole of the city lying below it on all sides'.[197]

Past the Hippodrome and through the Canobic Gate, they continued on to Kanopos (Canopus) on a tributary of the Nile in the Delta.[198] There they boarded a waiting ship and embarked on a once-in-a-lifetime cruise of the Nile River and its historic sites. The highlights of the tour are recorded in detail by Tacitus.[199] First among these was the confluence of the Nile at the Delta, where stood the Heracleum dedicated to Hercules, who, it was claimed, was born there.[200] A little way down the Nile, the travellers sailed past Babylon (Cairo), the former base of one of the three legions.[201] Further south, the party passed the deserted city of Heliopolis on the right bank, with its Nome and temple to Helios.[202] Two of its obelisks had been removed and shipped back for display in Rome just a few years before. Having toured the length of the Nile himself, forty-four years before Germanicus, Strabo observed:

> There is a ridge extending from the encampment even as far as the Nile, on which the water is conducted up from the river by wheels and screws; and one hundred and fifty prisoners are employed in the work; and from here, one can clearly see the pyramids on the far side of the river at Memphis, and they are near to it.[203]

In Pharaonic times, Memphis (Saqqara, Mit Rahina) was the royal residence, before its place was usurped by the Ptolemies, who relocated it 260km (162 miles) away to the north at Alexandria.[204] Here, Germanicus found temples to the Apis Bull, Hephaestus, and Serapis in one of the largest temple complexes in the country.[205] The Apis Bull was believed to be able to foresee the future. It was identified from its peers by several particular markings on its hide, including a crescent shape on its right side.[206] It was not allowed to live out the full length of its natural life, but was drowned in a sacred fountain amid great public mourning, and then replaced by a new animal after a time-consuming search. It lived in a chamber by itself and was treated with the utmost reverence. Germanicus approached the consecrated bull in person, as a supplicant hoping for favourable portents. He was surprised and disappointed when he offered the animal food and it turned away from him, which all took to mean that it prophesied misfortune in his future.[207]

From Memphis, the pyramids were just seven-and-a-half miles away.[208] At the Giza plateau, the visiting Romans saw 'the pyramids, rising up like mountains amid almost impassable wastes of shifting sand, raised by the emulation and vast wealth of kings'.[209] Even in Germanicus' time, the pyramids at Giza were already 2,570 years old and had become the subject of folklore.[210] Visitors of every age are awe-struck on their first sight of them, not least Strabo:

> One comes to a kind of mountain-brow; on it are numerous pyramids, the tombs of kings, of which three are noteworthy; and two of these are even numbered among the Seven Wonders of the World, for they are a *stadium* in height, are quadrangular in shape, and their height is a little greater than the length of each of the sides; and one of them is only a little larger than the other.[211]

As Herodotus had done before him, Strabo meticulously recorded the explanations the tour guides gave him, no matter how bizarre:

> One of the marvellous things I saw at the pyramids should not be omitted: there are heaps of stone-chips lying in front of the pyramids; and among these are found chips that are like lentils in both form and size; and under some of the heaps lie winnowings, as it were, as of half-peeled grains. They

say that what was left of the food of the workmen has petrified; and this is not improbable. Indeed, in my home-country, in a plain, there is a long hill which is full of lentil-shaped pebbles of porous stone; and the pebbles, both of the seas and of the rivers, present the same puzzling question; but while these latter find an explanation in the motion caused by the current of water, the speculation in that other case is more puzzling.[212]

Germanicus also stopped to see 'the lake hollowed out of the earth to be a receptacle for the Nile's overflow'.[213] Strabo had seen it, too, and admired this 'wonderful lake called the Lake of Moeris, which is an open sea in size and like a sea in colour'.[214] Some 400 years earlier, Herodotus mistakenly deduced that it was an artificial lake, fed by a canal.[215] The lake (nowadays called Birket Qarun), which is located north-west of the Fayum Oasis, is both natural and ancient and has since shrunk in size.

After several days sailing (plate 33), Germanicus reached Thebes (Luxor and Karnak), also known by its Greek name Diospolis Megale ('Great City of God') for its vast buildings, and he was treated to a feast from the local people.[216] Once the capital of Egypt, 'the city of 100 gates' was the city of Amon-Ra.[217] His temple was begun two millennia before, but the standing remains Germanicus saw dated from the time of Amenhotep (Amenophis) III (c.1390–c.1352 BCE) and it was still the most important temple in Egypt, even at the time of his visit.[218] The place did not fail to impress the visitors in Germanicus' party. Even today, guide-books recommend that visitors allow half a day to walk around the many precincts, which cover over 100 hectares (247 acres).[219] The Roman tourists wandered around the temple complex, enthralled by the immensity of the place. Germanicus was deeply aware of the antiquity of the buildings, which pre-dated the foundation of Rome by almost 1,200 years. On the south wall of the Peristyle Court:

> there yet remained on the towering piles Egyptian inscriptions, with a complete account of the city's past grandeur. One of the aged priests, who was desired to interpret the language of his country, related how once there had dwelt in Thebes seven hundred thousand men of military age, and how with such an army King Ramesses conquered Libya, Ethiopia, Media, Persia, Bactria, and Scythia, and held under his sway the countries inhabited by the Syrians, the Armenians, and their neighbours, the Cappadocians, from the Bithynian to the Lycian sea. There was also to be read what tributes were imposed on these nations, the weight of silver and gold, the tale of arms and horses, the gifts of ivory and perfumes to the temples, with the amount of grain and supplies furnished by each people, a revenue as magnificent as is now exacted by the might of Parthia or the power of Rome.[220]

Having negotiated with the king of Parthia himself, the story would not have been lost on the second most powerful man in Rome.

On the other side of the Nile at Western Thebes (Kom el-Hetan) lay the remains of some thirty-six temples, the most famous of which was the mortuary temple of Amenhotep III. The area bounded by his rectangular sanctuary was larger even than the temple complex across the river at Thebes. Little remains of it today, on account of damage caused by the Nile periodically flooding, but at the time of Germanicus' visit the foundations may have been visible. Guarding the entrance were two colossal statues of the seated pharaoh, each nearly 18m (59ft) high.[221] Germanicus was eager to see for himself these images of the great builder and warrior king.[222] In 27 BCE, an earthquake shattered one of the two statues from the waist up and split the lower half. A legend quickly sprang up, that the statue, 'when struck by the sun's rays, gives out the sound of a human voice'.[223] To explain it, some witty Greek-speaking tourist had given the northern statue the nickname Memnon, after the son of Aurora, Goddess of Dawn, and it stuck. Strabo recorded his own experience of seeing it first-hand:

> It is believed that, once each day, a noise, as of a slight blow, emanates from the part of the latter that remains on the throne and its base; and I, too, when I was present at the places with Aelius Gallus and his crowd of associates, both friends and soldiers, heard the noise at about the first hour, but whether it came from the base or from the colossus, or whether the noise was made on purpose by one of the men who were standing all round and near to the base, I am unable positively to assert; for, on account of the uncertainty of the cause, I am induced to believe anything rather than that the sound issued from stones thus fixed.[224]

What Germanicus made of the phenomenon is not recorded.

Some 15km (9.5 miles) south of Thebes, the Roman party passed Iuny, or Hermonthis (Armant) by its Greek name, where both Apollo and Zeus were worshipped. It was one of many riparian cities along the way with exotic religious associations, some familiar, others strange to the Romans' sensibilities: Oxyrhynkon Polis or Oxyrhynchus (el-Bahnasa), 'the city of the sharp-nosed fish'; Krokodilopolis or Ptolemais Euergetis, also known as Arsinoe (Medinet el-Fayum), which held the crocodile sacred; Aphroditopolis, in honour of Aphrodite; Latopolis (Esna), built for Athena and the *latus*, a fish of the Nile River; Eileithuia or Eileithyiaspolis (el-Kab) and its temple to the goddess of childbirth; Hierakonpolis, ancient Nekhen (Kom el-Ahmar), which revered the pre-dynastic falcon god Nekheny; and Apollonopolis (Qus), which despised the crocodile and waged an ongoing war against the reptile.[225]

Several weeks after the touring party had departed Alexandria, they came to Elephantine. It was an island set in the middle of the Nile, located just above the First Cataract. Historically, it marked the borders of the pharaohs' rule, and became an important crossing point for traders with Ethiopia and deeper Africa.[226] In the south-eastern corner of the island, the Romans had recently begun new quarrying operations to extract the much-prized rose-pink and black granites – the only place in Egypt where the stones are found.[227] The island was crowded with temples, and on the outer walls of the repurposed chapel of Mandulis – the local Nubian god at Kalabsha – there were reliefs in the stylized Egyptian fashion, depicting Caesar Augustus making offerings to the local deity and to Isis and Harpokrates.[228]

On the east bank of the Nile stood the busy commercial, industrial and touristic centre of Syene (Aswan). Tacitus noted that Syene then marked the limits of the Roman empire.[229] Its remote location encouraged a number of fantasies by writers who had not seen it for themselves, Tacitus being one. He regurgitated the claim he found in his references, of 'the river's narrow channel and profound depth, which no line of the explorer can penetrate', but he did not apparently check Strabo, who had actually seen this section of river for himself and rubbished the statement, calling it 'nonsense'.[230] One popular attraction for visitors was the Nilometer, a well which had marks cut along its length indicating the present depth of the Nile in relation to other recorded times. Its importance as a forecasting tool for the health of the river was one reason three cohorts were permanently stationed there to guard it, since the Roman *praefectus* could anticipate his revenue stream from reading its depth marks, 'for the greater rises indicate that the revenues also will be greater'.[231] Visitors who went at midday on the summer solstice and placed a gnomon beside the well were treated to the memorable sight of the disk of the sun reflecting in the waters below, but no shadow from the vertical staff on the ground above.[232] Germanicus may also have watched the local boatmen row upstream, then slide dramatically over the rocky edge of the cataract – a risky trick they had successfully performed years earlier for Aelius Gallus.[233]

The southern border of province Egypt was vulnerable to invasion. In 25 BCE, an army of 30,000 troops from Ethiopia led by Amanirensas, Kandake (Candace) of Kush, raided as far north as the Island of Elephantine.[234] They took Syene by storm, enslaved its inhabitants, destroyed buildings and property, and symbolically wrenched the bronze head off an over life-sized statue of Augustus and carted it to Meroë.[235] The region was eventually recaptured in 23 BCE by the new *praefectus Aegypti* C. Petronius, at the head of an army of 10,000 infantry and 800 cavalry. The Romans would not make the same mistake again and installed a permanent garrison in the Dodekashoinos, which remained for as long as they occupied Egypt. An inspection of the three cohorts stationed there was probably on Germanicus' itinerary: it was on the frontier, and he would want to see for himself the quality of the officers and men charged to guard it, since the units were not even at full strength.[236]

Beyond lay the Island of Philae (Anas el-Wagud) with its many temples and the world cult centre of Isis.[237] Tacitus does not record Germanicus as having gone that far south. In search of antiquities, Germanicus had already travelled a distance of some 1,210km (752 miles). Affairs of the present day now needed his attention. It was time to return to Alexandria, and it would take up to a month to make the journey, as long as the weather was favourable. He was, as yet, unaware of how much of a furor his unofficial tour had caused back in Rome.[238]

Tragedy in Epidaphnae
Germanicus returned to Syria and the tranquillity of the villa at Epidaphnae.[239] He discovered that, while he was spending the summer cruising the Nile, unbeknownst to him, Piso had taken it upon himself to repeal his civil directives and

military orders.[240] Suetonius records Germanicus' reaction, on discovering Piso's willful insubordination, as remarkably nonchalant:

> He was so extremely mild and gentle to his enemies, whoever they were, or on what account whatsoever they bore him enmity, that, although Piso rescinded his decrees, and for a long time severely harassed his dependents, he never showed the smallest resentment.[241]

Tacitus, in contrast, paints a very different picture. He reports a bitter exchange, as Germanicus threw 'grievous insults on Piso', and in return his deputy 'as savagely assailed Caesar'.[242] In a fit of pique, Piso announced that he was leaving Syria. He delayed his departure, however, when he received news that Germanicus Caesar had suddenly fallen sick.

The bad news quickly reached the streets of Antiocheia and the people turned to their temples, offering sacrifices and prayers for Germanicus' good health and safety. Incensed by the public reaction, Piso went into the streets with his lictors and demanded that the people disperse and go home. It was too late to stop the visiting merchants departing Syria, who would relay this news to the markets in Rome, where, upon hearing it, the people would wait with grave concern.[243] Reports then circulated in Antiocheia that Germanicus was recovering. The peoples' prayers had seemingly been answered. Within days, he relapsed, plunging the people into a gloomy mood. Rather than attending his commander at his bedside, instead Piso strangely departed for the nearby port at Seleucia on the Orontes. People began to speculate that Germanicus' worsening condition and Piso's bellicose behaviour and departure were somehow connected; indeed, that *he* was behind Germanicus' sickness. Rumours began to spread of poison, of a conspiracy to murder. Tacitus writes that, from his sick-bed, Germanicus responded to his predicament with fury as much as fear. At this point, he was still conscious and able to converse intelligibly with his assistants and family. As his condition worsened, he began to suspect, himself, that he was being slowly poisoned and that Piso was implicated in a plot to murder him; he even suspected that Piso had placed spies in the villa to relay back to him the progress of his illness.[244] Germanicus is reported as saying:

> If my doors are to be besieged, if I must gasp out my last breath under my enemies' eyes, what will then be the lot of my most unhappy wife, of my infant children? Poisoning seems tedious; he is in eager haste to have the sole control of the province and the legions. But Germanicus is not yet fallen so low, nor will the murderer long retain the reward of the fatal deed.[245]

It is entirely possible that one of Germanicus' adjutants recorded what he said, and Tacitus faithfully reproduced it, though equally the historian may have embellished the story to dramatize his narrative.

From his bed, Germanicus dictated a letter to Piso. In it, he formally renounced his friendship, a grave act conducted 'according to ancient custom'.[246] Several accounts Tacitus had access to – perhaps, among them, eyewitness testimony – also made reference to an order that Piso must leave the province.[247] In effect, Germanicus was firing him from his position. A courier rode off and hand-delivered the letter to Piso, who considered its sombre message. Boarding his ship, Piso ordered the captain to weigh anchor and set sail, but not to travel too fast, in case 'he might not have a long way to return should Germanicus' death leave Syria open to him'.[248]

The next few days passed agonizingly slowly. As Germanicus grew progressively weaker, his mind turned to dark thoughts. He implored his servants 'to avenge his death, if anything untoward should befall him'.[249] Momentarily, he seemed to recover, but the course of the sickness had drained him and he relapsed for a final time.[250] There now seemed no possibility of Germanicus returning to good health. Senior army commanders from Cyrrhus and several senators had since joined the staff and family at Epidaphnae.[251] When dawn broke on the morning of 10 October, the mood at the villa was grim.[252] There were reports that a shooting star with a trailing tail like a spear had been spotted in the sky, which many took to be a bad omen.[253]

Realizing that he was nearing his end, his family and friends gathered around his bed. Into the mouth of the dying man, Tacitus puts fighting words. Whether Germanicus really fingered Piso and his wife as the assassins, or exhorted those in the room with him to avenge him in the high court of the Senate, cannot be known for certain. 'Tears for Germanicus even strangers will shed', the historian records Germanicus as saying, 'vengeance must come from *you*, if you loved the man more than his fortune'.[254] These certainly sound like the words of a practised orator from years of appealing to juries – but are they truly Germanicus'? His friends clasped his right hand in turn and swore earnestly that they would sooner give up their lives than not pursue vengeance. Among them were his faithful friends Vibius Marsus, Cn. Sentius, Q. Veranius and P. Vitellius.

Germanicus reserved his last words for his beloved Agrippina. They had been a remarkable couple. Seemingly incompatible on the day they wed, they had stayed faithful and devoted to each other over fifteen years. He knew that she would not take his death well. He implored her, for the sake of his reputation and for the children, to swallow her rage and not to upset those in powerful places.[255] He said this loudly enough so that the others in the room could hear as witnesses. The public message was clear: he was ever loyal to Tiberius, even in his dying moments. Then, he drew Agrippina near and shared some private remarks with her quietly, so that the others could not hear. To the others in the room, he seemed to be pointing at something. They believed he was telling her his real feelings and of his secret fear of Tiberius.

He exhaled one last time. His body went limp.

Germanicus Iulius Caesar was dead. He was just 34 years old.[256]

Chapter 6

A Fine Roman in the Best Tradition
The Aftermath

Funeral Rites

Germanicus' body lay lifeless on the bed. As Agrippina grieved unconsolably, the stunned members of his staff debated quietly what to do next.[1] An official announcement had to be dispatched to Rome. A new governor had to be appointed to replace Piso. Germanicus' body had to be prepared for the funeral and his ashes shipped home. The cause of death had to be established, and, if found to be murder, the person responsible had to be found, arrested, and charged. The army commanders and senators considered who among them was best qualified to become interim governor, pending the *princeps'* decision about who should receive the official authority and a proper mandate. It was an uneasy discussion, coming so soon after their leader's death, and with his still-warm body only feet away, but Marsus and Sentius hotly debated the matter.[2] Age and vigour finally won, and Sentius accepted the position.

Even as the staff of the deceased Caesar considered the other issues, the tragic news was announced to the crowd waiting anxiously outside the villa. The outpouring of public grief was instant and passionate, and quickly spread to nearby Antiocheia.[3] The family began preparing the body. Tradition required that the dead man's body be washed with warm water, anointed with unguents, and a form of embalming be undertaken.[4] The body would normally be dressed in the finest attire from the man's wardrobe. Agrippina, however, insisted that Germanicus' body be left undressed, perhaps covered only by a simple sheet of cloth.[5] A coin would be slipped under the deceased's tongue to pay Charon the ferryman, who would carry his spirit across the River Styx to Elysium in the afterlife. Flowers, garlands and wreaths would be strewn over the body as it lay, while candles and lamps bathed the room in subdued light.

On the day of the funeral, laments were recited and sung as the body was made ready. Agrippina, her family and friends in mourning, each dressed in dark clothes (*vestes pullae*), assembled and performed a solemn ritual in which she would have called out Germanicus' name three times to the accompaniment of horns in a fanfare of death, and concluded with the words *conclamatio est!*[6] Each member of the family then said their personal final farewell (*extremum vale*) to him. Much as the family's and friends' grief was a deeply private affair, the funeral of this state official would be a very public event. Outside, the cortège began assembling. At the head of the line waited musicians – players of flutes, horns and lyres – followed by hired mourners (*praeficae*), who would sing dirges (*naeniae*).

Germanicus' body was now lifted carefully onto a waiting funeral couch. The attendants – perhaps chosen from among the officers or staff – carried the bier bearing Germanicus' body, feet first, upon their shoulders. They strode solemnly through the villa to their place in the line waiting outside, flanked by his twelve lictors, shouldering their *fasces* reversed to signify the death of the proconsul. Following immediately after Germanicus' corpse gathered his wife and children, his close friends and clients. On that sombre October day, as was customary for the wife of the deceased, Agrippina wore her hair dishevelled, and no jewellery. Then the musicians struck up their funereal tune, the mourners began their discordant wailing, and the solemn procession set off slowly along the road, from the villa to the forum, in the heart of the one of the greatest cities of the empire.

The funeral would lack some aspects required by ancient tradition: there could be no procession of the ancestral *imagines* of the *gens Antonii, Claudii Nerones* and *Iulii*, since they were locked up in cupboards in far-away Rome. The funerary procession, now joined by hundreds of ordinary people from the city and the surrounding country, gathered together in the forum. There, a wooden tribunal and a pyre had been erected. The funeral couch with Germanicus' body was set down before the tribunal. As befitted Rome's most popular commander, Germanicus' life and achievements were commemorated. Speaking from the raised platform, his oldest son present or closest friend – the sources do not say which – addressed the assembled crowd and gave a prepared funeral eulogy (*laudatio funebris*). As reported – or re-imagined – by Tacitus, the speaker told of Germanicus' many virtues and personal qualities. He drew the inevitable comparison with a young Macedonian hero of centuries past, who had similarly died young:

> Some there were who, as they thought of his beauty, his age, and the manner of his death, the vicinity, too, of the country where he died, likened his end to that of Alexander the Great. Both had a graceful person and were of noble birth; neither had much exceeded thirty years of age, and both fell by the treachery of their own people in strange lands. But Germanicus was gracious to his friends, temperate in his pleasures, the husband of one wife, with only legitimate children. He was, too, no less a warrior, though rashness he had none, and, though after having cowed Germany by his many victories, he was hindered from crushing it into subjection. Had he had the sole control of affairs, had he possessed the power and title of a king, he would have attained military glory as much more easily as he had excelled Alexander in clemency, in self-restraint, and in all other virtues.[7]

To gasps from the crowd, Agrippina pulled back the shroud and displayed her husband's naked body to show strange blue marks on his skin.[8] Agrippina was grief-stricken and the crowd pitied her awful situation.[9] The corpse was then carefully lifted onto the pyre. In accordance with custom, Agrippina ascended the pyre and kissed Germanicus in a final and public farewell. Family members and close friends tossed onto the pyre the personal belongings Germanicus had most cherished in his lifetime. Then, with a lighted torch, Agrippina or one of her close friends set the pyre alight. To the crackle and snap of burning kindling, the mourners stood aside and watched as the raging flames licked, and finally consumed, Germanicus' mortal body, and thick smoke curled up into the sky. After the fire had burned itself out, wine was poured onto the scorched bones and embers, and the ashes were gathered up, covered with oil or honey, and placed in a jar or casket.[10] Ordinarily, the body would be buried and then would begin a period called the 'Nine Days of Sorrow', and on the final day, a sacrifice (*sacrificium novendiale*) and a meal was offered to give the deceased a final send-off into the afterlife. However, Germanicus was not destined to be buried in Antiocheia. Agrippina was determined to see his casket of ashes placed 2,250km (1,400 miles) away in Rome.

By word of mouth, news of Germanicus Caesar's death passed from person to person and, within days, all Syria knew of it. Despite the great distances, merchants and travellers carried the news beyond the borders to neighbouring provinces, to client kingdoms, and far across the region. 'Foreign nations and kings grieved over him, so great was his courtesy to allies, his humanity to enemies', wrote Tacitus.[11] The shockwaves of the news from Syria led to the display of previously unthinkable marks of respect by foreign heads of state. Nations at war with each other or with Rome agreed to suspend hostilities for days of mourning.[12] Several regents of smaller kingdoms were reported to have shaved their beards and their wives' heads. Even the King of Parthia, the self-styled 'king of kings', suspended all business, including hunting and feasting, to commemorate his former adversary. Some of the accounts of events following Germanicus' death may be exaggerations by the Roman historians, but what is very likely true is that the unexpected death of Rome's emissary to the Orient now plunged her neighbours into a period of diplomatic uncertainty.

The news took several weeks to reach Rome. Spoken and written communications travelled only as fast as the physical mode of transportation, and delays were frequent and inevitable. More recent news could often arrive sooner than older news, creating confusion. The first news reports that Germanicus had died plunged the city into consternation and grief.[13] Initial accounts of Germanicus' death were both rejected and exaggerated, and 'the mourning of the people could neither be assuaged by consolation, nor restrained by edicts'.[14] The city was plunged into grief. Business in the city was suspended – shops were shuttered, the normally noisy courthouses were empty, the front doors of private houses were closed.[15] Even the Senate, without word from the prevailing speaker of the house or its magistrates, went into voluntary recess. 'Everywhere, there was a silence broken only by groans', writes Tacitus, 'nothing was arranged for mere effect; and though they refrained not from the emblems of the mourner, they sorrowed yet the more deeply in their hearts'.[16] Yet there were still those who – hoping against hope – were unwilling to believe the reports of Germanicus' death. They gathered at Ostia to quiz arriving merchants for updates on his condition. Then, one evening, a ship brought news – unconfirmed and source unknown – that Germanicus had actually recovered. Roused by the happy news, the crowd raced to the city, carrying lit torches and dragging sacrificial animals up to the Capitolinus Hill, all eager to fulfil their vows to the gods for having brought about Germanicus' recovery.[17] So many crowded onto the acropolis that they almost broke open the doors of the temple. On the neighbouring Palatinus Hill, Tiberius was awoken from his sleep by the incessant noise of the people in the streets, congratulating one another and chanting the words:

> Rome is safe,
> Our is country safe,
> Germanicus is safe![18]

Comfortably far from the madding crowd, Tiberius chose not investigate the reports and preferred to wait for the official announcement to arrive from Antiocheia.[19] Yet he could not afford to entirely ignore the situation in the streets below, which was getting rapidly out of hand. Confirmed reports arrived that, all the while the people had believed Germanicus was alive, he was long since dead. Jubilation now turned to abject despair. It was a cruel double blow, 'and so the people grieved the more bitterly, as though Germanicus was again lost to them'.[20] Suetonius reports that riots broke out. Stones were lobbed at temples, altars were cast down and broken, the statuettes of the cherished household gods were thrown into the streets by some, and some chose to expose their new born children to die, as though the world they would grow up in was not worthy without Germanicus.[21]

Causes and Culprits

In Syria, Veranius and Vitellius had been conducting an investigation to establish the cause of death. The sources do not relate if an autopsy was carried out on Germanicus' body, though it is not beyond the realm of possibility, since at least one is recorded as having taken place in Roman times.[22] The historian Velleius Paterculus, who of all the surviving historians' accounts wrote nearest in time to the events – his *Roman History* was completed by 30 CE – is oddly silent on the matter of Germanicus' death.[23] There evidently were several accounts in circulation soon after he passed away, since Flavius Josephus mentions the fact in passing. His is the earliest account we have that mentions Germanicus' death and offers a cause for it. He writes around 93 or 94 CE, 'when he had been in the East, and settled all affairs there, his life was taken away by the poison (φαρμάκῳ) which Piso gave him, as has been related elsewhere'.[24] Who those sources were, Josephus does not disclose. Suetonius reports, two decades or so later, that Germanicus died of 'a long drawn out disease (*diuturno morbo*)', adding that the visible signs after death were 'bluish spots (*livores*) that covered his entire body' and 'foaming at the mouth (*spuma*)'.[25] In his mind, based on these signs, poisoning was self-evident – a verdict confirmed for him by the fact that, after the cremation, Germanicus' heart was found still intact among the charred bones, which, according to widely-held belief at that time, was a clear indicator of poison (*veneno*).[26]

Writing about the same time as Suetonius, Tacitus gives us an inexact timeline, which puts the start of Germanicus' sickness (*valetudo*) after he had returned to

Antiocheia from Egypt.[27] The first symptoms of sickness probably would have revealed themselves in late September or the early part of October. Germanicus seems to have recovered; then he relapsed. Tacitus says that rumours of poisoning began to spread at that time. The sickness grew in intensity (*saevam vim morbi augebat*) and Germanicus himself began to believe Piso had poisoned him.[28] He appears not to have been delirious at that time, as he was able to converse with his friends and family. There is a hint that his condition improved again, but, by then, he was physically exhausted (*dein fesso corpore*) and unable to sustain a full recovery; not long after, he died (*neque multo post extinguitur*).[29] By this account, the sickness lasted under a month, and perhaps just a couple of weeks.

So what killed Germanicus? Modern doctors apply a systematic technique called 'differential diagnosis', in attempting to determine the cause of a sickness by comparing and contrasting clinical findings. A lingering sickness, bluish skin and foaming at the mouth – if Suetonius' and Tacitus' records are accurate – are the only three clues we have, with which to attempt to identify the cause of death. The duration of the condition clearly suggests a very serious sickness. The culprit could be one of several bacterial or viral infections, and Syria was a dangerous place, ending the lives of several Roman governors to infections of one type or another.[30] Typhoid is one candidate. It is caused by the bacterium *Salmonella Typhi* and is contracted by consuming food or drink that has been handled by a person shedding the bacteria, or it may be in water, used for drinking or washing food, that has come into contact with contaminated sewage.[31] It was certainly prevalent in Germanicus' day, and it affected parts of the Empire periodically, bringing Augustus close to death when he was in Spain, and his nephew Marcellus may even have died from it while in Campania.[32] Typhoidal fever typically lasts about a month, but in fatal cases it may be over in half that time. However, one fifth of people contracting it die from complications of the infection.[33] Its symptoms include high temperature, a feeling of weakness, stomach pains, headache, and loss of appetite. Alternatively, influenza might have been to blame, but as no others in his party are recorded as having come down with it, this seems an unlikely cause.[34] Similarly, malaria or West Nile Encephalitis, both spread by mosquitoes, could have been responsible for making Germanicus sick.[35] Without details about the accompanying symptoms – such as headache, fever, chills and sweating, bleeding, skin rashes, stomach pains or vomiting, diarrhoea, and the like – or information about the medications his doctor administered, any diagnosis today must needs be speculative.

Foaming or frothing at the mouth can occur while the patient is alive, such as during an epileptic fit or a seizure, and is quite natural before, or at the moment, a person dies.[36] It can occur when the patient has difficulty swallowing, which is caused by paralysis of the throat and mouth muscles, resulting in excessive salivation. Difficulty in breathing may also result from the restriction. The excess saliva mixed with air from rapid breathing forms bubbles – the foam or froth. It can also be a symptom of rabies. Alternatively, foaming occurs when the muscle which controls the opening and closing of the stomach finally relaxes and the gastric acid rises up the oesophagus, throat, and out of the mouth. Any of these could indicate a natural cause of death, though none of the accounts reveal Germanicus as having a history of epileptic attacks or having been bitten by a wild animal.

Bluish skin is called cyanosis in modern medical parlance. It usually indicates lack of oxygen in the blood, and can be an indicator of several serious medical problems.[37] It may develop suddenly, along with shortness of breath, such as in a seizure, but it can also indicate longer-term heart or lung problems. Causing the lack of oxygen can be a blood clot in the arteries of the lungs (pulmonary embolism), or asthma, chronic obstructive pulmonary disease (COPD), inflammation of the lungs (diffuse institial lung disease), or pneumonia. Any of these could provide adequate medical explanations for the natural cause of Germanicus' death. Thus, by itself, cyanosis does not indicate a particular naturally-induced cause of death – but neither is it a confirmation of poisioning, as Suetonius asserts.

Alternatively, a drug overdose, such as of a sedative administered by his own doctor, could equally well have been responsible. As a high-ranking official and member of the imperial family, Germanicus could have afforded the services of a private physician. Often a Greek by birth, he would have been trained to a high standard and been familiar with the works of Hippokrates.[38] Nevertheless, ignorance of the strength of medicaments did cause accidental deaths, and, with the frequency of Germanicus' travelling, it may have been difficult for a doctor accompanying him to obtain supplies of raw materials of a consistent potency or safety. Local alternatives may have been available, but Pliny the Elder warned especially about accepting drugs from herbalists and drug-pedlars as dancing with death by suicide.[39]

The Romans were aware of the toxic properties of many animals, minerals, and plants. Some were used in low dosages to induce euphoric trances for religious rites, rather than to kill. Indeed, some were used as remedies. These included aconite (wolfbane or monkshood), alcohol, belladonna, *cannabis sativa* (dagga), hemlock, hellebore, henbane, mandragora, opium, poisonous mushrooms, rhododendron, and thorn apple.[40] The most widely-used derived from plants. Problematic for modern scholars are the use of the terms for poison by ancient writers. The words φάρμακον and *venenum* are ambiguous. The Greek word, used by Josephus in his account, means a drug of any kind, and does not indicate whether its use is benign or malicious. Similarly, the Latin word, which originally meant a love potion, can mean poison, but can also be used for remedy, abortive or magic potion.[41] The Romans themselves recognized this ambiguity and, in later times, insisted that the user of the word should indicate whether beneficial or harmful effects were intended.[42] Tacitus uses the word *scelus* ('crime') specifically for murder by poison, but he does not in the case of Germanicus.[43] The precise meanings of the Greek and Latin terms depend on the context and, specifically, the dosage. Opium, for example, was known to aid digestion, and was also used as a soporific and analgesic; but, in large dosages, it was understood to be harmful and even kill.[44]

If Germanicus was poisoned by a single or repeated overdose of medication, his death was by misadventure. If, however, there was a plot to kill him, the murderer may have purposely administered several doses of one poison, or a variety of toxins, at different times, which would explain why he relapsed after having seemingly made a recovery. But the surviving accounts suggest not. Roman authors used the word *veneficium* to indicate poisoning or sorcery, and it is significant that neither Suetonius nor Tacitus uses it in describing the death of Germanicus. Indeed, Tacitus himself casts doubt on poisoning as the cause of his death. The body had lain uncovered in the forum at Antiocheia before it was burnt and, he writes, 'it is *doubtful* whether it exhibited the marks of poisoning (*veneficii*)'.[45]

If the death of Germanicus was not by accident or natural causes, but in fact *was* homicide, the question has to be asked who murdered him? There are several potential suspects. There are the known enemies of Germanicus to consider. If Tacitus' account is accurate, Germanicus himself believed that he was being poisoned by Cn. Calpurnius Piso and his wife Munatia Plancina. The couple's dislike of the young Caesar was well-known, and their personal actions were consistent with their low opinion of him. To convince a modern jury of guilt in a crime, however, police detectives look for three things in investigating a death: means, motive and opportunity. How would the husband or wife have benefited from murdering Germanicus? Their motive could not be financial: they were already extremely wealthy people. Perhaps it was power? There is a story that Augustus had described Piso as not unworthy of the throne, and under his successor he was a man of considerable influence, but there is no evidence that he had his eye on taking supreme power.[46] Was Piso settling an old score? Piso was a haughty, arrogant man and he had had bitter arguments with his superior, but there is no suggestion that he bore a festering grudge against Germanicus – at least, not one so great that he would have committed murder in order to find redress. Could the motivation have been the excitement of murder? It might seem an odd question, but modern studies have highlighted how risk-taking plays a part in a lot of criminal activity, and how, for some, the act of committing a crime is its own reward.[47] Were the Pisones thrill-seekers? Apparently not: far from finding pleasure in risky adventures, the couple are portrayed in the ancient literature as a pair of antisocial bores, who derived their pleasure from flaunting their wealth and status. Both husband and wife were undeniably callous towards Germanicus, but that would not necessarily drive them to murder him. If they were inclined to, they could certainly have provided the means and have paid for an assassin. Plancina was known to have an active personal interest in the arcane science of toxicology and befriended an experienced practitioner by the name of Martina.[48] Being co-located in Antiocheia, they also had the opportunity. Indeed, there is an allegation recorded by Tacitus that, at a dinner party, Piso reclined near Germanicus where he could have dropped poison in his host's food or drink at any moment.[49] Tacitus himself thought it implausible as, surrounded by other guests, he would likely have been seen doing it. Piso was also accused of using spies to note every unfavourable symptom and chart the progress of Germanicus' fatal illness, which did not cast him in a good light, but it was only an accusation.[50] Taken at face value, all this circumstantial evidence amounts to little of substance, and would probably be insufficient to secure a conviction. Other than removing someone they felt was below them socially, Piso and Plancina had little or nothing to gain personally from killing Germanicus.

Did they perhaps act in consort with another party? There is a suggestion recorded by Tacitus that Piso was operating under special instructions from Tiberius Caesar – or his mother.[51] These alleged instructions, if they existed at all, were never released for public scrutiny. The crux of this hypothesis is the premise that Tiberius had decided to eliminate his adopted son sooner rather than later. His motivation would have been the growing suspicion that his adopted son was driving an agenda of his own, becoming more arrogant and insubordinate in the knowledge that he was destined to rule. The main source for this theory is, again, Tacitus, and the historian provides examples of Tiberius' annoyance, such as Germanicus' insistence on continuing the war in Germania, or his disregard for policy preventing unauthorized high-ranking officials from visiting Egypt. Tiberius did not, himself, have the opportunity to kill his son, so he would have had to work secretly through agents, just as he was alleged to have done in the affair of Postumus Agrippa. In that role, the Calpurnii Pisones could have acted to carry out his instructions. If not them, there could have been other agents sufficiently removed from him for plausible deniability. These could have included trusted high-ranking military officers, such as the chief of his own Praetorian Cohorts, L. Aelius Seianus – of whom more later. Perhaps in the hope of advancement or favouritism, Seianus acted on his own initiative and commissioned Piso or Plancina or someone else to carry out the deed. Yet the logic seems flawed. The 'Tiberius as mastermind of Germanicus' death' theory fails to be convincing on two major counts. Firstly, if Tiberius was so upset about Germanicus' attitude or performance, or he felt so threatened by him, he could have simply recalled him and stripped him of his powers. As history shows, he did not. Secondly, the general impression left by a reading of the ancient accounts is that the *princeps* actually went out of his way to grant the man chosen by Augustus to be the third emperor considerable leeway in running his affairs, even publicly lavishing praise on the young Caesar for his achievements and promoting him with an ever-expanding portfolio of duties and powers.

If not Tiberius, then what about Livia? Initially, she had positive feelings about Germanicus. She approved of her grandson's marriage to Agrippina, seeing in it a union of the *gens Claudia* and *Iulia*, out of which would spring children carrying the mixed blood of the clans.[52] Yet she allegedly discouraged Augustus when he was actively considering the adoption of Germanicus as his primary heir.[53] Livia's supposed motive was to see her own eldest son follow Augustus first. If true, she had achieved her goal. But what would *she* gain by arranging the assassination of Germanicus? In explaining the many unfortunate premature deaths of Augustus' nominated heirs, some ancient historians have perceived a master assassin with a higher agenda at work. Stereotyping women as assassins whose preferred weapon was poison was a common literary device among Roman historians.[54] In the Augusta, such conspiracy theorists had a ready scapegoat. Indeed, historians and novelists alike have been unkind to Livia, branding her as a champion of her eldest son's advancement, ruthlessly eliminating anyone who stood in his way.[55]

The truth, however, is that the widely different circumstances of the deaths of M. Agrippa, Marcellus, Drusus the Elder, Caius and Lucius Caesar, Postumus Agrippa and Germanicus make it neither likely that a single criminal mind was at work, nor that Livia – or anyone else – schemed their demises.

Casting the net wider, among Germanicus' *amici*, advisors and adjutants, several men could have harboured secret grudges. The lust for power could have provided a motive for murder. Vibius Marsus and Cn. Sentius were quick to argue over who would take control of Syria and, with it, command of its four legions. Similarly, Q. Veranius and P. Vitellius might each have held private resentments. However, all of these men owed their recent advancements and current positions to Germanicus and had everything to gain from seeing him live a long and prosperous life, not dead. Nor is there a suggestion that his brother Drusus ever harboured any grudge – in fact, there was genuine fraternal affection between them. It is highly unlikely that his friends or members of staff produced a murderer. Intriguingly, Veranius and Vitellius, who were investigating the crime, did, however, have the opportunity to doctor the evidence and make it point to one or more individuals, whom they wanted to see brought down in fulfilment of their oath to their deceased patron.

Could Germanicus have been the victim of a foreign plot? During his tenure in the East, Germanicus had negotiated with a host of nations – Armenia, Cilicia, Commagene and Parthia. In advancing Rome's best interests there, he had probably hurt those of powerful local men and created enemies in the process – henchmen of Vonones, for instance. There were others, no doubt, who had much to gain if war broke out between Rome and Parthia. Any of these could have hired an assassin to pay back the chief Roman diplomat for his meddling in their affairs, or, by bringing about his death, to destabilize the region in order to realize their agendas. The Roman sources, however, give no indication of an agent working on behalf of the Parthians or their client states. Indeed, the response of potentates across the region was to mourn his passing, not to celebrate it.

In recent times, two other names have been suggested. These are L. Annaeus Seneca (Seneca the Younger) and, remarkably, Germanicus' own wife, Agrippina the Elder.[56] The theory is premised upon the idea that the young Seneca was staying in Alexandria at the time of Germanicus' visit, since he had been recuperating there from a serious sickness at the invitation of his uncle, C. Valerius, *praefectus* of Aegyptus. In the hope of advancing his career by making his mark, his supposed motive was to ingratiate himself with Tiberius by eliminating the man he had come to see as a threat. The author of the hypothesis presupposes that Agrippina is a wife in a rocky marriage. Seneca is portrayed as the seducer, providing the distraction of a short-term love affair, and the schemer, offering long-term fulfilment of her secret ambition to see her sons rule Rome before her husband. Agrippina is proposed as the willing accomplice and the executioner. While there were certainly opportunities aplenty for Agrippina to administer a lethal dose of poison at any time, it is a fanciful – if not an absurd – conjecture with absolutely no basis in fact. All the surviving evidence presents Agrippina as a devoted wife who was loyal to her husband, both during his life and well after his death. As for Seneca, in 19 CE, he was known only as a sickly teacher of rhetoric from Cordoba in southern Spain.

Forensic science was almost non-existent at this time. In the sincere belief that they were investigating a murder, Veranius and Vitellius conducted on-the-spot searches of the supposed crime scene for evidence, both at the villa at Epidaphnae and the residence of their prime suspects, Piso and Plancina. In the governor's property in Antiocheia, it is reported:

> certainly, there were found hidden in the floor and in the walls disinterred remains of human bodies, incantations and spells, and the name of Germanicus inscribed on leaden tablets, half-burnt cinders smeared with blood, and other horrors by which, in popular belief, souls are devoted to the infernal deities.[57]

The discovery of the use of black magic would reinforce the impression of the couple's wicked intentions. The little room of horrors may even have been stage-managed by friends of Germanicus, to ensure that there was enough evidence to secure a conviction. Many people had already made up their minds, no matter what any facts might prove, 'for men, according as they pitied Germanicus and were prepossessed with suspicion or were biased by partiality towards Piso, gave conflicting accounts'.[58] In the summary court of popular opinion – both in Antiocheia and Rome – the finger of accusation pointed straight at the former governor and his wife.[59] For Veranius, Vitellius and others, it was a foregone conclusion. They immediately began work on preparing the indictment, 'as if a prosecution had already been commenced'.[60] The task now was to find the accused, present the charges, and bring them to justice. Of deeper concern was the suspicion that the Pisones had not acted alone and that they were acting under direct orders from the emperor – or his mother.[61] In the meantime, a suspected accomplice – the woman named Martina, notorious for numerous poisonings in Syria – was taken into custody. The hunt for Piso and Plancina was on.

The former governor and his wife had long since left Syria and were already berthed at the Dodecanese island of Kos, just off the Carian coast.[62] It was there that they received news of Germanicus' death. The couple were jubilant. Piso celebrated his joy with sacrifices and prayers of thanks at the local temples. Plancina, who was in mourning for the loss of her sister, now expressed her happiness at Germanicus' passing, by wearing the brightest coloured clothes she could find. Among Piso's party were centurions who were still loyal to the former governor.[63] They hinted that the legions in Syria would come to his side if approached, and urged him to return and retake his office. His son, Marcus, urged him to go to Rome, however, saying he was not implicated in Germanicus' death since he had already left before it happened. Moreover, his return to Syria might provoke a civil war.[64] Domitius Celer, one of Piso's confidants, backed the centurions' motion, arguing that he had been appointed the governor by the emperor and that he was still entitled to lead the army stationed there.[65] More-over, he – or at least his wife – had the support of Livia, mother of Tiberius, who could exert considerable influence over the emperor. After weighing up his options, Piso decided his best interests lay in taking back command of Syria. He dispatched a letter to Tiberius, in which he accused Germanicus of living a life of luxury and arrogance and further stating that, having been forced out of office, he was resuming command of the army and the province.[66] Celer was sent on ahead aboard a trireme with orders to go directly to Antiocheia by the fastest route – open sea, not by hugging the coast. Meanwhile Piso's men began to assemble an army of deserters and armed the civilian camp-followers. They diverted a detachment of new recruits who were on their way to Syria, and also demanded that the client king of Cilicia should provide him with cohorts of auxiliary troops.

Meanwhile, leaving Sentius in charge in Syria, and accompanied by members of Germanicus' staff, Agrippina now set off with her children for Rome.[67] Carrying her husband's precious ashes, she was emotionally at her lowest ebb, worn out from grieving. Yet she was keen to hasten to Rome and see justice done.[68] In her wretched state, she was 'pitied by all', wrote Tacitus, but she had attained a heroic stature through her unwavering resolve:

> Here indeed was a woman of the highest nobility, and but lately because of her splendid union wont to be seen amid an admiring and sympathizing throng, now bearing in her bosom the mournful relics of death, with an uncertain hope of revenge, with apprehensions for herself, repeatedly at fortune's mercy by reason of the ill-starred fruitfulness of her marriage.[69]

The ships made steady progress along the coasts of Lycia and Pamphylia. By chance, her flotilla passed Piso's. Across the waves, there was a heated exchange. M. Vibius shouted that Piso should go to Rome and face charges. Piso is reported as replying that 'he would be there as soon as the *praetor* who had to try poisoning cases (*praetor qui de veneficiis quaereret*) had fixed a day for the accused and his prosecutors'.[70] He was determined to use every means available to him to come from a position of strength and appear in court on his own terms. The ships went their separate ways. Celer, meantime, had landed in Syria at Loadicea (Laodikeia, modern Latakia) and was heading for the winter camp of *Legio* VI *Ferrata*, which Tacitus remarks was particularly susceptible to revolutionary ideas. Its legate, Pacavius, had anticipated the visit and forestalled Piso's envoy. With the stakes rising, Sentius wrote a letter to Piso telling him to stay well away from the legions. If he did decide to wage war, Sentius would be at the head of a substantial force of men still loyal to the memory of Germanicus in Syria.[71]

His initial approaches having proved unsuccessful, Piso decided – wisely – against entering Syria. He took refuge, instead, in neighbouring Cilicia, in a fortified hill-top citadel called Celenderis. Combining the Cilician auxiliaries, the intercepted recruits and miscellaneous deserters, he cobbled together a legion.[72] In a show of force, they assembled, using the advantage of the terrain below the hill, where they faced Sentius' men deployed in battle array on the plain. When the order was given to engage, the veteran Roman soldiers and the reserves advanced up the slope of the hill and clashed with Piso's army of untested *tirones*, supplemented by a rag-tag band equipped with pitchforks and scythes. Seeing no chance of victory, the Cilician auxiliaries decided it was not worth risking their lives, and withdrew up the hill and back into the safety of the fortress. Piso attempted to attack a fleet that was waiting offshore, but that action also came to nought. In growing desperation, he tried to incite a mutiny of the troops on Sentius' side.[73] Riding up to their temporary camp, he called to men he knew by name, and shouted to them that a *signifer* of *Legio* VI had already come over to his side. Sentius would not stand for this behaviour and gave the order for his troops to besiege Celenderis. Faced with an all-out assault of tried and tested siege weaponry, Piso knew he could not win, and sued for time to write to Tiberius and consult about him the governorship of Syria. Sentius blankly refused, offering him only safe passage to the shore, where he could board a ship and return to Rome. Piso's revolt was over.

Honours for Germanicus
Outbreaks of civil disruption continued in Rome well into December.[74] On 16 December, the Senate decreed an extraordinary list of posthumous honours for Germanicus Iulius Caesar.[75] The decree of the Senate – *Senatus Consultum de supremis honoribus Germanici* – was later cast in plaques of bronze and posted in the portico of the Temple of Apollo on the Palatinus Hill in Rome, and on public buildings in the *municipiae* and *coloniae* of Italy and across the Empire, 'so that the devotion (*pietas*) of all orders toward the imperial household (*domus Augusta*) and unanimity of all citizens in honouring Germanicus' memory might be more easily visible'.[76] It decreed that the day of Germanicus' death was henceforth a day of remembrance on which neither legal cases could be heard, nor serious business could be conducted; no banquets, weddings, games or public entertainments could take place; and to accommodate for it, the theatrical games of Augustus (*ludi Augustales scaenici*), normally held on that day, should be postponed to the end of the month. It decreed that Germanicus' name was to be included in the song of the Salii, sung by the twelve priests of Mars Gradivus when they celebrated the ancient festival of Mars on the Kalends (1st) of March – an honour only a few mortal men ever received, the most recent being Augustus.[77] The chairs of state decorated with garlands of oak were to be set up in the places assigned to the priesthood of the *flamen divorum Augustalis* of which Germanicus had been its first chief priest. In the room used by Germanicus, no *flamen* or augur would henceforth be chosen, with the sole exception of those from the *gens Iulia*. His image, exquisitely carved in ivory, was to appear at the head of the ceremonial procession before the games (*ludi*) of the circus.

Three triumphal arches (*iani*) of marble were to be erected: in the Circus Flaminius in Rome, on the banks of the Rhine (probably at Mogontiacum), and on the slopes of Mount Amanus in Syria, where it would stand at the intersection of Syria, Cilicia, and Commagene – significantly all places and countries personally associated with Germanicus.[78] Each would display an inscription recording his lifetime's achievements and how he had died in the service of the Republic. The arch *in Circo Flaminio* in Rome would feature Germanicus riding in a decorated triumphator's chariot, flanked by the figures of Antonia, Agrippina and

Drusus the Elder.[79] The arch in Rome, specifically, would be raised to commemorate Germanicus' important mission to the East, 'because he died on behalf of the *Res Publica*'.[80] Thus, it was to be stated publicly that Germanicus had not died in vain, but – like his father, Drusus, before him – in the service of his country. The arch in Germania Superior would bear an inscription stressing the familial connection to Drusus the Elder, brother of Tiberius, where his reputation was still cherished.[81] Only in Syria, where the imperial family had no direct involvement before Germanicus, would the members of the *domus Augusta* not be represented on the triumphal arch. Its siting would, nevertheless, be at the discretion of the *princeps*.[82]

A high mound would be raised at Epidaphnae, where his life had ended, and a cenotaph (*sepulchrum*) was to be built at Antiocheia, where his body had been cremated.[83] A new bronze boundary marker was to be raised in Rome.[84] Statues were to be erected, and Tacitus remarks that there were finally so many that neither the number of them nor the places they were displayed in could be easily calculated. [85] Germanicus' famed skill as an orator also was to be celebrated, but, in the scale of its award, the Senate pushed its luck too far. When a remarkably large commemorative shield made of gold was voted him as *inter auctores eloquentiae*, 'a leader among orators', Tiberius – ever one for showing restraint (*moderatio*), the very quality for which Augustus chose him as his successor – overruled the decision. He declared that he would dedicate to his son one of the usual kind, similar to those issued to others, 'for in eloquence', he said, 'there was no distinction of rank, and it was a sufficient glory for him to be classed among ancient writers'.[86]

On the Capitolinus Hill, beside the Temple of Fides, honouring trust or faith, trophies of Germanicus' victories (*Tropaea Germanici*) were erected upon a tribunal, where they stood among others placed by notable Roman greats like C. Marius; it was a considerable honour for Germanicus, as only a decade or so before, Augustus had arranged for many of the historic monuments to be moved to other locations, to make the space more accessible for visitors.[87]

The lower orders, too, showed their respect to his memory. The *equites* changed the name given to the hemicycle of seats they occupied in the theatre, popularly known as 'the juniors' (*iuniores*), to 'Germanicus' row' (*cuneum Germanici*). Additionally, they arranged that their *turmae* would ride behind his effigy in their annual procession for the *transvectio equito* – a celebration held on the Ides (15th) of July by the Roman cavalry, which started at the Temple of Mars, then wound its way through Rome's streets, crossing the Forum, before finally halting at the Temple of the Dioscuri.[88] One of their number, C. Lutorius Priscus, composed a best-selling poem deploring the wasteful death of Germanicus, which pleased Tiberius greatly and, for it, he paid its author a cash reward.[89] Tiberius' own panegyric (*elogia*) for his son was set in bronze and put on public display.[90] The plebeian class also played its part by paying for statues of Germanicus in triumphal panoply and erecting them in the temples and altars that Augustus and Livia had formerly chosen for statues of Drusus the Elder, with dedicatory inscriptions from the thirty-five tribes.[91] To the ten voting centuries of the Caesars, five were to be added in honour of Germanicus Caesar.[92]

Individual cities across the empire also showed their appreciation for the life of their favourite member of the imperial family, each according to their means.[93] In Italy, the city of Gabii installed a marble statue (plate 39) in the forum, depicting Germanicus as a demi-god, his naked muscled body covered only around the waist and legs by a toga, while in Amelia, the city fathers repurposed an existing bronze statue (plate 40) by swapping the old head for a new one of Germanicus.[94]

On the banks of the Rhine, there was deep disaffection among the soldiers when they heard of the death – or, as some believed, the murder – of their beloved commander; the army remained calm, however, and began work on constructing the arch at Mogontiacum, as the Senate had ordered, and would later hold the first of many annual sacrifices on Germanicus' birthday.[95] On the coast of North Africa at Lepcis Magna, the city fathers were building a temple to *Roma et Augustus* in the Old Forum. In front of the main temple building, they erected a statue group honouring members of the imperial family, placing Germanicus and his brother Drusus, together in a triumphal chariot, prominently in the centre.[96] On mainland Greece, a day was dedicated to the 'Victory (*Nike*) of Germanicus' at the festival of the Kaisareia held at Gytheum (Gythion) near Sparta.[97] Several Greek-speaking cities of Asia – for example, in Bithynia et Pontus, Isauria, Paphlagonia – voluntarily changed their names to Γερμανικόπολις (*Germanikopolis*), 'city of Germanicus'. In mourning for him, the world had gone crazy for Germanicus.[98]

Amid all of the private and public grieving, new life had, meantime, come bawling into the world. In the imperial family, Drusus' wife Livilla had given birth to two sons. One of them was named Ti. Claudius Caesar Germanicus Gemellus (Ti. Germanicus, for short), and the other was Ti. Iulius Caesar Nero Gemellus (commonly known as Gemellus, 'the twin'). The news of the birth of twins would have normally been cause for joyous celebration; but, instead, it brought the opposite reaction, as people quickly speculated that the prospects for Germanicus' surviving children were now diminished by the additions to his brother's family.[99] Tiberius, for one, found reason to be cheerful, and boasted of his new grandsons to the Senate at every opportunity.[100]

By the end of the year, Agrippina's flotilla finally reached the island of Corcyra (Corfu). She was still distraught – 'wild with grief and knew not how to endure it' – yet determined to press on.[101] The crew and passengers disembarked for a few days' respite, but the stop was also calculated to ensure that news of her imminent arrival reached Italy and that a good-sized crowd would turn up. Just 300km (186 miles) across the Adriatic Sea, people began to gather at Brundisium, waiting expectantly for the famed widow of Germanicus Caesar.[102] Intimate friends, officers, men who had served under Germanicus, and strangers who just wanted to pay their respects and offer their condolences, all kinds of people crowded into the busy port city. Every vantage point was taken. Unaccustomed to welcoming home a deceased V.I.P., many on the quayside quizzed the people standing next to them about whether they should show respectful silence or freely express their grief. Then, someone saw the ships approaching on the horizon and cried out, and the general mood suddenly turned at once to excitement and gloom. The oarsmen carefully manoeuvred the ship bearing the imperial family along the dockside. Retracting their oars, the hawsers were cast and tied off at the piers. Dockhands carefully positioned the ramp, stood discreetly aside, and bowed their heads out of respect. It was a memorable scene. As reported by Tacitus:

> When Agrippina descended from the vessel with her two children, clasping the funeral urn, with eyes rivetted to the earth, there was one universal groan. You could not distinguish kinsfolk from strangers, or the laments of men from those of women; only the attendants of Agrippina, worn out as they were by long sorrow, were surpassed by the mourners who now met them, fresh in their grief.[103]

She was met by civic officials and two units of *Cohors Praetoria* – sent on Tiberius' direct orders – who would provide a ceremonial escort from the coast all the way to Rome.[104] The official welcomes and condolences having been given, the procession set off at a slow march along the ancient *Via Appia*. Ahead of the column marched the standard-bearers with their *signa* unadorned: this was not a time for celebration. Then came Germanicus' twelve lictors carrying their *fasces* reversed. The tribunes and centurions followed, carrying the urn with Germanicus' ashes on a bier upon their shoulders, and behind them walked Agrippina, her children, attendants and friends.[105] The 570km (354 mile) journey which lay ahead would take them across the breadth of Italy, through the *coloniae* and *municipiae* of Calabria, Campania and Latium. People turned out in strength to witness the funeral cortège. The *equites* dressed in their finest robes, the plebs wearing the best they could find in black, burned offerings of clothes and spices according to their means along the roadside. Even citizens of towns not directly on the route travelled to pay their respects, offering sacrifices and prayers, erecting altars, shedding tears and wailing their own sorrows, as the sad entourage rolled past. Many could recall how Germanicus' father, Nero Claudius Drusus, had been similarly welcomed home after his tragic death in 9 BCE.[106] Germanicus' brothers, Drusus the Younger and Claudius, and the other children of Agrippina met the mourners at Tarracina (Terracina), a full day's ride – 76km (47 miles) – south-east of Rome.[107] It was an emotional meeting: Drusus and Agrippina had not met since the spring of the previous year, when it had been under happier circumstances in Dalmatia; for Claudius, it was longer still. None could have imagined the tragedy causing this reunion. By now, Agrippina and her party had been travelling for weeks. As they approached Rome, people thronged the roadsides. The consuls, M. Valerius Messalla and M. Aurelius Cotta, came out to officially receive the cortège. All present shed tears at the overwhelming emotion of the event.

Conspicuously absent from the welcoming party were Tiberius, the Augusta (Livia) and Antonia. It did not go unnoticed. Tacitus offers alternative explanations for their absence. They may not have felt comfortable showing their grief in public, he says, or they believed people might see through their crocodile tears for the hypocrisy that it was. 'I do not find, in any historian or in the daily register, that Antonia, Germanicus' mother', he wrote:

> rendered any conspicuous honour to the deceased, though besides Agrippina, Drusus, and Claudius, all his other kinsfolk are mentioned by name. She may either have been hindered by illness, or with a spirit overpowered by grief she may not have had the heart to endure the sight of so great an affliction.[108]

Nevertheless, even here, he suspects the ill will of Tiberius and Livia at work, 'that their sorrow might seem equal to hers, and that the grandmother and uncle might be thought to follow the mother's example in staying at home'.[109]

There was to be no state funeral. Tacitus describes the actual day as 'desolate in its silence, distracted by lamentations'.[110] Rome's narrow streets were packed with mourners on their way to the *Via Flaminia*. Outside the city walls, lit torches blazed across the wide, open space of the Campus Martius. Soldiers turned out in their arms and armour, as if prepared for inspection by their commander. State officials and magistrates did not carry their badges of office, as if to appear as humble citizens. The crowds gathered on the parkland consecrated to Mars in front of the great Mausoleum of Augustus (fig. 9). The Roman historians do not record if a speech was given, but two fragments of an *eloquium* believed to have been for Germanicus have been found, carved on blocks belonging to the facing from the base of the monumental tomb.[111] Beneath the tree-covered earthen tumulus, deep within its concentric circles of arched vaults, were the caskets containing the ashes of Marcellus, Agrippa, Octavia, Nero Claudius Drusus, the brothers Caius and Lucius, and, most recently, Augustus himself. Agrippina led

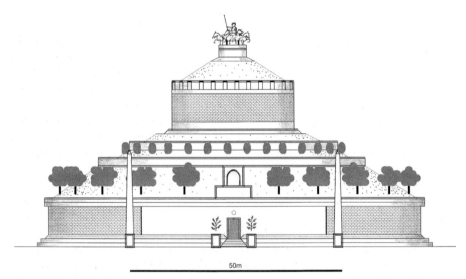

50m

Figure 9. Germanicus' ashes were placed in Augustus' mausoleum, Rome by his wife Agrippina after a long voyage from Syria. (Reconstructed by the author after H. von Hesburg)

her children silently past the two great obelisks and the bronze tablets, upon which were inscribed her grandfather's lifetime achievements. They walked slowly through the single doorway and down the dark, echoing passageway, illuminated only by flickering oil lamps. She reached a niche, which had been prepared in advance, and she carefully placed the urn in the dark space, uttered a prayer, and stood reflecting upon her loss. Then, she turned about and left Germanicus to rest for the ages. Outside, the people openly spoke of her as 'the glory of the country, the sole surviving offspring of Augustus, the solitary example of the old times'; and they looked up to heaven and the gods and 'prayed for the safety of her children and that they might outlive their oppressors'.[112]

Since dawn, the mood of the people had been sombre and resentful. Many had gone expecting a grand state funeral and were disappointed by what they saw. Others, who had attended the funeral of Drusus the Elder, compared what they had just witnessed with what they had seen some three decades before. They recalled the grandeur of that occasion, and the moving speech Augustus had given when he lauded the man's life and achievements, and compared it with Tiberius' present silence. They contrasted the aged Augustus, and his willingness to travel in winter from Ticinum to receive the body as the cortège made the long journey from Germania to Rome, with Tiberius, who now stayed at home. All the ceremony and trappings of a patrician funeral given to Drusus *pater* – the parade of the *imagines* of the Claudii and Iulii, the panegyrics spoken from the *Rostra*, even the pathetic laments of the crowd – were missing on this cold winter's day in January 20 CE.[113] They also contrasted the honours heaped upon Drusus and the meagre few granted to Germanicus. Yet, seen in the wider context, these criticisms seem unfair. After the death of Drusus, Tiberius had walked the entire journey on foot in front of the hearse, because it was a mark of *pietas* for his brother. He had attended his funeral and delivered the eulogy from the *Rostra* before the burning of the body, because it was in keeping with tradition for high-ranking Romans, such as accorded to Sulla, Agrippa and Augustus. He was not intentionally being disrespectful to his adopted son, whose body had been burned overseas. Tiberius had sent the *Cohors Praetoria* and officials to receive Germanicus' cremated ashes at Brundisium and ordered that they accompany them all the way to Rome. As for the claim of meagre posthumous honours, the Senate had already decreed them on 16 December, and they were fine distinctions for Rome's most popular citizen. Tacitus himself notes, 'granted that his body, because of the distance of the journey, was burnt in any fashion in foreign lands'.[114] This, therefore, was not intended to be a state funeral. In Tiberius' view, the family members were simply placing the urn in the family tomb. It was, in effect, a private ceremony. There were recent precedents for this. Caius and Lucius Caesar had each been cremated far from Rome and had not received funerals in the city, and the honours granted to Germanicus were just as substantial as theirs.[115] Tiberius was, thus, meticulously following standard protocol. His error was to misjudge the mood of the people. The people needed a response that reflected their pain, an assurance that the *princeps* cared. By staying out of view and not shedding tears in public, the head of state and his family were seen as cold and remote. The public responded to the perceived snub by turning their sorrow for the loss of Germanicus into scathing criticism of his adoptive father.[116]

The foul mood festered for weeks after the event. Finally, in late March or early April of that year, Tiberius was compelled to issue a public statement:

> Many eminent Romans had died for their country and none had been honoured with such passionate regret [as Germanicus]. This regret was a glory both to himself and to all, provided only a due mean were observed; for what was becoming in humble homes and communities, did not befit princely personages and an imperial people. Tears and the solace found in mourning were suitable enough for the first burst of grief; but now they must brace their hearts to endurance, as in former days the Divine Iulius after the loss of his only daughter, and the Divine Augustus when he was bereft of his grandchildren, had thrust away their sorrow. There was no need of examples from the past, showing how often the Roman people had patiently endured the defeats of armies, the destruction of generals, the total extinction of noble families. Princes were mortal; the State was everlasting. Let them then return to their usual pursuits, and, as the shows of the festival of the Great Goddess were at hand, even resume their amusements.[117]

The message was clear. The time for mourning was over. Romans must get on with their lives. He had done so himself when his own brother had died.[118] The proclamation had the intended effect. Businesses reopened and people went back to work.[119] The festival of the Magna Mater – the Megalensia – took place, as it always did, between 4 and 12 April: her temple was consecrated on the Palatinus Hill and her image was paraded through the streets to the Circus Maximus, followed by chariot races.[120] Yet Germanicus was not so easily forgotten. The public had a new spectacle to focus their minds on: the impending trial of Cn. Calpurnius Piso.[121]

The Trial

M. Piso had arrived ahead of his father to meet separately with Tiberius and Drusus.[122] The *princeps* received the man with courtesy. His son, however, was concerned about the allegations of Piso's involvement in Germanicus' death, and, while he professed he did not believe them, nevertheless, the meeting did not dismiss his concerns. Piso senior had arrived at Ancona and was making his way along the *Via Flaminia*. At one point on the journey, he intercepted *Legio* VIIII *Hispana* redeploying from Dalmatia to Africa, and he used the opportunity to flaunt his superior rank on the marching troops. Eventually, he took a ship down the Tiber to Rome, where, to everyone's consternation, he disembarked alongside the Mausoleum of Augustus.[123] It was a deliberately provocative act. In full daylight, Piso and Plancina and their retinue made their way through the crowds on the Campus Martius, arrogantly flashing their smiles at their joy to be back. They processed through the city to their lavish home on the Palatinus Hill, conspicuously located high above the Forum. Their house had been made all the more prominent by being decked out in garlands for a celebration. The wafting savoury aromas of cooking advertised the banquet being prepared for Piso's friends and followers.

The team seeking to prosecute Piso wasted no time. Normally, a case involving the allegation of poisoning would have been tried in the *quaestio de veneficiis*.[124] The following day, Veranius and Vitellius sought to file the application for the prosecution, but found themselves beaten to it by Fulcinius Trio.[125] As one of the new breed of legal professionals, he was keen to win the case and build his reputation. He had already asked the consuls for permission to file the indictment. Hardly had he finished filing the application than he was reproached by Germanicus' friends, who argued that, as accusers representing the deceased, it was *their* role, not Trio's, to file. Trio withdrew the application and sought to file a new case based on Piso's earlier career. The main case was given back to Veranius and Vitellius to present to the consuls. The consuls then asked Tiberius to take the case. He summoned his circle of close friends and advisers, and listened to the arguments presented by the prosecution and the defence, with Piso representing himself. Tiberius was apparently not yet aware of the convoluted nature of the case and of the many rumours circulating that implicated him in the death of Germanicus. Tiberius decided to refer the case to the Senate – not the *quaestio de veneficiis* – where Piso would be tried by his peers. Tiberius announced that he would personally attend the hearing, though not presiding as a judge. He had long been dissatisfied by the way in which cases were handled and, only five years earlier, chose to oversee them himself.[126] Even before that time, he had sat in on every known case involving the crime of *maiestas* – short for *maiestas minuta populi Romani*, 'the diminution of the majesty of the Roman people' – securing the defendant's aquittal in most cases, in a gesture of clemency (*clementia*). Knowing this, Piso would have had every reason to be optimistic about his own trial's outcome. Piso had assembled a defence counsel comprising some of Rome's great names, including M. Aemilius Lepidus, Livineius Regulus, and his own brother L. Calpurnius Piso – others having politely declined to represent him.[127] Drusus the Younger now decided to join the prosecution.[128] He joined with fellow advocates Servaeus, Trio, Veranius and Vitellius, and prepared his case notes.

The scene was set: the two sides had their teams in place and were eager to proceed. Outside the *curia* in the Forum Romanum, the crowds buzzed with excitement as they wondered how loyal Germanicus' friends would prove to be, speculating on the basis of their case against Piso, and how impartial Tiberius would remain during the hearings. Sentiment negative to Tiberius had never been so freely and publicly expressed.

Uniquely in recorded Roman history, we have both an official version of the trial and a reputable historian's account of it. A document survives, known to modern historians as the *Senatus Consultum de Cn. Pisone patre*, or 'Decree of the Senate Concerning Cn. Piso Senior', which summarizes the judgement of the conscript fathers at the end of the trial.[129] Like a set of meeting minutes, it provides an exceptional but contemporary account of the trial, and captures the authentic language used by the trial lawyers. In contrast, the account of Cornelius

Tacitus – prepared using his recollection of oral traditions he heard as a boy, and reference to official reports of the Roman senate (*acta senatus*) – was written some fifty years after the hearing.[130]

On the first day of the trial, the senators crowded into the high-ceilinged hall of the *curia* and took their seats across the wide aisle, according to their seniority. A composed Tiberius arrived and took his seat on the raised dais at the far end of the chamber.[131] Opening the proceedings, Tiberius gave a prepared speech (*oratio*). It was the very model of reason. The words recorded by Tacitus may be the actual words Tiberius spoke, since it is possible that he copied them directly from the official record. He began by stating that Piso had been Augustus' friend and representative. Tiberius reminded the senators that Piso had been appointed by him – on the advice of the Senate – to assist Germanicus in the administration of the East.[132] He quickly separated the matter of insulting behaviour by the accused towards his deceased son from the charge of his murder:

> Whether he [Piso] there had provoked the young prince by wilful opposition and rivalry, and had rejoiced at his death or wickedly destroyed him, is for you to determine with minds unbiased. Certainly, if a subordinate oversteps the bounds of duty and of obedience to his commander, and has exulted in his death and in my affliction, I shall hate him and exclude him from my house, and I shall avenge a personal quarrel without resorting to my power as emperor. If, however, a crime is discovered which ought to be punished, whoever the murdered man may be, it is for you to give just reparation both to the children of Germanicus and to us, his parents.[133]

Tiberius urged the conscript fathers, first, to consider whether Piso had committed treason (*maiestas*) by inveigling his way into the confidence of the troops, to incite the army to rebellion in an attempt to take Syria by force, causing civil war, or, in the words of the *Senatus Consultum*, diminishing the majesty of the Roman people. The second point was to prove whether Germanicus, a magistrate of the Roman state holding *imperium*, had, in fact, been murdered.[134] 'For my part,' he said:

> I sorrow for my son and shall always sorrow for him; still I would not hinder the accused from producing all the evidence which can relieve his innocence or convict Germanicus of any unfairness, if such there was'.[135]

The last charge was extortion. Standing accused with Piso were his wife, son and aides as accessories.

Tiberius sought an impeccably fair trial: this was not to be seen as a show trial with a foregone conclusion.[136] He urged the senators, of whom almost 300 were present, to keep an open mind as they considered the evidence to be presented. But there were harsh words, too, for Germanicus' friends. Tiberius criticized them for the manner in which they had displayed Germanicus' naked body – a humiliating act, in his opinion – to the non-Roman public in the forum at Antiocheia, and for spreading rumours that he had been poisoned, questioning pointedly 'if all this is still doubtful and requires investigation?'[137] He urged

1. Germanicus' father, Nero Claudius Drusus (Drusus the Elder), is shown on an *aureus*. The legend adds his imperatorial acclamation and war title, which his son adopted as his first name.

2. Germanicus' mother, Antonia Minor, was the daughter of M. Antonius. A beautiful and levelheaded woman she raised her son with an appreciation of tradition and family values.

3. Caesar Augustus saw great potential in Germanicus, and insisted that Tiberius adopt him to establish his place in the dynastic line of succession.

4. Tiberius was a fine soldier but a reluctant *princeps*. He treated Germanicus as fairly as his own son, Drusus Iulius Caesar (Drusus the Younger). Nevertheless rumours persisted of a strained relationship between Tiberius and Germanicus.

5. Agrippa Postumus, M. Agrippa's last surviving son, blew his chance at succeeding Augustus when he proved to be a wastrel and was sent into exile.

6. Handsome and good-natured, Germanicus was a patriot and loyal to his adoptive father.

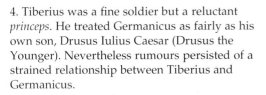

7. The earliest known depiction of Germanicus was unveiled at the consecration of the Ara Pacis on 30 January 9 BCE when he was five years old. While he holds his mother's hand Germanicus is presented as a confident and well-behaved patrician Roman boy.

8. Agrippina Maior (Agrippina the Elder) was the proud daughter of M. Vispanius Agrippa and granddaughter of Augustus. A confident and opinionated women, she was a devoted wife to Germanicus and a protective mother of their children.

9. Drusus the Younger was a quick-tempered man with a cruel streak, but enjoyed a close personal relationship with his adopted brother Germanicus.

10. Tiberius Claudius Nero was devoted to his older brother Germanicus. When he became Emperor, Claudius celebrated his brother's memory with coins and performances of his plays.

11. Nero Iulius Caesar was Germanicus' oldest son and most like him in looks and temperament.

12. Caius Iulius Caesar was Germanicus' youngest son. Raised in the camps of the Rhine legions, he was given the nickname Caligula, 'bootsy' and succeeded Tiberius as emperor.

13. *Legionarius* of the late first century BCE in a Montefortino-type helmet and chain mail shirt with oval shield and unsheathed *gladius* ready for action.

14. Scale armour offered better protection than chain mail and was often worn by middle-ranking officers, musicians and standard bearers.

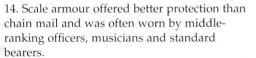

15. Replacing chain mail in the first century CE was articulated plate armour. The rectangular *scutum* also replaced the oval design.

16. Lightly armed Germanic warriors, often equipped only with a *framea* and shield, could still inflict damage on heavily armoured Roman troops by using agility, surprise, terrain and numbers.

17. The *centuria* of eighty men, led by the *centurio*, aided by his *optio*, was the basic combat unit in the Roman legion. Other officers relayed commands by music and motions of a *signum* or *vexillum* standard. A legion comprised sixty centuries.

18. For his amphibious invasion of Germania Magna, Germanicus ordered a fleet of a thousand ships of different designs to be built to carry men, matériel and livestock. This scene from Trajan's Column shows the range of vessels which might have been used to support the amphibious campaign.

19. The thick stonewalls of Salona protected the city's loyalist inhabitants from siege by Illyrian and Pannonian rebels during the War of the Batos of 6–9 CE.

20. Germanicus began his military career by commanding a unit of irregular troops during the War of the Batos. He led them to victory over the Mazaei, whose territory in Pannonia was nourished by the Vrbas River, in 7 CE.

21. Despite difficult terrain, Germanicus led successful assaults on rebel cities located among mountain range of the Dinarides in 8 CE.

22. Germanicus stands prepared for war as Tiberius descends from his triumphal chariot under the auspices of Augustus on the *Gemma Augustea*.

23. Germanicus and his wife Agrippina the Elder face his brother Claudius and his wife Agrippina the Younger on the *Gemma Claudia*.

24. Before setting off to take up his new assignment as governor general, Germanicus is depicted hailing Tiberius on the 'Grand Camée de France'. Agrippina and Caligula stand either side of him.

25. Deep inside Germania Magna, Germanicus' troops were subject to ambushes from the local Germanic nations who used the cover of trees to mask their movements.

26. Germanicus' fleet ran aground on the coastal mudflats of the Wadden Sea when he misjudged its tides.

27. The double Arch of C. Iulius Rufus in Saintes, France, is dedicated to Tiberius, Drusus the Younger and Germanicus Caesar.

28. At Nikopolis, Epirus, Germanicus stopped to visit the Actian War memorial and view the site of the sea battle in which both his grandfathers, Augustus and M. Antonius, had faced each other as adversaries.

29. *En route* to Syria Germanicus visited several of the coastal Greek-speaking cities of Asia Minor like opulent Apameia.

30. At Ilium Germanicus visited the site of the Trojan War which he had studied when reading Homer during his school days.

31. Germanicus established Cappadocia as a province within the Roman Empire in 18 CE without force of arms.

32. Germanicus travelled overland from Antiocheia to Artaxata, Armenia, perhaps even using this surviving section of Roman road at Tall 'Aqibrin in Syria.

33. Following in his grandfather Antonius' footsteps, Germanicus toured Egypt, taking a cruise down the Nile.

34. 'I have been sent by my father to set in order the overseas provinces' state lines 10–11 of P. Oxy 2435 (Recto), a contemporary account of Germanicus' actual address to the people of Alexandria on his arrival in Egypt.

35. On his accession in 37 CE, Caligula promoted his filial association with Germanicus on coins.

36. To celebrate the twentieth anniversary of Germanicus' triumph for his campaigns in Germania Magna and the recovery of the standards lost by Varus at Teutoburg, Caligula minted a commemorative *dupondius*.

37. Germanicus' profile graced the small change (*aes*) of Caligula's reign.

38. This *as* minted under Claudius imitates the one issued by his predecessor, with the profile of Germanicus reversed. The hole drilled in antiquity suggests it was worn as an amulet.

39. After his death in 19 CE, statues of Germanicus were erected all over the Roman Empire. This semi-nude figure from Gabii imitates statues of gods and heroes.

40. The spectacular 'Germanicus of Amelia' is the most complete bronze statue of the Roman commander in full military regalia to survive from the ancient world.

41. *Le Mort de Germanicus* by Nicolas Poussin began a new trend in Classical period art.

42. Benjamin West's *Agrippina Landing at Brundisium with the Ashes of Germanicus* depicts the scene vividly described by Tacitus in Book 3 of the *Annals*. Britain's King George III much admired the painting.

43. J.M.W. Turner's fantastical *Ancient Rome: Agrippina Landing with the Ashes of Germanicus* was first exhibited in 1839 to critical acclaim. Agrippina stands on the right bank.

44. King Ludwig II of Bavaria inspired Carl Theodor von Piloty to paint *Thusnelda im Triumphzug des Germanicus*. Germanicus is the silhouetted figure on the far left in the chariot.

those who could to speak eloquently in defence of Piso; and equally, he expected the prosecution to pursue their case robustly and with persistence:

> In this, and in this only, will we place Germanicus above the laws, by conducting the inquiry into his death in this house instead of in the forum, and before the Senate instead of before a bench of judges. In all else, let the case be tried as simply as others. Let no one heed the tears of Drusus or my own sorrow, or any stories invented to our discredit.[138]

Having established his expectations, it was now for the trial lawyers to argue their cases.

Two days were allocated for the prosecution to lay out the charges.[139] The court would recess for six days to consider the evidence. Piso would then be given three days to conduct his defence. Fulcinius Trio spoke first. Perhaps intending to portray Piso as a dishonourable man, the sort no respectable Roman would trust, he presented a rambling, somewhat irrelevant list of accusations about the defendant's term as governor in Hispania. Then Servaeus, Veranius and Vitellius each rose and spoke in turn. They delivered their words with earnest hearts, but Vitellius was notably eloquent in laying out the case against Piso. On the count of treason, he said the accused had been motivated by personal hatred (*odium*) of Germanicus. He had gone out of his way to incite the legions to revolt, to oppress the allies, and to be savagely cruel (*crudelitas*) to the commander's companions, friends and an officer of the Roman army, showing a complete lack of humanity (*humanitas*).[140] The prosecution now launched their accusation that Piso was the murderer. The word they used to describe Piso was *feritas*, meaning 'half-animal' – an extremely pejorative term to apply to a Roman nobleman. As to the method used, Vitellius alleged that he had poisoned Germanicus' food at a banquet. He explained that Piso had the opportunity as the man laying beside him on the lead couch, and he had the motive. Circumstantial evidence pointed to Martina as the source of the poison, because she had been a close friend of Plancina.[141] She had since been transported to Italy under guard on Cn. Sentius' orders to await the trial. Unfortunately for the prosecution team, she never reached Rome. She had apparently concealed poison of her own concoction in a knot of her hair, and died while in custody in Brundisium, though Tacitus adds that 'no symptoms of suicide were discovered on her person'.[142] In the absence of solid forensic science or a star witness, the murder charge was always going to be hard to prove. In summing up the case for the prosecution, Vitellius said that Piso 'destroyed Germanicus himself by sorceries and poison, and hence came those ceremonies and horrible sacrifices made by himself and Plancina; then he had threatened the *res publica* with war, and had been defeated in battle, before he could be tried as a prisoner'.[143]

When his turn came, Piso responded with a vigorous defence. His dislike of Germanicus was well-known, he said, and not a secret. However, the charge of murder levelled agianst him was preposterous. He even offered up his own household slaves for torture – standard Roman procedure when questioning slaves as witnesses – and insisted it be done.[144] The inference was that they would break

under pain and fully confess what they had seen, which was nothing. Throughout the proceedings, Piso was often seen to be holding a scroll. He did not, at
any time, disclose the contents of this document, but it nevertheless aroused
curiosity.[145] His friends repeatedly declared that it was a letter from the *princeps*
himself, in which he gave instructions referring to Germanicus. Piso, they said,
intended to produce it before the Senate and use it to scold Tiberius in the event
that he did not come to Piso's rescue.[146] For the moment, he kept its contents
concealed.

Outside the Senate House, the public were in a foul mood. In their minds, Piso
was guilty of Germanicus' murder and they wanted justice. The doors to the
Senate House were firmly shut to them, but they loudly shouted their threats
that, if Piso was acquitted, they would resort to violence.[147] The people found
a way to vent their anger and daubed the walls of many public buildings with
graffiti exclaiming:

GIVE US BACK GERMANICUS!

and people in all districts of the city shouted out these words through the night
until their voices were hoarse.[148] Some, impatient with the speed and direction of
the trial, carried out their own kind of summary justice by trashing Piso's statues.
Toppling them from their plinths, the rioters dragged them to the Gemonian
Steps (*Scalae Gemoniae*) – the so-called 'Stairs of Mourning', which led down
steeply from the Arx on the Capitolinus to the Forum Romanum below – and
began smashing them up. Hearing about the fracas, Tiberius quickly dispatched
men from the Praetorian Cohorts to bring a halt to the wanton destruction,
and had the statues restored to their bases.

For the time being, the husband-and-wife team of Piso and Plancina held
steadfast; but the trial was not going at all well for Piso. It seemed to him that the
senators would probably accept the prosecution's accusations of treason. That
meant a humiliating end for Piso. Sensing she was at threat of her own life,
Plancina now distanced herself from her husband and prepared an independent
defence.[149] In her favour, she enjoyed the protection of Livia, the *princeps'*
mother, and to her she appealed for help. Whether she actually did so or not, it
was widely believed at the time that the Augusta was secretly interceding on her
behalf. Her decision was a crushing blow to Piso. He was now left to defend
himself alone. He hesitated as to what to do next; but, at his sons' urging, he
returned to the Senate one last time to continue his defence. The senators railed
against him, pouring scorn on his reputation. Piso took all this in his stride, but
hard to bear was seeing his mentor and friend Tiberius, sitting icily cool, listening
unemotionally to the tirades launched at his deputy. At the end of that gruelling
day, he was carried in his litter back to his sanctuary on the Palatinus Hill.[150]
There, he retired to his private office, where it seemed to those in the house that
he continued to work on his closing statement. He wrote on a fresh sheet of
papyrus, rolled it up, and sealed it using his signet ring to indicate that it was
authentic. He gave the letter to one of his freedmen. Piso took some time to relax
with his wife and, after she left his bedroom late that night, he ordered the doors

to the room closed. An uneasy stillness fell upon the great house. At daybreak, Piso's manservant knocked on the door. Hearing no sound inside, he entered timidly. He found his master dead, laying in a pool of blood. Examining his body, it was found that his throat had been cut. An army issue sword was found lying on the floor close by.[151] Was it the handiwork of one of Seianus' men, or perhaps of Plancina, hoping to make it look like his work? The extant sources are silent on the matter.

That morning, the Senate assembled once again. A visibly saddened – perhaps dissembling – Tiberius lamented the death of Piso. His melancholy, however, may have had as much to do with the loss of a friend as with politics: he complained that it now made *him* look like the villain.[152] He repeatedly asked how Piso had spent his last night, and listened to the various sycophantic replies. Finally, he read out the suicide note, which the freedman had produced. In it, Piso explained that, against an overwhelming conspiracy of his enemies and the universal hatred it incited, he had decided he had no chance of proving his innocence. He stressed his loyalty to Tiberius and his predecessor Augustus, and begged the current *princeps* to spare the lives his sons, Cnaeus and Marcus. In the letter, he conspicuously made no mention of his wife. Many, both in the Senate House and outside, questioned whether it was a suicide. The weapon – a military-issue *gladius* – and the manner of the death-blow – a strike to the neck – seemed odd to Romans, for whom the more typical method was to slash the wrists and lay in a hot bath. It was never satisfactorily resolved.

On 10 December 20 CE – over a year since the Senate had voted honours for Germanicus – the conscript fathers assembled to give their verdicts. On the count of *maiestas*, the court found Piso guilty. The charge of murder, however, did not stick. The senators were unconvinced that Germanicus had been murdered by poisoning at Piso's hand as alleged by the prosecutors.[153] Plancina, meanwhile, benefited from her connection with Livia. She was pardoned – much to the chagrin of Tiberius, who was annoyed by the interference of his mother in affairs of state.[154] Whether Plancina was ever culpable would not now be proved in court.

Outside the Senate House, the verdict on Germanicus' murder was met with dismay. 'What the laws secure on behalf of every citizen', they grumbled, 'had to Germanicus alone been denied. The voices of Vitellius and Veranius had bewailed a Caesar, while the emperor and Augusta had defended Plancina'.[155]

The senators now considered the sentences. Piso was dead by his own hand, but the consul, Aurelius Cotta, moved that his name should be expunged from the public register (*fasti*). Prominent people in the Roman world worried a great deal about their reputation and of being forgotten (*oblivio*) after their deaths.[156] Piso's removal from the *fasti* was to deny his very existence as a noble man in the public memory (*memoriae*) forever. The shame of it would also be borne by the family members who survived him. His estate should be dissolved: half would go to the public purse, the other to Piso's son Cnaius, who was probably never in the East, but would be required to change his name.[157] For his complicity in the act of treason, Piso's son Marcus was to be stripped of his rank and banished from

Rome with an allowance of 5 million *sestertii*.[158] The Calpurnii Pisones, however, would be spared the ignominy of banishment and extinction. Piso's suicide provided Tiberius with an unexpected opportunity to show clemency (*clementia*). Through his intercession, the sentences were mitigated: Calpurnius Piso's name was not to be erased from the record, citing the examples of M. Antonius, who had waged war on Rome, and Iulius Antonius, who had dishonoured Augustus' house, and yet whose names had both remained in the register.[159] The estate was not broken up, and M. Piso, who was acquitted, inherited his father's entire household.[160]

The advocates for Germanicus – Valerius Messalinus and Caecina Severus – proposed that an altar and golden statue of Vengeance be erected in the Temple of Mars Ultor.[161] This, too, Tiberius overruled, saying that such honours were intended only for victories over foreigners, not over fellow Romans, and that it would be better for all to grieve silently. Messalinus proposed that the avengers of Germanicus – Agrippina, Antonia, Drusus, Livia, and Tiberius himself – be publicly thanked for their restraint (*moderatio*).[162] The absence of the name of Germanicus' brother, Ti. Claudius Nero, was pointedly noted by L. Asprenas to his peers. It was duly added. Finally, in recognition of their service in representing the case for the prosecution, the *princeps* proposed to the Senate that Servaeus, Veranius and Vitellius be appointed to the priesthood (*sacerdotia tribuendi*).[163] Ambitious Fulcinius Trio was not overlooked, either, in this distribution of accolades: he received a promise of imperial support for his promotion, but with a polite warning not to spoil his eloquence by harbouring resentfulness.

Based on the *acta senatus* recorded by the scribe, the official wording of the proceedings from the trial were agreed for publication, and copies cast in bronze of the *Senatus Consultum* were made for distribution across the Empire, to be displayed in its principal cities and all army bases, and 'in whatever place seemed best to Ti. Caesar Augustus'.[164] It served as a clear warning to government officials of the punishments which would be meted out to traitors. Significantly, the decree omitted any reference to the formal charge of the murder of Germanicus. It was, in effect, a whitewash. With time for reflection, the Senate may have decided that there was nothing to be gained by reminding readers of the decree of the mysterious demise of its young prince. They deemed it better to gloss over the matter, rather than to raise more questions and prompt speculations, especially those beloved of conspiracy theorists which might point the finger of suspicion at the *princeps*. In fact, the cause of his death was never properly determined. As far as Tiberius was concerned, the matter was now closed. The memory of Germanicus Iulius Caesar had been honoured. To emphasize the point, the Senate duly recorded in cast bronze tablets that Tiberius had 'exceeded the devotion (*pietas*) of all parents' in showing his grief for Germanicus, which was 'so great and so constant'.[165] Most people took their cue from this, but not all. 'This was the end of avenging the death of Germanicus', writes Tacitus, 'a subject of conflicting rumours, not only among the people then living, but also in after times'.[166] Important to Tiberius and the Senate was that the threat of civil war had been averted, the supremacy of the imperial family had been acknowledged, and the unity of the Roman state had been preserved.[167] The bronze tablets memorialized Germanicus for as long as the Roman Empire endured.

Around the Roman world, some people began worshipping the *genius* or departed spirit of Germanicus. In Anticaria in the Spanish province of Baetica, the *pontifex Caesarum* Cornelius Proculus paid for an inscription to be erected that confirms the worship of Germanicus.[168] The existence of *flamines* of the cult of Germanicus is also attested by inscriptions found in Lusitania (modern Portugal) and Vienna (Vienne on the Rhône).[169]

Early in the following year, the Senate received a letter from the chief of the Chatti nation, Adgandestrius, with a promise to eliminate Arminius, if the Romans would only provide the means.[170] Tiberius dismissed the offer outright, saying that the Romans avenged themselves on their enemies, not by secret deceptions, but openly using 'spades and spears'.[171] Tiberius' new policy of strategic patience with his Germanic neighbours would yet prove effective. With the region free of direct Roman rule for twelve years, and Marboduus having since found asylum at Ravenna, Arminius had grown arrogant and sought to be king over his coalition allies. It was an unpopular move. In a violent struggle, he was killed by one of his own kinsmen. Arminius died aged 37, within a year of his nemesis' passing.[172]

Chapter 7

The Fall of the House of Germanicus

Sons and Daughters

The years immediately following Germanicus' death were critical for his family. In 20 CE, Nero Iulius Caesar (plate 11) marked his official declaration of manhood on his fifteenth birthday.[1] Tiberius proposed that he be fast-tracked through the *cursus honorum*, with an exemption from the requirement for service on the board of junior magistrates (*vigintiviri*), citing the exceptions that Augustus had made for him and his brother Drusus, and suggesting that he start as *quaestor*, five years before the stipulated time. The sacred position of pontiff was also awarded to him at that time. These were conspicuous honours, indeed, to be heaped onto such young shoulders. On the first day in his elevated positions, as he entered the Forum in his official capacity, a cash donative was distributed to the plebs, who were overjoyed to witness the eldest son of Germanicus reach manhood and begin his public career so auspiciously. To bind the families closer, Nero was married to Drusus the Younger's daughter, Iulia.

Following in his brother Nero's footsteps, in 22 CE, Drusus Iulius Caesar completed his ceremony of manhood and was inscribed in the official rolls as a citizen, and donned his *toga virilis*. All the honours previously accorded by consent of the Senate to his elder brother were now granted to him.[2] The mood between leading members of the family was amiable and fraternal. During the discussion in the Senate House, Tiberius praised his own son Drusus the Younger for showing the same kindly manner he himself displayed towards the young sons of Germanicus. Drusus would grow up to be a very different man from his elder brother, Nero. He was impetuous, had a wild temper, and harboured a lust for power, which led to frequent fights between the siblings. It was partly explained by jealousy, borne of his belief that his mother really preferred Nero to himself.[3]

The youngest of the boys, Caius 'Caligula' – who disliked the nickname, but liked his *praenomen* even less – was still at school.[4] He lived with his mother and was the darling of the family; but, already, there were disturbing rumours of his odd behaviour. One of these was that he habitually committed incest with his under-age sisters, while still himself a minor.[5] On one occasion, when staying at his grandmother's house, Antonia found him lying naked in bed with Iulia Drusilla. Despite the efforts of Agrippina and Antonia, the absence of a father-figure left the impressionable boy vulnerable to a life of indiscipline and self-indulgent behaviour.

Germanicus' daughters enjoyed rather mixed fortunes. Agrippina the Younger inherited her mother's beauty along with her strong personality, but earned a reputation for ruthlessness, ambitiousness and domineering behaviour. Into her young teens, she lived with her mother. Tacitus reports that he found a copy of Agrippina's personal memoirs, which were not widely circulated, but whose contents revealed all the secret goings-on in lurid detail, as the fortunes of her family changed.[6] In 28 CE, on her thirteenth birthday, Agrippina was betrothed to her paternal second cousin, Cn. Domitius Ahenobarbus, the son of the former governor of Germania. The Domitii were an old and respected Roman patrician family. Through his mother, Antonia the Elder (sister of Germanicus' mother), Domitius was a great-nephew of Augustus, first cousin to Claudius, and thus second cousin to Agrippina and Caligula. He was a man of considerable means, but had a reputation for being extravagant, haughty and excessively cruel.[7] The couple divided their time between the up-market resort town of Antium and Rome.

Her sister Iulia Drusilla was brought up under the supervision of her mother. Her reputation was tarnished, however, by the rumours of improper relations with her brother Caius. In 33, at the age of seventeen, she was married to L. Cassius Longinus, a respected friend of Tiberius, who had served as consul three years earlier.[8]

Iulia Livilla shared her older sisters' company at home as a child. She was betrothed to P. Quinctilius Varus, son of the ill-fated governor of Germania province. However, he was prosecuted for treason in 27 and the marriage did not proceed. Five years later, she married M. Vinicius, a mild-mannered but talented orator from a small town outside Rome, who rose to be consul in 30 and served with L. Cassius Longinus.[9]

Agrippina the Elder devoted herself to raising her children, just as Germanicus would have wanted. She jealously championed their cause, both in private and in public. The mass of the Roman population still remembered her affectionately as the grand-daughter of Augustus, the devoted wife of Germanicus, and the glory of her country.[10] To the reigning *princeps*, however, she came to be perceived as an irritation. A catalytic event, which permanently damaged her reputation in Tiberius' eyes, was the obdurate stance she took in supporting her cousin Claudia Pulchra in a case against her husband, Domitius Afer.[11] He had accused his wife of infidelity with another man, and for plotting against Tiberius using poison and sorcery. Agrippina was impetuous by nature, and, while he lived, her husband provided a moderating influence over her. On his deathbed, Germanicus had even warned her to hold her tongue when moved to anger, and for years, she had done precisely that. On the occasion of the trial of her friend, however, and without a thought to the consequences, she burst upon a sacred ritual being conducted by Tiberius as he was offering sacrifice to the Divine Augustus. She accused him of siding with the husband, merely because Pulchra and Agrippina were friends. Tiberius rebuked her sternly with a line chosen from Greek poetry, reminding her that 'she was not wronged because she was not a queen'.[12] Her friend and her paramour were still found guilty. Tacitus pinpoints this as the pivotal event causing the deterioration in their relationship. Her emotional state did not help. As the years passed, she had gradually come to terms with the loss of

Germanicus, but she could no longer bear the loneliness widowhood imposed on her.[13] Unfortunately for her, Tiberius did not respond well to irrational demands. When she pleaded in a hysterical state – Tacitus states that she was with suffering some kind of sickness at the time – with Tiberius to find her a husband, he avoided the request by leaving the room without giving her an answer. Some said he feared that, should she marry again, the pair could become political rivals in opposition to him.

Indeed, there was already talk of an emerging opposition to Tiberius, calling itself the *partium Agrippinae*, 'the party of Agrippina'.[14] Sensitive to the rumours, Tiberius became increasingly wary of his daughter-in-law. In this frame of mind, her seemingly innocent remarks could be misconstrued. In 24 CE, during a prayer ceremony, the pontiffs offered prayers for Tiberius' health, but added the names of Germanicus' sons Nero and Drusus.[15] Their motives, asserts Tacitus, were sycophantic rather than inspired by love, but, learning after the event about the addition of his grandsons' names, Tiberius summoned the pontiffs and demanded to know if Agrippina had put them up to it. They flatly denied the accusation, but the *princeps* nevertheless rebuked them, even the ones who were related to him or were prominent individuals.

While he lived, Germanicus provided a counterbalance to the *princeps*, through his respect and awe of him.[16] 'Tiberius changed so much after the death of Germanicus', Dio writes, 'that, whereas previously he had been highly praised, he now caused even greater amazement'.[17] In the early years of his principate, he busied himself with the work of state, taking little time off.[18] He ruled diligently and fairly, and did not exceed his powers, using the courts to settle disputes with private citizens like everyone else.[19] In time, however, he came to rely more and more on the willing assistance of his Praetorian Cohort commander. His extraordinary rise to prominence would see the final demise of Germanicus' surviving sons – all except one.

The son of Seius Strabo, prefect of Egypt in the early teens CE, L. Aelius Seianus was born in the small Etruscan town of Vulsinii into an equestrian family.[20] He rose through the ranks to become *praefectus* of the Praetorian Cohorts. He ingratiated himself to C. Caesar and quickly gained the trust and confidence of Tiberius. He was a tough and ruthless soldier, but one able to feign humility when the situation called for it. Perhaps it was these qualities which appealed to the *princeps*, himself a soldier, who felt able to speak openly and freely with Seianus in a way he could not with others. Driving Seianus may have been a lust for power, though his true motive is not known and he carefully hid it behind a mischievous and hypocritical mind. He gradually won the confidence of prominent senators through the high praise of Tiberius, who referred to him as 'the partner of his toils' (*socium laborum*).[21] Soon, statues were being erected to the man in the *fora*, the theatres, and even the headquarters buildings of the legionary bases around the empire. One of his most consequential decisions was to bring all the *Cohortes Praetoriae*, up to that time scattered across Italy, into a single, purpose-built base camp located in Rome.[22] He exploited the proximity of the Praetorians to his advantage. A natural networker, he took great pains to get to know key officers and men, and earned their trust and loyalty.

Blocking his rise to ultimate power, however, were Tiberius' sons and grandsons.[23] First and foremost of these was Drusus the Younger. Tiberius' own son was the one man who would stand up to his upstart rival from Tuscany.[24] In a casual dispute, the irascible and hot-tempered Drusus retorted by punching Seianus in the face. Never one to forgive or forget a slight, to avenge himself, Seianus ingratiated himself with Drusus' wife Livilla and, not long after, was sharing her bed while her husband was away. He had no particular love for the woman, but anyway convinced her of his intention to marry her, seducing her into his scheme to share power with him – and involving her in a plot to kill Drusus. To show he meant what he said, he divorced Apicata, his wife and the mother of his three children. The second obstacle to power was Seianus' class. He was a member of the *ordo equester* and not a patrician, which meant he did not have the social and political status to succeed the *princeps*. Marriage to Livilla was one way he could raise himself up and join the patriciate.

With the consent of the Senate, in 22 CE, Drusus the Younger was granted the tribunician power.[25] Germanicus had never received it, perhaps on account of his age. At 35, Drusus was about the same age as Tiberius when Augustus had granted him this important power.[26] Drusus was now the second most powerful man in Rome, but he was not being marked out as heir apparent. Indeed, his role seems to have been one of guardian to the sons of Germanicus, who were the true heirs of Tiberius, in keeping with Augustus' wish to see their father rule.[27] Again, Tiberius was following precedent, when Augustus had appointed him as guardian of Caius and Lucius twenty-five years earlier. Yet, even as Seianus pretended to be an upright official of state and a loyal servant of the *princeps*, his mind turned to how he could eliminate this obstacle to his ambitions.[28] Tacitus suggests that he chose a slow-acting poison, the effects of which could be interpreted as death by natural causes.[29] To administer the poison, a eunuch by the name of Lygdus was chosen.[30] The assassin carried out the plan exactly according to instructions. The toxins gradually took hold of Drusus and he succumbed to a long drawn-out sickness. The doctor apparently failed to diagnose poisoning. Drusus finally died on 14 September 23 CE. Tiberius was distraught by the loss of his son, but, when faced by grieving consuls at a meeting of the Senate, he reminded them of the decorum required of their office, and recovered his composure. The same civil and military honours earlier granted to Germanicus were now accorded Drusus the Younger, augmented by several new ones.[31] The general population, by whom Drusus had never been truly loved, observed the formalities of grieving, but did no more.[32] If there was an investigation into the cause of his death, it was either inconclusive or deliberately suppressed by Seianus. The murderers were not pursued. Tiberius believed the cause of death was disease due to his bad lifestyle.[33] For the moment, Seianus had got away with murder.

Yet, if he thought Drusus' removal would advance his cause, Seianus was to be disappointed. Two years after her husband's death, Livilla, now enthralled by her gutsy paramour, insisted that Seianus marry her and, obligingly, he petitioned

Tiberius for permission to do so.[34] The *princeps* asked for time to consider the request, and then, to Seianus' great disappointment, declined it.[35] At issue was his social class, which, as a man of the equestrian order, was lower than Livilla's. It must then have been clear to the pretender to the throne – if, indeed, that is what he aspired to be – that, short of assassinating Tiberius, he would never attain supreme power. Unthwarted, however, Seianus connived to increase his power and influence by other means. His chosen weapon was access. Much of Rome's political business was done during the early morning *salutatio*, at which friends and petitioners greeted their patron and asked for help.[36] Every day, crowds gathered outside the *princeps*' house for the call *Caesarem iam salutari!* – 'Caesar is receiving callers!' – and lists of visitors were published. To be denied an audience was considered ominous. Who compiled the list had considerable influence. Seianus now assumed that role, isolating Tiberius from visitors and lobbyists, and permitting him to meet only those who did not threaten his interests. Growing more confident in his position, Seianus now encouraged Tiberius to move from Rome to a less public place.[37] Tiberius, now of a mind to retire, agreed. At first he relocated to Campania, but crowds of people from the local towns gathered every day, hoping to catch a glance of their emperor.[38] Tiberius issued an edict, warning the people not to disturb him, and posted soldiers around and about to enforce it. It was to no avail and, finally, he retreated across the 3-mile wide strait off the coast of Surrentum and retired to the island of Capreae (Capri). There he built an immense palace consisting of twelve houses upon a crag overlooking the Bay of Naples.[39] Seianus now had what he wanted. Tiberius' absence from Rome meant that he could exclusively control who had access to the emperor and what he could know about affairs in the city. All written correspondence, too, would have to pass through his hands.

Without their guardian, Tiberius made new arrangements for the care of the two eldest sons of Germanicus. Before he left Rome, when speaking of Drusus the Younger's death to the Senate, Tiberius is reported as having said:

> Senators, when these boys lost their father, I committed them to their uncle, and begged him, though he had children of his own, to cherish and rear them as his own offspring, and train them for himself and for posterity. Drusus is now lost to us, and I turn my prayers to you, and before heaven and your country I adjure you to receive into your care and guidance the great-grandsons of Augustus, descendants of a most noble ancestry. So fulfill your duty and mine. To you, Nero and Drusus, these senators are as fathers. Such is your birth that your prosperity and adversity must alike affect the State.[40]

The boys became more prominent public figures. Nero Iulius Caesar Germanicus was seen as a trusted and empathetic figure. On the occasion of successful impeachment, for abusing their positions, of the procurator of Asia, Lucilius Capito, and his predecessor C. Silanus, the provincials responded gratefully by erecting a temple to Tiberius, the Augusta and the Senate. On the Asian cities' behalf, Nero spoke in praise of the senators' support. The senators' response was affectionate, motivated in part by their fond memory of Germanicus, and many saw in the young man's face and heard in his voice his illustrious father's.[41] 'The youth, too, had a modesty and a grace of person worthy of a prince', writes Tacitus, adding ominously, 'the more charming because of his peril from the notorious enmity of Seianus'.[42]

Victims of Seianus

Increasingly, a personal connection with Germanicus or Agrippina became a liability. Seianus launched attacks on C. Silius and T. Sabinus.[43] Silius had been Germanicus' commander and went on to see over seven years' active service on campaign in Germania, winning a triumph for his victories. He boasted that his legions were more loyal than the other commanders', whose men seemed inclined to mutiny – a claim hardly designed to instill confidence in an already suspicious-minded Tiberius. Silius' wife, Sosia Galla, was a close friend of Agrippina. Silius was prosecuted on trumped-up charges of complicity in a rebellion and of extortion, and a treason case was brought before the Senate.[44] Silius denied his accusers their entertainment, when he took his own life. Sosia was banished and part of her property confiscated.[45]

In 28 CE, Sabinus was dragged off to jail, merely because of his friendship with Germanicus. Even as Seianus' agents made life uncomfortable for Agrippina and her children, Sabinus remained a loyal friend – one of the few left, by that time – by frequently visiting them at their home and accompanying them in public.[46] He was tricked by one of the Praetorian Cohort commander's agents, a man named Latinius Latiaris, into believing that he was a trusted companion and confidant, though, all the while, his criticisms of Seianus and Tiberius were meticulously recorded and relayed back. Finally, Latiaris arranged for certain senators to hide in the attic of what Sabinus had been lulled into believing was a safe place where he could speak his mind freely.[47] To his horror, his words came back to haunt him when Tiberius addressed the people in his New Year's letter and accused Sabinus of plotting against him.[48] The man was hauled off for execution. The *princeps* wrote to thank the people for having brought an enemy of the Roman state to justice, adding that he lived in constant fear of his life from the treachery of foes – a coded reference to Agrippina and Nero. Agrippina's nephew Asinius Gallus then submitted a motion in the Senate that Tiberius should reveal what he knew, but Seianus intervened to pacify him and, for the moment, nothing was disclosed.[49] By then, even trouble caused by barbarians on Rome's frontiers did not worry the Senate as much as the fear they had of Seianus.[50] Germanicus' old general, Seius Tubero, was also dragged before the courts despite his poor health, but was acquitted.[51]

Seianus' machinations against Agrippina increased in intensity and cruelty. Through his agents who were in Agrippina's confidence, he convinced her that she would be murdered by poison, and that, when dining with Tiberius, she should avoid eating at his table.[52] Unable to disguise her abject fear at a family dinner, one evening, she ate nothing. Tiberius noticed her demeanour and offered her fruit with his own hand. Now even more suspicious, she passed the fruit directly to one of her slaves. Bemused but annoyed by the slight, Tiberius turned to his mother reclining next to him and whispered that no one should be surprised if he meted out harsh punishment to someone who implied that he was a poisoner. A rumour also circulated at the time that there was a plan to kill Agrippina, and that Tiberius would act in secret to carry out the deed, which only heightened her anxiety.

Her sons, too, found themselves the focus of attention from Seianus' wicked intentions. Nero, in particular, as next in succession to Tiberius, was the subject of false accusations. His youth and natural modesty, but lack of experience of the real world, made him susceptible to accepting guidance from men acting with ulterior motives.[53] They urged him to speak up and display his self-confidence. Though not motivated by ambition, Nero would occasionally make ill-considered comments, which Seianus' spies dutifully reported, then took out of context and exaggerated, to implicate the young man in conspiracies.[54] They tried to embarrass and belittle him in public. One agent of Seianus would avoid meeting him; another, having exchanged greetings, would suddenly turn away; others would open a conversation, then suddenly break it off; while others would laugh at him from a distance. It mattered not whether Nero spoke or remained silent: all his reactions were noted and deemed suspicious, and implicated him in one imaginary crime or another. His wife revealed to her mother Livilla how he lay awake at night and talked, and she promptly passed along the information to Seianus.

His brother Drusus had since become ensnared in Seianus' web of intrigue.[55] Tiberius's first minister cynically engineered a rift between mother and brother, promising Drusus the throne if he would assist him in bringing down Nero. Drusus seemed amenable to the offer; but he was naïve if he thought that Seianus was acting out of any love for him. Even his wife was complicit in his downfall. Drusus had married Aemilia Lepida, the great-granddaughter of L. Sulla and Cn. Pompeius, and daughter of M. Aemilius Lepidus, his second cousin.[56] Lepidus was an independent-minded senator who had defended Calpurnius Piso at his trial, and rejected the emperor's offer of the governorship of Africa in 21 CE. The marriage was fraught from the outset and she pursued her husband with endless accusations.[57] In 36, she was accused of having committed adultery with a slave, and, rather than subject herself to the humiliation of a public trial, she took her own life. Perhaps as a result of her accusations, Drusus was declared a public enemy.[58]

Emboldened by his powerful place in society, and with the *princeps* safely away in his island palace, growing ever more suspicious of his daughter-in-law and her eldest son, Seianus now openly taunted Agrippina and Nero.[59] Wherever they went, Seianus' soldiers followed them. Every word they spoke was recorded. Every person they met was reported. Agents paid by Seianus urged them to flee Rome and seek sanctuary with the army of Germania. When they entered the crowded Forum, they were mockingly advised to embrace the statue of the Divine Augustus and appeal to the people and Senate for protection. Mother and son bravely tried to shrug off these malicious taunts, but, having ignored them, they were then accused of *considering* acting upon them. Rome had become unbearable. For a while in 27 CE, she retreated to her luxury villa in the seaside town of Herculaneum (Ercolaneo) in Campania, but even there she was kept under guard during her stay.[60] Adding to the pressure on Agrippina, she was cruelly separated from her son. In 29, Nero was declared a public enemy, taken into custody, and imprisoned on the island of Pontia (Ponza).[61] There, he was constantly threatened with torture, but, four years after his arrest and before being subjected to the final horrors of the noose and hooks, he committed suicide.[62]

In 28 CE, Tiberius agreed that Germanicus' daughter Agrippina could marry.[63] The man chosen was Cn. Domitius Ahenobarbus, son of the man who had taken Rome's army beyond the Elbe River. The choice was significant and quite deliberate. By marrying into the old Domitii family, Tiberius could claim a connection as great-nephew to Augustus through Domitius' grandmother Octavia. Meanwhile, relations between her mother and Livia had never been easy. Tacitus reports:

> Feminine animosities increased the tension as Livia had a stepmother's irritable dislike of Agrippina, whose own temper was not without a hint of fire, though purity of mind and wifely devotion kept her rebellious spirit on the side of righteousness.[64]

However, while she was alive, Agrippina came to no physical harm. That was about to change. The following year, Livia died a natural death on Capri, aged 87.[65] At her simple funeral, Germanicus' youngest son Caius – now 17 years old and still not yet having officially reached manhood – delivered the panegyric from the *Rostra* in the Forum Romanum, his first public speech in the city.[66] Tiberius made excuses and did not attend in person and overruled many of the posthumous honours the Senate voted her.[67] While Tiberius' mother lived, Seianus had felt constrained to keep his real intentions hidden.[68] Now that she was dead, the full force of his wickedness was unleashed against the House of Germanicus.[69] A letter was delivered to the Senate – believed to have been held back while Livia was alive – containing words pointedly directed against Agrippina and Nero. It accused them not of the grave crime of treason against the Roman State, but absurdly charged Agrippina of using insolent language and having a defiant spirit, and Nero of having unnatural passions and behaving in a profligate manner. The conscript fathers, now in awestruck terror of Tiberius' favourite, proceeded to debate the matter in the House. One senator, Iunius Rusticus, moved that trivial matters often led to greater crimes and that the fall of the House of Germanicus 'might one day move the old man's remorse'.[70] Word of the proceedings spread outside into the Forum, and ordinary people gathered hot-temperedly outside the *curia* carrying images of Germanicus' wife and eldest son. They shouted their blessings upon the emperor, mingled with cries that the letter was a forgery and that it was not Tiberius' wish to see his daughter-in-law and her son implicated in a plot to bring him down. Tensions rose. Inside the building, the Senate continued to debate the matter, while outside, the people carried on their protest. The two sides finally did not come to blows. Not long after, copies of speeches – probably works of fiction – making various allegations against Seianus were circulated.[71] Word of them reached Tiberius. Sensing trouble, he published an edict, in which he repeated his censure of Agrippina and Nero, but he also reprimanded the Roman people, stating that his dignity had been violated, and insisted that he alone should be permitted to rule on the matter.[72] The Senate responded immediately with a statement that they were prepared to exact vengeance, but they were held back in acting upon it by the *princeps'* strong hand. A stalemate had been reached. Nothing more ensued.

For Germanicus' wife and children, these were extremely dangerous times. With his brother Nero out of the way, Seianus now sought to bring down Drusus, until recently a compliant puppet in his mischievous schemes. Seianus filed charges that the young man had had illicit relations with the wives of all the leading men of Rome with promises to marry them, and, over the ensuing pillow talk, had learned what their husbands thought and said, with an intention to blackmail them.[73] Tiberius ordered Drusus to Rome, but there was a short-lived rumour – apparently spread, among others, by Tiberius' freedmen – that Drusus Caesar had fled to the Cycladic Islands and had then been seen on the Greek mainland.[74] He was intercepted, but was reported as having escaped custody and was intent on travelling to Egypt or Syria to lead the army of his father. Rallying to his cause were young men who believed in a better future and, together, they momentarily enjoyed wide popular support. But Seianus' agents quickly found out about of his scheme. A cat-and-mouse chase ensued, as he crossed the Aegean Islands, landed at Piraeus, sailed on to Corinth, and traversed the narrow Isthmus to arrive at Nikopolis, where he was finally caught and questioned by men sent by the governor of Achaea, Poppaeus Sabinus. The man they interviewed professed to be the son of M. Silanus, and, without more proof to confirm he was not who he claimed to be, he was released. Sabinus sent a report on to Tiberius.[75] Wherever Drusus actually was the whole time, it was to be his last dalliance with freedom. He was declared a public enemy, arrested, dragged back to Rome, and locked up in a room in the *princeps'* house on the Palatinus.[76]

In 30 CE, Tiberius finally consented for Seianus to marry Livilla – sister of Germanicus – and, in so doing, to become his son-in-law, as well as making him a patrician in the process.[77] Since Drusus the Younger's death, Seianus had become Tiberius' most trusted confidant and partner in running the affairs of state.[78] The men of the Praetorian Cohorts still loved him.[79] The Senate, too, had fallen under his spell. During the course of the following year, however, Seianus' fortunes changed dramatically. The surviving accounts are somewhat confused about the reason why. In Tiberius' own sketchy autobiography, which Suetonius had access to seven decades later, he offers another reason when he writes, 'I have punished Seianus, because I have found him bent upon the destruction of the children of my son Germanicus' – a testament to the popular affection which his adopted son and family still had, and its usefulness as a cover for extreme action.[80] It was a blatantly revisionist view of history. The imperial biographer did not believe the claim, for, as he pointed out, Tiberius had, himself, already put one of Germanicus' boys to death.[81] Tacitus is silent on the matter. Valerius Maximus, the contemporary apologist for Tiberius, cites a plot to commit parricide and to overthrow the *princeps*.[82] Inscriptions surviving from the time indicate that the officially-sanctioned version of events was that Seianus was planning to assassinate Tiberius.[83] Juvenal also repeated the claim, in one of his *Satires*.[84] In modern times, however, some doubt has been cast on this explanation. Seianus had much to lose by removing Tiberius. His power base was relatively weak, as he had neither status in law, nor the support of the aristocracy, the people, or the legions – he no longer even had direct control of the Praetorian Cohorts, as they were now under the command of Naevius Sertorius Macro.[85] Seianus demonstrably had soft power, standing at the centre of a network of informers motivated by favours and fears: everyone seeking advancement illuminated his world with reports of everything the emperor and their friends did and said, while Seianus kept the *princeps* on his island home completely in the dark.[86] One possibility is that Seianus was actually plotting against Germanicus' youngest son, Caligula, as part of the broader plan to remove Agrippina's children. His scheme may actually have worked, had it not been for the alertness of a senior member of the imperial family. Germanicus' mother, Antonia, seems to have detected a conspiracy of some kind, and wrote a letter to Tiberius about it.[87] He still held the wife of his deceased brother in the highest esteem. Perhaps, as a direct response to receiving the letter, Tiberius requested the 19-year-old Caligula join him in Capreae from the start of September 30 CE.[88] Tiberius was evidently now deeply suspicious of his partner and of his motives. He may have come to realize, just before it was too late, that Seianus was not so much devoted to him as to promoting his own agenda. Cassius Dio suggests that Tiberius now actively set out to ensnare his prime minister, using the enticement of the consulship to trick him into thinking that he was 'Sharer of my Cares', and the use of the affectionate form of address in letters and pronouncements as 'my Seianus'.[89] On 1 January 31 CE, Seianus was sworn in as consul jointly with Tiberius Caesar, his fifth time in this role.[90] Seianus had now risen to the highest public office: his birthday was publicly celebrated, his gilded statues received offerings, and people referred to him as 'Tiberius' colleague'.[91] All he lacked to make him the *princeps*' equal was the tribunician power, and, perhaps to lull him into a false sense of security, Tiberius even encouraged a rumour that this honour was being planned for him.[92] His fall would be all the more spectacular for it.

Caligula's career had since begun in earnest. Tiberius appointed him to the priesthood and indicated that the young man would become his successor.[93] As fast as doors opened for Germanicus' youngest surviving son, Seianus' options were suddenly closing. There were already clues that Tiberius was withdrawing his favour from his first minister. As often as his dispatches praised Seianus, he wrote others criticizing him.[94] Certain of his friends were honoured, while others were disgraced. Seianus grew increasingly concerned at these confusing signals. Dio suggests that he might have considered fomenting rebellion among the army, since it was likely that the soldiers would obey him, but he soon realized how dangerous that strategy was, when he saw how genuinely pleased the Roman people were at the words of praise directed at Caligula, 'out of reverence for the memory of Germanicus, his father'.[95] Men who had once supported Seianus now began deserting him and clustered around the new rising star of Tiberius' grandson.

When Seianus asked the *princeps* for permission to visit him in Capreae, Tiberius declined, ordering him to stay in Rome and advising that he would be travelling to the city in person soon.[96] It was a ploy to keep him in Rome while he planned his demise. The story of Seianus' downfall is preserved by Dio and reads like a climax to a modern thriller. Arriving unannounced on a dark mid-October night in Rome, the newly appointed *praefectus praetorio*, Sertorius Macro, explained the *princeps'* plan to Memmius Regulus (the other one of the two consuls, still loyal to Tiberius) and Graecinius Laco (commander of the night watch).[97] At dawn next morning, Macro went to the Palatinus, where he found Seianus and alerted him to expect the award of tribunician power and to attend that day's session of the Senate to receive it; the importance of the day was emphasized by reports that a shooting star had been seen.[98] The conscript fathers were meeting at the Temple of Apollo on the Hill and Seianus raced inside.[99] The trap was set. Leaving the night watch guarding the temple under the command of Laco, Macro then went to the Praetorian Camp, where he revealed his new authority, promised bonuses for their loyalty, and stayed to ensure that they stayed out of trouble as the events of the day unfolded.[100] In the temple, Tiberius' seal was broken and the letter was read out.[101] Seianus' face beamed as he imagined his great future. His supporters among the conscript fathers cheered him in anticipation of the honour about to be granted him. The letter began innocuously enough, but, as the reading proceeded, there was censure of his conduct, two senators were singled out for criticism, and finally, instructions were issued that Seianus must be kept under guard. Then, formal charges were read out. The trap was sprung. Realizing the danger they now faced by being seen with him, his supporters slipped out of the temple. The praetors and tribunes now surrounded Seianus to prevent him from sneaking away. Regulus then requested Seianus to step forward.[102] At first, he did not appear to understand. 'Seianus, come here!' he demanded, raising his voice. It was only after the third time that Tiberius' former favourite replied, 'me? you are calling me?' Laco now stood by his side. As the senators booed him, he was escorted out of the building and down into the Mamertine Prison in the Forum Romanum.[103] As word spread of his downfall, the common people pelted him and jeered him, venting their frustrations at the man whose agents had abused them over years of terror. At a secret meeting of the Senate in the Temple of Concord, just feet away from the jail, he was condemned to death. On 18 October 31 CE, Seianus suffered a traitor's death: strangulation with a cord and the disgrace of having his body tossed down the Gemonian Steps.[104] His children were also executed – his young daughter having been raped first, so that she would not die a virgin – before being thrown down the Steps.[105] His wife Apicata was spared, but learning about her childrens' fates, she composed a letter with a statement concerning the truth about the death of Drusus the Younger directed at Livilla, sent it to Tiberius, then took her own life.[106] The revelation of Seianus' and Livilla's culpability for

Drusus' murder by poison exasperated and tormented him until the last days of his life.[107]

Seianus having been eliminated, Agrippina and her surviving sons hoped for better times. Rumours circulated that there might even be a reconciliation between daughter-in-law, grandson and Tiberius – but the bitter old man's hatred of them still raged.[108] Drusus, still in confinement in 33 CE, suffered terribly. It was reported that, after eight days of continuously being fed the most meagre prison-grade rations, he resorted to chewing on the stuffing of his mattress.[109] He was driven nearly mad by regular beatings at the hand of the sadistic centurion, Attius, assigned to ensure that he did not escape. Before the year was over, he was dead. It was a tragic end to the career of a man once seen as Germanicus reborn. According to accounts available to Tacitus, one version told of how, in the event of Seianus attempting a *coup d'état*, Macro was to immediately release Drusus from house arrest and put him at the head of the Roman people, to lead a popular counter-revolution.[110] The coup did not take place, however, and the young man was never called upon to save the state. Instead, he died miserably and ignominiously through starvation, alone in a room on the Palatinus. Even death would not free him. Tiberius was intent on defaming his grandson's memory. The Senate was subjected to a daily reading of the tediously mundane details of Drusus' harassed life, even of his most intimate and rambling mutterings, carefully extracted from household slaves and reported by the men who guarded his prison room, looking for evidence of treasonous thoughts.[111] The Senate, which had once been enamoured of the young man, now feigned horror at what it heard about his treasonous comments from the steady stream of unedited gossip, but was equally awestruck by Tiberius' willingness to expose his own kin in this wretched way. The revelation that a son of Germanicus had met such a miserable end, nevertheless, led to an outpouring of popular grief among the common folk.

Agrippina was now, herself, arrested on a charge of attempting to flee and taking refuge, and she was banished to Pandataria (Ventotene) – the same bleak, rocky island to which the elder Iulia had been banished by her father, Augustus.[112] She reproached Tiberius for it, but his response was to order the centurion guarding her to beat her – so brutally, in fact, Suetonius records that she lost one eye.[113] Unbowed and unbroken, the proud mother of Germanicus' children vowed to starve herself to death, but the duty guard had orders to force-feed her: she must be made to live and suffer. In the end, her wish was fulfilled and she died of starvation on 18 October 33.[114] When news of the loss of the bold-spirited grand-daughter of Augustus and loyal wife of Germanicus reached Rome, the populace plunged once again into mourning. Away on his island home, Tiberius showed neither sympathy nor remorse. For him, the irritating thorn in his side had been plucked out. Perhaps to salve his conscience, or to deflect criticism levelled at him, he alleged that she had had sexual relations with Asinius Gallus, a man he deeply despised because he had married his former wife, Vipsania Agrippina, the only woman he ever truly loved.[115] The truth of it was never proved, but the allegation was a calculated slur on her good name. Tiberius also observed that the day she died, by an uncanny coincidence, was the second anniversary of the execution of Seianus, and he noted that he had shown her clemency by not insisting that she suffer the same public humiliation as his former first minister.[116] The Senate passed a vote of thanks in favour of the *princeps* and decreed that this ill-omened day of double deaths should be marked in perpetuity, and golden offerings were to be given to Iupiter Capitolinus to propitiate him. Shortly after, Plancina (the wife of Piso implicated in Germanicus' murder and who had been subject of various criminal charges, herself) took her own life.[117]

After Agrippina's death, Caligula and his sisters were taken into the care of their grandmother, Antonia. That year, Tiberius finally decided upon the men Agrippina's daughters could take as husbands.[118] His chosen fiancées for them were conservative but respectable men. Drusilla was now married to L. Cassius Longinus, a man from an old but honourable plebeian clan. Iulia was given the hand of M. Vinicius, a respectable man from an up-and-coming family from the provinces. In a letter to the Senate, Tiberius actually complimented the young men. Caligula married Iunia Claudia, daughter of M. Silanus, a man known for having learned how to disguise a fierce temper.[119] Caligula was now the last remaining male heir of the House of Germanicus. The lonely *princeps* had taken a liking to the young man, even over his other grandson Tiberius (Gemellus). By now, Tiberius had lost interest in affairs of state.[120] He appointed Caligula *quaestor* in 33 and promised to advance him through the *cursus honorum* five years earlier than the stipulated age, as had been done for his father and brothers.[121] The following year, he announced that Caligula and Gemellus would be his joint heirs, with equal shares of his estate.[122] He never returned to Rome, preferring the comforts of his luxurious island home or his private estates on the mainland in Campania.[123] There were scandalous rumours that the emperor indulged in dark perversions, which involved cavorting with sexual athletes (*spintriae*) and young boys, humiliating guests at drinking parties, and gloating over summary executions.[124] While staying at the Villa of Lucullus, he was taken ill.[125] Tiberius died on 16 March 37, aged 78. He had reigned for twenty-three years. He may have died a quite natural death, but soon there were rumours that Caligula was somehow involved – by administering a slow wasting poison, or denying him food during his convalescence, or suffocating him with a pillow.[126] For many, it mattered not: they were just glad that the long tyranny of Tiberius was finally over.[127]

The New Germanicus

The Senate hailed Caligula as the new *princeps* on 18 March and, ten days later, he entered Rome to a hero's welcome. With the arrival of the young C. Caesar, there was great optimism that a bright new era had begun. 'On account of his connection to Germanicus', writes Suetonius, 'the fondness with which they remembered his father and the pity they felt for the terrible fate of his family, the people of the Roman Empire had high hopes for their new *princeps*'.[128] The 24-year-old began his reign by leading the funeral of Tiberius on 3 April. It was a magnificent occasion and Caligula personally delivered the eulogy, bringing many onlookers to tears with his rhetoric – a talent inherited from his expert father.[129] Tiberius's body was ceremonially burned and his ashes were deposited in the Mausoleum of Augustus. Presenting the will of his predecessor to the Senate, Caligula declared it null and void – thereby cutting his cousin Gemellus off from his inheritance – on the basis that Tiberius had not been of sound mind and body at the time he wrote it.[130] Nevertheless, he respected Tiberius' wishes with regard to the other benefactors, not only paying bonuses to the army and the night watch, but to actors and gladiators too, and gained popularity by doing so.[131] A year later, Gemellus was dead.

Caligula hurried off to Pandataria and Pontia to gather up the neglected ashes of his mother and brother Nero. Almost a decade had passed since her ignominious death. According to Suetonius' account, Caligula turned the occasion of his return into a major spectacle. He arrived at Ostia aboard a bireme, displaying a banner flag (*vexillum*) flying from the stern, and cruised up the Tiber to Rome. Disembarking at the quayside along the Campus Martius at midday, when the crowds were at their largest, the casket containing Agrippina's ashes was placed on two biers, and carried ceremoniously upon the shoulders of the city's most illustrious men and members of the equestrian order to the Mausoleum of Augustus.[132] With his own hands, Caligula placed her casket in the nîche beside her beloved Germanicus'. On the large, plain slab – which is now on view in the Tabularium al Campidoglio, Rome – were carved in beautifully formed letters, the obituary:

THE BONES OF
AGRIPPINA, DAUGHTER OF M. AGRIPPA,
GRAND-DAUGHTER OF THE DIVINE AUGUSTUS, WIFE OF
GERMANICUS CAESAR
MOTHER OF C. CAESAR AUGUSTUS
GERMANICUS, PRINCEPS[133]

He authorized sacrifices to be made to his mother's memory each year in the Circus Maximus, paying for a carriage to bear her *imago* and tour the chariot racetrack at the start of sporting events.[134]

Tapping into the deep vein of good will still felt towards his father, Caligula was keen to emphasize his filial connection. He renamed September the month of Germanicus – significant, because it immediately followed the month named after Augustus (fig. 10).[135] He issued gold and silver coins (plate 35), which the more affluent members of society used to settle their accounts, showing his own profile with a laurel wreath on the obverse and his father's unadorned head on the reverse.[136] In the lower denomination bronze or copper *aes*, which shoppers and soldiers used to buy their daily snacks and draughts of wine at the *thermopolia* or market stalls, Caligula's moneyers at the Temple of Iuno Moneta in Rome produced a coin (plate 37) with a profile of Germanicus gazing out to the left.[137] He is boldly presented as a confident, vigorous and youthful man. Surrounding

XVIIKGERMANĠS

Figure 10. An extremely rare inscription showing the name Germanicus in use for the month of September following an edict by Caligula. The date '17 days before the Kalends of Germanicus' is 16 September.

his exquisitely engraved portrait with its strong facial features, finely detailed hair and muscular neck, the inscription reads:

GERMANICUS CAESAR, SON OF TIBERIUS AUGUSTUS, GRANDSON OF THE DIVINE AUGUSTUS.

Here is a Roman in the finest tradition with the best of family connections.

The most dramatic coin issued with the consent of the Senate by the mint in Rome for Caligula in honour of his father, however, was a large medallion-like bronze *dupondius* (plate 36), weighing over 15g (0.53 ounces.).[138] Likely minted in the year of the twentieth anniversary of Germanicus' triumph of May 17 CE, it shows him standing in a finely-decorated triumphator's four-horse chariot on the obverse, while the reverse bears an image of Germanicus advancing to the left in the full regalia of an *imperator*, with his right arm outstretched (fig. 7, plate 36).[139] His left arm supports a legionary *aquila* and the full figure of the military commander stands between the inscription:

STANDARDS RECOVERED, THE GERMANS DEFEATED

While it did not show the new *princeps'* head or name, no one could be left in any doubt that Caligula – a man completely lacking any military credentials, but whose very name was given to him by the soldiers of the Rhine army – was descended from a true Roman hero, who restored the nation's honour in the forests of *barbaricum*.

In the east, where Germanicus had been a popular imperial supervisor, cities minted their own commemorative coins. In Asia, one leading city minted a silver *drachm* showing the diademed head of Augustus on one side and Germanicus' profile – complete with stubble – on the other.[141] The officials of Smyrna in Ionia issued a low denomination piece showing the draped bust of Agrippina facing her bare-headed husband, with their son's profile on the obverse.[142] Across the sea on the island of Crete, the *duoviri* Dossennus Pulcher and Varius at Knossos issued a bronze coin showing Caligula's head on one side and Germanicus' on the other.[143] Not to be outdone, the nearby town of Gortyn minted its own coin showing the laureate head of Caligula on the 'heads' side and his father's on the 'tails'.[144]

To the surviving members of his family, Caligula was remarkably respectful. In the same year he assumed the throne, he made Germanicus' brother Claudius a suffect consul to serve alongside himself.[145] He conducted himself in the most dutiful manner towards his sisters, but paid particular respects to his grand-mother Antonia, in whose care he had been brought up for part of his life.[146] He saluted her as Augusta – the title formerly granted to Livia Drusilla – and appointed her to be priestess of Augustus. He also granted to her and his three sisters all the privileges of the Vestal Virgins.

His reign started well enough, but it did not last.[147] The pressure of living as a favourite in the household of his manic-depressive Uncle Tiberius, perhaps witnessing terrible things a child should never see, had apparently affected him psychologically.[148] Then, quite suddenly, he fell ill. People held their breath and prayed for his swift recovery. After his convalescence, he emerged a different man – headaches tormented him and he believed that he was now a god to rival Jove.

His grandmother, the Augusta Antonia, was now 73 years old, and she had been Drusus the Elder's widow for forty-six of those. Though honoured by her grandson, she witnessed the monster he had become.[149] She had been widowed early, outlived her son Germanicus, and witnessed the death of her rogue daughter Livilla. Her sole surviving son, Claudius, was a disappointment to her. In September or October 37 CE, she finally passed away. Rumour had it that Caligula did not attend the funeral, preferring to watch the flames consume her body from the comfort of his *triclinium* while he dined.[150]

Many saw Caligula's erratic behaviour as insanity.[151] There were summary arrests, confiscations, exiles and executions. Caligula never fitted the mould of his grandfather or father as a soldier, but military operations were carried out under his auspices. There was a successful march into Germania, apparently as far as the territory of the Suebi, in 39 or 40 CE, imitating what his father had done after the infamous mutinies of the Rhine army.[152] It was while in Germania Superior that he exacted revenge for the events of twenty-six years earlier:

> Before he left the province, he formed a design of the most horrid cruelty to massacre the legions which had mutinied upon the death of Augustus, for seizing and detaining his father, Germanicus, their commander, and himself, then an infant, in the camp. Though he was with great difficulty dissuaded from this rash attempt, yet neither the most urgent entreaties nor repre-sentations could prevent him from persisting in the design of decimating these legions. Accordingly, he ordered them to assemble unarmed, without so much as their swords, and then surrounded them with armed horse. But finding that many of them, suspecting that violence was intended, were making off to arm in their own defence, he quitted the assembly as fast as he could, and immediately marched for Rome, bending now all his fury against the Senate, whom he publicly threatened, to divert the general attention from the clamour excited by his disgraceful conduct.[153]

That same year, there was a farcical attempt at an invasion of Britannia, in which the troops allegedly picked up sea-shells from a Gallic beach and claimed them as trophies of war against the sea god Neptunus.[154] In the mockery of a triumph that followed, Gauls were dressed up as Germanic warriors in a display which convinced no one.[155] The reign of terror was too much even for members of the Praetorian Cohorts, the wing of the army which derived many exclusive privileges from its *princeps*. Cassius Chaerea, a former centurion who had served under Germanicus and since been promoted as a tribune of the Praetorians, felt that he had been routinely humiliated over particular words Caligula chose as passwords for the watch, and led a plot to murder him.[156] On 24 January 41 CE, the assassins struck. Germanicus' youngest son, once the darling of the soldiers, fell to the ground bleeding to death, slain by an officer of his own élite body-guard.[157] When the population learned of the news, they were at first too terrified to believe it, fearing that it was a trick to expose traitors.

The assassins were thorough in extinguishing the bloodline of Caligula. They also slew his wife, Milonia Caesonia, and smashed their only child's head against a wall, killing her instantly.[158]

Chapter 8

The Germanicus Tradition

The Memory of Germanicus

Caligula's death left a dangerous vacuum at the apex of Roman society. Soldiers stormed through the houses of the imperial family hunting for the murderers. What they found was the timid and terrified figure of Caligula's uncle. Rather than slaying him, the soldiers decided that he should now be their *princeps*.[1] Germanicus' brother, the lame and stammering Ti. Claudius Nero, unexpectedly found himself ruler of the Roman world.[2] Presented with a man they had often considered a fool to replace another they had considered insane, the Senate at first resisted.[3] When the Praetorian Cohorts demonstrated their support of Claudius, the Senate finally relented.[4] As with his nephew before him, he lacked credibility in the eyes of the Senate and the people, but in particular, the army of Rome. The reluctant *princeps* Claudius needed to quickly gain their confidence, to avoid meeting the same fate as his deeply flawed predecessor. His fraternal relationship to Germanicus certainly helped, and Suetonius notes that Claudius took every opportunity of honouring his brother.[5] On a trip to Neapolis (Naples), he attended a drama contest and brought out a Greek comedy in honour of his brother – by which he probably means one of the several comedies Germanicus penned.[6] The so-called *Gemma Claudia* (plate 23), a five-layer sardonyx cameo, made in around 49 CE and now in the collection of the Kunsthistorisches Museum Vienna which may have been commissioned by a member of the imperial family, appears to show Claudius and his wife Agrippina the Younger, facing Germanicus and his wife Agrippina the Elder.[7] He also issued coins to emphasize the connection. The mint produced large quantities of the low-value copper or bronze *aes*, the ancient equivalent of small change, which closely replicated the style struck by Caligula five years earlier, except in one detail.[8] Curiously, the portrait on the obverse (plate 38) faces right: it is as though Claudius' coin-makers felt compelled to engrave an all-new style bust. Furthermore, compared with the portrait engraved by Caligula's moneyers, the Claudian Germanicus is a noticeably bulkier, less athletic figure – visually more like Claudius, in fact. Yet it was truly to his father, Nero Claudius Drusus – the first Germanicus – that he looked for an endorsement.[9] In a society that championed paternal virtues, Caligula had proved the value of exploiting the connection to *his* father, and Claudius copied the idea. Nevertheless, there was benefit to him in setting his own story in a wider context, by promoting the entire imperial family. An altar at Ravenna features just such an example: the frieze appears to show the figures of Antonia, Drusus, Germanicus, Livia and the Divine Augustus. Drusus wears the panoply of a commander, but Germanicus is shown clad in a toga, stripped to the waist exactly like the figure of Augustus, sporting the same exquisite musculature.[10] The intention was clearly to make Germanicus appear god-like to the provincial onlooker.[11]

Claudius initially gave the name Germanicus to his son from his fateful marriage to Valeria Messalina, but, following his invasion of Britain, two years later he renamed him Britannicus.[12] Claudius surprised everyone when he married his brother's daughter Agrippina the Younger and adopted her son by Cn. Domitius Ahenobarbus, renaming him Nero Claudius Caesar Drusus Germanicus.[13] Thus, the knotty branches of Germanicus' family tree entwined, such that his grandson by adoption was now destined to become *princeps* jointly with his nephew Britannicus. In the meantime, Claudius tried and had executed the daughters of Drusus the Younger and Germanicus – both called Iulia – on unsupported charges, and denied them the right to a defence.[14] Claudius himself died in 54 CE – possibly by poisoning – and Britannicus' life ended tragically months later, just one day before his fourteenth birthday.[15] Nero was sole ruler, Agrippina's ambition having been a large factor in securing the throne for him. Nero privately schemed to remove her from his life, but it would be no easy task. The daughter of Germanicus was clever and popular. When his advisor Seneca the Younger proposed to approach the military to carry out the assassination, his colleague Sex. Afranius Burrus suggested that they would flinch from carrying out the order, because of their loyalty to the memory of her father (*memoria Germanici*).[16] Agrippina the Younger eventually died – under mysterious circumstances – in 59 CE at the age of 43.[17] Her life's work had been in vain, for his twelve-year reign turned out to be an epic failure.[18] Nero's only child, Claudia Augusta, died three months after birth and when he committed suicide on 9 June 68 CE – after being declared a public enemy by decree of the Senate – the direct bloodline of Germanicus ended.[19]

The men who immediately followed Nero – Galba, Otho, Vitellius and Vespasian – were keen to distance themselves from the dynasty of Augustus. It was the Flavian emperor Titus who finally re-evoked the glories of the Julio-Claudian past, in a series of 'restoration' coins, which began to appear from 79 or 80 CE. One of these great Romans was Germanicus Caesar, highlighting the fact that, even sixty years after his death, the man still had a reputation worth celebrating. The engraver of the new coin chose, as his model, the *aes* of Caligula's time with the left-facing Germanicus.[20] He reproduced the same physical features – the confident gaze, the hair grown long at the back, and the muscular neck – and even the inscription of the original. It is only on the reverse that the name of Titus is discreetly revealed.

Enjoying the patronage of the Flavian emperors in the 70s and 80s CE, Josephus began work on his encyclopaedic *Antiquities of the Jews* (*Antiquitates Iudaicae*). In writing the history of his own people, he faithfully reported on Germanicus' activities in the region. He was able to refer to other earlier accounts describing the Roman's life, and cited the widely-held belief that Germanicus had been poisoned.[21] None of these earlier accounts survives.

A few years earlier, Pliny the Elder, who had served with the Roman army across the Rhine, published his twenty volume *History of the German Wars*

(*Bellorum Germaniae*), the catalyst for which, he later related to his nephew, was a visit by the ghost of Nero Claudius Drusus, who implored him to save his name from oblivion. This was an account of 'all the wars we have waged against the Germans', and would probably have covered Germanicus' campaigns of 14–16 CE.[22] Sadly, none of it survives. We know it was one of the sources that his friend Cornelius Tacitus consulted in composing his own *Annals of Rome from the Death of the Divine Augustus* (*Ab Excessu Divi Augusti*), because he acknowledges referring to it.[23] Of all the extant accounts, it is Tacitus' *Annals* that presents the most in-depth political and military history of Germanicus' life. He covers the period of the mutiny of the Rhine army, the campaigns in Germania Magna, his travels around Greece, Asia Minor, the near East and Egypt, the final tragic hours of his premature life, the emotional aftermath that saw Agrippina bring his ashes to Rome, and the trial of Piso. It was published during the confident and tolerant reign of Trajan (98–117 CE), whom the Romans called *optimus* – 'best' – and the book enjoyed great acclaim while the author lived. Its popularity thereafter waned, and it was only temporarily restored when the Emperor Tacitus (275–276 CE) – who claimed to be connected by direct lineage to Rome's greatest historian – issued an order to make copies to save it from neglect (*incuria*). By the sixth century, Tacitus' fame had sunk even further into obscurity, as evidenced by Cassiodorus, who made reference in his own work merely to 'a certain Cornelius'.[24] Nevertheless, it was Tacitus' account of events of the early principate that would come to dominate the historical and artistic portraits of Germanicus painted in the post-Roman period.

Tacitus' near contemporary, Suetonius Tranquillus, prefaced his biography of Caligula in the *Lives of the Caesars* (*De Vita Caesarum*) with an account of the life of his father.[25] It is the most complete of the surviving accounts, in that it follows the arc of Germanicus' life from birth to death – albeit cursorily – and reveals the attractive personality of the man. By pairing father and son, Suetonius dramatically contrasted the life of a worthy man against that of a young wastrel. His influential book was published during the reign of Hadrian (117–138 CE) and it continued in circulation well into the fourth century, when other authors used it as a model to produce biographies of the later Roman emperors.

Writing in the 190s and 200s CE, Cassius Dio presented Germanicus as a central figure in Books 56 and 57 of his annalistic panorama of 1,400 years of Roman history. Dio introduced Germanicus in the context of the 'Wars of the Batos', followed him back to Rome, and thence to Germania, to put down the mutiny and avenge the blot of humiliation at Teutoburg, recalling an omen that 'doubtless had a bearing' on his fate, and briefly covered the trial of Calpurnius Piso.[26] His monumental history in eighty books remained influential and was copied and abridged by various individuals as late as the twelfth century.[27]

While historians preserved accounts of Germanicus' deeds and achievements, popular legend and state occasions also kept alive the memory of the young Caesar. Tacitus could recall, from his youth, stories told by elders about the letter Calpurnius Piso allegedly clutched in his hand during his trial, and inferred that it contained instructions from Tiberius to his deputy to rid him of Germanicus.[28]

Commenting on the distinctions created for Germanicus immediately following the news of his death, Tacitus writes that 'many of these honours still remain' (i.e. in the early second century CE), though he qualifies his statement by adding, 'some were at once dropped, or became obsolete with time'.[29] Yet, well into the reign of Severus Alexander (222–235 CE) – fully two centuries after his death – military units were still required to observe that, '9 days before the Kalends of June', public prayers should be held for the birthday of Germanicus Caesar.[30]

Antiquity Revived

After the Roman Empire collapsed, its books were preserved by the monks of western Europe and the Byzantine Empire. Within them, the name of Germanicus Caesar survived. Word by word, line by line, the monks copied entire manuscripts. By this means, the *Aratus Phaenomena* ascribed to Germanicus was saved. The earliest known 'modern' copies date to the ninth century, but the poem gained in popularity only in the fifteen, when printed editions appeared in 1474, by Benincontrius in Bologna, and in 1488, by Pisanus in Venice.[31] The poem has been in print almost continuously since then and it can still be found, with a little effort, in a French translation by A. Le Boeuffle and in English by D.B. Gain.[32] It is an impressive achievement, considering that Augustus' own *Res Gestae* only first appeared – incomplete – in an edition by the Dutch scholar Buysbecche, following his visit to the Sultan Soliman at Amasia in Asia Minor in 1555, at the request of Ferdinand II.[33] Other than his own and Germanicus', no other works penned by Augustus' family members have come down to us.

Copies of Tacitus' *Annals* also survived – strangely, in two parts. One portion, dating to the ninth century, was copied in Fulda in Germany. It contained books 1–6 (covering the life of Germanicus) and acquired the name 'First Medicean'.[34] The other part, containing the remaining ten books of the *Annals* (called the 'Second Medicean'), were copied in the eleventh century, in the Benedictine monastery of Monte Casino in Italy. Some 600 years later, Pope Leo X (1475–1521) purchased the First Medicean and brought it to the Vatican, where, with his blessing, the printed edition of books 1–6 of the *Annals* appeared in 1515.[35] Initially, it was seen as a dull chronicle, compared to the popular works of Cicero and Livy, then in wide circulation, which were considered to be uplifting reading; but Tacitus enjoyed a surge of public interest from the later part of the sixteenth century. At a time when the Roman Catholic Church preached absolutism and the Inquisition held sway, many free thinkers saw in Tacitus a fellow champion of liberty, no more so than in northern Europe. His book covering the early principate, and the life and death of Germanicus, became a source of material for an extraordinary group of painters, sculptors, dramatists, composers, and authors over the next four centuries, who told and retold what came to be known as the 'Germanicus Tradition'.

Germanicus' patriotism and moral virtue provided grand themes for poems and plays. Among the earliest productions of modern times, Edmé Boursault (1638–1701) staged his *Germanicus: tragédie* at the Théâtre du Marais, in a performance by Comédiens du Roi on 25 May 1673, which earned the approval of the great French dramatist Jean Racine (1639–1699).[36] Another tragedy of *Germanicus* was written in 1694 by Jacques Pradon (1632–1698) – a playwright supported by Pierre Corneille – which intentionally mocked his rival Racine.[37] Across the Channel in England, in 1731, Thomas Cooke wrote *Germanicus: A tragedy in verse*, but it was, apparently, never performed on stage.[38] An unnamed 'Gentleman of the University of Oxford' had better luck with his own *Germanicus: a tragedy*, seeing his work make it into print in 1775.[39] In the Netherlands, Lucretia Wilhelmina Merk Van Winter (1721–1789) published her *magnum opus* about the Roman commander and published it in Amsterdam in 1779, care of Pieter Meijer.[40] Assisted by her husband, she was the first Dutch woman to write epic poems, and she set the great story of Germanicus' campaigns across the Rhine, which included his relationship with the Batavians, in 10,350 lines of Dutch verse, set in rhyming couplets. Compared to her earlier *David* (1768), it was a modest success, partly on account of its more severe and cold style, but it gained a readership beyond the Low Countries when it was reprinted in a French translation in 1787 as *Germanicus, Poème En Seize Chants*.[41] Indeed, it may have inspired Antoine-Vincent Arnault (1766–1834) to write his *Germanicus, Tragédie En Cinq Actes Et En Vers* in 1817. His play became famous for the lines:

> *On craint, quand on connaît le peuple et ses caprices,*
> *Les vertus d'un rival tout autant que ses vices.*[42]

The bloody French Revolution was then still recent history, and, at the first performance of *Germanicus*, a disturbance broke out on the *parterre* outside, which threatened serious political complications for its playwright. Arnault went into exile for two years.

Later, in 1869, against the backdrop of the French Second Empire and the Imperial Bonapartist regime of Napoléon III, Charles-Ernest Beulé (1826–1874) published *Le Sang de Germanicus*. It was a florid biography of the House of Germanicus, spanning the lives of his parents down to the last days of Nero. Beulé attempted to understand how the seemingly noblest and most excellent of parents – Drusus and Antonia, Germanicus and Agrippina – could produce such disreputable and immoral children. In his introduction, he proposes that, 'in decadent times, virtue itself is only a beginning of easement and popularity becomes a poison that turns against the homeland'.[43] In his conclusion, he imagines Augustus and Livia bemoaning the dynasty they have bequeathed to the world. Germanicus and Agrippina turn their heads in dismay as they contemplate Nero, saying 'we dreamed of omnipotence for the happiness of the world, and the world exhausted, debased, degraded by the monstrous power, will he curse forever the blood of Germanicus?'[44] In Beulé's France meanwhile, confidence in the imperial *régime* vanished as the country was gripped with strikes and civil disturbances, and suffered international reverses. Perhaps *Le Sang de Germanicus* was less a treatise on the Roman imperial family than it was a warning from history about the dangers of dynastic power and the 'Napoléonic Idea'.

The Roman hero's life was also set to music. In Vienna, at the turn of the eighteenth century, a serenata was composed for the Habsburg Archduke Joseph.

Described as a handsome man with blue eyes and blond hair, as well as forward-looking and a reformer, he was destined to become the future Holy Roman Emperor Joseph I, King of the Romans. Perhaps performed under the title *Il Trionfo* (or *Il Sogno*) *di Germanico*, it set an Italian libretto based on Tacitus' *Annales* to a richly orchestrated score comprising of arias and recitatives for six voices with an opening sinfonia.[45] At face value, the piece with its languid melodies told of the triumphal return of Germanicus to Rome in 16 CE after campaigning in Germania, but seen as an allegory it celebrated the young prince's victorious arrival back from the successful Siege of Landau in the Palatinate in 1704. Georg Friedrich Händel (1685–1759) has been proposed as the serenata's composer, but the attribution is doubted by many and the names of both the musical talent and the librettist remain obscure.[46]

At almost the same time in Germany the aspiring 23-year-old composer Georg Philipp Telemann (1681–1767) took on a new commission. Shortly after marrying the pastor of Regensburg, the poetess Christine Dorothea Lachs (c.1672–1716?) wrote a libretto in German to her own opera entitled *Germanicus: Oper in drei Akten*. Her fictional story of love, lust and political intrigue set in Ara Ubiorum and among the German forests, is very loosely based on historical truth after the events of 15 CE. Telemann composed the score for an orchestra comprising trumpet, two horns, two flutes, two oboes, two bassoons, two violins, viola and basso continuo. In 1704, he completed an overture, forty-one arias, and recitatives for a cast that included Agrippina, Arminius, the boy Caligula, Florus, Germanicus, and Segestes. The opera was first staged at the Leipziger Oper, proved popular with audiences also in Hamburg two years later, and was revised in 1710. During his prolific musical career, Telemann wrote scores for some fifty operas, and *Germanicus* was eventually forgotten and lost. Remarkably, the overture and arias were rediscovered in a Frankfurt archive in the twenty-first century and given a modern première at the *Bachfest Leipzig* on 11 June 2007, in a performance by the Sächsisches Barockorchester.[47] One of Telemann's very earliest works, it reveals, even then, his talent for colourful instrumentation and the stylistic influence of his contemporary Mr Händel. The aria sung by Agrippina, *Komm o Schlaf, und laß mein Leid*, 'Come, o sleep, and let my cares', with its sweet melody sustained by two flutes amid glowing orchestration, has since gained a popularity of its own, independent of the opera.

Among the first painters to find inspiration in Germanicus' story was the Flemish protestant Peter Paul Rubens (1577–1640). In 1614, he painted *Agrippina and Germanicus*, a pair of portraits with an almost cameo-like quality.[48] Indeed, Rubens was a collector of antiquities, and numbered engraved gems among his collection. He intended to illustrate a publication of these items but did not complete the project. Germanicus' profile, with his aquiline nose, arched brows and rounded chin, differs from extant Roman busts or coins, and may have been styled after one of the pieces in his collection he believed to be the commander. He returned to Germanicus twelve years later. His painting, *The Glorification of Germanicus* of 1626, is a large-scale reproduction of the *Gemma Tiberiana*, which was actually discovered by his friend Nicolas-Claude de Peiresc, in the sacristy of the Sainte-Chapelle, Paris, six years earlier.[49] The modern master Rubens faithfully reproduced in oils the detail of the original Roman sardonyx cameo, engraved by an unknown master of the ancient world.

Two years later, a young French painter called Nicolas Poussin (1594–1665) created his first masterpiece (plate 41) entitled *La Mort de Germanicus*.[50] He was commissioned by Cardinal Francesco Barberini in Rome to recreate the scene of Germanicus' death in Epidaphne, as related in Tacitus' *Annals*.[51] The painting, which may have been a companion to *La Continence de Scipion* (The Continence of Scipio), presents, in rich gold, blue, brown and ochre coloured oils, the powerful themes of death, suffering, injustice, grief, loyalty and revenge. Poussin shows the Roman commander just after he expires for the last time. The vigorous Germanicus is now a gaunt figure, his pale, lifeless head turned to the side, away from the viewer. His deputies and soldiers stand around the foot of the bed, silently contemplating the pathos of the moment. One man – likely Sentius – standing in the centre of the painting, dressed in cuirass and *pteryges*, looks straight at Agrippina and, with his arm raised, appears to be taking command of the situation. Agrippina covers her face with a handkerchief in grief, while a calm, boyish Caligula clutches her hand, seeming not to understand that his father has just died. Composed like the decorative carving on an ancient sarcophagus, it is baroque in its emotional intensity and rich flowing gowns, but neo-classical in its architectural setting and sparse staging. It was an instant hit and became the model for historical death-bed scenes, studied and imitated by many artists in France, Germany and Italy – among them 'the Dutch Poussin' Gerard de Lairesse (1675–1680), Pierre Mignard (1720), Friedrich Heinrich Füger (1795) and Theodore Gericault (1811).[52]

In England, the sculptor Thomas Banks (1735–1805) carved a white marble bas-relief entitled *Death of Germanicus* in 1773–1774 to evoke the dignified solemnity of a family grieving.[53] Lying on the ground, his athletic naked body and disproportionately long legs reveal nothing of his sickness. Mourners and soldiers huddle around him. Their grief is controlled. Agrippina sits in a chair behind him, lovingly supporting her husband's neck, while two young children try to hug her in consolation.

The aftermath of Germanicus' death and the story of Agrippina's unswerving loyalty to his memory also became a favorite subject of artists. In response to a commission by Robert Hay Drummond (1711–1776), Archbishop of York, the American-born Benjamin West (1738–1820) painted *Agrippina Landing at Brundisium with the Ashes of Germanicus* (plate 42), first as a preparatory painting on paper in 1766, before completing the finished canvas around 1768.[54] West interpreted the mournful scene described by Tacitus.[55] Against the dramatic architectural backdrop of the port at Brundisium, the figures of Agrippina, her son Caligula, daughter Agrippina the Younger, and servants walk along the quayside. They stand out from the shadow cast by a colonnaded temple portico on account of their white gowns, which cover the heads of the adults. Leading the group, Agrippina clutches the urn containing Germanicus' ashes. The ships, which have brought them from Antiocheia, are berthed on the right, while a crowd of mourners – soldiers, citizens, young and old – look on with sad eyes from the left. The painting is neo-classical in its treatment of the subject, sublimating the intense emotions of the characters and using subdued colours, unfussy architectural features and subtle lighting, to illuminate a key moment in history. The painting deeply impressed King George III, who granted West lifelong patronage, and he became a painter to the royal court – that, despite the Pennsylvania-born artist's undisguised American patriotism.

The subject appealed to Gavin Hamilton (1723–1798), who began work on his interpretation in 1765. He took seven years to complete the *Agrippina Landing at Brundisium with the Ashes of Germanicus*.[56] In his painting, Hamilton focuses on the central figure of Agrippina holding the urn close to her breast. In contrast to West's sombre colours, Hamilton uses bright primary colours. Agrippina wears a scarlet tunic partially covered by a dark blue, almost grey *stola*. She stands calmly, head bowed, while two young children in front of here are keen to move on. Behind her, a young Agrippina is stepping lively up on to the quayside. She wears a golden yellow tunic, the effect of which is almost to draw the eye away from the central figure of Agrippina, her mother. Balance is restored by a seated figure on the left wearing clothing in both yellow and red. A soldier holding an eagle standard leans forward precariously trying to hold back the throng of mourners in the background.

Joseph Mallord William Turner (1775–1851) reimagined the same occasion in a way that only he could. His painting (plate 43), grandly titled *Ancient Rome: Agrippina Landing with the Ashes of Germanicus. The Triumphal Bridge and Palace of the Caesars restored*, was first exhibited in 1839.[57] The painting is classic Turner. He moves the action from Brundisium to Rome and presents the city as a fantastical backdrop of arches, columns, temples and towers. The palest shades of yellow blend mistily on the horizon, obscuring buildings on the Palatinus (or Capitolinus) Hill. The pale yellow hues grow progressively deeper and richer as they reach the bridge over the Tiber in the middle distance, turning to gold and amber as they move into the foreground. A massing crowd of people board a flotilla of boats and begin to set off from the left bank across the wide, mirror-like surface of the river towards the small, isolated figures of Agrippina, her children and servants on the other side. Dark shadows cast by walls in black and brown emphasize the bright but diminutive figures who are mostly faceless – perhaps a metaphor for life transcending death. Germanicus' urn is nowhere to be seen, yet he is the entire reason for the occasion.

By Turner's time, the Age of the Industrial Revolution was already transforming Britain.[58] Rising purchasing power among the burgeoning consumer middle class, who wished to appear educated and of discerning taste to their friends, created a demand for decorative ornaments, modelled after finds from the classical world. The entrepreneur Josiah Wedgwood saw potential sales in Germanicus-themed home decorations, adding a bust of the young Caesar (fig. 1) 'about 16 inches high' to a collection of pieces purchased from Oliver and Hoskins, and an intaglio polished to 'have exactly the effect of fine black basaltes or jasper' in a series of 'Antique Subjects', which sold from 1787 and became standard catalogue items.[59] They sold so well, in fact, that they were still featured in the original catalogue reprinted in 1873. Bizarrely, by this time, the name Germanicus became the *de facto* name for any statue or bust of a handsome but unidentified young Roman.[60]

On the Continent, the emergence of a nationalist movement in Germany was spurred on by literature telling a new version of history, inspired in part by the heroism of the barbarian who had stood up to, and beaten, Rome. Some 200 years earlier, Martin Luther had cleverly rebranded the Cheruscan prince Arminius into the freedom-fighter Hermann and promoted him as a poster boy for resistance against the Roman Catholic Church. It worked. In the Age of the Enlightenment, German theatre-goers thrilled to staged historical dramas, such as Heinrich von Kleist's *Die Hermannsschlacht* (1808/1821) – written after Napoléon Bonaparte's defeat of the Prussians, and perhaps a thinly disguised call for resistance to the French invader – and Friedrich de la Motte Fouqués' *Herrmann* (1818).[61] Arminius had defeated Varus, but in Germanicus he found a worthy opponent who had faced him on the battlefield and caused him to withdraw. In 1816, Dr Friedrich Hoffmann published *Die Vier Feldzüge des Germanicus*, describing the campaigns in which the Roman hunted down the Cheruscan leader. The mania for a broader pro-Germanic treatment of the emerging nation-state spurred Heinrich Luden to publish his influential, patriotic narrative history *Geschichte des teutschen Volkes* in 1825. Luden cast the Romans as imperialists bent on crushing the free and independent Germanic peoples at any cost. Thus he writes emotively of Germanicus' first punitive foray across the Rhine after he had quelled the mutiny of the legions:

> And even then in those wild people remained so burning a heat, and so overwhelming a desire to draw sword and blood, that Germanicus thought it necessary to conduct these frenzied people across the Rhine into Germany's peaceful districts, so they could cool their glow, taking their pleasure in the killing of Teutonic people, who under all circumstances the Romans took for enemies.[62]

Here, Germanicus is portrayed not as the brave Roman commander of history, but as the perpetrator of war crimes in a national foundation myth. However, Germanicus was not always a hate-figure in Germany. In 1826, Wilhelm Huscher published a tragic stageplay that was sympathetic to the man.[63] *Germanicus: Ein Trauerspiel* respun Tacitus' carefully crafted Latin prose tale of events leading to the death of the Roman commander and the machinations of Piso and Plancina into high German verse. It was an ambitious production with a large cast, numbering among them Tiberius, Livia, Drusus the Younger, Seianus, Sabinus, Silius, Martina, a magician, various soldiers, a veteran, and even a Gallic rider. The campaigns of Gemanicus in Germania Magna spawned several learned works by academics and doctoral theses by their students, each inspired by the story of Arminius/Hermann, the Battle of Teutoburg, and the Roman response – such as Friedrich Hoffmann (1816), Ludwig Reinking (1855), Alfred August Bernhard Breysig (1865 and 1892), Anton Linsmayer (1875), Paul Höfer (1885), Friederich

Knoke (1887), Anton Viertel (1901), Gerhard Kessler (1905), and O. Dörrenberg (1909), to cite but a few examples.[64] In his lectures during the 1880s, the great German classical historian Theodor Mommsen (1818–1903) presented the Arminius-Germanicus conflict story with notable balance and dispassion.[65]

Just as there were historians, like Luden, who were rewriting the prehistory of the emerging nation-state of Germany for a new age, so the themes of bravery, nobility, betrayal and shame occupied the minds of German-speaking painters. In Vienna in 1873, Munich-born Carl Theodor von Piloty (1826–1886) unveiled his great historical painting *Thusnelda im Triumphzug des Germanicus* (plate 44), after King Ludwig II had originally suggested the idea to him ten years earlier.[66] It evokes the scene from Tacitus' *Annals* and Ovid's *Epistula Ex Ponto*, describing the events of 26 May 17 CE.[67] Germanicus is a minor figure in the romantically theatrical painting. He stands in his victor's chariot adored by the crowds, but he is placed far to the left in the middle distance, almost as a silhouette. The focus is Thusnelda, Arminius' captured wife, spot-lit in the centre of the composition. Beside her stands her son, Thumelicus, his face seething with anger. Tiberius surveys the scene from on high, scowling. Beside him slouches Thusnelda's father, Segestes, who cannot even bring himself to look at her. The other Germanic captives are there – Segemundus, handcuffed Cheruscan chieftains, and old Libes the priest, who is dragged by his long white beard by a grinning Roman soldier with no more dignity than the brown bear which precedes him. The buxom blond Thusnelda is presented not just as a tragic heroine, but as a model for the good German woman of all ages. As the art historian at the Neue Pinatotek, Munich, notes, 'in the eyes of contemporaries, she appeared as a moral example of the German character who proudly confronts her destiny unbroken at the hour of doom'.[68]

History textbooks of the time – English as well as German – often included black and white engravings of these dramatic history paintings. A popular one was *Fighting Scene During the Retreat of Germanicus* by Ferdinand Leeke (1874–1923).[69] In this work, Leeke conveys the drama and tumult of an ambush at the edge of a forest, beside a marsh or stream. Germanicus is actually hard to spot: he is the figure on the far left of the picture in the crested helmet on a white horse, desperately waving his sword. It is the heroic standard-bearer who dominates the centre of the composition. In the retreat, he vainly tries to rally his men. Even as he waves the flag standard topped by an eagle, he is attacked by a sword-wielding German, who already has his fist firmly on the wooden staff. Roman soldiers scatter as the German warriors press down upon them. They are overwhelmed, unable to use their superior weapons, their legs are caught among the roots of trees and the long grass, and their escape is hampered by the narrowness of the wooden bridge formed by fallen tree trunks, forcing some to crawl humiliatingly through the swamp.

Germanicus in Our Times

In the twentieth century, there has been a more balanced reappraisal of Germany's ancient past and the role that Arminius and Germanicus played in it.[70] It turns out that there were many years of peace amidst the years of war. Field archaeology today has revealed a far more complex picture of interactions between cultures. Germans and Romans traded with each other for goods and slaves. Germans served with the Roman army, travelling to far-away lands. But Germanicus' association with Germany was one of war. By contrast, his diplomatic achievements in the Near East, which demonstrably avoided war with Rome's nemesis Parthia, have been largely forgotten or left under-reported.[71] Indeed, in quite recent times, Germanicus has been hidden under the shadows of members of his own extended family. His grandfather Augustus, his father Drusus, his mother Antonia, his uncle and adopted father Tiberius, his brother Claudius, his son Caligula, his grandson Nero, and even his daughter Agrippina, have all been the subjects of biographies and works of fiction. The story of Germanicus' life and achievements has been overlooked in favour of those of others, who were often considered lesser men even in his own time. The man who evoked admiration and sympathy among ordinary people, historians, and artists for 1,900 years has sadly since gone out of fashion.

Gone he is, yet not completely forgotten. Unsolved crimes and mysteries appeal to readers, and the suggestion of foul play behind Germanicus' death still inspires modern writers, especially historical novelists writing in English. Germanicus appears as a sympathetic figure in Robert Graves' best-selling novel *I, Claudius* (1934), based on Cassius Dio, Suetonius, and Tacitus, with a large dose of poetic licence.[72] In the excellent BBC television adaptation of the book by Jack Pullman (1976), the actor David Robb portrayed him as a handsome, good-natured 'golden boy', naïvely unaware that his family was being systematically murdered by Livia until told so by his brother, before finally being poisoned himself by his own son, Caligula. In *Germanicus* (2002), Livia is the one who commissions David Wishart's fictional Roman gumshoe, M. Corvinus, to investigate the death of her grandson in his first case, and he quickly uncovers a web of betrayal and deceit.[73] Beyond Britain's shores, the drama *Germanicus* by celebrated South African author, poet and intellectual N.P. van Wyk Louw represents one of the high points of Afrikaans dramatic art. Written in 1956, the historical play deals with the issues of heroism, tradition and absolute power told through key events in the life of the Roman general, from the mutiny on the Rhine to his death in Syria. Written in concise verse with deliberate archaisms, it was awarded the Hertzog Prize for Drama in 1960 and continues to be studied by university students in Namibia and South Africa.[74] In the non-fiction genre, Australian-born Stephen Dando-Collins creatively knits together facts and suppositions to propose how the murder (and he is convinced it was murder by poisoning) of Germanicus led to the fall of Roman Empire in *Blood of the Caesars* (2008).[75] As with the ancient writers, even today the boundaries between fact and fiction can become blurred.

Science too has found a place for Rome's most popular general. On 30 August 1997 an astronomer was observing the night sky at the Osservatorio Astrometrico Santa Lucia Stroncone, the Santa Lucia Stroncone Astronomical Observatory in northern Italy. The scientist, Antonio Vagnozzi, recorded a minor planet with its own satellite in the main asteroid belt between Mars and Jupiter. Provisionally designated '1997 QN' it was later renamed '10208 Germanicus', in honour of the man whose bronze statute was found just 6km (3 miles) away in the city of Terni. For as long as the asteroid circles the solar system, Germanicus will enjoy a kind of celestial immortality. As the Latin translator of Aratos' astronomical poem, Germanicus would certainly have approved.[76]

Chapter 9

Assessment

Talents and Temperament

Germanicus Iulius Caesar, née Nero Claudius Drusus, had the good fortune to be descended from two distinguished clans and to be adopted into a third that was the most powerful of the time. His genetic heritage equipped him well for his life of public service and his position afforded him many privileges in Rome's hierarchical society. No idler or spoilt brat, however, he honed his innate talents and leveraged his good nature to contribute his full measure to his nation at an extraordinary period in world history. In short, he was one of Rome's finest men.

From his Claudian birth father he inherited his honorific war title, which he adopted for his first name. He had hardly known the man, but the long shadow of his father's reputation reached well into his twenties. In many ways, Nero Claudius Drusus and his son were alike – in their affable personalities, tolerance for taking great personal risks, unswerving loyalty to family and country, but also their intractability and recklessness which led them to near disaster on occasions. The men of *gens Claudia* had long established a reputation for their spirit of scornful defiance, disdain for the law and hardness of heart. The soldiery and civil population who remembered Drusus with affection transferred their happy sentiment to his son. It might have overawed him and made him arrogant, but Germanicus learned to bear his heritage with humility and leveraged it to good effect during his career. Yet it was only after he had proved himself in Drusus the Elder's old stomping grounds that Germanicus truly established his own reputation independent of his father's.

After Germanicus' father died, his mother played a key role in his upbringing. A woman of great principle and sober temperament, she was loyal to her husband's memory and was still a 'one man woman' (*univira*) when she died aged 73.[1] She was descended from *gens Antonia* and was the youngest daughter of *triumvir* M. Antonius. Germanicus grew up aware of his grandfather's life and legend and it may have predisposed him to take a personal interest in public speaking and Rome's eastern dominions – Egypt in particular. Through his grandfather he was related to several important men in Asia Minor, giving him a ready-made political network in the region.

While his bloodlines and family tree gave him many advantages, the world Germanicus grew up in was dominated by the figure of C. Iulius Caesar Augustus and it was ultimately this connection which launched the young man to prominence. Augustus was a ruthless and uncompromising politician with a soft spot for family and tradition – an ancient world Roman mafia-style boss – who used his head to plan and scheme and the brawn of others, like his stepsons, to do the dangerous work. His great project had been to rescue the *Res Publica* from a generation of destructive civil wars and, under the guise of restoring it, to reform its institutions for the future. While Augustus was neither a king nor an emperor he strived to establish an autocratic dynasty which would follow after him and continue his life's work as steward of the *Pax Romana*. Germanicus, like his cousins and nephews, was an unwitting pawn in a great game of succession being played out in the emerging imperial system. In a plan which had taken a quarter century to shape, Caius and Lucius were destined to succeed the *princeps*. Their premature deaths meant Augustus had to radically rethink it. Augustus saw potential in Germanicus – as indeed he had with his father – but he finally could not bring himself to adopt him for reasons which are unclear, but seem to have been played up by his grandmother Livia Drusilla. Instead he placed Germanicus in the legal care of his primary heir Tiberius, and next in succession with Postumus Agrippa. It brought Germanicus into the powerful and prestigious *gens Iulia* – and with it a direct connection to the great Caesar – but he would still have to prove himself through deeds, which meant completing service in the military and politics. That was the Roman way.

Germanicus was recognized in his own time as a talented military leader, able to take on increasing responsibility and span of control. He came to the military relatively late for a Roman. At age 21 he was charged by Augustus with forming a unit of irregular troops of citizens and freed slaves for deployment during the emergency in Illyricum. The challenge was to shape a disparate group of men and train them into a battle-ready fighting unit. In its first operational season in 7 CE, the unit proved effective in defeating the Mazaei in the lowlands of Bosnia Herzegovina. It was a singular achievement considering Germanicus had no leadership training for the role he was asked to perform. Having impressed his adoptive father, Germanicus was given greater responsibility and placed in charge of regular legions and cohorts the following year. With them he successfully besieged cities in the valleys and mountains of Croatia. During the campaign he was acclaimed *imperator* by his troops as a mark of their gratitude to him. After the war he was among the victorious senior commanders honoured with a triumph. Immediately after the disaster at Teutoburg in 9 CE, Germanicus was placed in command of the remaining Rhine army units while Tiberius sought guidance from Augustus. Having won his adoptive father's confidence, his mentorship under Tiberius continued when he accompanied him on a foray into Germania Magna in 11.

Augustus promoted Germanicus to governor of the Tres Galliae from 13 CE, following in the footsteps of Drusus and Tiberius. During his tenure he put down a rebellion of Gauls, restoring order to the province. As *legatus Augusti pro praetore* he assumed full responsibility for the army in the two Germanies, representing a third of all Rome's legionary troops and perhaps the same again in auxiliary cohorts. After Augustus' death, he acted quickly to face down a mutiny of Roman citizen soldiers in his jurisdiction. He listened to their grievances and dealt with the issues of pay and conditions. With bad feeling lingering in the ranks, he recognized that the need to rebuild unit cohesion was urgent and led them in a punitive raid across the Rhine. The spilling of barbarian blood had the desired effect. The raid became the precursor to a larger mission. It is not clear from the sources whether an invasion was planned before the mutiny or if Germanicus acted opportunistically. It is reasonable to assume that the decision to make war against the Germanic nations was Germanicus' and that he was the commissioner and architect of the new plan. Invested with *imperium maius* he had the power to take such actions as necessary to safeguard the borders of his territory. The war was evidently conducted under the auspices of Tiberius despite the advice he had received from Augustus not to expand the boundaries of the empire. The fact that he disregarded that counsel and allowed Germanicus to instigate a new war indicates the level of confidence he had in his son to get the job done. It may be that what began at the outset of the first phase in 14–15 CE as a punitive action or pre-emptive strike – to restore lost honour – had expanded by the second into a campaign of regime change – by capturing or ousting Arminius – or outright conquest. Only at the end of 16 CE did Tiberius intervene to prevent further actions after he decided the investment was too high for the gains achieved and those being promised. Germanicus' stout resistance to the request shows his commitment to the mission but his final acceptance of the order confirms his loyalty once again to his commander-in-chief and *princeps*.

For the campaign strategy Germanicus looked to his father's example, after whom he replicated the amphibious invasion and multi-pronged attacks over land. The required military infrastructure – the forts, fortresses and their supply lines, plus the canal – which facilitated his expedition was already in place to which he added a new fleet of ships. Under his direct command were legates – Anteius, Caecina, Silius, Stertinius and Vitellius – each one a competent and seasoned war fighter hand picked by Augustus or Tiberius, to whom Germanicus delegated specific missions. But the war was nevertheless to prove difficult and the costs of victory high in blood and treasure. The unreliability of their alliance partners – in particular the Angrivarii and Chauci who were friend one season and foes the next – and guerilla warfare tactics of the disparate Germanic nations put the Romans at a disadvantage, especially on the march. Only in the pitched battles did the balance tip in the Romans' favour, but even at Idistaviso and the Angrivarian Wall Germanicus could still not deliver the final blow which would decisively knock-out his opponent. The German leadership escaped to fight another day, but the encounters do seem to have been enough to deter them from invading Roman territory for several years. Some scholars have dismissed the campaigns as futile punitive expeditions, but if the purpose of the mission was to restore Roman honour and confidence after Teutoburg in that Germanicus succeeded. He had proved Roman forces could still enter the lands across the Rhine at will and that Arminius could be beaten. Furthermore, two of the three eagles lost under Quinctilius Varus were retrieved, Rome's ally Segestes was rescued, Arminius' wife and son were captured, and they and several high profile war captives were later exhibited in Germanicus' triumph in May 17 CE. The decision to continue the war was finally not his to make and Tiberius – as commander-in-chief – decided to suspend operations in the region indefinitely, preferring a doctrine of strategic patience over direct military intervention.

The surviving ancient accounts of the battles Germanicus fought in are too vaguely described to enable us to judge whether his technical skills as a commander – in operational planning, battlefield communications, delivery of force and other aspects – showed flair in comparison to other acclaimed military leaders.[2] The inevitable favourable comparison between him and Alexander the Great was made at his funeral and he was judged as having the greater score in terms of 'clemency, self-restraint and in all other virtues'.[3] His scope for choosing his direct reports was limited as they had been chosen for him by Augustus or Tiberius, but the men in place complemented Germanicus' skills and he managed them well. His principal leadership attribute was *virtus* – a Latin word which translates as 'manliness', but conveys 'courage' and 'strength'. As defined by Carl von Clausewitz, Germanicus showed both the physical courage to face personal danger and moral courage to accept responsibility for his actions.[4] He led his troops from the front exposing himself to great personal risk, even dramatically removing his helmet at the Battle of the Angrivarian Wall so his men could see him in the midst of the mêlée at a critical moment when he needed to rally them to fight on. Germanicus' fearless, almost reckless, behaviour on the battle-field was, perhaps, inspired by stories of Drusus the Elder or his distant ancestor Claudius Marcellus, whose zeal to win the rich spoils – *spolia opima* – stripped from his opponent was well known. There is no evidence to suggest that Germanicus ever succeeded in winning this accolade, but the fact he put himself in the thick of battle won him the respect of his troops who rewarded him with two acclamations.

Determination – a trait Romans understood in terms of firmness of mind (*animi firmitas*) and perseverance (*constantia*) – was his other virtue. He revealed this trait when a youngster. Believing his legs to be too slender he worked out by riding his horse to build them up. As an adult, he applied himself to all the projects delegated to him with vigour – which cannot be said of Augustus' much favoured adopted son C. Caesar who on his first military assignment on the Danube shirked his responsibilities, or Postumus Agrippa who frittered away his time in drinking and gambling. Germanicus proved his commitment to completing his mission in Armenia in 18 CE even when his deputy Calpurnius Piso refused to obey orders and left him without the backing of his army. Germanicus could have balked and declined to go, but he did not hesitate and made the arduous and potentially dangerous trip to Artaxata, putting his duty above all else. His determination was rewarded when he completed the mission without bloodshed and crowned Artaxias III himself. It was rightly regarded by his peers as one of the most important achievements of his career.

Germanicus could be creative and decisive and held his nerve under pressure. The rapidly conceived snatch raid to rescue Segestes was well planned and achieved its objective with no reported losses on the Roman side. Recognizing the danger posed to his infantry by crossing the Weser River without the security of a bridge, he used his cavalry led by Aemilius and Stertinius to create a diversion to enable the crack Batavi units under Chariovalda to drive the main thrust into Arminius' centre. When the gambit failed, Germanicus quickly pulled his men out to conserve his resouces for more favourable conditions on another day. Germanicus' swift action also saved a cohort of cavalry from annihilation during an ambush led by Arminius after leaving the cenotaph at Teutoburg.

His bold attitude on the battlefield was tempered by his mild manner off it. Suetonius writes of his 'unexampled kindliness, and a remarkable desire and capacity for winning men's regard and inspiring their affection'.[5] Dio ascribes to Germanicus a quality of saintly incorruptibility, saying 'he was one of the few men of all time who have neither sinned against the fortune allotted to them nor been destroyed by it'.[6] Tacitus highlights Germanicus' ability to win men's trust:

> he inspired reverence alike by look and voice, and while he maintained the greatness and dignity of the highest rank, he had escaped the hatred that waits on arrogance.[7]

For Germanicus a man's word was his bond. Loyalty or trustworthiness (*fides*) was a quality he greatly valued. He demanded it of himself and he expected it from others. He was supremely loyal to his commander-in-chief and when, on the death of Augustus in 14 CE, the Rhine army mutineers proposed Germanicus take power, he adamantly refused and 'held them to their allegiance'.[8] There were other opportunities when he could have usurped power, but 'he refused to do so'.[9]

There was, however, a hard edge to Germanicus' character. He could be a tough negotiator. In his diplomatic dealings with the Parthian king, Artabanus II, he realized the relative strength of his bargaining position and, in a calculated snub, declined an invitation to meet the king in person. As a concession he agreed only to move Vonones so that he would not pose a threat to the king. When famine threatened the population of Alexandria, Germanicus arranged for distributions of grain, but coldly excluded several communities, including the Jews. In grinding down his enemy's morale and will to fight, he was not above committing acts of cruelty and genocide. The men, women and children of the Marsi were ruthlessly slaughtered in a raid in 14 CE and the following year the Chatti witnessed their capital at Mattium reduced to ashes and the surrounding territory devastated for miles around. He was deaf to the pleas of those Chatti warriors seeking to negotiate terms.

Germanicus made his share of mistakes. During the mutiny of the Rhine legions in 14 CE he thought he could trick his soldiers into a settlement with a fabricated letter. It may not have been his idea, but on the counsel of his leadership team he nevertheless proceeded with it. It was a bad call. In the eyes of his troops he had tried to dupe them. From that moment he lost his authenticity and credibility and he paid for it dearly during the ensuing prolonged negotiations. When the mutiny had finally been broken, he gave orders for Caecina Severus to round up the ringleaders. In his written communication, however, he also failed to make his orders crystal clear. His officers interpreted his orders in the broadest terms. The bloodbath which followed led to unnecessary deaths of both the innocent and guilty alike. Germanicus was mortified to discover his error, but by then it was too late.

Following the example of many of his Antonian and Claudian ancestors Germanicus was quite prepared to disregard protocol when circumstances demanded it. In picking up human bones and turfs to raise a monument to the fallen at Teutoburg, Germanicus committed an act of sacrilege because, as augur, he was prevented by custom and religious law from doing so. The exceptional circumstances called for a compassionate response. His need to connect with his men at a time of emotional stress transcended any political niceties. Nevertheless Tiberius disapproved. More gravely, as a senator he did not first seek permission to visit Egypt as required in a directive laid down – for good reason – by Augustus and upheld by Tiberius. By taking the broadest interpretation of his remit, Germanicus seems to have understood Aegyptus was a province and, as such, under his care as governor general in the eastern Empire. Alternatively, he may have felt able to disregard the rule as he was making a private trip to see the nation's famed antiquities. If so it was naïve of him: a man of his consular status could not simply sneak in to Egypt and hope not to be noticed. Indeed, he was mobbed as a 'rockstar' on his arrival in Alexandria. Making matters worse, once in the country, discovering its population faced famine, on his own initiative he ordered the warehouses opened and selectively issued grain to the needy. This unauthorized intervention may have been welcomed as a humanitarian act locally, but it risked starving the plebs in Rome and bringing its attendant dire consequences. Responding to what he saw as a serious breach of protocol, Tiberius issued his deputy with a written reprimand for his meddling.

The way in which Germanicus managed his difficult deputy, Cn. Calpurnius Piso, reveals how he handled interpersonal conflicts. Most people responded warmly to Germanicus' good-natured amiability – Piso was not one of them. He had made it plainly known that in his opinion Germanicus was his social inferior and he saw no reason to kow-tow to him. He was the authorized governor of Syria with complete jurisdiction over its internal affairs. As *praepositus Orienti*, Germanicus' role was that of an emissary or minister with special portfolio, but without direct control of any particular province. Piso felt no compunction about disobeying an order or countermanding instructions issued by him, because he likely regarded them only as advisories. On his return from Armenia, Germanicus confronted his deputy for failing to mobilize his army for the mission. In the account of that meeting preserved by Tacitus, emotions were high, and there was considerable posturing, but the issues between the two men were not brought out on to the table and no resolution was reached. Bad feelings remained to fester. But what was Germanicus to do? He was in an awkward position, both constitutionally and socially. On paper, he was Piso's superior, but the legate had been appointed by Tiberius with the consent of the Senate. Piso was a friend of his adoptive father and his wife was connected to his grandmother Livia. Custom demanded that the older aristocrat received respect from the younger, despite his uncouth behaviour. Germanicus' strategy for dealing with him seems to have been one of tolerance or blocking. At the dinner held in honour of the king of the

Nabataeans, Germanicus simply ignored Piso's intolerably bad manners. Upon his return from Egypt and discovering that his deputy had rescinded his orders, the sources give diametrically opposing versions about his reaction. In Suetonius' account Germanicus takes the news calmly. By contrast, Tacitus portrays Germanicus as reacting angrily. Which is closer to the truth is now impossible to say. A year into the job, Germanicus decided he could tolerate the disrespect no longer. Believing he had been poisoned by Piso, Germanicus formally renounced his friendship with him and dismissed the man from his post.

In a crisis, Germanicus felt unabashed about revealing his sensitive side – or was willing to fake it. It is reported that as he watched his fleet smashing against the Frisian shore and his men struggling in their wretched state, he repeatedly blamed himself and threatened to throw himself into the sea. It might be seen as overemotional by some, but this is surely only the heart-felt reaction of a man of moral courage, a general totally invested in his mission who cared deeply about the welfare of his men and who was devastated by the catastrophe he had brought upon them. A modern historian has described Germanicus' threat to commit suicide when faced with mutinous troops who demanded he take the throne as 'histrionic'.[10] But was it a genuinely emotional outburst? Another way to view the episode is this was Germanicus speaking as orator. Suetonius comments on Germanicus' 'surpassing ability in the oratory and learning of Greece and Rome'.[11] Trained by Salanus, a teacher of rhetoric respected by Ovid, Germanicus learned to perform with 'fiery eloquence'.[12] His widely acknowledged gift for public speaking helped him convince juries in favour of his clients at court and to rouse his troops to fight in battle. It was a talent the Senate recognized when it posthumously voted him a *clipeus* of gold to hang in the *curia*. Addressing the mutinous troops from the tribunal, Germanicus would have mustered all his skill as a performer. Declamation, the use of florid language and theatrical gestures were all tools in trade of the orator. He well knew how to work an audience. Threatening suicide with the flourish of a sword would be precisely the sort of grand gesture he would use to evoke an emotional – specifically a sympathetic 'no, don't do it' – response from his listeners. Indeed, many tried to grab his sword so he would not go through with the threat. He had not reckoned that one of the soldiers would offer his own weapon claiming it was sharper, which stole some of his thunder. It did not blunt his style, however, and he would use the technique again. Later when Agrippina and Caius were about to leave the danger of the mutineers' camp, Germanicus embraced his wife tearfully on the tribunal where he could be seen and said his farewell. Seeing the popular couple separated in this cruel manner, the men responded emotionally – just as he had calculated they would. Quickly injecting an appeal to patriotism, achievements and duty, he succeeded in swinging them to his side and broke the mutiny.

Germanicus was a man of culture (*humanitas*) and a cosmopolitan. His traditional education based on the study of Greek and Latin literature instilled in Germanicus a great love of drama, history, philosophy and poetry. Ovid considered him a poet in his own right. With his talent for the written word he crafted stage-worthy comedies (which were performed) and translated works of cosmology (which have survived). His choice of genres may reveal something of his personality and beliefs. Comedy brings joy by making people laugh and to do it well takes considerable talent. His decision to translate Aratos' *Phaenomena* – a work of 'stoic cosmologising, practical know how with moral uplift' – from Greek into Latin may have been a project Germanicus undertook just for his own amusement.[13] Or it may have been out of a genuine intellectual interest in the subjects it covered. There is nothing in Germanicus' lifestyle to suggest he was a practising stoic or a follower of any other Greek philosophy. If one word best describes his outlook on life it is 'traditional'.

Germanicus was a keen observer of the *mos maiorum*, the 'ways of the elders'. He was a prominent figure in the institutions which nourished Rome's religious life. He served willingly as an Arval Brother and as Chief Priest of the Cult of the Divine Augustus and observed the religious blood games as a sponsor. As augur he learned how to interpret bird flight and declare the auguries. It made a difference at Idistaviso where he deftly used the appearance of eagles in the sky to rally his men before giving the order to charge. He believed unquestioningly in the power of prophecy, going out of his way to visit the oracles at Claros and Memphis, and he would have visited Samothrace also had bad weather not prevented him landing on the island. To what degree their unfavourable predictions affected him personally is not recorded in the sources, but it is reasonable to suspect it was unsettling to him.

Germanicus was lucky in love. Arranged marriages were commonplace in the imperial household and divorces were frequent as political alliances shifted (as Tiberius discovered when he was made to divorce Vispania and marry Iulia). Germanicus married the strong-willed grand-daughter of Augustus, with whom he had nine children, five of whom survived him. He was faithful to Agrippina throughout the fourteen years of their marriage. There was no scandal while Germanicus lived and there is not a single suggestion in the surviving accounts that he was anything other than heterosexual. She repaid his loyalty by seeking justice for her husband after his mysterious death and by promoting the interests of their children. During their life together Germanicus and Agrippina were the glamourous celebrity couple par excellence. Along with their children, they were seen as the youthful and energetic faces of the next generation of the imperial family, a point Augustus himself made when he tried to enforce his policy on marriage by displaying the children on his knee in public. The couple was mobbed by crowds wherever they went – a clear sign of their widespread popularity with the common people.

Relationship with Tiberius

There remains the vexing issue of Germanicus' relationship with Tiberius. The story according to the so-called 'Germanicus Tradition' is largely based on Tacitus' account in the *Annals*.[14] At face value, Tacitus' Tiberius is a complex and flawed man who thrives on contradictions: his self-deprecating manner disguises his deceitful nature, his deference to the Senate is passive-aggressive control, his generosity is motivated by hypocritical self-interest, his upholding of the law enables him to abuse it. He inherits Augustus' form of benign autocracy and over the course of his reign degrades it into unbridled despotism. Germanicus is presented as the balancing force, preventing Tiberius from the descent into cruelty and oppression. While his adopted son lives, he rules much as Augustus intended – he defends the frontiers of empire more by diplomacy than force, upholds the law through the courts (*iustitia*), shows modesty (*modestia*) and clemency (*clementia*) even to wrong-doers. But he harbours a deep-rooted fear of his adopted son. He seems unable to believe Germanicus is genuinely loyal to him and that he must be concealing some scheme to overthrow him. When Germanicus asks to continue the war in Germania, his request for a troop surge is denied. Tiberius buys him off with a triumph and the promise of a second consulship. Then he is hurriedly dispatched to the Orient, where he is paired with Calpurnius Piso, a despicable man bent on making life difficult for his senior officer. On his death-bed Germanicus accuses Piso of poisoning him, while many see the hand of Tiberius in what they believe to have been an assassination. It is a real case of 'some rise by sin, and some by virtue fall'.[15]

Why would Tacitus choose to portray Tiberius as the schemer and Germanicus as the victim? Most modern historians agree that Tacitus twisted the story of Tiberius to portray him as an unpleasant individual.[16] In the *Annals*, Tacitus 'presents a detailed pathology of power under the Roman emperors' from Augustus to Nero.[17] He acknowledged that in the wake of civil war the institutions of the Republic collapsed and in the interests of peace all power had to reside in one man, but he did not concede that it had to be permanent. His view of history was that the *Pax Romana* established by the benign dictatorship of Augustus became 'the dreadful peace' of his successors, paid for in lost freedom and spilled blood, and which got dramatically worse with each new emperor.[18] Tiberius was the reluctant heir to the First Citizen and through his increasingly disengaged management style he facilitated the slow descent into despotism. Having adopted this editorial stance, to accentuate the hypocrisy of the tyrant and tell his story, Tacitus needed a foil in the form of a good and moral man, and found him in Germanicus. It is quite apparent to a modern reader of his work that Germanicus was a hero-figure for the Roman historian.[19] He deliberately slanted his presentation of the historical truth, assigning malicious intent to Tiberius' actions while portraying his adopted son as the innocent object of his designs. The tension between the two protagonists became the central story in Books 1 and 2 of the *Annals*.[20] Portraying the young man in the best light was essential to his telling of the story of decline and fall. Some have argued that Tacitus played down his idol's flaws and exaggerated his achievements, with one historian summing up the difference between the two men starkly as Germanicus 'pure white' and Tiberius 'jet black'.[21]

The problem for historians studying this period is that there are so few extant sources against which to compare Tacitus' version for accuracy – in fact for most parts of the story his is the only surviving account – but that does not absolve us of the duty to attempt to uncover the real truth. Tacitus claims in the introduction to the *Annals* to write 'without rancour or bias'.[22] But he was reliant on already decades-old source material on which to base his own version of events. Velleius Paterculus, who was partisan to Tiberius, neither makes mention of any bad feeling between the two men – indeed he lauds the *princeps* for the way he promoted his son – nor does he mention Germanicus' death. However, by the time Josephus wrote his *Antiquities* six decades later he was reporting Germanicus' poisoning as accepted fact. Thus, when Tacitus began writing his great work on the early principate the story of the hateful uncle and the murder of the irreproachable nephew-cum-son had become immutable lore.[23] While his expressed doubts that Germanicus was poisoned suggest he did not believe it himself, however, with the benefit of knowing the history of Seianus' conspiracies and the treason trials during the emperor's final years Tiberius' paranoid behaviour may have been explicable to him.

Strip away Tacitus' more obvious editorial bias, read between the lines, and what is revealed is rather different. Tiberius had reluctantly agreed to his own adoption by Augustus for the sake of the nation. When Augustus required Tiberius to adopt his nephew, Tiberius took on the solemn duty with the intention of seeing it through. In power he remained loyal to Augustus' vision of a Julio-Claudian dynasty, which meant Germanicus must succeed him. Tiberius may never have had a particularly strong paternal love for his adopted son, but Germanicus was the son of Tiberius' beloved brother and his treatment of him underlines a relationship based on respect not disdain.[24] Upon the death of Augustus, Tiberius acted quickly to ensure his adopted son in the Tres Galliae was granted *imperium maius* for five years, giving him the authority to run the military in the region which he had lacked up to that point. Through religious posts, and importantly the *flamen divorum Augustalis*, Tiberius raised his prestige. His treatment of Germanicus seems at times to actually have favoured him over his own son, Drusus. It was Germanicus he singled out for particular praise after quelling the mutiny on the Rhine, not Drusus who was still wrestling with the mutiny on the Danube. After his campaign in Germania, Tiberius agreed to a triumph for Germanicus and a second term as consul. The only legal power not granted to Germanicus was the tribunician. This was probably only on account of his age: had he lived he would almost certainly have received it within a year or two of taking on his next assignment.[25]

Germanicus was promoted by Tiberius to the important office of governor general of the eastern Empire – an honour previously accorded to M. Agrippa and C. Caesar – with the mission 'to restore order in the Orient' and granted *imperium maius* for a further five years to carry it out.[26] Rome's provinces closest to its frontier with Parthia were plagued with bad government at the hands of corrupt officials and the debilitating after-effects of natural disasters. Tiberius needed a man who could address the problems and stand up to the Parthians if the need arose. Tiberius could not risk the situation Augustus had found himself in when, as a young *triumvir*, he was obliged to go to war with M. Antonius who had become a dissolute potentate and a threat to Roman interests. In Germanicus, Tiberius had a safe pair of hands. For the most part, he toed the line.

Germanicus was not a free agent, however. Everything he did was under the auspices of the emperor. Whenever Germanicus failed to follow the agreed rules, as his mentor and superior – in the interests of maintaining the dignity of his office – Tiberius pointed out the error of his ways. He also knew better than most that power was seductive and it opened a man up to many temptations. In the East there were many enticements and Germanicus would be constantly fêted by special interests who would distract him from his mission – distractions which had finally seduced his grandfather, M. Antonius, and brought him into catastrophic conflict with Rome. With that in mind Tiberius dispatched Piso – his opinionated former co-consul – to Syria in the full knowledge that the crusty old patrician would challenge his son without hesitation. Indeed, it might have been a perceptive insight about his nephew. When Germanicus visited Athens and Alexandria he 'went native': he dispensed with his lictors who bore the traditional symbols of his consular status, and he dressed in a Greek *chiton* and sandals, eschewing the Roman tunic and toga – much to Tiberius' distaste and he chided him for it. Perhaps Germanicus' behaviour was intended to show sensitivity to local customs, but then, perhaps it was blatant self-promotion – conscious manipulation of his image intended to increase his popularity with his eye on the day when he would assume supreme power. The partnership of two men, in which each knew the younger would succeed the older, but not when, encouraged both parties to be on their best behaviour and thus provided a natural check and balance. While his son lived, Tiberius kept strictly to the straight and narrow. When Germanicus died, Tiberius lost his moral and political counterweight. Aided by men with personal agendas who he had promoted and a Senate fawning for his favour or living in fear of his retribution, he tipped inexorably into despotism.[27] Among the casualties were Germanicus' wife Agrippina and their sons Nero and Drusus. Germanicus could not have imagined his son Caius (Caligula) succeeding Tiberius, nor the bizarre lifestyles both men would lead.

Tiberius was not as black as Tacitus portrayed, but Germanicus was certainly *greyer*. There were actually striking parallels between the two men. Though temperamentally dissimilar – arguably even opposites – the two men were bound by the blood of the Claudians and shared similar backgrounds and life stories. They were both eldest sons who had lost their fathers at a young age, and were brought up by their strong willed mothers; both were highly educated men with interests in poetry and philosophy; both were thrust into leadership positions with much expected of them in their youths; both were self-starters, able to make decisions on their own initiative; and they were each mindful of their duty and willing to take great personal risks in the fulfilment of it. The main difference between them was the attractiveness of their personalities. Germanicus was popular with almost everyone, stranger and familiar alike; Tiberius was generally liked only by those in the military and Senate who had served with him and knew him personally. It has been said that Germanicus had *clementia* and *humanitas* in abundance, while Tiberius did not.[28] Tiberius could show clemency and generosity on occasions, but his cardinal virtue – and the one Augustus had chosen him as his successor for – was *moderatio*.[29] For most people, Germanicus was simply the most charismatic of the two men. If the great but reluctant leader was perceived to be brooding, cold and mean, any junior relative with some humanity would, in contrast, be seen as warm and approachable. It turned out that Drusus the Younger was as unpopular as his father. Thus, without much effort on his part, Germanicus became the friendly face in the palace – a person ordinary people, and even public figures such as Ovid, felt they could appeal to for help. With successive tellings of the story by historians, the contrasts between the men would become starker, painting Tiberius blacker and Germanicus whiter than either probably deserved.

Germanicus Caesar's unexpected death on 10 October 19 CE was ancient Rome's 'JFK moment'. It was a tremendous shock to the population whose response was nothing short of hysterical. Romans clamoured for every piece of news arriving by ship at Rome's great port and reacted to every rumour they heard. Even today, it is still unclear if Germanicus was murdered and if there was a conspiracy behind it, or if he died naturally from an unidentified disease of unknown origin, or accidentally by overdose of medication. Despite the allegations of Josephus and Suetonius, it is significant that Tacitus never actually verifies that Piso had poisoned Germanicus, and even expresses his own doubt about the charge.[30] Having reviewed the evidence provided by the prosecution, even the Senate recorded at the time only that Germanicus himself had identified Piso as the cause of his death, in response to which he renounced his friendship. The absence of an autopsy report or forensic evidence and the long interval of time which has since passed now makes impossible a definite identification of the cause of death. Germanicus' death will likely forever remain a mystery and the continuing subject of speculation. He would certainly not be the last prominent Roman official to die in Syria.[31]

Achievements

What, then, of his achievements? In his obituary of Germanicus, Suetonius lists his quelling of the mutiny of the Rhine legions and refusal to betray his emperor, the campaigns in Germania Magna, his two consulships, his assignment in the Orient as Tiberius' special envoy in which role he 'vanquishing the king of Armenia' and, finally, reduced Cappadocia 'to the form of a province'.[32] He was acclaimed *imperator* twice by his soldiers, granted an ovation, triumphal ornaments and finally rewarded with a full triumph. In death the Senate voted him honours far exceeding those accorded Augustus' popular adopted sons Caius and Lucius Caesar and rivalling those of his own birth father Nero Claudius Drusus. For many Germanicus embodied what it meant to be Roman: he demonstrated through his deeds the virtues of courage, loyalty, trustworthiness, restraint, dignity, humanity, patriotism, equity, dutifulness and respect for tradition. He burst with youthful energy and offered the promise that Rome could be strong and vigorous again, a place where the common people had a champion who stood up for their interests against the powerful and corrupt few. With his premature death, and the subsequent demise of his eldest son Nero who was most likely to realize it after him, that vision of the future was lost. But the memory of Germanicus continued to be celebrated each year by people from Dura Europos to Vindolanda for hundreds of years, some even using his name for the month of September, until the Roman Empire itself fell.

Over the centuries, historians, dramatists, novelists, painters and sculptors have accepted and rehashed the 'Germanicus Tradition' but that narrow version of his life has obscured the real man. From his self consciousness about his slender legs as a teenager to his irrational fear of chickens throughout his adult life; from his tearful farewell to his wife before mutinous troops to his sense of awe standing before the pyramids of Egypt; from the comedies he wrote to make men laugh to his translation of a cosmological treatise to make men think; from charging headlong into the thick of battle to laying the first sod on the cenotaph to the Roman dead at Teutoburg; from his willingness to flout regulations to save lives during a humanitarian crisis to his curiosity to know his fate from oracles, and in so many other ways, Germanicus emerges from the ancient world as an attractive, romantic and very human figure. To his contemporaries, the flesh-and-blood Germanicus was a Roman hero in the finest tradition. From his father, Nero Claudius Drusus Germanicus, he inherited an iconic name and a heady legacy. He lived up to it remarkably well through his own lifetime's deeds and achievements and was building a formidable reputation which many believed eclipsed it. Augustus recognized in his adoptive grandson a charismatic leader with innate talents for war fighting and diplomacy, but that he had much to learn and some maturing to do. With more experience and mentoring he believed Germanicus would one day be ready to become *princeps*. In his plan of succession he saw to it that Tiberius adopted him, intending Germanicus to one day be the third man on the throne.[33] Germanicus Caesar's tragically premature death, however, ended that dream and today we are left to ponder what might have been.

Appendix

Decree of the Senate Granting Honours for Germanicus

Senatus Consultum de Honoribus Germanici Decernendis ('Tabula Siarensis')

Fragment 1:
[…]n[… for the purpose of preserving the memory of Germanicus Caesar who] ought never [to have died … the Senate decided that a decree of the Senate should be passed concerning the d]eserved [honours of] Germanicus Caesar [… and moreover, it pleased the Senate that it should act concerning] this matter with the advice of Tiberius Caesar Augustus [our] *prin[ceps]* and that a copy [of the opinions that had been written down] should be given to him and that he, with his accustomed [moderation] should choose [from amongst all those] honours, that the Senate thought should be passed, [and whatever ones he wishes and] Augusta his mother, Drusus Caesar, and the mother of Germanicus Ca[esar and, if possible] bringing [his wife] into their deliberation, think are appropriate. [It was decreed concerning this matter:] that it pleased the Senate a marble arch be erected in the *circus Flaminius* [with public money, and pl]aced in the place where the statues to the Divine Augustus and the Augustan house [have already be]en erected by Caius Norbanus Flaccus, with representations of conquered nations and with an [inscription in golden] letters on the front of this arch saying that the Roman Senate and people dedicated this [marble] monum[ent] to the memory of Germanicus Caesar, since he, having conquered the Germans in war [and then] removed them from Gaul and recovered the military standards, avenged the treacher[ous massacre] of the army of the Roman people, and set Gaul in order, was sent as proconsul into the transmarine pro[vinces] to set the kingdoms of that region in order according to the instructions of Tiberius C⟨a⟩esar Au[gustus, imposing a ki]ng upon Armenia, and not ceasing from his labor before an [ovation] was [granted to him], died on behalf of the *Res Publica*. On top of this arch a statue [of] Ger[manicus Caesar] should be placed in a triumphal chariot, and around its sides statues [of] D[rusus Germanicus his father], the natural brother of Tiberius Caesar Augustus and of Antonia [his] mother [and of his wife Agrippina and] of [Li]via his sister and of Tiberius Germanicus his brother and of his sons and da[ughters].

Another arch should be placed on the slope of Mount Amanus, which is in [the province of Syria, or in wherever, if some] other spot should [seem] better to

Tiberius Caesar Augustus our *princeps* [in those regions of which] the care and government came to Germanicus Caesar upon the authority [of Tiberius Caesar Augustus and of this order]. A statue should be placed upon it and an inscription appropriate [to the deeds of Germanicus Caesar] should be carved upon it. A third arch should be erected either at [the winter camp of the army of the Roman people or next to the tumulus] which [the mourning army began] for Drusus, the brother of Tiberius Caesar Augustus [our *princeps*], and then [completed] with the permission of the divine Augustus, [and on top of that arch a statue of Germanicus Caes]ar should be placed, receiving [the standards recovered from the Germans, and the Ga]uls and Germans who [live] on this side of the Rhine, [the same states who were instructed by the Divine] Augustus [to make] sacrifice at the tumulus [of Drusus should be ordered to make a similar] sacrifice [at public expense in the same place] to the gods of the underworld [every year on the day that Germanicus Caesar died] and when [an army of the Roman people] should be in that region [it should offer sacrifice on that day, or on the birthday] of Germanicus Caesar [and it should march through the arch that is erected in accordance with this decree of the Senate]. It is pleasing to the Senate that a marble [sepulchre should be build in memory of Germanicus Caesar] in the forum of [Antiocheia where the body of Germanicus Caesar was cremated . . . and at Epidaphnae where Germanicus Caesar died, a tribunal should be erected].

Fragment 2, Column a:
[that every year, six days before the Ides of October at that altar] which is [before the tumulus of Germanicus Caesar public sacrifices should be made in his memory] to the gods of the underworld for his *Manes* [by the magistrate of the Augustan [brotherhood] wearing dark togas, as it is [right and proper for them to have] togas of that color on that day, and to sacrifice according to that rite by which [public sacrifices are made to the gods of the Underworld] on behalf of the *Manes* of Caius and Lucius Caesar, and a bronze boundary marker should similarly be inscribed next to that [tumulus of Germanicus Caesar] so that the decrees of the Senate that [pertain to his honours] should be inscribed upon it. And furthermore that it should not [be permitted for magistrates or those who administer justice in] a municipality or colony of Roman citizens or Latins to conduct any serious business in public, nor [may public banquets be given on that day ever afterwards] nor may weddings or engagements of Roman citizens take place nor [may someone] borrow or lend [money] nor should games take place [or be watched or anything be exhibited at games]. It pleases the Senate the theatrical Augustan games [which] are ordinarily held [six days before the Ides of October in memory of the Divine Augustus] should be postponed to five days before the Kalends of November, so that by this [delay of two *nundinae* after] that day upon which Germanicus Caesar died, the day of the theatrical games [will not be saddened by the funeral rite].

Fragment 2, Column b:
[six lines are too badly damaged for translation] [It is pleasing to the Senate that the urban plebs erect statues] of [Germa]nicus Caesar in triumph[al] dress [at

public expense in those temples and on] those public altars on which the Divine Augus]tus and Augusta] placed [them for Drusus Caesar his father] with an inscription [of the thirty-five tribes] of the urban plebs. [Also that the p]oem that Tiberius Caesar Augustus delivered to that body [about the dead Germanicus], be inscribed on bronze in a public place [that] pleases [his father]. Furthermore, the Senate thinks that it would be even more just, because the intimate [communication of Tiberius] Caesar Augustus does not contain greater praise of his son Germanicus Caesar than was true testimony about the order of his life and virtue, and he himself said, in this same intimate communication that he did not dissimulate his desire to hand it on to eternal memory and he judged that it would be useful to the children of our children and posterity. Also, so that the piety of Drusus Caesar should be better known, it pleases the Senate that the communication, which he recited in the next meeting of the Senate, should be inscribed on bronze and erected in the place that seems fitting to himself and his father. Also that this decree of the Senate should be inscribed on bronze with that decree of the Senate that was passed seventeen days before the Kalends of January, and that the bronze tablet be set up in the portico of the temple of Apollo on the Palatinus, where the meeting of the Senate was held. Also, the Senate wishes, and thinks that it is reasonable, so that the piety of all orders towards the Augustan house and the consensus of all citizens about honouring Germanicus Caesar should be plain, that the consuls should post this decree of the Senate with their own edict, and order the magistrates and ambassadors of the colonies and municipalities to send a copy to the municipalities and colonies in Italy and to those colonies that are in the provinces, and that those who govern the provinces will be acting correctly and properly if they take care that this decree of the Senate is displayed in as prominent a place as possible. Also that when Marcus Messalla and Marcus Antonius Cotta Maximus, the consuls designate, take office, they should, on the first possible occasion that the auspicies permit, without a delay of two or three *nundinae*, bring the law concerning honours for the deceased Germanicus to a vote by the people.

It was so voted.

There were 285 senators present when this decree of the Senate was made one by a second vote.

Fragment 2, Column c:
And [it is pleasing to the Senate] that on the Palatinus [in the portico by the Temple of Apollo, in which the Senate] is accustomed to meet, [among the images of men of illustrious character shall be placed those of Germanicus Caesar] and Drusus Ger[manicus his natural father and brother of Tiberius Caesar Augustus,] who was also himself (i.e. Drusus Germanicus) [a fecund genius, (the images shall be placed) on the capitals] of the columns [of that pediment by which the statue of Apollo is protected.] And [it is pleasing to the Senate] that the Salii [shall place] in their *hymns* [the name of Germanicus Caesar to honour] his memory, [which honour was also granted to Caius and Lucius Caesar, brothers of Tiberius] Caesar Augus[tus, and that to the ten centuries of

the Caesars, which are accustomed to cast their vote for the *desinatio]* of consuls and praetors, [shall be added five centuries named in honour of Germanicus Caesar...]

Translated by David S. Potter.

Fragment 1

1. [—]*minio[— Germanici Caesaris qui]* | [*mortem obire nu]nquam debuit v* [*— de*] | [*honoribus m*]*eritis Germanici Caesar*[*is —*] |

4. [*deque*] *ea re consilio Ti(beri) Caesaris Aug(usti) prin*[*cipis nostri — uti*] | *copia sententiarum ipsi fieret atque is adsueta sibi* [*— ex omnibus iis*] | *honoribus quos habendos esse censebat senatus leger⟨e⟩t eo*[*s quoscumque ipse et Iulia*] | *Augusta mater eius et Drusus Caesar materque Germanici Ca*[*esaris, uxore eius, si posset,*] |

8. *adhibita ab eis e⟨i⟩ deliberationi, satis apte posse haberi existu*[*marent, d(e) e(a) r(e)* | *i(ta) c(ensuere):*] | *placere uti ianus marmoreus extrueretur in circo Flaminio pe*[*cunia publica posi-*] | *tus ad eum locum, in quo statuae diuo Augusto domuique Augus*[*tae statutae es-*] | *sent ab C(aio) Norbano Flacco, cum signis deuictarum gentium ins*[*culpereturque*] |

12. *in fronte eius iani, senatum populumque Romanum id monum*[*entum — dedi-*] | *casse memoriae Germanici Caesaris, cum iis, Germanis bello superatis v* [*et —*] | *a Gallia summotis receptisque signis militaribus et uindicata frau*[*dulenta clade*] | *exercitus p(opuli) R(omani), ordinato statu Galliarum pro co(n)s(ule) missus in transmarinas pro*[*uincias atque*] |

16. *in conformandis iis regnisque eiusdem tractus ex mandatis Ti(berii) C⟨a⟩esaris Au*[*g(usti), dato etiam re-*] | *g⟨e⟩ Armeniae, non parcens labori suo priusquam decreto senatus*[*ouans urbem ingre-*] | *deretur ob rem p(ublicam) mortem obisset; supraque eum ianum statua Ger*[*manici Caesaris po*] | *neretur in curru triumphali et circa latera eius statuae D*[*rusi Germanici partris ei*] |

20. *us naturalis, fratris Ti(berii) Caesaris Aug(usti), et Antoniae matris ei*[*us et Agrippinae uxoris et Li-*] | *uiae sororis et Ti(berii) Germanici fratris eius et filiorum et fi*[*liarum eius; vacat*] | *alter ianus fieret in montis Amani iugo quod est in* [*Syria — siue quis*] | *alius aptior locus Ti(berio) Caesari Aug(usto) principi nostr* [*o uideretur in iis regionibus quarum*] |

24. *curam et tutelam Germanico Caesari ex auctori*[*tate senatus ipse mandasset;*] | *item statua eius poneretur et titulus conue*[*niens rebus gestis Germanici Caesaris in-*] | *sculperetur; vvvvv tertius ianus uel ad*[*strueretur uel iuxta eum tumulum fieret,*] | *quem Druso fratri Ti(beri) Caesaris Aug(usti) p*[*rimo sua sponte excitare coepisset exerci-*] |

28. *tus, deinde permissu diui Aug(usti) per*[*fecisset — Germanici Cae*] | *saris constitueretur recipienti*[*s signa militaria ab Germanis; et praeciperetur Gal-*] | *lis Germanisque qui citra Rhen*[*um incolunt, quorum ciuitates iussae sunt ab diuo*] | *Aug(usto) rem diuinam ad tumulu*[*m Drusi facere, —*] |

32. *le sacrificium, parentant*[*es quotannis eo die quo Germanicus Caesar defunctus esset;* | *vacat*] | *et cum esset in ea regio*[*ne qua tumulus Drusi est — die nata-*] |

li Germanici Caesar[is — ex hoc s(enatus) c(onsulto) factus;] | [ite]m placere uti m [onumentum — Anti-] |

36. *[ochi]ae in foro [ubi corpus Germanici Caesaris crematum esset —] | [item]qu[e epi Daphne ubi Germanicus Caesar expirasset tribunal constitueretur —]*

Fragment 1

[— uxo-] | re[eius — Fla-] | mi[nio — gen-] | tium[— supe-] | ratis et[—] | p⟨ro⟩ co(n)s(ule) mis[sus —] | non parce⟨n⟩s[—] | Caesaris pone[retur —] | Antoniae mat[ris —] | alter ianus fieret[—] | regionibus qu[arum —] | conueniens re[bus —] | tertius ianus ue[l — exer-] | citus deinde per[missu — Ger-] | manis et praec[ipue — tumu-] | lum Drusi facer[e —] | et cum esset in e[a —] | ex hoc s(enatus) c(onsulto) factus[—] | Caesaris cremat[um — expi-] | rasset trib[unal —]

Fragment 2, Col. a:

1. *[— utique a(nte) d(iem) (sextum) id(us) Oct(obres) quotannis apud eam aram] quae es[t] | [ante tumulum — in memoriam eius publice i]nferiae manibus | [eius mitterentur per magistros sodaliu]m Augustalium p[ullis] amictos togis, quibus eo- |*

4. *[rum — ius fasque erit habere] eo die sui coloris togam, eodem ritu sacrifici quo | [publice inferiae mittuntur] manibus C(ai) et L(uci) Caesarum; cippusque aeneus prope eum | [tumulum poneretur inque eo hoc s(enatus)] c(onsultum) similiter incideretur ut ea s(enatus) c(onsulta) incisa essent quae | [in C(ai) et L(uci) Caesarum honorem facta] essent; neue quid eo die rei seriae publice agere |*

8. *[liceret mag(istratibus) p(opuli) R(omani) iisque qui i(ure) d(icundo) p(raerunt) in] municipio aut colonia c(iuium) R(omanorum) aut Latinorum neue eo | [die qua conuiuia publica posth]ac neue quae nuptiae c(iuium) R(omanorum) fierent aut sponsalia ne- | [ue quis pecuniam creditam ab alio] sumeret aliue daret neue ludi fierent aut | [spectacula neue — au]diretur; vvv utique ludi Augustales sca⟨e⟩nici,*

12. *[qui a(nte) d(iem) (sextum) id(us) Oct(obres) antehac commit]ti solerent, ut a(nte) d(iem) (quintum) no⟨n⟩⟨as⟩ committerentur, qua | [—] eum diem quo Germanicus Caesar extinctus | [esset —] dies ludorum scaenicorum. vacat*

Fragment 2

[— p]erque domestica[sacra —] | [— T]i(berius) Caesar Aug(ustus) [—] | [—]mare se[—] | [—]u[—]

Fragment 2, Column b:

1. *[—]m | [— p]rinci- | [—]r quod dies etiam | [—]ori et adlocutioni- | [bus — studi] umque eius probare | [— uti ad]essent tribus urbanae et | [rusticae — uidere]tur pollicita esset; itaque place |*

8. *[re uti statuae — Germa]nici Caesaris cum ueste triumpha- | [li sumptu plebis urbanae ponerentur] i[n] eis ar⟨e⟩is publicis, in quibus diuus Aug- | [ustus et — statuas Drusi G]er(manici) posuissent, cum inscriptione plebis urbanae | [—; itemque uolu]men, quod Ti(berius) Caesar Aug(ustus) in eo ordine a(nte) d(iem) (septimum decimum) k(alendas) Ian(uarias) |*

12. [*recitasset et sub edicto*]*suo proposuisset, in aere incisum figeretur loco publico* |
[*quo —*] *placeret; idque eo iustius futurum arbitrari senatum, quod* | [*animus Ti(beri)*] *Caesaris Aug(usti) intumus et Germanici Caesaris f(ili) eius non magis laudatio* | *nem quam uitae totius ordinem et uirtut⟨is⟩ eius uerum testimonium contineret* |

16. *aeternae tradi memoriae, et ipse se uelle non dissimulare eodem libello testatus* |
esset et esse utile iuuentuti liberorum posteriorumque nostrorum iudicaret; | *item quo testatior esset Drusi Caesaris pietas placere uti libellus quem is proxu* | *mo senatu recitasset in aere incideretur eoque loco figeretur quo patri eius ipsique placuisset;* |

20. *itemque hoc s(enatus) c(onsultum) in aere incideretur cum eo s(enatus) c(onsulto)*
quod factum est a(nte) d(iem) (septimum decimum) kal(endas) Ian(uarias) idque aes in Palatio in | *porticu quae est ad Apollinis in templo quo senatus haberetur figeretur; vvv item senatum uel-* | *le atque aequom censere, quo facilius pietas omnium ordinum erga domum Augustam et consen-* | *su⟨s⟩ uniuersorum ciuium memoria honoranda Germanici Caesaris appareret, uti co(n)s(ules) hoc* |

24. *s(enatus) c(onsultum) sub edicto suo proponerent iuberentque mag(istratus) et legatos municipiorum et coloniar* | *um descriptum mittere in municipia et colonias Italiae et in eas colonias quae essent in* | *⟨p⟩rouinciis; eos quoque qui in prouinci⟨i⟩s praessent recte atque ordine facturos si hoc s(enatus) c(onsultum) de-* | *disse⟨n⟩t operam ut quam celeberrumo loco figeretur; vv utique M(arcus) Messalla M(arcus) Aurelius* |

28. *Cotta Maximus co(n)s(ules) designati cum magistratum inissent primo quoque tempore cum per* | *auspicia liceret sine binum trinumue nundinum prodictione legem ad populum de* | *honoribus Germanici Caesaris ferendam cur⟨ar⟩ent. cens (uere.) i(n) s(enatu) f(uerunt) (ducenti octoginta quinque). h(oc) s(enatus) c(onsultum) per relatio-* | *nem secundam factum est unum. vacat*

Fragment 2, Column c:
[*— a*]*rbitrar*[*i senatum —*] | [*—*]*+ aliquam* [*—*] | [*—t*]*ur in Palatio*[*—*] | [*— *]*in eodem libro*[*—*] | [*— Germ*]*anicum arbitra*[*ri —*] | [*—*] *senatui placere, uti*[*—*] | [*— im*]*agines ponerentur supr*[*a —*] | [*— e*]*aquae ex s(enatus) c(onsulto) honorandi c*[*ausa —*] | [*—*]*m, qui inter alia eodem uol*[*umine —*] | [*— trans*]*mar(inarum) prouinciarum Asia*[*e —*] | [*— gr*]*atias agere et adgnosc*[*ere —*] | [*— u*]*ocarentur fieren*[*t —*] | [*—*]*ris, cum honore*[*s —*] | [*C*]*acsarum, qu*[*ae —*] | [*— desti*]*narent*[*—*]/ [*—*]*un*[*—*]

Glossary

Acies – 'Line of troops', battle order.
Aedile – Magistrate in charge of public works.
Aes – 'Copper'.
Ala – 'Wing', legionary cavalry on wings of battle formation (*alae* pl.).
Amphora – Tall jar in which olive oil, fish sauce, wine and other products were
    carried and stacked in the holds of ships.
Annona – Personification of the grain supply of Rome.
Apex – Spiked cap worn by a *flamen*.
Aquila – 'Eagle', the eagle standard of a legion.
Aquilifer – Standard-bearer carrying the *aquila*.
Ara – Altar.
Armatura – Weapons training.
As – 'Copper', Roman coin worth half of one *dupondius* (*asses* pl.).
Augur – Soothsayer specializing in interpretation of bird flight.
Augustus – 'Revered One', honorific title voted to C. Iulius Caesar (Octavianus)
    and his successor Ti. Caesar.
Aureus – 'Gold', highest denomination gold coin worth 25 *denarii* (*aurei* pl.).
Auspex – Soothsayer specializing in interpreting flight of birds.
Auxilia – Support troops of non-Roman citizens.
Ballista – Artillery weapon throwing bolts or stones.
Bellator – 'Warrior', Roman war fighter (*bellatores* pl.).
Beneficiarius – Soldier given a special duty to perform (*beneficiarii* pl.).
Campidoctor – Drill sergeant.
Campus Martius – 'Field of Mars', a large park and recreation ground in Rome.
Capitolinus – Hill in Rome on which was built the Temple of Iupiter.
Carrus triumphalis – Decorated chariot used in a triumph.
Catapulta – Artillery weapon throwing bolts.
Censor – Magistrate in charge of the *census*.
Census – Assessment of taxable assets carried out every 5 years (*lustum*).
Centuria – 'Century', unit of 8 *contubernia*, 80 men; sixty centuries formed a
    Legio.
Centurio – 'Centurion', officer in charge of a *centuria*.
Clementia – 'Clemency', the Roman virtue of showing mercy.
Cohors – 'Cohort', unit of six centuries or twelve in a First Cohort (*cohortes* pl.).
Cohors Praetoria – 'Praetorian Cohort', Praetorian Guard.
Cohors Urbanus – Paramilitary police guarding the mint.
Colonia – 'Colony', town founded for retired legionaries.

Commilitio – 'Fellow soldier', a form of address to legionaries usually by a senior office (*commilitiones* pl.).

Confarreatio – Traditional form of wedding.

Consul – One of the two highest magistrates of the *res publica*, elected annually.

Contio – 'Meeting', an address by a magistrate to the people or the commander to his troops to present a proposal.

Contubernales – Form of address for men sharing a tent.

Contubernium – Unit of eight men sharing a tent (*contubernia* pl.).

Cornicen – Horn player, one of the *principales* in a *centuria*.

Cornu – Circular horn for relaying commands played by a *cornicen*.

Cuneus – 'Wedge', attack formation used by Roman army.

Curia – Senate House.

Cursus honorum – Career ladder leading to entry into the Senate as a senator.

Denarius – Silver coin, worth four *sestertii* (*denarii* pl.).

Doctor Armorum – Instructor in the use of the *gladius*, *pilum* and *scutum*.

Dupondius – Bronze coin, worth two *asses* or half a *sestertius* (*dupondii* pl.).

Dux – Leader (*duces* pl.).

Editor – Sponsor of the *ludi* or *munera*.

Equites – 'Knights', the middle or business class of Roman society.

Evocatus – Reservist, a *miles* who had served his time, been honorably discharged and volunteered to serve again at the request of a consul or military commander (*evocati* pl.).

Exercitus – Army.

Fabrica – Workshop (*fabricae* pl.).

Fasces – The tied bundle of rods around an axe carried by *lictores* as a symbol of the *praetor*'s high office.

Feliciter – 'Good luck', a wish shouted at weddings.

Feria – Public holiday and festival day (*feriae* pl.).

Flamen – Priest (*flamines* pl.).

Flammeum – Orange veil worn by the bride at a *confarreatio*.

Fossa – 'Fosse', a ditch or trench, used to mean a canal (*fossae* pl.).

Framea – Germanic spear or javelin (*frameae* pl.).

Frater – 'Brother', a form of address used by soldiers (*fratres* pl.).

Frumentarius – Commissary responsible for the military grain supply (*frumentarii* pl.).

Forum Romanum – Roman Forum in Rome.

Gladius – Short stabbing and thrusting weapon used by legionaries (*gladii* pl.).

Haruspex – Soothsayer specializing in interpreting animal entrails.

Hasta – Javelin used by Roman *auxilia* and cavalry.

Honesta – 'Honesty', the Roman virtue of respectability.

Humanitas – 'Humanity', the Roman virtue associated with being cultured from having a good education.

Ianus – 'Arch', triumphal arch.

Imago – Mask of wax made during the lifetime of a Roman citizen; military standard bearing a small statue bust of the *princeps*.

Imagnifer – Standard-bearer responsible for carrying the *imago*.
Immunis – Soldier exempt from certain duties, often a bookkeeper or clerk (*immunes* pl.).
Impedimenta – Baggage train.
Imperator – 'Commander', a title shouted by troops to a victorious leader.
Imperium maius – 'Supreme power', originally given to consuls, including the right to wage war.
Industria – Roman virtue of working hard.
Iumentarius – Soldier or slave responsible for baggage and animals that carried it.
Kalendae – 'Calends', first day of the month.
Laudatio – Eulogy.
Legatus Legionis – Commander of a *Legio* 'delegated' the *imperium* by Augustus.
Legio – Unit of ten *cohortes*, approximately 6,000 men (*Legiones* pl.).
Libertas – Roman virtue of independence, freedom of speech.
Liburna – 'Liburnian', type of ship, usually with two rows of oarsmen.
Lictor – Bodyguard of a senior magistrate: a *consul* had twelve, a *praetor* six, a *propraetor* five, and an *aedile* two (*lictores* pl.).
Lituus – Crooked staff used by an augur when interpreting bird flight.
Lorica hamata – Body armour made of chain or ring mail.
Lorica squamata – Body armour made of scales attached to a backing of cloth or leather.
Lorica segmentata – Body armour made of articulated metal plates (a non-Roman term coined in the sixteenth century).
Ludi – Roman blood games, held for religious observance and increasingly used to further political ends.
Maiestas – 'Majesty', short for *maiestas minuta populi Romani*, 'the diminution of the majesty of the Roman people', i.e. treason.
Medicus – 'Medic', doctor.
Miles – Common soldier, *miles gregarius* (*milites* pl.).
Moderatio – 'Moderation', Roman virtue of restraint from excess.
Modius – Measure of grain equivalent to a third of an *amphora*.
Mos maiorum – 'The ways of the elders', traditional values and forms of worship.
Munera – Roman blood games held for political and entertainment purposes.
Municipium – Chartered provincial Roman city.
Navis longa – 'Long ship', name of a bireme or trireme.
Officium – 'Service', the staff responsible for record keeping.
Oppidum – Town or defensible settlement often on a hill.
Onager – 'Wild ass', artillery weapon throwing stones.
Ovatio – Lower form of triumph awarded to a victorious commander who was permitted to ride on a horse through the streets of Rome.
Palatinus – Hill in Rome, location of homes for the Roman élite.
Paterfamilias – Legal master of the household.
Pes – 'Foot'.

Pes Drusianus – 'Drusian Foot', longer than a standard Roman foot.

Pes Monetalis – 'Monetan Foot', standard Roman unit of measuring length.

Pietas – Roman virtue of respect for the natural order of things.

Pilum – Roman javelin used by legionaries (*pila* pl.).

Pompa – Procession in a religious rite or funeral.

Pompa triumphalis – Full triumph in which the *triumphator* rode in a chariot followed by floats displaying the captive and spoils of war.

Pontifex Maximus – 'Chief bridge builder', chief priest.

Praefectus – 'Prefect', senior officer or magistrate.

Praefectus Castrorum – 'Camp Prefect', third in command of a *Legio*.

Praefectus Equitum – 'Prefect of Horse', senior officer in command of a *turma*.

Praefectus Praetorio – Commander of the *Cohors Praetoria*.

Praepositus – 'Overseer', special envoy or governor general.

Praetor – Senior magistrate responsible for administering law, the *ludi* and *feriae*.

Praetor Urbanus – Chief *praetor* in charge of administration of law in Rome.

Praetorium – 'Praetor's building', house of the senior officer of a *Legio*.

Primus Pilus – 'First javelin', the most senior *centurio* of a *Legio*.

Princeps – 'The First One', the title adopted by Augustus to describe his leadership position.

Princeps Praetorii – Officer in charge of the army unit's *officium*.

Principalis – Non-commissioned officer of a *centuria*, e.g. *cornicen*, *signifer* (*principales* pl.).

Principia – 'Front line', headquarters building in a Roman fort.

Proconsul – 'Former consul', governor of a senatorial province.

Propraetor – 'Former praetor', governor of an imperial province.

Pugio – Short, leaf-shaped dagger worn by legionaries.

Quaestor – Junior magistrate in charge of law courts and public financial accounting.

Rostra – Tribunal, speaker's platform in *Forum Romanum*.

Res publica – 'Public Things', the commonwealth of the Roman state.

Sacerdos – Priest (*sacerdotes* pl.).

Salutatio – Morning visit by clients to the patron.

Scutum – Roman shield (*scuta* pl.).

Semis – Roman coin worth half of one *as*.

Senatus Consultum – Decree of the Senate.

Sestertius – Brass coin, equal in value to one-quarter *denarius* (*sestertii* pl.).

Signifer – Standard-bearer carrying the centurial *signum*.

Signum – Unit standard (*signa* pl.).

Spatha – Long double-edged slashing sword used by cavalry.

Speculator – Military escort, often carrying out clandestine missions and executions (*speculatores* pl.).

Spolia opima – Prized spoils taken from an enemy after armed combat.

Suovetaurilia – Religious rite involving the sacrifice of a pig, sheep and bull.

Testudo – 'Tortoise', battle formation using shields raised over the heads.

Toga praetexta – White toga with a broad purple stripe along the curved edge.

Toga virilis – 'Manly gown', the all-white toga worn by Roman adult men.

Tresvir – 'Three Man', a board responsible for a state function, e.g. *tresviri monetales*, who were responsible for managing the coin supply.

Tribunus – Tribune: *tribunus plebis*, a representative of the people elected annually; *tribunus laticlavius*, the second in command of a *Legio* was accompanied by five junior *tribuni angusticlavii*.

Triumphator – The military commander awarded an *ovatio* or *pompa triumphalis*.

Triumvir – Commission of three political leaders (*triumviri* pl.).

Tropaeum – 'Trophy' made of captured weapons (*tropaea* pl.).

Tumulus – Cenotaph shaped like a raised circular dome (*tumuli* pl.).

Turma – Unit of Roman cavalry (*turmae* pl.).

Vexillum – Flag standard.

Vexillarius – Standard-bearer of the *vexillum*.

Via Praetoria – Cross road in a Roman camp leading to *principia*.

Via Principalis – Main street of a Roman camp.

Via Sacra – 'Sacred Way', the main road running through the *Forum Romanum*.

Virtus – 'Manliness', Roman virtue of courage.

Place Names

Cities and Towns

Actium Aktion (Preveza)
Alexandria Alexandria
Amelia Terni
Amisos Samsun
Andetrium Gornji Muč
Antiocheia Antakya
Antium Anzio
Apollonia Pojani
Ara Ubiorum Cologne, Köln (after 1 CE)
Argentorate Strasbourg
Ariminium Rimini
Artaxata Artashat
Asciburgium Moers-Asberg
Assos Behramkale
Athenae Athens, Athenai
Augusta Treverorum Trier
Augusta Vindelicorum Augsburg
Batavodurum Nijmegen
Bonna Bonn
Brundisium Brindisi
Burnum Camp near modern Kistanje, Croatia
Byzantium Istanbul, Constantinople
Caesarea Maritima Caesarea
Carnuntum (Karnuntum) Camp halfway between modern Vienna and Bratislava
Cibalae Vinkovici
Colonia Augusta Buthrotum Butrint
Colonia Copia Munatia Felix Lyon (Fourvière)
Colonia Laus Iulia Corinthiensis Corinth, Korinthos
Colonia Obsequens Iulia Pisana Pisa
Colophon Değirmendere

Condate Lyon (La Croix-Rousse)
Confluentes Koblenz
Dyrrhachium Durrës
Emona Ljubljana
Ephidaphnae Suburb of Antiocheia, modern Beit el-ma or Harbiye
Epidaurum Cavtat
Fectio Vechten
Gabii Roman town near modern Osteria dell'Osa
Hierosylima Jerusalem
Ilium (Ilion) Hisarlik, Troy
Laodikeia Loadikya
Lugdunum Lyon (after mid-first century CE)
Massalia Marseille
Mazaca (Caesarea) Kayseri
Mediolanum Santonum Saintes
Melitene Malatya
Memphis Helwan, Cairo
Metulum Viničica
Mogontiacum Mainz
Mursa Osijek
Nicopolis Nikopolis
Nissus Niš
Novaesium Neuss
Noviomagus Speyer
Oppidum Ubiorum Cologne, Köln (prior to 1 CE)
Pola Pula
Rhegium Reggio di Calabria
Roma Rome, Roma
Salona Solin
Samosata Samsat
Scupi Skopje
Sinope Sinop
Sirmium Mitrovica

Siscia Sisak
Surrentum Sorrento
Syene Aswan
Tarsus Tarsus
Tergeste Trieste
Tibur Tivoli
Ticinum Pavia
Tomis Constanţa
Tropaeum Drusi *Uncertain: Dresden?*
   Magdeburg? Poppenburg?
Vetera Xanten
Vienna Vienne on the Rhône
Vindobona Vienna, Austria

Islands
Capreae Capri
Corcyra (Korcyra) Corfu
Pandateria Ventotene
Planasia Pianosa
Rhodos Rhodes

Mountains
Mons Alma Fruska Gora
Mons Claudius Papuk Hills

Rivers
Albis Elbe
Amisia, Amisius Ems
Arar Saône

Bathinus Bosnar
Danuvius Danube, Donau
Dravus Drava, Drave
Drinus Drina
Eliso *Uncertain: Alme?*
Ister Danube, Donau
Lupia Lippe
Moenus Main
Mosa Meuse
Mosella Moselle, Mosel
Nilus Nile
Pyramus Ceyhan
Rhenus Rhine, Rhein
Rhodanus Rhône
Sala Saal
Savus Sava, Save, Száva
Vahalis Waal
Visurgis Weser

Seas
Mare Aegaeum Aegean Sea
Mare Germanicum North Sea
Mare Internum Mediterranean Sea
Pontus Euxinus Black Sea
Oceanus Germanicus North Sea
Sinus Ambracius Ambracian Gulf
Sinus Arabicus Red Sea
Sinus Hadriaticus Adriatic Sea

Ancient Sources

The evidence from which it is possible to piece together the life and exploits of Germanicus Caesar is scattered across several types of source material. These include written accounts and inscriptions. From coins and sculptures we have a good idea of how he looked.

1. Authors

Written sources from the ancient world pose particular problems for modern historians. The approach to writing history then was very different from today's. In *Ancient History: Evidence and Models* (1985), Sir Moses Finley observed that modern scholars tend to treat ancient authors' works with a reverence and lack of criticism that they do not accord material of other ages. It is particularly problematic for anyone studying the principates of Augustus and Tiberius. If Germanicus wrote an autobiography – and many famous Roman generals, such as C. Marius and M. Agrippa, did – it is completely lost. Few of the primary – that is to say, contemporary or eye-witness – accounts, of which several were written in antiquity (such as by Aufidius Bassus), have come down to us. The surviving accounts are Velleius Paterculus' brief history of the Roman Empire, Strabo's sprawling geographical treatise, and the poems of Albinovanus Pedo and Ovid. All the other extant accounts which mention Germanicus were written decades or centuries later. The most complete biography is Suetonius' introduction to the *Life of Caligula*. The most continuous in-depth narrative is the annalistic history of Tacitus, which is notably biased in favour of Germanicus and was written eighty years after he died. There is also the derivative history of Cassius Dio, which he wrote two centuries after the events, and, for his source material, he drew on earlier accounts, including Tacitus. In studying these accounts for evidence of the life and exploits of Germanicus, we have to be mindful of the difficulties posed by the literature, and understand the motives of their authors and the times in which they wrote, compare their claims against what is known from archaeological, epigraphical and numismatic sources. Futhermore, few of the ancient writers had personal military experience and thus lacked the insights a soldier learned from actual combat, which means that their accounts of expeditions, campaigns and battles are often flawed or difficult to interpret.

Albinovanus Pedo, late first century BCE–mid-first century CE – Pedo was a *praefectus equitum* leading a unit of Frisian cavalry in Germanicus' army in Germania Magna during the campaigns of 15 and 16 CE (Tac., *Ann.* 1.60, 2.23). Off duty he was a highly regarded raconteur (Ov., *Pont.* 4.10). His epic poem of the war in Germania was cited by Seneca the Elder as a fine example of Latin literature. It is preserved as an extract in his collection of exercises in deliberative oratory (*Suas.* 1.15), which describes the terrifying ordeal of the Roman army in 16 CE as it is tossed about by the stormy North Sea.

Ammianus Marcellinus, c. 325/330–after 391 CE – A former soldier turned historian, Marcellinus wrote a history of the Roman Empire, continuing the work of Tacitus, covering the years 96–378 CE (*Res Gestae a Fine Corneli Taciti*). In passing, he records Germanicus' visit to the shrine of the Apis bull on the Nile and the bad omen that was given him during the visit (22.14.7–8).

Cassius Dio (L. or Cl. Dio Cassius Cocceianus), c. 155 or 163/164–after 229 CE – Dio was a senator and consul who wrote one of the most complete histories of Roman civilization that has come down to us. Written in Greek in eighty volumes, it took Dio twenty-two years to research and assemble his material for Ῥωμαϊκὴ Ἱστορία (*Roman History*). One of his sources may have been Tacitus.

Germanicus appears in Books 56 and 57 of *Roman History*. Dio describes his campaigns in Illyricum (56.11–17) and his award of triumphal ornaments (56.17.2), his popularity as an advocate in Rome (56.24.7), his first consulship (56.26.1), Augustus' liking of his adoptive grandson (56.26.2), his first forays in Germania Magna with Tiberius (56.25.2), his sponsorship of the *Ludi Martiales* (56.27.6), his governorship of Tres Galliae and the two military districts of Germania (57.3.1), the mutiny of the Rhine legions (57.5.1–7), his invasions of Germania Magna (57.6 and 57.18.1), his refusal to usurp power (57.6.2–4), his role as a counterbalance to Tiberius' tyranny (57.13.6, 19.8), his amiable person- ality (57.18.6–8), his death in Antiocheia (57.18.9), the composition of a com- memorative ode to him (57.20.3), and finally the trial of Piso (57.18.10).

Josephus (Yosef Ben Matityahu or T. Flavius Josephus), 37–100 CE – The erstwhile leader of the resistance at Yodfat (Jotapata) during the First Jewish War of 66–73 CE, Josephus was a prolific writer under his Flavian benefactors, to whom he owed his life. In *Against Apion* (*Contra Apionem* 2.63–64), he describes the response of the Alexandrian Jewish community to Germanicus' selective dis- tribution of grain in the face of spreading famine. In his *Antiquities of the Jews* (*Antiquitates Iudaicae*), published around 75 CE, he mentions Germanicus' house on the Palatinus Hill (*Ant. Iud.* 19.1.15), confirming that he had his own resi- dence in Rome, and gives the earliest suggestion of all the surviving accounts that Germanicus was poisoned (*ibid.* 18.54).

Ovid (P. Ovidius Naso), 43 BCE–17 CE – Ovid was Rome's most popular poet who managed to upset Augustus – for reasons which remain obscure – and found himself banished to Tomis on the Black Sea. From Ovid, we learn that Salanus was Germanicus' teacher of rhetoric (*Pont.* 2.5.5–8, 41–46). Considering Germanicus a kindred spirit in the poetic art, Ovid invokes the reader of his *Epistle* to supplicate his imperial hero to intervene and advocate to have his exile rescinded (*Pont.* 4.8). He dedicated his *fasti* to Germanicus (*Fast.* 1.3–26) and, later in the same work, praises him for bringing peace to the Rhine (*ibid.* 1.227–301). He acknowledges Germanicus' role in the Batonian War (*Pont.* 2.1.45–52), and comments how he had brought Germania to its knees (*Tr.* 4.2.25–26). Ovid never returned to Rome and died in Tomis.

Pliny the Elder (C. Plinius Secundus), 23–79 CE – The polymath Pliny the Elder began his career as an active soldier in the Rhine army, seeing three tours of duty (45–51 CE), including one as a *praefectus equitum* – as a result of which he wrote a single-volume book on throwing the javelin while riding on horseback, which has been lost. Sadly, Pliny's history of Rome's wars in Germania (*Bella Germaniae*) in twenty volumes has also not survived, although we know that it, in turn, provided source material for other Roman historians, notably Tacitus (*Ann.* 1.69). Pliny is best known for his encyclopaedic *Naturalis Historia* (*Natural History*), which, among its many topics, describes the people and territories of the known world, and locates the cities named Germanikopolis in the Hellespont and Mysia (*Nat. Hist.* 5.40). He records the extraordinary games laid on by Germanicus, during which elephants danced and a meteor was seen in the sky (*Nat. Hist.* 2.25; 8.2), and mentions that he wrote a poem in honour of Augustus' deceased horse (*ibid.* 8.62).

Plutarch (Plutarchos, L. Mestrius Plutarchus), c. 46–120 CE – The Greek-speaking biographer, essayist and historian wrote a number of works, most famously Οἱ Βίοι Παράλληλοι (*Parallel Lives*), which compared the lives of famous Greek and Roman soldiers and statesmen. Plutarch did not write a book about Germanicus *per se*, but he mentions him as a grandson of M. Antonius via Antonia Minor (*Ant.* 87.3). He also mentions Germanicus' alektorophobia in his *de Invidia et Odio* (*On Envy and Hate*).

Seneca the Younger (L. Annaeus Seneca), c. 4 BCE–65 CE – The playright, Stoic philospher, statesman, tutor and later advisor to the Emperor Nero recorded that a shooting star appeared before Germanicus' death (*Quaestiones Naturales* 1.3), which was taken to be a portent.

Strabo (Strabonos), 63/64 BCE–c. 24 CE – The historian, geographer and philosopher Strabo is best known for his Γεωγραφικά (*Geography*), a seventeen-volume descriptive survey of the world known to the Romans. Begun some time around 20 BCE, Strabo gives us a valuable insight into the intelligence base that Germanicus and his legates had available to them at the time they planned their campaigns (*Geog.* 4.4.2). He provides us with near-contemporary descriptions of the cities, lands and rivers of the nations Germanicus visited. His descriptions of the cities and monuments of Egypt – Alexandria, Nikopolis, Memphis, Thebes and Syene – are particularly notable, as he visited these himself forty-four years before Germanicus. Strabo recorded the names of each of the captives humiliatingly displayed in Germanicus' triumph (*Geog.* 7.1.4).

Suetonius (C. Suetonius Tranquillus), c. 69/75–after 130 CE – Suetonius wrote the *Lives of the Caesars* (*De Vita Caesarum*), in which he collected biographical facts, rumours and tidbits about Iulius Caesar and the eleven men who followed him. In the *Life of Caligula*, he provides the only complete biography of Germanicus, his cultural, military and political achievements, his personality and temperament, his marriage to Agrippina, their family, and his death (*Calig.* 1–7). It is from him that we learn that Augustus actively considered him as his successor (*Calig.* 4). From the other *Lives*, we learn of his adoption by Tiberius (*Tib.* 15.2), the Rhine army's desire to see Germanicus take the throne (*ibid.* 25.2), Tiberius' indifference to both his sons (*ibid.* 52.1–3) and Germanicus' death in Syria (*ibid.* 39). He also mentions Caligula's decision to rename September after his father (*Calig.* 15.2) and that his brother Claudius staged performances of his plays in his memory (*Div. Claud.* 11.2).

Tacitus (P. or C. Cornelius Tacitus), 56–117 CE – Tacitus was a senator who wrote several books during the reign of the Emperor Trajan. He writes in the 'solemn' and 'dignified' style of a Roman orator (Pliny, *Ep.* 2.11.17) using terms and phrases which challenge translation into modern languages. He followed in the tradition of the historians of the Republic – notably, Sallust (C. Sallustius Crispus, 86–35 BCE) and Livy (T. Livius, 59 BCE–17 CE) – but presented his material in such a way as to stress how different life had become in Imperial times. He arranged his material by year, covering the period 14–96 CE. The story of Germanicus is told in Books 1 and 2 and the early chapters of Book 3 of his *Ab Excessu Divi Augusti* (more conveniently nowadays referred to as the *Annales*, or *Annals*), published in 117 CE. It is apparent that Tacitus used a number of primary sources (such as the *Senatus Consultum de Cn. Pisone patre*) and public records (*publica acta*), as well as oral histories and works of other authors who wrote at the time of the events or some while after them (such as Pliny the Elder). He also tells us that he had access to the memoirs of Agrippina the Younger, daughter of Germanicus, and speeches of Tiberius. Yet he invented speeches (such as Germanicus' to the mutinous troops) and borrowed material from earlier historians which have little or nothing to do with the Julio-Claudian emperors. Modern historians continue to debate the degree to which Tacitus' presentation of Germanicus' and Tiberius' relationship is based on fact or manipulated by him to serve a deeper purpose.

His editorial bias and poetic licence notwithstanding, Tacitus is a key source of information about Germanicus' life and death. From him, we have details of his adoption by Tiberius (*Ann.* 1.3), his appointment to command of the Rhine legions (*ibid.* 1.3), his handling of the mutiny (*ibid.* 1 31–49), the ensuing expeditions in Germania Magna (*ibid.* 1.50–52, 55–71; 2.5–26), the award and celebration of his triumph (*ibid.* 1.55; 2.41), his second consulship (*ibid.* 2.53), his travels to the Orient (*ibid.* 2.43, 53–58), sojourn in Egypt (*ibid.* 2.59–61, 64, 69), and, finally, his end in Syria (*ibid.* 2.69–72). Tacitus is also the most important source on the immediate aftermath, including Germanicus' funeral in Antiocheia (*ibid.* 2.73), the reaction of the Roman people to the news (*ibid.* 2.82–83), the honours accorded by the Senate (*ibid.* 2.83), Agrippina's journey to bring her husband's ashes to Rome (*ibid.* 2.75; 3.1–5), and the trial of Calpurnius Piso (*ibid.* 3.10–18). Finally, Tacitus describes Germanicus' personality, compares his achievements to Alexander the Great's and argues that they surpassed the Macedonian king's (*ibid.* 2.72–73).

Velleius Paterculus (C. or M. Velleius Paterculus), c. 19 BCE–c. 31 CE – Paterculus saw eight years of active service under Tiberius, serving first in Illyricum as a *praefectus equitum* during the Batonian War, and then in Germania as a *legatus legionis*. His *Historiae Romanae* (*Compendium of Roman History*) is regarded as that of a courtly annalist rather than a critical historian, particularly as it offers a gushing eulogy of Tiberius' exploits in Book 2. He includes a short but flattering description of Germanicus' achievements in the Illyrian Revolt (2.116), confirms his deployment to Germania on Augustus' orders (2.123), his role in the mutiny of the Rhine legions (2.125.1–4), and his successes against the Germanic nations, and lauds Tiberius' decision to send him to the East and the manner in which he did it (2.219.1–4).

2. Coins

No coins were produced by the official mints in Rome or Lugdunum during Germanicus' lifetime which mention the man by name or show his portrait. However, several communities in the provinces struck commemorative and definitive issues while he was alive and serving as *praepositus* under Tiberius. Coins issued for C. Caesar Augustus Germanicus should not be confused with Caligula's father, Germanicus Iulius Caesar.

(a) *Imperial Mints*

From 15 BCE, the imperial mint at Lugdunum struck gold (*aurei*) and silver (*denarii*) coins, while the mint at the Temple of Iuno Moneta in Rome minted lower denomination brass (*sestertii*) and bronze (*dupondii, asses, semis*) coins.

(i) Caligula:
- Gold *aureus* struck 37–38 CE in Lugdunum. Obverse: C CAESAR AVG GERM P M TR POT, bare head of Caligula facing right. Reverse: GERMANICVS CAES P C CAES AVG GERM, bare head of Germanicus facing right. (Numismatic references: *BMCRE* 18, Calicó 321, *C* 6 and *RIC* I, 17.)
- Silver *denarius* struck 37–38 CE in Lugdunum (plate 35). Obverse: C CAESAR AVG GERM P M TR POT, bare head of Caligula facing right. Reverse: GERMANICVS CAES P C CAES AVG GERM, bare head of Germanicus facing right. This is a silver version of the *aureus*, maybe using the same dies. (Numismatic references: *BMCRE* 13, *BN* 15–16, Lyon 165, 4 (D68/R68), *RIC* I, 12 and *RSC* 4.)
- Silver *denarius* struck 37–38 CE in Lugdunum? Obverse: GERMANICVS CAES P C CAES AVG GERM, bare head of Germanicus facing right. Reverse: AVGVST below capricorn facing right, cornucopia over shoulder. (Numismatic references: Giard, Lyon, R63, pl. XXXVIII, 164/4a (obverse) and *RIC* I, 126 (reverse).)

- Silver *denarius* struck 37–38 CE in Lugdunum? Obverse: GERMANICVS CAES P C CAES AVG GERM, bare head of Germanicus facing right. Reverse: M PLAETORI to right, SEST EX SC to left of caduceus. (Numismatic references: reverse type of M. Plaetorius Cestianus; Giard, Lyon, R63, pl. XXXVIII, 164/4a (obverse) and Crawford 405/5 (reverse).)
- Bronze *dupondius* struck 37 CE in Rome to commemorate the twentieth anniversary of Germanicus' triumph and the return of the legionary standards lost by Varus in the battle at Teutoburg in 9 CE (plate 36). Obverse: GERMANICVS CAESAR, Germanicus standing in toga with eagle-tipped sceptre in a triumphal *quadriga* facing right. Reverse: SIGNIS DEVICTIS S | RECEPT GERM C across flan separated by figure of Germanicus in full military panoply advancing left, holding *aquila* in left hand. (Numismatic references: *C* 7, *S* 1820 and *RIC* I, 57.)
- Bronze *as* struck 37–38 CE in Rome (plate 37). Obverse: GERMANICVS CAESAR TI AVGVST F DIVI AVG N, bare head of Germanicus facing left. Reverse: C CAESAR AVG GERMANICVS PON M TR POT around large S C. (Numismatic references: *C* 1, *BMCRE* 49; *RIC* I, 35; *RCV* 1821 and *RSC* 1.)
- Bronze *as* struck 40–41 CE in Rome. Obverse: GERMANICVS CAESAR TI AVGVST F DIVI AVG N, bare head of Germanicus facing left. Reverse: C CAESAR DIVI AVG PRON AVG P M TR POT IIII P P around large S C. (Numismatic references: *RIC* I, 43 and *SR* 1821.)

(ii) Claudius:
- Bronze *as* struck 41–54 CE in Rome (plate 38). Obverse: GERMANICVS CAESAR TI AVG F DIVI AVG N, bare head of Germanicus facing right. Reverse: TI CLAVDIVS CAESAR AVG GERMANI IMP P P around large S C. (Numismatic references: *BMCRE* 215, *CBN* 241, *C* 9, *RIC* I, 43 and 106.)

(iii) Titus:
- Bronze *as* struck 80–81 CE in Rome. Obverse: GERMANICVS CAESAR TI AVG F DIVI AVG N, bust of Germanicus facing left. Reverse: IMP T CAES DIVI VESP F AVG REST around large S C. (Numismatic references: *BMCRE* 293, *BN* 306, *C* 12 and *RIC* II.1, 442.)

(b) *Provincial Mints*

Several cities throughout the empire – particularly in Spain and Asia Minor – minted low denomination bronze (*aes*) and copper (*asses*) coins for local circulation. A few of the largest cities in the East minted silver coins (*didrachmai*, *drachmai*).

(i) Tiberius:
- Silver *drachm* struck c. 33–38 CE in Caesarea, Cappadocia. Obverse: GERMANICVS CAES TI AVGV COS II G M, bare head of Germanicus facing right. Reverse: DIVVS AVGVSTVS, radiate head of Augustus facing left. (Numismatic references: *RPC* I, 3623b, *RSC* 2 and Sydenham 52.)
- Bronze *as* struck c. 18–20 CE in Pergamum, Mysia. Obverse: ΓΕΡΜΑΝΙΚΟΣ ΚΑΙΣΑΡ ΚΤΙΣΤΗΣ, bare head of Germanicus facing right. Reverse:

ΔΡΟΥΣΟΣ ΚΑΙΣΑΡ, bare head of Drusus facing right. (Numismatic reference: *RPC* 2367.)

- Bronze *as* struck c. 18–20 CE in Tabae, Caria. Obverse: ΓΕΡΜΑΝΙΚΟΣ ΔΡΟΥΣΟΣ ΦΙΛΑΔΕΛΦΟΙ, confronted bare heads of Germanicus and Drusus. Reverse: ΤΑΒΗ | ΝΩΝ Α | ΦΗΝΑΓ | ΟΡΑΣ Σ | Ε, legend in four lines within wreath. (Numismatic references: *BMCRE* 61 and *RPC* 2871.)
- Bronze *as* struck c. 20 CE in Caesarea Germanica, Bithynia. Obverse: ΓΕΡΜΑΝΙΚΟΣ ΚΑΙΣΑΡ ΚΤΙΣΤΗΕ, bare head of Germanicus facing right. Reverse: ΚΑΙΣΑΡΗΑ ΓΕΡΜΑΝΙΚΗ, view of city gate with statue between four towers; monogram in exergue. (Numismatic references: Rec Gen 1 and *RPC* 2017.)
- Bronze *as* struck c. 28–29 CE under C. Asinius Pollio (proconsul, *anthypatos*) in Sardes, Lydia. Obverse: ΑΡΟΥΣΟΣ ΚΑΙ ΓΕΡΜΑΝΙΚΟΣ ΚΑΙΣΑΡΕΣ, Germanicus and Drusus the Younger togate sitting in curule chairs facing left. Reverse: ΓΑΙΩ ΑΣΙΝΝΙΩ ΠΩΛΛΙΩΝΙ ΝΟΨΥΡΑΤΩ | ΚΟΙΝΟΥ ΑΣΙΑΣ, in two rows around wreath. (Numismatic references: *BMCRE* 104, *RPC* 2994. This interesting coin is actually re-struck with two intricate ring-shaped 'countermarks'.)
- Bronze *as* struck c. 23–36 CE in Sardes, Lydia. Obverse: ΓΕΡΜΑΝΙΚΟΣ ΚΑΙΣΑΡΕΩΝ; bare head of Germanicus facing right. Reverse: ΔΡΟΥΣΟΣ ΣΑΡΔΙΑΝΩΝ; bare head of Drusus the Younger facing right. (Numismatic references: *BMCRE* 110, *RPC* I, 489 and 2992.)
- Bronze *as* struck c. 23–36 CE under C. Heius Pollio and C. Mussius Priscus *duumviri* in Corinth. Obverse: GERMANICVS CAESAR COR, bare head of Germanicus facing right. Reverse: C MVSSIO PRISCO IIVIR HEIO POLLIONE ITER, legend in four lines within wreath. (Numismatic reference: *RPC* 1142. The names in the reverse legend can appear in a different order.)
- Bronze *as* struck c. 20–36 CE under magistrate Mnaseas in Sardes, Lydia. Obverse: ΓΕΡΜΑΝΙΚΟΣ ΚΑΙΣΑΡ, bare head of Germanicus facing left. Reverse: ΣΑΡΔΙΑΝΩΝ ΜΝΑΣΕΑΣ, Athena standing left, holding phiale. (Numismatic references: *BMCRE* 113 corr. and *RPC* 2993.)
- Bronze *as* struck c. 23–36 CE in Tanagra, Boeotia. Obverse: ΓΕΡΜΑΝΙΚΟΣ, bare head of Germanicus facing right. Reverse: ΤΑΝΑ, Apollo standing facing forward holding branch and bow. (Numismatic references: *RPC* 1318 and *SNG Copenhagen* 239.)
- Bronze *as* struck c. 23–36 CE in Carteia, Spain. Obverse: GERMANICO ET DRVSO, turreted head of city goddess facing right. Reverse: CART CAESARIBVS IIII VIR, around rudder. (Numismatic references: Lindgren II 82, *RPC* 123 and SGI 363.)
- Bronze *semis* struck c. 23–36 CE in Romula, Spain. Obverse: GERMANICVS CAESAR TI AVG F, bare head of Germanicus facing left. Reverse: PERM AVG COL ROM, circular shield inside laurel wreath. (Numismatic references: *RPC* 75 and SGI 352.)

- Bronze *tessera* struck c. 20–37 CE at an unknown mint. Obverse: GER-MANICVS CAESAR, laureate head of Germanicus facing right. Reverse: captive kneeling right kneeling right at foot of trophy, hands tied behind back, helmet and shield left. (Numismatic reference: Buttrey 17 and *CNG* 120–47.)

(ii) Caligula:
- Bronze *as* struck 37–41 CE in Aezanis, Phrygia. Obverse: ΓΕΡΜΑΝΙΚΟΣ; bare head of Germanicus facing right. Obverse: ΑΓΡΙΠΠΙΝΑ ΑΙΖΑΝΙΩΝ ΕΠΙ ΜΗΔΗΟΥ, draped bust of Agrippina the Elder. (Numismatic reference: *RPC* 3077.)
- Bronze *as* struck 37–41 CE by magistrate Lollius Classicus in Aezanis, Phrygia. Obverse: ΓΕΡΜΑΝΙΚΟΣ, laureate head of Germanicus facing right. Reverse: ΑΓΡΙΠΠΙΝΑ ΕΠΙ ΚΛΑΕΣΙΚΟΥ ΑΙΖΑΝΙΤΩΝ, draped bust of Agrippina the Elder facing right. (Numismatic reference: *RPC* 3081.)
- Bronze *as* struck 37–41 CE by magistrate C. Iulius Kallikles in Apameia, Bithynia. Obverse: ΓΕΡΜΑΝΙΚΟΣ ΚΑΙΣΑΡ, bare head facing right. Reverse: ΙΟΥΛΙΟΣ ΚΑΛΛΙΚΛΗΣ ΑΡΑΜΕΩΝ, stag standing right. (Numismatic reference: *RPC* 3134.)
- Bronze *as* struck 37–41 CE by *duumvir* Pulcher and *triumvir* Varius in Knossos, Crete. Obverse: C CAESAR AVG GERMANICVS, laureate head of Caligula facing right. Reverse: GERM CAESAR PVLCHRO III VARIO II VIR, bare head of Germanicus facing right. (Numismatic reference: Sear 408.)
- Bronze *as* struck 37–41 CE in Gortyna, Crete. Obverse: ΓΑΙΟΝ ΚΑΙΣΑΡΑ ΓΕΡΜΑΝΙΚΩΝ ΣΕΒΑΣΟΝ, bare head of Caligula facing right. Reverse: ΓΕΡΜΑΝΙΚΩΝ ΚΑΙΣΡΑ ΕΡΙ ΑΥΓΟΥΡΕΙΝΩ bare head of Germanicus facing right. (Numismatic references: *RPC* 1022, *SNG Copenhagen* 462 and Svoronos 193.)
- Bronze *as* struck 37–41 CE in Italica, Spain. Obverse: GERMANICVS CAES TI AVG, bare head of Germanicus facing left. Reverse: PI R AVG across field, *aquila* between two *signa*. (Numismatic references: *RPC* 70 and *SNG Copenhagen* 418.)
- Bronze *as* struck 37–41 CE in Senior Philadelpheia, Lydia. Obverse: ΓΑΙΟΣ ΚΑΙΣΑΡ, laureate head of Caligula facing right with star behind head. Reverse: ΦΙΛΑΔΕΛΦΕΩΝ ΕΡΜΟΓΕΝΗΣ ΟΛΥΜΠΙΟΝΙΚΗΣ, bare heads of Agrippina the Elder and Germanicus offset behind facing right. (Numismatic references: *BMCRE* 52 and *RIC* I, 3023.)
- Bronze *as* struck 37–41 CE in Thessaloniki, Macedonia. Obverse: ΓΑΙΟΝ ΣΕΒΑΣΤΟΝ laureate head of Caligula facing left. Reverse: ΘΕΣΣΑΛΟΝΙ-ΚΕΩΝ ΓΕΡΜΑΝΙΚΩΝ, bare head of Germanicus facing left. (Numismatic references: *RPC* 1572, Touratsoglou 1–2.)

(iii) Claudius:
- Bronze *as* struck c. 48–49 CE in Anazarbos, Cilicia. Obverse: ΓΕΡΜΑΝΙΚΟΣ ΚΑΙΣΑΡ, bare head of Germanicus facing right. Reverse: ΚΑΙΣΑΡΕΩΝ ΠΡΟΡ Τ ΑΝΑΖΑΡΒΟΣ, bust of Zeus right, behind Acropolis of Anazarbos on a rock,

ΕΤΟΥΣ ΖΧ (= year 67 of the local era starting 19 BCE) in exergue. (Numismatic references: *RPC* I, 4060 and *SNG Levante* 1366.)

3. Inscriptions

Several inscriptions survive which specifically mention Germanicus. The greater number mention him as *Germanicus Caesar Ti. Avg. f.* Examples include *CIL* II, 1517, 2039, 2198, 3104 (all from the province of Baetica); III, 334 (Apamea); V, 4308 (Brixia), 6416.3 (Ticinum); VI, 921b, 923, 924 (all Rome); X, 460 (Lucania), 513 (Salernum), 1415 (Herculaneum); XI, 3306, 3308 (Forum Clodi), 3786 (Veii), 4776 (Spoletium), 5224 (Fulginiae), 6321 (Pisaurum); XIII, 1036 (Aquitania); XIV, 83 (Ostia), 3942 (Nomentum); XV, p. 995.1 (lead tessera, found in the Tiber); *IGR* III, 715 (Lycia); IV, 11 (Eresus), 326 (Pergamum). *CIL* X, 6639 (Antium) also names Tiberius and Germanicus as consuls, at the same time giving the name of the consul Tubero, elected to take the place of Tiberius after he had withdrawn. At least two inscriptions of that year bear the names of Germanicus and Tubero as consuls: *CIL* XI, 3196 (Nepet): *Cereri August.* | *matri agr.* | *L. Bennius Primus* | *mag. pagi I Bennia Primigenia* | *magistra fecer.* | *Germanico Caesare II I L. Seio Tuberone cos.* | *dies sacrifici XIII. K. Mai*; also IX, 3664 (Marruvium).

Following Germanicus' successful governorship of Tres Galliae, there is the inscription on the attic of the triumphal arch (plate 27) at Mediolanum Santonum (Saintes), dedicated by C. Iulius Rufus to Germanicus, Tiberius, and Drusus, son of Tiberius (*CIL* XIII, 1036 = *ILTG* 148 = *AE* 1980, 623): *Germanico [Caesa]r[i] Ti(beri) Aug(usti) f(ilio)* | *divi Augusti nep(oti) divi Iuli pronep(oti) auguri* | *flam(ini) August(ali) co(n)s(uli) II imp(eratori) II* || *Ti(berio) Caesar[i divi Aug(usti) f(ilio) divi Iuli nep(oti) Aug(usto)]* | *pontif(ici) max(imo sic) [co(n)s(uli) III?] imp(eratori) VIII [tri]b(unicia) pot(estate) [XXI?]* || *Dr[us]o Caesari [Ti(beri) Aug(usti)] f(ilio)* | *[divi Augusti] nep(oti) divi Iuli* | *[pronep(oti) co(n)s(uli)?] pontifici auguri.* And *C(aius) Iulius C(ai) Iuli Catuaneuni f(ilius) Rufus [C(ai) Iul(i) Agedomopatis nepos Epotsorovidi pronep(os) Volt(inia)]* | *sacerdos Romae et Augusti ad aram [quae est ad Confluentem praefectus fabrum d(e) s(ua) p(ecunia) f(ecit)]* ||*C(aius) Iuli[us] C(ai) Iuli C[a]tuaneuni f(ilius) Rufus C(ai) Iulii Agedomo[patis] nepos Epotsorovidi pron(epos) V[olt(inia)]* | *[sacerdos Romae et Au]gusti [ad a]ram qu[a]e est ad Confluent[em praefectus fab]ru[m] d(e) [s(ua) p(ecunia) f(ecit)].*

Recognising Germanicus' imperatorial salutations *ILS* 176 ff erected after his death shows him as *Imp. II.*

Inscriptions recording honorary magistracies, including the post of *praefectus* or *praefectus quinquennalis* have been found at Caesaraugusta, Heiss (1870), p. 270, no. 13; Colonia Augusta Buthrotum (Butrint) dated to 12 CE, *Germanico Iulio Ti. F.* | *Augusti. N. Caesari* | *Cos* | *C. Iulius C. F. Sirabo Praefect* | *Quinquen Eieus*; Fulginiae, *CIL* XI, 5224; Hispellum, *CIL* XI, 5289; Interpromium, *CIL* IX, 3044 = *ILS* 2689; Priene, *Ipriene* no. 142; and Regium Lepidum, *CIL* XI, 969. Germanicus with Drusus together have been found at Acci, Heiss (1870), p. 257, no. 12; Aqua Flaviae, *CIL* II, 5617 = I, 2479; ?Carteia, Heiss (1870), p. 332, no. 29 and 334); and Praeneste, *CIL* XIV, 2964.

Confirming Germanicus' presence in the East: *I. Olympia* 221 = *SIG*[3] 792 erected by M. Antonius Peisanus to his patron attests Germanicus as *Olympionikes* at Olympia, Greece in 17 CE. *CIL* III, 334 (Apamea), 426 (Ephesus); *IGR* III, 715 (Lycia); IV, 11 (Eresus), 326, 327 (Pergamum), 979 (Samos). In *CIL* XII, 3180, 3207 (Nemausus), and in Curtius and Adler (1897), p. 372, Germanicus and Drusus are associated, the first two inscriptions being dedicated each to a *flamen* of both Germanicus and Drusus, the third recording the honour paid to them both by the city of the Eleans and the Olympic Council. *CIL* II, 194 (Lusitania), and XII, 1872 (Vienne on the Rhône), are each dedicated to a *flamen* of Germanicus. An inscription dedicated to him has been found at Alexandria (*CIL* III, 12047): *Germanico Caesari Ti. Aug.f.* | *L. Valerius* | *L. Tonneius le* ... | *A. Mevius...* | *magistri larum Aug.* | *anno V. Ti. Caesam Aug. CIL* XI, 3786 (Veii) is dedicated also to Germanicus.

On his death in Syria, the *Fasti Antiates* mark 10 October as *Infer. Germanic.* (*CIL* I[2], p. 249), corroborating the day of his death with the *Tabula Siarensis*; being so interpreted, it means the Ostian calendar should be read: *inferiae actae ob excessum Germanici*: *CIL* XIV, 244. In connection with Tiberius' alleged attitude towards Germanicus, it is notable that, although the *Fasti Antiates* and *Ostienses* record the day of Germanicus' death, the *Fasti Amiternini*, written in Tiberius' reign, do not. In addition to the inscriptions of Germanicus already cited, a few suggest the general goodwill toward him. *CIL* VI, 909 (Rome): *plebs urbana quinque et* | *triginta tribuum* [*Germanico Caesari* | *Ti. Augusti f., I divi Augusti n.,* | *auguri, flamini Augustali,* | *cos. iterum, imp. iterum,* | *aere conlato.* Also *CIL* X, 6649 (Antium): *Germanico Caesari Ti. Caesaris f., divi Augusti n.* | *C. Iulius Chimarus; idem statuas et aediculam* | *refecit, sedes marmoreas posuit*; and *CIL* VI, 911 (Rome), the fragments of a *senatus consultum* decreeing honours to him after his death.

In 1982, three badly damaged bronze tablets were discovered at Siara, near Sevilla in southern Spain, the former province of Baetica. The reassembled fragments, which are now in the Vatican Museum (*CIL* VI, 31199), preserve a decree of the Senate (*Senatus Consultum de Honoribus Germanici Decernendis*) concerning a letter to Tiberius Caesar, asking him to help the Senate provide adequate honours for Germanicus after his death in Syria at the end of 19 CE. Parts of this decree – nowadays called the *Tabula Siarensis* – are preserved on the first two tablets (see Appendix). The third tablet appears to contain part of the final decree in honour of Germanicus, portions of which are also known from a bronze tablet found in pieces at Magliano (ancient Heba, in Etruria) in Italy in 1947 and 1951, and known as the *Tabula Hebana*.

Many inscriptions connect him to members of his family. The funerary inscription of Agrippina states she was 'wife of Germanicus' (*CIL* VI, 886, 31192 = *ILS* 180): *Ossa* | *Agrippinae M. Agrippae* [*f.*], | *divi Aug. neptis, uxoris* | *Germanici Caesaris,* | *matris C. Caesaris Aug.* | *Germanici, principis.* Several mention Germanicus as father to Nero or Drusus. One of Nero from Rome fully names his offices (*CIL* VI, 913): *Neroni Caesari* | *Germanici Caesaris f.,* | *Ti. Caesaris Augusti n.,* | *divi Augusti pron.,* | *flamini Augustali,* | *sodali Augustali,* | *sodali Titio,* *fratri Arvali,* | *fetiali, quaestori,* | *ex s. c.* Also *CIL* VI, 31274 (Rome, dedicated also to his father Germanicus, and to his brother Drusus); X, 5393 (Aquinum); XI, 3336 (Blera), 3789 (Veii); *IGR* IV, 74–75 (Mytilene), 1300 (Aeolia, calling him simply the 'son of Germanicus and Agrippina', without mention of either Tiberius or Augustus). One of Drusus from the Troad (*CIL* III, 380): *Druso Caesari | Germanici Caesaris | filio, | Ti. August. nepoti, | divi Augusti pronepoti, | pontifici | d. d.* Also *IGR* IV, 75 (Mytilene, designating him as 'son of Germanicus and Agrippina').

One inscription mentions the month of September renamed Germanicus by Caligula, mentioned by Suetonius (*Calig.* 15.2): *CIL* XI, 5745 (Foligno, Umbria), dedicated by C. Aetrius Naso, son of Caius, *praefectus* of *Coh.* I *Germanorum* and former *tribunus militum* of *Legio* I *Italica*, who ordered in his will that a stele be erected to the citizens of Sentium to commemorate the donation of 120,000 *sestertii* for a banquet to be given on the 'seventeenth of the *Kalends* of Germanicus', *quod XVII K. Germanicas | daretur | HS CXX legavit*.

4. Sculptures

Germanicus appears to have been a popular subject for ancient sculptors, particularly during the years 4–37 CE. Several carvings and busts have been identified as Germanicus, though the identifications of some can be – and have been – disputed. In 1940, Meriwether Stuart counted fifty-two portrait inscriptions of Germanicus surviving from ancient times, and others have come to light since then. For surveys of early Principate portraiture and the issues associated with identification, see Boschung (1993); Fittschen (1987); and Kiss (1975).

(a) *Ara Pacis Augustae, Rome*

On the south facing enclosure wall is the earliest official depiction of Germanicus (no. S-36). It was unveiled at the time of the inauguration on 30 January 9 BCE on the occasion of his grandmother Livia Drusilla's birthday when he was six years old. He is shown as a confident and relaxed boy in the company of his father and mother. Germanicus holds the hand of Antonia Minor and stares out from the frieze. He wears a child's *toga praetexta* and *bulla*.

(b) *Portrait Busts and Statues*

Characteristic of the busts are the clean-shaven, inverted V-shaped profile of the face with a strong chin, the pleasantly proportioned but sturdy nose, the small, thin lips, the large, clear eyes beneath gently arched eyebrows, prominent ears, the fringe of feathered curls falling over the broad forehead, and the thick head of hair dropping to the base of the neck. The best preserved are discussed here.

The most complete bronze statue of Germanicus to survive from antiquity is now on display at the Archaeological Museum of Amelia (Museo Archeologico di Amelia) in Umbria, Italy (plate 40). Fragments of the exquisitely and expensively cast statue were discovered in 1963, during the construction of a mill on the Via Rimembranze, outside Porta Romana on what was probably an army parade ground. Now attached to a steel frame, the statue stands some 2m (6.6ft) high. Art historians suggest that the statue did not start out as Germanicus, but most likely began as his son Caligula. When his memory was damned (*damnatio memoriae*) by the Senate in 41 CE, the city of Amelia was left with a statue of a hated man. Rather than scrap the costly piece, the head was replaced with that of the ever-popular Germanicus. A testament to the skill of a master craftstman of the ancient world, Germanicus is shown as *imperator*, walking casually, captured mid-stride, with a slight turn to the right. His head is uncovered and he is dressed in an elaborately decorated muscled cuirass with *pteryges*. On the upper part of the body armour is the sea monster Scylla. On the upper half is a homo-erotic scene from Homer's *Iliad* in which Achilles – the valiant Achaean hero – ambushes the young Trojan prince Troilus and drags him from his horse. Two exquisitely modelled winged victories bring Achilles arms as a reward for his feat. The raised decoration continues around to the back of the cuirass, ending in a religious rite in which two women dance before a candelabrum, a symbol of eternal imperial power. The first row of *pteryges* is decorated with lions' heads and the second features the faces of satyrs alternating with gorgons. His right arm is outstretched, his index finger pointing to some object in the distance. On his left side hangs a *parazonium*, while in his left hand he holds a staff, and his forearm is covered by the end of his commander's *paludamentum*.

The Museo Nazionale Romano at the Palazzo Massimo alle Terme, Rome has the only other bronze bust of Germanicus to survive from ancient times. It was probably part of a statue, like the one found in Amelia, designed to grace a building or public space. The head survives complete, but the base of the neck shows evidence of it having been torn from the upper torso. The surface of the cast bronze is badly pitted and the features are heavily worn, suggesting exposure to the elements in antiquity. The face gazes emotionlessly, capturing Germanicus in a moment of concentration.

A full body marble statue of Germanicus is on display at the Musée du Louvre, Paris (inv. Ma 1238 (MR 210)). It was one of a cache of 38 statues of Roman celebrities discovered by the Scottish antiquarian and painter Gavin Hamilton in 1792 in the forum of Gabii, a spa town located 18km (11 miles) due east of Rome along the *Via Praenestina*, where it formed a pair with a statue of Claudius on the opposite side of the gallery (plate 39). It was initially part of the Borghese Collection, but then moved to Paris in 1807. Standing 1.8m (5.9ft) high, Germanicus is portrayed as a demi-god or hero. He is shown semi-nude with a fine athletic upper body, while his waist and legs are covered by a toga. The right arm is missing and, while the left arm is preserved complete, it is covered by the draped toga. The left hand holds the pommel and grip of a *parazonium*, the sheathed blade of which is broken off. The base, the support and parts of the legs are modern replacements.

Most of the marble representations of Germanicus to survive are busts. Some of them were inserted into sockets in 'standard' bodies carved separately, while others were intended to be displayed as stand-alone busts. The portraits were probably copied from a common reference model sent out from Rome, but each differs slightly in the detailing of hair or eyes, according to the skill of the sculptor. The most attractive bust to come down to us is in the collection of the Louvre (inv. Ma 3135 (MND 968)), acquired in 1912 from Cordova (plate 6). It measures 50cm (19.7 ins) in height and is carved from a single block of marble, and the cut of the neck suggests this was a free-standing bust. Despite some damage to the nose, the bust is well-preserved. The portrait is more strongly individualized than many others which survive, showing a vigorous and confident young man in the style of busts of Augustus. The hair is cut in a heavy, feathered style, tumbling over the forehead with curly sideburns, and runs almost to the base of the neck.

A second bust in the Louvre collection (inv. MNE 937 (Ma 4712)), which was acquired in 1988, was carved in Greek marble to a very high standard, possibly while Germanicus was alive. It appears to have been part of a display mounted against a wall. The back of the bust is flat and roughly finished, and the top and right side of the head show tooling marks, indicating it was perhaps cut away to fit a niche. The head measures 30cm (11.8 ins) in height.

The Museo Nazionale Romano is fortunate also to have a marble bust of Germanicus that originally came from Mentana. The cut of the base of the neck suggests this was originally intended to fit into the torso of a statue. The bust bears a strong resemblance to the one in the Louvre, but the hair is more finely detailed and the look is less intense, more contemplative. The nose is chipped on the right side and there is a minor, purple-coloured blemish in the marble in the upper right cheek. It was discovered in Nomentanum.

The Museo Capitolino (Capitoline Museum), Rome has a fine portrait (inv. MC415) that is Augustan in style. It measures 44cm (17.3 ins) high. The sculptor has caught Germanicus gazing slightly up and to the right. The hair is the familiar feathered cut over the forehead, but notably longer at the back.

The magnificent bust in the Jamahiriya (Red Castle) Museum, Tripoli, Libya is more angular, the top of the head flatter in profile than other extant portraits, and is reminiscent of the face of the Augustus of Prima Porta. The hair is heavily tousled, the arch of the eyebrows flatter, and the flairs radiating out from the nose along the cheeks more prominent than in other sculptures identified as Germanicus. The lips are slightly parted as if the Roman general is about to speak. Like the Museo Nazionale Romano bust, the shape of the base of the neck suggests this was originally intended to fit into the body of a statue.

The collection of the British Museum, London has a striking bust (inv. GR 1872.6–5.1 (Sculpture 1883)) made of green-basanite igneous rock, found in Egypt. It may have been carved during Germanicus' lifetime in Egypt. The shoulders with carvings of shoulder straps of a muscled cuirass suggest this was a free-standing bust. It bears all the characteristics of Germanicus' portraiture, but is more stylized than either the Louvre or Museo Nazionale Romano busts and has glass-like polish, echoing a long tradition of idealized sculptures of pharaonic art. Measuring 44.5cm (17.5 ins) high, the face gazes upwards, accentuating the strong chin. The nose was accidentally broken or deliberately hacked off, sometime in the past, and at some unknown date it was also desecrated with a Christian cross carved crudely into the forehead. Religious fanatics believed that such marks were the only means of quelling the demons which they believed inhabited statues.

The Ny Carlsberg Glyptotek, Copenhagen has two portrait busts. One (inv. 633) bears a resemblance to the Palazzo Massimo sculpture, but with a less intense expression. Purchased in 1891, it is almost complete, save for a broken nose and chipped ears. The other bust (inv. 760), measuring 41cm (16.1 ins) high, was one of several imperial portraits found at the sanctuary of Diana in the Alban Hills outside Rome. Caligula had a particular affection for the place and had two giant ships built to cruise on nearby Lake Nemi. Another, closely resembling it stylistically, is in the Altes Schloß, Stuttgart. Similar in appearance are the busts found in the Roman Baths of Smyrna – now on display in the Archaeological Museum of Izmir, Turkey – and in the Museo de Cádiz (Arqueología y Bellas Artes), Spain. The eyebrows seem more angled at the temples and the nose thicker and more prominent than either bust in the Louvre or Museo Nazionale Romano. These and other busts identified as Germanicus not described here may, indeed, all be of him, and the differences between them may only highlight the variation in skills of local craftsmen making copies from an officially sanctioned reference model. However, busts of unidentified clean-shaven youthful Roman males of the first century CE are frequently labelled Germanicus, rather than as 'unidentified' or 'unknown Julio/Claudian prince' in several collections around the world.

(c) *Cameos*

In its collection, The Boston Museum of Fine Arts has a sardonyx cameo (inv. 98.753) believed to have been carved between 4 and 14 CE while Germanicus was alive. The side profile in white, contrasting dramatically with the black of the background, closely resembles the portraits of Germanicus on the coins of Caligula and the Ny Carlsberg bust, inv. 760. The hair is thick, but, unusually, the face is shown with a light beard (which may have been engraved later). The piece has restorations in gold to the lower neck and shoulders, which are not original.

The so-called *Gemma Augustea* (inv. IX A 79) in the Kunsthistorisches Museum, Vienna shows Tiberius' triumph of 12 CE (plate 22). Dating to the second or third decade of the first century CE, it is cut from double-layered Arabian onyx and is roughly square in shape, measuring 19cm (7.5 ins) high by 23cm (9 ins) wide. The engraver, believed to be master craftsman Dioskurides or one of his pupils, carefully cut the top white layer down to the bluish-brown stone beneath, leaving low-relief figures in high contrast. The engraver created two tiers of parallel scenes. In the upper tier, Augustus appears as Iupiter, seated on a curule chair holding a long staff. The gem commemorates Tiberius' triumph, but clearly communicates that it was won under the auspices of Augustus. The *princeps* is being crowned with a *corona civica* of oak leaves – for saving Roman lives – by Oikumene, the personification of the inhabited universe. Oceanus (or Neptunus) and Gaia sit beside her. The three figures are personifications of the world and the surrounding seas over which Rome has dominion, and the world yet unconquered beyond. To Augustus' right sits Roma, wearing a helmet and clasping a spear, but she is lightly touching a sword, as if to indicate that Rome is always ready to defend herself. To her right stands a man wearing the armour and distinctive *paludamentum* of a commanding officer. Most scholars identify this youthful military figure as Germanicus Caesar. To his right, Tiberius descends from a chariot, clutching a staff in one hand, as a winged victory stands behind him. In the lower tier, soldiers heave as they hoist up a *trophaea*, while bound barbarian captives look on dejectedly. This overt piece of propaganda art may have been given as a gift to a wealthy friend of the *princeps* or to a client king, after Tiberius' day of public recognition.

The *Grand Camée de France* (inv. CdM Paris Bab 264), or *Gemma Tiberiana*, in the Bibliothèque Nationale in Paris may have been commissioned on the occasion of Germanicus' appointment as *Orienti praepositus* in 17 CE (plate 24). Who placed the order for the work is not known, but the quality of the piece and the likely high cost of its manufacture suggests someone very important. It is an extraordinary engraved five-layered sardonyx cameo. Scholars have long debated the significance of the symbolic imagery on the gem – the largest ancient cameo to survive from the ancient world, measuring 31cm (12 ins) by 25.5cm (10.25 ins). Many believe it depicts the central figure of the enthroned Tiberius bidding farewell to Germanicus, who wears the panoply of a military commander, as he sets off on his new mission. Standing behind Germanicus are Agrippina and Caligula, the boy depicted in a child-size cuirass, *pteryges*, *paludamentum* and greaves. Behind Tiberius are Livia and Drusus the Younger. Below them, Asiatic-looking figures sit or lie down passively, while overhead fly the spirits of the deceased Augustus flanked by C. Caesar and Drusus the Elder or L. Caesar on the winged-horse Pegasus – the precise identifications depending on whether the cameo was carved in 17 CE or, as some argue 23 CE, or later.

The second item in the Kunsthistorisches Museum collection is the so-called *Gemma Claudia* (inv. IX A 63). Made around 49 CE, it is a five-layer sardonyx cameo, set within a gold rim (plate 23). It appears to show Claudius and his wife Agrippina the Younger facing Germanicus and his wife, Agrippina the Elder, set in *cornucopiae*. It is a striking pairing of couples, especially as one of the women is Germanicus' wife, the other is his daughter, married incestuously to his brother. An eagle with outstretched wings and its head facing Claudius connects the two brothers.

The British Museum has a rare *phalera* (registration number 1870,0224.2), a type of military award or medallion worn on a leather harness by a centurion. It was discovered in Colchester, England and acquired by the Trustees of the Museum in 1870. In a damaged circular bronze mounting, measuring 4.5cm (1.8 ins) in diameter, is a moulded disk of the deepest blue glass. In the centre of the disk is a raised bust of Germanicus, shown bare-headed, wearing a cuirass with *pteryges*. The heads of three young boys – presumably his sons, Nero, Drusus and Caius – appear around him, one on each shoulder, the third on his chest.

There are similar pieces in the Historisches Museum der Pfalz Speyer (still in its circular metalwork mounting with harness fixture) and Kunsthistorisches Museum, Vienna (inv. XI.b.8). Examples of a man and just two smaller figures of children – perhaps of Tiberius with Drusus and Germanicus as boys – are in the collection of the Rijksmuseum van Oudheden, Leiden (inv. U 1931/2.61) and Metropolitan Museum of Art, New York (acc. no. 17.194.18, measuring $1^7/_{16}$ inch × ¼ inch (3.7cm × 0.7cm)).

During the excavations of the St Josephhof, Nijmegen in 2005, an exquisite cobalt-blue glass phalera was found. Measuring 4cm in diameter, it features a remarkably naturalistic portrait in high relief of Germanicus wearing a cuirass, facing forward and slightly to the right.

Notes

Abbreviations

(a) *Modern*

AE	*L'Année Epigraphique.*
BMCRE	H.B. Mattingly *et al.*, *Coins of the Roman Empire in the British Museum* (London, 1923–62).
BMCRR	H.A. Grueber, *Coins of the Roman Republic in the British Museum* (London, 1910).
C	H. Cohen, *Description historique des monnaies frappées sous l'Empire Romain* (Paris, 1880–92).
CAH	A.K. Bowman *et al.*, *The Cambridge Ancient History, Volume X: The Augustan Empire, 43BC–AD69* (Cambridge, 1996).
Calicó	X. and F. Calicó, *Catálogo de Monedas Antiguas de Hispania* (Barcelona, 1979).
CBN	*Catalogue des monnaies de l'empire romaine, Bibliothèque nationale* (Paris, 1976–88).
CIG	*Corpus Inscriptionum Graecarum* (Berlin, 1828–77).
CIL	T. Mommsen *et al.*, *Corpus Inscriptionem Latinarum* (Berlin, 1863–).
CRA	P. Erdkamp, *A Companion to the Roman Army* (Oxford, 2007).
EJ	V. Ehrenberg and A.H.M. Jones, *Documents Illustrating the Reigns of Augustus and Tiberius* (Oxford, 1949; Second revised edition, 1955).
Eph. Epig.	*Ephemeris Epigraphica.*
IGR	*Inscriptiones Graecae et res Romanas pertinentes.*
ILS	*Inscriptiones Latinae Selectae.*
ILTG	P. Wuilleumier, *Inscriptions Latines des Trois Gaules* (Paris, 1963).
JbSGU	*Jahrbuch (Jahresbericht) der Schweizerischen Gesellschaft für Urgeschichte.*
JRA	*Journal of Roman Archaeology.*
JRMES	*Journal of Roman Military Equipment Studies.*
JRS	*Journal of Roman Studies.*
Klose	D.O.A. Klose, *Die Münzprägung von Smyrna in der römischen Kaiserzeit* (Berlin, 1987).
MDAI(I)	*Mitteilungen des Deutschen Archäologischen Instituts (Abteiling Instanbul).*
RIC	H.B. Mattingly and E.A. Sydenham, *Roman Imperial Coinage* (London, 1913–56).
RIL	*Rendiconti del Instituto Lombardo di scienza e lettere, Classe di Lettere,*
RPC	A. Burnett *et al.*, *Roman Provincial Coinage*, Vol. I (London, 1992).
RSC	H.A. Seaby *et al.*, *Roman Silver Coins* (London, 1978–87).
S	D.R. Sear, *Roman Coins and Their Values* (Fifth revised edition, London, 2000).
SCPP	*Senatus Consultum de Cn. Pisonem patre.*
SIG³	W. Dittenberger, *Sylloge Inscriptionum Graecarum* (Third revised edition, Leipzig, 1883).
SNG Aulock	H. von Aulock, *Sylloge Nummorum Graecorum, Deutschland*, Cilicia (Berlin, 1981).
SNG Copenhagen	*Sylloge Nummorum Graecorum, Danish National Museum* (Copenhagen, 1942–79).
SNG Levante	E. Levante, *Sylloge Nummorum Graecorum, Switzerland 1: Cilicia* (Bern, 1986).
Svoronos	J. Svoronos, *Ta Nomismata tou Kratous ton Ptolemaion* (Athens, 1904–08).

(b) *Ancient Authors*

Amm. Marc.	Ammianus Marcellinus, *Res Gestae.*
App., *Bell. Civ.*	Appian, *Bellum Civile.*

App., *Ill.*	Appian, *Illyrike.*
Athen., *Deipn.*	Athenaeus, *Deipnosophistai.*
Aul. Gell., *Noct. Att.*	Aulus Gellius, *Noctes Atticae.*
Caes., *Bell. Alex.*	Caesar, *Bellum Alexandrinum.*
Caes., *Bell. Gall.*	Caesar, *Bellum Gallicum.*
Cato, *Agr.*	Cato the Elder, *De Agricultura.*
Cic., *Att.*	Cicero, *Ad Atticum.*
Cic., *Brut.*	Cicero, *Brutus.*
Cic., *Div.*	Cicero, *De Divinatione.*
Cic., *Font.*	Cicero, *Pro Fonteio.*
Cic., *Prov. Cons.*	Cicero, *De Provinciis Consularibus.*
Cic., *Tusc. Disp.*	Cicero, *Tusculanae Disputationes.*
Dio	Cassius Dio, *Romaiki Historia.*
Diog. Laert.	Diogenes Laertius, *Lives of Eminent Philosophers.*
Diod. Sic.	Diodorus Siculus, *Bibliotheka Historika.*
Ennius, *Ann.*	Ennius, *Annales.*
Eutrop., *Brev.*	Eutropius, *Breviarium.*
Frontin., *Aq.*	Frontinus, *De Aquis.*
Hdt.	Herodotus, *Istorian.*
Hor., *Carm.*	Horace, *Carmina.*
Joseph., *Ant. Iud.*	Josephus, *Antiquitatae Iudaicae.*
Joseph., *Ap.*	Josephus, *Contra Apionem.*
Juv., *Sat.*	Juvenal, *Saturae.*
Lib., *Or.*	Libanius, *Orationes.*
Livy	Livy, *Ab Urbe Condita.*
Livy, *Per.*	Livy, *Periochae.*
Mart., *Epig.*	Martial, *Epigrammata.*
Ov., *Fast.*	Ovid, *Fasti.*
Ov., *Pont.*	Ovid, *Epistulae Ex Ponto.*
Ov., *Tr.*	Ovid, *Tristia.*
Paus.	Pausanias, *Ellados Periegisis.*
Pliny, *Ep.*	Pliny the Younger, *Epistulae.*
Pliny, *Nat. Hist.*	Pliny the Elder, *Naturalis Historia.*
Plut., *Ant.*	Plutarch, *Antonius.*
Plut., *Caes.*	Plutarch, *Caesar.*
Plut., *Mar.*	Plutarch, *Marius.*
Polyb.	Polybius, *Istorian.*
Ptol., *Geog.*	Ptolemy, *Geography.*
Sen., *Constant.*	Seneca the Younger, *De Constantia Sapientis.*
Sen., *Ep.*	Seneca the Younger, *Epistulae Morales.*
Sen., *Nat. Qu.*	Seneca the Younger, *Quaestiones Naturales.*
Sen., *Ira*	Seneca the Younger, *De Ira.*
Sen., *Polyb.*	Seneca the Younger, *De Consolatione ad Polyhium.*
Sen., *Suas.*	Seneca the Elder, *Suasoriae.*
Strab., *Geog.*	Strabo, *Geographika.*
Suet., *Calig.*	Suetonius, *Caligula.*
Suet., *Div. Aug.*	Suetonius, *Divus Augustus.*
Suet., *Div. Claud.*	Suetonius, *Divus Claudius.*
Suet., *Div. Iul.*	Suetonius, *Divus Iulius.*
Suet., *Div. Vesp.*	Suetonius, *Divus Vespasianus.*
Suet., *Ner.*	Suetonius, *Nero.*
Suet., *Tib.*	Suetonius, *Tiberius.*
Tac., *Agr.*	Tacitus, *Agricola.*
Tac., *Ann.*	Tacitus, *Annales.*

Tac., *Germ.*	Tacitus, *Germania.*
Tac., *Hist.*	Tacitus, *Historiae.*
Val. Max.	Valerius Maximus, *Facta et Dicta Memorabilia.*
Vell. Pat.	Velleius Paterculus, *Historiae Romanae.*
Xen., *Anab.*	Xenophon, *Anabasis.*
Zonar.	Zonaras, *Epitome Istorian.*

Chapter 1: In the Name of the Father

1. This reconstruction is based on the account of Drusus the Elder's funeral in Tacitus, (*Annales* 3.5) with details taken from much earlier funerals witnessed by Polybius (6.53.1–10), Propertius (1.17.19–24; 2.24.35–8, 49–52) and Tibullus (3.2.9–22), supplemented by the research findings of Favro and Johanson (2010) and Powell (2011a), pp. 111–14.
2. Based on Suet., *Div. Vesp.* 19.2. For use of *imagines*, see Flower (1996), pp. 32–59.
3. The clothes of the murdered Iulius Caesar were displayed in this way at his funeral: Suet., *Div. Iul.* 84.1–5; App., *Bell. Civ.* 2.146–7.
4. The *Rostra Augusti* was used at the funerals of his step-aunt Octavia Maior at which his father had spoken and later step-grandfather Augustus; Dio 54.35.5; Suet., *Div. Aug.* 100.
5. A boundary line, the *pomerium* (meaning 'the post behind the wall'), traced the original outer limit of the Four Regions of the city of Rome, but was later extended by Sulla and Iulius Caesar.
6. Polybius specifically cites the wearing of ancestral masks and delivery of eulogies: Polyb. 6.53.5–7. See also Flower (1996), pp. 91–127.
7. Polyb. 6.53.4.
8. Dio 55.1.1.
9. Livy, *Per.* 142; Dio 55.1.3; Florus 2.30.23–4; Val. Max. 5.5.3.
10. Suet., *Div. Claud.* 1.3.
11. Suet., *Tib.* 7.3; Livy, *Per.* 142.
12. Tac., *Ann.* 3.5; Suet., *Tib.* 6.4. On *laudationes*, see Flower (1996), pp. 128–58.
13. Ov., *Fast.* 1.597–8: *et mortem et nomen Druso Germania fecit; | me miserum, virtus quam brevis illa fuit!*
14. Polyb. 6.53.8.
15. Paoli (1963), p. 130.
16. Dio 55.2.2–3.
17. Polyb. 6.53.8.
18. *Consolatio ad Liviam* 177.
19. Suet., *Div. Claud.* 1.5: *Augustus ... et defunctum ita pro contione laudaverit, ut deos precatus sit, similes ei Caesares suos facerent sibique tam honestum quandoque exitum darent quam illi dedissent.*
20. Augustus, *Res Gestae* 2.12.
21. Paoli (1963), p. 131.
22. Paoli (1963), p. 131.
23. Suet., *Div. Claud.* 1.3–4.
24. The year is generally accepted as 16 BCE, based on Germanicus' death occurring at 34 years of age, as stated by Suetonius (*Div. Claud.* 1.6), though some argue for 15 BCE; e.g. Seager (1972), p. xv.
25. In 9 BCE, Lyon was still known by the name its founder gave it, rather than the Lugdunum of later years.
26. For a detailed review of the campaign, see Powell (2011a), pp. 33–4 and 38–48.
27. Powell (2011a), p. 48.
28. Powell (2011a), pp. 50–1; Powell (2015), p. 140.
29. Powell (2011a), pp. 18–19.
30. Powell (2011a), pp. 61–7.
31. Dio 54.35.4.
32. *Inscriptiones Italiae* 13.2.117.
33. Augustus, *Res Gestae* 2.12.

34. Fragments of the altar were discovered in the silt in 1568 and reassembled under Benito Mussolini in 1938. A controversial cover building designed by Richard Meier and opened in 2006 now houses the Ara Pacis.
35. Staccioli (1986), pp. 347–8.
36. Staccioli (1986), p. 348.
37. One interpretation of the event depicted in the frieze is that it represents the *suovetaurilia* Augustus ordered to be offered annually at the site, on the anniversary of the day the senate commissioned the altar, marking his return (*reditus*) from his extended stay in the Tres Galliae and Hispaniae in 13 BCE. However, an equally plausible explanation is that the frieze shows the actual consecration ceremony for the altar (*dedicatio*) in 9 BCE.
38. An alternative interpretation is that the woman is Iulia, Agrippa's wife.
39. The identification of the figures continues to be controversial; for example, see Crawford (1922), citing Domaszewski (1903), pp. 57ff; Mrs. Arthur Strong, *Roman Sculpture from Augustus to Constantine* (1907), pp. 39ff; J. Sieveking, 'Zur Ara Pacis Augustae', *Jh. Oest. Arch. I.* 10 (1907), pp. 175ff.; F. Studniczka, 'Zur Ara Pacis', *Abh. Sächs. Ges.* 27 (1909), Phil.-Hist. Kl., pp. 911ff.; and E. Petersen, *Ara Pacis Augustae* (1902). Most authors agree that the figure – S-38 – in *caligae* and wearing the *paludamentum* is Drusus the Elder: see Powell (2011), p. 167.
40. Powell (2011a), p. 135.
41. Suet., *Div. Claud.* 1.6; Kokkinos (2002), p. 11.
42. Val. Max. 4.3.3.
43. Dio 50.26; Plut., *Ant.* 31.
44. Plut., *Ant.* 87.3; Val. Max. 4.3.3; see also Goethert-Polaschek (1973); Kokkinos (2002), p. 28.
45. Suet., *Div. Aug.* 83.
46. Suet., *Div. Aug.* 64.3.
47. Suet., *Div. Aug.* 64.3.
48. Suet., *Tib.* 1.1; Tac., *Ann.* 11.23.
49. Suet., *Tib.* 1.2.
50. Suet., *Tib.* 2.1.
51. Livy 11.29.
52. Diod. Sic. 23.3.
53. Suet., *Tib.* 2.2: *Claudius Pulcher apud Siciliam non pascentibus in auspicando pullis ac per contemptum religionis mari demersis, quasi ut biberent quando esse nollent, proelium nauale iniit; superatusque, cum dictatorem dicere a senatu iuberetur, uelut iterum inludens discrimini publico Glycian uiatorem suum dixit.*
54. Livy 27.41–51.
55. Suet., *Tib.* 4.3.
56. Cic., *Att.* 6.6.
57. Caes., *Bell. Alex.* 25; Dio 42.40.
58. Suet., *Tib.* 6.4.
59. E. Huzar, *Mark Antony: A Biography* (1978), pp. 12–13.
60. Livy 3.35.11.
61. Livy 3.38.5, 41.10, 42.2–3; 4.42.3.
62. Huzar (1978), pp. 13–14.
63. Huzar (1978), p. 143.
64. Huzar (1978), p. 15–16.
65. Huzar (1978), p. 12. The day and month of his birth are securely attested as 14 January; see Suet., *Div. Claud.* 11.3. Claudius argued it was the same as his father's birthday, but Ovid (*Fast.* 1.587ff.) clearly suggests 13 January; Sen., *Polyb.* 16.1f. Plutarch (*Ant.* 86.8) records two traditions that he was 53 or 56 at his death in 30 BCE. It may be supposed that Antonius falsified his age in later life, following the example of his political mentor Iulius Caesar, to make himself three years younger; Caesar himself cut two years off his own age.
66. Huzar (1978), pp. 16–19; P. Southern, *Mark Antony: A Life* (2010), p. 35.
67. Huzar (1978), pp. 17–18.
68. Plut., *Ant.* 2.3; the sum was equivalent to 6 million *sestertii*.

69. Plut., *Ant.* 2.5.
70. Plut., *Ant.* 3.1–6. The proconsul of Syria was the same A. Gabinius who was later impeached by Ti. Claudius Nero.
71. Huzar (1978), p. 23.
72. Huzar (1978), pp. 68–72.
73. Plut., *Ant.* 14.3. Huzar (1978), pp. 84–7.
74. Plut., *Ant.* 21.4–22.4. Huzar (1978), pp. 125–8.
75. Plut., *Ant.* 25.1; 31.1. Huzar (1978), p. 139.
76. Plut., *Ant.* 63.1–68.3. Huzar (1978), pp. 216–22.
77. Plut., *Ant.* 76.4–78.1. Huzar (1978), p. 226.
78. Suet., *Div. Aug.* 13.5; Plut., *Ant.* 36.3; 54.4–6; 81.1–82.2. Huzar (1978), pp. 230–1. M. Antonius' eldest son was killed in a squabble with Octavianus' soldiers.
79. Paoli (1963), p. 169.
80. Two elaborate examples are shown in the *Pompeii AD 79* exhibition catalogue, Royal Academy of Arts 1977, item 48.
81. Balsdon (1969), p. 120.
82. Suet., *Div. Aug.* 84.1.
83. Ov., *Pont.* 2.5.5–8.
84. Ov., *Pont.* 2.5.41–6: *Te iuuenum princeps, cui dat Germania nomen, | participem studii Caesar habere solet. | Tu comes antiquus, tu primis iunctus ab annis | ingenio mores aequiperante places. | Te dicente prius studii fuit impetus illi | teque habet elicias qui sua uerba tuis.*
85. Paoli (1963), p. 170.
86. Suet., *Gramm.* 7.
87. Suet., *Div. Aug.* 89.1.
88. Paoli (1963), p. 192.
89. Suet., *Div. Aug.* 74.
90. Suet., *Div. Aug.* 20–1.1.
91. Dio 54.28.3–5.
92. Dio 54.31.2.
93. Dio 55.6.2–3.
94. Dio 55.6.3; Tac., *Ann.* 2.26; Augustus, *Res Gestae* 6.32.
95. Pliny, *Nat. Hist.* 3.136–137.
96. Dio 55.1, 55.8.2.
97. Dio 55.6.5–6. Rowe (2002), p. 22.
98. Dio 55.9.4; 55.10.20.
99. Suet., *Tib.* 11.1. The reasons for Tiberius' retirement have perplexed historians both ancient and modern. Suetonius (*Tib.* 11.5) suggests he left Rome to avoid the suspicion of rivalry with Caius and Lucius Caesar. Dio (55.9.7–8) suggests other explanations, such as he wanted to put some distance between himself and Caius and Lucius, fearing their anger or that he was too prominent, or to get away from his wife, or that he was angry at not being made Caesar, or even that he had been ordered to leave by Augustus, or that he was plotting against the *princeps* or his sons. The Roman sources are inconclusive. For a full discussion of points raised see Levick (1972a).
100. Suet., *Tib.* 12.2; Tac., *Ann.* 1.4.
101. Suet., *Div. Claud.* 1.5.
102. Dio 55.9.7.
103. Suet., *Div. Aug.* 65.
104. Aul. Gell., *Noct. Att.* 15.7.3.
105. Suet., *Div. Aug.* 54.1; the procedure involved touching a pair of scales with a copper *as* three times in the presence of a *praetor*.
106. In the letter quoted by Aulus Gellius (*Noct. Att.* 15.7.3), dated 23 September 1 CE, his sixty-third birthday, Augustus addresses his son as *mi Gai, meus asellus iucundissimus, quem semper medius fidius desidero, cum a me abes*, 'my Caius, my darling little donkey, whom the Heavens know I miss when you are away'.
107. Suet., *Div. Aug.* 29.4; 43.5.

108. Dio 55.10.19. Coins: *aureus*: *RIC* 209 (R3); *C* 42; Calicó 177; *denarius*: *BMCRE* 540; *C* 43; *RIC* II, 210.
109. Dio 55.9.3–4.
110. Dio 55.9.4.
111. Dio 55.9.9; Suet., *Div. Aug.* 26.2; Tac., *Ann.* 1.3.
112. Dio 55.9.10.
113. Dio 55.9.1–2.
114. Dio 55.10.17.
115. Dio 55.10a.9. Rowe (2002), p. 17, citing Kornemann (1930), notes the development of parallel careers, and assigning different theatres to pairs of his sons and stepsons was a characteristic of establishing Augustus' dynastic intentions.
116. Dio 55.10.18; Florus 2.32.
117. Dio 55.10.18.
118. Dio (55.10.18) states that 'he did not dare send out any other influential man'.
119. Suet., *Div. Aug.* 54.1; *Tib.* 12.2.
120. Dio 55.10.18; note also 53.13.2. She is also known by the name Livia.
121. Suet., *Tib.* 12.2 : *Comes et rector*.
122. Vell. Pat. 2.97.1; Hor., *Carm.* 4.9.37f.
123. Dio (55.10.19) says Chios; Suetonius (*Tib.* 12.2) says Samos.
124. Dio 55.10.19.
125. Lollius' behaviour towards Tiberius would later come back to haunt him with a censure in the Senate: Tac., *Ann.* 3.48.
126. Dio 55.10.19; Suet., *Div. Aug.* 93.
127. Dio 55.10.20–1; Florus 2.32.
128. Dio 55.10a.4–6.
129. See *denarius BMCRE* 500; *C* 40; *RIC* II, 199.
130. Dio 55.10a.9.
131. Pliny, *Nat. Hist.* 9.118.
132. Tac., *Ann.* 3.48.
133. Dio 55.10a.5.
134. Dio 55.10a.6–8.
135. Dio 55.10.19.
136. Dio 55.10a.6.
137. Dio 55.10a.7; Vell. Pat. 2.102.2.
138. Florus 2.32. The Parthian attacker committed suicide when surrounded by many angry Roman soldiers.
139. Dio 55.10a.8; Vell. Pat. 2.102.3.
140. Dio 55.10a.8.
141. Suet., *Div. Aug.* 65.1; Dio 55.10a.9. *ILS* 140. C. Caesar was widely mourned (*CIL* XI, 1421; *ILS* 140). Many honours were heaped upon him in death by citizens and city officials of the Empire, including Colonia Obsequens Iulia Pisana (Pisa), where it was decreed that the proper rites must be observed for matrons to lament his passing. Temples, public baths and shops shut their doors as women wept. Gordon (1983), p. 106, no. 31.
142. Vell. Pat. 2.102.3. An inscription was erected in the Portico that bore his and his brother's names in the *Forum Romanum*, next to an arch that straddled a newly-constructed spur of the *via Sacra*: Suet., *Div. Aug.* 29.4; Dio 56.27.5; Gordon (1983), p. 105, no. 30. A marble inscription found in Kempten is dedicated to L. Caesar; see Wamser *et al.* (2004), p. 15 (fig. 12).
143. Suet., *Div. Aug.* 65.1; Dio 55.10a.9–10.
144. Dio 55.12.1. For the honours voted to Caius, see *ILS* 140; for those voted to Lucius, see *ILS* 139, from the Roman *colonia* at Pisa. The honours to Lucius were passed in response to a decree of the Senate, in the form of a letter to Augustus asking him about proper honours for his son. The honours were not of equal measure, however. David S. Potter notes: 'the vastly more elaborate celebration of Caius probably reflects the final decree of the senate in Lucius' case, and a number of honors that were only granted at Rome. Assuming that the senate will suggest similar

measures in honor of Caius, the Pisans are adopting those provisions for their own city, and to do for Caius at their city what the senate would do at Rome'. Further, he notes: 'the funeral honors for Lucius and his brother Caius are of great importance because they illustrate the development of the concept of the imperial house defined in terms of relationship to Augustus'.

145. Suet., *Div. Aug.* 55.2; Suet., *Tib.* 23; Vell. Pat. 2.103.2–3.
146. Suet., *Div. Aug.* 61; *Tib.* 15; Dio 55.13.2; Vell. Pat. 2.103.2–3; Powell (2015), p.193.
147. Suet., *Tib.* 13.2; Vell. Pat. 2.103.1.
148. Suet., *Calig.* 4.1: *Quarum virtutum fructum uberrimum tulit, sic probatus et dilectus a suis, ut Augustus – omitto enim necessitudines reliquas – diu cunctatus an sibi successorem destinaret.*
149. Tac., *Ann.* 4.57.
150. Suet., *Div. Aug.* 55.1. Tiberius' son by his marriage to Vipsania Agrippina, named Nero Claudius Drusus, now became, in turn, Drusus Iulius Caesar (Drusus the Younger).
151. Suet., *Tib.* 21.3: *Rei publicae causa*; Vell. Pat. 2.104.1. Levick (1966).
152. Dio 55.13.2; Suet., *Tib.* 16; Tac., *Ann.* 1.10; Vell. Pat. 2.103.3.
153. Vell. Pat. 2.103.3.
154. Suet., *Div. Aug.* 55.2. See Jameson (1975), Levick (1972b) and Pappano (1941).
155. Suet., *Div. Aug.* 55.1; *Tib.* 15.2; Tac., *Ann.* 1.3; 4.57.
156. Kornemann (1930), pp.24ff.
157. Gruen (2005), p.48.
158. Kienast (2009), pp.138–9.
159. Suet., *Calig.* 3.2: *Formae minus congruebat gracilitas crurum, sed ea quoque paulatim repleta assidua equi vectatione post cibum.*
160. Tac., *Ann.* 1.33: *nam iuveni civile ingenium, mira comitas.*
161. Suet., *Calig.* 3.1: *Omnes Germanico corporis animique virtutes, et quantas nemini cuiquam, contigisse satis constat: formam et fortitudinem egregiam … benivolentiam singularem conciliandaeque hominum gratiae ac promerendi amoris mirum et efficax studium.*
162. Plut., *De Invidia et Odio* 3 (*Mor.* 537b): 'Germanicus could endure neither the crowing nor the sight of a cock'.
163. Tac., *Ann.* 1.33; Suet., *Div. Aug.* 64.1.
164. Suet., *Calig.* 7; Powell (2015), p.194.
165. Ironically, such micro-managing had unintended negative effects on his daughter, Iulia.
166. Suet., *Div. Aug.* 64.2.
167. Suet., *Div. Aug.* 73.
168. Suet., *Div. Aug.* 64.2–3.
169. Tac., *Ann.* 1.33.
170. Balsdon (1962), p.211.
171. Carcopino (1940), p.81.
172. Balsdon (1969), p.66; Paoli (1963), p.116.
173. Carcopino (1940), pp.81–2; Paoli (1963), pp.116–17.
174. Carcopino (1940), pp.81–2; Paoli (1963), pp.116–17.
175. Carcopino (1940), pp.81–2; Paoli (1963), pp.116–17.
176. Suet., *Tib.* 50. Fantham (2006), p.90.
177. Joseph., *Ant. Iud.* 19.1.15.
178. Tac., *Ann.* 5.1: *nullam posthac subolem edidit sed sanguini Augusti per coniunctionem Agrippinae et Germanici adnexa communis pronepotes habuit*; contrast this assessment with allegations of simmering 'feminine jealousies' mentioned in 1.33. See Chapter 7, note 64.
179. Dio 55.22.30.
180. Livy 35.10.12; 40.51.6; 41.27.

Chapter 2: First Steps to Glory

1. Dio 55.26.3.
2. Dio 55.26.2.
3. Dio 55.26.1.
4. Dio 55.26.3.

5. For a survey of famines in the ancient world, see Garnsey (1988).
6. Juv., *Sat.* 10.77–81.
7. Carcopino (1940), p. 18.
8. Carcopino (1940), p. 18 and 175.
9. Carcopino (1940), p. 16 and 18, citing Aurelius Victor and Josephus. For a survey of the *annona*, see Erdkamp (2005).
10. Carcopino (1940), p. 175.
11. Dio 55.26.3.
12. Dio 55.31.4.
13. Dio 55.26.4.
14. e.g. Dio 55.12.4.
15. Dio 55.26.4–5.
16. Dio 55.27.1.
17. Or Plautius Rufus in Suet., *Div. Aug.* 19.
18. Dio 55.27.2.
19. Dio 55.33.4.
20. Dio 55.27.3–4; Pliny, *Nat. Hist.* 8.2.
21. Futrell (1997), pp. 33–38.
22. Suet., *Tib.* 6.4.
23. Beacham (1999), p. 13.
24. Dio 55.33.4.
25. Claridge (1998), p. 264.
26. Suet., *Div. Aug.* 44.3–4.
27. For a detailed description of the different types of gladiators, see Shadrake (2005), p. 127–211.
28. Estimates are based on known contests by Georges Ville, cited by Shadrake (2005), p. 95.
29. Cic., *Tusc. Disp.* 2.41: *gladiatores, aut perditi homines aut barbari, quas plagas perferunt! quo modo illi, qui bene instituti sunt, accipere plagam malunt quam turpiter vitare! quam saepe apparet nihil eos malle quam vel domino satis facere vel populo! mittunt etiam vulneribus confecti ad dominos qui quaerant quid velint; si satis eis factum sit, se velle decumbere. Quis mediocris gladiator ingemuit, quis vultum mutavit umquam? quis non modo stetit, verum etiam decubuit turpiter? quis, cum decubuisset, ferrum recipere iussus collum contraxit? Tantum exercitatio, meditatio, consuetudo valet. Ergo hoc poterit 'Samnis, spurcus homo, vita illa dignus locoque,' vir natus ad gloriam ullam partem animi tam mollem habebit, quam non meditatione et ratione conroboret? Crudele gladiatorum spectaculum et inhumanum non nullis videri solet, et haud scio an ita sit, ut nunc fit. Cum vero sontes ferro depugnabant, auribus fortasse multae, oculis quidem nulla poterat esse fortior contra dolorem et mortem disciplina.*
30. Shadrake (2005), p. 27.
31. Dio 55.33.4.
32. Pliny, *Nat. Hist.* 8.2: *Germanici Caesaris munere gladiatorio quosdam etiam inconditos meatus edider saltantium modo. Vulgare erat per auras iacere, non auferentibus ventis, atque inter se gladiatorios congressus edere aut lascivienti pyrriche conludere. Postea et per funes incessere, lecticis etiam ferentes quaterni singulos puerperas imitantes, plenisque homine tricliniis accubitum iere per lectos ita libratis vestigiis, ne quis potantium attingeretur.* Compare Pliny's account with the embellished version in Ael., *Nat. Animal.* 2.11.
33. Dio 55.27.4; cf. 55.33.4.
34. Dio 55.27.4. The addition of -ianus to the *nomen gentile* indicated adoption, as in, e.g., Octavianus, the boy C. Octavius Thurinus, who was adopted by C. Iulius Caesar in 44 BCE.
35. Cic., *Div.* 2.37.
36. *Augur* or *auspex* derives from the Latin *avis*, 'bird'.
37. Livy 6.41.4: *auspiciis hanc urbem conditam esse, auspiciis bello ac pace, domi militiaeque omnia geri quis est, qui ignoret?*
38. Livy 1.18.5–10; Cic., *Div.* 2.33.
39. Cic., *Div.* 2.36.
40. Aul. Gell., *Noct. Att.* 6.7.
41. Rüpke (2008), p. 156.

42. Strab., *Geog.* 5.3. The festival occurred on 17, 19, and 20 May, or 27, 29, and 30 May.

43. An inscription preserves an account of the different ceremonies of this festival. It was written in the first year of the reign of the Emperor Heliogabalus (218 CE), who was elected a member of the college under the name of M. Aurelius Antoninus Pius Felix.

44. Pliny, *Nat. Hist.* 18.2.

45. Th. Mommsen, *History of Rome*, Book 1, Chapter 15, notes that the Romans of Augustus' time regarded the document to be the oldest existing in their language. This hints at an origin of the religious rite going back to at least the founding of the City, with legend suggesting Romulus was the founding member of the order.

46. He is called Nero Caesar in *CIL* III, 2808 (Scardona, Dalmatia); V, 23 (Pola, Gallia Cisalpina), 4374 (Brixia); VI, 887, 914 (= *ILS* 184), and 31274 (Rome); X, 5393 (Aquinum), 6101 (Formiae); XI, 3336 (Blera), 3789 (Veii); XIV, 3017 (Praeneste). His name appears in the Ostian Calendar (XIV, 244, lines 8–9) simply as Nero: *VII Idus Iun. Nero to[gam virilem] | sumpsit. Cong. di[visit]*. His full name, Nero Iulius Caesar, appears in Suet., *Calig.* 15; *IGR* IV, 1300 = *CIG* 3528 (near Cyme, Asia); *CIL* V, 6416 = *ILS* 107 (Ticinum); and possibly in the very fragmentary inscription *CIL* V, 853 (Aquileia). His official titles were *flamen Augustalis*: *CIL* III, 3808; VI, 887, 913; X, 798; XI, 3336; *quaestor*: VI, 887, 913; X, 798; XI, 3336; XIV, 2965; *sodalis Augustalis*: VI, 913; X, 798; XI, 3336; *duovir quinquennalis*: XIV, 2965 (Praeneste); *sodalis Titius*: VI, 913; *frater Arvalis*: VI, 913; *fetialis*: VI, 913. All of these titles (except *IIvir quinquennalis*) are recorded in *CIL* VI, 913: *Neroni Caesari | Germanici Caesaris f., | Ti. Caesaris Augusti n., I divi Augusti pro n., | flamint Augustali, | sodali Augustali, I sodali Titio, frdtri Arvdli, | fetiali, quaestori | ex s. c.* This inscription was dedicated between the years 27 CE – in which he held the quaestorship (Tac., *Ann.* 3.29) – and 29 CE – the year of his condemnation before the senate (Tac., *Ann.* 5.3). Tacitus records (*Ann.* 3.9) that the pontificate was decreed to Nero in the year 20 CE.

47. Suet., *Tib.* 1.2.

48. Examples of writers living during the Late Republic who exerted influence on their Augustan successors are the orator, philosopher and statesman M. Tullius Cicero, the orator M. Porcius Cato, the poets P. Valerius Cato and C. Valerius Catullus, and the grammarian M. Terentius Varro. Horace was a personal friend of the *princeps* and a willing contributor to the public relations apparatus manufacturing the image of Augustus as the bringer of peace after years of civil strife, the founder of a new epoch (*saeculum*) in the history of mankind, and the restorer of traditional Roman values. Horace composed the *Carmen Saeculare* for the spectacular Secular Games of 17 BCE, as well as *Carmen* IV that celebrated the exploits of Drusus the Elder and Tiberius during the Alpine and Norican Wars of 15 BCE.

49. Ovid was exiled to Tomis on the Black Sea in 8 CE – see Preston (1918).

50. Suet., *Calig.* 3.1–3: *atque inter cetera studiorum monimenta reliquit et comoedias Graecas.*

51. Ov., *Pont.* 4.8.73.

52. Pliny, *Nat. Hist.* 8.68: *fecit et Divus Augustus equo tumulum, de quo germanici caesaris carmen est.*

53. Gain (1976), p. 13.

54. Gain (1976), p. 13.

55. Possanza (2004), pp. 1–19, 99, 105–9, 13–38, 219–43, makes a compelling case for Germanicus as the author of the work.

56. Suet., *Calig.* 3.1–3. Possanza (2004), pp. 131–38, argues that Germanicus paid a debt to Ovid, Vergil, and Cicero, who had himself completed a translation of *Aratus*, but also places him firmly in the tradition of learned poetry.

57. Gain (1976), p. 16.

58. Suet., *Tib.* 6.4.

59. Dio 58.8.2.

60. Suet., *Tib.* 70.1. Fragment VI of the *Aratus* states that, while Greek may be a rich language in terms of its vocabulary, the word *triangula* was a perfectly acceptable native alternative to use in Latin.

61. Suet., *Tib.* 69.1, 70.2–3.

62. *Aratus* 1–16.

63. *Aratus* 558–560.

64. Possanza (2004), pp. 219–43, makes a strong case for Germanicus as the author of the work.
65. Gain (1976), p. 20.
66. Suet., *Calig.* 1.1.
67. Dio 54.26; the number was originally twenty-six, but was reduced to twenty (*vigintiviri*) while Augustus was away from Rome in 16–13 BCE.
68. For example, an inscription in the Berlin-Brandenburgische Akademie der Wissenschaften attests the presence of P. Quinctilius Varus, probably as *quaestor*, in Pergamon. It was presumably erected for an act of generosity on his part to the citizens: http://www.lwl.org/varus-download/presse_imperium/Presseinformation_I_eng.pdf.
69. Suet., *Tib.* 8.
70. Dio 55.2.5–6; 53.13.2.
71. Pliny, *Ep.* 7.31.
72. Drinkwater (1983), p. 132.
73. Dio 55.10a.2; Suet., *Ner.* 4.
74. Dio 55.10a.3.
75. Dio 55.28.5; Vell. Pat. 2.105.1–3.
76. Dio 55.28.6; Vell. Pat. 2.105.1. Saturninus was the son of the commander of the same name who had served in the region before him. For Saturninus, see Kokkinos (1995).
77. *Fossa Drusiana* is quoted by Tac., *Ann.* 2.8.1. Suetonius (*Div. Claud.* 1) uses the term *Fossae Drusinae* suggesting there was more than one canal.
78. Evidence suggests that Lacus Flevo was originally landlocked and the open end of the lake did not exist until 1163, when the sea broke through and changed freshwater Lake Flevo into briney Zuider Zee. The landscape of the Netherlands may have changed just too much in the last two millennia to make possible a certain identification of the location of the *fossa Drusiana* (or *fossae Drusianae*) and reveal how its structures worked. Until better evidence is found, the Drusus Canal – or system of canals – remains an enigma. What can be said with certainty is that it was considered important enough in Roman times to be maintained as late as the third century CE when the nearby fort at Fectio is known from inscriptions to have still been in service as a naval base. For a full review of the evidence, see Powell (2011a), pp. 64–67.
79. Vell. Pat. 2.106.3.
80. Vell. Pat. 2.106.1: *receptae Cauchorum nationes: omnis eorum iuventus infinita numero, immensa corporibus, situ locorum tutissima, traditis armis una cum ducibus suis saepta fulgenti armatoque militum nostrorum agmine ante imperatoris procubuit tribunal.*
81. Vell. Pat. 2.106.2.
82. Vell. Pat. 2.106.2: *Fracti Langobardi, gens etiam Germana feritate ferocior; denique quod numquam antea spe conceptum, nedum opere temptatum erat.*
83. Vell. Pat. 2.106.2; Eutrop., *Brev.* 7.9. Contrast the Roman response to the Langobardi with the Sugambri: in 8 BCE, Tiberius negotiated the surrender of the Sugambri and their war-chief Maelo, who had led the invasion of Gaul in 17 BCE – triggering Augustus's war of conquest – and relocated 40,000 of them to live on the Roman side.
84. Dio 55.27.3; Ov., *Fast.* 1.705ff.
85. Vell. Pat. 2.106.1: *Perlustrata armis tota Germania est, victae gentes paene nominibus incognitae.* Cf. Dio 55.28.5, whose verdict is altogether more sober, saying Tiberius achieved nothing worthy of record.
86. Vell. Pat. 2.108.1.
87. Strab., *Geog.* 7.1.3; Vell. Pat. 2.108.2.
88. Vell. Pat. 2.108.3–9.2.
89. Vell. Pat. 2.106.3.
90. Seager (1972), p. 40.
91. Vell. Pat. 2.109.3.
92. For a discussion of the organization and equipment of the Roman army, see Appendix 1. Tiberius was to lead at least eight legions (VIII *Augusta* from Pannonia, XV *Apollinaris* and XX *Valeria Victrix* from Illyricum, XXI *Rapax* from Raetia, and XIII *Gemina*, XIV *Gemina* and

XVI *Gallica* from Gallia Belgica, and an unknown unit), while Saturninus was to lead at least five legions (I *Germanica*, V *Alaudae*, XVII, XVIII and XIX).

93. Wells (1984), p. 80.
94. For a full discussion of Varus and *Legio* XIX, see Powell (2011a), pp. 42, 44 and 48.
95. Vell. Pat. 2.110.1: *Rumpit interdum, interdum moratur proposita hominum fortuna.*
96. App., *Ill.* 6. Later Roman writers, Dio among them, differentiate between Dalmatia and Pannonia, which were the names given to the two provinces created out of the larger when it was split.
97. Pliny, *Nat. Hist.* 3.26; Florus 2.25. In modern terms, it would cover parts of Albania, Croatia, Bosnia-Herzegovina and Montenegro.
98. Pliny, *Nat. Hist.* 3.28; Florus 2.24. In today's terms, it would cover parts of Austria, Croatia, Serbia, Slovenia, Slovakia and Bosnia-Herzegovina.
99. App., *Ill.* 22.
100. Wilkes (1992), pp. 203–5.
101. Mallory (1989), pp. 73–76.
102. Dzino (2010), p. xi.
103. Wilkes (1992), p. 206; J.-M. Rodaz, *Marcus Agrippa* (Paris, 1984), pp. 140–5.
104. Pliny (*Nat. Hist.* 3.28) mentions 'Serretes, Serrapilli, Jasi, and Sandrozetes: Saus through the Colapiani and Breuci. And these are the chief of the People. Moreover, the Arivates, Azali, Amantes, Belgites, Catari, Corneates, Aravisci, Hercuniates, Latovici, Oseriates, and Varciani. The Mountain Claudius (*Mons Claudius*), in the Front of which are the Scordisci, and upon the Back, the Taurisci'. On the construction of Illyricum, see Dzino (2010), p. 178.
105. Dzino (2005), pp. 141, 159–60.
106. Dio 54.34.2.
107. Dio 54.33.3; App., *Ill.* 15.
108. Dio 54.34.2; 53.12.7.
109. Powell (2015), p. 178. For a full discussion of rebellions and wars of conquest in Illyricum and Pannonia, see Dzino (2005), pp. 117–37.
110. Dio 54.31.3. Tiberius' brutal approach contrasts starkly with that of his brother Drusus, who saw value in the war-fighting skills of the men he defeated, such as the Ligures and Raeti, and recruited them into the Roman army as national units, deploying them into other theatres of war.
111. Iulius Caesar's army took this sea crossing in 48 BCE; his impatience at the speed of its progress, leading to a rare example of his humbling by the ferocious waves of the Adriatic Sea, is recorded by Valerius Maximus (9.8.2).
112. Strab., *Geog.* 7.5.10; cf. Pliny, *Nat. Hist.* 3.25–8.
113. Vell. Pat. 2.108.3–9.1.
114. Dio 56.16.3.
115. Dio 55.29.1.
116. Dio 55.29.3.
117. Dzino (2005), p. 146.
118. Dio 55.29.3. Strabo (*Geog.* 7.5.1) catalogues 'the tribes of the Pannonii are: the Breuci, the Andizetii, the Ditiones, the Peirustae, the Mazaei, and the Daesitiatae, whose leader is Bato, and also other small tribes of less significance which extend as far as Dalmatia and, as one goes south, almost as far as the land of the Ardiaei'.
119. Dio 55.29.3.
120. Dzino (2005), p. 147. Compare to Appian's estimate (*Ill.* 22) that the Pannonians could field 100,000 men.
121. Strab., *Geog.* 7.5.4.
122. For a full discussion of Iron Age Celtic society, arms, armour and modes of combat, see Powell (2011a), pp. 34–8.
123. See Wilkes (1992), p. 199, fig. 23, for an inscription from Ribic, Bosnia.
124. Ennius, *Ann.* 5.540.
125. On Illyrian arms and armour, see Wilkes (1992), pp. 238–41.

126. App., *Ill.* 22.
127. Pliny, *Nat. Hist.* 3.26.
128. Of these fortifications, the eastern section of the town walls – built out of huge stone blocks with the door surrounded by octagonal towers (Porta Caesarea) dating from the time of Augustus – still stands to the present day.
129. Dio 55.29.4; cf. Cowan (2010).
130. Dio 55.29.4.
131. Vell. Pat. 2.111.1: *Habiti itaque dilectus, revocati undique et omnes veterani, viri feminaeque ex censu libertinum coactae dare militem. Audita in senatu vox principis, decimo die, ni caveretur, posse hostem in urbis Romae venire conspectum. Senatorum equitumque Romanorum exactae ad id bellum operae, pollicitati.*
132. Vell. Pat. 2.111.2: *Itaque ut praesidium ultimum res publica ab Augusto ducem in bellum poposcit Tiberium.*
133. Dio 55.30.1–2. The home base of *Legio* XX was Burnum in Dalmatian Illyricum.
134. Suet., *Tib.* 26.
135. Swan (2004), p. 247.
136. Dio 55.30.2.
137. Dio 55.30.3.
138. Dio 55.30.3–4.
139. Dio 55.30.4.
140. Dio 55.30.4; 55.33.2.
141. Vell. Pat. 2.111.3.
142. Vell. Pat. 2.111.4.
143. Vell. Pat. 2.112.2.
144. Vell. Pat. 2.112.2.
145. Suet., *Tib.* 20; Vell. Pat. 2.112.2: *ornamenta* took the form of an *ovatio* rather than a full triumph.
146. Vell. Pat. 2.112.3.
147. Dio 55.30.5; Vell. Pat. 2.112.1.
148. Dio 55.30.5–6.
149. Dio 55.30.5–6.
150. Vell. Pat. 2.111.1.
151. Dio 55.31.1.
152. Suet., *Tib.* 21.4ff.
153. Tac., *Ann.* 1.4; Vell. Pat. 2.112.7.
154. Dio 55.32.1–2; Suet., *Div. Aug.* 65.4. On the dire ramifications of his involuntary abdication see Levick (1972b).
155. Dio 55.31.1.
156. The most famous example is Iulius Caesar's *Commentarii de Bello Gallico*, 'Commentaries on the Gallic War'.
157. A compound word comprising *strategos*, 'army', and *agein*, 'to lead'.
158. Frontinus, selected from the introductions to Books 2 and 4.
159. Suet., *Tib.* 37.1. The Praetorian Cohorts did not yet have a dedicated camp but were quartered in the city; cf. Rankov (1994), pp. 4–5.
160. Mart., *Epig.* 6.76; Tac., *Ann.* 16.27; *Hist.* 1.38.
161. Augustus made the change in 2 BCE, setting the term of service at twelve years, compared to sixteen for the regular legions: Rankov (1994), pp. 4–5.
162. Dio 55.31.1; cf. Brunt (1974).
163. Vell. Pat. 2.110.6: *Quin etiam tantus huius belli metus fuit, ut stabilem illum et firmatum tantorum bellorum experientia Caesaris Augusti animum quateret atque terreret.*
164. Dio 55.31.4.
165. Dio 55.31.2.
166. Th. Mommsen, *History of Rome*, translated by William Purdie Dickson (New York, 1894), Volume 3, Book 4, p. 244.
167. Dio 55. 32.3.

168. Vell. Pat. 2.113.1: *unctis exercitibus, quique sub Caesare fuerant quique ad eum venerant, contractisque in una castra decem legionibus, septuaginta amplius cohortibus, decem alis et pluribus quam decem veteranorum milibus, ad hoc magno voluntariorum numero frequentique equite regio, tanto denique exercitu.* Suetonius (*Tib.* 26) states that fifteen legions and an equal number of auxiliaries were involved; Seager (1972), p. 42, asserts that this is 'far more than he really needed', but this underestimates the difficulty of the terrain and the refusal of the rebels to fight in the open.

169. Vell. Pat. 2.113.1: *quantus nullo umquam loco post bella fuerat civilia, omnes eo ipso laeti erant maximamque fiduciam victoriae in numero reponebant.*

170. Tac., *Agr.* 5: *Nec Agricola licenter, more iuvenum qui militiam in lasciviam vertunt, neque segniter ad voluptates et commeatus titulum tribunatus et inscitiam rettulit.*

171. Vell. Pat. 2.112.4–5: *apud signa quoque legionum trepidatum.*

172. Vell. Pat. 2.112.6.

173. Vell. Pat. 2.112.5: *Sed Romani virtus militis plus eo tempore vindicavit gloriae quam ducibus reliquit, qui multum a more imperatoris sui discrepantes ante in hostem inciderunt, quam per explora,tores, ubi hostis esset, cognoscerent.*

174. Vell. Pat. 2.112.6: *Iam igitur in dubiis rebus semet ipsae legiones adhortatae, …invasere hostes nec sustinuisse contenti perrupta eorum acie ex insperato victoriam vindicaverunt.*

175. Dio 55.32.3.

176. Dio 55.32.3.

177. Dio 55.32.3–4.

178. Vell. Pat. 2.112.3; Pliny (*Nat. Hist.* 3.28) places Mons Claudius between the Scordisci and Taurisci.

179. Dio's account for 7 CE is lightweight, so our understanding of events may miss important events.

180. Dio 55.32.4.

181. Strab., *Geog.* 7.5.1.

182. Dio 55.32.4.

183. Tac., *Agr.* 5: *nosci exercitui, discere a peritis, sequi optimos, nihil adpetere in iactationem, nihil ob formidinem recusare, simulque et anxius et intentus agere.*

184. Dio 55.33.3.

185. Dio 56.11.1. The exact identity of this location is not known.

186. Evans (1883), pp. 11–12.

187. Mount Igman rises to its highest point at Vlahinja Ridge, 1,502m (4,928ft) high. Today it is a popular hiking and skiing resort.

188. Dio 56.11.1.

189. Dio 56.11.1.

190. Dio 56.11.2.

191. Dio 56.11.2.

192. Dio 56.11.1; 56.11.3. Raetinium may be the Rataneum of Pliny the Elder (*Nat. Hist.* 3.26). The modern location might be Bihać on the Una River.

193. Dio 56.11.3–7.

194. Swan (2004), p. 247, argues for eight legions.

195. Dio 56.12.2.

196. Dio 55.34.5–6.

197. Dio 55.34.6.

198. Wilkes (1969), p. 553.

199. Dio 55.34.7.

200. Dio 56.12.3.

201. Dio 56.12.4.

202. Dio 56.12.5.

203. Suet., *Tib.* 26.

204. Dio 55.33.1.

205. Dio 55.33.2; 56.15. On the Pannonian deserters, see Dzino (2005), pp. 154–5.

206. Dio 56.13.1.

207. Dio 56.13.2.
208. Dio 56.13.3.
209. Dio 56.13.4.
210. Dio 56.14.1.
211. Dio 56.14.5.
212. Dio 56.14.6.
213. Dio 56.14.7.
214. Dio 56.14.7.
215. Dio 56.15.1.
216. Dio 56.15.1–2.
217. Dio 56.15.2.
218. Dio 56.15.3.
219. Dio 56.16.1.
220. Dio 56.16.2.
221. Dzino (2005), p.155.
222. Dio 56.16.2–3.
223. Dio 56.16.2.
224. Suet., *Tib.* 16.
225. Dio 56.16.4.
226. Dio 55.28.7.
227. Dio 55.29.6–7.
228. Augustus, *Res Gestae* 30: *Pannoniorum gentes, quas ante me principem populi Romani exercitus nunquam adit.*
229. Dio 56.17.1; Ov., *Pont.* 2.1. On the meaning of the title *imperator* see Dio 52.41.3–4. Augustus normally assumed the battle honours won by his deputies for himself. He had refused Tiberius before, and also his brother Drusus the Elder's use of the title in 11 BCE, despite his troops having acclaimed him at the end of the campaign: see Dio 54.33.5.
230. Dio 56.17.1.
231. Ov., *Pont.* 2.75–126.
232. Levick (1976/1999), p.111.
233. Dzino (2005), p.154, n.74: *Cohortes Breucorum* are attested by several extant inscriptions, e.g. *CIL* III, 5613, 11781; XVI, 89; XLIII = *Eph.* VII, n.670, 671. For a full discussion, see Bogaers (1969).
234. Dio 54.31.3.
235. Wilkes (1995), p.207.
236. Vell. Pat. 2.116: *Magna in bello Delmatico experimenta virtutis in incultos ac difficilis locos praemissus Germanicus dedit; celebri etiam opera diligentique.*
237. Dio 56.17.2. *Ornamenta triumphalia* entitled Germanicus to ride on horseback through the streets of Rome; his father Drusus the Elder had been so honoured in 11 BCE (Dio 54.33.5).
238. Vell. Pat. 2.116.1: *Magna in bello Delmatico experimenta virtutis in incultos ac difficilis locos praemissus Germanicus dedit.*

Chapter 3: Law and Disorder
1. The units known or deduced to have remained in the region were *Legio* VIII *Augusta*, *Legio* VIIII *Hispana*, residing at Siscia (Sisak), and *Legio* XV *Apollinaris* at Ljubljana and/or Vindobona (modern Vienna) in Pannonia; while *Legio* XI *Claudia Pia Fidelis* was stationed in Dalmatia, possibly at Burnum (located 2.5km north of modern Kistanje, Croatia).
2. Vell. Pat. 2.117.1.
3. Dio 56.18.1.
4. Vell. Pat. 2.117.1.
5. Tac., *Ann.* 1.57.
6. Dio 56.22.2.
7. Dio 56.22.4.
8. Dio 56.22.2.

9. Suet., *Div. Aug.* 23.2: *Quintili Vare, legiones redde!*; Dio 56.23.1.
10. Dio 56.23.1.
11. Vell. Pat. 2.119.5.
12. On the *Germani Corporis Custodes*, see Rankov (1994), pp. 11–12.
13. Dio 56.23.4.
14. Dio 56.22.2.
15. Dio 56.23.2–3: ὄφελος ἦν, ἐκεκάκωτο. ὅμως δ᾽ οὖν τά τε ἄλλα ὡς ἐκ τῶν παρόντων παρεσκευάσατο, καὶ ἐπειδὴ μηδεὶς τῶν τὴν στρατεύσιμον ἡλικίαν ἐχόντων καταλεχθῆναι ἠθέλησεν, ἐκλήρωσεν αὐτούς, καὶ τῶν μὲν μηδέπω πέντε καὶ τριάκοντα ἔτη γεγονότων τὸν πέμπτον, τῶν δὲ πρεσβυτέρων τὸν δέκατον ἀεὶ λαχόντα τήν τε οὐσίαν ἀφείλετο καὶ ἠτίμωσε. καὶ τέλος, ὡς καὶ πάνυ πολλοὶ οὐδ᾽ οὕτω τι αὐτοῦ προετίμων, ἀπέκτεινέ τινας. ἀποκληρώσας δὲ ἔκ τε τῶν ἐστρατευμένων ἤδη καὶ ἐκ τῶν ἐξελευθέρων ὅσους ἠδυνήθη, κατέλεξε, καὶ εὐθὺς σπουδῇ μετὰ τοῦ Τιβερίου ἐς τὴν Γερμανίαν.
16. Dio 56.24.1.
17. Suet., *Tib.* 17.2.
18. For the contractual relationship between gods and men, see Powell (2010).
19. Dio 56.24.1.
20. Dio 56.24.4.
21. Dio 56.24.1: πολλαχῇ ἑώκει, ἀστέρες τε κομῆται συχνοὶ ἅμα κατεφαίνοντο, καὶ δόρατα ἀπ᾽ ἄρκτου φερόμενα πρὸς τὰ τῶν Ῥωμαίων στρατόπεδα προσπίπτειν ἐδόκει, μέλισσαί τε περὶ τοὺς βωμοὺς αὐτῶν κηρία ἀνέπλασσον, καὶ Νίκης τι ἄγαλμα ἔν τε τῇ Γερμανίᾳ ὂν καὶ πρὸς τὴν πολεμίαν βλέπον. Remarkably, the gilt bronze head of a horse from a statue of Augustus on horseback was discovered at Waldgirmes in the Lahn Valley in 2009: http://www.dainst.org/index_0824b37863dd14a91601001c3253dc21_de.html.
21. Dio 56.24.6: Τιβέριος διαβῆναι τὸν Ῥῆνον οὐκ ἔκρινεν, ἀλλ᾽ ἠτρέμιζεν ἐπιτηρῶν μὴ οἱ βάρβαροι τοῦτο ποιήσωσιν. ἀλλ᾽ οὐδ᾽ ἐκεῖνοι διαβῆναι ἐτόλμησαν γνόντες αὐτὸν παρόντα.
22. Dio 56.22.4.
23. Dio 56.25.4.
24. Dio 55.33.4; 56.27.2–3.
25. Metzger (2004), pp. 249–52.
26. Cic., *Verr.* 4.66.148.
27. Crook (1967), pp. 73–5; Paoli (1963), pp. 194–5.
28. Paoli (1963), pp. 193–4. Paoli notes that Germanicus' brother Claudius, as emperor, put a ceiling of 10,000 *sesterces* on fees that lawyers could charge their clients.
29. Metzger (2004), pp. 252–3, suggesting that the Romans did not have a system based on case law, but that it was based on formulary procedure, and 'the decision of a Roman judge did not make law for future decisions'.
30. Cic., *Brut.* 43.158.
31. Suet., *Calig.* 3.1: *ingenium in utroque eloquentiae doctrinaeque genere praecellens.*
32. Dio 56.24.7.
33. Dio 56.24.7: ἔδεισεν ὁ κατήγορος αὐτοῦ μὴ ἐλαττωθῇ διὰ τοῦτο παρὰ τοῖς δικασταῖς ἐφ᾽ οἷσπερ εἰώθει τὰ τοιαῦτα κρίνεσθαι, καὶ παρὰ τῷ Αὐγούστῳ δικασθῆναι μάτην ἠθέλησεν: οὐ γὰρ ἐκράτησεν.
34. Dio 56.24.7.
35. Dio 56.24.7: ὅτι ὁ Γερμανικὸς ἐκ πολλῶν ᾠκειοῦτο τῷ πλήθει, καὶ ὅτι ὑπερεδίκει τινῶν, οὐχ ὅπως ἐπὶ τῶν ἄλλων δικαστῶν ἀλλὰ καὶ ἐπ᾽ αὐτοῦ τοῦ Αὐγούστου. διὸ καὶ ταμίᾳ τινὶ φόνου αἰτίαν ἔχοντι τοῦ Γερμανικοῦ συναγορεύειν μέλλοντος.
36. Suet., *Div. Aug.* 33.1; Everitt (2006), p. 249.
37. Suet., *Tib.* 8.
38. Tac., *Ann.* 1.41; 2.43: *insigni fecunditate.*
39. Suet., *Calig.* 7. Several inscriptions mention Drusus Iulius Caesar. He is called Drusus Caesar in *CIL* II, 609; III, 380 = *ILS* 185; V, 4953 = *ILS* 187; 7567; X, 6101; XI, 3788; *ILS* 186; *IGR* IV, 75 = *IG* XII.2, 213; Drusus Iulius: *CIL* II, 1553; Drusus: *CIL* VI, 5201 = *ILS* 1837, which is one relating to his childhood; *CIL* VI, 31274, which is a fragment of marble surviving from a

monument that seems to have been dedicated *ob honorem Augustalitatis* by a *municipium* close to Rome, and reads *Druso Germanici Caesaris f.*; and *IGR* IV, 78 = *IG* XII.2, 172 = *ILS* 8789, from Mytilene, which mentions *Drusi* in Greek. The variations of his name are similar to those of his brother Nero (see Chapter 2, note 46) and the full name, Drusus Iulius Germanicus, appears in *CIL* V, 6416 no. 9 = *ILS* 107 no. 9. The clan name Iulius, which was usually omitted in the house of Augustus, recurs here not among his sons, but among his grandsons and great-grandsons. Drusus held fewer public offices than his older brother, Nero: known from inscriptions are *praefectus urbi* and *sodalis Augustalis*: *ILS* 186 (Bordeaux); *pontifex*: *CIL* III, 380; *duovir quin-quennalis*: XIV, 2965 (Praeneste); cf. 3017. One P. Vergilius is implied as *praefectus* of Drusus in *CIL* V, 7567; and P. Plautius Pulcher as *comes Drusi* in XIV, 3607. Tacitus (*Ann.* 6.40.4) reports that Drusus was married to Aemilia Lepida, to whom *CIL* VI, 9449 apparently refers.

40. Suet., *Calig.* 7.
41. *CIL* VI, 888: *Ti. Caesar | Germanici Caesaris f. | hic crematus est.* It was found in 1777 near the Mausoleum of Augustus from the crematory (*ustrinum domus Augustae*) along with five other epitaphs of members of the *princeps'* household.
42. http://www.utexas.edu/depts/classics/documents/Life.html. For a statistical survey, see Scheidel (2009), which shows that infant deaths peaked during the months of late summer and early autumn.
43. Suet., *Calig.* 8.2.
44. Suet., *Div. Aug.* 34.2; *Calig.* 7, 8.2. *CIL* VI, 889 = *ILS* 181, found at the sepulchral monument near the Mausoleum of Augustus on the *via Flaminia*, reads *C. Caesar | Germanici Caesaris f. | hic crematus est.*
45. Suet., *Calig.* 7, 8.2.
46. Suet., *Calig.* 7.
47. Suet., *Div. Aug.* 34: *accitos Germanici liberos receptosque partim ad se partim in patris gremium ostentavit, manu vultuque significans ne gravarentur imitari iuvenis exemplum.*
48. Dio 56.25.2: Τιβέριος μὲν καὶ Γερμανικὸς ἀντὶ ὑπάτου ἄρχων ἔς τε τὴν Κελτικὴν ἐσέβαλον καὶ κατέδραμόν τινα αὐτῆς. The claim that Germanicus was proconsul seems anachronistic; he had not yet served a term as consul. The trip in 11 CE was Germanicus' first visit to the region.
49. Dio 56.25.2: οὐ μέντοι οὔτε μάχῃ τινὶ ἐνίκησαν ᾿ἐς γὰρ χεῖρας οὐδεὶς αὐτοῖς ἤει οὔτε.
50. Dio 56.25.3: ἔθνος τι ὑπηγάγοντο· δεδιότες γὰρ μὴ καὶ συμφορᾷ αὖθις περιπέσωσιν, οὐ πάνυ πόρρω τοῦ Ῥήνου προῆλθον. Dio's comment overlooks the fact that Tiberius' patient but methodical approach had been key to winning the *Bellum Batonianum*. Augustus himself was fond of the Greek maxim, 'the cautious commander is better than the bold': Suet., *Div. Aug.* 25.
51. Dio 56.25.3: ἀλλὰ αὐτοῦ που μέχρι τοῦ μετοπώρου μείναντες καὶ τὰ τοῦ Αὐγούστου γενέθλια ἑορτάσαντες καί τινα ἱπποδρομίαν ἐν αὐτοῖς διὰ τῶν ἑκατοντάρχων ποιήσαντες ἐπανῆλθον.
52. Timpe (1968), p. 37; cf. p. 45, proposes that, for this campaign, Germanicus was acclaimed *imperator*. Syme (1978), p. 60 n. 3, thinks this 'cannot be correct'.
53. Suet., *Calig.* 1.1: *et post eam consulatum statim gessit.*
54. Dio 56.1; Suet., *Calig.* 8.
55. Cic., *Font.* 18, cited by Weinstock (1950).
56. Dio 56.1.
57. Cowell (1962), pp. 166–71.
58. Everitt (2001), p. 87.
59. Everitt (2006), pp. 209 11.
60. Dio 53.12.1.
61. Dio 56.26.1.
62. *Consules suffecti* were traditional replacements for men who had died or resigned from office. Suffects were elected in each of the following years of his lifetime since birth: 16, 12, 5, 4, 2 and 1 BCE, and 1, 2, 3, 4, 5, 6, 7, 8, 9, 10, 11 and 12 CE.
63. Varro was a later deputy of Tiberius in the province of Germania Inferior: Tac., *Ann.* 3.41.
64. Dio 56.26.1: Γερμανικὸς... καὶ αὐτὸς μὲν οὐδὲν ἄξιον μνήμης ἔπραξε, πλὴν ὅτι καὶ τότε ὑπερεδίκησεν, ἐπεί γε ὁ συνάρχων αὐτοῦ Γάιος Καπίτων καὶ πάνυ τὴν ἄλλως ἠριθμεῖτο.
65. Dio 56.26.2.

66. Dio 56.27.4.
67. Dio 56.27.4.
68. Dio 56.27.5.
69. Beacham (1999), p. 115.
70. Cato, *Agr.* 141.4.
71. Shadrake (2005), p. 236.
72. Dio 54.2.4.
73. Sen., *Ep.* 70.20, says that the *bestiarii* were generally a feature of the morning show, and, as they were usually condemned criminals or prisoners, they were considered of lesser status than gladiators.
74. Futrell (1997), p. 45; Shadrake (2005), p. 25.
75. Dio 56.27.5.
76. Pliny, *Nat. Hist.* 2.25.
77. Suet., *Calig.* 8.1, 5: he argues strongly for Antium, a seaside resort town located along the western coast of Italy some 64km (40 miles) south of Rome, based on an entry in the proceedings of the Senate, and against other contemporaries who argued for Tibur.
78. Suet., *Calig.* 8.1.
79. Suet., *Calig.* 7.
80. Ov., *Pont.* 4.13.47f.
81. Seager (1972), p. 45 n. 6, points out that the day is certain but the year is not, though there is more evidence in support of 12 CE.
82. Dio 56.17.1; Suet., *Tib.* 17.2.
83. Dio 56.18.1; Vell. Pat. 2.112.2; 121.3; Suet., *Tib.* 20.
84. Suet., *Tib.* 20; Ov., *Pont.* 2.1, 2; 3.3.85ff.
85. Dio 55.8.2.
86. Ov., *Pont.* 2.1.25ff.
87. Suet., *Tib.* 17. A silver *denarius* minted in Lugdunum in 13 CE shows Tiberius standing to the right in a triumphal *quadriga*, holding an eagle-tipped sceptre: *RIC* 222; *RSC* 300; *BMCRE* 512.
88. Ov., *Pont.* 2.1.45–6; Suet., *Tib.* 20.
89. M. Grant, *Caesar* (London, 1974), p. 160.
90. Dio 56.12.5.
91. Suet., *Tib.* 20.
92. Suet., *Tib.* 16: *Ac perseuerantiae grande pretium tulit, toto Illyrico, quod inter Italiam regnumque Noricum et Thraciam et Macedoniam interque Danuuium flumen et sinum maris Hadriatici patet, perdomito et in dicionem redacto.*
93. Suet., *Tib.* 20.
94. The *Gemma Augustea* is now in the Collection of Greek and Roman Antiquities in the Kunsthistorisches Museum, Vienna (inventory number IX A 79).
95. On the arguments about the dating of the gem and what its images represent, see Zanker (1990), pp. 230–3; Galinsky (1996), pp. 120–1.
96. An alternative interpretation sees the reclining woman as Italia Turrita, the personification of the Italian nation.
97. Suet., *Tib.* 21.1. The tribunician power had been granted to him for the second time before the Batonian War: Suet., *Tib.* 16.1.
98. Ov., *Pont.* 2.1.57–68.
99. Suet., *Tib.* 20.
100. Tac., *Ann.* 1.3, 14.
101. Lintott (1993), p. 22.
102. Suet., *Calig.* 8.3.
103. Barrett (1989), p. 7.
104. A.K. Bowman, 'Provincial Administration and Taxation', *CAH*, pp. 344–5.
105. Powell (2011a), pp. 52–7.
106. Dio 54.25.1; Drinkwater (1983), pp. 228–30; Wolff (1998), p. 121.
107. Tac., *Ann.* 1.11.7.

108. On the paucity of evidence for these magistracies in the Gallic *civitates*, see Drinkwater (1983), p. 108.
109. Goudineau, in *CAH*, pp. 498–9; Wightman (1971), p. 37.
110. Wolff (1998), p. 33.
111. Tac., *Agr.* 21.
112. Tac., *Agr.* 21.
113. Tac., *Agr.* 11.
114. In the settlement with the Senate in 27 BCE, Augustus took over all imperial provinces and the army located in them, which left the Senate with control of the other territories, but no means to enforce it: Dio 55.23.1–5.6.
115. Dio 55.23.2–6; Tac., *Ann.* 1.31; in 1.56, he states that there were at least '5,000 auxiliaries' under Caecina in Germania Inferior.
116. Tac., *Ann.* 1.7.
117. Erdkamp (2007), p. 102.
118. Erdkamp (2007), p. 103.
119. P. Herz, 'Finances and Costs of the Roman Army', *CRA*, p. 317.
120. Brunn (1999), p. 24, cites the example of *RIC* I, 25; Sutherland (1978), pp. 65–6.
121. Brunn (1999), p. 24. Copper *aes* and bronze *dupondii* coins continued to be minted in Rome.
122. Grant (1958), p. 79.
123. Mattingly (1960), pp. 104–5.
124. For a full discussion, see Powell (2011a), pp. 56–7 and 96–9.
125. Wightman (1971), p. 36; Powell (2015), pp. 139–40.
126. Dio 55.10a.3.
127. Tac., *Ann.* 1.39, 57.2.
128. Drinkwater (1983), p. 21.
129. Dio 54.25.1.
130. Augustus, *Res Gestae* 2.8; Livy, *Per.* 134.
131. Tac., *Ann.* 1.31; 2.6.
132. Ulpian, *Digesta* 50.15.4, cited in Levick (1985), pp. 72–4, no. 63.
133. The best known example of a census is that recorded in the Gospel of St Luke 2:1–6; see Braunert (1957).
134. *ILS* 1514, cited in Mommsen and Demandt (1996), p. 291 n. 495.
135. Suet., *Calig.* 8.1.
136. Suet., *Calig.* 7.
137. Suet., *Calig.* 8.1: *OB AGRIPPINAE PUERPERIUM.* He writes that Agrippina had nine children, two of whom – an unnamed boy and Caius – died in infancy and one boy died entering boyhood, plus three girls who lived, who were born in successive years, which would be 15, 16 and 18 CE. This leaves one child unaccounted for, which I place at Ambitarvium. See Lindsay (1995).
138. Suet., *Calig.* 8.4: see the interpretation of the context in Barrett (1989), p. 7.
139. *Tabula Siarensis*, lines 13–14: *Germanici Caesaris, cum[i]is Germanis bello supe[ratis] [–] a Gallia sum⟨m⟩otis.* See Rowe (2002), p. 3; Levick (1976/1999), p. x.
140. Vell. Pat. 2.121.1.
141. See Syme (1978), pp. 58 with notes 5 and 6. Syme believes that the epigram celebrates Germanicus' later victories in Germania, rather than a Gallic insurrection. In Syme (1979), p. 318, he again points out that the Greek poet may mean Germans, 'alluding to the subsequent campaigns of Germanicus Caesar', but also suggests he might be referring to the campaigns of the man's father, Drusus the Elder.
142. As noted by Syme (1978), pp. 58–61, Germanicus is known to have been acclaimed as imperator twice during his lifetime. The first occasion is still the subject of debate amongst scholars.
143. Vell. Pat. 2.123: *Quippe Caesar Augustus cum Germanicum nepotem suum reliqua belli patraturum misisset in Germaniam.*
144. Vell. Pat. 2.123; Tac., *Ann.* 1.5.3; Suet., *Div. Aug.* 97.3; *Tib.* 21.1.
145. Suet., *Div. Aug.* 97.3. On the shooting star see Sen. *Nat. Qu.* 1.3.
146. Tac., *Ann.* 1.33.

147. Suet., *Div. Aug.* 50. See also Simpson (2005), pp. 180–8.
148. Tac., *Ann.* 1.7.
149. Dio 56.30.1; 30.5; Suet., *Div. Aug.* 98.5–100.1; Tac., *Ann.* 1.9.
150. Suet., *Div. Aug.* 101.2; Eutrop., *Brev.* 7.10.
151. Tac., *Ann.* 1.14: *at Germanico Caesari pro consulare imperium petivit, missique legati qui deferrent, simul maestitiam eius ob excessum Augusti solarentur.*
152. Life: Dio 56.30.5. *Princeps Senatus*: Augustus, *Res Gestae* 1.7.
153. Dio 56.32.1; Suet., *Div. Aug.* 101.2; *Tib.* 23; Tac., *Ann.* 1.8 (mentions the breviary listing imperial revenues and military dispositions). Only Dio (56.33.1) states that there was a fourth document in which Augustus advised against expanding the empire's borders. On the discrepancy between the number of documents and its significance, see Ober (1982).
154. Dio 56.32.2; Suet., *Div. Aug.* 101.2.
155. Dio 57.18.11.
156. Dio 56.32.2; Suet., *Div. Aug.* 101.2–3.
157. Will: Dio 56.33.1–4; Suet., *Div. Aug.* 101.4; *Tib.* 23. Dio mentions Tiberius and Drusus the Younger as present during the meeting of the Senate and at the funeral, but not Germanicus. Limits to Empire: Dio 56.33.5–6; Tac., *Ann.* 1.9, 11.
158. Gruen (2005), p. 50.
159. Suet., *Tib.* 21; Vell. Pat. 2.121.1. On the importance of creating and maintaining the façade of Republican legitimacy, see Ehrenberg (1953), pp. 113–36.
160. Dio 57.2.1; Suet., *Tib.* 23–4; Tac., *Ann.* 1.7.
161. Dio 56.44.3; Tac., *Ann.* 1.2, 12.
162. Tac., *Ann.* 1.33.
163. Suet., *Tib.* 50.1.
164. Dio 56.43.4. This era of peace was symbolically represented by closing the doors of the Temple of Janus, an achievement boasted of by Augustus in his *Res Gestae* (2.13), and the consecration of the *Ara Pacis Augustae* in the Campus Martius in January 9 BCE. On the *rei publicae causa*, see Chapter 1, n. 151.
165. Dio 56.43.4.
166. Tac., *Ann.* 1.6: *eam condicionem esse imperandi, ut non aliter ratio constet quam si uni reddatur.*
167. Dio 56.45.1–2.
168. Dio 56.41.1.
169. Dio 56.41.9: τοιγαροῦν διὰ ταῦτα εἰκότως καὶ προστάτην αὐτὸν καὶ πατέρα δημόσιον ἐποιήσασθε, καὶ ἄλλοις τε πολλοῖς καὶ ὑπατείαις πλείσταις ἐπεγαυρώσατε, καὶ τὸ τελευταῖον καὶ ἥρωα ἀπεδείξατε καὶ ἀθάνατον ἀπεφήνατε. οὔκουν οὐδὲ πενθεῖν αὐτὸν ἡμῖν πρέπει, ἀλλὰ τὸ μὲν σῶμα αὐτοῦ τῇ φύσει ἤδη ἀποδοῦναι, τὴν δὲ ψυχὴν ὡς καὶ θεοῦ ἀεὶ ἀγάλλειν.
170. Dio 56.46.1.
171. Tac., *Ann.* 1.54. See also Rüpke (2008), p. 9.
172. Tac., *Ann.* 1.54.
173. Rüpke (2008), p. 161.
174. Dio 51.19; 54.34; Tac., *Ann.* 1.54.
175. Tac., *Ann.* 1.13, 15; Dio 56.46.
176. Dio 54.34; Suet., *Div. Aug.* 98.
177. Dio 56.29.1.
178. *Augustalia* of 14 CE: Tac., *Ann.* 1.54. Content of the *Augustalia*: Suet., *Claud.* 11.2; cf. Dio 56.46.1–47.2. Tiberius' complex personality: Dio 57.1.1–6; Tac., *Ann.* 1.33. Actors' dispute: Dio 56.47.2.
179. Dio 56.47.2; Tac., *Ann.* 1.54.
180. Dio 57.8.2: καὶ πολλάκις γε ἔλεγεν ὅτι 'δεσπότης μὲν τῶν δούλων, αὐτοκράτωρ δὲ τῶν στρατιωτῶν.
181. Tac., *Ann.* 1.7.
182. Suet., *Tib.* 22; Tac., *Ann.* 1.5–6, 53. See Allen (1947). Postumus had been banished to Surrentum in 6 CE and to Planasia in 7 CE – Levick (1972b), pp. 692 and 694–95.

183. Suet., *Tib.* 25. Detweiler (1970), pp. 289–295. See also Allen (1947), who argues that Postumus may have died a natural death.
184. Dio 57.18.1; Tac., *Ann.* 1.53.
185. Suet., *Div. Aug.* 101.3.
186. Tac., *Ann.* 1.7: *ausa praecipua ex formidine, ne Germanicus, in cuius manu tot legiones, immensa sociorum auxilia, mirus apud populum favor, habere imperium quam exspectare mallet.*
187. Suet., *Tib.* 24; Tac., *Ann.* 1.7.
188. L. Scribonius Libo: Suet., *Tib.* 25.
189. Suet., *Tib.* 25: *Quem maxime casum timens, partes sibi quas senatui liberet, tuendas in re p. depoposcit, quando uniuersae sufficere solus nemo posset nisi cum altero uel etiam cum pluribus.*
190. Tac., *Ann.* 1.14.3.
191. Syme (1978), p. 57, citing Tac., *Ann.* 1.31.
192. Tac., *Ann.* 1.34; Suet., *Tib.* 25.
193. Tac., *Ann.* 1.34.
194. Vell. Pat. 2.125; Tac., *Ann.* 1.31.
195. Tac., *Ann.* 1.34.
196. Tac., *Ann.* 1.16.
197. Dio 57.4.1.
198. Tac., *Ann.* 1.31.
199. Pliny, *Ep.* 3.5.4: *'Bellorum Germaniae viginti'; quibus quae cum Germanis gessimus bella collegit. Incohavit cum in Germania militaret, somnio monitus: adstitit ei quiescenti Drusi Neronis effigies, qui Germaniae latissime victor ibi periit, commenadabat memoriam suam orabatque ut se iniuria oblivionis aderet.*
200. Tac., *Ann.* 3.41; 4.73; 13.53. The region covers what is now North Rhine-Westfalia, Luxembourg, and the southern part of the Netherlands.
201. Tac., *Ann.* 3.41; 4.73; 13.53. The region covers what is now western Switzerland, Jura and Alsace in France, and Bavaria.
202. Tac., *Ann.* 1.31, 37–39, 45.
203. Tac., *Ann.* 1.34.
204. Tac., *Ann.* 1.34.
205. Rowe (2002), p. 163.
206. Tac., *Ann.* 1.35. Rowe (2002), p. 163, notes similarities to the speech recorded by Tacitus in the *Tabula Siarensis*, which records his actual words to the troops against Piso.
207. Tac., *Ann.* 1.35.
208. Tac., *Ann.* 1.35.
209. Tac., *Ann.* 1.35. Cassius Chaerea would become famous in history as the assassin of Caligula.
210. Tac., *Ann.* 1.35.
211. Tac., *Ann.* 1.35: *mox indiscretis vocibus pretia vacationum, angustias stipendii, duritiam operum ac propriis nominibus incusant vallum, fossas, pabuli materiae lignorum adgestus, et si qua alia ex necessitate aut adversus otium castrorum quaeruntur. atrocissimus veteranorum clamor oriebatur, qui tricena aut supra stipendia numerantes, mederetur fessis, neu mortem in isdem laboribus, sed finem tam exercitae militiae neque inopem requiem orabant.*
212. Dio 55.23.1.
213. Dio 57.4.2; cf. Vell. Pat. 2.125, noting that the men 'demanded a new leader, a new constitution, a new republic; they even had the confidence to threaten that they would give laws to the Senate, and to the *princeps*; and they attempted to fix the amount of their pay and of their service' (*Quippe exercitus, qui in Germania militabat . . ., rabie quadam et profunda confudendi omnia cupiditate novum ducem, novum statum, novam quaerebant rem publicam; quin etiam ausi sunt minaridaturos se senatui, daturos principi leges; modum stipendii, finem militiae sibi ipsi constituere conati sunt*).
214. Dio 55.25.1.
215. Dio 55.24.9–55.25.1.
216. Augustus, *Res Gestae* 3.

217. Dio 55.25.3; Suet., *Div. Aug.* 49. The tax on auctions was reduced by Tiberius to half of one per cent (*ducentesima*), and abolished altogether by Caligula in Italy (Tac., *Ann.* 1.78; 2.42; Suet., *Calig.* 16).
218. Dio, 55.23–35; Augustus, *Res Gestae* 17.
219. The *praetores aerarii* were chosen by lot: Frontin., *Aq.* 100; Suet., *Div. Aug.* 36; Tac., *Ann.* 1.75; 13.2, 28–9.
220. Dio 55.23.1: χαλεπῶς δὲ δὴ τῶν στρατιωτῶν πρὸς τὴν τῶν ἄθλων σμικρότητα διὰ τοὺς πολέμους τοὺς τότε ἐνεστηκότας οὐχ ἥκιστα ἐχόντων, καὶ μηδενὸς ἔξω τοῦ τεταγμένου τῆς στρατείας σφίσι χρόνου ὅπλα λαβεῖν ἐθέλοντος, ἐψηφίσθη τοῖς μὲν ἐκ τοῦ δορυφορικοῦ πεντακισχιλίας δραχμάς, ἐπειδὰν ἑκκαίδεκα ἔτη, τοῖς δὲ ἑτέροις τρισχιλίας, ἐπειδὰν.
221. Dio 55.24.8.
222. Dio 55.24.8: καὶ εἰσὶ καὶ νῦν σύστημα ἴδιον, ῥάβδους φέροντες ὥσπερ οἱ ἑκατόνταρχοι.
223. Tac., *Ann.* 1.35.
224. Tac., *Ann.* 1.31: *igitur audito fine Augusti vernacula multitudo, nuper acto in urbe dilectu, lasciviae sueta, laborum intolerans, implere ceterorum rudes animos: venisse tempus quo veterani maturam missionem, iuvenes largiora stipendia, cuncti modum miseriarum exposcerent saevitiamque centurionum ulciscerentur.* The levy followed the emergency to raise troops to defend Italy after the disaster at Teutoburg in 9 CE.
225. Tac., *Ann.* 1.31.
226. They may not necessarily have been in one giant circumvallated camp, but two camps of the legions, paired up and located in close proximity. Co-billeting of legions on this scale, however, was common in the reigns of Augustus and Tiberius.
227. Tac., *Ann.* 1.32.
228. Tac., *Ann.* 1.31: *sua in manu sitam rem Romanam, suis victoriis augeri rem publicam, in suum cognomentum adscisci imperatores.*
229. Tac., *Ann.* 1.35.
230. Dio 57.5.1.
231. Tac., *Ann.* 1.31: *Isdem ferme diebus isdem causis Germanicae legiones turbatae, quanto plures tanto violentius, et magna spe fore ut Germanicus Caesar imperium alterius pati nequiret daretque se legionibus vi sua cuncta tracturis.*
232. Dio 57.5.2; Tac., *Ann.* 1.35; Suet., *Tib.* 25.
233. Dio 57.5.2; Tac., *Ann.* 1.35.
234. Dio 57.5.3: ὁ οὖν Γερμανικὸς ἰδὼν ὅποι 1 τὸ πρᾶγμα προεληλύθει, ἀποκτεῖναι μὲν ἑαυτὸν οὐκ ἐτόλμησε διά τε τἆλλα καὶ ὅτι στασιάσειν αὐτοὺς οὐδὲν ἧττον ἤλπισε, γράμματα δὲ δή τινα ὡς καὶ παρὰ τοῦ Τιβερίου πεμφθέντα συνθείς, τήν τε δωρεὰν τὴν ὑπὸ τοῦ Αὐγούστου καταλειφθεῖσάν σφισι διπλῆν ὡς καὶ παρ' ἐκείνου ἔδωκε, καὶ τοὺς.
235. Tac., *Ann.* 1.35.
236. Tac., *Ann.* 1.36.
237. Tac., *Ann.* 1.36.
238. Tac., *Ann.* 1.36: *igitur volutatis inter se rationibus placitum ut epistulae nomine principis scriberentur: missionem dari vicena stipendia meritis, exauctorari qui sena dona fecissent ac retineri sub vexillo ceterorum inmunes nisi propulsandi hostis, legata quae petiverant exsolvi duplicarique.* The same episode is repeated in Dio 57.5.1.
239. Dio 57.5.1–2; Tac., *Ann.* 1.37.
240. Dio 57.5.3; Tac., *Ann.* 1.37.
241. Dio 57.5.4: ἔξω τῆς ἡλικίας ἀφῆκε: καὶ γὰρ ἐκ τοῦ ἀστικοῦ ὄχλου, οὓς ὁ Αὔγουστος μετὰ τὴν τοῦ Οὐάρου συμφορὰν προσκατέλεξεν, οἱ πλείους αὐτῶν ἦσαν.
242. Tac., *Ann.* 1.45.
243. A vexillation may also have been stationed 40.6km (28.6 miles) away in Novaesium, which had been the original home of *Legiones* XVIII and XIX – with forward bases possibly at Oberaden and confirmed at Haltern – before they were annihilated in 9 CE.
244. Tac., *Ann.* 1.37. There was considerable movement of legionary units in the aftermath of the disaster at Teutoburg. *Legio* II Augusta was based, at this time, at Mogontiacum (Mainz); *Legio* XIII *Gemina* may have been stationed at Augusta Vindelicorum (Augsburg) or Mogontiacum,

before finally settling at Vindonissa (Windisch); and *Legio* XVI *Gallica* is attested at Mogontiacum in 14 CE, alongside XIV *Gemina*.

245. Tac., *Ann.* 1.37.
246. Tac., *Ann.* 1.38.
247. Tac., *Ann.* 1.38.
248. Dio 57.5.4; Tac., *Ann.* 1.39.
249. Dio 57.5.4–5: ὕστερον δὲ πρεσβευτῶν παρὰ τοῦ Τιβερίου βουλευτῶν ἐλθόντων, οἷς ἐκεῖνος ἐν ἀπορρήτῳ μόνα εἶπεν ὅσα τὸν Γερμανικὸν μαθεῖν ἠθέλησεν ˙ εὖ τε γὰρ ἠπίστατο πάντως σφᾶς ἐροῦντάς οἱ πάντα τὰ ἑαυτοῦ διανοήματα, καὶ οὐκ ἠβουλήθη παρὰ ταῦτα οὐδέν, ὡς καὶ μόνα ὄντα, οὔτε ἐκείνους οὔτε τὸν Γερμανικὸν πολυπραγμονῆσαί, τούτων οὖν ἀφικομένων οἱ στρατιῶται τό τε τοῦ Γερμανικοῦ στρατήγημα μαθόντες, καὶ τοὺς βουλευτὰς ὡς καὶ ἐπὶ τῇ τῶν πεπραγμένων ὑπ᾽ αὐτοῦ καταλύσει παρόντας ὑποπτεύσαντες, ἐθορύβησαν.
250. Tac., *Ann.* 1.39.
251. Tac., *Ann.* 1.39.
252. Dio 57.5.6.
253. Dio 57.5.6; Suet., *Calig.* 9; Tac., *Ann.* 1.39.
254. Dio 57.5.6; Tac., *Ann.* 1.39.
255. On the importance of the legion's *aquila*, see Dio 40.18.1–2; 43.35.4.
256. Tac., *Ann.* 1.39.
257. Tac., *Ann.* 1.39.
258. Tac., *Ann.* 1.40.
259. Augustus exacted the strictest discipline in the legions: 'it was with great reluctance that he allowed even his *legati* to visit their wives, and then only in the winter season' (Suet., *Div. Aug.* 24.1). Upon enlistment in the army, married men below the rank of centurion were automatically granted divorce. For the presence of women in military bases, see Barrett (2006); Campbell (2010).
260. Tac., *Ann.* 3.33: *Inter quae Severus Caecina censuit ne quem magistratum cui provincia obvenisset uxor comitaretur, multum ante repetito concordem sibi coniugem et sex partus enixam, seque quae in publicum statueret domi servavisse, cohibita intra Italiam, quamquam ipse pluris per provincias quadraginta stipendia explevisset. haud enim frustra placitum olim ne feminae in socios aut gentis externas traherentur: inesse mulierum comitatui quae pacem luxu, bellum formidine morentur et Romanum agmen ad similitudinem barbari incessus convertant. non imbecillum tantum et imparem laboribus sexum sed, si licentia adsit, saevum, ambitiosum, potestatis avidum; incedere inter milites, habere ad manum centuriones.*
261. Tac., *Ann.* 1.40.
262. Suet., *Calig.* 9.
263. Tac., *Ann.* 1.41.
264. Tac., *Ann.* 1.40. Tacitus wryly comments that they wept as much for her departure as for their own insecurity at being left behind.
265. Tac., *Ann.* 1.41.
266. Suet., *Calig.* 9.
267. Tac., *Ann.* 1.42–3.
268. Dio 57.5.7; Suet., *Calig.* 9; Tac., *Ann.* 1.44.
269. Tac., *Ann.* 1.44.
270. Dio 57.5.7; Tac., *Ann.* 1.44.
271. Tac., *Ann.* 1.44.
272. Tac., *Ann.* 1.45.
273. Tac., *Ann.* 1.48.
274. Tac., *Ann.* 1.48.
275. Tac., *Ann.* 1.49: *mox ingressus castra Germanicus, non medicinam illud plurimis cum lacrimis sed cladem appellans, cremari corpora iubet.*
276. Tac., *Ann.* 1.35.3.
277. Dio 57.6.1; Tac., *Ann.* 1.44, 49.
278. Tac., *Ann.* 1.43.

279. Tac., *Ann.* 1.49: *sequitur ardorem militum Caesar iunctoque ponte tramittit duodecim milia e legionibus, sex et viginti socias cohortis, octo equitum alas, quarum ea seditione intemerata modestia fuit*; cf. Dio 57.6.1. The bridge was probably erected at Vetera.
280. Tac., *Ann.* 1.50.
281. Tac., *Ann.* 1.50: *at Romanus agmine propero silvam Caesiam limitemque a Tiberio coeptum scindit, castra in limite locat, frontem ac tergum vallo, latera concaedibus munitus.* It is not at all clear where and what this barrier was, and so far nothing has been discovered through archaeology.
282. Tac., *Ann.* 1.50.
283. Tac., *Ann.* 1.50: *ac ne pax quidem nisi languida et soluta inter temulentos.*
284. Tac., *Ann.* 1.51: *non sexus, non aetas miserationem attulit: profana simul et sacra et celeberrimum illis gentibus templum quod Tanfanae vocabant solo aequantur. sine vulnere milites, qui semisomnos, inermos aut palantis ceciderant.*
285. Tac., *Ann.* 1.51: *quod gnarum duci incessitque itineri et proelio. pars equitum et auxiliariae cohortes ducebant, mox prima legio, et mediis impedimentis sinistrum latus unetvicesimani, dextrum quintani clausere, vicesima legio terga firmavit, post ceteri sociorum.*
286. Tac., *Ann.* 1.51: *pergerent, properarent culpam in decus vertere.*
287. Suet., *Calig.* 4.
288. Suet., *Calig.* 4: *e Germania vero post compressam seditionem revertenti praetorianas cohortes universas prodisse obviam, quamvis pronuntiatum esset, ut duae tantum modo exirent, populi autem Romani sexum, aetatem, ordinem omnem usque ad vicesimum lapidem effudisse se.*
289. Tac., *Ann.* 1.46, 52.
290. News of the mutiny by the Pannonian legions only reached Rome well after it had been settled: Tac., *Ann.* 1.46.
291. Tac., *Ann.* 1.46.
292. Suet., *Tib.* 38.
293. Suet., *Tib.* 21.
294. Suet., *Tib.* 28: *in ciuitate libera linguam mentemque liberas esse debere.*
295. Tac., *Ann.* 1.46; cf. 1.33. Tacitus also manages to belittle Drusus the Younger and Germanicus in the same statement for their approach to the mutiny, which 'could not be quelled by the yet imperfectly-matured authority of two striplings' (*dissideat interim miles neque duorum adulescentium nondum adulta auctoritate comprimi queat*).
296. Tac., *Ann.* 3.56.
297. Dio 57.6.2.
298. Tac., *Ann.* 1.52; cf. 1.46; Dio 57.6.4.
299. Suet., *Calig.* 1: *Germanicus, … ad exercitum in Germaniam, excessu Augusti nuntiato, legiones universas imperatorem Tiberium pertinacissime recusantis et sibi summam rei p. deferentis incertum pietate an constantia maiore compescuit.*
300. Tac., *Ann.* 1.52; Dio 57.4.2, 6.4–5.
301. Tac., *Ann.* 1.46–7, 78.2.

Chapter 4: Up Against the Angrivarian Wall

1. Ov., *Pont.* 2.1.57–68.
2. Tac., *Ann.* 1.55.1. Some argue that Tiberius granted the triumph as much to gently admonish as to reward: see Syme (1978), p. 60 and Syme (1979), p. 323.
3. Tac., *Ann.* 2.41.1.
4. Tac., *Ann.* 1.55.
5. Strab., *Geog.* 7.1.3. For a survey of current knowledge of the Chatti, see Powell (2011a), pp. 82–83.
6. Tac., *Germ.* 30: *Duriora genti corpora, stricti artus, minax vultus et maior animi vigor.*
7. Tac., *Ann.* 1.56.
8. Tac., *Germ.* 30: *Omne robur in pedite, quem super arma ferramentis quoque et copiis onerant: alios ad proelium ire videas, Chattos ad bellum.*
9. Tac., *Germ.* 30: *Rari excursus et fortuita pugna. Equestrium sane virium id proprium, cito parare victoriam, cito cedere: velocitas iuxta formidinem, cunctatio propior constantiae est.*

10. Tac., *Ann.* 1.55. Tacitus says the opportunity arose *in aestatem*, 'at the beginning of spring'.
11. Tac., *Ann.* 1.56: *et tumultuarias catervas Germanorum cis Rhenum colentium*. The auxiliaries were probably levied from among the recently relocated Sugambri (now known by the name Ciberni or Cugerni), and the Treveri and Ubii nations, resettled by Iulius Caesar and M. Agrippa respectively, the Ubii having been specifically moved there to defend that section of the river.
12. Tac., *Ann.* 1.56; 2.17. The *cohors Raetorum* and *Vindelicorum* had been established by Drusus the Elder following the Alpine War of 15 BCE.
13. Tac., *Ann.* 1.56.
14. Tac., *Ann.* 1.56: *positoque castello super vestigia paterni praesidii in monte Tauno expeditum exercitum in Chattos rapit, L. Apronio ad munitiones viarum et fluminum relicto. nam (rarum illi caelo) siccitate et amnibus modicis inoffensum iter properaverat.*
15. Tac., *Ann.* 1.56: *ut quod imbecillum aetate ac sexu statim captum aut trucidatum sit.*
16. This is the first mention of *flumen Adrana* in Latin literature.
17. Tac., *Ann.* 1.56: *dein tormentis sagittisque pulsi.*
18. Tac., *Ann.* 1.56: *temptatis frustra condicionibus pacis, cum quidam ad Germanicum perfugissent, reliqui omissis pagis vicisque in silvas disperguntur.*
19. Tac., *Ann.* 1.56. The exact location of Mattium is not known for certain, though the Fritzlar or Maden – with its basalt mound known locally as the Maderstein rising 265m – in the Schwalm-Eder district of northern Hessen is suspected. It is one of the few Germanic place names cited in Latin literature of the time.
20. Tac., *Ann.* 1.56.
21. Grote (2005); http://www.grote-archaeologie.de/roemer.html.
22. Tac., *Ann.* 1.56: *non auso hoste terga abeuntium lacessere, quod illi moris, quotiens astu magis quam per formidinem cessit.*
23. Caes., *Bell. Gall.* 6.10.
24. Dio 55.1.2.
25. Or Armenius: Strab., *Geog.* 7.1.4.
26. Tac., *Ann.* 1.56.
27. Tac., *Ann.* 1.56; 2.25.
28. Tac., *Ann.* 1.57.
29. Tac., *Ann.* 1.57.
30. Tac., *Ann.* 1.58.
31. Tac., *Ann.* 1.58.5: *exercitum reduxit nomenque imperatoris auctore Tiberio accepit*. For a discussion of the significance of this, see Syme (1978), p. 61 and Syme (1979), pp. 322–3, noting Tiberius did not add this acclamation to his own titulature, and his declining of it may be seen as an act of 'admonition, still amicable'. Germanicus is recorded as *Imp. II* on *ILS* 176 ff erected after his death.
32. Tac., *Ann.* 1.60.
33. Tac., *Ann.* 1.61.
34. For a discussion of the canal, see Powell (2011a), pp. 64–6.
35. Sen., *Suas.* 1.15: *Latini declamatores in descriptione Oceani non nimis viguerunt, nam aut tumi(de) descripserunt aut curiose. nemo illorum potuit tanto spiritu dicere quanto PEDO, qui (in) navigante Germanico dicit.* For Pedo, see Tac., *Ann.* 1.60.
36. Sen., *Suas.* 1.15: *Iam pridem post terga diem solemque relictum | iamque vident noti se extorres finibus orbis, | per non concessas audaces ire tenebras | Hesperii metas extremaque litora mundi. | nunc illum, pigris immania monstra sub undis | qui ferat, Oceanum, qui saevas undique pristis | aequoreosque canes, ratibus consurgere prensis, | accumulat fragor ipse metus, iam sidere limo | navigia et rapido desertam flamine classem, | seque feris credunt per inertia fata marinis | iam non felici laniandos sorte relinqui. | atque aliquis prora caecum sublimis ab alta | aera pugnaci luctatus rumpere visu, | ut nihil erepto valuit dinoscere mundo, | obstructo talis effundit pectore voces: | 'quo ferimur?' fugit ipse dies orbemque relictum | ultima perpetuis claudit natura tenebris. | anne alio positas ultra sub cardine gentes | atque alium bellis intactum quaerimus orbem? | di revocant rerumque vetant cognoscere finem | mortales oculos. aliena quid aequora remis | et sacras violamus aquas divumque quietas | turbamus sedes?* The splendidly evocative

English translation was generously offered by Bob Durrett and received by the author with sincere thanks.

37. See the excavation report on Bentumersiel online at http://www.nihk.de/index.php?id=2234.
38. Strahl (2009b), pp. 12–15.
39. Tac., *Ann.* 1.60.
40. Tac., *Germ.* 33.
41. Strab., *Geog.* 7.1.3: ὧν ἐν τῷ Ἀμασίᾳ Δροῦσος Βρουκτέρους κατεναυμάχησε.
42. Tac., *Ann.* 1.60.
43. Tac., *Ann.* 1.60: *interque caedem et praedam repperit undevicesimae legionis aquilam cum Varo amissam.*
44. Tac., *Ann.* 1.60.
45. Tac., *Ann.* 1.61.
46. Tac., *Ann.* 1.61: *incedunt maestos locos visuque ac memoria deformis.*
47. Tac., *Ann.* 1.62.
48. Suet., *Calig.* 3.2.
49. Tac., *Ann.* 1.62: *Igitur Romanus qui aderat exercitus sextum post cladis annum trium legionum ossa, nullo noscente alienas reliquias an suorum humo tegeret, omnis ut coniunctos, ut consanguineos, aucta in hostem ira, maesti simul et infensi condebant.*
50. Tac., *Ann.* 1.62.
51. Military commanders apparently frequently flouted rules of augury: see Cic., *Div.* 2.36.
52. For an account of the Battle of Arbalo, see Powell (2011a), pp. 88–9.
53. Tac., *Ann.* 1.63.
54. Tac., *Ann.* 1.63: *inde hostibus terror, fiducia militi.*
55. Tac., *Ann.* 1.63.
56. Tac., *Ann.* 1.63.
57. Tac., *Ann.* 1.64: *Et cuncta pariter Romanis adversa, locus uligine profunda, idem ad gradum instabilis, procedentibus lubricus, corpora gravia loricis; neque librare pila inter undas poterant.*
58. Tac., *Ann.* 1.64.
59. Tac., *Ann.* 1.64.
60. Tac., *Ann.* 1.64.
61. Tac., *Ann.* 1.65.
62. Tac., *Ann.* 1.65: *infectos caeno aut cruore cibos dividentes funestas tenebras et tot hominum milibus unum iam reliquum diem lamentabantur.*
63. Tac., *Ann.* 1.66.
64. Tac., *Ann.* 1.67.
65. Tac., *Ann.* 1.68.
66. Tac., *Ann.* 1.69.
67. Tac., *Ann.* 1.69: *Sed femina ingens animi munia ducis per eos dies induit, militibusque, ut quis inops aut saucius, vestem et fomenta dilargita est. tradit C. Plinius Germanicorum bellorum scriptor, stetisse apud principium ponti laudes et grates reversis legionibus habentem.*
68. Tac., *Ann.* 1.70.
69. Tac., *Ann.* 1.70: *sternuntur fluctibus, hauriuntur gurgitibus; iumenta, sarcinae, corpora exanima inter-fluunt, occursant. permiscentur inter se manipuli, modo pectore, modo ore tenus extantes, aliquando sub-tracto solo disiecti aut obruti. non vox et mutui hortatus iuvabant adversante unda; nihil strenuus ab ignavo, sapiens ab inprudenti, consilia a casu differre: cuncta pari violentia involvebantur.*
70. The reference to the Visurgis is odd, given that Germanicus' fleet was in the Amisia, as reported by Tacitus (*Ann.* 1.63). Perhaps Tacitus confused the rivers or just intended to mean that the men were marching generally in an easterly direction.
71. Tac., *Ann.* 1.70.
72. Tac., *Ann.* 1.71.
73. Tac., *Ann.* 1.57, 71.
74. Tac., *Ann.* 1.71.

75. Tac., *Ann.* 1.71: *Quorum laudato studio Germanicus, armis modo et equis ad bellum sumptis, propria pecunia militem iuvit. utque cladis memoriam etiam comitate leniret, circumire saucios, facta singulorum extollere; vulnera intuens alium spe, alium gloria, cunctos adloquio et cura sibique et proelio firmabat.*
76. Tac., *Ann.* 1.72. Syme (1979), p. 323, argues that the granting of *ornamenta* to the consular legates – since Germanicus already had triumphal honours, as yet uncelebrated – implies that the German Wars were to be regarded as terminated.
77. Tac., *Ann.* 1.72, 76.
78. Tac., *Ann.* 1.76.
79. Barrett (1996), p. xix; Freisenbruch (2010), p. 100.
80. Tac., *Ann.* 12.27. Under Claudius, the settlement was also elevated in status and renamed Colonia Claudia Ara Agrippinensium (CCAA).
81. Iulia Agrippina is commonly known to history as Agrippina Minor, or Agrippina the Younger.
82. Tac., *Ann.* 2.5: *fundi Germanos acie et iustis locis, iuvari silvis, paludibus, brevi aestate et praematura hieme.* For a full discussion of Germanic arms, equipment, training, military strategies and combat doctrine, see Powell (2011), pp. 84–8 and Powell (2014).
83. Tac., *Ann.* 2.5: *suum militem haud perinde vulneribus quam spatiis itinerum, damno armorum adfici.* For a full discussion of Germanic arms, equipment, training, military strategies and combat doctrine, see Powell (2011), pp. 26–33 and Powell (2014).
84. Tac., *Ann.* 2.5: *defensantibus iniquum.*
85. Tac., *Ann.* 2.5: *At si mare intretur, promptam ipsis possessionem et hostibus ignotam, simul bellum maturius incipi legionesque et commeatus pariter vehi; integrum equitem equosque per ora et alveos fluminum media in Germania fore.*
86. Tac., *Ann.* 2.6.
87. Tac., *Ann.* 2.6: *Mille naves sufficere visae properataeque, aliae breves, angusta puppi proraque et lato utero, quo facilius fluctus tolerarent; quaedam planae carinis, ut sine noxa siderent; plures adpositis utrimque gubernaculis, converso ut repente remigio hinc vel illinc adpellerent; multae pontibus stratae, super quas tormenta veherentur, simul aptae ferendis equis aut commeatui; velis habiles, citae remis augebantur alacritate militum in speciem ac terrorem.* This is the first time that Tacitus mentions Anteius.
88. Pitassi (2011), pp. 123–6 and plan 16.
89. Czysz *et al.* (1995), pp. 493–4; http://www2.rgzm.de/navis/ships/ship037/ship037Engl.htm.
90. *Victoria*: the reconstruction of 'Oberstimm 1' was built between January 2007 and March 2008 by historians from the University of Hamburg and boatbuilders from the shipyard of Jugend in Arbeit Hamburg e.V. At launch, it was named *Victoria*. See Asskamp and Schäfer (2009). Tests: *Terra X-Schliemanns Erbe: Der Limes* (ZDF), broadcast 5 April 2009: http://terra-x.zdf.de/ZDFde/inhalt/11/0,1872,7552299,00.html.
91. http://www2.rgzm.de/navis/Ships/Ship101/Navisnachbau1Engl.htm.
92. Measurements are based on the lines of Mainz 5 and the shape of Mainz 1. Unlike ships built for the Mediterranean, the Mainz ships had no keelson, but instead had a mast-frame, which is cut thicker in the middle and features a hole for the mast. In the ancient world, mast-frames were often placed in ships north of the Alps. The museum notes that 'besides the measuring unit of the *Pes Drusianus* the mast frame proves that the Roman shipbuilders who built the Mainz ships belonged to the provincial population north of the Alps'.
93. Tac., *Ann.* 2.6: *citae remis augebantur alacritate militum in speciem ac terrorem.*
94. Willems (1991).
95. Tac., *Ann.* 2.6: *insula Batavorum in quam convenirent praedicta, ob facilis adpulsus accipiendisque copiis et transmittendum ad bellum opportuna. nam Rhenus uno alveo continuus aut modicas insulas circumveniens apud principium agri Batavi velut in duos amnis dividitur, servatque nomen et violentiam cursus, qua Germaniam praevehitur, donec Oceano misceatur: ad Gallicam ripam latior et placidior adfluens (verso cognomento Vahalem accolae dicunt), mox id quoque vocabulum mutat Mosa flumine eiusque inmenso ore eundem in Oceanum effunditur.*
96. Tac., *Ann.* 2.7.
97. Tac., *Ann.* 2.7.

98. Tac., *Ann.* 2.7; compare this to Claudius' force of 45,000 men under Aulus Plautius' for the invasion of Britain.

99. Tac., *Ann.* 2.7: *et cuncta inter castellum Alisonem ac Rhenum novis limitibus aggeribusque permunita.*

100. Wells (1972), pp. 152–153. The discovery and preliminary excavation of the supply base at Olfen in October 2011 hints that other military bases remain to be discovered along the Lippe River.

101. Tac., *Ann.* 2.7.

102. Tac., *Ann.* 2.7.

103. Dio 55.1.3; Florus 2.30.23–4; Val. Max. 5.5.3.

104. Ptol., *Geog.* 2.10.

105. Poppenburg in Lower Saxony on the Hellweg has recently been proposed by Jürgen Martin Regel: http://zocher-regel.gmxhome.de/ArbaloSchlacht/register.html.

106. Tac., *Ann.* 2.7.

107. Tac., *Ann.* 2.7: *restituit aram honorique patris princeps ipse cum legionibus decucurrit*; cf. Dio 56.25.3 (see Chapter 3, note 51), on the horse race held by Tiberius and Germanicus to celebrate the birthday of Augustus in 11 CE.

108. Tac., *Ann.* 2.7: *ingressus precatusque Drusum patrem ut se eadem ausum libens placatusque exemplo ac memoria consiliorum atque operum iuvaret.*

109. Tac., *Ann.* 2.7. Compare *novis limitibus aggeribusque* to the reference in Tac., *Ann.* 1.50 to a barrier apparently erected beyond the Caesian Forest between the Lippe and IJssel rivers, begun by Tiberius and added to by Germanicus in 14 CE.

110. Tac., *Ann.* 2.8.

111. Tac., *Ann.* 2.8.

112. Tac., *Ann.* 2.8: *aut transposuit militem dextras in terras iturum; ita plures dies efficiendis pontibus absumpti.*

113. Tac., *Ann.* 2.8: *et eques quidem ac legiones prima aestuaria, nondum adcrescente unda, intrepidi transiere: postremum auxiliorum agmen Batavique in parte ea, dom insultant aquis artemque nandi ostentant, turbati et quidam hausti sunt.*

114. Tac., *Ann.* 2.8.

115. Tac., *Germ.* 32–33.

116. Tac., *Ann.* 2.8: *missus ilico Stertinius cum equite et armatura levi igne et caedibus perfidiam ultus est.*

117. Strab., *Geog.* 1.2: much of the research was likely on account of the expeditions of Drusus the Elder, 12–9 BCE.

118. e.g. Baehr (1887), p. 11.

119. Tac., *Ann.* 2.9.

120. Tac., *Ann.* 2.9: *erat is in exercitu cognomento Flavus, insignis fide et amisso per vulnus oculo paucis ante annis duce Tiberio.*

121. Tac., *Ann.* 2.9–10.

122. Tac., *Ann.* 2.9.

123. Tac., *Ann.* 2.10.

124. Tac., *Ann.* 2.11.

125. As W. Hamilton Fyfe notes in the 'Introduction' to his translation of Tacitus' *Histories*, published by Clarendon Press in 1912, 'Tacitus is not a 'bad military historian'. He is not a 'military' historian at all. Botticelli is not a botanist, nor is Shakespeare a geographer' (p. 11).

126. Tac., *Ann.* 2.11.

127. Tac., *Ann.* 2.11.

128. Tac., *Ann.* 2.11: *qua celerrimus amnis*; cf. 2.8, where the Batavi lost men during this same manoeuvre.

129. Tac., *Ann.* 2.11.

130. Tac., *Ann.* 2.12.

131. Tac., *Ann.* 2.12.

132. Tac., *Ann.* 2.12.

133. Tac., *Ann.* 2.13: *cum hic nobilitatem ducis, decorem alius, plurimi patientiam, comitatem, per seria per iocos eundem animum laudibus ferrent reddendamque gratiam in acie faterentur, simul perfidos et ruptores pacis ultioni et gloriae mactandos.*

134. Tac., *Ann.* 2.13.
135. Tac., *Ann.* 2.14.
136. Recounting of dreams and dream visions was also a literary trope used by ancient historians to reveal a deeper truth or lend credibility to a prediction or as a way for a god to deliver a message. See Kelsey (1991), pp. 57–79.
137. Tac., *Ann.* 2.14: *Si taedio viarum ac maris finem cupiant, hac acie parari: propiorem iam Albim quam Rhenum neque bellum ultra, modo se patris patruique vestigia prementem isdem in terris victorem sisterent.*
138. Tac., *Ann.* 2.13: *tertia ferme vigilia adsultatum est castris sine coniectu teli*; cf. 2.17, where Tacitus says the battle lasted from nine in the morning until nightfall, *quinta ab hora diei ad noctem.*
139. Tac., *Ann.* 2.14. See Baehr (1887), p. 11: 'Fast alle Forscher sind darüber einig, dass der *Campus Idistaviso* auf dem rechten Ufer der Weser in der näheren Umgegend der *Porta westfalica* zu suchen sei. Eine Hauptfrage aber, die zu entscheiden sein wird, ist die: befand sich das Schlachtfeld oberhalb oder unterhalb der Porta? Die Urteile hierüber gehen weit auseinander. Um nun diese Aufrabe zu lösen, ist es, wie gesagt, unbedingt notwendig, denjenigen Weg nachzuweisen, auf welchem die Römer von der Ems bis zur Weser marschiert sind'.
140. Tac., *Ann.* 2.16: *Sic accensos et proelium poscentis in campum, cui Idistaviso nomen, deducunt. is medius inter Visurgim et collis, ut ripae fluminis cedunt aut prominentia montium resistunt, inaequaliter sinuatur. Pone tergum insurgebat silva editis in altum ramis et pura humo inter arborum truncos. campum et prima silvarum barbara acies tenuit: soli Cherusci iuga insedere ut proeliantibus Romanis desuper incurrerent.* The name Idistaviso apparently means 'place of the Maidens'.
141. Tac., *Ann.* 2.16: *Noster exercitus sic incessit: auxiliares Galli Germanique in fronte, post quos pedites sagittatii; dein quattuor legiones et cum duabus praetoriis cohortibus ac delecto equite Caesar; exim totidem aliae legiones et levis armatura cum equite sagittario ceteraeque sociorum cohortes. intentus paratusque miles ut ordo agminis in aciem adsisteret.*
142. Tac., *Ann.* 2.17: *exclamat irent, sequerentur Romanas avis, propria legionum numina.*
143. Tac., *Ann.* 2.17.
144. Tac., *Ann.* 2.17: *quidam adgnitum a Chaucis inter auxilia Romana agentibus emissumque tradiderunt.*
145. Tac., *Ann.* 2.17: *et plerosque tranare Visurgim conantis iniecta tela aut vis fluminis, postremo moles ruentium et incidentes ripae operuere. quidam turpi fuga in summa arborum nisi ramisque se occultantes admotis sagittariis per ludibrium figebantur, alios prorutae arbores adflixere.*
146. Tac., *Ann.* 2.18: *Magna ea victoria neque cruenta nobis fuit. quinta ab hora diei ad noctem caesi hostes decem milia passuum cadaveribus atque armis opplevere.*
147. Syme (1978), p. 61 with n. 4.
148. Tac., *Ann.* 2.19.
149. Tac., *Ann.* 2.19. The comparison with the zig-zag earthwork found at Kalkriese, believed by many to be the site of the Battle of Teutoburg but disputed by some, is compelling.
150. Tac., *Ann.* 2.20.
151. Tac., *Ann.* 2.20: *Seio Tuberoni legato tradit equitem campumque; peditum aciem ita instruxit ut pars aequo in silvam aditu incederet, pars obiectum aggerem eniteretur; quod arduum sibi, cetera legatis permisit.* This is the first time Tacitus mentions Tubero.
152. Tac., *Ann.* 2.20.
153. Tac., *Ann.* 2.20: *utrisque necessitas in loco, spes in virtute, salus ex victoria.*
154. Tac., *Ann.* 2.21.
155. Suet., *Calig.* 3: *Hostem comminus saepe percussit.* For a discussion of Drusus the Elder's reputation for fighting to win the *spolia opima*, see Powell (2011a), pp. 94–6.
156. Tac., *Ann.* 2.21.
157. Tac., *Ann.* 2.22: *debellatis inter Rhenum Albimque nationibus exercitum Tiberii Caesaris ea monimenta Marti et Iovi et Augusto sacravisse.* At this time the troops also acclaimed Tiberius *imperator* which was added to his titulature as *Imp. VIII*: Tac. *Ann.* 2.18.2. See commentary in Syme (1979), pp. 322–5 in which he notes that while Germanicus was victorious in the field, Idistaviso was to be seen as the victory of the *princeps.*
158. Tac., *Ann.* 2.22: *de se nihil addidit, metu invidiae an ratus conscientiam facti satis esse.*
159. Tac., *Ann.* 2.22.

160. Strab., *Geog.* 7.1.4; cf. Caes., *Bell. Gall.* 4.13.
161. Tac., *Ann.* 2.22.
162. Tac., *Ann.* 2.23: *ac primo placidum aequor mille navium remis strepere aut velis inpelli: mox atro nubium globo effusa grando, simul variis undique procellis incerti fluctus prospectum adimere, regimen inpedire; milesque pavidus et casuum maris ignarus dum turbat nautas vel intempestive iuvat, officia prudentium corrumpebat omne dehinc caelum et mare omne in austrum cessit, qui tumidis Germaniae terris, profundis amnibus, immenso nubium tractu validus et rigore vicini septentrionis horridior rapuit disiecitque navis in aperta Oceani aut insulas saxis abruptis vel per occulta vada infestas. quibus paulum aegreque vitatis, postquam mutabat aestus eodemque quo ventus ferebat, non adhaerere ancoris, non exhaurire inrumpentis undas poterant: equi, iumenta, sarcinae, etiam arma praecipitantur quo levarentur alvei manantes per latera et fluctu superurgente.*
163. Tac., *Ann.* 2.24: *Quanto violentior cetero mari Oceanus et truculentia caeli praestat Germania, tantum illa clades novitate et magnitudine excessit, hostilibus circum litoribus aut ita vasto et profundo ut credatur novissimum ac sine terris mare. pars navium haustae sunt, plures apud insulas longius sitas eiectae; milesque nullo illic hominum cultu fame absumptus, nisi quos corpora equorum eodem elisa toleraverant.*
164. Tac., *Ann.* 2.24: *quem per omnis illos dies noctesque apud scopulos et prominentis oras, cum se tanti exitii reum clamitaret, vix cohibuere amici quo minus eodem mari oppeteret.*
165. Tac., *Ann.* 2.24.
166. Tac., *Ann.* 2.24: *ut quis ex longinquo revenerat, miracula narrabant, vim turbinum et inauditas volucris, monstra maris, ambiguas hominum et beluarum formas, visa sive ex metu credita.*
167. Tac., *Ann.* 2.25.
168. Tac., *Ann.* 2.25.
169. Tac., *Ann.* 2.25: *quippe invictos.*
170. Tac., *Ann.* 2.25: *nullis casibus superabilis Romanos praedicabant, qui perdita classe, amissis armis, post constrata equorum virorumque corporibus litora eadem virtute, pari ferocia et velut aucti numero inrupissent.*
171. Tac., *Ann.* 2.26.
172. Suet., *Tib.* 32.
173. The inscription – *AE* 1973, 501 = 1975, 806 = 1978, 790 = J.M. Cook, *The Troad* (Oxford, 1973), Appendix, no. 50 = C. Ricl, *The Inscriptions of Alexandreia Troas* (Bonn, 1997), 34 (Alexandria Troas, Asia) – was discovered in the Troad in 1959 and reads *hasta pura et corona aurea donatus est a Germanico Caesare imp[eratore] bello Germanico d[ecreto] d[ecurionem]*. Cf. Brunt (1974); Orth (1978); Speidel (1976).
174. Suet., *Vit.* 2.3.
175. The sword and scabbard were found in Mainz, Germany.
176. British Museum, London, inventory number GR 1866.8–6.1 (Bronze 867).
177. The British Museum interprets the figures to be Augustus receiving Tiberius. Zanker argues for Tiberius receiving Germanicus: http://www.britishmuseum.org/explore/highlights/highlight_objects/gr/t/the_sword_of_tiberius.aspx.
178. Zanker (1988), p. 233.
179. Several inscriptions mention Drusilla: one these dates from her childhood, *CIL* VI, 5201 = *ILS* 1837, which reads *C. Papius Asclepiades | Papia Erotis l., | Iulia Iucunda nutrix | Drusi et Drusillae.* She is usually addressed as *diva Drusilla*, though in at least two inscriptions she is called Iulia Drusilla: *CIL* V, 5722 = *ILS* 194 (Ager Mediolanensis, Gallia Cisalpina); XII, 1026 = *ILS* 195 (Avennio, Gallia Narbonensis). In *CIL* VI, 8822 = *ILS* 1655, a *dispensator* of Claudius with the name of Cinnamus Drusillianus is mentioned, which suggests that he took his *cognomen* from the name Drusilla. Cf. *CIL* VI, 8823. In time, Drusilla became the favourite sister of Caligula.
180. Dio (57.14.5) records that, in 15 CE, Tiberius introduced measures to require new provincial governors to have departed Rome by 1 June of their year of appointment, because their tardiness in leaving was causing the men they were replacing to have to serve beyond their designated terms of office. However, Tacitus records (*Ann.* 2.36) that, in 16 CE, Tiberius resisted a proposal from Asinius Gallus on the Senate floor that the magistrates should be elected every five years, the legionary legates who had not yet been appointed as praetors should become praetors-elect,

and that the *princeps* should nominate twelve candidates annually; he cited subversion of laws stipulating terms of service and frequency of elections.

181. Suet., *Div. Aug.* 34.
182. Suetonius (*Tib.* 32) notes that the emperor rebuked some ex-consuls for not submitting their campaign reports.
183. Tac., *Ann.* 2.26.
184. Tac., *Ann.* 2.26: *satis iam eventuum, satis casuum.*
185. Tac., *Ann.* 2.26: *gravia tamen et saeva damna intulissent.*
186. Tac., *Ann.* 2.26: *Se novies a divo Augusto in Germaniam missum plura consilio quam vi perfecisse.*
187. This was stretching a point: the break-out of revolt in Illyricum effectively forced Tiberius, at the time located in Germania, into negotiating terms so that he could take his army to the Balkans.
188. Dio 56.33.5–6.
189. Tac., *Ann.* 2.26: *Haud cunctatus est ultra Germanicus, quamquam fingi ea seque per invidiam parto iam decori abstrahi intellegeret.*
190. Tac., *Ann.* 2.41.
191. Seager (1972), p. 81.
192. Syme (1978), p. 62, notes that Augustus established the precedent that only he could possess the *auspicia*. Since 13 CE, the war in Germania had been fought *auspiciis Tiberii Caesaris*, when Tiberius was granted the *auspicia* over the army and provinces by Augustus as joint ruler.
193. Boatwright (2000), pp. 60–1, n. 15. Germanicus at Caesaraugusta: Heiss (1870), p. 270, no. 13; Colonia Augusta Buthrotum (Butrint) dated to 12 CE; Fulginiae, *CIL* XI, 5224; Hispellum, *CIL* XI, 5289; Interpromium, *CIL* IX, 3044 = *ILS* 2689; Priene, *IPriene* no. 142; and Regium Lepidum, *CIL* XI, 969. Germanicus with Drusus together at Acci: Heiss (1870), p. 257, no. 12; Aqua Flaviae, *CIL* II, 5617 = I, 2479; ?Carteia: Heiss (1870), p. 332, no. 29 and 334); and Praeneste, *CIL* XIV, 2964. By the end of their lives, Drusus the Younger held ten honorary magistracies to Tiberius' ten.

Chapter 5: Travels and Tribulations in the Orient
1. Suet., *Calig.* 3.2.
2. *CIL* VI, 909 = *ILS* 176; Rüpke (2008), p. 179.
3. Beard *et al.* (1998), p. 50; Weinstock (1971), pp. 291–6; Fishwick (1987), p. 51.
4. Tac., *Ann.* 2.49.
5. Tac., *Ann.* 2.49. He lists temples of Ceres, Flora, Ianus, Liber and Libera; cf. Suet., *Tib.* 69.1, in which the biographer notes that Tiberius was neglectful of the gods, preferring to believe in astrology and fate.
6. Ov., *Fast.* 2.549–52.
7. Ov., *Fast.* 1.3–6: *excipe pacato, Caesar Germanice, voltu | hoc opus et timidae derige navis iter, | officioque, levem non aversatus honorem, | en tibi devoto numine dexter ades.* See also Allen (1922).
8. Green (1982).
9. The poet, who once enjoyed wide popularity in Rome, died a homesick and unforgiven man in his bleak Getic township in 17 CE or the following year.
10. Tac., *Ann.* 2.41: *C. Caelio L. Pomponio consulibus Germanicus Caesar a. d. VII. Kal. Iunias triumphavit*; Suet., *Calig.* 1. See also Beard (2007), pp. 107–14.
11. Strab., *Geog.* 7.1.4.
12. Tac., *Ann.* 2.41: *de Cheruscis Chattisque et Angrivariis quaeque aliae nationes usque ad Albim colunt.*
13. Ov., *Tr.* 4.2.3–4: *altaque velentur fortasse Palatia sertis, | turaque in igne sonent inficiantque diem.*
14. On coins, *C* 81; *BMCRE* 401 var.; *RIC* 98; *CBN* 1199.
15. Pliny, *Nat. Hist.* 33.111–2.
16. Bronze and orichalcum *dupondii* minted in Rome by Caligula, 37–41 CE, show Germanicus standing in a *quadriga* bearing an eagle-tipped sceptre on the obverse, with the legend GERMANICVS CAESAR, while on the reverse, he stands in full military panoply, right arm outstretched, with the sceptre over his left shoulder, with the legend SIGNIS RECEPT[IS] DEVICTIS GERM[ANIS] S C: *RIC* I, 57; *BMCRE* 93; *CBN* 140; *C* 7.

17. Tac., *Ann.* 2.41: *Vecta spolia, captivi, simulacra montium, fluminum, proeliorum; bellumque, quia conficere prohibitus erat, pro confecto accipiebatur. augebat intuentium visus eximia ipsius species currusque quinque liberis onustus.*

18. Vell. Pat. 2.129: *Quibus iuventam eius exaggeravit honoribus, respondente cultu triumphi rerum, quas gesserat, magnitudini!.*

19. Tac., *Ann.* 2.41: *Vecta spolia, captivi, simulacra montium, fluminum, proeliorum*; cf. Ov., *Tr.* 4.2.19–24; *Pont.* 2.1.37–44.

20. Strab., *Geog.* 7.1.4: Σεγιμοῦντός τε Σεγέστου υἱός, Χηρούσκων ἡγεμών, καὶ ἀδελφὴ αὐτοῦ, γυνὴ δ᾽ Ἀρμενίου τοῦ πολεμαρχήσαντος ἐν τοῖς Χηρούσκοις ἐν τῇ πρὸς Οὐᾶρον Κουιντίλλιον παρασπονδήσει καὶ νῦν ἔτι συνέχοντος τὸν πόλεμον, ὄνομα Θουσνέλδα, καὶ υἱὸς τριετὴς Θουμέλικος: ἔτι δὲ Σεσίθακος, Σεγιμήρου υἱὸς τῶν Χηρούσκων ἡγεμόνος, καὶ γυνὴ τούτου Ῥαμίς, Οὐκρομήρου θυγάτηρ ἡγεμόνος Χάττων, καὶ Δευδόριξ, Βαιτόριγος τοῦ Μέλωνος ἀδελφοῦ υἱός, Σούγαμβρος. Σεγέστης δὲ ὁ πενθερὸς τοῦ Ἀρμενίου καὶ ἐξ ἀρχῆς διέστη πρὸς τὴν γνώμην αὐτοῦ καὶ λαβὼν καιρὸν ηὐτομόλησε καὶ τῷ θριάμβῳ παρῆν τῶν φιλτάτων, ἐν τιμῇ ἀγόμενος. ἐπόμπευσε δὲ καὶ Λίβης τῶν Χάττων ἱερεύς, καὶ ἄλλα δὲ σώματα ἐπομπεύθη ἐκ τῶν πεπορθημένων ἐθνῶν, Καούλκων Καμψανῶν Βρουκτέρων Οὐσίπων Χηρούσκων Χάττων Χαττουαρίων Λανδῶν Τουβαττίων. The 'Sougambros' were called Sicambri or Sugambri by the Romans, the 'Tubattioi' were called Tubanti. Segimountos is the Segimundus of Tac., *Ann.* 1.57. Segimerus surrendered to Stertinius in Tac., *Ann.* 1.71. Melonos or Melo, who surrendered to Tiberius, is spelled Maelo in Augustus, *Res Gestae* 6.32. Ukroumiruos or Acrumerus or Ucromerus is Actumerus or Catumerus in Tac., *Ann.* 11.16–17.

21. Ov., *Tr.* 4.2.25–6: *et cernet vultus aliis pro tempore versos, | terribiles aliis inmemoresque sui. | quorum pars causas et res et nomina quaeret, | pars referet, quamvis noverit illa parum.*

22. Tac., *Ann.* 2.42.

23. Ov., *Tr.* 4.2.5–8: *candidaque adducta collum percussa securi | victima purpureo sanguine pulset humum, | donaque amicorum templis promissa deorum | reddere victores Caesar uterque parent.*

24. Tac., *Ann.* 2.41: *bellumque, quia conficere prohibitus erat, pro confecto accipiebatur.*

25. Ov., *Tr.* 4.2.1–1–2: *Iam fera Caesaribus Germania, totus ut orbis, | victa potest flexo succubuisse genu.*

26. Ov., *Fast.* 1.285–6: *pax erat, et vestri, Germanice, causa triumphi, | tradiderat famulas iam tibi Rhenus aquas.*

27. Rosso (2000), online at http://labyrinthe.revues.org/index805.html. The author notes that dating the monument is difficult, other than to say it was at a key moment of Tiberius' principate. Grimal (1947), p. 134, supports the 18 CE date. For a date after Germanicus' death, see *CIL* XIII, 1036, p. 137, and Grenier (1931), p. 568, both citing Tac., *Ann.* 2.83.2.

28. Tac., *Ann.* 2.54: *nec ideo sincerae caritatis fidem adsecutus amoliri iuvenem specie honoris statuit struxitque causas aut forte oblatas arripuit.*

29. Suet., *Calig.* 1: *Consul deinde iterum creatus ac prius quam honorem iniret ad componendum Orientis statum expulsus*; cf. Joseph., *Ant. Jud.* 18.2.5.

30. Augustus, *Res Gestae* 32.2; Tac., *Ann.* 2.1.

31. Joseph., *Ant. Jud.* 18.39. In return for the Parthian King's sons, Augustus handed over an Italian slave-girl, Thermusa of Parthia, who later became Queen Musa, also known as Thea Urania (Astarte).

32. Tac., *Ann.* 2.2; Joseph., *Ant. Jud.* 18.39.

33. Seager (1972), p. 96.

34. Tac., *Ann.* 2.4.

35. Tac., *Ann.* 2.3.

36. Joseph., *Ant. Jud.* 18.39.

37. Tac., *Ann.* 2.42; Suet., *Tib.* 37.4; Dio 57.17.1; Strab., *Geog.* 12.1.4.

38. For a fuller discussion of the relationship and rift between Tiberius and Archelaus, see Romer (1985).

39. Tac., *Ann.* 2.42.

40. Dio 57.17.6.

41. Dio 57.17.7.

42. Dio 57.17.7; Eutrop., *Brev.* 7.11; Strab., *Geog.* 12.1.4; Tac., *Ann.* 2.42.

43. Eutrop., *Brev.* 7.11.
44. Shaw (1990).
45. Joseph., *Ant. Jud.* 18.53; Tac., *Ann.* 2.42.
46. Tac., *Ann.* 2.42: *et provinciae Syria atque Iudaea, fessae oneribus, deminutionem tributi orabant.*
47. Tac., *Ann.* 2.43: *Igitur haec et de Armenia quae supra memoravi apud patres disseruit, nec posse motum Orientem nisi Germanici sapientia conponi: nam suam aetatem vergere, Drusi nondum satis adolevisse. tunc decreto patrum per missae Germanico provinciae quae mari dividuntur, maiusque imperium, quoquo adisset, quam iis qui sorte aut missu principis obtinerent.*
48. A legal definition of Germanicus' *imperium maius* is set out in the *Senatus Consultum de Cn. Pisone patre*, lines 30–7.
49. Vell. Pat. 2.129: *Quanto cum honore Germanicum suum in transmarinas misit provincias!*
50. Tac., *Ann.* 2.5: *Ceterum Tiberio haud ingratum accidit turbari res Orientis, ut ea specie Germanicum suetis legionibus abstraheret novisque provinciis impositum dolo simul et casibus obiectaret.*
51. The disposition of the legions in the East in 14 CE: in Syria, III *Gallica*, VI *Ferrata*, X *Fretensis* and XII *Fulminata*; in Aegyptus, III *Cyrenaica* and XXII *Deiotariana*.
52. The *sacramentum* reproduced here is a composite of Dionysius' and Vegetius' versions in Watson (1969), p. 49; see also Nock (1952).
53. Two cohorts of Praetorians were dispatched on the orders of Tiberius to meet Agrippina on her return from the East in 20 CE, but there is no mention of any bodyguards arriving with her: Tac., *Ann.* 3.2.
54. Suet., *Calig.* 1.
55. Dio 57.14.5.
56. Babelon 264. Barrett (1989), pp. 12–13.
57. For a recent review, see Giuliani and Schmidt (2010). The jewel may have been reworked during the fourth century, making the identification of the original central figure difficult.
58. Tac., *Ann.* 2.43.
59. Tac., *Ann.* 2.43: *ingenio violentum et obsequii ignarum.*
60. Tac., *Ann.* 3.12.2: *patris sui legatum atque amicum Pisonem fuisse adiutoremque Germanico datum a se auctore senatu rebus apud Orientem administrandis*; cf. 2.43.3.
61. Tac., *Ann.* 2.43: *nec dubium habebat se delectum qui Syriae imponeretur ad spes Germanici coercendas.*
62. Tac., *Ann.* 2.5; see n. 59, above.
63. Suet., *Tib.* 50.1.
64. Suet., *Tib.* 52.1.
65. Tac., *Ann.* 2.43.
66. Tac., *Ann.* 2.43: *sed fratres egregie concordes et proximorum certaminibus inconcussi.*
67. Marsus: Tac., *Ann.* 2.74. Sentius: *ibid.* 2.74. Servaeus: *ibid.* 2.56. Silius: *ibid.* 1.31. Suillius: *ibid.* 4.31. Veranius: *ibid.* 2.56. Vitellius: *ibid.* 1.70.
68. Tac., *Ann.* 3.2. Barrett (1996), p. 29.
69. Tacitus (*Ann.* 2.55) specifically describes the ships as *triremis*. For dimensions and crew size based on two reliefs from Pozzuoli, see Pitassi (2011), pp. 119–23 and plan 14.
70. Tac., *Ann.* 2.53. This was in fulfillment of Tiberius' wish to expand Drusus' military experience in that theatre of war; cf. Tac., *Ann.* 2.26.
71. Horden and Purcell (2000), p. 139.
72. Cic., *Prov. Cons.* 12.31.
73. Horden and Purcell (2000), pp. 137–8; the authors draw upon the work of John H. Pryor, *Geography, Technology, and War: Studies in the Maritime History of the Mediterranean, 649–1571* (Cambridge, 1988), who studied the records of connectivity in Genoese ships' logs, 1351–1370.
74. Tac., *Ann.* 2.53.
75. Suet., *Calig.* 1; Tac., *Ann.* 2.53.
76. Seager (1972), p. 99. Note Tacitus' comment (*Ann.* 3.31) that Tiberius was not agreeable to the partnership.
77. Strab., *Geog.* 7.7.6: ἡ μὲν οὖν Νικόπολις εὐανδρεῖ καὶ λαμβάνει καθ' ἡμέραν ἐπίδοσιν, χώραν τε ἔχουσα πολλὴν καὶ τὸν ἐκ τῶν λαφύρων κόσμον, τό τε κατασκευασθὲν τέμενος ἐν τῷ προαστείῳ τὸ μὲν εἰς τὸν ἀγῶνα τὸν πεντετηρικὸν ἐν ἄλσει ἔχοντι γυμνάσιόν τε καὶ στάδιον,

τὸ δ᾽ ἐν τῷ ὑπερκειμένῳ τοῦ ἄλσους ἱερῷ λόφῳ τοῦ Ἀπόλλωνος. ἀποδέδεικται δ᾽ ὁ ἀγὼν
Ὀλύμπιος, τὰ Ἄκτια, ἱερὸς τοῦ Ἀκτίου Ἀπόλλωνος, τὴν δ᾽ ἐπιμέλειαν ἔχουσιν αὐτοῦ
Λακεδαιμόνιοι. αἱ δ᾽ ἄλλαι κατοικίαι περιπόλιοι τῆς Νικοπόλεώς εἰσιν. ἤγετο δὲ καὶ πρότερον
τὰ Ἄκτια τῷ θεῷ, στεφανίτης ἀγών, ὑπὸ τῶν περιοίκων· νυνὶ δ᾽ ἐντιμότερον ἐποίησεν ὁ
Καῖσαρ.

78. Strab., *Geog.* 7.7.6: καὶ ἱερὸν τοῦ Ἀκτίου Ἀπόλλωνος ἐνταῦθά ἐστι πλησίον τοῦ στόματος,
λόφος τις ἐφ᾽ ᾧ ὁ νεώς, καὶ ὑπ᾽ αὐτῷ πεδίον ἄλσος ἔχον καὶ νεώρια, ἐν οἷς ἀνέθηκε Καῖσαρ τὴν
δεκαναΐαν ἀκροθίνιον, ἀπὸ μονοκρότου μέχρι δεκήρους· ὑπὸ πυρὸς δ᾽ ἠφανίσθαι καὶ οἱ
νεώσοικοι λέγονται καὶ τὰ πλοῖα.

79. Dio 51.1; Suet., *Div. Aug.* 18.2. For a discussion of the significance of the monument, see Gurval (1995), pp. 65–72.

80. Suet., *Div. Aug.* 96.2. Tac., *Ann.* 2.53: *magnaque illic imago tristium laetorumque.*

81. The inscription on *SIG*³ 792 in Sherk (1988) 33 p. 59 reads 'Germanicus Caesar, son of *Imperator* Ti. Caesar Augustus, | victorious in the Olympic Games with his chariot drawn by four fully-grown horses. | [This monument was erected by] M. Antonius Peisanus, || to his own patron. To Olympian Zeus'. See also Pleket and Stroud (2012).

82. Tac., *Ann.* 2.53: *magnaque illic imago tristium laetorumque.*

83. Dio 51.5.2. The *Diolkos* was an ancient trackway or proto-railway used to drag ships overland across the narrowest part of the Isthmus of Corinth. Just 6.4km (4 miles) long, the *Diolkos* connected the Corinthian Gulf to the Saronic Gulf, representing a considerable saving over the 400km (250 miles) long journey around the Peloponnese. It also reduced the risk of encountering a dangerous weather event, which could be 25–35 per cent in summer and up to 40 per cent in winter. It was built from immense blocks of stone, forming a continuous roadway 3.5–5.0m (10–16.5ft) wide, with two parallel tracks engraved in it, spaced 1.5m apart for trolley wheels. The gradient is just 0.023 per cent, or 70m (230ft) in 3km (1.9 miles). The *Diolkos* was in operation in the first century and was last recorded in use in 883 CE. See Engels (1990), pp. 58–9; Pettegrew (2011); Werner (1997). According to Suetonius (*Calig.* 21), Germanicus' son later stated his intention to dig a canal through the Isthmus and dispatched a centurion to survey the work. His son Drusus Caesar was rumoured to have gone in the reverse direction *en route* to Nikopolis, while escaping the clutches of Seianus' agents: Tac., *Ann.* 5.10.

84. Green (1982).

85. Tac., *Ann.* 2.53.

86. Tac., *Ann.* 2.53: *hinc ventum Athenas, foederique sociae et vetustae urbis datum ut uno lictore uteretur.*

87. Suet., *Calig.* 3.2.

88. Tac., *Ann.* 2.53: *excepere Graeci quaesitissimis honoribus, vetera suorum facta dictaque praeferentes quo plus dignationis adulatio haberet.*

89. Tac., *Ann.* 2.55. Tiberius was well-known to dislike the encroachment of Greek words and phrases in the Latin language, where there were already suitable native words available that fitted the intended purpose: Suet., *Tib.* 56; 71.

90. Tac., *Ann.* 2.55: *At Cn. Piso quo properantius destinata inciperet civitatem Atheniensium turbido incessu exterritam oratione saeva increpat, oblique Germanicum perstringens quod contra decus Romani nominis non Atheniensis tot cladibus extinctos, sed conluviem illam nationum comitate nimia coluisset: hos enim esse Mithridatis adversus Sullam, Antonii adversus divum Augustum socios. etiam vetera obiectabat, quae in Macedones inprospere, violenter in suos fecissent, offensus urbi propria quoque ira quia Theophilum quendam Areo iudicio falsi damnatum precibus suis non concederent.*

91. Paus. 1.3–30.

92. Suet., *Calig.* 3.

93. Tac., *Ann.* 2.54.

94. Tac., *Ann.* 2.54.

95. Diog. Laert. 1.79.

96. Tac., *Ann.* 2.54; 6.15; Dio 60.8.27. Although all three of the sisters of Caligula were called Iulia, she seems to be the one indicated in *CIL* VI, 3998 (*Hymnus* | *paedagogus* | [*I*]*uliae Germanici* | *filiae*) and VI, 10563 (*Acuto* | *Iuliae Germanici Caesar* (sic) *filiae ser.*); cf. VI, 4352; *IGR* IV, 328, 464, 476 (Pergamum). The extant Greek inscriptions and coins (Cohen I, p. 249, n. 1; pp. 236, 237, 248)

lend support for Tacitus' statement (*Ann.* 2.54) that she was born on Lesbos. For epigraphic evidence for the name Livilla: *CIL* VI, 891 = *ILS* 188 (*Livilla* [*M. Vinici*] | *Germanici C*[*aesaris f.*] | *hic sita* [*est*]), which is her sepulchral inscription and therefore to be dated after Caligula's death; cf. Suet., *Div. Claud.* 29; Dio 60.8.27; Sen., *Apocol.* 10. Theodor Mommsen identified her husband's name from Tac., *Ann.* 6.15. She is probably referred to in *CIL* VI, 8711 = *ILS* 7803 (*Secunda* | *Livillaes* | *medica* ...); cf. XIV, 3661; J. Eckhel, *Doctrina Numorum Veterum* VI, 219, 233. Tacitus describes her as ungainly as a child (*Ann.* 4.3) and compared her unfavourably to Agrippina the Elder (*ibid.* 2.43).

97. *ILS* 8788 = *EJ* 95, cited by Seager (1972), p. 100, n. 1.
98. Tac., *Ann.* 2.54: *tum extrema Asiae ... intrat.*
99. Tac., *Ann.* 2.54. Perinthus is mentioned as the home of Thracians also by Xen., *Anab.* 2.6.
100. Tac., *Ann.* 2.64. Ovid dedicated *Pont.* 2.9 to Kotys.
101. Tac., *Ann.* 2.64–7.
102. Tac., *Ann.* 2.67. The three most powerful tribes of Thrace – Coelaletae, Dii and Odrusae – later took up arms against the Romans, but were beaten by P. Villaeus, who sent infantry and cavalry to defeat them: Tac., *Ann.* 3.38–39.
103. Tac., *Ann.* 2.54.
104. Tac., *Ann.* 2.54: *cupidine veteres locos et fama celebratos noscendi*; Ov., *Tr.* 1.8.1–50.
105. Conjectural visit based on an interpretation of Tac., *Ann.* 2.56.
106. Dio 49.33.2; 40.2; 44; Plut., *Ant.* 53.6; Zonar. 10.27.
107. Tac., *Ann.* 2.54.
108. Tac., *Ann.* 2.54; Strab., *Geog.* 1.2.
109. Archaeologists refer to this level as Troy IX.
110. Tac., *Ann.* 2.54: *igitur adito Ilio quaeque ibi varietate fortunae et nostri origine veneranda.*
111. P. Frisch, *Die Inschriften von Ilion* (Bonn, 1975), 88 = *ILS* 8787 = *IGR* IV, 206. See Carter and Morris (1995), p. 471.
112. *IGR* IV, 251; Decree of Assos, translated in *Papers of the Archaeological Institute of America*, 1881, pp. 134–5.
113. Coins of Aezanis, Phrygia: *RPC* I 3074, 3081, shown with Agrippina on the reverse. Apameia, Phrygia: *RPC* I 3134, struck by magistrate C. Iulius Kallikles. Pergamon, Mysia: *RPC* I 2367, shown with Drusus the Younger on the reverse. Sardes, Lydia: *RPC* I 2292, shown with Germanicus' head on the obverse and Drusus Caesar's on the reverse, possibly struck under Tiberius; 2993, possibly struck under Caligula. Smyrna: *RPC* I 2471, showing Germanicus' profile facing that of Agrippina on the reverse. For surveys of the cities mentioned, see Bean (1979).
114. Tac., *Ann.* 2.54: *pariterque provincias internis certaminibus aut magistratuum iniuriis fessas refovebat*; cf. Vell. Pat. 2.126.
115. Tac., *Ann.* 2.47. Tacitus lists the cities as Sardis, Magnesia under Mount Sipylus, Temnus, Philadelpheia, Aegae, Apollonis, the Mostenians and Hyrcanian Macedonians, with the towns of Hierocaesarea, Myrina, Cyme and Tmolus.
116. Tac., *Ann.* 2.54. For a survey of Colophon, see Bean (1979), pp. 151–4.
117. For a survey of Claros, see Bean (1979), pp. 155–60.
118. Tac., *Ann.* 2.54.
119. Tac., *Ann.* 2.54: *non femina illic, ut apud Delphos, sed certis e familiis et ferme Mileto accitus sacerdos numerum modo consultantium et nomina audit; tum in specum degressus, hausta fontis arcani aqua, ignarus plerumque litterarum et carminum edit responsa versibus compositis super rebus quas quis mente concepit.*
120. Tac., *Ann.* 2.54: *et ferebatur Germanico per ambages, ut mos oraculis, maturum exitum cecinisse.* Woodman (2004), p. 67, n. 92, notes that the word *exitum* means 'death' or 'departure' (natural or otherwise) and is the same word used by Germanicus in his last speech recorded by Tacitus (*Ann.* 2.71.1). Thus, the prophecy can also be translated as 'an early doom'.
121. Horden and Purcell (2000), p. 139.

122. Strab., *Geog.* 14.2.5: ἡ δὲ τῶν Ῥοδίων πόλις κεῖται μὲν ἐπὶ τοῦ ἑωθινοῦ ἀκρωτηρίου, λιμέσι δὲ καὶ ὁδοῖς καὶ τείχεσι καὶ τῇ ἄλλῃ κατασκευῇ τοσοῦτον διαφέρει τῶν ἄλλων ὥστ' οὐκ ἔχομεν εἰπεῖν ἑτέραν ἀλλ' οὐδὲ πάρισον, μή τί γε κρείττω ταύτης τῆς πόλεως.

123. Strab., *Geog.* 14.2.5.

124. Pliny, *Nat. Hist.* 34.41; Strab., *Geog.* 14.2.5. For a full discussion of scholarly research on the Colossus of Rhodes, see Clayton and Price (1988), pp. 124–37.

125. See Chapter 1, n. 99.

126. Tac., *Ann.* 2.55.

127. Tac., *Ann.* 2.55.

128. Tacitus does not say how Germanicus reached Armenia. He may have landed at Seleuda in Lycia, Tarsus in Cilicia, or Seleucia, the port of Antiocheia in Syria.

129. Tac., *Ann.* 2.56. Vonones was subsequently taken into custody by the Romans and held in Syria: Tac., *Ann.* 2.58.

130. Tac., *Ann.* 2.57.

131. Bertrandy and Rémy (2000).

132. Florus 1.40.27–8.

133. Tac., *Ann.* 2.56.

134. Suet., *Calig.* 1: *cum Armeniae regem devicisset.* Suetonius listed the conquest of Armenia among Germanicus' supreme achievements.

135. In the same announcement, Drusus was similarly recognized for his recent success in securing the surrender of the Marcomannic king Marboduus: Tac., *Ann.* 2.64: *decrevere patres ut Germanicus atque Drusus ovantes urbem introirent. structi et arcus circum latera templi Martis Vltoris cum effigie Caesarum.* On Drusus' exploits in Germania, see Tac., *Ann.* 2.62–3.

136. Tac., *Ann.* 2.64: *laetiore Tiberio quia pacem sapientia firmaverat quam si bellum per acies confecisset.*

137. A coin minted at around this time at Anazarbus in Cilicia shows a profile which appears to be Germanicus, set within the inscription showing Tiberius' full name in Greek characters: *RPC* 4060; *SNG Levante* 1366.

138. Tacitus (*Ann.* 2.56) states that 'Q. Servaeus was appointed to Commagene, then first put under a *praetor*'s jurisdiction'.

139. Tac., *Ann.* 2.56: *quo mitius Romanum imperium speraretur.*

140. Tac., *Ann.* 2.57: *Cunctaque socialia prospere composita non ideo laetum Germanicum habebant ob superbiam Pisonis.*

141. Tac., *Ann.* 2.57: *sed amici accendendis offensionibus callidi intendere vera, adgerere falsa ipsumque et Plancinam et filios variis modis criminari.* These friends presumably included P. Vitellius, P. Suillius Rufus, Cn. Sentius, C. Silius, and Vibius Marsus.

142. Tac., *Ann.* 2.57: *firmato vultu, Piso adversus metum, Germanicus ne minari crederetur.*

143. Tac., *Ann.* 2.57: *postremo paucis familiarium adhibitis sermo coeptus a Caesare, qualem ira et dissimulatio gignit, responsum a Pisone precibus contumacibus.*

144. Tac., *Ann.* 2.57: *discesseruntque apertis odiis.*

145. Tac., *Ann.* 2.57: *post quae rarus in tribunali Caesaris Piso, et si quando adsideret, atrox ac dissentire manifestus. vox quoque eius audita est in convivio, cum apud regem Nabataeorum coronae aureae magno pondere Caesari et Agrippinae, leves Pisoni et ceteris offerrentur, principis Romani, non Parthi regis filio eas epulas dari; abiecitque simul coronam et multa in luxum addidit quae Germanico quamquam acerba tolerabantur tamen.*

146. Tac., *Ann.* 2.58. Presumably, Aretas IV Philopatris, who was king of the Nabataeans from roughly 9 BCE to 40 CE.

147. Tac., *Ann.* 2.58: *daturumque honori Germanici ut ripam Euphratis accederet.*

148. Seager (1972), p. 103.

149. Tac., *Ann.* 2.58.

150. Tac., *Ann.* 2.58: *Datum id non modo precibus Artabani, sed contumeliae Pisonis cui gratissimus erat ob plurima oficia et dona quibus Plancinam devinxerat.*

151. Tac., *Ann.* 2.68.

152. Suet., *Calig.* 3.

153. Pliny, *Nat. Hist.* 5.79.

154. Maas (2000).
155. Lib., *Or.* 11.124 (Oration 11 is known as *Antiochikos*).
156. Lib., *Or.* 11.125.
157. Pliny, *Nat. Hist.* 5.79.
158. Athen., *Deipn.* 2.59b.
159. Norman (2000).
160. Tac., *Ann.* 2.83; *Tabula Siarensis*, Fragment 1; Pliny, *Nat. Hist.* 5.79. Pliny spells the place name as two words, 'Epi Daphnae'. Josephus (*Ant. Jud.* 14.13.1) refers to the place as Daphe by Antioch.
161. Butcher (2003), pp. 100, 108, 131.
162. Joseph., *Ant. Jud.* 14.13.1, 15.11, 17.3.
163. Tac., *Ann.* 2.69; cf. 2.42, 54.
164. Tac., *Ann.* 2.70.
165. Butcher (2003), p. 193.
166. Dio 57.18.3–5: Μάρκου δὲ δὴ Ἰουνίου Λουκίου τε Νωρβανοῦ μετὰ ταῦτα ἀρξάντων τέρας ἐν αὐτῇ τῇ νουμηνίᾳ οὐ σμικρὸν ἐγένετο, ὅπερ που ἐς τὸ Γερμανικοῦ πάθος ἀπεσήμαινεν· ὁ γὰρ Νωρβανὸς ὁ ὕπατος σάλπιγγι ἀεὶ προσκείμενος, καὶ ἐρρωμένως τὸ πρᾶγμα ἀσκῶν, ἠθέλησε καὶ τότε ὑπὸ τὸν ὄρθρον, πολλῶν ἤδη πρὸς τὴν οἰκίαν αὐτοῦ παρόντων, σαλπίσαι. καὶ τοῦτό τε πάντας ὁμοίως ἐξετάραξε καθάπερ ἐμπολέμιόν τι σύνθημα τοῦ ὑπάτου σφίσι παραγγείλαντος, καὶ ὅτι καὶ τὸ τοῦ Ἰανοῦ ἄγαλμα κατέπεσε. λόγιόν τέ τι ὡς καὶ Σιβύλλειον, ἄλλως μὲν οὐδὲν τῷ τῆς πόλεως χρόνῳ προσῆκον, πρὸς δὲ τὰ παρόντα ᾀδόμενον, οὐχ ἡσυχῇ σφας ἐκίνει· ἔλεγε γὰρ ὅτι· τρὶς δὲ τριηκοσίων περιτελλομένων ἐνιαυτῶν Ῥωμαίους ἔμφυλος ὀλεῖ 1 στάσις, χἀ Συβαρῖτις ἀφροσύνα.
167. Tac., *Ann.* 2.70.
168. Tac., *Ann.* 2.59: *Germanicus Aegyptum proficiscitur cognoscendae antiquitatis. sed cura provinciae praetendebatur*; cf. 2.62. For a detailed study, see Weingärtner (1969).
169. Tac., *Ann.* 2.59: *Dum ea aestas Germanico pluris per provincias transigitur*. Coins from Crete issued during the reign of Caligula hint that he visited there. Knossos: *RPC* I, 992/993, minted by *duoviri* Dossennus and Pulcher; *RPC* I, 999, minted by *triumvir* Pulcher and *duovir* Varius. Gortyn: *RPC* I, 1022; *BMCRE* 81; cf. Baldwin Bowsky (2004).
170. Strab., *Geog.* 17.1.6.
171. Strab., *Geog.* 17.1.6. See map in Marlowe (1971), p. 229.
172. Strab., *Geog.* 17.1.7.
173. Strab., *Geog.* 17.1.6.
174. Strab., *Geog.* 17.1.6.
175. Marlowe (1971), p. 30.
176. Strab., *Geog.* 17.1.8.
177. Strab., *Geog.* 17.1.9.
178. Strab., *Geog.* 17.1.12. See Brunt (1975). Valerius replaced Seius Strabo, father of L. Aelius Seianus, the current *praefectus* of the *Cohors Praetoria*. Seneca the Younger (L. Annaeus Seneca) may also have resided as a guest of his Aunt Marcia, while he recovered from an extended illness.
179. Strab., *Geog.*, 17.1.9.
180. The papyrus *P. Oxy.* 2435 is now held in the Papyrology Rooms, Sackler Library, Oxford. For a translation see Sherk (1988) 34A pp. 60.
181. Plut., *Ant.* 60.1; 62.1.
182. *EJ* 320. For a translation of the second edit see Sherk (1988) 34B pp. 60–1. See *Acta Alexandrinorum* in Lobel and Turner (1959), pp. 102 ff.; Oliver (1989).
183. Tac., *Ann.* 2.59: *sine milite incedere, pedibus intectis et pari cum Graecis amictu.*
184. Tac., *Ann.* 2.59.
185. Tac., *Ann.* 2.59: *nam Augustus inter alia dominationis arcana, vetitis nisi permissu ingredi senatoribus aut equitibus Romanis inlustribus, seposuit Aegyptum ne fame urgeret Italiam quisquis eam provinciam claustraque terrae ac maris quamvis levi praesidio adversum ingentis exercitus insedisset.* Indeed, the price of grain became an issue in Rome in the following year (Tac., *Ann.* 2.87). Tiberius

responded by fixing the price of grain to be paid by the purchaser, offset by adding two *sestertii* on every *modius* for the sellers.

186. Lobel and Turner (1959), p. 110, n. 10; Tac., *Ann.* 2.43, 59, 60; Seager (1972), p. 104.
187. Suet., *Tib.* 52.2.
188. Tac., *Ann.* 2.59: *sed cura provinciae praetendebatur, levavitque apertis horreis pretia frugum multaque in vulgus grata usurpavit.*
189. Joseph., *Ap.* 2.5.63: *si uero Germanicus frumenta cunctis in Alexandria commorantibus metiri non potuit, hoc indicium est sterilitatis ac necessitatis frumentorum, non accusatio Iudaeorum.*
190. Joseph., *Ap.* 2.5.63–4: *quid enim sapiant omnes imperatores de Iudaeis in Alexandria commorantibus, palam est; nam amministratio tritici nihilo minus ab eis quam ab aliis Alexandrinis translata est.*
191. Isaac (2006), pp. 440–91, 510–11. See Dio 57.18.5, for Tiberius's expulsion from Rome of the Jews who had 'flocked to Rome in great numbers and were converting many of the natives to their ways'.
192. Strab., *Geog.* 17.1.10. Scholars still debate the identity and location of the suburb founded by Octavianus on the site of his defeat of Antonius' army: see Hanson (1980), pp. 249–54. A *stadium* was about 185m (625ft) in length.
193. For a discussion of the significance of the monument, see Gurval (1995), pp. 72–4.
194. Strab., *Geog.* 17.1.10.
195. Strabo (*Geog.* 17.1.35) notes that olive trees did not grow in Egypt, except here.
196. Strab., *Geog.* 17.1.10.
197. Strab., *Geog.* 17.1.10: ἔστι δὲ καὶ Πάνειον, ὕψος τι χειροποίητον στροβιλοειδὲς ἐμφερὲς ὄχθῳ πετρώδει διὰ κοχλίου τὴν ἀνάβασιν ἔχον· ἀπὸ δὲ τῆς κορυφῆς ἔστιν ἀπιδεῖν ὅλην τὴν πόλιν ὑποκειμένην αὐτῷ πανταχόθεν.
198. Strab., *Geog.* 17.1.10, 16; Tac., *Ann.* 2.60. Tacitus and Strabo both record that the place was named after the pilot Canobus, who guided the Spartans led by Menelaus back from Troy and was buried there. It had a reputation as a party town with nightly revelries, according to Strabo (*Geog.* 17.1.17).
199. Kelly (2010) notes the places are not listed in the correct order. They are rearranged here to fit their actual geographic locations.
200. Tac., *Ann.* 2.60; Strab., *Geog.* 17.1.17; cf. Hdt. 2.43, 113.
201. Strab., *Geog.* 17.1.30. Strabo (*Geog.* 17.1.12) records: 'There are also three legions of soldiers, one of which is stationed in the city and the others in the country; and apart from these there are nine Roman cohorts, three in the city, three on the borders of Aethiopia in Syenê, as a guard for that region, and three in the rest of the country. And there are also three bodies of cavalry, which likewise are assigned to the various critical points'. By the time of Germanicus' visit, the complement of three legions had been reduced to two.
202. Strab., *Geog.* 17.1.27.
203. Strab., *Geog.* 17.1.30: ῥάχις δ᾽ ἐστὶν ἀπὸ τοῦ στρατοπέδου καὶ μέχρι Νείλου καθήκουσα, δι᾽ ἧς ἀπὸ τοῦ ποταμοῦ τροχοὶ καὶ κοχλίαι τὸ ὕδωρ ἀνάγουσιν, ἀνδρῶν ἑκατὸν πεντήκοντα ἐργαζομένων δεσμίων· ἀφορῶνται δ᾽ ἐνθένδε τηλαυγῶς αἱ πυραμίδες ἐν τῇ περαίᾳ ἐν Μέμφει καὶ εἰσὶ πλησίον.
204. Strab., *Geog.* 17.1.31.
205. Strab., *Geog.* 17.1.31–32. The remains of the Ptah temple complex and the House of the Apis Bulls can still be seen at Mit Rahina: see Wilkinson (2000), pp. 114–15.
206. Amm. Marc. 22.14.7.
207. Amm. Marc. 22.14.8. This was now the third bad omen, coming after Colophon and Rome – the fourth, if the failure to land at Samothrace is considered one – in just over a year.
208. Pliny, *Nat. Hist.* 36.16.
209. Tac., *Ann.* 2.61: *vix pervias arenas instar montium eductae pyramides certamine et opibus regum.*
210. Hdt. 2.124.
211. Strab., *Geog.* 17.1.33: τετταράκοντα δ᾽ ἀπὸ τῆς πόλεως σταδίους προελθόντι ὀρεινή τις ὀφρύς ἐστιν, ἐφ᾽ ᾗ πολλαὶ μέν εἰσι πυραμίδες, τάφοι τῶν βασιλέων, τρεῖς δ᾽ ἀξιόλογοι· τὰς δὲ δύο τούτων καὶ ἐν τοῖς ἑπτὰ θεάμασι καταριθμοῦνται· εἰσὶ γὰρ σταδιαῖαι τὸ ὕψος, τετράγωνοι τῷ σχήματι, τῆς πλευρᾶς ἑκάστης μικρῷ μεῖζον τὸ ὕψος ἔχουσαι; cf. Hdt. 2.149. The Great

286   *Germanicus*

Pyramid, or Pyramid of Khufu (Cheops), originally stood 146.5m (481ft) high and was the tallest man-made structure for over 3,800 years: see Wilkinson (2000), pp. 116–17.

212. Strab., *Geog.*, 17.1.34: "εν δέ τι τῶν ὁραθέντων ὑφ᾽ ἡμῶν ἐν ταῖς πυραμίσι παραδόξων οὐκ ἄξιον παραλιπεῖν. ἐκ γὰρ τῆς λατύπης σωροί τινες πρὸ τῶν πυραμίδων κεῖνται· ἐν τούτοις δ᾽ εὑρίσκεται ψήγματα καὶ τύπῳ καὶ μεγέθει φακοειδῆ· ἐνίοις δὲ καὶ ὡς ἂν πτίσμα οἷον ἡμιλεπίστων ὑποτρέχει· φασὶ δ᾽ ἀπολιθωθῆναι λείψανα τῆς τῶν ἐργαζομένων τροφῆς· οὐκ ἀπέοικε δέ· καὶ γὰρ οἴκοι παρ᾽ ἡμῖν λόφος ἐστὶν ἐν πεδίῳ παραμήκης, οὗτος δ᾽ ἐστὶ μεστὸς ψήφων φακοειδῶν λίθου πωρείας· καὶ αἱ θαλάττιαι δὲ καὶ αἱ ποτάμιαι ψῆφοι σχεδόν τι τὴν αὐτὴν ἀπορίαν ὑπογράφουσιν· ἀλλ᾽ αὗται μὲν ἐν τῇ κινήσει τῇ διὰ τοῦ ῥεύματος εὑρεσιλογίαν τινὰ ἔχουσιν, ἐκεῖ δ᾽ ἀπορωτέρα ἡ σκέψις· cf. Hdt. 2.12.

213. Tac., *Ann.* 2.61: *lacusque effossa humo, superfluentis Nili receptacula.*

214. Lake Moeris or Moiris: Strab., *Geog.* 17.1.35: θαυμαστὴν δὲ καὶ τὴν λίμνην ἔχει τὴν Μοίριδος καλουμένην, πελαγίαν τῷ μεγέθει καὶ τῇ χρόᾳ θαλαττοειδῆ.

215. Hdt. 2.149.

216. Hdt. (2.9) reckoned the journey from Memphis to Thebes took nine days by river. A receipt (Sherk (1988) 34C p. 61) survives from a savings and loan bank at Thebes dated to 25 January 20 CE issued by Menedoros to Phatres, son of Psenthotes, in settlement of a payment 'for the price of wheat from the granary for the visit of Germanicus Caesar'. It seems Phatres could not initially pay the public granary for the food and had to pay a financial penalty to the local bank.

217. Strab., *Geog.*, 17.1.46, quoting Homer.

218. Fletcher (2004), pp. 16–21.

219. Wilkinson (2000), p. 154.

220. Tac., *Ann.* 2.60: *et manebant structis molibus litterae Aegyptiae, priorem opulentiam complexae: iussusque e senioribus sacerdotum patrium sermonem interpretari, referebat habitasse quondam septingenta milia aetate militari, atque eo cum exercitu regem Rhamsen Libya Aethiopia Medisque et Persis et Bactriano ac Scytha potitum quasque terras Suri Armeniique et contigui Cappadoces colunt, inde Bithynum, hinc Lycium ad mare imperio tenuisse. legebantur et indicta gentibus tributa, pondu.s argenti et auri, numerus armorum equorumque et dona templis ebur atque odores, quasque copias frumenti et omnium utensilium quaeque natio penderet, haud minus magnifica quam nunc vi Parthorum aut potentia Romana iubentur.* For a description of the complex, see Oakes (2001), pp. 142–3. Cf. Strab., *Geog.* 17.1.28. The Great Hypostyle Hall contains 134 columns of open or bundled papyrus form, some 21m (69ft) tall: see Wilkinson (2000), pp. 154–61. Barbaric though its style may have been to Strabo's taste, it was bigger than any covered building the Romans had built, up to Germanicus' day.

221. Wilkinson (2000), pp. 188–9.

222. Tac., *Ann.* 2.61: *Ceterum Germanicus aliis quoque miraculis intendit animum, quorum praecipua fuere Memnonis saxca effigie.*

223. Tac., *Ann.* 2.61: *ubi radiis solis icta est, vocalem sonum reddens.*

224. Strab., *Geog.* 17.1.46: πεπίστευται δ᾽ ὅτι ἅπαξ καθ᾽ ἡμέραν ἑκάστην ψόφος ὡς ἂν πληγῆς οὐ μεγάλης ἀποτελεῖται ἀπὸ τοῦ μένοντος ἐν τῷ θρόνῳ καὶ τῇ βάσει μέρους· κἀγὼ δὲ παρὼν ἐπὶ τῶν τόπων μετὰ Γάλλου Αἰλίου καὶ τοῦ πλήθους τῶν συνόντων αὐτῷ φίλων τε καὶ στρατιωτῶν περὶ ὥραν πρώτην ἤκουσα τοῦ ψόφου· εἴτε δὲ ἀπὸ τῆς βάσεως εἴτε ἀπὸ τοῦ κολοσσοῦ εἴτ᾽ ἐπίτηδες τῶν κύκλῳ καὶ περὶ τὴν βάσιν ἱδρυμένων τινὸς ποιήσαντος τὸν ψόφον, οὐκ ἔχω διισχυρίσασθαι· διὰ γὰρ τὸ ἄδηλον τῆς αἰτίας πᾶν μᾶλλον ἐπέρχεται πιστεύειν ἢ τὸ ἐκ τῶν λίθων οὕτω τεταγμένων ἐκπέμπεσθαι τὸν ἦχον. The mention of C. Aelius Gallus, who was *praefectus* of Egypt from 26–24 BCE, gives us a *terminus post quem* for Strabo's visit.

225. Strab., *Geog.* 17.1.38–47. On Oxyrhynchus, see Parsons (2007).

226. Strab., *Geog.* 1.17.48. See Jackson (2002), pp. 112–15.

227. In a reply to Lawley (2002), Ole Nielsen says the rocks quarried here and in neighbouring Syene were called collectively by the name 'syenite'. The term is still used by geologists, but to denote a different kind of rock. Both monumental 'red' (pinkish) and monumental 'black' (hornblende) granites were quarried there. The granites were transported down the Nile River to Giza, Edfu, Karnak and Luxor to grace the sanctuaries and temples. Egyptian granite obelisks can be seen in London, New York, Paris and Rome.

228. Hawass (2005), pp. 29–39; Wright (1977).
229. Tac., *Ann.* 2.60. He notes of his own day the frontier 'which now extends to the Red Sea'. See Jackson (2002), pp. 112–15.
230. Tac., *Ann.* 2.61: *atque alibi angustiae et profunda altitudo, nullis inquirentium spatiis penetrabilis*; cf. Strab., *Geog.* 1.17.52.
231. Strab., *Geog.* 1.17.48. See Jackson (2002), pp. 115–18.
232. Strab., *Geog.* 1.17.48. Ancient scientists believed – erroneously – that Syene was directly under a tropic. Aswan actually lies just above the Tropic of Cancer. It was here that Eratosthenes conducted his experiment on 21 June 250 BCE, from which he calculated the circumference of the Earth with 98 per cent accuracy, and the planet's tilt. See Bean (1979), Appendix 1, pp. 231–232.
233. Strab., *Geog.* 1.17.49.
234. Strabo, *Geog.* 17.1.54: he suggests that while Gallus was trying to annex Arabia Felix (17.1.53), the Kushites seized the area north of the First Cataract, though this seems more of a coincidence than a coordinated attack. Gallus was replaced by Petronius in 24 BCE. The Kandake is mentioned in the Bible in *Acts* 8:26–27. Her full name and title was *Amnirense qore li kdwe li* ('Amanirensas, Qore and Kandake').
235. The masterful portrait bust, with its glass and stone eyes, is now on display in the British Museum, London (accession number GR 1911.9–1.1). The statue was buried in the steps of the temple of the Kushite god of victory, which meant that worshippers would tread upon the Roman emperor's head as they entered and left the building, as a mark of disrespect.
236. Strab., *Geog.* 17.1.53.
237. Wilkinson (2000), pp. 213–14. Philae now lies under water, having been flooded as part of the Aswan Dam works; the buildings were rescued and reassembled on the nearby island of Agilkia.
238. Tac., *Ann.* 2.60: *Sed Germanicus nondum comperto profectionem eam incusari Nilo subvehebatur* ('Germanicus, however, who had not yet learnt how much he was blamed for his expedition'); cf. Suet., *Tib.* 52.2.
239. Tac., *Ann.* 2.83; *Tabula Siarensis*, Fragment 1.
240. Suet., *Calig.* 3; Tac., *Ann.* 2.62: *Dum ea aestas Germanico pluris per provincias transigitur.*
241. Suet., *Calig.* 3: *Obtrectatoribus etiam, qualescumque et quantacumque de causa nanctus esset, lenis adeo et innoxius, ut Pisoni decreta sua rescindenti, clientelas divexanti non prius suscensere in animum induxerit, quam veneficiis quoque et devotionibus impugnari se comperisset.*
242. Tac., *Ann.* 2.69: *hinc graves in Pisonem contumeliae, nec minus acerba quae ab illo in Caesarem intentabantur.* On the suggestion that Tacitus presents, that Germanicus 'invents and believes in the cause of his own death', see Haynes (2003), p. 11.
243. Tac., *Ann.* 2.72.
244. Tac., *Ann.* 2.69.
245. Tac., *Ann.* 2.70: *si limen obsideretur, si effundendus spiritus sub oculis inimicorum foret, quid deinde miserrimae coningi, quid infantibus liberis eventurum? lenta videri veneficia: festinare et urgere, ut provinciam, ut legiones solus habeat. sed non usque eo defectum Germanicum, neque praemia caedis apud interfectorem mansura.*
246. Tac., *Ann.* 2.70: *componit epistulas quis amicitiam ei renuntiabat: addunt plerique iussum provincia decedere*; cf. Suet., *Calig.* 3.
247. Tac., *Ann.* 2.70.
248. Tac., *Ann.* 2.70: *nec Piso moratus ultra navis solvit moderabaturque cursui quo propius regrederetur si mors Germanici Syriam aperuisset.*
249. Suet., *Calig.* 3: *mandaretque domesticis ultionem, si quid sibi accideret.*
250. Tac., *Ann.* 2.71.
251. Tac., *Ann.* 2.74.
252. *Tabula Siarensis*, Fragment 2, Col. a: 'six days before the Ides of October'.
253. Sen. *Nat. Qu.* 1.3. A shower of meteors (possibly the Perseids) presaged the death of Germanicus' father, Drusus the Elder: see Powell (2011), p. 105.
254. Tac., *Ann.* 2.71: *lebunt Germanicum etiam ignoti: vindicabitis vos, si me potius quam fortunam meam fovebatis.* Savage (1942) sees parallels between Germanicus' words on his death-bed and Vergil, *Aeneid* 12.435 ff.

255. Tac., *Ann.* 2.72.
256. Suet., *Calig.* 1: *annum agens aetatis quartum et tricensimum ... obiit.*

Chapter 6: A Fine Roman in the Best Tradition
1. Tac., *Ann.* 2.74–5.
2. Tac., *Ann.* 2.74.
3. Tac., *Ann.* 2.72.
4. Paoli (1963), p. 128.
5. Tac., *Ann.* 2.73: *corpus antequam cremaretur nudatum.*
6. Paoli (1963), p. 128.
7. Tac., *Ann.* 2.73: *et erant qui formam, aetatem, genus mortis ob propinquitatem etiam locorum in quibus interiit, magni Alexandri fatis adacquarent. nam utrumque corpore decoro, genere insigni, haud multum triginta annos egressum, suorum insidiis externas inter gentis occidisse: sed hunc mitem erga amicos, modicum voluptatum, uno matrimonio, certis liberis egisse, neque minus proeliatorem, etiam si temeritas afuerit praepeditusque sit perculsas tot victoriis Germanias servitio premere. quod si solus arbiter rerum, si iure et nomine regio fuisset, tanto promptius adsecuturum gloriam militiae quantum clementia, temperantia, ceteris bonis artibus praestitisset.* Alexander was well-known for killing his friends (Klitos, Parmenio, Kallisthenes), for excessive drinking, and for having unconfirmed illegitimate heirs (including Herakles with his mistress Barsine and the posthumous Alexander IV with his queen Roxana). For other examples of Tacitus' *comparatio* with the 'Alexander tradition', see Borzsák (1982); Gissel (2001).
8. Tac., *Ann.* 2.73; 3.12; Suet., *Calig.* 1.
9. Tac., *Ann.* 2.75.
10. Paoli (1963), pp. 131–2.
11. Tac., *Ann.* 2.72: *indoluere exterae nationes regesque: tanta illi comitas in socios, mansuetudo in hostis.*
12. Suet., *Calig.* 5.
13. Suet., *Calig.* 6; Tac., *Ann.* 2.82.
14. Suet., *Calig.* 6: *Et ut demum fato functum palam factum est, non solaciis ullis, non edictis inhiberi luctus publicus potui.*
15. Tac., *Ann.* 2.82. The front doors of private houses were normally kept open during the daytime for the *salutatio,* for clients to drop in and meet their patron before noon.
16. Tac., *Ann.* 2.82: *hos vulgi sermones audita mors adeo incendit ut ante edictum magistratuum, ante senatus consultum sumpto iustitio desererentur fora, clauderentur domus.*
17. Suet., *Calig.* 6.
18. Suet., *Calig.* 6: *Salva Roma,| salva patria, | salvus est Germanicus.*
19. Tac., *Ann.* 2.82.
20. Tac., *Ann.* 2.82: *et populus quasi rursum ereptum acrius doluit.*
21. Suet., *Calig.* 5.
22. After his assassination, Iulius Caesar's body was examined by a doctor, who deduced that only one of the twenty-three stab wounds was fatal; see Suet., *Div. Iul.* 82.3.
23. Paterculus' compendium of history is dedicated to M. Vinicius in the year of his consulship.
24. Joseph., *Ant. Jud.* 18.54: καὶ ψηφίζεται ἡ σύγκλητος Γερμανικὸν πέμπειν διορθώσοντα τὰ κατὰ τὴν ἀνατολὴν πραγματευομένης αὐτῷ τῆς τύχης εὐκαιρίαν τοῦ θανάτου: καὶ γὰρ γενόμενος κατὰ τὴν ἀνατολὴν καὶ πάντα διορθώσας ἀνῃρέθη φαρμάκῳ ὑπὸ Πείσωνος, καθὼς ἐν ἄλλοις δεδήλωται.
25. Suet., *Calig.* 1: *diuturno morbo ... obiit. Nam praeter livores, qui toto corpore erant, et spumas.*
26. Suet., *Calig.* 1: *quae per os fluebant, cremati quoque cor inter ossa incorruptum repertum est, cuius ea natura existimatur, ut tinctum veneno igne confici nequeat.*
27. Tac., *Ann.* 2.69.
28. Tac., *Ann.* 2.69.
29. Tac., *Ann.* 2.71.
30. Syme (1981) documents twenty-five consular legates who died in Syria in the period October 19–August 117 CE.

31. http://www.cdc.gov/nczved/divisions/dfbmd/diseases/typhoid_fever/ and http://www.mayoclinic.com/health/typhoid-fever/DS00538.
32. Dio 53.25.7, 30.1- 4.
33. http://www.cdc.gov/nczved/divisions/dfbmd/diseases/typhoid_fever/.
34. http://www.mayoclinic.com/health/influenza/DS00081.
35. WNE has been proposed as the cause of Alexander the Great's death by Marr and Calisher (2003), available online in full at http://wwwnc.cdc.gov/eid/article/9/12/03–0288_article.htm.
36. http://en.diagnosispro.com/differential_diagnosis-for/foaming-frothing-at-the-mouth/34376–154.html.
37. http://www.nlm.nih.gov/medlineplus/ency/article/003215.htm.
38. Scarborough (1968), p. 257, cites Plut., *Mar.* 6.3. Davies (1989), pp. 214–15.
39. Pliny, *Nat. Hist.* 29.8.
40. Cilliers and Retief (2000), p. 90 n. 3, citing Rutten (1997); Mayor (2009), pp. 67–73.
41. Kaufman (1932).
42. Ulpian, *Digesta* 50.16.236.
43. For examples of the use of *scelus*, see Tac., *Ann.* 1.5.2; 4.10.2; 6.33.1; 12.66.3.
44. Cilliers and Retief (2000), p. 98 citing Dioscorides, *Materia Medica* 4.64.
45. Tac., *Ann.* 2.73: *corpus antequam cremaretur nudatum in foro Antiochensium, qui locus sepulturae destinabatur, praetuleritne veneficii signa parum constitit.*
46. Tac., *Ann.* 1.13.
47. Wood *et al.* (1994), available at http://www.doc.state.ok.us/offenders/ocjrc/94/940650G.htm.
48. Tac., *Ann.* 2.74.
49. Tac., *Ann.* 3.14.
50. Tac., *Ann.* 2.69.
51. Tac., *Ann.* 3.16; Suet., *Tib.* 52.3. Tacitus remarks that he recalled hearing old men in his youth mentioning the letter.
52. Tac., *Ann.* 5.1.
53. Tac., *Ann.* 4.57.
54. Chery Golden, 'Women and Poison in Ancient Rome', Visiting Lecture, Western Illinois University, 12 October 2006.
55. Along with Tacitus' general portayal of Livia as a villainess is Robert Graves' influential novel *I, Claudius*. For a rational assessment, see Dennison (2010), pp. 268–9.
56. Dando-Collins (2008), pp. 223–233.
57. Tac., *Ann.* 2.69: *et reperiebantur solo ac parietibus erutae humanorum corporum reliquiae, carmina et devotiones et nomen Germanici plumbeis tabulis insculptum, semusti cineres ac tabo obliti aliaque malefica quis creditur animas numinibus infernis sacrari.* The context infers the room was in Piso's residence.
58. Tac., *Ann.* 2.73: *nam ut quis misericordia in Germanicum et praesumpta suspicione aut favore in Pisonem pronior, diversi interpretabantur.*
59. Suet., *Calig.* 2; Tac., *Ann.* 2.82.
60. Tac., *Ann.* 2.74: *postulantibus Vitellio ac Veranio ceterisque qui crimina et accusationem tamquam adversus receptos iam reos instruebant.*
61. Suet., *Calig.* 2; Tac., *Ann.* 2.82.
62. Tac., *Ann.* 2.75.
63. Tac., *Ann.* 2.76.
64. Tacitus thus acknowledges that Germanicus had secured the loyalty of the Syrian legions. See Chapter 5, n. 60.
65. Tac., *Ann.* 2.77.
66. Tac., *Ann.* 2.78.
67. Tac., *Ann.* 2.78.
68. Tac., *Ann.* 2.75.
69. Tac., *Ann.* 2.75: *At Agrippina, quamquam defessa luctu et corpore aegro, omnium tamen quae ultionem morarentur intolerans ascendit classem cum cineribus Germanici et liberis, miserantibus cunctis quod femina nobilitate princeps, pulcherrimo modo matrimonio inter venerantis gratantisque aspici solita, tunc feralis reliquias sinu ferret, incerta ultionis, anxia sui et infelici fecunditate fortunae totiens obnoxia.*

70. Tac., *Ann.* 2.79.
71. Presumably *Legiones* III *Gallica*, X *Frentensis* and XII *Fulminata*.
72. Tac., *Ann.* 2.80.
73. Tac., *Ann.* 2.81.
74. Suet., *Calig.* 6.
75. Tac., *Ann.* 2.83; cf. *Tabula Siarensis* in Appendix 2.
76. *Tabula Siarensis*, Fragment 2b, 20–7: *Item senatum uel- | le atque aequom censere, quo facilius pie|t|as omnium ordinum erga domum Augustam et consen- | su|s| uniuersorum ciuium memoria honoranda Germanici Caesaris appareret, uti co(n)s(ules) hoc | s(enatus) c(onsultum) sub edicto suo proponerent . . . [et] ut quam celeberrumo loco figeretur.*
77. *Tabula Hebana* 1–6; Augustus, *Res Gestae* 10.
78. *Tabula Siarensis*, Fragment 1, 22–23. Sánchez-Ostiz Gutiérrez (1999), pp. 138–9. Lebek (1991), discusses the textual evidence for the arches in depth.
79. *Tabula Siarensis*, Fragment 1, 22–6.
80. *Tabula Siarensis*, Fragment 1, 13, 18: *cum . . . ob rem p(ublicam) mortem obisset*; cf. Tac., *Ann.* 2.83.2; *CIL* VI, 31199.
81. *Tabula Siarensis*, Fragment 1, 22–6: *Druso, fratri Ti(beri) Caesaris Aug(usti)*.
82. *Tabula Siarensis*, Fragment 1, 22–6: 'or another place in those areas that seemed more suitable to Tiberius Caesar Augustus, our *princeps*' (*[siue qui] | alius aptior locus Ti(berio) Caesari Aug(usto) principi nostro [uideretur in iis regionibus]*). For the placement of the arch in Syria, see Potter (1987), pp. 271–6.
83. *Tabula Siarensis*, Fragment 1, 35–7; Tac., *Ann.* 2.83.2.
84. *Tabula Siarensis*, Fragment 2a, 1–14. Curiously, none of these are mentioned by Tacitus.
85. Tac., *Ann.* 2.83. Stuart (1940), p. 64, n. 4, counted fifty-two portrait inscriptions of Germanicus surviving from ancient times.
86. Tac., *Ann.* 2.83.3: *neque enim eloquentiam fortuna discerni et satis inlustre si veteres inter scriptores haberetur*. On Tiberius' virtue of *moderatio*, see Tac., *Ann.* 3.56.2.
87. The *Tropaea Germanici* is known from inscriptions (*CIL* XVI, 32, 33) on the location of military diplomas – issued from the time of Claudius on – which state *post tropahea Germanici in trubunali quae sunt ad aedem Fidei*. This part of the temple complex was crowded with votive monuments: Plut., *Caes.* 6; Suet., *Div. Iul.* 11; *Calig.* 34.
88. McCall (2002), p. 7, n. 35.
89. Tac., *Ann.* 3.49.
90. *Tabula Siarensis*, Fragment 2b, 12–13.
91. *Tabula Siarensis*, Fragment 2b, 1–10.
92. *Tabula Hebana* 6–7.
93. An inscription from Rome dedicated, without doubt, after his death, demonstrates the esteem in which Germanicus was held: *CIL* VI, 909 = *ILS* 176: *Pleps urbana quinque et | triginta tribuum | Germanico Caesari | Ti. Augusti f., I divi Augusti n., | auguri, flamini Augustali, | cos. iterum, imp. iterum, | aere conlato*. See also *CIL* VI, 31274 (Rome); X, 6638 (p. 665), 6649 (Antium); XIV, 244 (Ostia).
94. For the eventful history of the statue, see 'Ancient Sources: 4. Sculptures (b) Portrait Busts and Statues'. On the mythological associations, see Dares, *De Exidio Troiae Historia* 33.
95. Tac., *Ann.* 3.40. For a reconstruction of the arch at Mainz, after Hans G. Frenz, see Cüppers *et al.* (1990), p. 85, fig. 42. For a review of literary evidence for the Germanicus arch, see Lebek (1991), pp. 54, 69–71: Lebek argues that the arch would have been located close to the *tumulus* of Drusus, and that the foundations of the triumphal arch which have been found on the right bank of the river, beside the Mainz-Kastel, date from the time of Domitian.
96. The temple was erected between 23 and 31 CE. The members represented in the group were (from left to right) Augustus, Roma, Tiberius, Livia, Augustus (again), Agrippina (wife of Germanicus), Livilla (sister of Germanicus); Germanicus and Drusus (son of Tiberius) standing together in a chariot; and Antonia (mother of Germanicus), Vipsania Agrippina and Claudius: Flower (2006), pp. 176–9.
97. Flower (2006), p. 176.

98. Caesarea Germanicopolis, or Tahtali on the Gebes River in Bithynia, see Pliny, *Nat. Hist.* 5.40, on the Hellespont and Mysia: 'we then come to the river Gelbes; and, in the interior, the town of Helgas, or Germanicopolis, which has also the other name of Booscoete Apamea [or Booscoetes], now more generally known as Myrlea of the Colophonians'. Germanikopolis or Clibanus or Ermenek in Isauria, see Mitchell, 'Map 66 Taurus', in Talbert (2000), p. 1016. Gangra Germanicopolis or Çankırı in Paphlagonia, see Head (1888).

99. Tac., *Ann.* 2.84.

100. A brass *sestertius* was minted showing the twins, the head of each popping out of a *cornucopia*: *RIC* I, 42.

101. Tac., *Ann.* 3.1: *violenta luctu et nescia tolerandi.*

102. Tac., *Ann.* 3.1.

103. Tac., *Ann.* 3.1: *neque satis constabat quid pro tempore foret, cum classis paulatim successit, non alacri, ut adsolet, remigio sed cunctis ad tristitiam compositis. postquam duobus cum liberis, feralem urnam tenens, egressa navi defixit oculos, idem omnium gemitus; neque discerneres proximos alienos, virorum feminarumve planctus, nisi quod comitatum Agrippinae longo maerore fessum obvii et recentes in dolore antibant.*

104. Tac., *Ann.* 3.2.

105. There is no suggestion in the extant accounts that she opted to go by litter or carriage.

106. Suet., *Tib.* 7.3; *Consolatio ad Liviam* 177.

107. Tac., *Ann.* 3.2.

108. Tac., *Ann.* 3.3: *matrem Antoniam non apud auctores rerum, non diurna actorum scriptura reperio ullo insigni officio functam, cum super Agrippinam et Drusum et Claudium ceteri quoque consanguinei nominatim perscripti sint, seu valetudine praepediebatur seu victus luctu animus magnitudinem mali perferre visu non toleravit.*

109. Tac., *Ann.* 3.3: *facilius crediderim Tiberio et Augusta, qui domo non excedebant, cohibitam, ut par maeror et matris exemplo avia quoque et patruus attineri viderentur.* Seager (1972), pp. 110–11.

110. Tac., *Ann.* 3.4: *per silentium vastus, modo ploratibus inquies.*

111. *CIL* VI, 894 = 31194. Cordingley and Richmond (1927).

112. Tac., *Ann.* 3.4: *cum decus patriae, solum Augusti sanguinem, unicum antiquitatis specimen appellarent versique ad caelum ac deos integram illi subolem ac superstitem iniquorum precarentur.*

113. Tac., *Ann.* 3.5.

114. Tac., *Ann.* 3.5: *sane corpus ob longinquitatem itinerum externis terris quoquo modo crematum.*

115. Levick (1976/1999), p. 156.

116. Tac., *Ann.* 3.6.

117. Tac., *Ann.* 3.6: *utque premeret vulgi sermones, monuit edicto multos inlustrium Romanorum ob rem publicam obisse, neminem tam flagranti desiderio celebratum. idque et sibi et cunctis egregium si modus adiceretur. non enim eadem decora principibus viris et imperatori popolo quae modicis domibus aut civitatibus. convenisse recenti dolori luctum et ex maerore solacia; sed referendum iam animum ad firmitudinem, ut quondam divus Iulius amissa unica filia, ut divus Augustus ereptis nepotibus abstruserint tristitiam. nil opus vetustioribus exemplis, quotiens populus Romanus cladis exercituum, interitum ducum, funditus amissas nobilis familias constanter tulerit. principes mortalis, rem publicam aeternam esse. proin repeterent sollemnia, et quia ludorum Megalesium spectaculum suberat, etiam voluptates resumerent.*

118. Sen., *Polyb.* 15.4–16.4.

119. Tac., *Ann.* 3.7.

120. Livy 29.14.10–14.

121. Tac., *Ann.* 3.7.

122. Tac., *Ann.* 3.8.

123. Tac., *Ann.* 3.9.

124. Tac., *Ann.* 2.79.1.

125. Tac., *Ann.* 3.10.

126. For example, the cases of Falanius and Rubrius (Tac., *Ann.* 1.73.1–4), Granius Marcellus (*ibid.* 1.72.2), and Libo Drusus in 16 CE (*ibid.* 2.29.2). Interestingly, in the case of P. Suillius, Germanicus' *quaestor*, Tiberius insisted he be exiled for having been found guilty of corruption: Tac., *Ann.* 4.31.

127. Tac., *Ann.* 3.11.
128. Tac., *Ann.* 3.11.
129. In the late 1980s, fragments of several copies of the *Senatus Consultum de Cn. Pisone patre* (*SCPP*) inscribed on bronze came to light near Seville, in the former Roman province of Baetica. Discovered as a result of unofficially sanctioned searches by metal detectorists, by the early 1990s, the Archaeological Museum in Seville had acquired all the extant fragments for restoration, study and eventual publication. Running to 176 lines of text, it is one of the longest Latin inscriptions to survive down to our own day. After careful study, and some carefully considered interpretation of missing letters and words in places by experts, we now have an excellent master text and evidence of six copies, all from Baetica.
130. Tac., *Ann.* 3.16.1.
131. Tac., *Ann.* 3.15.2.
132. Tac., *Ann.* 3.12, possibly the speech referred to in *SCPP*, lines 168–70.
133. Tac., *Ann.* 3.12: *illic contumacia et certaminibus asperasset iuvenem exituque eius laetatus esset an scelere extinxisset, integris animis diiudicandum. 'nam si legatus officii terminos, obsequium erga imperatorem exuit eiusdemque morte et luctu meo laetatus est, odero seponamque a domo mea et privatas inimicitias non vi principis ulciscar: sin facinus in cuiuscumque mortalium nece vindicandum detegitur, vos vero et liberos Germanici et nos parentes iustis solaciis adficite.*
134. Tacitus emphasizes the murder charge, whereas, in distinct contrast, the *SCPP* subsumes it.
135. Tac., *Ann.* 3.12: *defleo equidem filium meum semperque deflebo: sed neque reum prohibeo quo minus cuncta proferat, quibus innocentia eius sublevari aut, si qua fuit iniquitas Germanici, coargui possit, vosque oro ne, quia dolori meo causa conexa est, obiecta crimina pro adprobatis accipiatis.*
136. This is consistent with Tiberius' wish to be seen as exhibiting the virtues of *aequitas* ('impartiality') and *iustitia* ('justice').
137. Tac., *Ann.* 3.12: *si incerta adhuc ista et scrutanda sunt?*
138. Tac., *Ann.* 3.12: *id solum Germanico super leges praestiterimus, quod in curia potius quam in foro, apud senatum quam apud iudices de morte eius anquiritur: cetera pari modestia tractentur. nemo Drusi lacrimas, nemo maestitiam meam spectet, nec si qua in nos adversa finguntur.*
139. Tac., *Ann.* 3.13.
140. Cooley (1989), pp. 200–1.
141. Tac., *Ann.* 2.74.
142. Tac., *Ann.* 3.7: *nec ulla in corpore signa sumpti exitii reperta.*
143. Tac., *Ann.* 3.13: *sacra hinc et immolationes nefandas ipsius atque Plancinae, peritam armis rem publicam, utque reus agi posset, acie victum.*
144. Tac., *Ann.* 3.14.
145. Tac., *Ann.* 3.16; Suet., *Tib.* 52.3. Tacitus remarks he recalled hearing old men in his youth mentioning the letter.
146. Tac., *Ann.* 3.16.
147. Tac., *Ann.* 3.14.
148. Suet., *Tib.* 72.3: *Redde Germanicum!*
149. Tac., *Ann.* 3.15.
150. Tac., *Ann.* 3.14.
151. Tacitus specifically calls the weapon a *gladius*: Tac., *Ann.* 3.15.
152. Tac., *Ann.* 3.16.
153. Tac., *Ann.* 3.14.
154. Tac., *Ann.* 3.17; *SCPP*, lines 109–20; at line 114, the document states as the basis for the pardon *iustissimus causas.*
155. Tac., *Ann.* 3.17: *quod pro omnibus civibus leges obtineant uni Germanico non contigisse. Vitellii et Veranii voce defletum Caesarem, ab imperatore et Augusta defensam Plancinam.*
156. Flower (2006), pp. 132–8.
157. *SCPP* differs in that it records only that the Senate rewarded the younger Cn. Piso *half* of his father's property, suggesting that Tacitus consulted the actual document in the course of his research; the only condition imposed for the younger Cn. Piso (*SCPP*, lines 90–100) is to change his name: *si praenomen patris mutasset.*

158. *SCPP*, lines 100–1, records that Marcus received half of his father's property, but makes no mention of the proposed banishment. On Tiberius' appeal to spare Marcus, lines 4–8.
159. Tac., *Ann.* 3.18. Flower (1996), p. 155; (2006), pp. 136–7, argues that this is a case of *damnatio memoria*. An inscription dated to 5/6 CE in the forum at Leptis Magna in the province of Africa, where Piso had been proconsul, does survive where his name has been chipped away: *ILS* 95 = *EJ* 39.
160. *SCPP*, lines 100–101.
161. Tac., *Ann.* 3.18.
162. Antonia, the mother of Germanicus, is cited in the *SCPP*, lines 140–2. Tacitus (*Ann.* 3.2) comments, in contrast, that Antonia was not seen in public during the trial, highlighting one difference between the official and the historian's version of events, perhaps indicative of his bias. See Flower (1996), pp. 250–2.
163. Tac., *Ann.* 3.19.
164. *SCPP*, lines 169–70, specifies *quo loco Ti. Caes(ari) Aug(usto) vide-* | *retur.*
165. *SCPP*, lines 123–5: *item cum iudicaret senatus omnium parentium pietatem antecessisse Ti. Caesarem Aug(ustum) principem nostrum tant|i| et |t|am aequali⟨s⟩ dolor|is| ⟨eius indicis⟩ totiens conspectis.* Compare to Tiberius' display of *pietas* by walking in front of his brother Drusus' hearse all the way from Germania Magna to Rome.
166. Tac., *Ann.* 3.19: *is finis fuit ulciscenda Germanici morte, non modo apud illos homines qui tum agebant etiam secutis temporibus vario rumore iactata.*
167. *SCPP*, lines 12–14, *Senatum populumq(ue) Romanum ante omnia dis immortalibus gratias agere,| quod nefaris consilis Cn.Pisonis patris tranquillitatem praesentis status | r(ei) p(ublicae), quo melior optari non pote |e|t quo beneficio principis nostri frui contigit.* Cooley (1989), pp. 201–2, noting that the Senate thanks the Gods for protecting the State from Piso's wicked plots (*nefaris consilis*).
168. *Eph. Epig.* VIII, 2039, cited by Fiske (1900), p. 107.
169. *CIL* II, 194 (Lusitania); XII, 1872 (Vienna); both are dedicated to a *flamen* of Germanicus.
170. Tac., *Ann.* 2.88.
171. Tac., *Ann.* 2.88: *non fraude neque occultis, sed palam et armatum populum Romanum hostis suos ulcisci.*
172. Tac., *Ann.* 2.88. Tacitus notes that he ruled for twelve years and 'assuredly he was the deliverer of Germany; one, too, who had defied Rome, not in her early rise, as other kings and generals, but in the height of her empire's glory, had fought, indeed, indecisive battles; yet, in war, remained unconquered' (*petitusque armis cum varia fortuna certaret, dolo propinquorum cecidit: liberator haud dubie Germaniae et qui non primordia populi Romani, sicut alii reges ducesque, sed florentissimum imperium lacessierit, proeliis ambiguus, bello non victus*).

Chapter 7: The Fall of the House of Germanicus

1. Tac., *Ann.* 3.29.
2. Tac., *Ann.* 4.4.
3. Tac., *Ann.* 4.60.
4. Sen., *Constant.* 18.2–5; Suet., *Calig.* 9.
5. Suet., *Calig.* 24.
6. Tac., *Ann.* 4.53.
7. Suet., *Ner.* 4.3.
8. Suet., *Calig.* 24.
9. Tac., *Ann.* 6.15.1; Dio 58.21.1.
10. Tac., *Ann.* 3.4.
11. Tac., *Ann.* 4.52.
12. Tac., *Ann.* 4.52: *non ideo laedi quia non regnaret*; Suet., *Tib.* 53.1.
13. Tac., *Ann.* 4.53.
14. Tac., *Ann.* 4.17.
15. Tac., *Ann.* 4.17.
16. Suet., *Calig.* 6.2: *Auxit gloriam desideriumque defuncti et atrocitas insequentium temporum, cunctis nec temere opinantibus reverentia eius ac metu repressam Tiberi saevitiam, quae mox eruperit.*

17. Dio 57.19.8: τὸ μὲν οὖν σύμπαν οὕτω μετὰ τὸν τοῦ Γερμανικοῦ θάνατον μετεβάλετο ὥστε αὐτὸν μεγάλως καὶ πρότερον ἐπαινούμενον πολλῷ δὴ τότε μᾶλλον θαυμασθῆναι.

18. Tac., *Ann.* 4.13.

19. Tac., *Ann.* 4.7.

20. Tac., *Ann.* 4.1; 6.8. The site of Vulsinii – or Velzna, as it is spelled in Etruscan – is still debated, with Bolsena in Lazio or Orvieto in Umbria proposed as candidates. The people of the region are mentioned by Pliny (*Nat. Hist.* 3.8).

21. Tac., *Ann.* 4.1.

22. Tac., *Ann.* 4.2; Suet., *Tib.* 37.1.

23. Tac., *Ann.* 4.3.

24. Tac., *Ann.* 4.7.

25. Tac., *Ann.* 3.56.

26. Tac., *Ann.* 3.52. Augustus gave Tiberius the tribunician power in 6 CE, at the age of 36, after which he retired to Rhodes.

27. Drusus' role as guardian is inferred by Dio (57.22.4). Barrett (1996), p. 32; Shotter (1992), p. 40.

28. Tac., *Ann.* 4.7.

29. Tac., *Ann.* 4.8.

30. The fact was only revealed eight years later.

31. Tac., *Ann.* 4.9: *memoriae Drusi eadem quae in Germanicum decernuntur, plerisque additis, ut ferme amat posterior adulatio.*

32. Tac., *Ann.* 4.12.

33. Suet., *Tib.* 62.1.

34. Tac., *Ann.* 4.39.

35. Tac., *Ann.* 4.40.

36. Balsdon (1969), p. 21.

37. Tac., *Ann.* 4.41.

38. Tac., *Ann.* 4.67.

39. Tac., *Ann.* 4.67.

40. Tac., *Ann.* 4.8: *quibus adprensis 'patres conscripti, hos' inquit 'orbatos parente tradidi patrno ipsorum precatusque sum, quamquam esset illi propria suboles, ne secus quam suum sanguinem foveret attolleret, sibique et posteris coniormaret. erepto Druso preces ad vos converto disque et patria coram obtestor: Augusti pro nepotes, clarissimis maioribus genitos, suscipite regite, vestram meamque vicem explete. hi vobis, Nero et Druse, parentum loco. ita nati estis ut bona malaque vestra ad rem publicam pertineant.*

41. Tac., *Ann.* 4.15.

42. Tac., *Ann.* 4.15: *aderantque iuveni modestia ac forma principe viro digna, notis in eum Seiani odiis ob periculum gratiora.*

43. Tac., *Ann.* 4.18.

44. Tac., *Ann.* 4.19.

45. Tac., *Ann.* 4.20.

46. Tac., *Ann.* 4.68.

47. Tac., *Ann.* 4.68.

48. Tac., *Ann.* 4.70.

49. Tac., *Ann.* 4.71.

50. Tac., *Ann.* 4.74.

51. Tac., *Ann.* 4.29.

52. Tac., *Ann.* 4.54.

53. Tac., *Ann.* 4.59.

54. Tac., *Ann.* 4.60.

55. Tac., *Ann.* 4.60.

56. Tac., *Ann.* 3.22.

57. Tac., *Ann.* 6.40.

58. Suet., *Tib.* 54.2; *Calig.* 7.

59. Tac., *Ann.* 4.67.

60. Sen., *Ira* 3.21.5; Tac., *Ann.* 4.67.6.

61. Suet., *Tib.* 54.2.
62. This was a coded sign that his execution had been ordered – the noose to strangle him, the hook to drag his body to the Tiber River.
63. Tac., *Ann.* 4.75.
64. Tac., *Ann.* 1.33: *accedebant muliebres offensiones novercalibus Liviae in Agrippinam stimulis, atque ipsa Agrippina paulo commotior, nisi quod castitate et mariti amore quamvis indomitum animum in bonum vertebat.*
65. Tac., *Ann.* 5.1; Suet., *Tib.* 51.
66. Barrett (1989), p. 24.
67. Tac., *Ann.* 5.2.
68. Tac., *Ann.* 4.70.
69. Tac., *Ann.* 5.3. Freisenbruch (2010), p. 93, argues that, while the Augusta lived, Agrippina came to no harm.
70. Tac., *Ann.* 5.4: *posse quandoque domus Germanici exitium paenitentiae esse seni.*
71. Tac., *Ann.* 5.4.
72. Tac., *Ann.* 5.5.
73. Dio 58.5.8.
74. Tac., *Ann.* 5.10. Dio (58.25) puts this event in the twentieth year of Tiberius' reign, i.e. 34 CE.
75. Tacitus professes not to know anything about the origins of the story.
76. Suet., *Tib.* 64.2; Tac., *Ann.* 6.23.
77. Tac., *Ann.* 5.6; 6.8. Dio (58.3.9) states that Seianus was actually betrothed to Drusus the Younger's daughter, but Tacitus' reference to him as Tiberius' son-in-law (*Ann.* 5.6; 6.8) only makes sense if he was married to Livilla.
78. Dio 58.4.3.
79. Dio 58.4.2.
80. Suet., *Tib.* 61.1: *etsi commentario, quem de uita sua summatim breuiterque composuit, ausus est scribere Seianum se punisse, quod comperisset furere aduersus liberos Germanici filii sui.*
81. Nero Iulius Caesar Germanicus.
82. Val. Max. 9.11.ext.4.
83. Seager (1972), pp. 214–15, citing *ILS* 157, 158, 159 (= *EJ* 51, 52, 85).
84. Juv., *Sat.* 10.74 ff.
85. Seager (1972), pp. 215–16. On Macro, see Tac., *Ann.* 6.15; Joseph., *Ant. Jud.* 18.179.
86. Dio 58.4.2.
87. Joseph., *Ant. Jud.* 18.179 f.
88. Suet., *Calig.* 10.1.
89. Dio 58.4.4.
90. Dio 58.5.5; Suet., *Tib.* 65.1.
91. Suet., *Tib.* 65.1; Dio 58.4.4, 6.2.
92. Seager (1972), pp. 214, 219; Dio 58.9.2; Suet., *Tib.* 65.1.
93. Dio 58.8.1.
94. Dio 58.6.4.
95. Dio 58.8.2: εἰ μὴ τὸν δῆμον ἰσχυρῶς τοῖς περὶ τοῦ Γαΐου λεχθεῖσι πρὸς τὴν τοῦ Γερμανικοῦ τοῦ πατρὸς αὐτοῦ μνήμην ἡσθέντα εἶδε.
96. Dio 58.7.4.
97. Dio 58.9.3.
98. Dio 58.9.4. On the shooting star see Sen. *Nat. Qu.* 1.3.
99. Dio 58.9.5.
100. Dio 58.9.5–6.
101. Dio 58.10.1–5.
102. Dio 58.10.6.
103. Dio 58.10.8.
104. Dio 58.10–11.5; Suet., *Tib.* 53.2; Tac., *Ann.* 6.25.
105. Dio 58.10–11.5; Suet., *Tib.* 61.5.
106. Dio 58.10–11.6.

107. Suet., *Tib.* 72.1.
108. Tac., *Ann.* 6.23.
109. Suet., *Tib.* 54.2.
110. Dio 58.9.2; Suet., *Tib.* 65.2; Tac., *Ann.* 6.23.
111. Tac., *Ann.* 6.24.
112. Pliny, *Nat. Hist.* 8.145; Suet., *Tib.* 53.2; 54.2; 64; *Calig.* 7.
113. Suet., *Tib.* 53.2.
114. Suet., *Tib.* 53.2; Tac., *Ann.* 6.25.
115. Tac., *Ann.* 6.25. Tiberius harboured a deep resentment towards Gallus, as he was the man who married Vipsania, the *princeps'* first wife.
116. Suet., *Tib.* 53.2; Tac., *Ann.* 6.25.
117. Tac., *Ann.* 6.25.
118. Dio 58.21.1; Tac., *Ann.* 6.15.
119. Tac., *Ann.* 6.20.
120. Suet., *Tib.* 41.
121. Dio 58.23.1.
122. Suet., *Tib.* 76.
123. Suet., *Tib.* 72.1.
124. Suet., *Tib.* 42.1; 43.1–45; 60; according to 42.2, he established an office of Minister of Pleasures, the *officium a volumptatibus*, run by the equestrian T. Caesonius Priscus.
125. Suet., *Tib.* 73.1.
126. Suet., *Tib.* 73.2.
127. Eutrop., *Brev.* 7.11.
128. Suet., *Calig.* 13.1: *Sic imperium adeptus, populum Romanum, vel dicam hominum genus, voti compotem fecit, exoptatissimus princeps maximae parti provincialium ac militum, quod infantem plerique cognoverant, sed et universae plebi urbanae ob memoriam Germanici patris miserationemque prope afflictae domus.*
129. Suet., *Calig.* 15.1.
130. Dio 59.1.1–2.
131. Dio 59.1.5–59.2.1.
132. Suet., *Calig.* 15.2.
133. *CIL* VI, 886 = 31192 = *ILS* 180: *Ossa | Agrippinae M. Agrippae [f.] | divi Aug. neptis, uxoris | Germanici Caesaris, | matris C. Caesaris Aug. | Germanici, principis.*
134. Suet., *Calig.* 15.2. A brass *sestertius* (*RIC* I, 55) was minted showing the two-wheeled *carpentum*, which carried the *imago* of Agrippina on the reverse, and the inscription *MEMORIAE AGRIPPINAE*; on the obverse is a finely-detailed portrait of the lady with the legend *AGRIPPINA M F MAT C CAESARIS AVGVSTI.*
135. Suet., *Calig.* 15.2. At least one inscription attests the renamed month: see *CIL* XI, 5745 (Foligno, Umbria) of C. Aetrius Naso (*praefectus* of *Cohors* I *Germanorum, tribunis militum* of *Legio* I *Italica*). The name appears to have still been in use in the fifth century, at the time Macrobius was writing his *Saturnalia: Mensis September principalem sui retinet appellationem: quem Germanici appellatione* (*Sat.* 1.12.36). The call to rename September echoes the proposal to rename November, cited by Dio: 'The senate urged upon Tiberius the request that the month of November, on the sixteenth day of which he had been born, should be called Tiberius: "What will you do, then, if there are thirteen Caesars?"' (Dio 57.18.2).
136. Gold *aureus: BMCRE* I.18, *RIC* I, 17. Silver *denarius: BMCRE* I.19, *RIC* I, 18; the obverse inscription on both coins reads *C CAESAR AVG GERM P M TR POT*, while the reverse reads *GERMANICVS CAES P C CAES AVG GERM.* It continues to be a highly sought after coin among modern numismatists.
137. *RIC* I, 35: obverse, bust of Germanicus surrounded by the legend *GERMANICVS CAESAR TI AVG F DIVI AVG N*; reverse, capitals *S C*, surrounded by the legend *C CAESAR DIVI AVG PRON AVG P M TR P IIII P P.*
138. *RIC* I, 57; *BMCRE* 93, 94.

139. Whether the coin was minted during the reign of Tiberius or of Caligula has been the subject of debate. According to the noted numismatist Curtis Clay of Chicago-based Harlan J. Berk, Ltd, '[Francis] Hobler, writing around 1860, shared the universal assumption of his time that the Germanicus *dupondii* were struck during Germanicus' lifetime, and the Agrippa *asses* during Agrippa's lifetime. There is, after all, nothing on the coins to indicate that a later emperor had struck them or that the honorees had already died! It was only during the twentieth century that these coins were redated to Caligula's reign. The chief arguments are: (1) The countermarks that are found on these middle bronzes, specifically TI AV and TI CAESAR ligate, are ones that otherwise occur on bronzes of Caligula, but not on bronzes of Tiberius. (2) Tiberius' bronze coins were struck with their die axes either upright or inverted, but Caligula's mint introduced a change: his bronze coins show the inverted die axis only. The Germanicus *dupondii* and Agrippa *asses* followed the Caligulan practice: axes inverted only. That seems to be powerful evidence that these coins were struck not by Tiberius, but by Caligula. (3) During the reign of Caligula, the mint of Caesaraugusta in Spain copied various obverse types from Caligula's bronze coinage, including the obv. type of the Agrippa *asses*. Those copied obv. types were: bare head l. of Caligula, radiate head l. of Divus Augustus, bare head l. of Germanicus, draped bust r. of Agrippina I, and finally head of Agrippa l. wearing rostral crown (*RPC* 373–386). But if the Agrippa *asses* were struck by Caligula, the Germanicus *dupondii* probably were too'. Clay also proposes an intriguing new explanation of these two commemorative bronze coins, which he has kindly permitted me to publish here, that 'Caligula may have allowed the Senate to melt down the bronze coins of Tiberius, whom the Senate hated, just as Claudius later allowed the Senate to melt down the bronze coins of Caligula himself. The metal from the melted down Tiberius bronzes was then used to strike coins for Caligula's great grandfather Agrippa and his father Germanicus, who, had they only lived longer, would have been the successors of Augustus instead of Tiberius and, by implication, would have been better emperors! Caligula didn't add his own name to the coins because that would have spoiled the impression they were intended to give of having been struck long before his accession to the throne. An interesting attempt to rewrite history, or at least to express dissatisfaction with the course it had actually taken'. (http://www.forumancientcoins.com/board/index.php?topic=70716.0). Compare to the bronze statue of Germanicus found at Amelia.

140. *SIGNIS RECEPT[IS] DEVICTIS GERM[ANIS]*. It was pure propaganda; cf. Tac., *Ann.* 1.60. The third and last of the eagle standards lost at Teutoburg was not recovered until 40 CE, when it was found among the Chauci: Dio 60.8.7.

141. *RIC* I, 61; *RSC* 2b.

142. *RPC* 2471, *SNG Aulock* 2201, *S* 413, Klose 29. The obverse shows the inscription ΓΑΙΟΝ ΚΑΙΣΑΡΑ [ΓΕΡΜΑΝΙΚΟΝ ΕΠΙ ΟΥΙΟΛΑ], with a laureate head of Caligula facing right; the reverse shows the draped bust of Agrippina facing the bare head of Germanicus, surrounded by the legend ΓΕΡΜΑΝΙΚΟΣ ΑΓΡΙΠΠΕΙΝΑΝ ΖΜΥΡΝΑΙΩ ΜΗΝΟΦΑΝΗΣ.

143. *RPC* 991, 994; Svoronos 202.

144. *BMCRE* 81; *RPC* 1022.

145. Suet., *Calig.* 15.2.

146. Dio 59.3.3.

147. Plut., *Ant.* 87.3.

148. Suet., *Calig.* 10.2.

149. Suet., *Calig.* 10.1; 24.1.

150. Suet., *Calig.* 23.2.

151. Suet., *Calig.* 50.2–3; 51.1.

152. Eutrop., *Brev.* 7.12.3; Levick (1990), p. 152.

153. Suet., *Calig.* 48.1–2: *Prius quam prouincia decederet, consilium iniit nefandae atrocitatis legiones, quae post excessum Augusti seditionem olim mouerant, contrucidandi, quod et patrem suum Germanicum ducem et se infantem tunc obsedissent, uixque a tam praecipiti cogitatione reuocatus, inhiberi nullo modo potuit quin decimare uelle perseueraret. uocatas itaque ad contionem inermes, atque etiam gladiis depositis, equitatu armato circumdedit. sed cum uideret suspecta re plerosque dilabi ad resumenda si qua*

uis fieret arma, profugit contionem confestimque urbem omnem petit, deflexa omni acerbitate in senatum, cui ad auertendos tantorum dedecorum rumores palam minabatur.

154. Suet., *Calig.* 19.3; 46.
155. Suet., *Calig.* 47.
156. Sen., *Constant.* 18.2; Suet., *Calig.* 56.2; Dio 59.29.1.
157. Suet., *Calig.* 58.1–3.
158. Joseph., *Ant. Jud.* 19.190–200; Suet., *Calig.* 59. The child was named Iulia Drusilla.

Chapter 8: The Germanicus Tradition
1. Dio 60.1.1–4; Suet., *Div. Claud.* 10.1–2.
2. Eutrop., *Brev.* 7.13.1.
3. Suet., *Div. Claud.* 10.4.
4. Levick (1990), pp. 31–9.
5. Suet., *Div. Claud.* 11.2. Suetonius records that, during his second consulship, Claudius presided at games sponsored by Caligula and was received by the spectators with the greeting *Germanici fratri!* ('all hail to the brother of Germanicus!') (*Div. Claud.* 7.1).
6. Suet., *Div. Claud.* 11.2; *Calig.* 3.2; Dio 60.6.1–2.
7. AS Inv. No. IX A 63. It measures 12cm high and is set in a gold rim.
8. *RIC* I, 105–6; *C* 9; *S*1905: the obverse shows a profile of Germanicus, surrounded by the words *GERMANICVS CAESAR TI AVG F DIVI AVG N*, while the reverse shows the large letters *S C* in the centre, surrounded by the inscription *TI CLAVDIVS CAESAR AVG GERM P M TR P IMP P P.*
9. Suet., *Div. Claud.* 11.2.
10. The frieze is in the collection of the Museo Nazionale, Ravenna. The figure of Germanicus bears comparison with the statue in the Louvre.
11. Osgood (2011), p. 65.
12. Suet., *Div. Claud.* 27.1; Tac., *Ann.* 12.25. Griffin (1984), pp. 27.
13. Plut., *Ant.* 87.3; Suet., *Ner.* 5.2; Tac., *Ann.* 25. On Nero's name after his adoption by Claudius, see Griffin (1984), p. 29, citing *ILS* 224 and *BMCRE*, Nero, nos. 84 and 90.
14. Suet., *Div. Claud.* 29.1.
15. Claudius: Galatas (2008). Britannicus: Barrett (1996), pp. 137–9, cf. pp. 171–2, questioning whether it was murder or by accident.
16. Tac., *Ann.* 14.7; Suet., *Ner.* 5.2. She had no other children and the direct bloodline of Germanicus ended with her.
17. Dio, Suetonius and Tacitus all give different and incompatible accounts of how she died. For an assessment of the sources, see Barrett (1996), pp. 181–95; Griffin (1984), pp. 73–6.
18. Eutrop., *Brev.* 7.14.
19. Claudia: Suet., *Ner.* 35.3. Nero: *ibid.* 49, 57. See also Griffin (1984), pp. 189–96.
20. *RIC* II, 442; *C* 12; *BMCRE* 293: the obverse shows the bare head of Germanicus facing left, with the inscription *GERMANICVS CAESAR TI AVG F DIVI AVG N*; the reverse shows the large letters *S C* and the inscription *IMP T CAES DIVI VESP F AVG REST.*
21. Joseph., *Ant. Iud.* 18.53. Copies of C. Lutorius Priscus' poem deploring the wasteful death of Germanicus were probably still in circulation: Tac., *Ann.* 3.49.
22. Pliny, *Ep.* 3.5.4: *quibus omnia quae cum Germanis gessimus bella collegit.*
23. Tac., *Ann.* 1.69.
24. Cassiodorus, *Chronica* 45.4–5.
25. Suet., *Calig.* 1–7.
26. Dio 57.18.3.
27. John Xiphilinus, a monk in the eleventh century, was commissioned to provide a précis of Cassius Dio's *Roman History* by the Byzantine emperor Michael VII Doukas. The annals of the twelfth-century Byzantine chronicler Joannes Zonaras also contain many extracts from Dio.
28. Tac., *Ann.* 3.16: *neque tamen occulere debui narratum ab iis qui nostram ad iuventam duraverunt.*
29. Tac., *Ann.* 2.83: *pleraque manent: quaedam statim omissa sunt aut vetustas oblitteravit.*

30. Hekster (2008), p.128. The *Feriale Duranum* is named after Dura, the fort of *cohors* XX *Palmyrenorum*, where the document was found in a room in the Temple of Artemis Azzanathkona. For a full discussion, see Fishwick (1988).
31. Gain (1976), pp.1–13.
32. Le Boeuffle (1975/2003); Gain (1976).
33. Shipley (1924), p.334.
34. Barrett and Yardley (2008), pp.xxvi–xxvii. See also Oliver (1951).
35. The first complete edition, uniting all sixteen books, did not appear in print until 1607.
36. Boursault (1694), reported in *Théâtre de Feu Monsieur Boursault* (2nd edn, Paris, 1725), pp.51–134. The whole stage play can be read at http://www.theatre-classique.fr/pages/programmes/edition.php?t=../documents/boursault_germanicus.xml
37. Jacques Pradon is also known as Nicolas Pradon: http://www.theatre-classique.fr/pages/programmes/edition.php?t=../documents/boursault_germanicus.xml
38. According to Baker *et al.* (1812), p.264, 'this piece was neither acted nor printed, but was left in a finished state by the author, and the manuscript was in the possession of the late Sir Joseph Mawbey' – a curious conclusion, as separately reported by Hipwell (1890): 'Report XI, part vii. p.43 of the Hist. MSS. Commission, will form a fitting addition to the account of Cooke found in 'Dict. Nat. Biog.' Vol. xii, p.95 – 'The Manuscripts of the Duke of Leeds at Hornby Castle, Yorkshire. Cooke, Thomas. Germanicus, a tragedy. A note is prefixed by the Duke of Leeds, dated Feb. 25, 1796, that he believes the dedication is to his father, and that it must have been written about 1731; of the author he knew nothing. Pp. 145, 4to".
39. The play is listed in Baker *et al.* (1812), p.264.
40. Smit (1975–1983), pp.757–758: http://www.dbnl.org/tekst/smit021kall01_01/smit021kall01_01_0061.php.
41. Rabbe *et al.* (1836), p.1599; Smit (1975–1983), p.758.
42. Antoine Vincent Arnault, *Germanicus* (1817), Act I, Scene 1: the quotation roughly translates as 'One believes that when one knows the people and their whims, | One knows the virtues of a rival as well as his vices'.
43. Charles-Ernest Beulé, *Le sang de Germanicus* (Paris, 1869): 'Il semble que, dans les époques de décadence, la vertu elle-même ne soit qu'une amorce de la servitude et que la popularité devienne un poison qui se tourne contre la patrie'.
44. Beulé, *ibid.*: 'Nous rêvions la toute-puissance pour le bonheur du monde, et le monde entier épuisé, avili, dégradé par cette puissance monstrueuse, maudira-t-il à jamais le sang de Germanicus?'
45. See Carlo Vitali, 'Handel – True or False', *Classical Voice* magazine, (translated at http://www.operatoday.com/content/2011/05/handel_true_or_.php: the libretto is based on *Annales* 2.14–16 and 41.
46. Italian conductor and musicologist Ottaviano Tenerani came across a copy of a 'serenata' that was signed with the name of 'Hendl' in the Conservatorio Cherubini in Florence in 2007. His initial hypothesis was that *Germanico* must be one of the first works written by the young Händel during his stay in Italy (1706–1709). Others dispute this and suggest either of two composers who wrote celebratory serenatas for the court of Vienna, Attilio Ariosti or Giovanni Bononcini. The identity of the librettist has been suggested as imperial court poet Donato Cupeda or his vice Pietro Andrea Bernardoni.
47. The overture and arias were found by Dr Michael Maul at Frankfurt University Library and identified as coming from *Germanicus*.
48. The painting is now in the National Gallery of Art, Washington, DC: inventory number 1963.8.1. See *A Collector's Cabinet, National Gallery of Art, Washington, D.C.* (1998), no. 49, fig. 21.
49. Ashmolean Musem, Oxford: inv. no. WA 1989, 74; oil on canvas. See http://www.artfund.org/artwork/1615/the-gemma-tiberiana-cameo-of-the-glorification-of-germanicus. The printer Paulus Pontius made an engraving of the painting, which he used in an appendix on gems in *Dissertatio de Gemma Tiberiana* to Albert Rubens' *De Re Vestiaria Veterum* in 1665, published posthumously.
50. The painting is now in Minneapolis Institute of Art, Minneapolis: inventory number 58.28.

51. Tac., *Ann.* 2.71–5.
52. Gerard de Lairesse's (1641–1711) *La mort de Germanicus, victime de jalousie de Tibère* hangs in the Gemäldegalerie Alte Meister, Museumslandschaft Hessen Kassel, Germany. Friedrich Heinrich Füger's (1751–1818) *Death of Germanicus* hangs in the Oesterreichische Galerie im Belvedere, Vienna, Austria.
53. It is now in a private collection.
54. The painting is now in Yale University Art Gallery, New Haven: inventory number 1947.16. For a discussion of the painting, see Nemerov (1998); Staley (1965), pp. 16–17.
55. Tac., *Ann.* 3.1.
56. The painting is now in the Tate Collection, London: inventory number T03365; oil on canvas.
57. It is now in the Tate Gallery, London: inventory number N00523. It is catalogued in Thornbury (1862), Vol. 2, p. 381. In his biography of Turner, art critic Philip Gilbert Hamerton (1879, p. 279) writes: 'It is a fine composition of its class, giving a grand idea of the enormous palace of the Caesars, in which Tiberius and Augusta remained invisible whilst the people of Rome received Agrippina with the most touching demonstrations of sympathy and sorrow. The architectural invention in the palace is not very elaborate, and it may be open to the criticism of architects, but the ideas of vastness, majesty, and a haughty domination are conveyed very impressively. The smaller masses are not altogether so fortunate; they have an arranged look, like the architecture in Martin's pictures; and one of them, that above the bridge, is in very bad perspective. The scene is lighted by slanting rays of sunset, which, with the cast shadows and the mist in the atmosphere, afforded Turner an opportunity for one of his poetical effects of light, shadow, and reflection'. He noted, however, that 'the picture will not bear historical criticism'. Turner had placed the action in Rome, when, in fact, Agrippina had landed at Brundisium. Hamerton (*ibid.*, p. 280) continued: 'The whole description, as given by Tacitus, implies an imposing entry into Rome by land on an incomparably vaster scale than the few groups of figures in the picture. Turner, with his half-a-dozen people on the right, his four boats on the left, with people in balconies and on shore, renders the human interest of the scene so inadequately, that we are driven to imagine it over again for ourselves with the help of the Roman historian'.
58. Dawson (1972).
59. Bust: Farrer (2011), p. 72 (entry for Etruria, 24 June 1774). Intaglio: Wedgwood (1873), Section II, p. 29, item 25; the bust of young Germanicus also appears on p. 86, and the cameo of Caesar Germanicus (item 1614) on p. 25.
60. A naked statue in the Louvre (inventory number 1207) with its head inscribed with the artist's name Kleomenes of Kleone is popularly identified as Germanicus, as well as the alternatives Julius Caesar and Marcellus, despite having been dated to 50 BCE. An eighteenth-century copy of it stands in the grounds of Schloss Nordkirchen, 'the Westfalian Versailles', near Münster, Germany.
61. Kleist: Helbling (1975). Fouqué?s: Stockinger (2000).
62. Luden (1825), p. 264: 'Und auch dann noch blieb in den verwilderten Menschen eine so brennende Gluth und eine so wahnsinnige Lust zu Schwert und Blut, daß Germanicus für nöthig hielt, diese rasenden Menschen über den Rhein zu führen, in Teutschlands friedliche Gaue hinein, damit sie ihre Gluth kühleten, ihre Lust stilleten in der Ermordung teutscher Menschen, die den Römern unter allen Verhältnissen für Feinde galte'.
63. Huscher (1826). It may have been performed as early as 1812, as it appears in *Der Sammler* ('ein Unterhaltungsblatt') dated to that year.
64. Breysig (1865), (1892); Dörrenberg (1909); Höfer (1885); Hoffmann (1816); Huscher (1826); Kessler (1905); Knoke (1887); Linsmayer (1875); Reinking (1855); Viertel (1901). Many of these books are available to download as digital copies from the internet.
65. See the lecture notes of Sebastian and Paul Hensel, 1882–1886, reprinted as Mommsen and Demandt (1996), pp. 134–7. Also Mommsen (1878).
66. The painting hangs in Hall 13 of the Bayerische Staatsgemäldesammlungen/Neue Pinatotek, Munich: inventory number WAF 771; oil on canvas.
67. Tac., *Ann.* 2.41; Ov., *Pont.* 4.2 ff.

68. http://www.pinakothek.de/carl-theodor-von-piloty?curImg=2 ('In den Augen der Zeitgenossen erschien sie als moralisches Beispiel deutschen Wesens, das in der Stunde des Untergangs stolz und ungebrochen seinem Schicksal entgegensieht').
69. The painting hangs in the Nationalgalerie, Staatliche Museen, Berlin: inventory number A II 1001; oil on canvas. It is reproduced as an engraving in Horne (1901), Müller-Baden (1904), and here, in fig. 4.
70. e.g. Christ (1956); Norkus (1963); Lindemann (1967); Timpe (1968); Dreyer (2009); Wolters (2009). Of particular note is Wamser *et al.* (2004), which brings together the latest insights from archaeological surveys across Germany.
71. Germanicus appears in Isaac (1992) on just one page in a volume of 510 pages, and in Millar (1993) on just two pages in a tome of 587.
72. Graves (1934).
73. Wishart (2002).
74. See Claassen (2006) on the challenges of translating van Wyk Louw's work from Afrikaans into English.
75. Dando-Collins (2008).
76. http://ssd.jpl.nasa.gov/sbdb.cgi?sstr=10208 and http://89.202.249.94:81/ricerca_asteroidi.asp. It was subsequently linked to observations from 1987. My brother Martin J. Powell, an archaeo-astronomer writes in an email, 8 October 2012: 'Asteroid "10208 Germanicus" comes closest to the Earth about every 521 days on average (1.42 years). The interval between each close approach isn't always the same because Germanicus moves at a varying speed as it orbits the Sun (the Earth's speed also varies during the year, but not as much as Germanicus'). The dates when it next comes closest to us are 15 April 2013, 30 October 2014, 8 March 2016, 8 August 2017. Of these, the 2017 encounter will be the best, i.e. the closest and brightest. Germanicus will then be 75.3 million miles (121.3 million kms) from Earth, though it will still be fainter than Pluto. After 2017 the next date will be 31 January 2019, when it will be positioned in Cancer, but it will be rather more distant and fainter then. The information was derived using NASA-JPL's Small-Body Database Browser.'

Chapter 9: Assessment

1. Val. Max. 4.3.3.
2. Vermillion (1987).
3. Tac., *Ann.* 2.73: *quantum clementia, temperantia, veteris bonis artibus praestitisset.*
4. Clausewitz (1832), Book 1, Chapter 3: 'Der Mut ist doppelter Art: einmal Mut gegen die persön-liche Gefahr, und dann Mut gegen die Verantwortlichkeit, sei es vor dem Richterstuhl irgend-einer äußeren Macht oder der inneren, nämlich des Gewissens'.
5. Suet., *Calig.* 3: *benivolentiam singularem conciliandaeque hominum gratiae ac promerendi amoris mirum et efficax studium.*
6. Dio 57.18.8: Τιβέριον ἐπαίτιον ἔπραττεν, ἀλλὰ συνελόντι εἰπεῖν ἐν ὀλίγοις τῶν πώποτε οὔτ᾽ ἐξήμαρτέ τι ἐς τὴν ὑπάρξασαν αὐτῷ τύχην οὔτ᾽ αὐτὸς ὑπ᾽ ἐκείνης διεφθάρη: δυνηθεὶς γοῦν πολλάκις καὶ παρ᾽ ἑκόντων, οὐχ ὅτι τῶν στρατιωτῶν ἀλλὰ καὶ τοῦ δήμου τῆς τε βουλῆς, τὴν αὐτοκράτορα λαβεῖν.
7. Tac., *Ann.* 2.72: *visuque et auditu iuxta venerabilis, cum magnitudinem et gravitatem summae fortunae retineret, invidiam et adrogantiam effugerat.*
8. Suet., *Calig.* 1; cf. Dio 57.18.8.
9. Dio 57.18.8.
10. Shotter (1992), p. 36.
11. Suet., *Calig.* 3.
12. Ov., *Pont.* 2.5.45–6: *Te dicente prius studii fuit impetus illi | teque habet elicias qui sua uerba tuis.*
13. Green (1989), p. 265.
14. For a discussion of the Germanicus Tradition, see Liebenam (1891); Hurley (1989).
15. W. Shakespeare, *Measure for Measure*, Act II, scene 1, 43.
16. See Bowden (1913), p. 162 and Woodman (1998), p. 40.

17. Krebs (2011), online at http://www.historytoday.com/christopher-krebs/tacitus-continuing-message.
18. Tac., *Hist.* 1.50: *nec iam recentia saevae pacis exempla.* Brown (1981).
19. e.g. Syme (1958), Vol. 1, pp. 254, 418.
20. Shotter (1968).
21. Daitz (1960). There may have been an allegorical dimension to Tacitus' story-telling, also: see Shannon (2011).
22. Tac., *Ann.* 1.1: *sine ira et studio*; cf. Tac., *Hist.* 1.1, 'without partiality or without hatred'.
23. Downey (1983), pp. 109–10. Bowden (1913), p. 166 argues that Tacitus 'did not traduce the character of Tiberius, but portrayed it essentially as it was known to the Roman world at the time of the writing of the *Annals.* Unfortunately for Tiberius this estimate was based largely on his conduct during the latter and unhappy part of his reign and did not, apparently, give due consideration to the early and successful part of his reign'.
24. Tiberius treated his own son impeccably fairly, giving him the same legal powers as Germanicus at the same points in his career. Drusus the Younger received the *tribunicia potestas* when he reached the age of 35; Germanicus died aged 34.
25. Suet., *Calig.* 1: *ad componendum Orientis statum expulsus.*
26. Foremost of whom were the Praetorian Cohort commanders L. Aelius Seianus and Naevius Sertorius Macro.
27. Green (1989), p. 216.
28. Levick (1976/1999), pp. 66, 68, and 207, n. 29. See also Sutherland (1938).
29. See especially Tac., *Ann.* 2.73.3, 3.14.1–2; cf. 2.69.3, 79.1, 3.12.4, 13.2.
30. Syme (1981) believes the cause of Germanicus' death was an infection he brought with him from Egypt or caught in Syria.
31. Suet., *Calig.* 1: *Cappadociam in provinciae formam redegisset.*
32. Tac., *Ann.* 4.57; Kienast (2009), pp. 138–9.

Bibliography

Ancient Authors

Ammianus Marcellinus, *Res Gestae a Fine Corneli Taciti* (*Roman History*).

Augustus, *Res Gestae* (*Deeds of Augustus*).

Aulus Gellius, *Noctes Atticae* (*Attic Nights*).

Caesar, *Commentarii de Bello Gallico* (*The Gallic War*).

Cassiodorus, Χρονικῶν (*Chronicles*).

Cassius Dio, Ῥωμαϊκὴ Ἱστορία (*Roman History*).

Diodorus Siculus, Διόδωρου Σικελιώτου Βιβλιοθήκη Ἱστορική (*Library of History*).

Eutropius, *Breviarium Historiae Romanae* (*Brief History of the Romans*).

Florus, *Epitome de T. Livio Bellorum Omnium Annorum* (*Epitome of Livy*).

Frontinus, *Strategemata* (*Stratagems*).

Germanicus Caesar, *Aratus – Phaenomena*.

Hippokrates of Kos, *Peri Agmon* (*On Fractures*).

Horace, *Carmina* (*Odes*).

Josephus, *Antiquitates Iudaicae* (*Antiquities of the Jews*).

Josephus, *Contra Apionem* (*Against Apion*).

Josephus, Ἱστορία Ἰουδαϊκοῦ πολέμου πρὸς Ῥωμαίους (*Wars of the Jews* or *The History of the Destruction of Jerusalem*).

Livy, *Ab Urbe Condita* (*History from the Foundation of Rome*).

Livy, *Periochae* (*Extracts*).

Obsequens, *Ab Anno Urbis Conditae Du Prodigiorum Liber* (*Book of Prodigies Since the Foundation of the City*).

Ovid (?), *Consolatio ad Liviam* (*Poem of Consolation to Livia on the Death of Her Son, Drusus Nero*).

Ovid, *Epistulae Ex Ponto* (*Letters from Pontus*).

Ovid, *Fasti* (*Holy Days*).

Ovid, *Tristia* (*Sorrows*).

Pliny the Elder, *Naturalis Historia* (*Natural History*).

Pliny the Younger, *Epistulae Selectae* (*Selected Letters*).

Plutarch, *Antonios* (*Life of Antonius*).

Plutarch, *De Invidia et Odio* (*On Envy and Hate*).

Polybius, Οι Ιστορίες (*The Histories*).

Propertius, *Elegiae* (*Elegies*).

Ptolemy, Γεωγραφικὴ Ὑφήγησις (*Geography, Cosmographia*).

Senatus Consultum de Cn. Pisone Patre.

Seneca the Younger, *De Consolatione ad Marciam* (*To Marcia on Consolation*).

Seneca the Younger, *De Consolatione ad Polybium* (*To Polybius on Consolation*).

Seneca the Younger, *De Constantia Sapientis* (*On the Constancy of the Wise Man*).

Strabo, Γεωγραφικά (*Geography*).

Suetonius, *De Vita Caesarum* (*Lives of the Caesars*).

Suetonius, *De Grammaticis et Rhetoribus* (*On Teachers of Grammar and Rhetoric*).

Tabula Hebana.

Tabula Siarensis.

Tacitus, *Ab Excessu Divi Augusti* (*Annales, The Annals*).

Tacitus, *De Origine et Situ Germanorum* (*Germania*).

Ulpian, *Digesta* (*Digest*).
Valerius Maximus, *Factorum ac Dictorum Memorabilium* (*Memorable Deeds and Sayings*).
Velleius Paterculus, *Historiae Romanae* (*Compendium of Roman History*).
Zonaras, Ἐπιτομὴ Ἱστοριῶν (*Extracts of History*).

Modern Authors

Aalders, G.J.D. (1961), 'Germanicus und Alexander der Grosse', *Historia* 10, pp. 382–4.
Abbott, F.F. and Johnson, A.C. (1926), *Municipal Administration in the Roman Empire*, Princeton.
Adler, W. (1993), *Studien zur germansichen Bewaffnung: Waffenmitgabe und Kampfesweise im Niederel-begebiet und im Freien Germanien um Christi Geburt*, Bonn.
Africa, T.W. (1971), 'Urban Violence in Imperial Rome', *Journal of Interdisciplinary History* 2.1, pp. 3–21.
Akveld, W.F. (1961), *Germanicus, Historische studies uitgegeven vanwege het Instituut voor Geschiedenis der Rijksuniversiteit te Utrecht. no. 18*, Groningen.
Alföldy, G. (1974), *Noricum*, London.
Allen, K. (1922), 'The *fasti* of Ovid and the Augustan Propaganda', *The American Journal of Philology* 43.3, pp. 250–66.
Allen, S. (2001), *Celtic Warrior, 300BC–AD100*, Oxford.
Allen, W. Jr. (1947), 'The Death of Agrippa Postumus', *Transactions and Proceedings of the American Philological Association* 78, pp. 131–9.
Asskamp, R. and Schäfer, C. (eds) (2009), *Projekt Römerschiff: Nachbau und Erprobung für die Ausstellung Imperium – Konflikt – Mythos. 2000 Jahre Varusschlacht*, Hamburg.
Austin, N.E. and Rankov, N.B. (1995), *Exploratio: Military and Political Intelligence in the Roman World from the Second Punic War to the Battle of Adrianople*, London.
Baatz, D. and Herrmann, F.-R. (eds) (2002), *Die Römer in Hessen*, revised edition, Hamburg.
Baehr, P. (1887), *Die Örtlichkeit der Schlacht auf Idistaviso*, Halle.
Baker, D.E., Reed, I. and Jones, S. (eds) (1812), *Biographia Dramatica: or A Companion to the Playhouse, Vol. 2 – Names of dramas: A–L*, London.
Baldwin Bowsky, M.W. (2004), 'Of Two Tongues: Acculturation at Roman Knossos', in G. Salmeri, A. Raggi and A. Baroni (eds), *Colonie romane nel mondo Greco*, Rome, pp. 133–4.
Balsdon, J.P.V.D. (1962), *Roman Women: Their History and Habits*, London.
Balsdon, J.P.V.D. (1969), *Life and Leisure in Ancient Rome*, London.
Balsdon, J.P.V.D. (1979), *Romans and Aliens*, London.
Bannon, C.J. (1997), *The Brothers of Romulus: Fraternal Pietas in Roman Law, Literature, and Society*, Princeton.
Barnes, T.D. (1998), 'Tacitus and the *Senatus Consultum de Cn. Pisone* Patre', *Phoenix* 52, pp. 125–48.
Barrett, A.A. (1989), *Caligula: The Corruption of Power*, New Haven.
Barrett, A.A. (1996), *Agrippina: Sex, Power, and Politics in the Early Empire*, New Haven.
Barrett, A.A. (2002), *Livia: First Lady of Imperial Rome*, New Haven.
Barrett, A.A. (2006), 'Augustus and the Governor's Wives', *Rheinisches Museum für Philologie* 149, pp. 129–47.
Barrett, A.A. and Yardley, J.C. (2008), *The Annals: The Reigns of Tiberius, Claudius, and Nero*, Oxford.
Bartels, J. (2009), 'Der Tod des Germanicus und seine epigraphische Dokumentation: Ein neues Exemplar des *senatus consultum de Cn. Pisone patre* aus Genf', *Chiron* 39, pp. 1–9.
Beacham, R.C. (1999), *Spectacle Entertainments of Early Imperial Rome*, New Haven.
Bean, G.E. (1979), *Aegean Turkey*, second edition, London.
Beard, M. (2007), *The Roman Triumph*, Cambridge, Mass.
Beard, M., North, J.A. and Price, S.R.F. (1998), *Religions of Rome: A History*, Cambridge.
Bechert, T. and Willems, W.J.H. (1997), *De Romeinse rijksgrens tussen Moezel en Noordzeekust*, Utrecht.
Beesly, A.H. (1876), *Germanicus, or Extracts from the Annals of Tacitus*, London.
Berke, S. *et al.* (2009), *Corpus der römischen Funde im europäischen Barbaricum, Deutschland, 7: Land Nordrhein-Westfalen, Landesteile Westfalen und Lippe*, Bonn.
Bertrandy, G. and Rémy, B. (2000), '*Legio XII Fulminata*', in Y. Le Bohec (ed.), *Les légions de Rome sous le Haut-Empire*, Lyon, pp. 253–7.

Besteman, J.C., Bos, J.M., Gerrets, D.A., Heidinga, H.A. and de Koning, J. (1999), *The Excavations at Wijnaldum: Reports on Frisia in Roman and Medieval Times, Volume 1*, Rotterdam.

Betzig, L. (1992), 'Roman Monogamy', *Ethology and Sociobiology* 13, pp. 351–83.

Beulé, M. (1869), *Le Sang de Germanicus*, Paris.

Bishop, M.C. (2002), *Lorica Segmentata Volume 1: A Handbook of Articulated Plate Armour, JRMES* Monograph 1, Duns (available online at http://www.mcbishop.co.uk/armatura/vol1.htm).

Bishop, M.C. and Coulston, J.C.N. (2006), *Roman Military Equipment from the Punic Wars to the Fall of Rome*, Oxford.

Blumberg, C.G. (1697), *Der Eichelstein: das ist* Neronis Claudi Drusi monumentum, *Oder das zu Mainz berühmte ist zerstörte Ehren-Grab*, Chemnitz.

Boatwright, M.T. (2000), *Hadrian and the Cities of the Roman Empire*, Princeton.

Bodel, J.P. (1999), 'Punishing Piso', *American Journal of Philology* 120.1, pp. 43–63.

Bogaers, J.E. (1969), '*Cohortes Breucorum*', *Berichte van de Rijksdienst voor het Oudheidkundig Bodemonderzoek* 19, pp. 27–50.

Bonamente, G. and Segoloni, M.P. (eds) (1987), *Germanico. La persona, la personalità, il personaggio nel bimillenario dalla nascita: atti del convegno, Macerata-Perugia, 9–11 maggio 1986*, Rome.

Borzsák, S. (1969), 'Das Germanicusbild des Tacitus', *Latomus* 28, pp. 588–600.

Borzsák, S. (1982), 'Alexander der Grosse als Muster taciteischer Heldendarstellung', *Gymnasium* 89, pp. 37–56.

Boschung, D. (1993), 'Die Bildnistypen der iulisch-claudischen Kaiserfamilie: ein kritischer Forschungsbericht', *Journal of Roman Archaeology* 6, pp. 39–79.

Bosworth, A.B. (2004), 'Mountain and Molehill? Cornelius Tacitus and Quintus Curtius', *Classical Quarterly* 54, pp. 551–67.

Boursault, E. (1694), *Germanicus: tragédie*, Paris. (Full text at http://www.theatre-classique.fr/pages/ programmes/edition.php?t=../documents/Boursault_Germanicus.xml).

Bowden, E.P. (1913), 'Did Tacitus in the Annals Traduce the Character or Tiberius', *The Classical Weekly* 6.21, pp. 162–6.

Braccesi, L. (1991), *Alessandro e la Germania*, Rome.

Braund, D. (1996), *Ruling Roman Britain: Kings, Queens, Governors and Emperors from Julius Caesar to Agricola*, London.

Braund, D. (1984), *Rome and the Friendly King: The Character of Client Kingship*, Beckenham.

Braunert, H. (1957), 'Der römische Provinzialzensus und der Schätzungsbericht des Lukas-Evangeliums', *Historia* 6, pp. 192–214.

Breysig, A.A.B. (1865), *Emendationen zum Scholiasten des Germanicus*, Posen.

Breysig, A.A.B. (1892), *Germanicus*, Rome.

Bridger, C.J. (1984), 'The *Pes Monetalis* and *Pes Drusianus* in Xanten', *Britannia* 15, pp. 85–98.

Brouwer, M. (1993), *De Romeinse tijd in Nederland*, Amsterdam.

Brown, I.C. (1981), 'Tacitus and a Space for Freedom', *History Today* 31.4, pp. 11–15 (available online at http://www.historytoday.com/irene-brown/tacitus-and-space-freedom).

Brunt, P.A. (1974), 'C. Fabricius Tuscus and an Augustan Dilectus', *Zeitschrift für Papyrologie und Epigraphik* 13, pp. 161–85.

Brunt, P.A. (1975), 'The Administrators of Roman Egypt', *Journal of Roman Studies* 65, pp. 124–47.

Bruun, P. (1999), 'Coins and the Roman Imperial Government', in Paul and Ierardi (1999), pp. 19–40.

Burmeister, S. and Rottmann, J. (2015), *Ich Germanicus: Feldherr – Priester – Superstar*, Varusschlacht im Osnabrücker Land, Darmstadt.

Burn, A.R. (1952), *The Government of the Roman Empire from Augustus to the Antonines*, London.

Butcher, K. (2003), *Roman Syria and the Near East*, London.

Campbell, J.B. (1984), *The Emperor and the Roman Army, 31 BC–AD 235*, Oxford.

Campbell, J.B. (1994), *The Roman Army, 31 BC–AD 337: A Sourcebook*, London.

Campbell, D.B. (2006), *Roman Legionary Fortresses, 27 BC–AD 378*, Oxford.

Campbell, D.B. (2009), 'Secrets from the Soil: The archaeology of Augustus' military bases', *Ancient Warfare*, Special Issue 1, pp. 10–16.

Campbell, D.B. (2010), 'Women in Roman forts: residents, visitors or barred from entry?', *Ancient Warfare* 4.6, pp. 48–53.

Carcopino, J. (1940), *Daily Life in Ancient Rome. The People and the City at the Height of the Empire*, New Haven.

Carpenter, R. (1973), *Beyond the Pillars of Hercules: the classical world seen through the eyes of its discoverers*, London.

Carroll, M. (2001), *Romans, Celts and Germans: The German Provinces of Rome*, Stroud.

Carter, J.B. and Morris, S.P. (eds) (1995), *The Ages of Homer: A Tribute to Emily Townsend Vermeule*, Austin.

Casson, L. (1974), *Travel in the Ancient World*, Baltimore.

Chadwick, N. (1970), *The Celts*, London.

Champlin, E. (2009), 'Itinera Tiberi', *Princeton/Stanford Working Papers in Classics*, Paper no. 030901 (available online at http://dx.doi.org/10.2139/ssrn.1427462).

Chevalier, R. (1976), *Roman Roads*, London.

Christ, K. (1956), *Drusus und Germanicus: der Eintritt der Römer in Germanien*, Paderborn.

Christ, K. (1977), 'Zur augusteischen Germanienpolitik', *Chiron* 7, pp. 149–205.

Christopherson, A.J. (1968), 'The Provincial Assembly of the Three Gauls in the Julio-Claudian Period', *Historia* 17, pp. 351–66.

Cilliers, L. and Retief, F.P. (2000), 'Poisons, Poisoning and the Drug Trade in Ancient Rome', *Akroterion* 45, pp. 88–100.

Claassen, J.M. (2006), 'Rendering Caesar: Thoughts on the Translation into English of N.P. van Wyk Louw's *Germanicus*'. *Akroterion* 51, pp. 57–69.

Claridge, A. (1998), *Rome: An Oxford Archaeological Guide*, Oxford.

Clausewitz, C. von (1832), *Vom Kriege*, Berlin.

Clayton, P.A. and Price, M. (1988), *The Seven Wonders of the Ancient World*, London.

Connolly, P. (1975), *The Roman Army*, London.

Connolly, P. (1978), *Hannibal and the Enemies of Rome*, London.

Connolly, P. (1988), 'Experiments with the Roman Saddle', *Exercitus: The Bulletin of the Ermine Street Guard* 2.5, pp. 71–6.

Connolly, P. (1998), *Greece and Rome at War*, London.

Cooley, A. (1989), 'The Moralizing Message of the *Senatus consultum de Cn. Pisone patre*', *Greece and Rome* 45, pp. 199–212.

Cooper, F. (1979), *Roman Realities*, Detroit.

Cordingley, R.A. and Richmond, I.A. (1927), 'The Mausoleum of Augustus', *Papers of the British School at Rome* 10, pp. 23–35.

Cowan, R. (2003), *Roman Legionary, 58 BC–AD 69*, Oxford.

Cowan, R. (2007), *Roman Battle Tactics, 109 BC–AD 313*, Oxford.

Cowan, R. (2010), 'Sticks and Stones: 'Low-tech' and improvised weapons', *Ancient Warfare* 4.6, pp. 44–7.

Cowell, F.R. (1962), *Cicero and the Roman Republic*, second edition, London.

Crawford, J.R. (1922), 'Drusus Junior on the Ara Pacis', *American Journal of Archaeology* 26, pp. 307–15.

Crook, J.A. (1967), *Law and Life of Rome*, London.

Cuff, D.B. (2010), *The Auxilia in Roman Britain and the Two Germanies from Augustus to Caracalla: Family, Religion and 'Romanization'*, Unpublished Doctoral Thesis, University of Toronto.

Cunliffe, B.W. (1975), *Rome and the Barbarians*, London.

Cunliffe, B.W. (ed.) (1994), *Oxford Illustrated Prehistory of Europe*, Oxford.

Cunliffe, B.W. (1997), *The Ancient Celts*, Oxford.

Cunliffe, B.W. (1998), *Greeks, Roman and Barbarians: Spheres of Influence*, London.

Cunliffe, B.W. (2001), *Facing the Ocean: The Atlantic and its Peoples, 8000 BC–AD 1500*, Oxford.

Cunliffe, B.W. (2008), *Europe Between The Oceans: 9000 BC–AD 1000*, New Haven.

Cüppers, H., Bernhard, H. and Boppert, W. (eds) (1990), *Die Römer in Rheinland-Pfalz*, Stuttgart.

Czysz, W., Dietz, K., Fischer, T. and Kellner, H.-J. (1995), *Die Römer in Bayern*, Stuttgart.

D'Amato, R. (2009), *Imperial Roman Naval Forces, 31 BC–AD 500*, Oxford.

D'Amato, R. and Sumner, G. (2009), *Arms and Armour of the Imperial Roman Soldier: From Marius to Commodus*, Barnsley.

Daitz, S.G. (1960), 'Tacitus' Technique of Character Portrayal', *American Journal of Philology* 81, pp. 30–52.

Damon, C. (1999), 'The Trial of Cn. Piso in Tacitus' *Annals* and the *Senatus consultum de Cn. Pisone patre*: New Light on Narrative Technique', *American Journal of Philology* 120, pp. 143–62.

Dando-Collins, S. (2008), *Blood of the Caesars: How the Murder of Germanicus led to the Fall of Rome*, New Jersey.

David, J.-M. (1996), *The Roman Conquests of Italy*, Oxford.

Davies, P.J.E. (2004), *Death and the Emperor: Roman Imperial Funerary Monuments from Augustus to Marcus Aurelius*, Austin.

Davies, R. (1989), *Service in the Roman Army* (eds D. Breeze and V.A. Maxfield), Edinburgh.

Dawson, K. (1972), *The Industrial Revolution*, London.

Delbrück, H. (1990), *History of the Art of War. Volume 2: The Barbarian Invasions* (trans. W.J. Renfroe, Jr.), Lincoln.

Dennison, M. (2010), *Livia: Empress of Rome: a biography*, London.

Desbat, A. (2005), *Lugdunum: Naissance d'une Capitale*, Lyon-Fourvière.

Detweiler, R. (1970), 'Historical Perspectives on the Death of Agrippa Postumus', *Classical Journal* 65, pp. 289–95.

Dilke, O.A.W. (1962), 'The Roman Surveyors', *Greece and Rome* 9, pp. 170–80.

Dilke, O.A.W. (1985), 'Ground Survey and Measurement in Roman Towns', in F. Grew and B. Hobley (eds), *Roman Urban Topography in Britain and the Western Empire* (Council for British Archaeology Research Report 59), pp. 6–13.

Dilke, O.A.W. (1998), *Greek and Roman Maps*, Baltimore.

Dixon, K.R. and Southern, P. (1992), *The Roman Cavalry from the First to the Third Century AD*, London.

Domaszewski, A. von (1903), 'Die Familie des Augustus auf der Ara Pacis', *Jh. Oest. Arch. I.*, pp. 57–60.

Dörrenberg, O. (1909), *Römerspuren und Römerkriege im nordwestlichen Deutschland*, Leipzig.

Downey, G. (1975), 'Tiberiana', *Aufstieg und Niedergang der römischen Welt* II.2, pp. 95–130.

Dreyer, B. (2009), *Arminius und der Untergang des Varus: Warum die Germanen keine Römer wurden*, Stuttgart.

Drinkwater, J.F. (1983), *Roman Gaul: The Three Provinces, 58 BC–AD 260*, London.

Dušanić, S. (2004), 'Roman Mining in Illyricum: Historical Aspects', in G. Urso (ed.), *Dall' Adriatico al Danubio: L'Illirico nell'età greca e romana*, Pisa, pp. 247–70.

Dzino, D. (2005), *Illyrian Policy of Rome in the Late Republic and Early Principate*, Unpublished Doctoral Thesis, University of Adelaide (available online at http://digital.library.adelaide.edu.au/dspace/bitstream/2440/37806/1/02whole.pdf).

Dzino, D. (2008), 'Deconstructing Illyrians: Zeitgeist, changing perceptions and the identity of peoples from ancient Illyricum', *Croatian Studies Review* 5, pp. 43–55.

Dzino, D. (2010), *Illyricum in Roman Politics: 229 BC–AD 68*, Cambridge.

Earl, D.C. (1968), *The Age of Augustus*, London.

Ebel-Zepauer, W. (2003), 'Die augusteischen Marschlager in Dorsten-Holsterhausen', *Germania* 81, pp. 539–55.

Ebel-Zepauer, W. (2005), 'Römer und Germanen in Dorsten-Holsterhausen', in H.-G. Horn *et al.* (eds), *Von Anfang an. Archäologie in Nordrhein-Westfalen* (Schriften zur Bodendenkmalpflege in Nordrhein-Westfalen 8), pp. 367–8.

Eck, W. (2003), *The Age of Augustus* (trans. D.L. Schneider), Oxford.

Eck, W. (2009), *Augustus und seine Zeit*, fifth edition, Munich.

Eck, W., Caballos, A. and Fernández, F. (eds) (1996), *Das senatus consultum de Cn. Pisone Patre*, Munich.

Edwards, C. (2007), *Death in Ancient Rome*, New Haven.

Eggers, H.J. (1976), 'Zur absoluten Chronologie der römischen Kaizerzeit im freien Germanien', *Aufstieg und Niedergang der römischen Welt* II.5.1, pp. 3–64.

Ehrenberg, V. (1953), '*imperium maius* in the Roman Republic', *American Journal of Philology* 74, pp. 113–36.

Elbe, J. von (1977), *Die Römer in Deutschland: Ausgrabungen, Fundstätten, Museen*, Gütersloh.

Elton, H. (1996), *Frontiers of the Roman Empire*, Bloomington.

Enckevort, H. van and Willems, W.J.H. (1994), 'Roman cavalry helmets in ritual hoards from the Kops Plateau at Nijmegen, The Netherlands', *Journal of Roman Military Equipment Studies* 5, pp. 125–37.

Engels, D. (1990), *Roman Corinth: An Alternative Model for the Classical City*, Chicago.

Erdkamp, P. (2005), *The Grain Market in the Roman Empire: A Social, Political and Economic Study*, Cambridge.

Erdkamp, P. (ed.) (2007), *A Companion to the Roman Army*, Oxford.

Esmonde Cleary, S. (2007), *Rome in the Pyrenees. Lugdunum and the Convenae from the First Century B.C. to the Seventh Century A.D.*, London.

Eubel, P.K. (1906), *Geschichte der Kölnischen Minoriten-ordensprovinz*, Cologne.

Evans, Sir A.J. (1883), 'Antiquarian Researches in Illyricum, Part III. An investigation of the Roman road-lines from Salonae to Scupi, and of the municipal sites and mining centres in the old Dalmatian and Dardanian ranges', *Archaeologia* 49, pp. 1–78.

Evans, R. (2011), *Roman Conquests: Asia Minor, Syria and Armenia*, Barnsley.

Everitt, A. (2001), *Cicero: The Life and Times of Rome's Greatest Politician*, New York.

Everitt, A. (2006), *Augustus: The Life of Rome's First Emperor*, New York.

Fagan, G.F. (2011), *The Lure of the Arena: Social Psychology, Spectatorship and the Roman Games*, Cambridge.

Fantham, E. (2006), *Julia Augusti: The Emperor's Daughter*, London.

Farrer, K.E. (ed.) (2011), *Correspondence of Josiah Wedgwood, Volume 2: Letters of Josiah Wedgwood, 1772 to 1780*, Cambridge.

Favro, D. and Johanson, C. (2010), 'Death in Motion: Funeral Processions in the Roman Forum', *Journal of the Society of Architectural Historians* 69, pp. 12–37.

Feeny, D. (2007), *Caesar's Calender: Ancient Time and the Beginnings of History*, Berkeley.

Feldman, L.H. (1993), *Jew and Gentile in the Ancient World: Attitudes and Interactions from Alexander to Justinian*, Princeton.

Ferris, I.M. (2000), *Enemies of Rome: Barbarians Through Roman Eyes*, Stroud.

Fields, N. (2009), *The Roman Army of the Principate, 27 BC-AD 117*, Oxford.

Figuera, T.J., Brennan, T.C. and Sternberg, R.H. (2001), *Wisdom of the Ancients: Leadership Lessons from Alexander the Great to Julius Caesar*, New York.

Fiks, N. (2002), *Die Römer in Ostfriesland: Archäologische und literarische Spuren*, Leer (available online at http://www.ewetel.net/~norbert.fiks/ebooks/rio.pdf).

Fink, R.O. (1944), '*Feriale Duranum* I,1 and *Mater Castrorum*', *American Journal of Archaeology* 48, p. 17–19.

Finley, M.I. (1985), *Ancient History: Evidence and Models*, London.

Fischer, L. and Hasse, J. (2001), 'Historical and Current Perceptions of the Landscapes in the Wadden Sea Region', in M. Vollmer, M. Gulberg, M. Maluck, D. Marrewijk and G. Schlicksbier, *Landscape and Cultural Heritage in the Wadden Sea Region - Project Report (Wadden Sea Ecosystem no. 12)*, pp. 72–97 (available online at http://www.waddensea-secretariat.org/lancewad/report.html).

Fishwick, D. (1987), *The Imperial Cult in the Latin West: Studies in the Ruler Cult of the Western Provinces of the Roman Empire, Volume 1, Parts 1 and 2*, Boston.

Fishwick, D. (1988), 'Dated inscriptions and the *Feriale Duranum*', *Syria* 65, pp. 349–61.

Fishwick, D. (2002), *The Imperial Cult in the Latin West: Studies in the Ruler Cult of the Western Provinces of the Roman Empire, Volume 3, Part 1*, Boston.

Fishwick, D. (2003), *The Imperial Cult in the Latin West: Studies in the Ruler Cult of the Western Provinces of the Roman Empire, Volume 3, Part 3*, Boston.

Fiske, G.C. (1900), 'Notes on the worship of the Roman emperors in Spain', *Harvard Studies in Classical Philology* 11, pp. 101–39.

Fittschen, K. (1987), 'I Ritratti di Germanico', in Bonamente and Segoloni (1987), pp. 205–18.

Fletcher, J. (2004), *The Search for Nefertiti*, London.

Flower, H.I. (1996), *Ancestor Masks and Aristocratic Power in Roman Culture*, Oxford.

Flower, H.I. (1997), Review of Eck *et al.* (1996), *Bryn Mawr Classical Review* 97.7.22 (available online at http://bmcr.brynmawr.edu/1997/97.07.22.html).

Flower, H.I. (1998), 'Rethinking 'Damnatio Memoriae': The Case of Cn. Calpurnius Piso Pater in AD 20', *Classical Antiquity* 17, pp. 155–87.

Flower, H.I. (2000), 'The Tradition of the *spolia opima*: M. Claudius Marcellus and Augustus', *Classical Antiquity* 19, pp. 34–64.

Flower, H.I. (2006), *The Art of Forgetting: Disgrace and Oblivion in Roman Political Culture*, Chapel Hill.

Frank, T. (1933), 'On Augustus and the Aerarium', *Journal of Roman Studies* 23, pp. 143–8.

Freisenbruch, A. (2010), *Caesar's Wives: Sex, Power and Politics in Ancient Rome*, New York.

Frenz, H.G. (1985), 'Drusus maior und sein Monument zu Mainz', in *Jahrbuch des Römisch-Germanischen Zentralmuseums Mainz* 32, pp. 394–421.

Futrell, A. (1997), *Blood in the Arena: The Spectacle of Roman Power*, Austin.

Gabriel, R.A. (2006), *Soldiers' Lives through History: The Ancient World*, Santa Barbara.

Gain, D.B. (1976), *The Aratus ascribed to Germanicus Caesar*, London.

Galatas, C. (2008), 'Snow White's Apple and Claudius' Mushrooms: A look at the use of poison in the early Roman Empire', *Hirundo* 6, pp. 7–16.

Galinsky, K. (1996), *Augustan Culture: An Interpretive Introduction*, Princeton.

Galinsky, K. (ed.) (2005), *The Cambridge Companion to the Age of Augustus*, Cambridge.

Gallotta, B. (1987), *Germanico*, Rome.

Garnsey, P.D.A. (1988), *Famine and Food-supply in the Graeco-Roman World: Responses to Risk and Crisis*, Cambridge.

Garnsey, P.D.A. and Whittaker, C.R. (eds) (1978), *Imperialism in the Ancient World*, Cambridge.

Gissel, J.A.P. (2001), 'Germanicus as an Alexander Figure', *Classica et Mediaevalia* 52, pp. 277–301.

Giuliani, L. and Schmidt, G. (2010), *Ein Geschenk für den Kaiser. Das Geheimnis des großen Kameo*, Munich.

Goethert-Polaschek, G. (1973), *Studien zur Ikonographie der Antonia Minor* (*Studia archaeologica* 15), Rome.

Goldsworthy, A. (1996), *The Roman Army at War, 100 BC–AD 200*, Oxford.

Goldsworthy, A. (2000a) *Roman Warfare*, London.

Goldsworthy, A. (2000b) *The Punic Wars*, London.

Goldsworthy, A. (2003), *In the Name of Rome: The Men Who Won the Roman Empire*, London.

Golz Huzar, E. (1978), *Mark Antony: A Biography*, Minneapolis.

González, J. (1984), '*Tabvla Siarensis, Fortvnales Siarenses et Mvnicipia Civivm Romanorvm*', *Zeitschrift für Papyrologie und Epigraphik* 55, pp. 55–100.

González, J. (1999), 'Tacitus, Germanicus, Piso, and the *Tabula Siarensis*', *American Journal of Philology* 120, pp. 123–42.

Gordon, A.E. (1983), *Illustrated Introduction to Latin Epigraphy*, Berkeley.

Gordon, R., Reynolds, J., Beard, M. and Roueché, C. (1997), 'Roman Inscriptions 1991–95', *Journal of Roman Studies* 87, pp. 203–40.

Goudineau, C. and Rebourg, A. (eds) (1991), *Les villes augustéennes de Gaule: Actes du Colloque international d'Autun, 6–8 juin 1985*, Autun.

Grant, M. (1958), *Roman History from Coins*, Cambridge.

Grant, M. (1971), *Gladiators*, London.

Grant, M. (1974), *The Army of the Caesars*, New York.

Graves, R. (1934), *I, Claudius*, London.

Green, P. (1989), *Classical Bearings: Interpreting Ancient History and Culture*, Berkeley.

Green, P. (1982), 'Ovid in Tomis', *Grand Street* 2, pp. 116–25.

Grenier, A. (1931), *Manuel d'archéologie gallo-romaine*, Vol. I, Paris.

Griffin, M.T. (1984), *Nero: The End of a Dynasty*, London.

Griffin, M.T. (1997), 'The Senate's Story' (Review of Eck *et al.*, 1996), *Journal of Roman Studies* 87, pp. 249–63.

Grimal, P. (1947), 'Deux inscriptions de Saintes', *Revue des études anciennes* 49, pp. 130–8.

Grote, K. (2005), *Römerlager Hedemünden. Vor 2000 Jahren: Römer an der Werra* (*Sydekum-Schriften zur Geschichte der Stadt Münden* 34), Hann. Münden.

Grote, K. (2006a), 'Das Römerlager im Werratal bei Hedemünden (Ldkr. Göttingen). Ein neuentdeckter Stützpunkt der augusteischen Okkupationsvorstöße im rechtsrheinischen Germanien', *Germania* 84, pp. 27–59.

Grote, K. (2006b), 'Neue Forschungen und Funde im augusteischen Römerlager bei Hedemünden (Werra)', *Göttinger Jahrbuch* 54, pp. 5–19.

Grote, K. (2006c), 'Die Römer an der Werra. Das Militärlager aus der Zeit der augusteischen Germanienfeldzüge bei Hedemünden – Hessen in der Antike', in D. Rohde and H. Schneider (eds), *Hessen in der Antike. Die Chatten vom Zeitalter der Römer bis zur Alltagskultur der Gegenwart*, Kassel, pp. 70–87.

Grote, K. (2006d), 'Werra: augusteisches Lager Hedemünden', *Reallexikon der germanischen Altertumskunde* 33, pp. 485–9.

Grote, K. (2007a), 'Der römische Militärstützpunkt an der Werra bei Hedemünden', in G. Uelsberg (ed.), *Krieg und Frieden. Kelten – Römer – Germanen (Begleitbuch zur gleichnamigen Ausstellung im Rheinischen Landesmuseum Bonn 21.6.2007–6.1.2008)*, Bonn/Darmstadt, pp. 218–22.

Grote, K. (2007b), 'Das Römerlager Hedemünden (Werra). Die archäologischen Arbeiten bis Jahresende 2007', *Göttinger Jahrbuch* 55, pp. 5–17.

Grote, K. (2008), 'Der römische Stützpunkt bei Hedemünden an der Werra/Oberweser. Aspekte seiner logistischen Ausrichtung im Rahmen der augusteischen Germanienvorstöße', in *Rom auf dem Weg nach Germanien: Geostrategie, Vormarschtrassen und Logistik. Internationales Kolloquium in Delbrück-Anreppen vom 4. bis 6. November 2004 (Bodenaltertümer Westfalens 45)*, Mainz, pp. 323–43.

Gruen, E.S. (2003), 'The emperor Tiberius and the Jews', in T. Hantos (ed.), *Laurea internationalis. Festschrift für Jochen Bleicken zum 75 Geburtstag*, Stuttgart, pp. 298–312.

Gruen, E.S. (2005), 'Augustus and the Making of the Principate', in Galinsky (2005), pp. 33–51.

Grünewald, T. (ed.) (2000), *Germania inferior: Beiträge des deutschen-niederländischen Kolloquiums in Regionalmuseum Xanten 21.–24. September 1999*, Berlin.

Gurval, R.A. (1995), *Actium and Augustus: The Politics and Emotions of Civil War*, Ann Arbor.

Halbertsma, H. (1963), *Terpen tussen Vlie en Eems: Een geografisch-historische Benadering*, Groningen.

Haley, E.W. (2003), *Baetica Felix: People and Prosperity in Southern Spain from Caesar to Septimius Severus*, Austin.

Hamerton, P.G. (1879), *The Life of J.M.W. Turner, R.A.*, London and Boston.

Hanel, N. (1995), *Vetera I. Die Funde aus den römischen Lagern auf dem Fürstenberg bei Xanten (Rheinische Ausgrabungen 35)*, Cologne.

Hanson, A.E. (1980), 'Juliopolis, Nicopolis, and the Roman Camp', *Zeitschrift für Papyrologie und Epigraphik* 37, pp. 249–54.

Hanson, W.S. (ed.) (2009), *The Army and Frontiers of Rome (Journal of Roman Archaeology*, Supplementary Series 74), Portsmouth.

Harris, W. (1979), *War and Imperialism in Republican Rome 327–70 BC*, Oxford.

Harley, B. and Woodward, D. (1987), *The History of Cartography: Cartography in Prehistoric, Ancient and Medieval Europe and the Mediterranean, Vol. 1*, Chicago.

Hawass, Z.A. (2005), *The Island of Kalabsha*, Cairo.

Haynes, H. (2003), *The History of Make-Believe: Tacitus on Imperial Rome*, Berkeley.

Head, B.V. (1888), 'Germanicopolis and Philadelphia in Cilicia', *Numismatic Chronicle* 8, pp. 300–7.

Head, I.C. (1934), *Biography of Germanicus Caesar*, Unpublished Dissertation, University of Wisconsin, Madison. (Full text at http://minds.wisconsin.edu/handle/1793/21816).

Heinrichs, J. (1999), 'Zur Verwicklung ubischer Gruppen in den Ambiorix-Aufstand d. J. 54 v. Chr.: Eburonische und ubische Münzen im Hortfund Fraire-2', *Zeitschrift für Papyrologie und Epigraphik* 127, pp. 275–93.

Heinrichs, J. (2000), 'Römische Perfidie und germanischer Edelmut? Zur Umsiedlung proto-cugernischer Gruppen in den Raum Xanten 8 v. Chr.', in Grünewald (2000), pp. 54–92.

Heiss, A. (1870), *Description générale des monnaies antiques de l'Espagne*, Paris.

Hekster, O. (2008), *Rome and its Empire, AD 193–284*, Edinburgh.

Helbling, R. (1975), *The Major Works of Heinrich von Kleist*, New York.

Herm, G. (1977), *The Celts: The People Who Came Out of the Darkness*, New York.

Hersen, M., Turner, S.M. and Beidel, D.C. (eds) (2007), *Adult Psychopathology and Diagnosis*, Hoboken.

Herz, P. (1984), 'Das Kenotaph von Limyra. Kultische und juristische Voraussetzungen', *Mitteilung des deutschen archäologischen Instituts* (Istanbul) 35, pp. 178–92.

Hinge, G. and Krasilnikoff, J.A. (eds) (2009), *Alexandria: A Cultural and Religious Melting Pot* (*Aarhus Studies in Mediterranean Antiquity* 9), Aarhus.

Hipwell, D. (1890), 'Thomas Cooke', *Notes and Queries* 10 (no. 243), p. 146.

Höfer, P. (1885), *Der Feldzug des Germanicus im Jahre 16 n. Chr.*, Bernburg.

Hoffmann, F. (1816), *Die Vier Feldzüge des Germanicus in Deutschland*, Göttingen.

Holtzhausser, C.A. (1918), *An Epigraphic Commentary on Suetonius's Life of Tiberius*, Philadelphia.

Horden, P. and Purcell, N. (2000), *The Corrupting Sea: A Study of Mediterranean History*, London.

Horne, C.F. (1901), *Greatest Nations: Germany*, New York.

Horstmann, W. (1982), 'Die Römer an der Weser. Untersuchungen zum Germanicus-Feldzug des Jahres 16 n. Chr.', *Mitteilungen des Mindener Geschichtsvereins* 54, pp. 9–49.

Hübener, W. (1973), *Die römischen Metallfunde von Augsburg-Oberhausen*, Kallmünz.

Huisman, K. (1995), 'De Drususgrachten: een Nieuwe Hypothese', *Westerheem* 44, pp. 188–94.

Hurlet, F. (1997), *Les Collègues du prince au temps d'Auguste et de Tibère: de la légalité républicaine à la légitimité dynastique* (*Collection de l'École Française de Rome* 227), Rome.

Hurley, D.W. (1989), 'Caligula in the Germanicus Tradition', *American Journal of Philology* 110, pp. 316–38.

Huscher, W. (1826), *Germanicus: ein Trauerspiel in fünf Aufzügen*, Kibingen.

Huzar, E.G. (1978), *Mark Antony: A Biography*, Beckenham.

Huzar, E.G. (1995), 'Emperor Worship in Julio-Claudian Egypt', *Aufstieg und Niedergang der römischen Welt* II.18.5, pp. 3092–143.

Inker, P. (2008), *Caesar's Gallic Triumph: Alesia 52 BC*, Barnsley.

Issac, B. (1992), *The Limits of Empire: The Roman Army in the East*, revised edition, Oxford.

Isaac, B. (2006), *The Invention of Racism in Classical Antiquity*, Princeton.

Jackson, R.B. (2002), *At Empire's Edge: Exploring Rome's Egyptian Frontier*, New Haven.

Jankuhn, H. (1976), 'Siedlung, Wirtschaft und Gesellschaftsordnung der germanischen Stämme in der Zeit der römischen Angriffskriege', *Aufstieg und Niedergang der römischen Welt* II.5.1, pp. 65–126.

James, H. (1989), *A German Identity: 1770–1990*, New York.

Jameson, S. (1975), 'Augustus and Agrippa Postumus', *Historia: Zeitschrift für Alte Geschichte* 24, 2 (2nd Qtr.), pp. 287–314.

Jarrett, M.G. (2002), 'Early Roman Campaigns in Wales', in R.J. Brewer (ed.), *The Second Augustan Legion and the Roman Military Machine*, Cardiff, pp. 45–61.

Johne, K.-P. (2006), *Die Römer an der Elbe: Das Stromgebiet der Elbe im geographischen Weltbild und im politischen Bewusstsein der griechisch-römischen Antike*, Berlin.

Johnson, A. (1983), *Roman Forts of the First and Second Centuries AD in Britain and the German Provinces*, London.

Jones, A.H.M. (1950), 'The Aerarium and the Fiscus', *Journal of Roman Studies* 40, pp. 22–9.

Jorgensen, L. *et al.* (eds) (2003), *The Spoils of Victory: The North in the Shadow of the Roman Empire*, Copenhagen.

Kaufman, D.B. (1932), 'Poisons and Poisoning Among the Romans', *Classical Philology* 27, pp. 156–67.

Kavanagh, B. (2004), 'The Elder Corbulo and the Seating Incident', Historia 53, pp. 379–84.

Keegan, J. (2003), *Intelligence in War: From Napoleon to Al-Qaeda*, New York.

Kehne, P. (1998), 'Augustus und 'seine' *spolia opima*: Hoffnungen auf den Triumph des Nero Claudius Drusus?', in T. Hantos and G.A. Lehmann (eds), *Althistorisches Kolloquium aus Anlass des 70. Geburtstags von Jochen Bleicken*, Stuttgart, pp. 187–211.

Kelly, K. (2010), 'Tacitus, Germanicus and the Kings of Egypt (Tac. *Ann.* 2.59–61)', *Classical Quarterly* 60, pp. 221–37.

Kelsey, M.T. (1991), *God, Dreams and Revelation: A Christian Interpretation of Dreams*, Minneapolis.

Kennedy, D. (ed.) (1996), *The Roman Army in the East* (*Journal of Roman Archaeology*), Supplementary Series 18), Ann Arbor.

Keppie, L. (1984a) *The Making of the Roman Army. From Republic to Empire*, London.

Keppie, L. (1984b) 'Colonisation and Veteran Settlement in Italy in the First Century AD', *Papers of the British School at Rome* 52, pp. 77–114.

Kessler, G. (1905), *Die Tradition über Germanicus*, Berlin.

Kienast, D. (2009), *Augustus: Prinzeps und Monarch*, fourth edition, Darmstadt.

Kiessel, M. and Weidner, M. (2009), 'Defining Roman, Celtic and Germanic ethnicity through archaeological monuments. Examples from Roman provinces in north-western Europe', *Girne American University Journal of Social and Applied Sciences* 5, pp. 35–51.

King, A. (1990), *Roman Gaul and Germany*, London.

Kiss, Z. (1975), *L'iconographie des princes julio-claudiens au temps d'Auguste et de Tibère*, Warsaw.

Kleineburg, A. *et al.* (2010), *Germania und die Insel Thule: Die Entschlüsselung von Ptolemaios' 'Atlas der Oikumene'*, Darmstadt.

Knoke, F. (1887), *Die Kriegszüge des Germanicus in Deutschland*, Berlin.

Kokkinos, N. (1995), 'The Honorand of the Titulus Tiburtinus: C. Sentius Saturninus?', *Zeitschrift für Papyrologie und Epigraphik* 105, pp. 21–36.

Kokkinos, N. (2002), *Antonia Augusta: Portrait of a Great Roman Lady*, London.

Koepfer, C. (2009a), 'The Legionary's Equipment: Archaeological Evidence', *Ancient Warfare*, Special Issue 1, pp. 37–41.

Koepfer, C. (2009b), 'Arming the Warrior: Archaeological Evidence', *Ancient Warfare*, Special Issue 1, pp. 48–51.

Koestermann, E. (1957a), 'Die Mission des Germanicus im Orient', *Historia* 6, pp. 331–75.

Koestermann, E. (1957b), 'Die Feldzüge des Germanicus 14–16 n. Chr.', *Historia* 6, pp. 429–79.

Kondoleon, C. (ed.) (2000), *Antioch: The Lost Ancient City*, Princeton.

Kornemann, E. (1930), *Doppelprinzipat und Reichsteilung im Imperium Romanum*, Leipzig.

Kornemann, E. (1960), *Tiberius*, Stuttgart (repr. Frankfurt 1980).

Krebs, C.B. (2011), 'Tacitus: The Continuing Message', *History Today* 61.9 (available online at http://www.historytoday.com/christopher-krebs/tacitus-continuing-message).

Kruta, V. (ed.) (1999), *The Celts*, New York.

Kühlborn, J.S. (1989), 'Oberaden', in R. Asskamp (ed.), *2000 Jahre Römer in Westfalen*, Mainz.

Kühlborn, J.S. (ed.) (1995), *Germaniam pacavi: Germanien habe ich befriedet. Archäologische Stätten augusteischer Okkupation*, Münster.

Kühlborn, J.S. (1996), *Das römische Uferkastell* Beckinghausen, Lünen (available online at http://www.luenen.de/medien/archiv/dok/Uferkastell.pdf).

Kunić, A.D. (2006), 'Posljednja faza osvajanja Ju'ne Panonije', *Vjesnik Arheološkog muzeja u Zagrebu* 39, pp. 59–164.

Kurkjian, V.M. (1958), *A History of Armenia*, New York.

Kuttner, A.L. (1995), *Dynasty and Empire in the Age of Augustus: The Case of the Boscoreale Cups*, Berkeley.

Langguth, A.J. (1994), *A Noise of War: Caesar, Pompey, Octavian and the Struggle for Rome*, New York.

Lawley, E.A. (2002), 'Pink, Pink Everywhere!', *€U(RO)CK* (Newsletter of the Open University Geological Society, Mainland Europe).

Le Boeuffle, A. (1975), *Germanicus: Les Phénomènes d'Aratos*, Paris (second edition, 2003).

Le Bohec, Y. (1994), *The Imperial Roman Army*, London.

Lebek, W.D. (1986), 'Schwierige Stellen der Tabula Siarensis', *Zeitschrift für Papyrologie und Epigraphik* 66, pp. 31–48.

Lebek, W.D. (1987), 'Die drei Ehrenbögen für Germanicus: Tab. Siar. Frg. I 9–34; CIL VI 31199a 2–17', *Zeitschrift für Papyrologie und Epigraphik* 67, pp. 129–48.

Lebek, W.D. (1989a), 'Die Mainzer Ehrungen für Germanicus, den älteren Drusus and Domitian (Tab. Siar. Frg. I 26–34; Suet. Claud. 1,3)', *Zeitschrift für Papyrologie und Epigraphik* 78, pp. 45–82.

Lebek, W.D. (1989b), 'Die postumen Ehrenbögen und der Triumph des Drusus Caesar (CIL VI 31200 B Col. I, 1–4; Tac. Ann. 4,9,2)', *Zeitschrift für Papyrologie und Epigraphik* 78, pp. 83–91.

Lebek, W.D. (1991), 'Ehrenbogen und Prinzentod: 9 v.Chr.–23 n. Chr.', *Zeitschrift für Papyrologie und Epigraphik* 86, 1991, pp. 47–78.

Lehmann, G.A. (1991), 'Das Ende der römischen Herrschaft über das "westelbische" Germanien: von der Varus-Katastrophe zur Abberufung des Germanicus Caesar 16/7 n. Chr.', *Zeitschrift für Papyrologie und Epigraphik* 86, pp. 79–96.

Lendering, J. and Bosman, A. (2010), *De Rand van het Rijk: De Romeinen en de Lage Landen*, Amsterdam.

Lepper, F. and Frere, S. (1988), *Trajan's Column*, Gloucester.

Letta, C. (1976), 'La dinastia dei Cozii e la romanizzazione delle Alpi occidentali', *Athenaeum* 54, pp. 37–76.

Levick, B. (1966), 'Drusus Caesar and the Adoptions of A.D. 4', *Latomus* 25, pp. 227–44.

Levick, B. (1972a), 'Tiberius' Retirement to Rhodes in 6 B.C.', *Latomus* 31, pp. 779–813.

Levick, B.M. (1972b), 'Abdication and Agrippa Postumus', *Historia: Zeitschrift für Alte Geschichte* 21, 4, pp. 674–97.

Levick, B. (1976), *Tiberius the Politician*, London (revised edition, 1999).

Levick, B. (1985), *Government of the Roman Empire: A Source Book*, Beckenham.

Levick, B. (1990), *Claudius*, London.

Lewis, M.J.T. (2001), 'Railways in the Greek and Roman world', in A. Guy and J. Rees (eds), *Early Railways. A Selection of Papers from the First International Early Railways Conference*, London, pp. 8–19.

Liebenam, W. (1891), 'Bemerkungen zur Tradition über Germanicus', *Neue Jahrbücher für Philologie und Pedagogik* 143, pp. 717–36.

Limoges, S. (2008), 'The portrayal of Germanicus in Tacitus' *Annales* and the historicity of the Germanicus-Tiberius conflict', *Hirundo* 6, pp. 32–40.

Lindemann, K. (1967), *Der Hildesheimer Silberfund: Varus und Germanicus*, Hildesheim.

Lindsay, H. (1995), 'A fertile marriage: Agrippina and the chronology of her children by Germanicus', *Latomus* 54, pp. 3–17.

Linsmeyer, A. (1875), *Der Triumphzug des Germanicus*, Munich.

Lintott, A. (1993), *Imperium Romanum: Politics and Administration*, London.

Lobel, E. and Turner, E.G. (eds) (1959), *The Oxyrhynchus Papyri*, Part 25, London.

Luden, H. (1825), *Geschichte des teutschen Volkes*, Volume 1, Gotha.

Maas, M. (2000), 'People and Identity in Roman Antioch', in Kondoleon (2000), pp. 13–22.

MacKendrick, P. (1970), *Romans on the Rhine: Archaeology in Germany*, New York.

MacKendrick, P. (1971), *Roman France*, London.

MacMullen, R. (2000), *Romanization in the Time of Augustus*, New Haven.

Makaske, B., Maas, G.J. and van Smeerdijk, D.G. (2008), 'The age and origin of the Gelderse IJssel', *Netherlands Journal of Geosciences* 87–4, pp. 323–37.

Malissard, A. (1990), 'Germanicus, Alexandre et le début des Annales de Tacite. À propos de Tacite, Annales, 2, 73', in J.M. Croisille (ed.), *Neronia IV. Alejandro Magno, modelo de los emperadores romanos*, Brussels, pp. 328–38.

Malloch, S.J.V. (2004), 'The end of the Rhine mutiny in Tacitus, Suetonius, and Dio', *Classical Quarterly* 54, pp. 198–210.

Mallory, J.P. (1989), *In Search of Indo-Europeans: Language, Archaeology and Myth*, London.

Marlowe, J. (1971), *The Golden Age of Alexandria: from its foundation by Alexander the Great in 331 BC to its capture by the Arabs in 642 AD*, London.

Marr, J.S. and Calisher, C.H. (2003), 'Alexander the Great and West Nile Virus Encephalitis', *Emerging Infectious Diseases* 9, pp. 1599–603.

Matijević, K. (2006), *Zur augusteischen Germanienpolitik*, Osnabrück.

Mattern, S.P. (1999), *Rome and the Enemy: Imperial Strategy in the Principate*, Berkeley.

Mattingly, H. (1960), *Roman Coins: From the Earliest Times to the Fall of the Western Empire*, second edition, London.

Matyszak, P. (2006), *The Sons of Caesar: Imperial Rome's First Dynasty*, London.

Mayor, A. (2009), *Greek Fire, Poison Arrows and Scorpion Bombs: Biological and Chemical Warfare in the Ancient World*, New York.

Maxfield, V.A. (1981), *The Military Decorations of the Roman Army*, London.

McCall, J.B. (2002), *The Cavalry of the Roman Republic: Cavalry Combat and Elite Reputations in the Middle and Late Republic*, London.

McCullough, D.W. (ed.) (1998), *Chronicles of the Barbarians; Firsthand Accounts of Pillage and Conquest, From the Ancient World to the Fall of Constantinople*, New York.

McDonnell-Staff, P. (2009), 'The Other Invader Over the Alps: Watershed of the Second Punic War', *Ancient Warfare* 3.4, pp. 36–41.

McPherson, C. (2010), 'Fact and Fiction: Crassus, Augustus, and the *spolia opima*', *Hirundo* 8, pp. 21–34.

Mennella, G. (1978), 'Ipotesi sull'iscrizione dei re Cozi nel teatro di Augusta Taurinorum', *Rendiconti dell'Istituto Lombardo* 112, pp. 96–100.

Merriweather, S. (1940), 'Tacitus and the Portraits of Germanicus and Drusus', *Classical Philology* 35, pp. 64.

Metzger, E. (2004), 'Roman judges, case law, and principles of procedure', *Law and History Review* 22, pp. 243–75.

Mierow, C.C. (1943), '*Germanicus Caesar Imperator*', *Classical Journal* 39, pp. 137–55.

Millar, F. (1988), 'Imperial Ideology in the Tabula Siarensis', in J. González and J. Arce (eds), *Estudios sobre la Tabula Siarensis*, Madrid, pp. 11–19.

Millar, F. (1993), *The Roman Near East, 31 BC–AD 337*, London.

Mommsen, Th. (1878), 'Die Familie des Germanicus', *Hermes* 13, pp. 245–65.

Mommsen, T. and Demandt, A. (1996), *A History of Rome Under the Emperors*, London.

Monteil, M. (2008), *La France gallo-romaine*, Paris.

Mossé, C. (2004), *Alexander: Destiny and Myth*, Baltimore.

Mueller, H.-F. (2002), *Roman religion in Valerius Maximus*, London.

Müller-Baden, E. (ed.) (1904), *Bibliothek des allgemeinen und praktischen Wissens*, Vol. 1 (Berlin, Leipzig, Vienna, Stuttgart).

Murdoch, A. (2006), *Rome's Greatest Defeat: Massacre at the Teutoburg Forest*, Stroud.

Nemerov, A. (1998), 'The Ashes of Germanicus and the Skin of Painting: Sublimation and Money in Benjamin West's Agrippina', *Yale Journal of Criticism* 11, pp. 11–27.

Newark, T. (1985), *The Barbarians: Warriors and Wars of the Dark Ages*, Poole.

Newark, T. (1986), *Celtic Warriors 400 BC–AD 1600*, Poole.

Newark, T. (1998), *Celtic Warriors*, Hong Kong.

Nicolet, C. (1991), *Space, Geography, and Politics in the Early Roman Empire*, Ann Arbor.

Nony, D. (1982), 'Sur quelques monnaies impériales romaines', *Mélanges de l'Ecole française de Rome: Antiquité* 94, pp. 893–909.

Nock, A.D. (1952), 'The Roman army and the Roman religious year', *Harvard Theological Review* 45, pp. 187–252.

Norkus, J. (1963), *Die Feldzüge der Römer in Nordwestdeutschland in den Jahren 9–16 n. Chr. von einem Soldaten gesehen*, Hildesheim.

Norman, A.F. (2000), *Antioch as a Centre of Hellenic Culture Observed by Libianus*, Liverpool.

North, J.A. (1981), 'The Development of Roman Imperialism', *Journal of Roman Studies* 71, pp. 1–9.

Oakes, L. (2001), *Sacred Sites of Ancient Egypt: An Illustrated Guide to the Temples and Tombs of the Pharoahs*, London.

Ober, J. (1982), 'Tiberius and the political testament of Augustus', *Historia* 31, pp. 306–28.

Oberziner, G. (1900), *Le guerre di Augusto contro i populi Alpini*, Rome.

Oldfather, W.A. and Canter, H.V. (1916), *The Defeat of Varus and the German Frontier Policy of Augustus*, Urbana.

Oliver, J.H. (1989), *Greek Constitutions of Early Roman Emperors from Inscriptions and Papyri*, Philadelphia.

Oliver, J.H. and Palmer, R.E.A. (1954), 'Text of the Tabula Hebana', *American Journal of Philology* 75, pp. 225–49.

Oliver, R.P. (1951), 'The First Medicean MS of Tacitus and the Titulature of Ancient Books', *Transactions and Proceedings of the American Philological Association* 82, pp. 232–61.

Orth, W. (1978), 'Zur Fabricius-Tuscus-Inschrift aus Alexandreia/Troas', *Zeitschrift für Papyrologie und Epigraphik* 28, pp. 57–60.

Osgood, J. (2011), *Claudius Caesar: Image and Power in the Early Roman Empire*, Cambridge.

Panter, A. (2007), Der Drususstein in Mainz und dessen Einordnung in die römische Grabarchitektur seiner Erbauungszeit (*Mainzer Archäologische Schriften* 6), Mainz.

Pantle, C. (2009), *Die Varusschlacht: Der germanische Freiheitskrieg*, Berlin.

Paoli, U.E. (1963), *Rome: Its People, Life and Customs*, London.

Pappano, A.E. (1941), 'Agrippa Postumus', *Classical Philology* 36, 1, pp. 30–45.

Parsons, P. (2007), *City of the Sharp-Nosed Fish: Greek Lives in Roman Egypt*, London.

Paul, G.M. and Ierardi, M. (eds) (1999), Roman Coins and Public Life under the Empire (*E. Togo Salmon Papers II*), Ann Arbor.

Peddie, J. (1987), *Invasion: The Roman Conquest of Britain*, Gloucester.

Pelling, C. (1993), 'Tacitus and Germanicus', in T.J. Luce and A.J. Woodman (eds), Tacitus and the Tacitean Tradition, Princeton, pp. 59–85.

Perowne, S. (1956), *The Life and Times of Herod the Great*, London.

Petrikovits, H. (1960), *Das römische Rheinland: archäologische Forschungen seit 1945* (*Beihefte der Bonner Jahrbücher* 8), Cologne.

Pettegrew, D.K. (2011), 'The *Diolkos* of Corinth', *American Journal of Archaeology* 115, pp. 549–74.

Pietsch, M. (1993), 'Die Zentralgebäude des augusteischen Legionslagers von Marktbreit und die Principia von Haltern', *Germania* 71, pp. 355–68.

Pietsch, M., Timpe, D. and Wamser, L. (1991), 'Das augusteische Truppenlager Marktbreit. Bisherige archäologische Befunde und historische Erwägungen', *Bericht der Römisch-Germanischen Kommission* 72, pp. 263–324.

Pitassi, M. (2011), *Roman Warships*, Woodbridge.

Pleket, H.W. and Stroud, R.S. (2012), 'Olympia. Statue Base in Honor of Germanicus, Olympionikes, 17 A.D. (40–390)', *Supplementum Epigraphicum Graecum*.

Possanza, D.M. (2004), *Translating the Heavens: Aratus, Germanicus, and the Poetics of Latin Translation* (*Lang Classical Studies* 14), New York.

Potter, D.S. (1987), 'The *Tabula Siarensis*, Tiberius, the Senate, and the Eastern Boundary of the Roman Empire', *Zeitschrift für Papyrology und Epigraphik* 69, pp. 269–76.

Potter, D.S. (1998), '*Senatus Consultum de Cn. Pisone*' (Review of Eck *et al.*, 1996), *Journal of Roman Archaeology* 11, pp. 437–57.

Potter, D.S. (ed.) and Damon, C. (trans.) (1999), 'The *Senatus Consultum de Cn. Pisone patre*', *American Journal of Philology* 120, pp. 13–42.

Potter, T.W. (1987), *Roman Italy*, London.

Powell, L. (2009), '*Bella Germaniae*: The German Wars of Drusus the Elder and Tiberius', *Ancient Warfare*, Special Issue 1, pp. 10–16.

Powell, L. (2010), 'Fighting for the Gods: Historical Introduction', *Ancient Warfare* 4.5, pp. 2–5.

Powell, L. (2011a) *Eager for Glory: The Untold Story of Drusus the Elder*, Barnsley.

Powell, L. (2011b) 'The Last Clash of the Cimbri and Romans: The Battle of Vercellae, 101 BC', *Ancient Warfare* 5.1, pp. 27–33.

Powell, L. (2014), *Combat: Roman Soldier versus Germanic Warrior, 1st Century AD*, Oxford.

Powell, L. (2015), *Marcus Agrippa: Right-Hand Man of Caesar Augustus*, Barnsley.

Preston, K. (1918), 'An Author in Exile', *The Classical Journal* 13, 6, pp. 411–19.

Priuli, S. (1980), 'Osservazioni sul feriale di Spello', *Tituli* 2, 47–80.

Questa, C. (1957), 'Il Viaggio di Germanico in Oriente e Tacito', *Maia* 9, pp. 291–321.

Rabbe, A., Vieilh de Boisjolin, C.-A.-C. and de Sainte-Preuve, F.-G. (1836), *Biographie universelle et portative des contemporains, ou dictionnaire historique*, Paris.

Rankov, B. (1994), *The Praetorian Guard*, London.

Reed, N. (1975), 'Drusus and the "Classis Britannica"', *Historia* 24, pp. 315–23.

Reeve, M.D. (1976), 'The tradition of Consolatio ad Liviam', *Revue d'Histoire des Textes* 6, pp. 79–98.

Reinking, L. (1855), *Die Niederlage des Quintilius Varus und Germanicus Kriegszug durch das Bructererland: Eine Prüfung der bisherigen Ansichten*, Warendorf.

Rettinger, E. (ed.) (2001), *2000 Jahre Mainz: Geschichte der Stadt* (CD-ROM), Mainz.

Rich, J. and Shipley, G. (1993), *War and Society in the Roman World*, London.

Rihll, T. (2007), *The Catapult: A History*, Yardley.

Ritchie, W.F. and Ritchie, J.N.G. (1985), *Celtic Warriors*, Aylesbury.

Roddaz, J.-M. (1984), *Marcus Agrippa*, Rome.

Rogers, G.M. (2004), *Alexander: The Ambiguity of Greatness*, New York.

Rollo, W. (1938), 'The Franco-German Frontier', *Greece and Rome* 8, pp. 36–49.

Romer, F.E. (1985), 'A case of client-kingship', *American Journal of Philology* 106, pp. 75–100.

Rosborough, R.R. (1920), *An epigraphic commentary on Suetonius's Life of Gaius Caligula*, Philadelphia.

Ross, A. (1970), *Everyday Life of the Pagan Celts*, London.

Ross, D.O. (1973), 'The Tacitean Germanicus', Yale Classical Studies 23, pp. 209–27.

Rossini, O. (2006), *Ara Pacis*, Milan.

Rosso, E. (2000), 'Vie d'un groupe statuaire julio-claudien à *Mediolanum Santonum*', *Labyrinthe* 7, pp. 103–122 (available online at http://labyrinthe.revues.org/805).

Roth, J.P. (1999), *The Logistics of the Roman Army at War (264 BC- AD 235)*, Leiden.

Rowe, G. (2002), *Princes and Political Cultures: The New Tiberian Senatorial Decrees*, Ann Arbor.

Roymans, N. (2000), 'The Lower Rhine Triquetrum coinages and the ethnogenesis of the Batavi', in Grünewald (2000), pp. 93–145.

Roymans, N. (2004), *Ethnic identity and imperial power: the Batavians in the early Roman Empire*, Amsterdam.

Roymans, N. and Aarts, J. (2009), 'Coin use in a dynamic frontier region. Late Iron Age Coinages in the Lower Rhine area', *Journal of Archaeology in the Low Countries* 1 (available online at http://dpc.uba.uva.nl/jalc/01/nr01/a02).

Rozier, A. (ed.) (2009), 'Le Sanctuaire fédéral des Trois Gaules: Localisation Inconnue', *La Ficèlle* 9, Lyon, pp. 6–10.

Rüpke, J. (2008), *Fasti Sacerdotum: A Prosopography of Pagan, Jewish, and Christian Religious Officials in the City of Rome, 300 BC to AD 499*, Oxford.

Russell, J.B. (1995), *A History of Witchcraft: Sorcerers, Heretics, and Pagans*, London.

Rutland, L.W. (1987), 'The Tacitean Germanicus: Suggestions for a Re-evaluation', *Rheinisches Museum für Philologie* 130, pp. 153–64.

Rutten, A.M.G. (1997), *Ondergang in bedwelming: Drugs en giften in het West-Romeinse Rijk*, Rotterdam.

Sampson, G.C. (2007), *The Defeat of Rome in the East: Crassus, the Parthians and the Disastrous Battle of Carrhae, 53 BC*, Barnsley.

Sánchez-Ostiz Gutiérrez, A. (1999), *Tabula Siarensis. Edición, Traducción y Comentario*, Pamplona.

Santosuosso, A. (1997), *Soldiers, Citizens and the Symbols of War: from Classical Greece to Republican Rome, 500–167 BC*, Boulder.

Sauer, E. (1999), 'The Augustan coins from Bourbonne-les-Bains (Haute-Marne): a mathematical approach to dating a coin assemblage', *Revue numismatique* 6, pp. 145–82.

Savage, J.J. (1942), 'Germanicus and Aeneas again', *Classical Journal* 38, pp. 166–7.

Sayles, W.G. (2007), *Ancient Coin Collecting III: The Roman World – Politics and Propaganda*, Iola.

Scarborough, J. (1968), 'Roman Medicine and the Legions: a reconsideration', *Medical History* 12, pp. 254–61.

Scheidel, W., 2009, 'Disease and death in the ancient city of Rome', *Princeton/Stanford Working Papers in Classics* (available online at http://dx.doi.org/10.2139/ssrn.1347510).

Schiller, A.A. (1978), *Roman Law: Mechanisms of Development*, Berlin.

Schneider, H. (ed.) (2006), *Feindliche Nachbarn: Rom und die Germanen*, Vienna.

Schnurbein, S. von (1971), 'Ein Bleibarren der XIX. Legion aus dem Hauptlager von Haltern', *Germania* 49, pp. 132–6.

Schnurbein, S. von (1974), *Die römischen Militäranlagen bei Haltern: Bericht über die Forschungen seit 1899*, Münster.

Schnurbein, S. von (1985), 'Die Funde von Augsburg-Oberhausen und die Besetzung des Alpenvorlandes durch die Römer', in J. Bellot, W. Czysz and G. Krahe (eds), *Forschungen zur provinzial-römischen Archäologie in Bayerisch-Schwaben*, Augsburg, pp. 15–43.

Schnurbein, S. von (2000), 'The organization of the fortresses in Augustan Germany', in R.J. Brewer (ed.), *Roman Fortresses and their Legions: Papers in Honour of George C. Boon*, London, pp. 29–39.

Schnurbein, S. von (2002), 'Neue Grabungen in Haltern, Oberaden und Anreppen', in P. Freeman *et al.* (eds), *Limes XVIII: Proceedings of the XVIIIth International Congress of Roman Frontier Studies*, Oxford, pp. 527–33.

Schnurbein, S. von and Köhler, H.-J. (1994), 'Dorlar: Ein augusteisches Römerlager im Lahntal', *Germania* 72, pp. 193–703.

Schön, F. (1986), *Der Beginn der römischen Herrschaft in Rätien*, Sigmaringen.

Schönberger, H. (1969), 'The Roman frontier in Germany: an archaeological survey', *Journal of Roman Studies* 59, pp. 144–97.

Schönberger, H. and Simon, H.G. (1976), *Römerlager Rödgen (Limesforschungen* 15), Berlin.

Schußmann, M. (1993), *Die Kelten in Bayern*, Treuchtlingen-Berlin.

Seager, R. (1972), *Tiberius*, Berkeley.

Severy, B. (2000), 'Family and State in the Early Imperial Monarchy: the *Senatus Consultum de Pisone Patre*, Tabula Siarensis, and Tabula Hebana', *Classical Philology* 95, pp. 318–37.

Severy, B. (2003), *Augustus and the Family at the Birth of the Roman Empire*, London.

Shadrake, S. (2005), *The World of the Gladiator*, Stroud.

Shannon, K. (2011), 'Livy's Cossus and Augustus, Tacitus' Germanicus and Tiberius: a historio-graphical allusion', *Histos* 5, pp. 266–82.

Shaw, B.D. (1984), 'Bandits in the Roman Empire', *Past and Present* 105, pp. 3–52.

Shaw, B.D. (1990), 'Bandit highlands and lowland peace: the mountains of Isauria-Cilicia', *Journal of the Economic and Social History of the Orient* 33, pp. 199–233 and 237–70.

Sherk, R.T. (1974), 'Roman Geographical Exploration and Military Maps', *Aufstieg und Niedergang der römischen Welt* II.1, pp. 534–62.

Sherk, R.T. (1988), *The Roman Empire: Augustus to Hadrian*, Translated Documents of Greece and Rome 6, Cambridge.

Shipley, F.W. (1924), *Velleius Paterculus and Res Gestae Divi Augusti*, Cambridge, Mass.

Shirley, E. (2001), *Building a Roman Legionary Fortress*, Stroud.

Shotter, D.C.A. (1968), 'Tacitus, Tiberius and Germanicus', *Historia* 17, pp. 194–214.

Shotter, D.C.A. (1992), *Tiberius Caesar*, London.

Shotter, D.C.A. (2000), 'Agrippina the Elder: A Woman in a Man's World', *Historia* 49, pp. 341–57.

Sidnell, P. (2006), *Warhorse: Cavalry in Ancient Warfare*, London.

Signon, H. (1978), *Agrippa: Freund und Mitregent des Kaisers Augustus*, Frankfurt.

Simkins, M. (1984), *The Roman Army from Caesar to Trajan*, revised edition, London.

Simpson, C.J. (1988), 'The change in *praenomen* of Drusus Germanicus', *Phoenix* 42, pp. 173–5.

Simpson, C.J. (2005), 'Rome's 'Official Imperial Seal'? The Rings of Augustus and his first century successors', *Historia* 54, pp. 180–8.

Sitwell, N.H.H. (1986), *Outside the Empire: The World the Romans Knew*, revised edition, London.

Sommer, C.S. (2009), 'Why there? The positioning of forts along the riverine frontiers of the Roman Empire', in Hanson (2009), pp. 103–14.

Smit, W.A.P. (1975), *Kalliope in de Nederlanden: het Renaissancistisch-klassicistische epos van 1550 tot 1850*, Assen.

Smith, W. (ed.) (1867), *The Dictionary of Greek and Roman Biography and Mythology*, Boston.

Speidel, M.P. (1976), 'Citizen cohorts in the Roman imperial army. New data on the cohorts Apula, Campana, and III Campestris', Transactions of the American Philological Association 106, pp. 339–48.

Speidel, M.P. (1992), 'Exploratores: mobile elite units of Roman Germany', *Roman Army Studies* II (*Mavors* 8), pp. 89–104.

Speidel, M.P. (2004), *Ancient Germanic Warriors: Warrior Styles from Trajan's Column to Icelandic Sagas*, Abingdon.

Spencer, D. (2002), *The Roman Alexander: Reading a Cultural Myth*, Exeter.

Staccioli, R.A. (1986), *Guida di Roma Antica*, Milan.

Staley, A. (1965), 'The Landing of Agrippina at Brundisium with the Ashes of Germanicus', *Philadelphia Museum of Art Bulletin* 61 (287/288), pp. 10–19.

Starr, C.G. (1941), *The Roman Imperial Navy 31 BC–AD 324*, New York.

Steuer, H. (2006), 'Warrior bands, war lords, and the birth of tribes and states in the first millennium AD in middle Europe', in T. Otto, H. Thrane and H. Vandkilde (eds), *Warfare and Society: Archaeological and Social Anthropological Perspectives*, Aarhus, pp. 227–36.

Stockinger, C. (2000), *Das dramatische Werk Friedrich de la Motte Fouqués. Ein Beitrag zur Geschichte des romantischen Dramas*, Tübingen.

Strahl, E. (2009), 'Die Dame von Bentumersiel an der Ems – Römischer Luxus für das Jenseits', *Archäologie in Niedersachsen* 12, pp. 63–6.

Strahl, E. (2009), 'Germanische Siedler – Römische Legionäre. Die Siedlung Bentumersiel im Reiderland', *Varus-Kurier* 11, pp. 12–15.

Strassmeir, A. and Gagelman, A. (2009), *Das Heer des Arminius: Germanische Krieger zu Beginn des 1. nachchristlichen Jahrhunderts (Heere & Waffen)*, Berlin.

Strassmeir, A. and Gagelman, A. (2011), *Das Heer des Varus: Römische Truppen in Germanien 9 n. Chr. Teil 1: Legionen und Hilfstruppen, Bekleidung, Trachtzubehör, Schutzwaffen (Heere & Waffen)*, Berlin.

Strassmeir, A. and Gagelman, A. (2012), *Das Heer des Varus: Römische Truppen in Germanien 9 n. Chr. Teil 2: Waffen, Ausrüstung, Feldzeichen, Reiterei, Verbände und Einheiten (Heere & Waffen)*, Berlin.

Straube, H. (1996), *Ferrum Noricum und die Stadt auf dem Magdalensberg*, Vienna.

Strothmann, M. (2000), *Augustus – Vater der res publica: zur Funktion der drei Begriffe* restitutio – saeculum – pater patriae *im augusteischen Prinzipat*, Stuttgart.

Stuart, M. (1940), 'Tacitus and the portraits of Germanicus and Drusus', *Classical Philology* 35, pp. 64–7.

Sumi, G. (2005), *Ceremony and Power: Performing Politics in Rome between Republic and Empire*, Ann Arbor.

Sumner, G. (2009), *Roman Military Dress*, Stroud.

Sumner, G.V. (1967), 'Germanicus and Drusus', *Latomus* 26, pp. 421–33.

Sumner, G.V. (1970), 'The truth about Velleius Paterculus: prolegomena', *Harvard Studies in Classical Philology* 74, pp. 257–97.

Sutherland, C.H.V. (1938), 'Two 'virtues' of Tiberius: a numismatic contribution to the history of his reign', *Journal of Roman Studies* 28, pp. 129–40.

Sutherland, C.H.V. (1978), *Coinage in Roman Imperial Policy*, New York.

Swan, P.M. (2004), *The Augustan Succession: An Historical Commentary on Cassius Dio's Roman History Books 55–56 (9 BC–AD 14)*, Oxford.

Swoboda, E. (1932), *Octavian and Illyricum*, Vienna.

Syme, R. (1933), 'Some notes on the legions under Augustus', *Journal of Roman Studies* 23, pp. 14–33.

Syme, R. (1934), 'The northern frontier under Augustus', in J.B. Bury *et al.* (eds), *Cambridge Ancient History* Vol. 10, Cambridge, pp. 358–364.

Syme, R. (1958), *Tacitus*, Oxford.

Syme, R. (1978), *History in Ovid*, Oxford.

Syme, R. (1979), 'Some Imperial Salutations', *Phoenix* 33, No. 4, pp. 308–29.

Syme, R. (1981), 'Governors Dying in Syria', *Zeitschrift für Papyrologie und Epigraphik*, Bd. 41, pp. 125–44.

Syme, R. (1984), *Roman Papers III*, ed. A.R. Birley, Oxford.

Syme, R. (1999), *The Provincial at Rome and Rome and the Balkans 80 BC–AD 14*, ed. A.R. Birley, Exeter.

Talbert, R.J.A. (2000), *Barrington Atlas of the Greek and Roman World. Map-by-Map Directory*, Princeton.

Tameanko, M. (1999), *Monumental Coins: Buildings and Structures on Ancient Coins*, Iola.

Tarver, J.C. (1902), *Tiberius the Tyrant*, London.

Taylor, L.R. (1929), 'Tiberius' Refusals of Divine Honors', *Transactions and Proceedings of the American Philological Association* 60, pp. 87–101.

Taylor, M.J. (2009), 'Hit and Run: The Germanic Warrior in the First Century AD', *Ancient Warfare*, Special Issue 1, pp. 42–7.

Thompson, E.A. (1958), 'Early Germanic Warfare', *Past and Present* 14, pp. 2–22.

Thorburn, J.E., Jr. (2008), 'Suetonius' *Tiberius*: a proxemic approach', *Classical Philology* 103, pp. 435–448.

Thornbury, G.W. (1862), *The Life of J.M.W. Turner*, London.

Timpe, D. (1968), *Der Triumph des Germanicus: Untersuchungen zu den Feldzügen der Jahre 14–16 n. Chr. in Germanien*, Bonn.

Timpe, D. (1998), 'Germanen, Germania, Germanische Altertumskunde', *Reallexikon der germanischen Altertumskunde* 11, pp. 181–245.

Timpe, D. (2006), *Römisch-germanische Begegnung in der späten Republik und frühen Kaiserzeit. Voraussetzungen – Konfrontationen – Wirkungen. Gesammelte Studien*, Munich.

Trillmich, W. (1978), *Familienpropaganda der Kaiser Caligula und Claudius: Agrippina Maior und Antonia Augusta auf Münzen*, Berlin.

Van Merken, L.W. (1779), *Germanicus: In Zestien Boeken*, Amsterdam (available online at http://www.dbnl.org/tekst/merk001germ01_01/).

van Wyk Louw, N.P. (1963), *Germanicus*, Kaapstad.

Vanvinckenroye, W. (1985), *Tongeren: Romeinse Stad*, Tielt.

Vermillion, J.M. (1987), 'The Pillars of Generalship', *Parameters: The US Army's Senior Professional Journal* 17, pp. 2–17 (available online at http://www.au.af.mil/au/awc/awcgate/au-24/vermillion.pdf).

Viertel, A. (1901), *Tiberius und Germanicus: Eine Historische Studie*, Göttingen.

Wallace-Hadrill, A. (1982), 'The Golden Age and Sin in Augustan Ideology', *Past and Present* 95, pp. 19–36.

Wallace-Hadrill, A. (1993), *Augustan Rome*, London.

Wallace-Hadrill, J.M. (1952), *The Barbarian West, 400–1000*, London.

Walser, G. (1994), *Studien zur Alpengeschichte in antiker Zeit*, Stuttgart.

Wamser, L., Flügel, C. and Ziegaus, B. (eds) (2004), *Die Römer zwischen Alpen und Nordmeer*, Mainz.

Watson, A. (1992), *The Germans: Who Are They Now?*, London.

Watson, G.R. (1969), *The Roman Soldier*, London.

Wedgwood, J. (1873), *Wedgwood's Catalogue of Cameos, Intaglios, Medals, Bas-Reliefs, Busts and Small Statues; Reprinted from the Edition of 1787*, London.

Weingärtner, D.G. (1969), *Die Ägyptenreise des Germanicus*, Bonn.

Weinrib, E.J. (1968), 'The family connections of M. Livius Drusus Libo', *Harvard Studies in Classical Philology* 72, pp. 247–78.

Weinstock, S. (1950), 'C. Fonteius Capito and the *Libri Tagetici*', *Papers of the British School at Rome* 18, pp. 44–9.

Weinstock, S. (1957), 'The image and the chair of Germanicus', *Journal of Roman Studies* 47, pp. 144–54.

Weinstock, S. (1971), *Divus Julius*, Oxford.

Wells, C.M. (1970), 'The supposed Augustan base at Augsburg-Oberhausen: a new look at the evidence', *Saalburg-Jahrbuch* 27, pp. 63–72.

Wells, C.M. (1972), *The German Policy of Augustus: An Examination of the Archaeological Evidence*, Oxford.

Wells, C.M. (1984), *The Roman Empire*, Cambridge, Mass.

Wells, P.S. (1999), *The Barbarians Speak: How the Conquered Peoples Shaped Roman Europe*, Princeton.

Werner, W. (1997), 'The largest ship trackway in ancient times: the Diolkos of the Isthmus of Corinth, Greece, and early attempts to build a canal', *International Journal of Nautical Archaeology* 26, pp. 98–119.

Weski, T. (1982), *Waffe in germanischen Gräbern der älteren römischen Kaiserzeit südlich der Ostsee*, Oxford.

White, K.D. (1984), *Greek and Roman Technology*, Ithaca.

Whittaker, C.R. (1994), *Frontiers of the Roman Empire: A Social and Economic Study*, Baltimore.

Wightman, E.M. (1971), *Roman Trier and the Treveri*, New York.

Wilcox, P. (1982), *Rome's Enemies: Germanics and Dacians*, London.

Wilhelm, A.B. (1826), *Die Feldzüge des Nero Claudius Drusus in nördlichen Deutschland*, Halle.

Wilkes, J.J. (1969), *Dalmatia*, London.

Wilkes, J.J. (1992), *The Illyrians*, Oxford.

Wilkinson, R.H. (2000), *The Complete Temples of Ancient Egypt*, London.

Willems, W.J.H. (1980), 'Arnhem-Meinerswijk: een nieuw castellum aan de Rijn', *Westerheem* 29, pp. 334–48.

Willems, W.J.H. (1991), 'Early Roman Camps on the Kops Plateau at Nijmegen (NL)', in V.A. Maxfield and M.J. Dobson (eds), *Roman Frontier Studies 1989. Proceedings of the XVth International Congress of Roman Frontier Studies*, Exeter, pp. 210–14.

Willems, W.J.H. (1992), 'Roman face masks from the Kops Plateau, Nijmegen, The Netherlands', *Journal of Roman Military Equipment Studies* 3, pp. 57–66.

Willems, J. H.W. and Enckevort, H. van (2009), *Vlpia Noviomagus, Roman Nijmegen, The Batavian Capital at the Imperial Frontier* (*Journal of Roman Archaeology*, Supplementary Series 73), Portsmouth.

Williams, D. (1998), *Romans and Barbarians*, London.

Wishart, D. (2002), *Germanicus*, London.

Wolfram, H. (1997), *The Roman Empire and Its Germanic Peoples*, Berkeley.

Wolters, R. (1990), *Römische Eroberung und Herrschaftsorganisation in Gallien und Germanien*, Bochum.

Wolters, R. (2009), *Die Schlacht im Teutoburger Wald: Arminius, Varus und das römische Germanien*, revised edition, Munich.

Wood, P.B., Gove, W.R. and Cochran, J.K. (1994), 'Motivations for violent crime among incarcerated adults: a consideration of reinforcement processes', *Journal of the Oklahoma Criminal Justice Research Consortium* (online at http://www.doc.state.ok.us/offenders/ocjrc/94/940650G.htm).

Woodman, A.J. (1998), *Tacitus Reviewed*, Oxford.

Woodman, A.J. (2004), *Tacitus: The Annals*, Indianapolis.

Woolff, G. (1998), *Becoming Roman: The Origins of Provincial Civilization in Gaul*, Cambridge.

Wright, G.R.H. (1977), 'Ptolemaic remains from Kalabsha Temple reconstituted on Elephantine Island (1974–1975)', *Journal of Egyptian Archaeology* 63, pp. 156–58.

Zanier, W. (1994), 'Eine römische Katapultpfeilspitze der 19. Legion aus Oberammergau: Neues zum Alpenfeldzug des Drusus im Jahre 15 v. Chr.', *Germania* 72, pp. 587–96.

Zanker, P. (1990), *The Power of Images in the Age of Augustus*, Ann Arbor.

Musical Recordings

Germanico , attributed to Georg Friedrich Händel, restored by Ottaviano Tenerani (Sony recording 2011, 88697860452).

Germanicus: Oper in Drei Akten, Georg Philipp Telemann; libretto by Christine Dorothea Lachs, reconstructed by Michael Maul (CPO recording 2011, CPO7776022).

Index